1977

μένους,
γίστας

THE METHODS
OF ETHICS

by Henry Sidgwick

Dover Publications, Inc., New York

This Dover edition, first published in 1966, is an unabridged and unaltered republication of the seventh (1907) edition, as published by Macmillan and Company, Limited.

International Standard Book Number: 0-486-21608-X
Library of Congress Catalog Card Number: 64-15504

Manufactured in the United States of America
Dover Publications, Inc.
180 Varick Street
New York, N.Y. 10014

PREFACE TO THE FIRST EDITION

In offering to the public a new book upon a subject so trite as Ethics, it seems desirable to indicate clearly at the outset its plan and purpose. Its distinctive characteristics may be first given negatively. It is not, in the main, metaphysical or psychological: at the same time it is not dogmatic or directly practical: it does not deal, except by way of illustration, with the history of ethical thought: in a sense it might be said to be not even critical, since it is only quite incidentally that it offers any criticism of the systems of individual moralists. It claims to be an examination, at once expository and critical, of the different methods of obtaining reasoned convictions as to what ought to be done which are to be found—either explicit or implicit—in the moral consciousness of mankind generally: and which, from time to time, have been developed, either singly or in combination, by individual thinkers, and worked up into the systems now historical.

I have avoided the inquiry into the Origin of the Moral Faculty—which has perhaps occupied a disproportionate amount of the attention of modern moralists—by the simple assumption (which seems to be made implicitly in all ethical reasoning) that there is something [1] under any given circumstances which it is right or reasonable to do, and that this may be known. If it be admitted that we now have the faculty of knowing this, it appears to me that the investigation of the historical antecedents of this cognition, and of its relation to other

[1] I did not mean to exclude the supposition that two or more alternatives might under certain circumstances be equally right (1884).

elements of the mind, no more properly belongs to Ethics than the corresponding questions as to the cognition of Space belong to Geometry.[1] I make, however, no further assumption as to the nature of the object of ethical knowledge : and hence my treatise is not dogmatic : all the different methods developed in it are expounded and criticised from a neutral position, and as impartially as possible. And thus, though my treatment of the subject is, in a sense, more practical than that of many moralists, since I am occupied from first to last in considering how conclusions are to be rationally reached in the familiar matter of our common daily life and actual practice ; still, my immediate object—to invert Aristotle's phrase—is not Practice but Knowledge. I have thought that the predominance in the minds of moralists of a desire to edify has impeded the real progress of ethical science : and that this would be benefited by an application to it of the same disinterested curiosity to which we chiefly owe the great discoveries of physics. It is in this spirit that I have endeavoured to compose the present work : and with this view I have desired to concentrate the reader's attention, from first to last, not on the practical results to which our methods lead, but on the methods themselves. I have wished to put aside temporarily the urgent need which we all feel of finding and adopting the true method of determining what we ought to do ; and to consider simply what conclusions will be rationally reached if we start with certain ethical premises, and with what degree of certainty and precision.

I ought to mention that chapter iv. of Book i. has been reprinted (with considerable modifications) from the *Contemporary Review,* in which it originally appeared as an article on "Pleasure and Desire." And I cannot conclude without a tribute of thanks to my friend Mr. Venn, to whose kindness in accepting the somewhat laborious task of reading and criticising my work, both before and during its passage through the press, I am indebted for several improvements in my exposition.

[1] This statement now appears to me to require a slight modification (1884).

PREFACE TO THE SECOND EDITION

In preparing this work for the second edition, I have found it desirable to make numerous alterations and additions. Indeed the extent which these have reached is so considerable, that I have thought it well to publish them in a separate form, for the use of purchasers of my first edition. On one or two points I have to acknowledge a certain change of view; which is partly at least due to criticism. For instance, in chap. iv. of Book i. (on " Pleasure and Desire "), which has been a good deal criticised by Prof. Bain and others, although I still retain my former opinion on the psychological question at issue, I have been led to take a different view of the relation of this question to Ethics; and in fact § 1 of this chapter as it at present stands directly contradicts the corresponding passage in the former edition. So again, as regards the following chapter, on ' Free-Will,' though I have not exactly found that the comments which it has called forth have removed my difficulties in dealing with this time-honoured problem, I have become convinced that I ought not to have crudely obtruded these difficulties on the reader, while professedly excluding the consideration of them from my subject. In the present edition therefore I have carefully limited myself to explaining and justifying the view that I take of the practical aspect of the question. I have further been led, through study of the Theory of Evolution in its application to practice, to attach somewhat more importance to this theory than I had previously done; and also in several passages of Books iii. and iv. to substitute ' well-being ' for ' happiness,' in my exposition of that implicit reference to some further end and standard which reflection on the Morality of Common Sense continually brings into view. This latter change however (as I explain in the concluding chapter of Book iii.) is not ultimately found to have any practical effect. I have also modified my view of

' objective rightness,' as the reader will see by comparing Book i. chap. i. § 3 with the corresponding passage in the former edition; but here again the alteration has no material importance. In my exposition of the Utilitarian principle (Book iv. chap. i.) I have shortened the cumbrous phrase ' greatest happiness of the greatest number' by omitting—as its author ultimately advised —the last four words. And finally, I have yielded as far as I could to the objections that have been strongly urged against the concluding chapter of the treatise. The main discussion therein contained still seems to me indispensable to the completeness of the work; but I have endeavoured to give the chapter a new aspect by altering its commencement, and omitting most of the concluding paragraph.

The greater part, however, of the new matter in this edition is merely explanatory and supplementary. I have endeavoured to give a fuller and clearer account of my views on any points on which I either have myself seen them to be ambiguously or inadequately expressed, or have found by experience that they were liable to be misunderstood. Thus in Book i. chap. ii. I have tried to furnish a rather more instructive account than my first edition contained of the mutual relations of Ethics and Politics. Again, even before the appearance of Mr. Leslie Stephen's interesting review in *Fraser* (March 1875), I had seen the desirability of explaining further my general view of the ' Practical Reason,' and of the fundamental notion signified by the terms ' right,' ' ought,' etc. With this object I have entirely rewritten chap. iii. of Book i., and made considerable changes in chap. i. Elsewhere, as in chaps. vi. and ix. of Book i., and chap. vi. of Book ii., I have altered chiefly in order to make my expositions more clear and symmetrical. This is partly the case with the considerable changes that I have made in the first three chapters of Book iii.; but I have also tried to obviate the objections brought by Professor Calderwood [1] against the first of these chapters. The main part of this Book

---

[1] Cf. *Mind*, No. 2.

(chaps. iv.-xii.) has been but slightly altered; but in chap. xiii. (on 'Philosophical Intuitionism'), which has been suggestively criticised by more that one writer, I have thought it expedient to give a more direct statement of my own opinions; instead of confining myself (as I did in the first edition) to comments on those of other moralists. Chap. xiv. again has been considerably modified; chiefly in order to introduce into it the substance of certain portions of an article on 'Hedonism and Ultimate Good,' which I published in *Mind* (No. 5). In Book iv. the changes (besides those above mentioned) have been inconsiderable; and have been chiefly made in order to remove a misconception which I shall presently notice, as to my general attitude towards the three Methods which I am principally occupied in examining.

In revising my work, I have endeavoured to profit as much as possible by all the criticisms on it that have been brought to my notice, whether public or private.[1] I have frequently deferred to objections, even when they appeared to me unsound, if I thought I could avoid controversy by alterations to which I was myself indifferent. Where I have been unable to make the changes required, I have usually replied, in the text or the notes, to such criticisms as have appeared to me plausible, or in any way instructive. In so doing, I have sometimes referred by name to opponents, where I thought that, from their recognised position as teachers of the subject, this would give a distinct addition of interest to the discussion; but I have been careful to omit such reference where experience has shown that it would be likely to cause offence. The book is already more controversial than I could wish; and I have therefore avoided encumbering it with any polemics of purely personal interest. For this reason I have generally left unnoticed such criticisms as have been due to mere misapprehensions, against which I thought I could

---

[1] Among unpublished criticisms I ought especially to mention the valuable suggestions that I have received from Mr. Carveth Read; to whose assistance in revising the present edition many of my corrections are due.

effectually guard in the present edition. There is, however, one fundamental misunderstanding, on which it seems desirable to say a few words. I find that more than one critic has overlooked or disregarded the account of the plan of my treatise, given in the original preface and in § 5 of the introductory chapter: and has consequently supposed me to be writing as an assailant of two of the methods which I chiefly examine, and a defender of the third. Thus one of my reviewers seems to regard Book iii. (on Intuitionism) as containing mere hostile criticism from the outside: another has constructed an article on the supposition that my principal object is the 'suppression of Egoism': a third has gone to the length of a pamphlet under the impression (apparently) that the 'main argument' of my treatise is a demonstration of Universalistic Hedonism. I am concerned to have caused so much misdirection of criticism: and I have carefully altered in this edition the passages which I perceive to have contributed to it. The morality that I examine in Book iii. is my own morality as much as it is any man's: it is, as I say, the 'Morality of Common Sense,' which I only attempt to represent in so far as I share it; I only place myself outside it either (1) temporarily, for the purpose of impartial criticism, or (2) in so far as I am forced beyond it by a practical consciousness of its incompleteness. I have certainly criticised this morality unsparingly: but I conceive myself to have exposed with equal unreserve the defects and difficulties of the hedonistic method (cf. especially chaps. iii., iv. of Book ii., and chap. v. of Book iv.). And as regards the two hedonistic principles, I do not hold the reasonableness of aiming at happiness generally with any stronger conviction than I do that of aiming at one's own. It was no part of my plan to call special attention to this "Dualism of the Practical Reason" as I have elsewhere called it: but I am surprised at the extent to which my view has perplexed even those of my critics who have understood it. I had imagined that they would readily trace it to the source from which I learnt it, Butler's well-known Sermons. I hold with Butler that " Reasonable Self-love and Conscience are the two chief or superior principles in the nature of man," each of which we are under a " manifest obligation " to obey : and I do not (I believe) differ materially from Butler in my view either of reasonable self-love, or—theology apart—of its relation to conscience. Nor, again, do I differ from him in regarding conscience as essentially a function•of the practical Reason : "moral precepts," he says in the *Analogy* (Part II. chap. viii.),"are precepts the reason of which we see." My difference only begins when I ask myself, ' What among the precepts of our common conscience do we really see to be ultimately reasonable ? ' a question which Butler does not seem to have seriously put, and to which, at any rate, he has given no satisfactory answer. The answer that I found to it supplied the rational basis that I had long perceived to be wanting to the Utilitarianism of Bentham, regarded as an ethical doctrine : and thus enabled me to transcend the commonly received antithesis between Intuitionists and Utilitarians.

PREFACE TO THE THIRD EDITION

IN this third edition I have again made extensive alterations, and introduced a considerable amount of new matter. Some of these changes and additions are due to modifications of my own ethical or psychological views ; but I do not think that any of these are of great importance in relation to the main subject of the treatise. And by far the largest part of the new matter introduced has been written either (1) to remove obscurities, ambiguities, and _ninor inconsistencies in the exposition of my views which the criticisms[1] of others or my

[1] I must here acknowledge the advantage that I have received from the remarks and questions of my pupils, and from criticisms privately communi-

own reflection have enabled me to discover; or (2) to treat as fully as seemed desirable certain parts or aspects of the subject which I had either passed over altogether or discussed too slightly in my previous editions, and on which it now appears to me important to explain my opinions, either for the greater completeness of my treatise,—according to my own view of the subject,—or for its better adaptation to the present state of ethical thought in England. The most important changes of the first kind have been made in chaps. i. and ix. of Book i., chaps. i.-iii. of Book ii., and chaps. i., xiii., and xiv. of Book iii.: under the second head I may mention the discussions of the relation of intellect to moral action in Book i. chap. iii., of volition in Book i. chap. v., of the causes of pleasure and pain in Book ii. chap. vi., of the notion of virtue in the morality of Common Sense in Book iii. chap. ii., and of evolutional ethics in Book iv. chap iv. (chiefly).

I may add that all the important alterations and additions have been published in a separate form, for the use of purchasers of my second edition.

PREFACE TO THE FOURTH EDITION

THE chief alterations in this fourth edition are the following. (1) I have expanded the discussion on Free Will in Book i. chap. v. § 3, to meet the criticisms of Mr. Fowler, in his *Principles of Morals*, and Dr. Martineau, in his *Types of Ethical Theory*. (2) In consequence of the publication of the last-mentioned work, I have rewritten part of chap. xii. of Book iii., which deals with the Ethical view maintained by Dr. Martineau. (3) I have expanded the argument in Book

cated to me by others; among these latter I ought especially to mention an instructive examination of my fundamental doctrines by the Rev. Hastings Rashdall.

iii. chap. xiv., to meet objections ably urged by Mr. Rashdall in *Mind* (April 1885). (4) I have somewhat altered the concluding chapter, in consequence of an important criticism by Prof. v. Gizycki (*Vierteljahrsschrift für Wissenschaftliche Philosophie*, Jahrg. iv. Heft i.) which I had inadvertently overlooked in preparing the third edition. Several pages of new matter have thus been introduced : for which—I am glad to say—I have made room by shortening what seemed prolix, omitting what seemed superfluous, and relegating digressions to notes, in other parts of the work : so that the bulk of the whole is not increased.

For the index which forms a new feature in the present edition I am indebted to the kindness of Miss Jones of Girton College, the author of *Elements of Logic as a Science of Propositions*.

PREFACE TO THE FIFTH EDITION

SUCH criticisms of my Ethical opinions and reasonings as have come under my notice, since the publication of the fourth edition of this treatise,. have chiefly related to my treatment of the question of Free Will in Book i. chap. v., or to the hedonistic view of Ultimate Good, maintained in Book iii. chap. iv. I have accordingly rewritten certain parts of these two chapters, in the hope of making my arguments more clear and convincing : in each case a slight change in view will be apparent to a careful reader who compares the present with the preceding edition : but in neither case does the change affect the main substance of the argument. Alterations, in one or two cases not inconsiderable, have been made in several other chapters, especially Book i. chap. ii., and Book iii. chaps. i. and ii. : but they have chiefly aimed at removing defects of exposition, and do not (I think) in any case imply any material change of view.

My thanks are again due to Miss Jones, of Girton College, for reading through the proofs of this edition and making most useful corrections and suggestions : as well as for revising the index which she kindly made for the fourth edition.

PREFACE TO THE SIXTH EDITION

THE revision of *The Methods of Ethics* for this edition was begun by Professor Sidgwick and carried through by him up to p. 276, on which the last of his corrections on the copy were made. The latter portion of his revision was done under the pressure of severe illness, the increase of which prevented him from continuing it beyond the point mentioned; and by the calamity of his death the rest of the book remains without the final touches which it might have received from his hand. In accordance with his wish, I have seen pp. 277 to 509 through the press unchanged—except for a few small alterations which he had indicated, and the insertion on pp. 457-459 of the concluding passage of Book iv. chapter iii.[1] Such alterations as were made by Professor Sidgwick in this edition prior to p. 276 will be found chiefly in chapters i.-v. and ix. of Book i., and chapters iii. and vi. of Book ii.

The Appendix on "The Kantian Conception of Free Will," promised in note 1 on p. 58 of this edition, is substantially a reprint of a paper by Professor Sidgwick under that heading which appeared in *Mind*, vol. xiii. No. 51, and accurately covers the ground indicated in the note.

There is one further matter of importance. Among the MS. material which Professor Sidgwick intended to be referred to, in preparing this edition for the press, there occurs, as part of the MS. notes for a lecture, a brief history of the development in his thought of the ethical view which he has set

[1] Cf. note on p. 457, and Prefatory Note to the Seventh Edition.

forth in the *Methods of Ethics.* This, though not in a finished condition, is in essentials complete and coherent, and since it cannot fail to have peculiar value and interest for students of the book, it has been decided to insert it here. Such an arrangement seems to a certain extent in harmony with the author's own procedure in the Preface to the Second Edition ; and in this way while future students of the *Methods* will have access to an introductory account which both ethically and historically is of very exceptional interest, no dislocation of the text will be involved.

In the account referred to Professor Sidgwick says :—

"My first adhesion to a definite Ethical system was to the Utilitarianism of Mill : I found in this relief from the apparently external and arbitrary pressure of moral rules which I had been educated to obey, and which presented themselves to me as to some extent doubtful and confused ; and sometimes, even when clear, as merely dogmatic, unreasoned, incoherent. My antagonism to this was intensified by the study of Whewell's *Elements of Morality* which was prescribed for the study of undergraduates in Trinity. It was from that book that I derived the impression— which long remained uneffaced—that Intuitional moralists were hopelessly loose (as compared to mathematicians) in their definitions and axioms.

The two elements of Mill's view which I am accustomed to distinguish as Psychological Hedonism [that each man does seek his own Happiness] and Ethical Hedonism [that each man ought to seek the general Happiness] both attracted me, and I did not at first perceive their incoherence.

Psychological Hedonism—the law of universal pleasure-seeking —attracted me by its frank naturalness. Ethical Hedonism, as expounded by Mill, was morally inspiring by its dictate of readiness for absolute self - sacrifice. They appealed to different elements of my nature, but they brought these into apparent harmony : they both used the same words " pleasure," " happiness," and the persuasiveness of Mill's exposition veiled for a time the profound discrepancy between the natural end of action—private happiness, and the end of duty—general happiness. Or if a doubt assailed me as to the coincidence of private and general happiness, I was inclined to hold that it ought to be cast to the winds by a generous resolution.

But a sense grew upon me that this method of dealing with the conflict between Interest and Duty, though perhaps proper for practice could not be final for philosophy. For practical men who do not philosophise, the maxim of subordinating self-interest, as commonly conceived, to "altruistic" impulses and sentiments which they feel to be higher and nobler is, I doubt not, a commendable maxim ; but it is surely the business of Ethical Philosophy to find and make explicit the rational ground of such action.

I therefore set myself to examine methodically the relation of Interest and Duty.

This involved a careful study of Egoistic Method, to get the relation of Interest and Duty clear. Let us suppose that my own Interest is paramount. What really is my Interest, how far can acts conducive to it be known, how far does the result correspond with Duty (or Wellbeing of Mankind) ? This investigation led me to feel very strongly *this* opposition, rather than that which Mill and the earlier Utilitarians felt between so-called Intuitions or Moral Sense Perceptions, and Hedonism, whether Epicurean or Utilitarian. Hence the arrangement of my book—ii., iii., iv. [Book ii. Egoism, Book iii. Intuitionism, Book iv. Utilitarianism].

The result was that I concluded that no complete solution of the conflict between my happiness and the general happiness was possible on the basis of mundane experience. This [conclusion I] slowly and reluctantly accepted—cf. Book ii. chap. v., and last chapter of treatise [Book ii. chap. v. is on "Happiness and Duty," and the concluding chapter is on "The Mutual Relations of the Three Methods"]. This [was] most important to me.

In consequence of this perception, moral choice of the general happiness or acquiescence in self-interest as ultimate, became practically necessary. But on what ground ?

I put aside Mill's phrases that such sacrifice was "heroic" : that it was not "well" with me unless I was in a disposition to make it. I put to him in my mind the dilemma :—Either it is for my own happiness or it is not. If not, why [should I do it] ?— It was no use to say that if I was a moral hero I should have formed a habit of willing actions beneficial to others which would remain in force, even with my own pleasure in the other scale. I knew that at any rate I was not the kind of moral hero who does this without reason ; from *blind* habit. Nor did I even wish to be that kind of hero : for it seemed to me that that kind of hero, however admirable, was certainly not a philosopher. I must somehow *see* that it was right for me to sacrifice my happiness for the good of the whole of which I am a part.

Thus, in spite of my early aversion to Intuitional Ethics, derived from the study of Whewell, and in spite of my attitude of discipleship to Mill, I was forced to recognise the need of a fundamental ethical intuition.

The utilitarian method—which I had learnt from Mill—could

not, it seemed to me, be made coherent and harmonious without this fundamental intuition.

In this state of mind I read Kant's Ethics again : I had before read it somewhat unintelligently, under the influence of Mill's view as to its "grotesque failure."[1] I now read it more receptively and was impressed with the truth and importance of its fundamental principle :—*Act from a principle or maxim that you can will to be a universal law*—cf. Book iii. chap. i. § 3 [of *The Methods of Ethics*]. It threw the "golden rule" of the gospel ("Do unto others as ye would that others should do unto you") into a form that commended itself to my reason.

Kant's resting of morality on Freedom did not indeed commend itself to me,[2] though I did not at first see, what I now seem to see clearly, that it involves the fundamental confusion of using "freedom" in two distinct senses—"freedom" that is realised only when we do right, when reason triumphs over inclination, and "freedom" that is realised equally when we choose to do wrong, and which is apparently implied in the notion of ill-desert. What commended itself to me, in short, was Kant's ethical principle rather than its metaphysical basis. This I briefly explain in Book iii. chap. i. § 3 [of *The Methods of Ethics*]. I shall go into it at more length when we come to Kant.

That whatever is right for me must be right for all persons in similar circumstances—which was the form in which I accepted the Kantian maxim — seemed to me certainly fundamental, certainly true, and not without practical importance.

But the fundamental principle seemed to me inadequate for the construction of a system of duties ; and the more I reflected on it the more inadequate it appeared.

On reflection it did not seem to me really to meet the difficulty which had led me from Mill to Kant : it did not settle finally the subordination of Self-Interest to Duty.

For the Rational Egoist—a man who had learnt from Hobbes that Self-preservation is the first law of Nature and Self-interest the only rational basis of social morality—and in fact, its actual basis, so far as it is effective—such a thinker might accept the Kantian principle and remain an Egoist.

He might say, "I quite admit that when the painful necessity comes for another man to choose between his own happiness and the general happiness, he must as a reasonable being prefer his own, *i.e.* it is right for him to do this on my principle. No doubt, as I probably do not sympathise with him in particular any more than with other persons, I as a disengaged spectator should like

---

[1] Kant's *Fundamental Principles* (*Grundlegung zur Metaphysik der Sitten*), §§ 1, 2. Mill, *Utilitarianism*, pp. 5, 6 [7th edition (large print), 1879].

[2] Book i. chap. v. of *The Methods of Ethics*.

him to sacrifice himself to the general good : but I do not expect him to do it, any more than I should do it myself in his place."

It did not seem to me that this reasoning could be effectively confuted. No doubt it was, from the point of view of the universe, reasonable to prefer the greater good to the lesser, even though the lesser good was the private happiness of the agent. Still, it seemed to me also undeniably reasonable for the individual to prefer his own. The rationality of self-regard seemed to me as undeniable as the rationality of self-sacrifice. I could not give up this conviction, though neither of my masters, neither Kant nor Mill, seemed willing to admit it : in different ways, each in his own way, they refused to admit it.

I was, therefore, [if] I may so say, a disciple on the loose, in search of a master—or, if the term 'master' be too strong, at any rate I sought for sympathy and support, in the conviction which I had attained in spite of the opposite opinions of the thinkers from whom I had learnt most.

It was at this point then that the influence of Butler came in. For the stage at which I had thus arrived in search of an ethical creed, at once led me to understand Butler, and to find the support and intellectual sympathy that I required in his view.

I say to understand him, for hitherto I had misunderstood him, as I believe most people then misunderstood, and perhaps still misunderstand, him. He had been presented to me as an advocate of the authority of Conscience ; and his argument, put summarily, seemed to be that because reflection on our impulses showed us Conscience claiming authority therefore we ought to obey it. Well, I had no doubt that my conscience claimed authority, though it was a more utilitarian conscience than Butler's : for, through all this search for principles I still adhered for practical purposes to the doctrine I had learnt from Mill, *i.e.* I still held to the maxim of aiming at the general happiness as the supreme directive rule of conduct, and I thought I could answer the objections that Butler brought against this view (in the " Dissertation on Virtue " at the end of the *Analogy*). My difficulty was, as I have said, that this claim of conscience, whether utilitarian or not, had to be harmonised with the claim of Rational Self-love ; and that I vaguely supposed Butler to avoid or override [the latter claim].

But reading him at this stage with more care, I found in him, with pleasure and surprise, a view very similar to that which had developed itself in my own mind in struggling to assimilate Mill and Kant. I found he expressly admitted that "interest, my own happiness, is a manifest obligation," and that "Reasonable Self-love" [is "one of the two chief or superior principles in the nature of man"]. That is, he recognised a "Dualism of the

Governing Faculty"—or as I prefer to say "Dualism of the Practical Reason," since the 'authority' on which Butler laid stress must present itself to my mind as the authority of reason, before I can admit it.

Of this more presently: what I now wish to make clear is that it was on this side—if I may so say—that I entered into Butler's system and came under the influence of his powerful and cautious intellect. But the effect of his influence carried me a further step away from Mill: for I was led by it to abandon the doctrine of Psychological Hedonism, and to recognise the existence of 'disinterested' or 'extra-regarding' impulses to action, [impulses] not directed towards the agent's pleasure [cf. chap iv. of Book i. of *The Methods of Ethics*]. In fact as regards what I may call a Psychological basis of Ethics, I found myself much more in agreement with Butler than Mill.

And this led me to reconsider my relation to Intuitional Ethics. The strength and vehemence of Butler's condemnation of pure Utilitarianism, in so cautious a writer, naturally impressed me much. And I had myself become, as I had to admit to myself, an Intuitionist to a certain extent. For the supreme rule of aiming at the general happiness, as I had come to see, must rest on a fundamental moral intuition, if I was to recognise it as binding at all. And in reading the writings of the earlier English Intuitionists, More and Clarke, I found the axiom I required for my Utilitarianism [That a rational agent is bound to aim at Universal Happiness], in one form or another, holding a prominent place (cf. *History of Ethics*, pp. 172, 181).

I had then, theoretically as well as practically, accepted this fundamental moral intuition ; and there was also the Kantian principle, which I recognised as irresistibly valid, though not adequate to give complete guidance.—I was then an "intuitional" moralist to this extent : and if so, why not further ? The orthodox moralists such as Whewell (then in vogue) said that there was a whole intelligible system of intuitions : but how were they to be learnt ? I could not accept Butler's view as to the sufficiency of a plain man's conscience : for it appeared to me that plain men agreed rather verbally than really.

In this state of mind I had to read Aristotle again ; and a light seemed to dawn upon me as to the meaning and drift of his procedure—especially in Books ii., iii., iv. of the *Ethics*—(cf. *History of Ethics*, chap. ii. § 9, p. 58, read to end of section).

What he gave us there was the Common Sense Morality of Greece, reduced to consistency by careful comparison : given not as something external to him but as what "we"—he and others— think, ascertained by reflection. And was not this really the Socratic induction, elicited by interrogation ?

Might I not imitate this : do the same for *our* morality here and now, in the same manner of impartial reflection on current opinion ?

Indeed *ought* I not to do this before deciding on the question whether I had or had not a system of moral intuitions ? At any rate the result would be useful, whatever conclusion I came to.

So this was the part of my book first written (Book iii., chaps. i.-xi.), and a certain imitation of Aristotle's manner was very marked in it at first, and though I have tried to remove it where it seemed to me affected or pedantic, it still remains to some extent.

But the result of the examination was to bring out with fresh force and vividness the difference between the maxims of Common Sense Morality (even the strongest and strictest, *e.g.* Veracity and Good Faith) and the intuitions which I had already attained, *i.e.* the Kantian Principle (of which I now saw the only certain element in Justice—"treat similar cases similarly"—to be a particular application), and the Fundamental Principle of Utilitarianism. And this latter was in perfect harmony with the Kantian Principle. I certainly could will it to be a universal law that men should act in such a way as to promote universal happiness ; in fact it was the only law that it was perfectly clear to me that I could thus decisively will, from a universal point of view.

I was then a Utilitarian again, but on an Intuitional basis.

But further, the reflection on Common Sense Morality which I had gone through, had continually brought home to me its character as a system of rules tending to the promotion of general happiness (cf. [*Methods of Ethics*] pp. 470, 471).

Also the previous reflection on hedonistic method for Book ii. had shown me its weaknesses. What was then to be done ? [The] conservative attitude [to be observed] towards Common Sense [is] given in chapter v. of Book iv.: "Adhere generally, deviate and attempt reform only in exceptional cases in which,—notwithstanding the roughness of hedonistic method,—the argument against Common Sense is decisive."

In this state of mind I published my book : I tried to say what I had found : that the opposition between Utilitarianism and Intuitionism was due to a misunderstanding. There was indeed a fundamental opposition between the individual's interest and either morality, which I could not solve by any method I had yet found trustworthy, without the assumption of the moral government of the world : so far I agreed with both Butler and Kant.

But I could find no real opposition between Intuitionism and Utilitarianism. . . . The Utilitarianism of Mill and Bentham seemed to me to want a basis : that basis could only be supplied

by a fundamental intuition ; on the other hand the best examination I could make of the Morality of Common Sense showed me
no clear and self-evident principles except such as were perfectly
consistent with Utilitarianism.

Still, investigation of the Utilitarian method led me to see
defects [in it] : the merely empirical examination of the consequences of actions is unsatisfactory ; and being thus conscious of
the practical imperfection in many cases of the guidance of the
Utilitarian calculus, I remained anxious to treat with respect, and
make use of, the guidance afforded by Common Sense in these
cases, on the ground of the general presumption which evolution
afforded that moral sentiments and opinions would point to conduct
conducive to general happiness ; though I could not admit this
presumption as a ground for overruling a strong probability of the
opposite, derived from utilitarian calculations."

It only remains to mention that the Table of Contents and
the Index have been revised in accordance with the changes
in the text.

E. E. CONSTANCE JONES.

GIRTON COLLEGE,
CAMBRIDGE, *April* 1901.

PREFATORY NOTE TO THE SEVENTH EDITION

THIS Edition is a reprint of the Sixth, the only changes
(besides correction of a few clerical errors) being an alteration
of type in the passage which occurs on p. 457 in the Sixth
Edition and pp. 457-459 in this Edition, together with consequent changes (1) in paging and indexing, (2) in the
reference to the passage in question in the reprinted Preface
to the Sixth Edition, and (3) in the insertion of the note on
p. 457.

E. E. C. J.

December 1906.

CONTENTS

BOOK I

CHAPTER I

INTRODUCTION

CHAPTER II

ETHICS AND POLITICS

CHAPTER III

ETHICAL JUDGMENTS

CHAPTER IV

PLEASURE AND DESIRE

CHAPTER V

FREE WILL

CHAPTER VI

ETHICAL PRINCIPLES AND METHODS

CHAPTER VII

EGOISM AND SELF-LOVE

CHAPTER VIII

INTUITIONISM

CHAPTER IX

GOOD

BOOK II

EGOISM

CHAPTER I

THE PRINCIPLE AND METHOD OF EGOISM

CHAPTER II

EMPIRICAL HEDONISM

CHAPTER III

EMPIRICAL HEDONISM (*continued*)

CHAPTER IV

OBJECTIVE HEDONISM AND COMMON SENSE

CHAPTER V

HAPPINESS AND DUTY

CHAPTER VI

DEDUCTIVE HEDONISM

BOOK III

INTUITIONISM

CHAPTER I

INTUITIONISM

CHAPTER II

VIRTUE AND DUTY

CHAPTER III

THE INTELLECTUAL VIRTUES

CHAPTER IV

BENEVOLENCE

CHAPTER V

JUSTICE

CHAPTER VI

LAWS AND PROMISES

CHAPTER VII

CLASSIFICATION OF DUTIES. TRUTH

CHAPTER VIII

OTHER SOCIAL DUTIES AND VIRTUES

CHAPTER IX

SELF-REGARDING VIRTUES

CHAPTER X

COURAGE, HUMILITY, ETC.

CHAPTER XI

REVIEW OF THE MORALITY OF COMMON SENSE

CHAPTER XII

MOTIVES OR SPRINGS OF ACTION AS SUBJECTS OF MORAL JUDGMENT

BOOK IV

UTILITARIANISM

CHAPTER I

THE MEANING OF UTILITARIANISM

CHAPTER II

THE PROOF OF UTILITARIANISM

CHAPTER III

THE RELATION OF UTILITARIANISM TO THE MORALITY OF COMMON SENSE

CHAPTER IV

THE METHOD OF UTILITARIANISM

CHAPTER V

THE METHOD OF UTILITARIANISM (*continued*)

CONCLUDING CHAPTER

THE MUTUAL RELATIONS OF THE THREE METHODS

BOOK I

BOOK I

CHAPTER I

INTRODUCTION

§ 1. THE boundaries of the study called Ethics are variously and often vaguely conceived: but they will perhaps be sufficiently defined, at the outset, for the purposes of the present treatise, if a 'Method of Ethics' is explained to mean any rational procedure by which we determine what individual human beings 'ought'—or what it is 'right' for them—to do, or to seek to realise by voluntary action.[1] By using the word "individual" I provisionally distinguish the study of Ethics from that of Politics,[2] which seeks to determine the proper constitution and the right public conduct of governed societies: both Ethics and Politics being, in my view, distinguished from positive sciences by having as their special and primary object to determine what ought to be, and not to ascertain what merely is, has been, or will be.

The student of Ethics seeks to attain systematic and precise general knowledge of what ought to be, and in this sense his aims and methods may properly be termed 'scientific': but I have preferred to call Ethics a study rather than a science, because it is widely thought that a Science must necessarily

---

[1] The exact relation of the terms 'right' and 'what ought to be' is discussed in chap. iii. of this Book. I here assume that they may be used as convertible, for most purposes.

[2] I use 'Politics' in what I take to be its most ordinary signification, to denote the science or study of Right or Good Legislation and Government. There is a wider possible sense of the term, according to which it would include the greater part of Ethics : i.e. if understood to be the Theory of Right Social Relations. See chap. ii. § 2.

S

have some department of actual existence for its subject-matter. And in fact the term 'Ethical Science' might, without violation of usage, denote either the department of Psychology that deals with voluntary action and its springs, and with moral sentiments and judgments, as actual phenomena of individual human minds; or the department of Sociology dealing with similar phenomena, as manifested by normal members of the organised groups of human beings which we call societies. We observe, however, that most persons do not pursue either of these studies merely from curiosity, in order to ascertain what actually exists, has existed, or will exist in time. They commonly wish not only to understand human action, but also to regulate it; in this view they apply the ideas 'good' and 'bad,' 'right' and 'wrong,' to the conduct or institutions which they describe; and thus pass, as I should say, from the point of view of Psychology or Sociology to that of Ethics or Politics. My definition of Ethics is designed to mark clearly the fundamental importance of this transition. It is true that the mutual implication of the two kinds of study—the positive and the practical—is, on any theory, very close and complete. On any theory, our view of what ought to be must be largely derived, in details, from our apprehension of what is; the means of realising our ideal can only be thoroughly learnt by a careful study of actual phenomena; and to any individual asking himself 'What ought I to do or aim at?' it is important to examine the answers which his fellow-men have actually given to similar questions. Still it seems clear that an attempt to ascertain the general laws or uniformities by which the varieties of human conduct, and of men's sentiments and judgments respecting conduct, may be *explained*, is essentially different from an attempt to determine which among these varieties of conduct is *right* and which of these divergent judgments *valid*. It is, then, the systematic consideration of these latter questions which constitutes, in my view, the special and distinct aim of Ethics and Politics.

§ 2. In the language of the preceding section I could not avoid taking account of two different forms in which the fundamental problem of Ethics is stated; the difference between which leads, as we shall presently see, to rather important consequences. Ethics is sometimes considered as an investi-

gation of the true Moral laws or rational precepts of Conduct;
sometimes as an inquiry into the nature of the Ultimate End
of reasonable human action—the Good or ' True Good ' of man
—and the method of attaining it. Both these views are
familiar, and will have to be carefully considered : but the
former seems most prominent in modern ethical thought, and
most easily applicable to modern ethical systems generally.
For the Good investigated in Ethics is limited to Good in
some degree attainable by human effort; accordingly knowledge of the end is sought in order to ascertain what actions
are the right means to its attainment. Thus however
prominent the notion of an Ultimate Good—other than
voluntary action of any kind—may be in an ethical system,
and whatever interpretation may be given to this notion, we
must still arrive finally, if it is to be practically useful, at
some determination of precepts or directive rules of conduct.

On the other hand, the conception of Ethics as essentially
an investigation of the ' Ultimate Good ' of Man and the means
of attaining it is not universally applicable, without straining,
to the view of Morality which we may conveniently distinguish
as the Intuitional view; according to which conduct is held to
be right when conformed to certain precepts or principles of
Duty, intuitively known to be unconditionally binding. In
this view the conception of Ultimate Good is not necessarily
of fundamental importance in the determination of Right conduct except on the assumption that Right conduct itself—or
the character realised in and developed through Right conduct
—is the sole Ultimate Good for man. But this assumption
is not implied in the Intuitional view of Ethics : nor would
it, I conceive, accord with the moral common sense of modern
Christian communities. For we commonly think that the
complete notion of human Good or Well-being must include
the attainment of Happiness as well as the performance of
Duty; even if we hold with Butler that " the happiness of the
world is the concern of Him who is the Lord and the Pro-
prietor of it," and that, accordingly, it is not right for men to
make their performance of Duty conditional on their knowledge of its conduciveness to their Happiness. For those who
hold this, what men ought to take as the *practically* ultimate
end of their action and standard of Right conduct, may in some

cases have no logical connexion with the conception of Ultimate Good for man : so that, in such cases, however indispensable this latter conception may be to the completeness of an ethical system, it would still not be important for the methodical determination of Right conduct.

It is on account of the prevalence of the Intuitional view just mentioned, and the prominent place which it consequently occupies in my discussion, that in defining Ethics I have avoided the term ' Art of Conduct ' which some would regard as its more appropriate designation. For the term ' Art '— when applied to the contents of a treatise—seems to signify systematic express knowledge (as distinguished from the implicit knowledge or organised habit which we call skill) of the right means to a given end. Now if we assume that the rightness of action depends on its conduciveness to some ulterior end, then no doubt—when this end has been clearly ascertained—the process of determining the right rules of conduct for human beings in different relations and circumstances would naturally come under the notion of Art. But on the view that the practically ultimate end of moral action is often the Rightness of the action itself—or the Virtue realised in and confirmed by such action—and that this is known intuitively in each case or class of cases, we can hardly regard the term ' Art ' as properly applicable to the systematisation of such knowledge. Hence, as I do not wish to start with any assumption incompatible with this latter view, I prefer to consider Ethics as the science or study of what is right or what ought to be, so far as this depends upon the voluntary action of individuals.[1]

§ 3. If, however, this view of the scope of Ethics is accepted, the question arises why it is commonly taken to consist, to a great extent, of psychological discussion as to the ' nature of the moral faculty '; especially as I have myself thought it right to include some discussion of this kind in the present treatise. For it does not at first appear why this should belong to Ethics, any more than discussions about the mathematical faculty or the faculty of sense-perception belong to mathematics and physics respectively. Why do we not simply

---

[1] The relation of the notion of ' Good ' to that of ' Right' or ' what ought to be ' will be further considered in a subsequent chapter of this Book (ix.)

start with certain premises, stating what ought to be done or sought, without considering the faculty by which we apprehend their truth ?

One answer is that the moralist has a practical aim : we desire knowledge of right conduct in order to act on it. Now we cannot help believing what we see to be true, but we can help doing what we see to be right or wise, and in fact often do what we know to be wrong or unwise : thus we are forced to notice the existence in us of irrational springs of action, conflicting with our knowledge and preventing its practical realisation : and the very imperfectness of the connexion between our practical judgment and our will impels us to seek for more precise knowledge as to the nature of that connexion.

But this is not all. Men never ask, ' Why should I believe what I see to be true ? ' but they frequently ask, ' Why should I do what I see to be right ? ' It is easy to reply that the question is futile, since it could only be answered by a reference to some other recognised principle of right conduct, and the question might just as well be asked as regards that again, and so on. But still we do ask the question widely and continually, and therefore this demonstration of its futility is not completely satisfactory ; we require besides some explanation of its persistency.

One explanation that may be offered is that, since we are moved to action not by moral judgment alone, but also by desires and inclinations that operate independently of moral judgment, the answer which we really want to the question ' Why should I do it ? ' is one which does not merely prove a certain action to be right, but also stirs in us a predominant inclination to do the action.

That this explanation is true for some minds in some moods I would not deny. Still I think that when a man seriously asks ' why he should do ' anything, he commonly assumes in himself a determination to pursue whatever conduct may be shown by argument to be reasonable, even though it be very different from that to which his non-rational inclinations may prompt. And we are generally agreed that reasonable conduct in any case has to be determined on principles, in applying which the agent's inclination—as it exists apart from such determination—is only one element among several that have to be considered, and commonly not the most important element. But when we ask what these principles are, the diversity of answers which we find manifestly declared in the systems and fundamental formulæ of professed moralists seems to be really present in the common practical reasoning of men generally; with this difference, that whereas the philosopher seeks unity of principle, and consistency of method at the risk of paradox, the unphilosophic man is apt to hold different principles at once, and to apply different methods in more or less confused combination. If this be so, we can offer another explanation of the persistent unsatisfied demand for an ultimate reason, above noticed. For if there are different views of the ultimate reasonableness of conduct, implicit in the thought of ordinary men, though not brought into clear relation to each other,—it is easy to see that any single answer to the question 'why' will not be completely satisfactory, as it will be given only from one of these points of view, and will always leave room to ask the question from some other.

I am myself convinced that this is the main explanation of the phenomenon: and it is on this conviction that the plan of the present treatise is based. We cannot, of course, regard as valid reasonings that lead to conflicting conclusions; and I therefore assume as a fundamental postulate of Ethics, that so far as two methods conflict, one or other of them must be modified or rejected. But I think it fundamentally important to recognise, at the outset of Ethical inquiry, that there is a diversity of methods applied in ordinary practical thought.

§ 4. What then are these different methods? what are the different practical principles which the common sense of mankind is *prima facie* prepared to accept as ultimate? Some care is needed in answering this question: because we frequently prescribe that this or that 'ought' to be done or aimed at without any express reference to an ulterior end, while yet such an end is tacitly presupposed. It is obvious that such prescriptions are merely, what Kant calls them, Hypothetical Imperatives; they are not addressed to any one who has not first accepted the end.

For instance: a teacher of any art assumes that his pupil

wants to produce the product of the art, or to produce it excellent in quality: he tells him that he *ought* to hold the awl, the hammer, the brush differently. A physician assumes that his patient wants health: he tells him that he *ought* to rise early, to live plainly, to take hard exercise. If the patient deliberately prefers ease and good living to health, the physician's precepts fall to the ground: they are no longer addressed to him. So, again, a man of the world assumes that his hearers wish to get on in society, when he lays down rules of dress, manner, conversation, habits of life. A similar view may be plausibly taken of many rules prescribing what are sometimes called "duties to oneself": it may be said that they are given on the assumption that a man regards his own Happiness as an ultimate end: that if any one should be so exceptional as to disregard it, he does not come within their scope: in short, that the '*ought*' in such formulæ is still implicitly relative to an *optional* end.

It does not, however, seem to me that this account of the matter is exhaustive. We do not all look with simple indifference on a man who declines to take the right means to attain his own happiness, on no other ground than that he does not care about happiness. Most men would regard such a refusal as irrational, with a certain disapprobation; they would thus implicitly assent to Butler's statement[1] that "interest, one's own happiness, is a manifest obligation." In other words, they would think that a man *ought* to care for his own happiness. The word 'ought' thus used is no longer relative: happiness now appears as an ultimate end, the pursuit of which—at least within the limits imposed by other duties—appears to be prescribed by reason 'categorically,' as Kant would say, *i.e.* without any tacit assumption of a still ulterior end. And it has been widely held by even orthodox moralists that all morality rests ultimately on the basis of "reasonable self-love";[2] *i.e.* that its rules are ultimately binding on any individual only so far as it is his interest on the whole to observe them.

Still, common moral opinion certainly regards the duty or virtue of Prudence as only a part—and not the most

---

[1] See the Preface to Butler's *Sermons on Human Nature.*
[2] The phrase is Butler's.

important part—of duty or virtue in general. Common moral opinion recognises and inculcates other fundamental rules— *e.g.* those of Justice, Good Faith, Veracity—which, in its ordinary judgments on particular cases, it is inclined to treat as binding without qualification and without regard to ulterior consequences. And, in the ordinary form of the Intuitional view of Ethics, the "categorical" prescription of such rules is maintained explicitly and definitely, as a result of philosophical reflection : and the realisation of Virtue in act—at least in the case of the virtues just mentioned—is held to consist in strict and unswerving conformity to such rules.

On the other hand it is contended by many Utilitarians that all the rules of conduct which men prescribe to one another as moral rules are really—though in part unconsciously — prescribed as means to the general happiness of mankind, or of the whole aggregate of sentient beings; and it is still more widely held by Utilitarian thinkers that such rules, however they may originate, are only valid so far as their observance is conducive to the general happiness. This contention I shall hereafter examine with due care. Here I wish only to point out that, if the duty of aiming at the general happiness is thus taken to include all other duties, as subordinate applications of it, we seem to be again led to the notion of Happiness as an ultimate end categorically prescribed,—only it is now General Happiness and not the private happiness of any individual. And this is the view that I myself take of the Utilitarian principle.

At the same time, it is not necessary, in the methodical investigation of right conduct, considered relatively to the end either of private or of general happiness, to assume that the end itself is determined or prescribed by reason : we only require to assume, in reasoning to cogent practical conclusions, that it is adopted as ultimate and paramount. For if a man accepts any end as ultimate and paramount, he accepts implicitly as his "method of ethics" whatever process of reasoning enables him to determine the actions most conducive to this end.[1] Since, however, to every difference in the end accepted at least some difference in method will generally correspond : if all the ends which men are found practically to adopt as

---

[1] See the last paragraph of chap. iii. of this Book.

ultimate (subordinating everything else to the attainment of them under the influence of 'ruling passions'), were taken as principles for which the student of Ethics is called upon to construct rational methods, his task would be very complex and extensive. But if we confine ourselves to such ends as the common sense of mankind appears to accept as rational ultimate ends, the task is reduced, I think, within manageable limits ; since this criterion will exclude at least many of the objects which men practically seem to regard as paramount. Thus many men sacrifice health, fortune, happiness, to Fame ; but no one, so far as I know, has deliberately maintained that Fame is an object which it is reasonable for men to seek for its own sake. It only commends itself to reflective minds either (1) as a source of Happiness to the person who gains it, or (2) a sign of his Excellence, moral or intellectual, or (3) because it attests the achievement by him of some important benefit to society, and at the same time stimulates him and others to further achievement in the future : and the conception of " benefit " would, when examined in its turn, lead us again to Happiness or Excellence of human nature,—since a man is commonly thought to benefit others either by making them happier or by making them wiser and more virtuous.

Whether there are any ends besides these two, which can be reasonably regarded as ultimate, it will hereafter [1] be part of our business to investigate : but we may perhaps say that *prima facie* the only two ends which have a strongly and widely supported claim to be regarded as rational ultimate ends are the two just mentioned, Happiness and Perfection or Excellence of human nature—meaning here by ' Excellence ' not primarily superiority to others, but a partial realisation of, or approximation to, an ideal type of human Perfection. And we must observe that the adoption of the former of these ends leads us to two *prima facie* distinct methods, according as it is sought to be realised universally, or by each individual for himself alone. For though doubtless a man may often best promote his own happiness by labouring and abstaining for the sake of others, it seems to be implied in our common notion of self-sacrifice that actions most conducive to the general happiness do not—in this world at least—always tend

---

[1] See chap. ix. of this Book, and Book iii. chap. xiv.

also to the greatest happiness of the agent.[1] And among those who hold that " happiness is our being's end and aim " we seem to find a fundamental difference of opinion as to whose happiness it is that it is ultimately reasonable to aim at. For to some it seems that " the constantly proper end of action on the part of any individual at the moment of action is his real greatest happiness from that moment to the end of his life " ;[2] whereas others hold that the view of reason is essentially universal, and that it cannot be reasonable to take as an ultimate and paramount end the happiness of any one individual rather than that of any other—at any rate if equally deserving and susceptible of it—so that general happiness must be the " true standard of right and wrong, in the field of morals " no less than of politics.[3] It is, of course, possible to adopt an end intermediate between the two, and to aim at the happiness of some limited portion of mankind, such as one's family or nation or race : but any such limitation seems arbitrary, and probably few would maintain it to be reasonable *per se*, except as the most practicable way of aiming at the general happiness, or of indirectly securing one's own.

The case seems to be otherwise with Excellence or Perfection.[4] At first sight, indeed, the same alternatives present themselves :[5] it seems that the Excellence aimed at may be

[1] For a full discussion of this question, see Book ii. chap. v. and the concluding chapter of the work.

[2] Bentham, *Memoirs* (vol. x. of Bowring's edition), p. 560.

[3] Bentham again, *Memoirs*, p. 79. See note at the end of Book i. chap. vi. The Utilitarians since Bentham have sometimes adopted one, sometimes the other, of these two principles as paramount.

[4] I use the terms 'Excellence' and ' Perfection ' to denote the same ultimate end regarded in somewhat different aspects : meaning by either an ideal complex of mental qualities, of which we admire and approve the manifestation in human life : but using ' Perfection ' to denote the ideal as such, while ' Excellence' denotes such partial realisation of or approximation to the ideal as we actually find in human experience.

[5] It may be said that even more divergent views of the reasonable end are possible here than in the case of happiness : for we are not necessarily limited (as in that case) to the consideration of sentient beings : inanimate things also seem to have a perfection and excellence of their own and to be capable of being made better or worse in their kind ; and this perfection, or one species of it, appears to be the end of the Fine Arts. But reflection I think shows that neither beauty nor any other quality of inanimate objects can be regarded as good or desirable in itself, out of relation to the perfection or happiness of sentient beings. Cf. *post*, chap. ix. of this Book.

taken either individually or universally; and circumstances are conceivable in which a man is not unlikely to think that he could best promote the Excellence of others by sacrificing his own. But no moralist who takes Excellence as an ultimate end has ever approved of such sacrifice, at least so far as Moral Excellence is concerned; no one has ever directed an individual to promote the virtue of others except in so far as this promotion is compatible with, or rather involved in, the complete realisation of Virtue in himself.[1] So far, then, there seems to be no need of separating the method of determining right conduct which takes the Excellence or Perfection of the individual as the ultimate aim from that which aims at the Excellence or Perfection of the human community. And since Virtue is commonly conceived as the most valuable element of human Excellence—and an element essentially preferable to any other element that can come into competition with it as an alternative for rational choice—any method which takes Perfection or Excellence of human nature as ultimate End will *prima facie* coincide to a great extent with that based on what I called the Intuitional view: and I have accordingly decided to treat it as a special form of this latter.[2] The two methods which take happiness as an ultimate end it will be convenient to distinguish as Egoistic and Universalistic Hedonism: and as it is the latter of these, as taught by Bentham and his successors, that is more generally understood under the term 'Utilitarianism,' I shall always restrict that word to this signification. For Egoistic Hedonism it is somewhat hard to find a single perfectly appropriate term. I shall often call this simply Egoism: but it may sometimes be convenient to call it Epicureanism: for though this name more properly denotes a particular historical system, it has come to be commonly used in the wider sense in which I wish to employ it.

§ 5. The last sentence suggests one more explanation, which, for clearness' sake, it seems desirable to make: an explanation, however, rather of the plan and purpose of the

---

[1] Kant roundly denies that it can be my duty to take the Perfection of others for my end: but his argument is not, I think, valid. Cf. *post*, Book iii. chap. iv. § 1.

[2] See Book iii. chap. xiv., where I explain my reasons for only giving a subordinate place to the conception of Perfection as Ultimate End.

present treatise than of the nature and boundaries of the subject of Ethics as generally understood.

There are several recognised ways of treating this subject, none of which I have thought it desirable to adopt. We may start with existing systems, and either study them historically, tracing the changes in thought through the centuries, or compare and classify them according to relations of resemblance, or criticise their internal coherence. Or we may seek to add to the number of these systems : and claim after so many unsuccessful efforts to have at last attained the one true theory of the subject, by which all others may be tested. The present book contains neither the exposition of a system nor a natural or critical history of systems. I have attempted to define and unfold not one Method of Ethics, but several : at the same time these are not here studied historically, as methods that have actually been used or proposed for the regulation of practice ; but rather as alternatives between which—so far as they cannot be reconciled—the human mind seems to me necessarily forced to choose, when it attempts to frame a complete synthesis of practical maxims and to act in a perfectly consistent manner. Thus, they might perhaps be called natural methods rationalised ; because men commonly seem to guide themselves by a mixture of different methods, more or less disguised under ambiguities of language. The impulses or principles from which the different methods take their rise, the different claims of different ends to be rational, are admitted, to some extent, by all minds : and as along with these claims is felt the need of harmonising them—since it is, as was said, a postulate of the Practical Reason, that two con-flicting rules of action cannot both be reasonable—the result is ordinarily either a confused blending, or a forced and pre-mature reconciliation, of different principles and methods. Nor have the systems framed by professed moralists been free from similar defects. The writers have usually proceeded to synthesis without adequate analysis; the practical demand for the former being more urgently felt than the theoretical need of the latter. For here as in other points the development of the theory of Ethics would seem to be somewhat impeded by the preponderance of practical considerations; and perhaps a more complete detachment of the theoretical study

of right conduct from its practical application is to be desired
for the sake even of the latter itself: since a treatment which
is a compound between the scientific and the hortatory is apt
to miss both the results that it would combine; the mixture
is bewildering to the brain and not stimulating to the heart.
So again, I am inclined to think that here, as in other
sciences, it would be an advantage to draw as distinct a line
as possible between the known and the unknown; as the clear
indication of an unsolved problem is at any rate a step to its
solution.   In ethical treatises, however, there has been a continual tendency to ignore and keep out of sight the difficulties
of the subject; either unconsciously, from a latent conviction
that the questions which the writer cannot answer satisfactorily must be questions which ought not to be asked; or
consciously, that he may not shake the sway of morality over
the minds of his readers.   This last well-meant precaution
frequently defeats itself: the difficulties thus concealed in
exposition are liable to reappear in controversy: and then
they appear not carefully limited, but magnified for polemical
purposes.   Thus we get on the one hand vague and hazy
reconciliation, on the other loose and random exaggeration of
discrepancies; and neither process is effective to dispel the
original vagueness and ambiguity which lurks in the fundamental notions of our common practical reasonings.   To
eliminate or reduce this indefiniteness and confusion is the
sole immediate end that I have proposed to myself in the
present work.   In order better to execute this task, I have
refrained from expressly attempting any such complete and
final solution of the chief ethical difficulties and controversies
as would convert this exposition of various methods into the
development of a harmonious system.   At the same time I
hope to afford aid towards the construction of such a system;
because it seems easier to judge of the mutual relations and
conflicting claims of different modes of thought, after an
impartial and rigorous investigation of the conclusions to
which they logically lead.   It is not uncommon to find in
reflecting on practical principles, that—however unhesitatingly
they seem to command our assent at first sight, and however
familiar and apparently clear the notions of which they are
composed—nevertheless when we have carefully examined the

consequences of adopting them they wear a changed and somewhat dubious aspect. The truth seems to be that most of the practical principles that have been seriously put forward are more or less satisfactory to the common sense of mankind, so long as they have the field to themselves. They all find a response in our nature : their fundamental assumptions are all such as we are disposed to accept, and such as we find to govern to a certain extent our habitual conduct. When I am asked, "Do you not consider it ultimately reasonable to seek pleasure and avoid pain for yourself ? " " Have you not a moral sense ? " " Do you not intuitively pronounce some actions to be right and others wrong ? " " Do you not acknowledge the general happiness to be a paramount end ? " I answer ' yes ' to all these questions. My difficulty begins when I have to choose between the different principles or inferences drawn from them. We admit the necessity, when they conflict, of making this choice, and that it is irrational to let sometimes one principle prevail and sometimes another ; but the necessity is a painful one. We cannot but hope that all methods may ultimately coincide : and at any rate, before making our election we may reasonably wish to have the completest possible knowledge of each.

My object, then, in the present work, is to expound as clearly and as fully as my limits will allow the different methods of Ethics that I find implicit in our common moral reasoning ; to point out their mutual relations ; and where they seem to conflict, to define the issue as much as possible. In the course of this endeavour I am led to discuss the considerations which should, in my opinion, be decisive in determining the adoption of ethical first principles : but it is not my primary aim to establish such principles ; nor, again, is it my primary aim to supply a set of practical directions for conduct. I have wished to keep the reader's attention throughout directed to the processes rather than the results of ethical thought : and have therefore never stated as my own any positive practical conclusions unless by way of illustration : and have never ventured to decide dogmatically any controverted points, except where the controversy seemed to arise from want of precision or clearness in the definition of principles, or want of consistency in reasoning.

CHAPTER II

THE RELATION OF ETHICS TO POLITICS

§ 1. In the last chapter I have spoken of Ethics and Politics as being both Practical Studies, including in the scope of their investigation somewhat that lies outside the sphere of positive sciences—viz. the determination of ends to be sought, or rules to be unconditionally obeyed. Before proceeding further, it would seem desirable to determine in outline the mutual relations of these cognate studies, regarded from the point of view of Ethics.

As I have defined them, Ethics aims at determining what ought to be done by individuals, while Politics aims at determining what the government of a state or political society ought to do and how it ought to be constituted,—including under the latter head all questions as to the control over government that should be exercised by the governed.

At first sight it may seem that Politics, so conceived, must be a branch of Ethics. For all the actions of government are actions of individuals, alone or in combination, and so are all the actions of those who, obeying, influencing, or perhaps occasionally resisting government, maintain and from time to time modify the constitution of their state: and it would seem that if properly performed such actions must be determined on ethical principles or be capable of justification by such principles. But this argument is not decisive; for by similar reasoning Ethics would have to comprehend all arts, liberal and industrial. *E.g.* it is a main part of the moral duty of a sea-captain and his subordinates to navigate their ship properly; but we do not take Ethics to include a

15

study of the rules of navigation. It may be replied that every man is not a sailor, but—at least in a country under popular government—every citizen has important political duties, which he ought to perform according to knowledge, so far as possible; but, similarly, it is an important part of every adult's moral duty to take care of his health, and it is proverbial that "every man at forty is a fool or his own physician"; yet we do not consider Ethics to include the art of medicine.

The specially important connexion between Ethics and Politics arises in a different way. It is the business of government, by laying down and enforcing laws, to regulate the outward conduct of the governed, not in one department only, but in all their social relations, so far as such conduct is a proper subject for coercive rules. And not only ought this regulation to be in harmony with morality—for obviously people ought not to be compelled to do what they ought not to do—but further, to an important extent the Law of a man's state will properly determine the details of his moral duty, even beyond the sphere of legal enforcement. Thus we commonly regard it as an individual's moral duty, under the head of Justice, to "give every man his own," even when— through some accident—the other party has not the power of legally enforcing his right; but still, in considering what is the other's "own," we assume him generally to be guided by the law of his state; if that were changed, his moral duty would change with it. Similarly, the mutual moral duties of husbands and wives, and of children and parents, will vary in detail with the variations in their legal relations.

But when we look closer at the relation thus constituted between Ethics and Politics, we see that a distinction has to be taken between actual or Positive Law and Ideal Law or Law as it ought to be. It is for the latter that Political Theory lays down principles; but it is Positive, not Ideal, Law that primarily determines right conduct for an individual here and now, in the manner just exemplified. No doubt if Positive and Ideal Law appear to me to diverge very widely —if (*e.g.*) I am convinced by political theory that a fundamental change in the law of property is desirable—this conviction is likely to influence my view of my moral duty under the existing law; but the extent of this influence is vague and uncertain.   Suppose I am a slave-owner in a society in which slavery is established, and become convinced that private property in human beings should be abolished by law: it does not therefore follow that I shall regard it as my moral duty to set free my slaves at once.   I may think immediate general abolition of slavery not only hopeless, but even inexpedient for the slaves themselves, who require a gradual education for freedom: so that it is better for the present to aim at legal changes that would cut off the worst evils of slavery, and meanwhile to set an example of humane and considerate treatment of bondsmen.   Similar reasonings might be applied to the abolition of private property in the instruments of production, or in appointments to offices, civil or ecclesiastical. Speaking generally, the extent to which political ideals ought to influence moral duty would seem to depend partly on the apparent remoteness or nearness of the prospect of realising the ideal, partly on its imperativeness, or the expediency of immediate realisation: and the force attached to both these considerations is likely to vary with the political method adopted; so that it belongs to Politics rather than Ethics to determine them more precisely.

To sum up: we have to distinguish clearly between two questions: (1) how far the determination of right conduct for an individual here and now ought to be influenced by Positive Laws, and other commands of Government as actually established; and (2) how far it ought to be influenced by Political Theory, as to the functions and structure of Government as it ought to be.   As regards the former, it clearly belongs to Ethics to determine the grounds and limits of obedience to Government; and also the general conception of political duty, so far as it goes beyond mere obedience—with due recognition of the large variations due to the varying political conditions of different states.   (A "good citizen" in the United States will reasonably form a conception of his actual political duty widely divergent from that reasonably formed by a good citizen in Russia.[1])   And this will be the primary business of

---

[1] It may be doubted whether the latter ought properly to be termed a "good citizen," and not rather a "faithful subject of the Czar of Russia."   But this doubt only illustrates the divergence to which I am drawing attention.

Ethics so far as it deals with the political side of life. The discussion of political ideals will only come within its purview in a more indefinite and indirect way, so far as such ideals cannot but have some influence on the determination of political duty under existing conditions.

§ 2. I have stated the Relation of Ethics to Politics—regarded from an ethical point of view—that seems to me to accord with the definition of the former subject adopted in the preceding chapter. Some thinkers, however, take a view of Ethical Theory which involves a relation to Political Theory quite different from that just set forth ; regarding Theoretical or "Absolute" Ethics as properly an investigation not of what ought to be done here and now, but of what ought to be the rules of behaviour in a society of ideally perfect human beings. Thus the subject-matter of our study would be doubly ideal: as it would not only prescribe what ought to be done as distinct from what is, but what ought to be done in a society that itself *is* not, but only *ought* to be. In this view the conclusions of Theoretical or "Absolute" Ethics would have as indirect and uncertain a relation to the practical problems of actual life as those of Theoretical Politics :—or even more so, as in sober political theory it is commonly only the government and not the governed society that is conceived in an ideal condition. Still the two studies are not unlikely to blend in one theory of ideal social relations ;—unless the ideal society is conceived as having no need of government, so that Politics, in the ordinary sense,[1] vanishes altogether.

Those who take this view [2] adduce the analogy of Geometry

---

[1] Sometimes, as before observed, Politics appears to be used in a wider sense, to denote the theory of ideal social relations, whether conceived to be established through governmental coercion or otherwise.

[2] In writing this section I had primarily in view the doctrine set forth in Mr. Spencer's *Social Statics*. As Mr. Spencer has restated his view and replied to my arguments in his *Data of Ethics*, it is necessary for me to point out that the first paragraph of this section is not directed against such a view of 'Absolute' and 'Relative' Ethics as is given in the later treatise—which seems to me to differ materially from the doctrine of *Social Statics*. In *Social Statics* it is maintained not merely—as in the *Data of Ethics*—that Absolute Ethics which "formulates normal conduct in an ideal society" ought to "take precedence of Relative Ethics" ; but that Absolute Ethics is the only kind of Ethics with which a philosophical moralist can possibly concern himself. To quote Mr.

to show that Ethics ought to deal with ideally perfect human relations, just as Geometry treats of ideally straight lines and perfect circles.   But the irregular lines which we meet with in experience have spatial relations which Geometry does not ignore altogether ; it can and does ascertain them with a sufficient degree of accuracy for practical purposes : though of course they are more complex than those of perfectly straight lines.   So in Astronomy, it would be more convenient for purposes of study if the stars moved in circles, as was once believed : but the fact that they move not in circles but in ellipses, and even in imperfect and perturbed ellipses, does not take them out of the sphere of scientific investigation : by patience and industry we have learnt how to reduce to principles and calculate even these more complicated motions. It may be useful for purposes of instruction to assume that the planets move in perfect ellipses : but what we want, as astronomers, to know is the actual motion of the stars, and its causes : and similarly as moralists we naturally inquire what ought to be done in the actual world in which we live. In neither case can we hope to represent in our general reasonings the full complexity of the actual considerations : but we endeavour to approximate to it as closely as possible.   It is only so that we really grapple with the question to which mankind generally require an answer : ' What is a man's duty in his present condition ? '   For it is too paradoxical to say that the whole duty of man is summed up in the effort to attain an ideal state of social relations ; and unless we say this, we must determine our duties to existing men in view of

Spencer's words :—" Any proposed system of morals which recognises existing defects, and countenances acts made needful by them, stands self-condemned. . . . Moral law . . . requires as its postulate that human beings be perfect.   The philosophical moralist treats solely of the *straight* man . . . shows in what relationship he stands to other straight men . . . a problem in which a *crooked* man forms one of the elements, is insoluble by him."   *Social Statics* (chap. i.). Still more definitely is Relative Ethics excluded in the following passage of the concluding chapter of the same treatise (the italics are mine) :—" It will very likely be urged that, whereas the perfect moral code is confessedly beyond the fulfilment of imperfect men, some other code is needful for our present guidance . . . to say that the imperfect man requires a moral code which recognises his imperfection and allows for it, *seems at first sight reasonable.   But it is not really so* . . . a system of morals which shall recognise man's present imperfections and allow for them *cannot be devised ; and would be useless if it could be devised.*"

existing circumstances : and this is what the student of Ethics seeks to do in a systematic manner.

The inquiry into the morality of an ideal society can therefore be at best but a preliminary investigation, after which the step from the ideal to the actual, in accordance with reason, remains to be taken. We have to ask, then, how far such a preliminary construction seems desirable. And in answering this we must distinguish the different methods of Ethics. For it is generally held by Intuitionists that true morality prescribes absolutely what is in itself right, under all social conditions; at least as far as determinate duties are concerned : as (*e.g.*) that truth should always be spoken and promises kept, and ' Justice be done, though the sky should fall.' And so far as this is held it would seem that there can be no fundamental distinction drawn, in the determination of duty, between the actual state of society and an ideal state : at any rate the general definition of (*e.g.*) Justice will be the same for both, no less than its absolute stringency. Still even an extreme Intuitionist would admit that the details of Justice and other duties will vary with social institutions : and it is a plausible suggestion, that if we can clearly contemplate as a pattern the " absolute " Justice of an ideal community, we shall be better able to attain the merely " relative " Justice that is alone possible under existing conditions. How far this is so, we shall be in a better position to judge when we have examined the definition of Justice from an Intuitional point of view.

The question takes a simpler form in the case of the method which proposes as an ultimate end, and supreme standard, Universal Happiness.[1] Here we have merely to ask how far a systematic consideration of the social relations of an ideally happy group of human beings is likely to afford guidance in our efforts to promote human happiness here and now. I shall not at present deny that this task might usefully be included in an exhaustive study of this method.

---

[1] I omit, for the present, the consideration of the method which takes Perfection as an ultimate end : since, as has been before observed, it is hardly possible to discuss this satisfactorily, in relation to the present question, until it has been somewhat more clearly distinguished from the ordinary Intuitional Method.

But it can easily be shown that it is involved in serious difficulties.

For as in ordinary deliberation we have to consider what is best under certain conditions of human life, internal or external, so we must do this in contemplating the ideal society. We require to contemplate not so much the end supposed to be attained—which is simply the most pleasant consciousness conceivable, lasting as long and as uninterruptedly as possible —but rather some method of realising it, pursued by human beings ; and these, again, must be conceived as existing under conditions not too remote from our own, so that we can at least endeavour to imitate them.   And for this we must know how far our present circumstances are modifiable ; a very difficult question, as the constructions which have actually been made of such ideal societies show.   For example, the *Republic* of Plato seems in many respects sufficiently divergent from the reality, and yet he contemplates war as a permanent unalterable fact, to be provided for in the ideal state, and indeed such provision seems the predominant aim of his construction ; whereas the soberest modern Utopia would certainly include the suppression of war.   Indeed the ideal will often seem to diverge in diametrically opposite directions from the actual, according to the line of imagined change which we happen to adopt, in our visionary flight from present evils. For example, permanent marriage-unions now cause some unhappiness, because conjugal affection is not always permanent ; but they are thought to be necessary, partly to protect men and women from vagaries of passion pernicious to themselves, but chiefly in order to the better rearing of children. Now it may seem to some that in an ideal state of society we could trust more to parental affections, and require less to control the natural play of emotion between the sexes, and that ' Free Love ' is therefore the ideal ; while others would maintain that permanence in conjugal affection is natural and normal, and that any exceptions to this rule must be supposed to disappear as we approximate to the ideal.   Again, the happiness enjoyed in our actual society seems much diminished by the unequal distribution of the means of happiness, and the division of mankind into rich and poor.   But we can conceive this evil removed in two quite different ways : either by an increased disposition on the part of the rich to redistribute their share, or by such social arrangements as would enable the poor to secure more for themselves. In the one case the ideal involves a great extension and systematisation of the arbitrary and casual almsgiving that now goes on : in the other case, its extinction.

In short, it seems that when we abandon the firm ground of actual society we have an illimitable cloudland surrounding us on all sides, in which we may construct any variety of pattern states ; but no definite ideal to which the actual undeniably approximates, as the straight lines and circles of the actual physical world approximate to those of scientific geometry.

It may be said, however, that we can reduce this variety by studying the past history of mankind, as this will enable us to predict to some extent their future manner of existence. But even so it does not appear that we shall gain much definite guidance for our present conduct. For let us make the most favourable suppositions that we can, and such as soar even above the confidence of the most dogmatic of scientific historians. Let us assume that the process of human history is a progress of mankind towards ever greater happiness. Let us assume further that we can not only fix certain limits within which the future social condition of mankind must lie, but even determine in detail the mutual relations of the different elements of the future community, so as to view in clear outline the rules of behaviour, by observing which they will attain the maximum of happiness. It still remains quite doubtful how far it would be desirable for us to imitate these rules in the circumstances in which we now live. For this foreknown social order is *ex hypothesi* only presented as a more advanced stage in our social progress, and not as a. type or pattern which we ought to make a struggle to realise approximately at an earlier stage. How far it should be taken as such a pattern, is a question which would still have to be determined, and in the consideration of it the effects of our actions on the existing generation would after all be the most important element.[1]

[1] Some further consideration of this question will be found in a subsequent chapter. Cf. Book iv. chap. iv. § 2.

CHAPTER III

§ **1.** IN the first chapter I spoke of actions that we judge to be right and what ought to be done as being "reasonable," or "rational," and similarly of ultimate ends as "prescribed by Reason": and I contrasted the motive to action supplied by the recognition of such reasonableness with "non-rational" desires and inclinations. This manner of speaking is employed by writers of different schools, and seems in accordance with the common view and language on the subject. For we commonly think that wrong conduct is essentially irrational, and can be shown to be so by argument; and though we do not conceive that it is by reason alone that men are influenced to act rightly, we still hold that appeals to the reason are an essential part of all moral persuasion, and that part which concerns the moralist or moral philosopher as distinct from the preacher or moral rhetorician. On the other hand it is widely maintained that, as Hume says, "Reason, meaning the judgment of truth and falsehood, can never of itself be any motive to the Will"; and that the motive to action is in all cases some Non-rational Desire, including under this term the impulses to action given by present pleasure and pain. It seems desirable to examine with some care the grounds of this contention before we proceed any further.

Let us begin by defining the issue raised as clearly as possible. Every one, I suppose, has had experience of what is meant by the conflict of non-rational or irrational desires with reason : most of us (*e.g.*) occasionally feel bodily appetite prompting us to indulgences which we judge to be imprudent, and anger prompting us to acts which we disapprove as unjust or unkind. It is when this conflict occurs that the desires are said to be irrational, as impelling us to volitions opposed to our deliberate judgments; sometimes we yield to such seductive impulses, and sometimes not; and it is perhaps when we do *not* yield that the impulsive force of such irrational desires is most definitely felt, as we have to exert in resisting them a voluntary effort somewhat analogous to that involved in any muscular exertion. Often, again,—since we are not always thinking either of our duty or of our interest, —desires of this kind take effect in voluntary actions without our having judged such actions to be either right or wrong, either prudent or imprudent; as (*e.g.*) when an ordinary healthy man eats his dinner. In such cases it seems most appropriate to call the desires " non-rational " rather than " irrational." Neither term is intended to imply that the desires spoken of—or at least the more important of them— are not normally accompanied by intellectual processes. It is true that some impulses to action seem to take effect, as we say " blindly " or " instinctively," without any definite consciousness either of the end at which the action is aimed, or of the means by which the end is to be attained: but this, I conceive, is only the case with impulses that do not occupy consciousness for an appreciable time, and ordinarily do not require any but very familiar and habitual actions for the attainment of their proximate ends. In all other cases—that is, in the case of the actions with which we are chiefly concerned in ethical discussion—the result aimed at, and some part at least of the means by which it is to be realised, are more or less distinctly represented in consciousness, previous to the volition that initiates the movements tending to its realisation. Hence the resultant forces of what I call " non-rational " desires, and the volitions to which they prompt, are continually modified by intellectual processes in two distinct ways; first by new perceptions or representations of means conducive to the desired ends, and secondly by new presentations or representations of facts actually existing or in prospect—especially more or less probable consequences of contemplated actions—which rouse new impulses of desire and aversion.

The question, then, is whether the account just given of the influence of the intellect on desire and volition is not exhaustive; and whether the experience which is commonly described as a "conflict of desire with reason" is not more properly conceived as merely a conflict among desires and aversions; the sole function of reason being to bring before the mind ideas of actual or possible facts, which modify in the manner above described the resultant force of our various impulses.

I hold that this is not the case; that the ordinary moral or prudential judgments which, in the case of all or most minds, have some—though often an inadequate—influence on volition, cannot legitimately be interpreted as judgments respecting the present or future existence of human feelings or any facts of the sensible world; the fundamental notion represented by the word "ought" or "right,"[1] which such judgments contain expressly or by implication, being essentially different from all notions representing facts of physical or psychical experience. The question is one on which appeal must ultimately be made to the reflection of individuals on their practical judgments and reasonings: and in making this appeal it seems most convenient to begin by showing the inadequacy of all attempts to explain the practical judgments or propositions in which this fundamental notion is introduced, without recognising its unique character as above negatively defined. There is an element of truth in such explanations, in so far as they bring into view feelings which undoubtedly accompany moral or prudential judgments, and which ordinarily have more or less effect in determining the will to actions judged to be right; but so far as they profess to be interpretations of what such judgments mean, they appear to me to fail altogether.

In considering this question it is important to take separately the two species of judgments which I have distinguished as "moral" and "prudential." Both kinds might, indeed, be termed "moral" in a wider sense; and, as we saw, it is a strongly supported opinion that all valid moral rules have ultimately a prudential basis. But in ordinary thought we clearly distinguish cognitions or judgments of duty from

---

[1] The difference between the significations of the two words is discussed later.

cognitions or judgments as to what "is right" or "ought to be done" in view of the agent's private interest or happiness: and the depth of the distinction will not, I think, be diminished by the closer examination of these judgments on which we are now to enter.

This very distinction, however, suggests an interpretation of the notion of rightness which denies its peculiar significance in moral judgments. It is urged that "rightness" is properly an attribute of means, not of ends: so that the attribution of it merely implies that the act judged right is the fittest or only fit means to the realisation of some end understood if not expressly stated: and similarly that the affirmation that anything 'ought to be done' is always made with at least tacit reference to some ulterior end. And I grant that this is a legitimate interpretation, in respect of a part of the use of either term in ordinary discourse. But it seems clear (1) that certain kinds of actions—under the names of Justice, Veracity, Good Faith, etc.—are commonly held to be right unconditionally, without regard to ulterior results: and (2) that we similarly regard as "right" the adoption of certain ends—such as the common good of society, or general happiness. In either of these cases the interpretation above suggested seems clearly inadmissible.[1]

We have therefore to find a meaning for "right" or "what ought to be" other than the notion of fitness to some ulterior end. Here we are met by the suggestion that the judgments or propositions which we commonly call moral—in the narrower sense—really affirm no more than the existence of a specific emotion in the mind of the person who utters them; that when I say 'Truth ought to be spoken' or 'Truthspeaking is right,' I mean no more than that the idea of truthspeaking excites in my mind a feeling of approbation

---

[1] As, for instance, when Bentham explains (*Principles of Morals and Legislation*, chap. i. § i. note) that his fundamental principle "states the greatest happiness of all those whose interest is in question as being the right and proper end of human action," we cannot understand him really to *mean* by the word "right" "conducive to the general happiness," though his language in other passages of the same chapter (§§ ix. and x.) would seem to imply this; for the proposition that it is conducive to general happiness to take general happiness as an end of action, though not exactly a tautology, can hardly serve as the fundamental principle of a moral system.

or satisfaction. And probably some degree of such emotion, commonly distinguished as 'moral sentiment,' ordinarily accompanies moral judgments on real cases. But it is absurd to say that a mere statement of my approbation of truth-speaking is properly given in the proposition 'Truth ought to be spoken'; otherwise the fact of another man's disapproba-tion might equally be expressed by saying 'Truth ought not to be spoken'; and thus we should have two coexistent facts stated in two mutually contradictory propositions. This is so obvious, that we must suppose that those who hold the view which I am combating do not really intend to deny it: but rather to maintain that this subjective fact of my approbation is all that there is any *ground* for stating, or perhaps that it is all that any reasonable person is prepared on reflection to affirm. And no doubt there is a large class of statements, in form objective, which yet we are not commonly prepared to maintain as more than subjective if their validity is ques-tioned. If I say that 'the air is sweet,' or 'the food dis-agreeable,' it would not be exactly true to say that I mean no more than that I like the one or dislike the other: but if my statement is challenged, I shall probably content myself with affirming the existence of such feelings in my own mind. But there appears to me to be a fundamental difference between this case and that of moral feelings. The peculiar emotion of moral approbation is, in my experience, insepar-ably bound up with the conviction, implicit or explicit, that the conduct approved is 'really' right—*i.e.* that it cannot, without error, be disapproved by any other mind. If I give up this conviction because others do not share it, or for any other reason, I may no doubt still retain a sentiment prompt-ing to the conduct in question, or—what is perhaps more common—a sentiment of repugnance to the opposite conduct: but this sentiment will no longer have the special quality of 'moral sentiment' strictly so called. This difference between the two is often overlooked in ethical discussion: but any experience of a change in moral opinion produced by argument may afford an illustration of it. Suppose (*e.g.*) that any one habitually influenced by the sentiment of Veracity is convinced that under certain peculiar circumstances in which he finds himself, speaking truth is not right but wrong. He will probably still feel a repugnance against violating the rule of truthspeaking: but it will be a feeling quite different in kind and degree from that which prompted him to veracity as a department of virtuous action. We might perhaps call the one a 'moral' and the other a 'quasi-moral' sentiment.

The argument just given holds equally against the view that approbation or disapprobation is not the mere liking or aversion of an individual for certain kinds of conduct, but this complicated by a sympathetic representation of similar likings or aversions felt by other human beings. No doubt such sympathy is a normal concomitant of moral emotion, and when the former is absent there is much greater difficulty in maintaining the latter: this, however, is partly because our moral beliefs commonly agree with those of other members of our society, and on this agreement depends to an important extent our confidence in the truth of these beliefs.[1] But if, as in the case just supposed, we are really led by argument to a new moral belief, opposed not only to our own habitual sentiment but also to that of the society in which we live, we have a crucial experiment proving the existence in us of moral sentiments as I have defined them, colliding with the represented sympathies of our fellow-men no less than with our own mere likings and aversions. And even if we imagine the sympathies opposed to our convictions extended until they include those of the whole human race, against whom we imagine ourselves to stand as *Athanasius contra mundum;* still, so long as our conviction of duty is firm, the emotion which we call moral stands out in imagination quite distinct from the complex sympathy opposed to it, however much we extend, complicate and intensify the latter.

§ 2. So far, then, from being prepared to admit that the proposition 'X ought to be done' *merely* expresses the existence of a certain sentiment in myself or others, I find it strictly impossible so to regard my own moral judgments without eliminating from the concomitant sentiment the peculiar quality signified by the term 'moral.' There is, however, another interpretation of 'ought,' in which the likings and aversions that men in general feel for certain kinds of conduct are considered not as sympathetically represented in the

---

[1] See Book iii. chap. xi. § 1.

emotion of the person judging, and thus constituting the moral element in it, but as causes of pain to the person of whom 'ought' or 'duty' is predicated. On this view, when we say that a man 'ought' to do anything, or that it is his 'duty' to do it, we mean that he is bound under penalties to do it; the particular penalty considered being the pain that will accrue to him directly or indirectly from the dislike of his fellow-creatures.

I think that this interpretation expresses a part of the meaning with which the words 'ought' and 'duty' are used in ordinary thought and discourse. For we commonly use the term 'moral obligation' as equivalent to 'duty' and expressing what is implied in the verb 'ought,' thus suggesting an analogy between this notion and that of legal obligation; and in the case of positive law we cannot refuse to recognise the connexion of 'obligation' and 'punishment': a law cannot be properly said to be actually established in a society if it is habitually violated with impunity. But a more careful reflection on the relation of Law to Morality, as ordinarily conceived, seems to show that this interpretation of 'ought'—though it cannot be excluded—must be distinguished from the special ethical use of the term. For the ideal distinction taken in common thought between legal and merely moral rules seems to lie in just this connexion of the former but not the latter with punishment: we think that there are some things which a man ought to be compelled to do, or forbear, and others which he ought to do or forbear without compulsion, and that the former alone fall properly within the sphere of law. No doubt we also think that in many cases where the compulsion of law is undesirable, the fear of moral censure and its consequences supplies a normally useful constraint on the will of any individual. But it is evident that what we mean when we say that a man is "morally though not legally bound" to do a thing is not merely that he "will be punished by public opinion if he does not"; for we often join these two statements, clearly distinguishing their import: and further (since public opinion is known to be eminently fallible) there are many things which we judge men 'ought' to do, while perfectly aware that they will incur no serious social penalties for omitting them. In such cases, indeed, it would be commonly said that social disapprobation 'ought' to follow on immoral conduct; and in this very assertion it is clear that the term 'ought' cannot mean that social penalties are to be feared by those who do not disapprove. Again, all or most men in whom the moral consciousness is strongly developed find themselves from time to time in conflict with the commonly received morality of the society to which they belong: and thus—as was before said— have a crucial experience proving that duty does not mean *to them* what other men will disapprove of them for not doing.

At the same time I admit, as indeed I have already suggested in § 3 of chap. i., that we not unfrequently pass judgments resembling moral judgments in form, and not distinguished from them in ordinary thought, in cases where the obligation affirmed is found, on reflection, to depend on the existence of current opinions and sentiments as such. The members of modern civilised societies are under the sway of a code of Public Opinion, enforced by social penalties, which no reflective person obeying it identifies with the moral code, or regards as unconditionally binding: indeed the code is manifestly fluctuating and variable, different at the same time in different classes, professions, social circles, of the same political community. Such a code always supports to a considerable extent the commonly received code of morality: and most reflective persons think it generally reasonable to conform to the dictates of public opinion—to the code of Honour, we may say, in graver matters, or the rules of Politeness or Good Breeding in lighter matters—wherever these dictates do not positively conflict with morality; such conformity being maintained either on grounds of private interest, or because it is thought conducive to general happiness or wellbeing to keep as much as possible in harmony with one's fellow-men. Hence in the ordinary thought of unreflective persons the duties imposed by social opinion are often undistinguished from moral duties: and indeed this indistinctness is almost inherent in the common meaning of many terms. For instance, if we say that a man has been 'dishonoured' by a cowardly act, it is not quite clear whether we mean that he has incurred contempt, or that he has deserved it, or both: as becomes evident when we take a case in which the Code of Honour comes into conflict with

Morality.   If (*e.g.*) a man were to incur social ostracism anywhere for refusing a duel on religious grounds, some would say that he was 'dishonoured,' though he had acted rightly, others that there could be no real dishonour in a virtuous act.   A similar ambiguity seems to lurk in the common notion of 'improper' or 'incorrect' behaviour.   Still in all such cases the ambiguity becomes evident on reflection : and when discovered, merely serves to illustrate further the distinction between the notion of 'right conduct,' 'duty,' what we 'ought' or are under 'moral obligation' to do—when these terms are used in a strictly ethical sense—and conduct that is merely conformed to the standard of current opinion.

There is, however, another way of interpreting 'ought' as connoting penalties, which is somewhat less easy to meet by a crucial psychological experiment.   The moral imperative may be taken to be a law of God, to the breach of which Divine penalties are annexed; and these, no doubt, in a Christian society, are commonly conceived to be adequate and universally applicable.   Still, it can hardly be said that this belief is shared by all the persons whose conduct is influenced by independent moral convictions, occasionally unsupported either by the law or the public opinion of their community.   And even in the case of many of those who believe fully in the moral government of the world, the judgment " I ought to do this" cannot be identified with the judgment " God will punish me if I do not "; since the conviction that the former proposition is true is distinctly recognised as an important part of the grounds for believing the latter.   Again, when Christians speak —as they commonly do—of the 'justice' (or other moral attributes) of God, as exhibited in punishing sinners and rewarding the righteous, they obviously imply not merely that God *will* thus punish and reward, but that it is 'right'[1] for Him to do so: which, of course, cannot be taken to mean that He is 'bound under penalties.'

§ 3.   It seems then that the notion of 'ought' or 'moral obligation' as used in our common moral judgments, does not merely import (1) that there exists in the mind of the person judging a specific emotion (whether complicated or not by sympathetic representation of similar emotions in other minds);

---

[1] 'Ought' is here inapplicable, for a reason presently explained.

nor (2) that certain rules of conduct are supported by penalties which will follow on their violation (whether such penalties result from the general liking or aversion felt for the conduct prescribed or forbidden, or from some other source). What then, it may be asked, does it import ? What definition can we give of ' ought,' ' right,' and other terms expressing the same fundamental notion ? To this I should answer that the notion which these terms have in common is too elementary to admit of any formal definition. In so saying, I do not mean to imply that it belongs to the " original constitution of the mind "; *i.e.* that its presence in consciousness is not the result of a process of development. I do not doubt that the whole fabric of human thought—including the conceptions that present themselves as most simple and elementary—has been developed, through a gradual process of psychical change, out of some lower life in which thought, properly speaking, had no place. But it is not therefore to be inferred, as regards this or any other notion, that it has not really the simplicity which it appears to have when we now reflect upon it. It is some-times assumed that if we can show how thoughts have grown up—if we can point to the psychical antecedents of which they are the natural consequents—we may conclude that the thoughts in question are really compounds containing their antecedents as latent elements. But I know no justification for this trans-ference of the conceptions of chemistry to psychology ; [1] I know no reason for considering psychical antecedents as really con-stitutive of their psychical consequents, in spite of the apparent dissimilarity between the two. In default of such reasons, a psychologist must accept as elementary what introspection carefully performed declares to be so ; and, using this criterion, I find that the notion we have been examining, as it now exists in our thought, cannot be resolved into any more

---

[1] In Chemistry we regard the antecedents (elements) as still existing in and constituting the consequent (compound) because the latter is exactly similar to the former in weight, and because we can generally cause this compound to disappear and obtain the elements in its place. But we find nothing at all like this in the growth of mental phenomena : the psychical consequent is in no respect exactly similar to its antecedents, nor can it be resolved into them. I should explain that I am not here arguing the question whether the *validity* of moral judgments is affected by a discovery of their psychical antecedents. This question I reserve for subsequent discussion. See Book iii. chap. i. § 4.

simple notions : it can only be made clearer by determining as precisely as possible its relation to other notions with which it is connected in ordinary thought, especially to those with which it is liable to be confounded.

In performing this process it is important to note and distinguish two different implications with which the word "ought" is used; in the narrowest ethical sense what we judge 'ought to be' done, is always thought capable of being brought about by the volition of any individual to whom the judgment applies. I cannot conceive that I 'ought' to do anything which at the same time I judge that I cannot do. In a wider sense, however,—which cannot conveniently be discarded—I sometimes judge that I 'ought' to know what a wiser man would know, or feel as a better man would feel, in my place, though I may know that I could not directly produce in myself such knowledge or feeling by any effort of will. In this case the word merely implies an ideal or pattern which I 'ought'—in the stricter sense—to seek to imitate as far as possible.   And this wider sense seems to be that in which the word is normally used in the precepts of Art generally, and in political judgments : when I judge that the laws and constitution of my country 'ought to be' other than they are, I do not of course imply that my own or any other individual's single volition can directly bring about the change.[1]   In either case, however, I imply that what ought to be is a possible object of knowledge : *i.e.* that what I judge ought to be must, unless I am in error, be similarly judged by all rational beings who judge truly of the matter.

In referring such judgments to the ' Reason,' I do not mean here to prejudge the question whether valid moral judgments are normally attained by a process of reasoning from universal principles or axioms, or by direct intuition of the particular duties of individuals.   It is not uncommonly held that the moral faculty deals primarily with individual cases as they arise, applying directly to each case the general notion of

---

[1] I do not even imply that any combination of individuals could completely realise the state of political relations which I conceive ' ought to ' exist.   My conception would be futile if it had no relation to practice : but it may merely delineate a pattern to which no more than an approximation is practically possible.

duty, and deciding intuitively what ought to be done by this person in these particular circumstances. And I admit that on this view the apprehension of moral truth is more analogous to Sense-perception than to Rational Intuition (as commonly understood) :[1] and hence the term Moral Sense might seem more appropriate. But the term Sense suggests a capacity for feelings which may vary from A to B without either being in error, rather than a faculty of cognition :[2] and it appears to me fundamentally important to avoid this suggestion. I have therefore thought it better to use the term Reason with the explanation above given, to denote the faculty of moral cognition :[3] adding, as a further justification of this use, that even when a moral judgment relates primarily to some particular action we commonly regard it as applicable to any other action belonging to a certain definable class : so that the moral truth apprehended is implicitly conceived to be intrinsically universal, though particular in our first apprehension of it.

Further, when I speak of the cognition or judgment that ' X ought to be done '—in the stricter ethical sense of the term ought [4]—as a ' dictate ' or ' precept ' of reason to the persons to whom it relates, I imply that in rational beings as such this cognition gives an impulse or motive to action : though in human beings, of course, this is only one motive among others which are liable to conflict with it, and is not always—perhaps not usually—a predominant motive. In fact, this possible conflict of motives seems to be connoted by the term ' dictate ' or ' imperative,' which describes the relation of Reason to mere inclinations or non-rational impulses by comparing it to the

[1] We do not commonly say that particular physical facts are apprehended by the Reason : we consider this faculty to be conversant in its discursive operation with the relation of judgments or propositions : and the intuitive reason (which is here rather in question) we restrict to the apprehension of universal truths, such as the axioms of Logic and Mathematics.

[2] By cognition I always mean what some would rather call " apparent cognition "—that is, I do not mean to affirm the *validity* of the cognition, but only its existence as a psychical fact, and its claim to be valid.

[3] A further justification for this extended use of the term Reason will be suggested in a subsequent chapter of this Book (chap. viii. § 3).

[4] This is the sense in which the term will always be used in the present treatise, except where the context makes it quite clear that only the wider meaning—that of the political ' ought '—is applicable.

relation between the will of a superior and the wills of his subordinates. This conflict seems also to be implied in the terms 'ought,' 'duty,' 'moral obligation,' as used in ordinary moral discourse : and hence these terms cannot be applied to the actions of rational beings to whom we cannot attribute impulses conflicting with reason. We may, however, say of such beings that their actions are 'reasonable,' or (in an absolute sense) 'right.'

§ 4. I am aware that some persons will be disposed to answer all the preceding argument by a simple denial that they can find in their consciousness any such unconditional or categorical imperative as I have been trying to exhibit. If this is really the final result of self-examination in any case, there is no more to be said. I, at least, do not know how to impart the notion of moral obligation to any one who is entirely devoid of it. I think, however, that many of those who give this denial only mean to deny that they have any consciousness of moral obligation to actions without reference to their consequences ; and would not really deny that they recognise some universal end or ends—whether it be the general happiness, or well-being otherwise understood—as that at which it is ultimately reasonable to aim, subordinating to its attainment the gratification of any personal desires that may conflict with this aim. But in this view, as I have before said, the unconditional imperative plainly comes in as regards the end, which is— explicitly or implicitly—recognised as an end at which all men 'ought' to aim ; and it can hardly be denied that the recognition of an end as ultimately reasonable involves the recognition of an obligation to do such acts as most conduce to the end. The obligation is not indeed " unconditional," but it does not depend on the existence of any non-rational desires or aversions. And nothing that has been said in the preceding section is intended as an argument in favour of Intuitionism, as against Utilitarianism or any other method that treats moral rules as relative to General Good or Well-being. For instance, nothing that I have said is inconsistent with the view that Truthspeaking is only valuable as a means to the preservation of society : only if it be admitted that it *is* valuable on this ground I should say that it is implied that the preservation of society—or some further end to which this preservation, again, is a means—must be valuable *per se*, and therefore something at which a rational being, as such, ought to aim. If it be granted that we need not look beyond the preservation of society, the primary 'dictate of reason' in this case would be 'that society *ought* to be preserved': but reason would also dictate that truth ought to be spoken, so far as truthspeaking is recognised as the indispensable or fittest means to this end: and the notion "ought" as used in either dictate is that which I have been trying to make clear.

So again, even those who hold that moral rules are only obligatory because it is the individual's interest to conform to them—thus regarding them as a particular species of prudential rules—do not thereby get rid of the 'dictate of reason,' so far as they recognise private interest or happiness as an end at which it is ultimately reasonable to aim. The conflict of Practical Reason with irrational desire remains an indubitable fact of our conscious experience, even if practical reason is interpreted to mean merely self-regarding Prudence. It is, indeed, maintained by Kant and others that it cannot properly be said to be a man's duty to promote his own happiness; since "what every one inevitably wills cannot be brought under the notion of duty." But even granting [1] it to be in some sense true that a man's volition is always directed to the attainment of his own happiness, it does not follow that a man always does what he believes will be conducive to his own *greatest* happiness. As Butler urges, it is a matter of common experience that men indulge appetite or passion even when, in their own view, the indulgence is as clearly opposed to what they conceive to be their interest as it is to what they conceive to be their duty. Thus the notion 'ought'—as expressing the relation of rational judgment to non-rational impulses—will find a place in the practical rules of any egoistic system, no less than in the rules of ordinary morality, understood as prescribing duty without reference to the agent's interest.

Here, however, it may be held that Egoism does not properly regard the agent's own greatest happiness as what he "ought" to aim at: but only as the ultimate end for the realisation of which he has, on the whole, a predominant desire; which may be temporarily overcome by particular

---

[1] As will be seen from the next chapter, I do not grant this.

passions and appetites, but ordinarily regains its predominance when these transient impulses have spent their force.
I quite recognise that this is a view widely taken of egoistic action, and I propose to consider it in a subsequent
chapter.[1] But even if we discard the belief, that any end of
action is unconditionally or "categorically" prescribed by
reason, the notion 'ought' as above explained is not thereby
eliminated from our practical reasonings : it still remains in
the "hypothetical imperative" which prescribes the fittest
means to any end that we may have determined to aim at.
When (e.g.) a physician says, "If you wish to be healthy you
ought to rise early," this is not the same thing as saying
"early rising is an indispensable condition of the attainment
of health." This latter proposition expresses the relation of
physiological facts on which the former is founded; but it is
not merely this relation of facts that the word 'ought' imports : it also implies the unreasonableness of adopting an
end and refusing to adopt the means indispensable to its
attainment. It may perhaps be argued that this is not
only unreasonable but impossible : since adoption of an end
means the preponderance of a desire for it, and if aversion to
the indispensable means causes them not to be adopted
although recognised as indispensable, the desire for the end
is *not* preponderant and it ceases to be adopted. But this
view is due, in my opinion, to a defective psychological
analysis. According to my observation of consciousness, the
adoption of an end as paramount—either absolutely or within
certain limits—is quite a distinct psychical phenomenon from
desire : it is a kind of volition, though it is, of course,
specifically different from a volition initiating a particular immediate action. As a species intermediate between the two,
we may place resolutions to act in a certain way at some future
time : we continually make such resolutions, and sometimes
when the time comes for carrying them out, we do in fact act
otherwise under the influence of passion or mere habit, without
consciously cancelling our previous resolve. This inconsistency
of will our practical reason condemns as irrational, even
apart from any judgment of approbation or disapprobation
on either volition considered by itself. There is a similar

[1] Chap. ix. of this Book.

inconsistency between the adoption of an end and a general refusal to take whatever means we may see to be indispensable to its attainment: and if, when the time comes, we do not take such means while yet we do not consciously retract our adoption of the end, it can hardly be denied that we 'ought' in consistency to act otherwise than we do. And such a contradiction as I have described, between a general resolution and a particular volition, is surely a matter of common experience.

CHAPTER IV

PLEASURE AND DESIRE

§ 1. In the preceding chapter I have left undetermined the emotional characteristics of the impulse that prompts us to obey the dictates of Reason. I have done so because these seem to be very different in different minds, and even to vary much and rapidly in the same mind, without any corresponding variation in the volitional direction of the impulse. For instance, in the mind of a rational Egoist the ruling impulse is generally what Butler and Hutcheson call a "calm" or "cool" self-love: whereas in the man who takes universal happiness as the end and standard of right conduct, the desire to do what is judged to be reasonable as such is commonly blended in varying degrees with sympathy and philanthropic enthusiasm. Again, if one conceives the dictating Reason—whatever its dictates may be—as external to oneself, the cognition of rightness is accompanied by a sentiment of Reverence for Authority; which may by some be conceived impersonally, but is more commonly regarded as the authority of a supreme Person, so that the sentiment blends with the affections normally excited by persons in different relations, and becomes Religious. This conception of Reason as an external authority, against which the self-will rebels, is often irresistibly forced on the reflective mind: at other times, however, the identity of Reason and Self presents itself as an immediate conviction, and then Reverence for Authority passes over into Self-respect; and the opposite and even more powerful sentiment of Freedom is called in, if we consider the rational Self as liable to be enslaved by the usurping force of

39

sensual impulses. Quite different again are the emotions of Aspiration or Admiration aroused by the conception of Virtue as an ideal of Moral Beauty.[1]   Other phases of emotion might be mentioned, all having with these the common characteristic that they are inseparable from an apparent cognition—implicit or explicit, direct or indirect—of *rightness* in the conduct to which they prompt.   There are, no doubt, important differences in the moral value and efficacy of these different emotions, to which I shall hereafter call attention; but their primary practical effect does not appear to vary so long as the cognition of rightness remains unchanged.   It is then with these cognitions that Ethics, in my view, is primarily concerned: its object is to free them from doubt and error, and systematise them as far as possible.

There is, however, one view of the feelings which prompt to voluntary action, which is sometimes thought to cut short all controversy as to the principles on which such action ought to be regulated.   I mean the view that volition is always determined by pleasures or pains actual or prospective.   This doctrine—which I may distinguish as Psychological Hedonism —is often connected and not seldom confounded with the method of Ethics which I have called Egoistic Hedonism; and no doubt it seems at first sight a natural inference that if one end of action—my own pleasure or absence of pain—is definitely determined for me by unvarying psychological laws, a different end cannot be prescribed for me by Reason.

Reflection, however, shows that this inference involves the unwarranted assumption that a man's pleasure and pain are determined independently of his moral judgments: whereas it is manifestly possible that our prospect of pleasure resulting from any course of conduct may largely depend on our conception of it as right or otherwise: and in fact the psychological theory above mentioned would require us to suppose that this is normally the case with conscientious persons, who habitually act in accordance with their moral convictions.   The connexion of the expectation of pleasure from an act with the judgment that it is right may be different in different cases: we commonly conceive a truly moral man as one who finds pleasure

---

[1] The relation of the æsthetic to the moral ideal of conduct will be discussed in a subsequent chapter (ix.) of this Book.

in doing what he judges to be right because he so judges it : but, even where moral sensibility is weak, expectation of pleasure from an act may be a necessary consequent of a judgment that it is right, through a belief in the moral government of the world somehow harmonising Virtue and Self-interest.

I therefore conclude that there is no necessary connexion between the psychological proposition that pleasure or absence of pain to myself is always the actual ultimate end of my action, and the ethical proposition that my own greatest happiness or pleasure is for me the *right* ultimate end. It may, however, be replied that if the former proposition be accepted in the same quantitatively precise form as the latter —if it is admitted that I must by a law of my nature always aim at the greatest possible pleasure (or least pain) to myself —then at least I cannot conceive any aim conflicting with this to be prescribed by Reason. And this seems to me undeniable. If, as Bentham[1] affirms, " on the occasion of every act he exercises, every human being is " inevitably " led to pursue that line of conduct which, according to his view of the case, taken by him at the moment, will be in the highest degree contributory to his own greatest happiness," [2] then, to any one who knows this, it must become inconceivable that Reason dictates to him to pursue any other line of conduct. But at the same time, as it seems to me, the proposition that he ' ought ' to pursue *that* line of conduct becomes no less clearly incapable of being affirmed with any significance. For a psychological law invariably realised in my conduct does not admit of being conceived as ' a precept ' or ' dictate ' of reason : this latter must be a rule from which I am conscious that it is possible to deviate. I do not, however, think that the proposition quoted from Bentham would be affirmed without qualification by any of the writers who now maintain psychological Hedonism. They would admit, with J. S. Mill,[3] that men often, not from merely intellectual deficiencies, but from

---

[1] I here, as in chap. i., adopt the exact hedonistic interpretation of ' happiness ' which Bentham has made current. This seems to me the most suitable use of the term ; but I afterwards (Book i. chap. vii. § 1) take note of other uses.

[2] *Constitutional Code*, Introduction, § 2.

[3] *Utilitarianism*, chap. ii. p. 14.

"infirmity of character, make their election for the nearer good, though they know it to be less valuable : and this no less when the choice is between two bodily pleasures . . . they pursue sensual indulgences to the injury of health, though perfectly aware that health is the greater good."[1]

This being so, Egoistic Hedonism becomes a possible ethical ideal to which psychological Hedonism seems to point. If it can be shown that the ultimate aim of each of us in acting is always solely *some* pleasure (or absence of pain) to himself, the demonstration certainly suggests that each *ought* to seek his own *greatest* pleasure.[2] As has been said, no cogent inference is possible from the psychological generalisation to the ethical principle : but the mind has a natural tendency to pass from the one position to the other : if the actual ultimate springs of our volition are always our own pleasures and pains, it seems *prima facie* reasonable to be moved by them in proportion to their pleasantness and painfulness, and therefore to choose the greatest pleasure or least pain on the whole. Further, this psychological doctrine seems to conflict with an ethical view widely held by persons whose moral consciousness is highly developed : viz. that an act, to be in the highest sense virtuous, must not be done solely for the sake of the attendant pleasure, even if that be the pleasure of the moral sense ; so that if I do an act from the sole desire of obtaining the glow of moral self-approbation which I believe will attend its performance, the act will not be truly virtuous.

It seems therefore important to subject psychological Hedonism, even in its more indefinite form, to a careful examination.

§ 2. It will be well to begin by defining more precisely the question at issue. First, I will concede that pleasure is a kind of feeling which stim'lates the will to actions tending to sustain or produce it,—to sustain it, if actually present, and to produce it, if it be only represented in idea—; and similarly pain is a kind of feeling which stimulates to actions

---

[1] Mr. Leslie Stephen, who holds (*Science of Ethics*, p. 50) that "pain and pleasure are the sole determining causes of action," at the same time thinks that it "will be admitted on all hands" that "we are not always determined by a calculation of pleasure to come."

[2] Or, more precisely, 'greatest surplus of pleasure over pain.'

tending to remove or avert it.[1] It seems convenient to call the felt volitional stimulus in the two cases respectively Desire[2] and Aversion; though it should be observed that the former term is ordinarily restricted to the impulse felt when pleasure is not actually present, but only represented in idea. The question at issue, then, is not whether pleasure, present or represented, is normally accompanied by an impulse to prolong the actual or realise the represented feeling, and pain correspondingly by aversion: but whether there are no desires and aversions which have not pleasures and pains for their objects—no conscious impulses to produce or avert results other than the agent's own feelings.   In the treatise to which I have referred, Mill explains that "desiring a thing, and finding it pleasant, are, in the strictness of language, two modes of naming the same psychological fact." If this be the case, it is hard to see how the proposition we are discussing requires to be determined by "practised self-consciousness and self-observation"; as the denial of it would involve a contradiction in terms.   The truth is that an ambiguity in the word Pleasure has tended to confuse the discussion of

---

[1] The qualifications and limitations which this proposition requires, before it can be accepted as strictly true, do not seem to me important for the purpose of the present argument. See Book ii. chap. ii. § 2.

[2] In the present treatise 'Desire' is primarily regarded as a felt impulse or stimulus to actions tending to the realisation of what is desired.   There are, however, states of feeling, sometimes intense, to which the term 'desire' is by usage applicable, in which this impulsive quality seems to be absent or at least latent; because the realisation of the desired result is recognised as hopeless, and has long been so recognised.   In such cases the 'desire' (so-called) remains in consciousness only as a sense of want of a recognised good, a feeling no more or otherwise impulsive than the regretful memory of past joy.   That is, desire in this condition may develop a secondary impulse to voluntary day-dreaming, by which a bitter-sweet imaginary satisfaction of the want is attained; or, so far as it is painful, it may impel to action or thought which will bring about its own extinction: but its primary impulse to acts tending to realise the desired result is no longer perceptible.

With this state of mind
    —"the desire of the moth for the star,
Of the night for the morrow"—

I am not concerned in the present discussion.   I notice it chiefly because some writers (e.g. Dr. Bain) seem to contemplate as the sole or typical case of desire, "where there is a motive and no ability to act upon it"; thus expressly excluding that condition of desire (as I use the term) which seems to me of primary importance from an ethical point of view, i.e. where action tending to bring about the desired result is conceived as at once possible.

this question.[1] When we speak of a man doing something "at his pleasure," or "as he pleases," we usually signify the mere fact of voluntary choice : not necessarily that the result aimed at is some prospective feeling of the chooser. Now, if by "pleasant" we merely mean that which influences choice, exercises a certain attractive force on the will, it is an assertion incontrovertible because tautological, to say that we desire what is pleasant—or even that we desire a thing in proportion as it appears pleasant. But if we take "pleasure" to denote the kind of feelings, above defined, it becomes a really debateable question whether the end to which our desires are always consciously directed is the attainment by ourselves of such feelings. And this is what we must understand Mill to consider "so obvious, that it will hardly be disputed."

It is rather curious to find that one of the best-known of English moralists regards the exact opposite of what Mill thinks so obvious, as being not merely a universal fact of our conscious experience, but even a necessary truth. Butler, as is well known, distinguishes self-love, or the impulse towards our own pleasure, from "particular movements towards particular external objects—honour, power, the harm or good of another"; the actions proceeding from which are "no otherwise interested than as every action of every creature must from the nature of the case be; for no one can act but from a desire, or choice, or preference of his own," Such particular passions or appetites are, he goes on to say, "*necessarily presupposed by the very idea* of an interested pursuit; since the very idea of interest or happiness consists in this, that an appetite or affection enjoys its object." We could not pursue pleasure at all, unless we had desires for something else than pleasure ; for pleasure consists in the satisfaction of just these "disinterested" impulses.

Butler has certainly over-stated his case,[2] so far as my own

---

[1] The confusion occurs in the most singular form in Hobbes, who actually identifies Pleasure and Appetite—"this motion in which consisteth pleasure, is a solicitation to draw near to the thing that pleaseth."

[2] The same argument is put in a more guarded, and, I think, unexceptionable form by Hutcheson. It is perhaps more remarkable that Hume, too, shares Butler's view which he expresses almost in the language of the famous sermons. "There are," he says, "bodily wants or appetites, acknowledged by every one,

experience goes; for many pleasures,—especially those of sight, hearing and smell, together with many emotional pleasures,— occur to me without any perceptible relation to previous desires, and it seems quite *conceivable* that our primary desires might be entirely directed towards such pleasures as these. But as a matter of fact, it appears to me that throughout the whole scale of my impulses, sensual, emotional, and intellectual alike, I can distinguish desires of which the object is something other than my own pleasure.

I will begin by taking an illustration of this from the impulses commonly placed lowest in the scale. The appetite of hunger, so far as I can observe, is a direct impulse to the eating of food. Such eating is no doubt commonly attended with an agreeable feeling of more or less intensity; but it cannot, I think, be strictly said that this agreeable feeling is the object of hunger, and that it is the representation of this pleasure which stimulates the will of the hungry man as such. Of course, hunger is frequently and naturally accompanied with anticipation of the pleasure of eating: but careful intro- spection seems to show that the two are by no means in- separable. And even when they occur together the pleasure seems properly the object not of the primary appetite, but of a secondary desire which can be distinguished from the former; since the *gourmand*, in whom this secondary desire is strong, is often prompted by it to actions designed to stimulate hunger, and often, again, is led to control the primary impulse, in order to prolong and vary the process of satisfying it.

Indeed it is so obvious that hunger is something different from the desire for anticipated pleasure, that some writers have regarded its volitional stimulus (and that of desire generally) as a case of aversion from present pain. This, however, seems to me a distinct mistake in psychological classification. No

---

which necessarily precede all sensual enjoyment, and carry us directly to seek possession of the object. Thus hunger and thirst have eating and drinking for their end : and from the gratification of these primary appetites arises a pleasure, which may become the object of another species of inclination that is secondary and interested." Hence Hume finds that "the hypothesis which allows of a disinterested benevolence, distinct from self-love," is "conformable to the analogy of nature." See *Enquiry concerning the Principles of Morals* (Appendix II.).

doubt desire is a state of consciousness so far similar to pain, that in both we feel a stimulus prompting us to pass from the present state into a different one. But aversion from pain is an impulse to get out of the present state and pass into some other state which is only negatively represented as different from the present: whereas in desire as such, the primary impulse is towards the realisation of some positive future result. It is true that when a strong desire is, for any reason, baulked of its effect in causing action, it is generally painful in some degree: and so a secondary aversion to the state of desire is generated, which blends itself with the desire and may easily be confounded with it. But here, again, we may distinguish the two impulses by observing the different kinds of conduct to which they occasionally prompt: for the aversion to the pain of ungratified desire, though it may act as an additional stimulus towards the gratification of the desire, may also (and often does) prompt us to get rid of the pain by suppressing the desire.

The question whether all desire has in some degree the quality of pain, is one of psychological rather than ethical interest;[1] so long as it is admitted that it is often not painful in any degree comparable to its intensity as desire, so that its volitional impulse cannot be explained as a case of aversion to its own painfulness. At the same time, so far as my experience goes, I have no hesitation in answering the question in the negative. Consider again the case of hunger; I certainly do not find hunger as an element of my normal life at all a painful feeling: it only becomes painful when I am in ill health, or when the satisfaction of the appetite is abnormally delayed. And, generally speaking, any desire that is not felt to be thwarted in its primary impulse to actions tending to its satisfaction, is not only not itself a painful feeling—even when this attainment is still remote— but is often an element of a state of consciousness which as a whole is highly pleasurable. Indeed, the pleasures afforded by the consciousness of eager activity, in which desire is an essential element, constitute a considerable item in the total enjoyment of life. It is almost a commonplace to say that

---

[1] Some further discussion of it will be found in the note at the end of the chapter.

such pleasures, which we may call generally the pleasures of Pursuit, are more important than the pleasures of Attainment : and in many cases it is the prospect of the former rather than of the latter that induces us to engage in a pursuit.   In such cases it is peculiarly easy to distinguish the desire to attain the object pursued, from a desire of the pleasure of attainment : since the attainment only becomes pleasant in prospect because the pursuit itself stimulates a desire for what is pursued.   Take, for example, the case of any game which involves — as most games do — a contest for victory.   No ordinary player before entering on such a contest, has any desire for victory in it : indeed he often finds it difficult to imagine himself deriving gratification from such victory, before he has actually engaged in the competition. What he deliberately, before the game begins, desires is not victory, but the pleasant excitement of the struggle for it ; only for the full development of this pleasure a transient desire to win the game is generally indispensable.   This desire, which does not exist at first, is stimulated to considerable intensity by the competition itself : and in proportion as it is thus stimulated both the mere contest becomes more pleasurable, and the victory, which was originally indifferent, comes to afford a keen enjoyment.

The same phenomenon is exhibited in the case of more important kinds of pursuit.   Thus it often happens that a man, feeling his life languid and devoid of interests, begins to occupy himself in the prosecution of some scientific or socially useful work, for the sake not of the end but of the occupation. At first, very likely, the occupation is irksome : but soon, as he foresaw, a desire to attain the end at which he aims is stimulated, partly by sympathy with other workers, partly by his sustained exercise of voluntary effort directed towards it ; so that his pursuit, becoming eager, becomes also a source oi pleasure.   Here, again, it is no doubt true that in proportion as his desire for the end grows strong, the attainment of it becomes pleasant in prospect : but it would be a palpable mistake to say that this prospective pleasure is the object ot the desire that causes it.[1]

---

[1] Professor J. S. Mackenzie, in his *Manual of Ethics* (3rd edition, Book i. chap. ii. note), arguing for the universal painfulness of desire, urges that the so-called

When we compare these pleasures with those previously discussed, another important observation suggests itself. In the former case, though we could distinguish appetite, as it appears in consciousness, from the desire of the pleasure attending the satisfaction of appetite, there appeared to be no incompatibility between the two. The fact that a glutton is dominated by the desire of the pleasures of eating in no way impedes the development in him of the appetite which is a necessary condition of these pleasures. But when we turn to the pleasures of pursuit, we seem to perceive this incompatibility to a certain extent : a certain subordination of self-regard seems to be necessary in order to obtain full enjoyment. A man who maintains throughout an epicurean mood, keeping his main conscious aim perpetually fixed on his own pleasure, does not catch the full spirit of the chase ; his eagerness never gets just the sharpness of edge which imparts to the pleasure its highest zest. Here comes into view what we may call the fundamental paradox of Hedonism, that the impulse towards pleasure, if too predominant, defeats its own aim. This effect is not visible, or at any rate is scarcely visible, in the case of passive sensual pleasures. But of our active enjoyments generally, whether the activities on which they attend are classed as ' bodily ' or as ' intellectual ' (as well as of many emotional

"pleasures of pursuit" are really pleasures of "progressive attainment" ; what causes pleasure being the series of partial attainments that precede the final attainment. There seems to me much truth in this view, as regards some forms of pursuit ; but in other cases I can find nothing deserving the name in the course of the pursuit : the prominent element of the pleasure seems to be clearly the reflex of eager and hopeful, perhaps consciously skilful, activity. *E.g.* this is often the case in the pursuit of truth, scientific or historical. I have spent most pleasant hours in hunting for evidence in favour of a conjecture that had occurred to me as a possible solution of a difficult historical question, without any "progressive attainment" at all, as I found no evidence of any importance : but the pleasure had none the less been real, at any rate in the earlier part of the pursuit. Or take the common experience of deer-stalking, or the struggle for victory in an evenly balanced game of chess, or a prolonged race in which no competitor gains on the others till near the end. I find nothing like "progressive attainment" in these cases.

But even granting Mr. Mackenzie's view to be more widely applicable than I think it, the question it deals with seems to me in the main irrelevant to the issue that I am now discussing : since it remains true that the presence of antecedent desire is an essential condition of the pleasures of attainment—whether "progressive" or "catastrophic"—and that the desire is not itself perceptibly painful.

pleasures), it may certainly be said that we cannot attain them, at least in their highest degree, so long as we keep our main conscious aim concentrated upon them. It is not only that the exercise of our faculties is insufficiently stimulated by the mere desire of the pleasure attending it, and requires the presence of other more objective, 'extra-regarding,' impulses, in order to be fully developed: we may go further and say that these other impulses must be temporarily predominant and absorbing, if the exercise and its attendant gratification are to attain their full scope. Many middle-aged Englishmen would maintain the view that business is more agreeable than amusement; but they would hardly find it so if they transacted the business with a perpetual conscious aim at the attendant pleasure. Similarly, the pleasures of thought and study can only be enjoyed in the highest degree by those who have an ardour of curiosity which carries the mind temporarily away from self and its sensations. In all kinds of Art, again, the exercise of the creative faculty is attended by intense and exquisite pleasures: but it would seem that in order to get them, one must forget them: the genuine artist at work seems to have a predominant and temporarily absorbing desire for the realisation of his ideal of beauty.

The important case of the benevolent affections is at first sight somewhat more doubtful. On the one hand it is of course true, that when those whom we love are pleased or pained, we ourselves feel sympathetic pleasure and pain: and further, that the flow of love or kindly feeling is itself highly pleasurable. So that it is at least plausible to interpret benevolent actions as aiming ultimately at the attainment of one or both of these two kinds of pleasures, or at the averting of sympathetic pain from the agent. But we may observe, first, that the impulse to beneficent action produced in us by sympathy is often so much out of proportion to any actual consciousness of sympathetic pleasure and pain in ourselves, that it would be paradoxical to regard this latter as its object. Often indeed we cannot but feel that a tale of actual suffering arouses in us an excitement on the whole more pleasurable than painful, like the excitement of witnessing a tragedy; and yet at the same time stirs in us an impulse to relieve it, even when the process of relieving is painful and laborious and involves various sacrifices of our own pleasures. Again, we may often free our-selves from sympathetic pain most easily by merely turning our thoughts from the external suffering that causes it : and we sometimes feel an egoistic impulse to do this, which we can then distinguish clearly from the properly sympathetic impulse prompting us to relieve the original suffering. And finally, the much-commended pleasures of benevolence seem to require, in order to be felt in any considerable degree, the pre-existence of a desire to do good to others for their sake and not for our own. As Hutcheson explains, we may *cultivate* benevolent affection for the sake of the pleasures attending it (just as the glutton cultivates appetite), but we cannot produce it at will, however strong may be our desire of these pleasures : and when it exists, even though it may owe its origin to a purely egoistic impulse, it is still essentially a desire to do good to others for their sake and not for our own.

It cannot perhaps be said that the self-abandonment and self-forgetfulness, which seemed an essential condition of the full development of the other elevated impulses before noticed, characterise benevolent affection normally and permanently ; as love, when a powerful emotion, seems naturally to involve a desire for reciprocated love, strong in proportion to the in-tensity of the emotion ; and thus the consciousness of self and of one's own pleasures and pains seems often heightened by the very intensity of the affection that binds one to others.   Still we may at least say that this self-suppression and absorption of consciousness in the thought of other human beings and their happiness is a common incident of all strong affections : and it is said that persons who love intensely sometimes feel a sense of antagonism between the egoistic and altruistic elements of their desire, and an impulse to suppress the former, which occasionally exhibits itself in acts of fantastic and extravagant self-sacrifice.

If then reflection on our moral consciousness seems to show that " the pleasure of virtue is one which can only be obtained on the express condition of its not being the object sought," [1] we need not distrust this result of observation on account of the abnormal nature of the phenomenon. We have merely another illustration of a psychological law, which, as we have

[1] Lecky, *Hist. of European Morals*, Introduction.

seen, is exemplified throughout the whole range of our desires
In the promptings of Sense no less than in those of Intellect
or Reason we find the phenomenon of strictly disinterested
impulse : base and trivial external ends may excite desires of
this kind, as well as the sublime and ideal : and there are
pleasures of the merely animal life which can only be obtained
on condition of not being directly sought, no less than the
satisfactions of a good conscience.

§ 3. So far I have been concerned to insist on the felt incompatibility of ' self-regarding ' and 'extra-regarding' impulses
only as a means of proving their essential distinctness.   I do
not wish to overstate this incompatibility : I believe that most
commonly it is very transient, and often only momentary, and
that our greatest happiness—if that be our deliberate aim—is
generally attained by means of a sort of alternating rhythm of
the two kinds of impulse in consciousness.   A man's conscious
desire is, I think, more often than not chiefly extra-regarding ;
but where there is strong desire in any direction, there is commonly keen susceptibility to the corresponding pleasures ; and
the most devoted enthusiast is sustained in his work by the
recurrent consciousness of such pleasures.   But it is important
to point out that the familiar and obvious instances of conflict
between self-love and some extra-regarding impulse are not
paradoxes and illusions to be explained away, but phenomena
which the analysis of our consciousness in its normal state,
when there is no such conflict, would lead us to expect.   If we
are continually acting from impulses whose immediate objects
are something other than our own happiness, it is quite natural
that we should occasionally yield to such impulses when they
prompt us to an uncompensated sacrifice of pleasure.   Thus a
man of weak self-control, after fasting too long, may easily
indulge his appetite for food to an extent which he knows to
be unwholesome : and that not because the pleasure of eating
appears to him, even in the moment of indulgence, at all worthy
of consideration in comparison with the injury to health ; but
merely because he feels an impulse to eat food, which prevails
over his prudential judgment.   Thus, again, men have sacrificed
all the enjoyments of life, and even life itself, to obtain posthumous fame : not from any illusory belief that they would be
somehow capable of deriving pleasure from it, but from a direct

desire of the future admiration of others, and a preference of it
to their own pleasure.   And so, again, when the sacrifice is
made for some ideal end, as Truth, or Freedom, or Religion :
it may be a real sacrifice of the individual's happiness, and
not merely the preference of one highly refined pleasure (or of
the absence of one special pain) to all the other elements of
happiness.   No doubt this preference is possible ; a man may
feel that the high and severe delight of serving his ideal is a
" pearl of great price " outweighing in value all other pleasures.
But he may also feel that the sacrifice will not repay *him*, and
yet determine that it shall be made.

   To sum up : our conscious active impulses are so far from
being always directed towards the attainment of pleasure or
avoidance of pain for ourselves, that we can find everywhere in
consciousness extra-regarding impulses, directed towards something that is not pleasure, nor relief from pain ; and, indeed,
a most important part of our pleasure depends upon the existence of such impulses : while on the other hand they are in
many cases so far incompatible with the desire of our own
pleasure that the two kinds of impulse do not easily coexist
in the same moment of consciousness ; and more occasionally
(but by no means rarely) the two come into irreconcilable
conflict, and prompt to opposite courses of action.   And this
incompatibility (though it is important to notice it in other
instances) is no doubt specially prominent in the case of the
impulse towards the end which most markedly competes in
ethical controversy with pleasure : the love of virtue for its
own sake, or desire to do what is right as such.

   § 4. The psychological observations on which my argument
is based will not perhaps be directly controverted, at least to
such an extent as to involve my main conclusion : but there
are two lines of reasoning by which it has been attempted to
weaken the force of this conclusion without directly denying it.
In the first place, it is urged that Pleasure, though not the only
conscious aim of human action, is yet always the result to which
it is unconsciously directed.   The proposition would be difficult
to disprove ; since no one denies that pleasure in some degree
normally accompanies the attainment of a desired end : and
when once we go beyond the testimony of consciousness there
seems to be no clear method of determining which among the

consequences of any action is the end at which it is aimed. For the same reason, however, the proposition is at any rate equally difficult to prove. But I should go further, and maintain that if we seriously set ourselves to consider human action on its unconscious side, we can only conceive it as a combination of movements of the parts of a material organism : and that if we try to ascertain what the 'end' in any case of such movements is, it is reasonable to conclude that it is some material result, some organic condition conducive to the preservation either of the individual organism or of the race to which it belongs. In fact, the doctrine that pleasure (or the absence of pain) is the end of all human action can neither be supported by the results of introspection, nor by the results of external observation and inference : it rather seems to be reached by an arbitrary and illegitimate combination of the two.

But again, it is sometimes said that whatever be the case with our present adult consciousness, our original impulses were all directed towards pleasure [1] or from pain, and that any impulses otherwise directed are derived from these by "association of ideas." I can find no evidence that even tends to prove this : so far as we can observe the consciousness of children, the two elements, extra-regarding impulse and desire for pleasure, seem to coexist in the same manner as they do in mature life. In so far as there is any difference, it seems to be in the opposite direction ; as the actions of children, being more instinctive and less reflective, are more prompted by extra-regarding impulse, and less by conscious aim at pleasure. No doubt the two kinds of impulse, as we trace back the development of consciousness, gradually become indistinguishable : but this obviously does not justify us in identifying with either of the two the more indefinite impulse out of which both have been developed. But even supposing it were found that our earliest appetites were all merely appetites for pleasure, it

---

[1] I must ask the reader to distinguish carefully the question discussed in this chapter, which relates to the *objects* of desires and aversions, from the different question whether the *causes* of these impulses are always to be found in antecedent experiences of pleasure and pain. The bearing of this latter question on Ethics, though not unimportant, is manifestly more indirect than that of the question here dealt with : and it will be convenient to postpone it till a later stage of the discussion. Cf. *post*, Book ii. chap. vi. § 2, and Book iv. chap. iv. § 1.

would have little bearing on the present question. What I am concerned to maintain is that men do not *now* normally desire pleasure alone, but to an important extent other things also : some in particular having impulses towards virtue, which may and do conflict with their conscious desire for their own pleasure. To say in answer to this that all men *once* desired pleasure is, from an ethical point of view, irrelevant : except on the assumption that there is an original type of man's appetitive nature, to which, as such, it is right or best for him to conform. But probably no Hedonist would expressly maintain this ; though such an assumption, no doubt, is frequently made by writers of the Intuitional school.

NOTE.—Some psychologists regard Desire as essentially painful. This view seems to me erroneous, according to the ordinary use of the term : and though it does not necessarily involve the confusion—against which I am chiefly concerned to guard in the present chapter—between the volitional stimulus of desire itself and the volitional stimulus of aversion to desire as painful, it has some tendency to cause this confusion. It may therefore be worth while to point out that the difference of opinion between myself and the psychologists in question—of whom I select Dr. Bain as a leading example—depends largely, though not entirely, on a difference of definition. In chap. viii. of the second division of his book on *The Emotions and the Will*, Dr. Bain defines Desire as " that phase of volition where there is a motive and not ability to act on it," and gives the following illustration :—

" The inmate of a small gloomy chamber conceives to himself the pleasure of light and of an expanded prospect : the unsatisfying ideal urges the appropriate action for gaining the reality ; he gets up and walks out. Suppose now that the same ideal delight comes into the mind of a prisoner. Unable to fulfil the prompting, he remains under the solicitation of the motive : and his state is denominated craving, longing, appetite, desire. If all motive impulses could be at once followed up, desire would have no place . . . there is a bar in the way of acting which leads to the state of conflict and renders desire a more or less painful state of mind."

Now I agree that Desire is most frequently painful in some degree when the person desiring is inhibited from acting for the attainment of the desired object. I do not indeed think that even under these circumstances it is always painful, especially when it is accompanied with hope. Take the simple case of hunger. Ordinarily, when I am looking forward to dinner with a good appetite, I do not find hunger painful—unless I have fasted unusually long—although custom and a regard for my digestion prevent me from satisfying the appetite till the soup is served. Still I admit that when action tending to fruition is excluded, desire is very liable to be painful.

But it is surely contrary to usage to restrict the term Desire to this case. Suppose Dr. Bain's prisoner becomes possessed of a file, and sees his way to getting out of prison by a long process, which will involve, among other operations, the filing of certain bars. It would surely seem absurd to say that his desire finally ceases when the operation of filing begins. No doubt the concentration of attention on the complex activities necessary for the attainment of freedom is likely to cause the prisoner to be so absorbed by other ideas and feelings that the desire of freedom may temporarily cease to be present in his consciousness. But as the stimulus on which his whole activity ultimately depends is certainly derived from the unrealised idea of freedom, this idea, with the concomitant feeling of desire, will normally recur at brief intervals during the process. Similarly in other cases, while it is quite true that men often work for a desired end without consciously feeling desire for the end, it would be absurd to say that they never feel desire while so working: at any rate this restricted use of the term has never, I think, been adapted by ethical writers in treating of Desire. And in some passages Dr. Bain himself seems to adopt a wider meaning. He says, for instance, in the chapter from which I have quoted, that "we have a form of desire . . . *when we are working for distant ends.*" If, then, it be allowed that the feeling of Desire is at any rate sometimes an element of consciousness coexisting with a process of activity directed to the attainment of the desired object, or intervening in the brief pauses of such a process, I venture to think that when the feeling is observed under these conditions, it will not be found in accordance with the common experience of mankind to describe it as essentially painful.

Take, as a simple instance, the case of a game involving bodily exercise and a contest of skill. Probably many persons who take part in such exercises for sanitary or social purposes begin without any perceptible desire to win the game: and probably as long as they remain thus indifferent the exercise is rather tedious. Usually, however, a conscious desire to win the game is excited, as a consequence of actions directed towards this end: and—in my experience at least—in proportion as the feeling grows strong, the whole process becomes more pleasurable. If this be admitted to be a normal experience, it must surely be also admitted that Desire in this case is a feeling in which introspection does not enable us to detect the slightest quality of pain.

It would be easy to give an indefinite number of similar instances of energetic activity carried on for an end—whether in sport or in the serious business of life—where a keen desire for the attainment of the end in view is indispensable to a real enjoyment of the labour required to attain, and where at the same time we cannot detect any painfulness in the desire, however much we try to separate it in introspective analysis from its concomitant feeling.

The error that I am trying to remove seems to me partly due to overlooking these cases, and contemplating exclusively cases in which Desire is for some reason or other prevented from having its normal effect in stimulating activity directed to the attainment of the desired object. Partly, however, it seems to be due to the resemblance between Desire and Pain, to which I have drawn attention in the text of this chapter, *i.e.* the *unrestfulness* which is undoubtedly a characteristic of the state of desire, and—ordinarily—of pain. For the characteristic of "unrestfulness" requires some care to distinguish it from "uneasiness," in the sense in which this latter term signifies some degree of painfulness. The mistake is connected with the equally erroneous view—which Hobbes controverts in his usual forcible style—that "the Felicity of this life consisteth in the repose of a mind satisfied"; and it has also some affinity with the widespread view—which has left its mark on more than one European language—that labour, strenuous activity, is essentially painful. On both these points, it ought to be said, there is doubtless considerable divergence between the experiences of different individuals : but at any rate among Englishmen I conceive that a person who finds desire always painful—in the sense in which, as I have tried to show, the word is commonly used both by moralists and in ordinary discourse—is as exceptional a being as one who finds labour always painful.

CHAPTER V

§ 1. IN the preceding chapters I have treated first of rational, and secondly of disinterested action, without introducing the vexed question of the Freedom of the Will. The difficulties connected with this question have been proved by long dialectical experience to be so great, that I am anxious to confine them within as strict limits as I can, and keep as much of my subject as possible free from their perturbing influence. And it appears to me that we have no psychological warrant for identifying Disinterested with either "Free" or "Rational" action; while to identify Rational and Free action is at least misleading, and tends to obscure the real issue raised in the Free Will controversy. In the last chapter I have tried to show that action strictly disinterested, that is, disregardful of foreseen balance of pleasure to ourselves, is found in the most instinctive as well as in the most deliberate and self-conscious region of our volitional experience. And rational action, as I conceive it, remains rational, however completely the rationality of any individual's conduct may be determined by causes antecedent or external to his own volition : so that the conception of acting rationally, as explained in the last chapter but one, is not bound up with the notion of acting 'freely,' as maintained by Libertarians generally against Determinists. I say "Libertarians generally," because in the statements made by disciples of Kant as to the connexion of Freedom and Rationality, there appears to me to be a confusion between two meanings of the term Freedom, which require to be carefully distinguished in any discussion of Free Will. When a disciple of Kant [1] says that a man "is a free agent in so far as he acts under the guidance of reason," the statement easily wins assent from ordinary readers; since, as Whewell says, we ordinarily "consider our Reason as being ourselves rather than our desires and affections. We speak of Desire, Love, Anger, as mastering *us*, or of *ourselves* as controlling them. If we decide to prefer some remote and abstract good to immediate pleasures, or to conform to a rule which brings us present pain (which decision implies exercise of Reason), we more particularly consider such acts as our *own* acts." [2] I do not, therefore, object on the score of usage to this application of the term "free" to denote voluntary actions in which the seductive solicitations of appetite or passion are successfully resisted: and I am sensible of the gain in effectiveness of moral persuasion which is obtained by thus enlisting the powerful sentiment of Liberty on the side of Reason and Morality. But it is clear that if we say that a man is a "free" agent in so far as he acts rationally, we cannot also say—in the same sense—that it is by his own "free" choice that he acts irrationally, when he does so act; and it is this latter proposition which Libertarians generally have been concerned to maintain. They have thought it of fundamental importance to show the 'Freedom' of the moral agent, on account of the connexion that they have held to exist between Freedom and Moral Responsibility: and it is obvious that the Freedom thus connected with Responsibility is not the Freedom that is only manifested or realised in rational action, but the Freedom to choose between right and wrong which is manifested or realised equally in either choice. Now it is implied in the

[1] I have thought it expedient to exclude the Kantian conception of Free Will from the scope of the discussion in this chapter, partly on account of the confusion mentioned in the text; partly because it depends on the conception of a causality not subject to time-conditions, which appears to me altogether untenable, while it does not fall within the plan of the present treatise to discuss it. But considering the widespread influence of Kantian theory on current ethical thought, I have thought it desirable to give a brief discussion of his conception of Free Will in an Appendix (1.).

[2] *Elements of Morality*, Book i. chap. ii. At the same time, it is also true—as I afterwards say—that we sometimes identify ourselves with passion or appetite in conscious conflict with reason: and then the rule of reason is apt to appear an external constraint, and obedience to it a servitude, if not a slavery.

Christian consciousness of "wilful sin" that men do deliberately and knowingly choose to act irrationally. They do
not merely prefer self-interest to duty (for here is rather
a conflict of claims to rationality than clear irrationality); but (*e.g.*) sensual indulgence to health, revenge to
reputation, etc., though they know that such preference is
opposed to their true interests no less than to their duty.[1]
Hence it does not really correspond to our experience as a
whole to represent the conflict between Reason and passion
as a conflict between 'ourselves' on the one hand and a force
of nature on the other. We may say, if we like, that when
we yield to passion, we become 'the slaves of our desires and
appetites': but we must at the same time admit that our
slavery is self-chosen. Can we say, then, of the wilful wrongdoer that his wrong choice was 'free,' in the sense that he
might have chosen rightly, not merely if the antecedents of
his volition, external and internal, had been different, but
supposing these antecedents unchanged? This, I conceive, is
the substantial issue raised in the Free Will controversy;
which I now propose briefly to consider: since it is widely
believed to be of great Ethical importance.

§ 2. We may conveniently begin by defining more exactly
the notion of Voluntary action, to which, according to all
methods of Ethics alike, the predicates 'right' and 'what ought
to be done'—in the strictest ethical sense—are exclusively
applicable. In the first place, Voluntary action is distinguished as 'conscious' from actions or movements of the
human organism which are 'unconscious' or 'mechanical.'
The person whose organism performs such movements only
becomes aware of them, if at all, after they have been performed; accordingly they are not imputed to him as a person,

---

[1] The difficulty which Socrates and the Socratic schools had in conceiving
a man to choose deliberately what he knows to be bad for him—a difficulty
which drives Aristotle into real Determinism in his account of purposed action,
even while he is expressly maintaining the "voluntariness" and "responsibility" of vice—seems to be much reduced for the modern mind by the distinction between moral and prudential judgments, and the *prima facie* conflict
between 'interest' and 'duty.' Being thus familiar with the conception of
deliberate choice consciously opposed *either* to interest *or* to duty, we can without much difficulty conceive of such choice in conscious opposition to both
See chap. ix. § 3, of this Book.

or judged to be morally wrong or imprudent; though they may sometimes be judged to be good or bad in respect of their consequences, with the implication that they ought to be encouraged or checked as far as this can be done indirectly by conscious effort.

So again, in the case of conscious actions, the agent is not regarded as morally culpable, except in an indirect way, for entirely unforeseen effects of his voluntary actions. No doubt when a man's action has caused some unforeseen harm, the popular moral judgment often blames him for carelessness; but it would be generally admitted by reflective persons that in such cases strictly moral blame only attaches to the agent in an indirect way, in so far as his carelessness is the result of some wilful neglect of duty. Thus the proper immediate objects of moral approval or disapproval would seem to be always the results of a man's volitions so far as they were intended—*i.e.* represented in thought as certain or probable [1] consequences of his volitions:—or, more strictly, the volitions themselves in which such results were so intended, since we do not consider that a man is relieved from moral blame because his wrong intention remains unrealised through external causes.

This view seems at first sight to differ from the common opinion that the morality of acts depends on their 'motives'; if by motives are understood the desires that we feel for some of the foreseen consequences of our acts. But I do not think that those who hold this opinion would deny that we are blameworthy for any prohibited result which we foresaw in willing, whether it was the object of desire or not. No doubt it is commonly held that acts, similar as regards their foreseen results, may be 'better' or 'worse' [2] through the presence of certain desires or aversions. Still so far as these feelings

---

[1] It is most convenient to regard "intention" as including not only such results of volition as the agent *desired* to realise, but also any that, without desiring, he foresaw as certain or probable. The question how far we are responsible for all the foreseen consequences of our acts, or, in the case of acts prescribed by definite moral rules, only for their results within a certain range, will be considered when we come to examine the Intuitional Method.

[2] In a subsequent chapter (chap. ix. of this Book) I shall examine more fully the relation of the antithesis 'right' and 'wrong' to the vaguer and wider antithesis 'good' and 'bad,' in our practical reasonings.

are not altogether under the control of the will, the judgment of 'right' and 'wrong'—in the strictest sense of these terms— seems to be not properly applicable to the feelings themselves, but rather to the exertion or omission of voluntary effort to check bad motives and encourage good ones, or to the conscious adoption of an object of desire as an end to be aimed at—which is a species of volition.

We may conclude then that judgments of right and wrong relate properly to volitions accompanied with intention— whether the intended consequences be external, or some effects produced on the agent's own feelings or character. This excludes from the scope of such judgments those conscious actions which are not intentional, strictly speaking; as when sudden strong feelings of pleasure and pain cause movements which we are aware of making, but which are not preceded by any representation in idea either of the movements themselves or of their effects. For such actions, sometimes distinguished as 'instinctive,' we are only held to be responsible indirectly so far as any bad consequences of them might have been prevented by voluntary efforts to form habits of more complete self-control.

We have to observe further that our common moral judgments recognise an important distinction between *impulsive* and *deliberate* wrongdoing, condemning the latter more strongly than the former. The line between the two cannot be sharply drawn: but we may define 'impulsive' actions as those where the connexion between the feeling that prompts and the action prompted is so simple and immediate that, though intention is distinctly present, the consciousness of personal choice of the intended result is evanescent. In deliberate volitions there is always a conscious selection of the result as one of two or more practical alternatives.

In the case, then, of such volitions as are pre-eminently the objects of moral condemnation and approbation, the psychical fact 'volition' seems to include—besides intention, or representation of the results of action—also the consciousness of self as choosing, resolving, determining these results. And the question which I understand to be at issue in the Free Will controversy may be stated thus: Is the self to which I refer my deliberate volitions a self of strictly determinate moral qualities, a definite character partly inherited, partly formed by my past actions and feelings, and by any physical influences that it may have unconsciously received; so that my voluntary action, for good or for evil, is at any moment completely caused by the determinate qualities of this character, together with my circumstances, or the external influences acting on me at the moment—including under this latter term my present bodily conditions?—or is there always a possibility of my choosing to act in the manner that I now judge to be reasonable and right, whatever my previous actions and experiences may have been?

In the above questions a materialist would substitute 'brain and nervous system' for 'character,' and thereby obtain a clearer notion; but I have avoided using terms which suggest materialistic assumptions, because Determinism by no means involves Materialism. For the present purpose the difference is unimportant. The substantial dispute relates to the completeness of the causal dependence of any volition upon the state of things at the preceding instant, whether we specify these as 'character and circumstances,' or 'brain and environing forces.' [1]

On the Determinist side there is a cumulative argument of great force. The belief that events are determinately related to the state of things immediately preceding them is now held by all competent thinkers in respect of all kinds of occurrences except human volitions. It has steadily grown both intensively and extensively, both in clearness and certainty of conviction and in universality of application, as the human mind has developed and human experience has been systematised and enlarged. Step by step in successive departments of fact conflicting modes of thought have receded and faded, until at length they have vanished everywhere,

---

[1] It is not uncommon for Determinists to conceive of each volition as connected by uniform laws with our past state of consciousness. But any uniformities we might trace among a man's past consciousnesses, even if we knew them all, would yet give us very imperfect guidance as to his future action : as there would be left out of account—

(1) All inborn tendencies and susceptibilities, as yet latent or incompletely exhibited ;

(2) All past physical influences, of which the effects had not been perfectly represented in consciousness.

except from this mysterious citadel of Will. Everywhere else the belief is so firmly established that some declare its opposite to be inconceivable : others even maintain that it always was so. Every scientific procedure assumes it : each success of science confirms it. And not only are we finding ever new proof that events are cognisably determined, but also that the different modes of determination of different kinds of events are fundamentally identical and mutually dependent : and naturally, with the increasing conviction of the essential unity of the cognisable universe, increases the indisposition to allow the exceptional character claimed by Libertarians for the department of human action.

Again, when we fix our attention on human action, we observe that the portion of it which is originated unconsciously is admittedly determined by physical causes : and we find that no clear line can be drawn between acts of this kind and those which are conscious and voluntary. Not only are many acts of the former class entirely similar to those of the latter, except in being unconscious : but we remark further that actions which we habitually perform continually pass from the conscious class into the—wholly or partly—unconscious : and the further we investigate, the more the conclusion is forced upon us, that there is no kind of action originated by conscious volition which cannot also, under certain circumstances, be originated unconsciously. Again, when we look closely at our conscious acts, we find that in respect of such of them as I have characterised as 'impulsive'—acts done suddenly under the stimulus of a momentary sensation or emotion— our consciousness can hardly be said to suggest that they are not completely determined by the strength of the stimulus and the state of our previously determined temperament and character at the time of its operation : and here again, as was before observed, it is difficult to draw a line clearly separating these actions from those in which the apparent consciousness of 'free choice' becomes distinct.

Further, we always explain [1] the voluntary action of all

---

[1] I do not mean that this is the only view that we take of the conduct of others : I hold (as will presently appear) that in judging of their conduct morally, we ordinarily apply the conception of Free Will. But we do not ordinarily regard it as one kind of causation, limiting and counteracting the other kind.

men except ourselves on the principle of causation by character and circumstances. Indeed otherwise social life would be impossible: for the life of man in society involves daily a mass of minute forecasts of the actions of other men, founded on experience of mankind generally, or of particular classes of men, or of individuals; who are thus necessarily regarded as things having determinate properties, causes whose effects are calculable. We infer generally the future actions of those whom we know from their past actions; and if our forecast turns out in any case to be erroneous, we do not attribute the discrepancy to the disturbing influence of Free Will, but to our incomplete acquaintance with their character and motives. And passing from individuals to communities, whether we believe in a "social science" or not, we all admit and take part in discussions of social phenomena in which the same principle is assumed: and however we may differ as to particular theories, we never doubt the validity of the assumption: and if we find anything inexplicable in history, past or present, it never occurs to us to attribute it to an extensive exercise of free will in a particular direction. Nay, even as regards our own actions, however 'free' we feel ourselves at any moment, however unconstrained by present motives and circumstances and unfettered by the result of what we have previously been and felt, our volitional choice may appear: still, when it is once well past, and we survey it in the series of our actions, its relations of causation and resemblance to other parts of our life appear, and we naturally explain it as an effect of our nature, education, and circumstances. Nay we even apply the same conceptions to our future action, and the more, in proportion as our moral sentiments are developed: for with our sense of duty generally increases our sense of the duty of moral culture, and our desire of self-improvement: and the possibility of moral self-culture depends on the assumption that by a present volition we can determine to some extent our actions in the more or less remote future. No doubt we habitually take at the same time the opposite, Libertarian, view as to our future: we believe, for example, that we are perfectly able to resist henceforward temptations to which we have continually yielded in the past. But it should be observed that this belief is (as moralists of all

schools admit and even urge) *at any rate to a great extent*
illusory and misleading. Though Libertarians contend that
it is *possible* for us at any moment to act in a manner opposed
to our acquired tendencies and previous customs,—still, they
and Determinists alike teach that it is much less easy than
men commonly imagine to break the subtle unfelt trammels
of habit.

§ 3. Against the formidable array of cumulative evidence
offered for Determinism there is to be set the immediate
affirmation of consciousness in the moment of deliberate action.
Certainly when I have a distinct consciousness of choosing
between alternatives of conduct, one of which I conceive as
right or reasonable, I find it impossible not to think that I can
now choose to do what I so conceive,—supposing that there is
no obstacle to my doing it other than the condition of my
desires and voluntary habits,—however strong may be my
inclination to act unreasonably, and however uniformly I may
have yielded to such inclinations in the past.[1] I recognise
that each concession to vicious desire makes the difficulty of
resisting it greater when the desire recurs : but the difficulty
always seems to remain separated from impossibility by an
impassable gulf.   I do not deny that the experience of mankind includes cases in which certain impulses—such as aversion
to death or extreme pain, or morbid appetite for alcohol or
opium—have reached a point of intensity at which they have
been felt as irresistibly overmastering voluntary choice.   I
think we commonly judge that when this point is reached the
individual ceases to be morally responsible for the act done
under such overmastering impulse : but at any rate the moral
problem thus presented is very exceptional ; in ordinary cases
of yielding to temptation this consciousness of the irresistibility
of impulse does not come in.   Ordinarily, however strong may
be the rush of appetite or anger that comes over me, it does
not present itself as irresistible ; and, if I deliberate at such a
moment, I cannot regard the mere force of the impulse as a
reason for doing what I otherwise judge to be unreasonable.
I can suppose that my conviction of free choice *may* be illusory :

[1] It is not the possibility of merely indeterminate choice, of an "arbitrary
freak of unmotived willing," with which we are concerned from an ethical point
of view, but the possibility of choosing between rational and irrational motives.

that if I knew my own nature I *might* see it to be predetermined that, being so constituted and in such circumstances, I should act on the occasion in question contrary to my rational judgment.   But I cannot conceive myself seeing this, without at the same time conceiving my whole conception of what I now call " my " action fundamentally altered : I cannot conceive that if I contemplated the actions of my organism in this light I should refer them to my " self "—*i.e.* to the mind so contemplating—in the sense in which I now refer them. In this conflict of arguments, it is not surprising that the theoretical question as to the Freedom of the Will is still differently decided by thinkers of repute ; and I do not myself wish at present to pronounce any decision on it.   But I think it possible and useful to show that the ethical importance of deciding it one way or another is liable to be exaggerated ; and that any one who will consider the matter soberly and carefully will find this importance to be of a strictly limited kind.

It is chiefly on the Libertarian side that I find a tendency to the exaggeration of which I have just spoken.   Some Libertarian writers maintain that the conception of the Freedom of the Will, alien as it may be to positive science, is yet quite indispensable to Ethics and Jurisprudence ; since in judging that I " ought " to do anything I imply that I " can " do it, and similarly in praising or blaming the actions of others I imply that they " could " have acted otherwise.   If a man's actions are mere links in a chain of causation which, as we trace it back, ultimately carries us to events anterior to his personal existence, he cannot, it is said, really have either merit or demerit ; and if he has not merit or demerit, it is repugnant to the common moral sense of mankind to reward or punish— even to praise or blame—him.   In considering this argument, it will be convenient—for clearness of discussion—to assume in the first instance that there is no doubt or conflict in our view of what it is right to do, except such as may be caused by the present question.   It will also be convenient to separate the discussion of the importance of Free Will in relation to moral action generally from the special question of its importance in relation to punishing and rewarding ; since, in the latter species of action, what chiefly claims attention is not the present Freedom of the agent, but the past Freedom of the person now acted on.

As regards action generally, the Determinist allows that a man is only morally bound to do what is "in his power"; but he explains "in his power" to mean that the result in question will be produced if the man choose to produce it. And this is, I think, the sense in which the proposition "what I ought to do I can do" is commonly accepted: it means "can do if I choose," not "can choose to do." Still the question remains "*Can* I choose to do what in ordinary thought I judge to be right to do?" Here my own view is that—within the limits above explained—I inevitably conceive that I *can* choose; however, I can suppose myself to regard this conception as illusory, and to judge, inferring the future from the past, that I certainly shall not choose, and accordingly that such choice is not really possible to me. This being supposed, it seems to me undeniable that this judgment will exclude or weaken the operation of the moral motive in the case of the act contemplated: I either shall not judge it reasonable to choose to do what I should otherwise so judge, or if I do pass the judgment, I shall also judge the conception of duty applied in it to be illusory, no less than the conception of Freedom. So far I concede the Libertarian contention as to the demoralising effect of Determinism, if held with a real force of conviction. But I think the cases are rare in which it is even on Determinist principles legitimate to conclude it to be certain —and not merely highly probable—that I shall deliberately choose to do what I judge to be unwise.[1] Ordinarily the legitimate inference from a man's past experience, and from his general knowledge of human nature, would not go beyond

---

[1] I think that in most cases when a man yields to temptation, judging that it is "no use trying to resist," he judges in semi-conscious self-sophistication, due to the influence of appetite or passion disturbing the process of reasoning. I do not doubt that this self-sophistication is likely to take a Determinist form in the mind of one who has adopted Determinism as a speculative opinion : but I see no reason for thinking that a Libertarian is not in equal danger of self-sophistication, though in his case it will take a different form. *E.g.* where a Determinist would reason "I certainly shall take my usual glass of brandy to-night, so there is no use resolving not to take it," the Libertarian's reasoning would be "I mean to leave off that brandy, but it will be just as easy to leave it off to-morrow as to-day ; I will therefore have one more glass, and leave it off to-morrow."

a very strong probability that he would choose to do wrong: and a mere probability—however strong—that I shall not will to do right cannot be regarded by me in deliberation as a reason for not willing:[1] while it certainly supplies a rational ground for willing strongly—just as a strong probability of any other evil supplies a rational ground for special exertions to avoid it.   Indeed, I do not see why a Libertarian should not—equally with a Determinist—accept as valid, and find it instructive to contemplate, the considerations that render it probable that he will *not* choose to do right in any particular circumstances.   In all ordinary cases, therefore, it does not seem to me relevant to ethical deliberation to determine the metaphysical validity of my consciousness of freedom to choose whatever I may conclude to be reasonable, unless the affirmation or negation of the Freedom of the Will somehow modifies my view of what it would be reasonable to choose to do if I could so choose.

I do not think that any such modification of view can be maintained, as regards the ultimate ends of rational action which, in chap. i., I took as being commonly accepted.   If Happiness, whether private or general, be taken as the ultimate end of action on a Libertarian view, the adoption of a Determinist view affords no ground for rejecting it: and if Excellence is in itself admirable and desirable, it surely remains equally so whether any individual's approximation to it is entirely determined by inherited nature and external influences or not:—except so far as the notion of Excellence includes that of Free Will.   Now Free Will is obviously not included in our common ideal of physical and intellectual perfection: and it seems to me also not to be included in the common notions of the excellences of character which we call virtues: the manifestations of courage, temperance, and justice do not become less admirable because we can trace their antecedents in a happy balance of inherited dispositions developed by a careful education.[2]

---

[1] There is, however, a special case in which this probability may be indirectly a reason for not resolving to do what would otherwise be best ; *i.e.* where this resolution would only be right if followed by subsequent resolutions.   The problem thus presented is considered later, pp. 75, 76.

[2] I should admit, indeed, that the ordinary notion of merit becomes inapplicable (see pp. 71, 72).   But I do not see that Perfection becomes less an

Can, then, the affirmation or negation of Free Will affect our view of the fittest means for the attainment of either end? In considering this we have to distinguish between the case of a connexion between means and end believed to exist on empirical or other scientific grounds, and the case where the belief in such connexion is an inference from the belief in a moral government of the world. According to the received view of the moral government of the world, the performance of Duty is the best means of attaining the agent's happiness largely through its expected consequences in another world, in which virtue will be rewarded and vice punished by God: if, then, the belief in the moral government of the world and a future life for men is held to depend on the assumption of Free Will, this latter becomes obviously of fundamental ethical importance: not, indeed, in determining a man's Duty, but in reconciling it with his Interest. This, I think, is the main element of truth in the view that the denial of Free Will removes motives to the performance of Duty: and I admit the validity of the contention, so far as (1) the course of action conducive to an individual's Interest would be thought to diverge from his Duty, apart from theological considerations, and (2) in the theological reasoning that removes this divergence Free Will is an indispensable assumption. The former point will be examined in a subsequent chapter;[1] the latter it hardly falls within the scope of this treatise to discuss.[2]

If we confine our attention to such connexion between means and ends as is scientifically cognisable, it does not appear that an act now deliberated on can be less or more a means to any ulterior end, because it is predetermined. It may, however, be urged that in considering how we ought to act in any case, we have to take into account the probable future actions of others, and also of ourselves; and that with regard to these it is necessary to decide the question of Free Will, in order that we may know whether the future is capable

---

End to be aimed at, because we cease to regard its attainment as meritorious. The inapplicability of the notion of 'merit' to Divine action has never been felt to detract from the Perfection of the Divine Nature.

[1] See Book ii. chap. v. and the concluding chapter of the treatise.

[2] I ought, however, to point out that an important section of theologians who have held the belief in the moral government of the world in its intensest form have been Determinists.

of being predicted from the past. But here, again, it seems to me that no definite practical consequences would logically follow from this decision. For however far we may go in admitting Free Will as a cause, the actual operation of which may falsify the most scientific forecasts of human action, still since it is *ex hypothesi* an absolutely unknown cause, our recognition of it cannot lead us to modify any such forecasts : at most, it can only affect our reliance on them.

We may illustrate this by an imaginary extreme case. Suppose we were somehow convinced that all the planets were endowed with Free Will, and that they only maintained their periodic motions by the continual exercise of free choice, in resistance to strong centrifugal or centripetal inclinations. Our general confidence in the future of the solar system might reasonably be impaired, though it is not easy to say how much ; [1] but the details of our astronomical calculations would be clearly unaffected : the free wills could in no way be taken as an element in the reckoning. And the case would be similar, I suppose, in the forecast of human conduct, if psychology and sociology should ever become exact sciences. At present, however, they are so far from being such that this additional element of uncertainty can hardly have even any emotional effect.

To sum up : we may say that, in so far as we reason to any definite conclusions as to what the future actions of ourselves or others will be, we must consider them as determined by unvarying laws : if they are not completely so determined our reasoning is *pro tanto* liable to error : but no other is open to us. While on the other hand, when we are endeavouring to ascertain (on any principles) what choice it is reasonable to make between two alternatives of present conduct, Determinist conceptions are as irrelevant as they are in the former case inevitable. And from neither point of view does it seem practically important, for the general regulation of conduct, to decide the metaphysical question at issue in the Free-will Controversy : unless—passing from Ethics into Theology— we rest the reconciliation of Duty and Interest on a theological argument that requires the assumption of Free Will.

---

[1] In order to determine this we should require first to settle another disputed question, as to the general reasonableness of our expectation that the future will resemble the past.

§ 4. So far I have been arguing that the adoption of Determinism will not—except in certain exceptional circumstances or on certain theological assumptions—reasonably modify a man's view of what it is right for him to do or his reasons for doing it. It may, however, be said that—granting the reasons for right action to remain unaltered—still the motives that prompt to it will be weakened; since a man will not feel *remorse* for his actions, if he regards them as necessary results of causes anterior to his personal existence. I admit that so far as the sentiment of remorse implies self-blame irremovably fixed on the self blamed, it must tend to vanish from the mind of a convinced Determinist. Still I do not see why the imagination of a Determinist should not be as vivid, his sympathy as keen, his love of goodness as strong as a Libertarian's : and I therefore see no reason why dislike for his own shortcomings and for the mischievous qualities of his character which have caused bad actions in the past should not be as effective a spring of moral improvement as the sentiment of remorse would be. For it appears to me that men in general take at least as much pains to cure defects in their circumstances, organic defects, and defects of intellect— which cause them no remorse—as they do to cure moral defects ; so far as they consider the former to be no less mischievous and no less removable than the latter.

This leads me to the consideration of the effect of Determinist doctrines on the allotment of punishment and reward. For it must be admitted, I think, that the common retributive view of punishment, and the ordinary notions of " merit," " demerit," and " responsibility," also involve the assumption of Free Will : if the wrong act, and the bad qualities of character manifested in it, are conceived as the necessary effects of causes antecedent or external to the existence of the agent, the moral responsibility—in the ordinary sense—for the mischief caused by them can no longer rest on him. At the same time, the Determinist can give to the terms " ill-desert " and " responsibility " a signification which is not only clear and definite, but, from an utilitarian point of view, the only suitable meaning. In this view, if I affirm that A is responsible for a harmful act, I mean that it is right to punish him for it ; primarily, in order that the fear of punishment may prevent him and others from committing similar acts in future. The difference between these two views of punishment is theoretically very wide. I shall, however, when I come to examine in detail the current conception of Justice,[1] endeavour to show that this admission can hardly have any practical effect; since it is practically impossible to be guided, either in remunerating services or in punishing mischievous acts, by any other considerations than those which the Determinist interpretation of desert would include. For instance, the treatment of legal punishment as deterrent and reformatory rather than retributive seems to be forced upon us by the practical exigences of social order and wellbeing— quite apart from any Determinist philosophy.[2] Moreover, as I shall hereafter show, if the retributive view of Punishment be strictly taken—abstracting completely from the preventive view—it brings our conception of Justice into conflict with Benevolence, as punishment presents itself as a purely useless evil. Similarly, as regards the sentiments which prompt to the expression of moral praise and blame—I admit that in the mind of a convinced Determinist, the desire to encourage good and prevent bad conduct must take the place of a desire to requite the one or the other : but again I see no reason why the Determinist species of moral sentiments should not be as effective in promoting virtue and social wellbeing as the Libertarian species.

§ 5. It is, however, of obvious practical importance to ascertain how far the power of the will (whether metaphysically free or not) actually extends : for this defines the range within which ethical judgments are in the strictest sense applicable. This inquiry is quite independent of the question of metaphysical freedom ; we might state it in Determinist terms as an inquiry into the range of effects which it would be possible to cause by human volition, provided that adequate motives are not wanting. These effects seem to be mainly of three kinds : first, changes in

---

[1] See Book iii. chap. v.

[2] Thus we find it necessary to punish negligence, when its effects were very grave, even when we cannot trace it to wilful disregard of duty ; and to punish rebellion and assassination none the less although we know that they were prompted by a sincere desire to serve God or to benefit mankind.

the external world consequent upon muscular contractions; secondly, changes in the train of ideas and feelings that constitutes our conscious life; and thirdly, changes in the tendencies to act hereafter in certain ways under certain circumstances.

I. The most obvious and prominent part of the sphere of volitional causation is constituted by such events as can be produced by muscular contractions. As regards these, it is sometimes said that it is properly the muscular contraction that we will, and not the more remote effects; for these require the concurrence of other causes, and therefore we can never be absolutely certain that they will follow. But no more is it certain, strictly speaking, that the muscular contraction will follow, since our limb may be paralysed, etc. The immediate consequent of the volition is some molecular change in the motor nerves. Since, however, we are not conscious in willing of our motor nerves and their changes,— nor indeed commonly of the muscular contractions that follow them,—it seems a misuse of terms to describe either as the normal 'object' of the mind in willing: since it is almost always some more remote effect which we consciously will and intend. Still of almost all effects of our will on the external world some contraction of our muscles is an indispensable antecedent; and when that is over our part in the causation is completed.

II. We can control to some extent our thoughts and feelings. It would seem, indeed, that an important part of what we commonly call 'control of feeling' comes under the head just discussed. Our control over our muscles enables us to keep down the expression of the feeling and to resist its promptings to action: and as the giving free vent to a feeling tends, generally speaking, to sustain and prolong it, this muscular control amounts to a certain power over the emotion. But there is not the same connexion between our muscular system and our thoughts: and yet experience shows that most men (though some, no doubt, much more than others) can voluntarily determine the direction of their thoughts, and pursue at will a given line of meditation. In such cases, what is effected by the effort of will seems to be the concentration of our consciousness on a part of its content, so that this part grows more vivid and clear, while the rest tends to become obscure and ultimately to vanish. Frequently this voluntary exertion is only needed to initiate a train of ideas, which is afterwards continued without effort: as in recalling a series of past events or going through a familiar train of reasoning. By such concentration we can free ourselves of many thoughts and feelings upon which we do not wish to dwell: but our power to do this is very limited, and if the feeling be strong and its cause persistent, it requires a very unusual effort of will to banish it thus.

III. The effect of volition, however, to which I especially wish to direct the reader's attention is the alteration in men's tendencies to future action which must be assumed to be a consequence of general resolutions as to future conduct, so far as they are effective. Even a resolution to do a particular act —if it is worth while to make it, as experience shows it to be—must be supposed to produce a change of this kind in the person who makes it: it must somehow modify his present tendencies to act in a certain way on a foreseen future occasion. But it is in making general resolutions for future conduct that it is of most practical importance for us to know what is within the power of the will. Let us take an example. A man has been in the habit of drinking too much brandy nightly: one morning he resolves that he will do so no more. In making this resolve he acts under the belief that by a present volition he can so far alter his habitual tendency to indulgence in brandy, that some hours hence he will resist the full force of his habitual craving for the stimulant. Now whether this belief is well or ill founded is a different question from that usually discussed between Determinists and Libertarians: at the same time the two questions are liable to be confused. It is sometimes vaguely thought that a belief in Free Will requires us to maintain that at any moment we can alter our habits to any extent by a sufficiently strong exertion. And no doubt most commonly when we make such efforts, we believe at the moment that they will be completely effectual: we will to do something hours or days hence with the same confidence with which we will to do something immediately. But on reflection, no one, I think, will maintain that in such cases the future act appears

to be in his power in the same sense as a choice of alternatives
that takes effect immediately.   Not only does continual experience show us that such resolutions as to the future have
a limited and too frequently an inadequate effect : but the
common belief is really inconsistent with the very doctrine of
Free Will that is thought to justify it : for if by a present
volition I can fully determine an action that is to take place
some hours hence, when the time comes to do that act I
shall find myself no longer free.   We must therefore accept
the conclusion that each such resolve has only a limited effect :
and that we cannot know when making it how far this effect
will exhibit itself in the performance of the act resolved upon.
At the same time it can hardly be denied that such resolves
sometimes succeed in breaking old habits : and even when they
fail to do this, they often substitute a painful struggle for
smooth and easy indulgence.   Hence it is reasonable to suppose
that they always produce some effect in this direction ; whether
they operate by causing new motives to present themselves on
the side of reason, when the time of inner conflict arrives; or
whether they directly weaken the impulsive force of habit in
the same manner as an actual breach of custom does, though
in an inferior degree.[1]

If this account of the range of volition be accepted, it will,
I trust, dispel any lingering doubts which the argument of
the preceding section, as to the practical unimportance of the
Free Will controversy, may have left in the reader's mind.
For it may have been vaguely thought that while on the
Determinist theory it would be wrong, in certain cases, to
perform a single act of virtue if we had no ground for believing that we should hereafter duly follow it up ; on the
assumption of Freedom we should boldly do always what

---

[1] It should be observed that the same kind of change is sometimes brought
about, without volition, by a powerful emotional shock, due to extraneous
causes : and hence it might be inferred that in all cases it is a powerful impression of an emotional kind that produces the effect ; and that the will is only
concerned in concentrating our attention on the benefits to be gained or evils to
be avoided by the change of habit, and so intensifying the impression of these.
But though this kind of voluntary contemplation is a useful auxiliary to good
resolutions, it does not seem to be this effort of will that constitutes the resolution : we can clearly distinguish the two.   Hence this third effect of volition
cannot be resolved into the second, but must be stated separately.

would be best if consistently followed up, being conscious that such consistency is in our power.   But the supposed difference vanishes, if it be admitted that by any effort of resolution at the present moment we can only produce a certain limited effect upon our tendencies to action at some future time, and that immediate consciousness cannot tell us that this effect will be adequate to the occasion, nor indeed how great it will really prove to be.   For the most extreme Libertarian must then allow that before pledging ourselves to any future course of action we ought to estimate carefully, from our experience of ourselves and general knowledge of human nature, what the probability is of our keeping present resolutions in the circumstances in which we are likely to be placed.   It is no doubt morally most important that we should not tranquilly acquiesce in any weakness or want of self-control: but the fact remains that such weakness is not curable by a single volition: and whatever we can do towards curing it by any effort of will at any moment, is as clearly enjoined by reason on the Determinist theory as it is on the Libertarian.   On neither theory is it reasonable that we should deceive ourselves as to the extent of our weakness, or ignore it in the forecast of our conduct, or suppose it more easily remediable than it really is.

CHAPTER VI

ETHICAL PRINCIPLES AND METHODS

§ 1. THE results of the three preceding chapters may be briefly stated as follows :—

The aim of Ethics is to systematise and free from error the apparent cognitions that most men have of the rightness or reasonableness of conduct, whether the conduct be considered as right in itself, or as the means to some end commonly conceived as ultimately reasonable.[1] These cognitions are normally accompanied by emotions of various kinds, known as "moral sentiments": but an ethical judgment cannot be explained as affirming merely the existence of such a sentiment: indeed it is an essential characteristic of a moral feeling that it is bound up with an apparent cognition of something more than mere feeling. Such cognitions, again, I have called 'dictates,' or 'imperatives'; because, in so far as they relate to conduct on which any one is deliberating, they are accompanied by a certain impulse to do the acts recognised as right, which is liable to conflict with other impulses. Provided this impulse is effective in producing right volition, it is not of primary importance for ethical purposes to determine the exact characteristics of the emotional states that precede such volitions. And this remains true even if the

[1] As I have before said, the applicability of a method for determining right conduct relatively to an ultimate end—whether Happiness or Perfection—does not necessarily depend on the acceptance of the end as prescribed by reason : it only requires that it should be in some way adopted as ultimate and paramount. I have, however, confined my attention in this treatise to ends which are widely accepted as reasonable : and I shall afterwards endeavour to exhibit the self-evident practical axioms which appear to me to be implied in this acceptance. Cf. *post*, Book iii. chap. xiii.

force actually operating on his will is mere desire for the
pleasures that he foresees will attend right conduct, or aversion
to the pains that will result from doing wrong : though we
observe that in this case his action does not correspond to our
common notion of strictly virtuous conduct; and though there
seems to be no ground for regarding such desires and aversions
as the sole, or even the normal, motives of human volitions.
Nor, again, is it generally important to determine whether we
are always, metaphysically speaking, 'free' to do what we
clearly see to be right.   What I 'ought' to do, in the strictest
use of the word 'ought,' is always 'in my power,' in the sense
that there is no obstacle to my doing it except absence of
adequate motive; and it is ordinarily impossible for me, in
deliberation, to regard such absence of motive as a reason
for not doing what I otherwise judge to be reasonable.

What then do we commonly regard as valid ultimate
reasons for acting or abstaining?   This, as was said, is the
starting-point for the discussions of the present treatise:
which is not primarily concerned with proving or disproving
the validity of any such reasons, but rather with the critical
exposition of the different 'methods'—or rational procedures
for determining right conduct in any particular case—which
are logically connected with the different ultimate reasons
widely accepted.   In the first chapter we found that such
reasons were supplied by the notions of Happiness and
Excellence or Perfection (including Virtue or Moral Perfection
as a prominent element), regarded as ultimate ends, and Duty
as prescribed by unconditional rules.   This threefold difference
in the conception of the ultimate reason for conduct corresponds to what seem the most fundamental distinctions that
we apply to human existence; the distinction between the
conscious being and the stream of conscious experience, and
the distinction (within this latter) of Action and Feeling.
For Perfection is put forward as the ideal goal of the development of a human being, considered as a permanent entity;
while by Duty, we mean the kind of Action that we think
ought to be done; and similarly by Happiness or Pleasure
we mean an ultimately desired or desirable kind of Feeling.
It may seem, however, that these notions by no means exhaust
the list of reasons which are widely accepted as ultimate

grounds of action. Many religious persons think that the
highest reason for doing anything is that it is God's Will :
while to others ' Self-realisation ' or ' Self-development,' and to
others, again, ' Life according to nature ' appear the really
ultimate ends.   And it is not hard to understand why conceptions such as these are regarded as supplying deeper and
more completely satisfying answers to the fundamental question of Ethics, than those before named : since they do not
merely represent ' what ought to be,' as such ; they represent
it in an apparently simple relation to what actually is.   God,
Nature, Self, are the fundamental facts of existence ; the
knowledge of what will accomplish God's Will, what is,
' according to Nature,' what will realise the true Self in each
of us, would seem to solve the deepest problems of Metaphysics as well as of Ethics.   But just because these notions
combine the ideal with the actual, their proper sphere belongs
not to Ethics as I define it, but to Philosophy—the central
and supreme study which is concerned with the relations of
all objects of knowledge.   The introduction of these notions
into Ethics is liable to bring with it a fundamental confusion
between " what is " and " what ought to be," destructive of all
clearness in ethical reasoning : and if this confusion is avoided,
the strictly ethical import of such notions, when made explicit,
appears always to lead us to one or other of the methods
previously distinguished.

There is least danger of confusion in the case of the
theological conception of ' God's Will ' ; since here the connexion between ' what is ' and ' what ought to be ' is perfectly
clear and explicit.   The content of God's Will we conceive
as presently existing, in idea : its actualisation is the end to
be aimed at.   There is indeed a difficulty in understanding
how God's Will can fail to be realised, whether we do right or
wrong : or how, if it cannot fail to be realised in either case,
its realisation can give the ultimate motive for doing right.
But this difficulty it belongs to Theology rather than Ethics
to solve.   The practical question is, assuming that God wills
in a special sense what we ought to do, how we are to ascertain this in any particular case.   This must be either by
Revelation or by Reason, or by both combined.   If an external
Revelation is proposed as the standard, we are obviously

carried beyond the range of our study; on the other hand, when we try to ascertain by reason the Divine Will, the conception seems to present itself as a common form under which a religious mind is disposed to regard whatever method of determining conduct it apprehends to be rational; since we cannot know any act to be in accordance with the Divine Will, which we do not also, by the same exercise of thought, know to be dictated by reason. Thus, commonly, it is either assumed that God desires the Happiness of men, in which case our efforts should be concentrated on its production: or that He desires their Perfection, and that that should be our end: or that whatever His end may be (into which perhaps we have no right to inquire) His Laws are immediately cognisable, being in fact the first principles of Intuitional Morality. Or perhaps it is explained that God's Will is to be learnt by examining our own constitution or that of the world we are in: so that 'Conformity to God's Will' seems to resolve itself into 'Self-realisation,' or 'Life according to nature.' In any case, this conception, however important it may be in supplying new motives for doing what we believe to be right, does not—apart from Revelation—suggest any special criterion of rightness.

§ 2. Let us pass to consider the notions 'Nature,' 'Natural,' 'Conformity to Nature.' I assume—in order to obtain a principle distinct from 'Self-realisation,'[1]—that the 'Nature' to which we are to conform is not each one's own individual nature, but human nature generally, considered either apart from or in relation to its environment: that we are to find the standard of right conduct in a certain type of human existence which we can somehow abstract from observation of actual human life. Now in a certain sense every rational man must, of course, "conform to nature"; that is, in aiming at any ends, he must adapt his efforts to the particular conditions of his existence, physical and psychical. But if he is to go beyond this, and conform to 'Nature' in the adoption of an ultimate end or paramount standard

---

[1] The notion of 'Self-realisation' will be more conveniently examined in the following chapter: where I shall distinguish different interpretations of the term 'Egoism,' which I have taken to denote one of the three principal species of ethical method.

of right conduct, it must be on the basis—if not of strictly Theological assumptions, at any rate—of the more or less definite recognition of Design exhibited in the empirically known world.   If we find no design in nature, if the complex processes of the world known to us through experience are conceived as an aimless though orderly drift of change, the knowledge of these processes and their laws may indeed limit the aims of rational beings, but I cannot conceive how it can determine the ends of their action, or be a source of unconditional rules of duty.   And in fact those who use 'natural' as an ethical notion do commonly suppose that by contemplating the actual play of human impulses, or the physical constitution of man, or his social relations, we may find principles for determining positively and completely the kind of life he was designed to live.   I think, however, that every attempt thus to derive 'what ought to be' from 'what is' palpably fails, the moment it is freed from funda-mental confusions of thought.   For instance, suppose we seek practical guidance in the conception of human nature regarded as a system of impulses and dispositions, we must obviously give a special precision to the meaning of " natural "; since in a sense, as Butler observes, any impulse is natural, but it is manifestly idle to bid us follow Nature in this sense : for the question of duty is never raised except when we are conscious of a conflict of impulses, and wish to know which to follow. Nor does it help us to say that the supremacy of Reason is Natural, as we have started by assuming that what Reason prescribes is conformity to Nature, and thus our line of thought would become circular : the Nature that we are to follow must be distinguished from our Practical Reason, if it is to become a guide to it.   How then are we to distinguish 'natural impulses'—in the sense in which they are to guide rational choice — from the unnatural?   Those who have occupied themselves with this distinction seem generally to have interpreted the Natural to mean either the *common* as opposed to the rare and exceptional, or the *original* as opposed to what is later in development ; or, negatively, what is not the effect of human volition.   But I have never seen any ground for assuming broadly that Nature abhors the exceptional, or prefers the earlier in time to the later ; and when we take a retrospective view of the history of the human race, we find that some impulses which all admire, such as the love of knowledge and enthusiastic philanthropy, are both rarer and later in their appearance than others which all judge to be lower.   Again, it is obviously unwarrantable to eschew as unnatural and opposed to the Divine design all such impulses as have been produced in us by the institutions of society, or our use of human arrangements and contrivances, or that result in any way from the deliberate action of our fellow-men : for this were arbitrarily to exclude society and human action from the scope of Nature's purposes.   And besides it is clear that many impulses so generated appear to be either moral or auxiliary to morality and in other ways beneficial : and though others no doubt are pernicious and misleading, it seems that we can only distinguish these latter from the former by taking note of their effects, and not by any precision that reflection can give to the notion of ' natural.'   If, again, we fall back upon a more physical view of our nature and endeavour to ascertain for what end our corporeal frame was constructed, we find that such contemplation determines very little.   We can infer from our nutritive system that we are intended to take food, and similarly that we are to exercise our various muscles in some way or other, and our brain and organs of sense.   But this carries us a very trifling way, for the practical question almost always is, not whether we are to use our organs or leave them unused, but to what extent or in what manner we are to use them : and it does not appear that a definite answer to this question can ever be elicited, by a logical process of inference, from observations of the human organism, and the actual physical life of men.

If, finally, we consider man in his social relations—as father, son, neighbour, citizen—and endeavour to determine the " natural " rights and obligations that attach to such relations, we find that the conception ' natural ' presents a problem and not a solution.   To an unreflective mind what is customary in social relations usually appears natural ; but no reflective person is prepared to lay down " conformity to custom " as a fundamental moral principle : the problem, then, is to find in the rights and obligations established by custom in a particular society at a particular time an element that has a binding force beyond what mere custom can give. And this problem can only be solved by reference to the ultimate good of social existence — whether conceived as happiness or as perfection—or by appealing to some intuitively known principle of social duty, other than the principle of aiming at the happiness or perfection of society.

Nor, again, does it help us to adopt the more modern view of Nature, which regards the organic world as exhibiting, not an aggregate of fixed types, but a continuous and gradual process of changing life. For granting that this ' evolution '—as the name implies—is not merely a process from old to new, but a progress from less to more of certain definite characteristics; it is surely absurd to maintain that we ought *therefore* to take these characteristics as Ultimate Good, and make it our whole endeavour to accelerate the arrival of an inevitable future. That whatever is to be will be better than what is, we all hope; but there seems to be no more reason for summarily identifying ' what ought to be ' with ' what certainly will be,' than for finding it in ' what commonly is,' or ' what originally was.'

On the whole, it appears to me that no definition that has ever been offered of the Natural exhibits this notion as really capable of furnishing an independent ethical first principle. And no one maintains that ' natural ' like ' beautiful ' is a notion that though indefinable is yet clear, being derived from a simple unanalysable impression. Hence I see no way of extracting from it a definite practical criterion of the rightness of actions.

§ 3. The discussion in the preceding section will have shown that not all the different views that are taken of the ultimate reason for doing what is concluded to be right lead to practically different methods of arriving at this conclusion. Indeed we find that almost any method may be connected with almost any ultimate reason by means of some—often plausible— assumption. Hence arises difficulty in the classification and comparison of ethical systems; since they often appear to have different affinities according as we consider Method or Ultimate Reason. In my treatment of the subject, difference of Method is taken as the paramount consideration : and it is on this account that I have treated the view in which Perfection is taken to be the Ultimate End as a variety of the Intuitionism which determines right conduct by reference to axioms of duty intuitively known; while I have made as marked a separation as possible between Epicureanism or Egoistic Hedonism, and the Universalistic or Benthamite [1] Hedonism to which I propose to restrict the term Utilitarianism.

I am aware that these two latter methods are commonly treated as closely connected: and it is not difficult to find reasons for this. In the first place, they agree in prescribing actions as means to an end distinct from, and lying outside the actions; so that they both lay down rules which are not absolute but relative, and only valid if they conduce to the end. Again, the ultimate end is according to both methods the same in quality, i.e. pleasure; or, more strictly, the maximum of pleasure attainable, pains being subtracted. Besides, it is of course to a great extent true that the conduct recommended by the one principle coincides with that inculcated by the other. Though it would seem to be only in an ideal polity that 'self-interest well understood' leads to the perfect discharge of all social duties, still, in a tolerably well-ordered community it prompts to the fulfilment of most of them, unless under very exceptional circumstances. And, on the other hand, a Universalistic Hedonist may reasonably hold that his own happiness is that portion of the universal happiness which it is most in his power to promote, and which therefore is most especially entrusted to his charge. And the practical blending of the two systems is sure to go beyond their theoretical coincidence. It is much easier for a man to move in a sort of diagonal between Egoistic and Universalistic Hedonism, than to be practically a consistent adherent of either. Few men are so completely selfish, whatever their theory of morals may be, as not occasionally to promote the happiness of others from natural sympathetic impulse unsupported by Epicurean calculation. And probably still fewer are so resolutely unselfish as never to find "all men's good" in their own with rather too ready conviction.

Further, from Bentham's psychological doctrine, that every human being always does aim at his own greatest apparent happiness, it seems to follow that it is useless to point out to a man the conduct that would conduce to the general happiness,

[1] See Note at the end of the chapter.

unless you convince him at the same time that it would conduce to his own. Hence on this view, egoistic and universalistic considerations must necessarily be combined in any practical treatment of morality: and this being so, it was perhaps to be expected that Bentham[1] or his disciples would go further, and attempt to base on the Egoism which they accept as inevitable the Universalistic Hedonism which they approve and inculcate. And accordingly we find that J. S. Mill does try to establish a logical connexion between the psychological and ethical principles which he holds in common with Bentham, and to convince his readers that because each man naturally seeks his own happiness, therefore he ought to seek the happiness of other people.[2]

Nevertheless, it seems to me undeniable that the practical affinity between Utilitarianism and Intuitionism is really much greater than that between the two forms of Hedonism. My grounds for holding this will be given at length in subsequent chapters. Here I will only observe that many moralists who have maintained as practically valid the judgments of right and wrong which the Common Sense of mankind seems intuitively to enunciate, have yet regarded General Happiness as an end to which the rules of morality are the best means, and have held that a knowledge of these rules was implanted by Nature or revealed by God for the attainment of this end. Such a belief implies that, though I am bound to take, as *my* ultimate standard in acting, conformity to a rule which is for me absolute, still the natural or Divine reason for the rule laid down is Utilitarian. On this view, the *method* of Utilitarianism is certainly rejected: the connexion between right action and happiness is not ascertained by a process of reasoning. But we can hardly say that the Utilitarian principle is altogether rejected: rather the limitations of the human reason are supposed to prevent it from apprehending adequately the real connexion between the true principle and the right rules of conduct. This connexion, however, has always been to a large extent recognised by all reflective persons. Indeed, so clear is it

---

[1] See Note at the end of the chapter.
[2] We shall have occasion to consider Mill's argument on this point in a subsequent chapter. Cf. *post*, Book iii. chap. xiii.

that in most cases the observance of the commonly received moral rules tends to render human life tranquil and happy, that even moralists (as Whewell) who are most strongly opposed to Utilitarianism have, in attempting to exhibit the "necessity" of moral rules, been led to dwell on utilitarian considerations.

And during the first period of ethical controversy in modern England, after the audacious enunciation of Egoism by Hobbes had roused in real earnest the search for a philosophical basis of morality, Utilitarianism appears in friendly alliance with Intuitionism. It was not to supersede but to support the morality of Common Sense, against the dangerous innovations of Hobbes, that Cumberland declared "the common good[1] of all Rationals" to be the end to which moral rules were the means. We find him quoted with approval by Clarke, who is commonly taken to represent Intuitionism in an extreme form. Nor does Shaftesbury, in introducing the theory of a "moral sense," seem to have dreamt that it could ever impel us to actions not clearly conducive to the Good[1] of the Whole: and his disciple Hutcheson expressly identified its promptings with those of Benevolence. Butler, I think, was our first influential writer who dwelt on the discrepancies between Virtue as commonly understood and "conduct likeliest to produce an overbalance of happiness."[2] When Hume presented Utilitarianism as a mode of explaining current morality, it was seen or suspected to have a partially destructive tendency. But it was not till the time of Paley and Bentham that it was offered as a method for determining conduct, which was to overrule all traditional precepts and supersede all existing moral sentiments. And even this final antagonism relates rather to theory and method than to

---

[1] It should be observed that neither Cumberland nor Shaftesbury uses the term "Good" (substantive) in a purely and exclusively hedonistic sense. But Shaftesbury uses it mainly in this sense: and Cumberland's "Good" includes Happiness as well as Perfection.

[2] See Dissertation II. *Of the Nature of Virtue* appended to the *Analogy*. It may be interesting to notice a gradual change in Butler's view on this important point. In the first of his Sermons on Human Nature, published some years before the *Analogy*, he does not notice, any more than Shaftesbury and Hutcheson, any possible want of harmony between Conscience and Benevolence. A note to Sermon XII., however, seems to indicate a stage of transition between the view of the first Sermon and the view of the Dissertation.

practical results: practical conflict, in ordinary human minds, is mainly between Self-interest and Social Duty however determined. Indeed, from a practical point of view the principle of aiming at the "greatest happiness of the greatest number" is *prima facie* more definitely opposed to Egoism than the Common-Sense morality is. For this latter seems to leave a man free to pursue his own happiness under certain definite limits and conditions: whereas Utilitarianism seems to require a more comprehensive and unceasing subordination of self-interest to the common good. And thus, as Mill remarks, Utilitarianism is sometimes attacked from two precisely opposite sides: from a confusion with Egoistic Hedonism it is called base and grovelling; while at the same time it is more plausibly charged with setting up too high a standard of unselfishness and making exaggerated demands on human nature.

A good deal remains to be said, in order to make the principle and method of Utilitarianism perfectly clear and explicit: but it seems best to defer this till we come to the investigation of its details. It will be convenient to take this as the final stage of our examination of methods. For on the one hand it is simpler that the discussion of Egoistic should precede that of Universalistic Hedonism; and on the other, it seems desirable that we should obtain in as exact a form as possible the enunciations of Intuitive Morality, before we compare these with the results of the more doubtful and difficult calculations of utilitarian consequences.

In the remaining chapters of this Book I shall endeavour to remove certain ambiguities as to the general nature and relations of the other two methods, as designated respectively by the terms Egoism and Intuitionism, before proceeding to the fuller examination of them in Books ii. and iii.

NOTE.—I have called the ethical doctrine that takes universal happiness as the ultimate end and standard of right conduct by the name of Bentham, because the thinkers who have chiefly taught this doctrine in England during the present century have referred it to Bentham as their master. And it certainly seems to me clear—though Mr. Bain (cf. *Mind*, January 1883, p. 48) appears to doubt it—that Bentham adopted this doctrine explicitly, in its most comprehensive scope, at the earliest stage in the formation of his opinions; nor do I think that he ever consciously abandoned or qualified it. We find him writing in his common-place book, in 1773-4 (cf. *Works*, Bowring's edition, vol. x. p. 70), that Helvetius had "established a standard of rectitude for actions";—the standard being that "a sort of action is a right one, when the tendency of it is to augment the mass of happiness in the community." And we find him writing fifty years later (cf. *Works*, vol. x. p. 79) the following account of his earliest view, in a passage which contains no hint of later dissent from it:—"By an early pamphlet of Priestley's . . . light was added to the warmth. In the phrase 'the greatest happiness of the greatest number,' I then saw delineated, for the first time, a plain as well as a true standard for whatever is right or wrong . . . in human conduct, *whether in the field of morals or of politics.*"

At the same time I must admit that in other passages Bentham seems no less explicitly to adopt Egoistic Hedonism as the method of 'private Ethics,' as distinct from legislation: and in his posthumous 'Deontology' the two principles appear to be reconciled by the doctrine, that it is always the individual's true interest, even from a purely mundane point of view, to act in the manner most conducive to the general happiness. This latter proposition—which I regard as erroneous—is not, indeed, definitely put forward in any of the treatises published by Bentham in his lifetime, or completely prepared by him for publication: but it may be inferred from his common-place book that he held it (see his *Works*, vol. x. pp. 560, 561).

CHAPTER VII

EGOISM AND SELF-LOVE

§ 1. IN the preceding chapters I have used the term
"Egoism," as it is most commonly used, to denote a system
which prescribes actions as means to the end of the individual's
happiness or pleasure. The ruling motive in such a system
is commonly said to be "self-love." But both terms admit of
other interpretations, which it will be well to distinguish and
set aside before proceeding further.

For example, the term "egoistic" is ordinarily and not
improperly applied to the basis on which Hobbes attempted
to construct morality; and on which alone, as he held, the
social order could firmly rest, and escape the storms and
convulsions with which it seemed to be menaced from the
vagaries of the unenlightened conscience. But it is not
strictly the end of Egoism as I have defined it—greatest
attainable pleasure for the individual—but rather "self-
preservation," which determines the first of those precepts of
rational egoism which Hobbes calls "Laws of Nature," viz.,
"Seek peace and ensue it." And in the development of his
system we often find that it is Preservation rather than
Pleasure, or perhaps a compromise between the two,[1] that is
taken as the ultimate end and standard of right conduct.

Again, in Spinoza's view the principle of rational action
is necessarily egoistic, and is (as with Hobbes) the impulse of
self-preservation. The individual mind, says Spinoza, like

---

[1] Thus the end for which an individual is supposed to renounce the unlimited rights of the State of Nature is said (*Leviathan*, chap. xiv.) to be
"nothing else but the security of a man's person in this life, and the means of
preserving life so as not to be weary of it."

everything else, strives so far as it is able to continue in its state of being: indeed this effort is its very essence. It is true that the object of this impulse cannot be separated from pleasure or joy; because pleasure or joy is "a passion in which the soul passes to higher perfection." Still it is not at Pleasure that the impulse primarily aims, but at the mind's Perfection or Reality: as we should now say, at Self-realisation or Self-development. Of this, according to Spinoza, the highest form consists in a clear comprehension of all things in their necessary order as modifications of the one Divine Being, and that willing acceptance of all which springs from this comprehension. In this state the mind is purely active, without any admixture of passion or passivity: and thus its essential nature is realised or actualised to the greatest possible degree.

We perceive that this is the notion of Self-realisation as defined not only *by* but *for* a philosopher: and that it would mean something quite different in the case of a man of action —such, for example, as the reflective dramatist of Germany introduces exclaiming:

> Ich kann mich nicht
> Wie so ein Wortheld, so ein Tugend-Schwätzer
> An meinem Willen wärmen, und Gedanken . . .
> Wenn ich nicht wirke mehr, bin ich vernichtet.[1]

The artist, again, often contemplates his production of the beautiful as a realisation of self: and moralists of a certain turn of mind, in all ages, have similarly regarded the sacrifice of inclination to duty as the highest form of Self-development; and held that true self-love prompts us always to obey the commands issued by the governing principle—Reason or Conscience—within us, as in such obedience, however painful, we shall be realising our truest self.

We see, in short, that the term Egoism, so far as it merely implies that reference is made to self in laying down first principles of conduct, does not really indicate in any way the substance of such principles. For all our impulses, high and low, sensual and moral alike, are so far similarly related to self, that—except when two or more impulses come into con-

---

[1] Schiller's *Wallenstein.*

scious conflict—we tend to identify ourselves with each as it arises. Thus self-consciousness may be prominent in yielding to any impulse: and egoism, in so far as it merely implies such prominence, is a common form applicable to all principles of action.

It may be said, however, that we do not, properly speaking, 'develop' or 'realise' self by yielding to the impulse which happens to be predominant in us; but by exercising, each in its due place and proper degree, all the different faculties, capacities, and propensities, of which our nature is made up. But here there is an important ambiguity. What do we mean by 'due proportion and proper degree'? These terms may imply an ideal, into conformity with which the individual mind has to be trained, by restraining some of its natural impulses and strengthening others, and developing its higher faculties rather than its lower: or they may merely refer to the original combination and proportion of tendencies in the character with which each is born; to this, it may be meant, we ought to adapt as far as possible the circumstances in which we place ourselves and the functions which we choose to exercise, in order that we may "be ourselves," "live our own life," etc. According to the former interpretation rational Self-development is merely another term for the pursuit of Perfection for oneself: while in the latter sense it hardly appears that Self-development (when clearly distinguished) is really put forward as an absolute end, but rather as a means to happiness; for supposing a man to have inherited propensities clearly tending to his own unhappiness, no one would recommend him to develop these as fully as possible, instead of modifying or subduing them in some way. Whether actually the best way of seeking happiness is to give free play to one's nature, we will hereafter consider in the course of our examination of Hedonism.

On the whole, then, I conclude that the notion of Self-realisation is to be avoided in a treatise on ethical method, on account of its indefiniteness: and for a similar reason we must discard a common account of Egoism which describes its ultimate end as the 'good' of the individual; for the term 'good' may cover all possible views of the ultimate end of rational conduct. Indeed it may be said that Egoism in this sense was assumed in the whole ethical controversy of ancient Greece; that is, it was assumed on all sides that a rational individual [1] would make the pursuit of his own good his supreme aim: the controverted question was whether this Good was rightly conceived as Pleasure or Virtue, or any *tertium quid*. Nor is the ambiguity removed if we follow Aristotle in confining our attention to the Good attainable in human life, and call this Well-being (Εὐδαιμονία). For we may still argue with the Stoics, that virtuous or excellent activities and not pleasures are the elements of which true human Well-being is composed. Indeed Aristotle himself adopts this view, so far as to determine the details of Well-being accordingly: though he does not, with the Stoics, regard the pursuit of Virtue and that of Pleasure as competing alternatives, holding rather that the "best pleasure" is an inseparable concomitant of the most excellent action. Even the English term Happiness is not free from a similar ambiguity.[2] It seems, indeed, to be commonly used in Bentham's way as convertible with Pleasure,—or rather as denoting that of which the constituents are pleasures;—and it is in this sense that I think it most convenient to use it. Sometimes, however, in ordinary discourse, the term is rather employed to denote a particular kind of agreeable consciousness, which is distinguished from and even contrasted with definite specific pleasures—such as the gratifications of sensual appetite or other keen and vehement desires—as being at once calmer and more indefinite: we may characterise it as the feeling which accompanies the normal activity of a "healthy mind in a healthy body," and of which specific pleasures seem

---

[1] I shall afterwards try to explain how it comes about that, in modern thought, the proposition 'My own Good is my only reasonable ultimate end' is not a mere tautology, even though we define 'Good' as that at which it is ultimately reasonable to aim. Cf. *post*, chap. ix. and Book iii. chaps. xiii. xiv.

[2] Aristotle's selection of εὐδαιμονία to denote what he elsewhere calls "Human" or "Practicable" good, and the fact that, after all, we have no better rendering for εὐδαιμονία than "Happiness" or "Felicity," has caused no little misunderstanding of his system. Thus when Stewart (*Philosophy of the Active and Moral Powers*, Book ii. chap. ii.) says that "by many of the best of the ancient moralists . . . the whole of ethics was reduced to this question . . . What is most conducive on the whole to our happiness?" the remark, if not exactly false, is certain to mislead his readers; since by Stewart, as by most English writers, "Happiness" is definitely conceived as consisting of "Pleasures" or "Enjoyments."

to be rather stimulants than elements. Sometimes, again—
though, I think, with a more manifest divergence from common
usage—" happiness " or " true happiness " is understood in a
definitely non-hedonistic sense, as denoting results other than
agreeable feelings of any kind.[1]

§ 2. To be clear, then, we must particularise as the object
of Self-love, and End of the method which I have distinguished
as Egoistic Hedonism, Pleasure, taken in its widest sense, as
including every species of " delight," " enjoyment," or " satisfaction "; except so far as any particular species may be
excluded by its incompatibility with some greater pleasures, or
as necessarily involving concomitant or subsequent pains. It
is thus that Self-love seems to be understood by Butler [2] and
other English moralists after him ; as a desire of one's own
pleasure generally, and of the greatest amount of it obtainable,
from whatever source it may be obtained. In fact, it is upon
this generality and comprehensiveness that the ' authority ' and
' reasonableness' attributed to Self-love in Butler's system are
founded. For satisfaction or pleasure of some kind results
from gratifying any impulse ; thus when antagonistic impulses
compete for the determination of the Will, we are prompted
by the desire for pleasure in general to compare the pleasures
which we foresee will respectively attend the gratification of
either impulse, and when we have ascertained which set of

---

[1] Thus Green (*Prolegomena to Ethics*, Book iii. chap. iv. § 228) says, " It is the
realisation of those objects in which we are mainly interested, *not the succession
of enjoyments which we shall experience in realising them*, that forms the definite
content of our idea of true happiness, so far as it has such content at all." Cf.
also § 238. It is more remarkable to find J. S. Mill (*Utilitarianism*, chap. iv.)
declaring that "money"—no less than " power " or " fame "—comes by association of ideas to be " a part of happiness," an " ingredient in the individual's
conception of happiness." But this seems to be a mere looseness of phraseology,
venial in a treatise aiming at a popular style ; since Mill has expressly said that
"by happiness is intended pleasure and the absence of pain," and he cannot
mean that money is either the one or the other. In fact he uses in the same
passage—as an alternative phrase for "parts of happiness"—the phrases "sources
of happiness " and " sources of pleasure " : and his real meaning is more precisely
expressed by these latter terms. That is, the distinction which he is really concerned to emphasise is that between the state of mind in which money is valued
solely as a means of buying other things, and the state of mind—such as the
miser's—in which the mere consciousness of possessing it gives pleasure, apart
from any idea of spending it.

[2] See Sermon XI. ". . . the cool principle of self-love or general desire of
our own happiness."

pleasures is the greatest, Self-love or the desire for pleasure in general reinforces the corresponding impulse. It is thus called into play whenever impulses conflict, and is therefore naturally regulative and directive (as Butler argues) of other springs of action. On this view, so far as Self-love operates, we merely consider the *amount* of pleasure or satisfaction: to use Bentham's illustration, " quantity of pleasure being equal, push-pin is as good as poetry."

This position, however, seems to many offensively paradoxical; and J. S. Mill[1] in his development of Bentham's doctrine thought it desirable to abandon it and to take into account differences in quality among pleasures as well as differences in degree. Now here we may observe, first, that it is quite consistent with the view quoted as Bentham's to describe some kinds of pleasure as inferior in quality to others, if by ' a pleasure ' we mean (as is often meant) a whole state of consciousness which is only partly pleasurable ; and still more if we take into view subsequent states. For many pleasures are not free from pain even while enjoyed ; and many more have painful consequences. Such pleasures are, in Bentham's phrase, " impure ": and as the pain has to be set off as a drawback in valuing the pleasure, it is in accordance with strictly quantitative measurement of pleasure to call them inferior in kind. And again, we must be careful not to confound intensity of *pleasure* with intensity of *sensation* : as a pleasant feeling may be strong and absorbing, and yet not so pleasant as another that is more subtle and delicate. With these explanations, it seems to me that in order to work out consistently the method that takes pleasure as the sole ultimate end of rational conduct, Bentham's proposition must be accepted, and all *qualitative* comparison of pleasures must really resolve itself into quantitative. For all pleasures are understood to be so called because they have a common property of pleasantness, and may therefore be compared in respect of this common property. If, then, what we are seeking is pleasure as such, and pleasure alone, we must evidently always prefer the more pleasant pleasure to the less pleasant : no other choice seems reasonable, unless we are aiming at something besides pleasure. And often when we say

[1] *Utilitarianism*, chap. ii.

that one kind of pleasure is better than another—-as (*e.g.*) that the pleasures of reciprocated affection are superior in quality to the pleasures of gratified appetite—we mean that they are more pleasant. No doubt we may mean something else : we may mean, for instance, that they are nobler and more elevated, although less pleasant. But then we are clearly introducing a non-hedonistic ground of preference : and if this is done, the method adopted is a perplexing mixture of Intuitionism and Hedonism.

To sum up : Egoism, if we merely understand by it a method that aims at Self-realisation, seems to be a form into which almost any ethical system may be thrown, without modifying its essential characteristics. And even when further defined as Egoistic Hedonism, it is still imperfectly distinguishable from Intuitionism if quality of pleasures is admitted as a consideration distinct from and overruling quantity. There remains then Pure or Quantitative Egoistic Hedonism, which, as a method essentially distinct from all others and widely maintained to be rational, seems to deserve a detailed examination. According to this the rational agent regards quantity of consequent pleasure and pain to himself as alone important in choosing between alternatives of action ; and seeks always the greatest attainable surplus of pleasure over pain—which, without violation of usage, we may designate as his 'greatest happiness.' It seems to be this view and attitude of mind which is most commonly intended by the vaguer terms ' egoism,' ' egoistic ': and therefore I shall allow myself to use these terms in this more precise signification.

CHAPTER VIII.

§ 1. I HAVE used the term ' Intuitional ' to denote the view
of ethics which regards as the practically ultimate end of
moral actions their conformity to certain rules or dictates [1] of
Duty unconditionally prescribed. There is, however, considerable ambiguity as to the exact antithesis implied by the terms
' intuition,' ' intuitive,' and their congeners, as currently used
in ethical discussion, which we must now endeavour to remove.
Writers who maintain that we have ' intuitive knowledge ' of
the rightness of actions usually mean that this rightness is
ascertained by simply " looking at " the actions themselves, without considering their ulterior consequences. This view, indeed,
can hardly be extended to the whole range of duty ; since no
morality ever existed which did not consider ulterior consequences to some extent. Prudence or Forethought has
commonly been reckoned a virtue : and all modern lists of
Virtues have included Rational Benevolence, which aims at
the happiness of other human beings generally, and therefore
necessarily takes into consideration even remote effects of
actions. It must be observed, too, that it is difficult to draw
the line between an act and its consequences : as the effects
consequent on each of our volitions form a continuous series
of indefinite extension, and we seem to be conscious of causing
all these effects, so far as at the moment of volition we foresee
them to be probable. However, we find that in the common

---

[1] I use the term " dictates " to include the view afterwards mentioned (§ 2)
in which the ultimately valid moral imperatives are conceived as relating to
particular acts.

notions of different kinds of actions, a line is actually drawn between the results included in the notion and regarded as forming part of the act, and those considered as its consequences. For example, in speaking truth to a jury, I may possibly foresee that my words, operating along with other statements and indications, will unavoidably lead them to a wrong conclusion as to the guilt or innocence of the accused, as certainly as I foresee that they will produce a right impression as to the particular matter of fact to which I am testifying : still, we should commonly consider the latter foresight or intention to determine the nature of the act as an act of veracity, while the former merely relates to a consequence. We must understand then that the disregard of consequences, which the Intuitional view is here taken to imply, only relates to certain determinate classes of action (such as Truth-speaking) where common usage of terms adequately defines what events are to be included in the general notions of the acts, and what regarded as their consequences.

But again : we have to observe that men may and do judge remote as well as immediate results to be in themselves good, and such as we ought to seek to realise, without considering them in relation to the feelings of sentient beings. I have already assumed this to be the view of those who adopt the general Perfection, as distinct from the Happiness, of human society as their ultimate end ; and it would seem to be the view of many who concentrate their efforts on some more particular results, other than morality, such as the promotion of Art or Knowledge. Such a view, if expressly distinguished from Hedonism, might properly be classed as Intuitional, but in a sense wider than that defined in the preceding paragraph : *i.e.* it would be meant that the results in question are judged to be good *immediately*, and not by inference from experience of the pleasures which they produce. We have, therefore, to admit a wider use of ' Intuition,' as equivalent to ' immediate judgment as to what ought to be done or aimed at.' It should, however, be observed that the current contrast between ' intuitive ' or ' *a priori* ' and ' inductive ' or ' *a posteriori* ' morality commonly involves a certain confusion of thought. For what the ' inductive' moralist professes to know by induction, is commonly not the same thing as what the ' intuitive ' moralist professes to

know by intuition.   In the former case it is the conduciveness
to pleasure of certain kinds of action that is methodically ascertained : in the latter case, their rightness : there is therefore
no proper opposition.   If Hedonism claims to give authoritative
guidance, this can only be in virtue of the principle that pleasure
is the only reasonable ultimate end of human action : and this
principle cannot be known by induction from experience.
Experience can at most tell us that all men always do seek
pleasure as their ultimate end (that it does not support this
conclusion I have already tried to show): it cannot tell us that
any one ought so to seek it.   If this latter proposition is legitimately affirmed in respect either of private or of general
happiness, it must either be immediately known to be true,—
and therefore, we may say, a moral intuition—or be inferred
ultimately from premises which include at least one such moral
intuition ; hence either species of Hedonism, regarded from the
point of view primarily[1] taken in this treatise, might be legitimately said to be in a certain sense 'intuitional.'   It seems,
however, to be the prevailing opinion of ordinary moral persons,
and of most of the writers who have maintained the existence
of moral intuitions, that certain kinds of actions are unconditionally prescribed without regard to ulterior consequences :
and I have accordingly treated this doctrine as a distinguishing
characteristic of the Intuitional method, during the main[2] part
of the detailed examination of that method which I attempt
in Book iii.

§ 2. Further ; the common antithesis between 'intuitive'
and 'inductive' morality is misleading in another way : since
a moralist may hold the rightness of actions to be cognisable
apart from the pleasure produced by them, while yet his
method may be properly called Inductive.   For he may hold
that, just as the generalisations of physical science rest on
particular observations, so in ethics general truths can only be
reached by induction from judgments or perceptions relating to
the rightness or wrongness of particular acts.

For example, when Socrates is said by Aristotle to have

---

[1] I have explained in the concluding paragraph of chap. iii. that a different
view of hedonistic systems is admissible.

[2] The wider of the two meanings of 'Intuition' here distinguished is required
in treating of Philosophical Intuitionism.   See Book iii. chap. xiii.

applied inductive reasoning to ethical questions, it is this kind of induction which is meant.[1] He discovered, as we are told, the latent ignorance of himself and other men : that is, that they used general terms confidently, without being able, when called upon, to explain the meaning of those terms. His plan for remedying this ignorance was to work towards the true definition of each term, by examining and comparing different instances of its application. Thus the definition of Justice would be sought by comparing different actions commonly judged to be just, and framing a general proposition that would harmonise with all these particular judgments.

So again, in the popular view of Conscience it seems to be often implied that particular judgments are the most trustworthy. 'Conscience' is the accepted popular term for the faculty of moral judgment, as applied to the acts and motives of the person judging ; and we most commonly think of the dictates of conscience as relating to particular actions. Thus when a man is bidden, in any particular case, to 'trust to his conscience,' it commonly seems to be meant that he should exercise a faculty of judging morally this particular case without reference to general rules, and even in opposition to conclusions obtained by systematic deduction from such rules. And it is on this view of Conscience that the contempt often expressed for 'Casuistry' may be most easily justified : for if the particular case can be satisfactorily settled by conscience without reference to general rules, 'Casuistry,' which consists in the application of general rules to particular cases, is at best superfluous. But then, on this view, we shall have no practical need of any such general rules, or of scientific Ethics at all. We may of course form general propositions by induction from these particular conscientious judgments, and arrange them systematically : but any interest which such a system may have will be purely speculative. And this accounts, perhaps, for the indifference or hostility to systematic morality shown by some conscientious persons. For they feel that they can at any rate do without it : and they fear that the cultivation of it may place the mind in a wrong

---

[1] It must, however, be remembered that Aristotle regarded the general proposition obtained by induction as really more certain (and in a higher sense knowledge) than the particulars through which the mind is led up to it.

attitude in relation to practice, and prove rather unfavourable than otherwise to the proper development of the practically important faculty manifested or exercised in particular moral judgments.

The view above described may be called, in a sense, 'ultra-intuitional,' since, in its most extreme form, it recognises simple immediate intuitions alone and discards as superfluous all modes of reasoning to moral conclusions: and we may find in it one phase or variety of the Intuitional method,—if we may extend the term 'method' to include a procedure that is completed in a single judgment.

§ 3. But though probably all moral agents have experience of such particular intuitions, and though they constitute a great part of the moral phenomena of most minds, comparatively few are so thoroughly satisfied with them, as not to feel a need of some further moral knowledge even from a strictly practical point of view. For these particular intuitions do not, to reflective persons, present themselves as quite indubitable and irrefragable: nor do they always find when they have put an ethical question to themselves with all sincerity, that they are conscious of clear immediate insight in respect of it. Again, when a man compares the utterances of his conscience at different times, he often finds it difficult to make them altogether consistent: the same conduct will wear a different moral aspect at one time from that which it wore at another, although our knowledge of its circumstances and conditions is not materially changed. Further, we become aware that the moral perceptions of different minds, to all appearance equally competent to judge, frequently conflict: one condemns what another approves. In this way serious doubts are aroused as to the validity of each man's particular moral judgments: and we are led to endeavour to set these doubts at rest by appealing to general rules, more firmly established on a basis of common consent.

And in fact, though the view of conscience above discussed is one which much popular language seems to suggest, it is not that which Christian and other moralists have usually given. They have rather represented the process of conscience as analogous to one of jural reasoning, such as is conducted in a Court of Law. Here we have always a system of universal rules given, and any particular action has to be brought under one of these rules before it can be pronounced lawful or unlawful. Now the rules of positive law are usually not discoverable by the individual's reason : this may teach him that law ought to be obeyed, but what law is must, in the main, be communicated to him from some external authority. And this is not unfrequently the case with the conscientious reasoning of ordinary persons when any dispute or difficulty forces them to reason : they have a genuine impulse to conform to the right rules of conduct, but they are not conscious, in difficult or doubtful cases, of seeing for themselves what these are: they have to inquire of their priest, or their sacred books, or perhaps the common opinion of the society to which they belong. In so far as this is the case we cannot strictly call their method Intuitional. They follow rules generally received, not intuitively apprehended. Other persons, however (or perhaps all to some extent), do seem to see for themselves the truth [1] and bindingness of all or most of these current rules. They may still put forward ' common consent ' as an argument for the validity of these rules : but only as supporting the individual's intuition, not as a substitute for it or as superseding it.

Here then we have a second Intuitional Method : of which the fundamental assumption is that we can discern certain general rules with really clear and finally valid intuition. It is held that such general rules are implicit in the moral reasoning of ordinary men, who apprehend them adequately for most practical purposes, and are able to enunciate them roughly ; but that to state them with proper precision requires a special habit of contemplating clearly and steadily abstract moral notions. It is held that the moralist's function then is to perform this process of abstract contemplation, to arrange the results as systematically as possible, and by proper definitions and explanations to remove vagueness and prevent conflict. It is such a system as this which seems to be generally intended when Intuitive or *a priori* morality is mentioned, and which will chiefly occupy us in Book iii.

§ 4. By philosophic minds, however, the ' Morality of

---

[1] Strictly speaking, the attributes of truth and falsehood only belong formally to Rules when they are changed from the imperative mood ("Do X") into the indicative ("X ought to be done").

Common Sense ' (as I have ventured to call it), even when made as precise and orderly as possible, is often found unsatisfactory as a system, although they have no disposition to question its general authority. It is found difficult to accept as scientific first principles the moral generalities that we obtain by reflection on the ordinary thought of mankind, even though we share this thought. Even granting that these rules can be so defined as perfectly to fit together and cover the whole field of human conduct, without coming into conflict and without leaving any practical questions unanswered,—still the resulting code seems an accidental aggregate of precepts, which stands in need of some rational synthesis. In short, without being disposed to deny that conduct commonly judged to be right is so, we may yet require some deeper explanation *why* it is so. From this demand springs a third species or phase of Intuitionism, which, while accepting the morality of common sense as in the main sound, still attempts to find for it a philosophic basis which it does not itself offer : to get one or more principles more absolutely and undeniably true and evident, from which the current rules might be deduced, either just as they are commonly received or with slight modifications and rectifications.[1]

The three phases of Intuitionism just described may be treated as three stages in the formal development of Intuitive Morality: we may term them respectively Perceptional, Dogmatic, and Philosophical. The last-mentioned I have only defined in the vaguest way : in fact, as yet I have presented it only as a problem, of which it is impossible to foresee how many solutions may be attempted : but it does not seem desirable to investigate it further at present, as it will be more satisfactorily studied after examining in detail the Morality of Common Sense.

It must not be thought that these three phases are sharply distinguished in the moral reasoning of ordinary men : but then no more is Intuitionism of any sort sharply distinguished from either species of Hedonism. A loose combination or confusion of methods is the most common type of actual moral reasoning. Probably most moral men believe that their moral sense or

---

[1] It should be observed that such principles will not necessarily be "intuitional" in the narrower sense that excludes consequences ; but only in the wider sense as being self-evident principles relating to 'what ought to be.'

instinct in any case will guide them fairly right, but also that there are general rules for determining right action in different departments of conduct : and that for these again it is possible to find a philosophical explanation, by which they may be deduced from a smaller number of fundamental principles. Still for systematic direction of conduct, we require to know on what judgments we are to rely as ultimately valid.

So far I have been mainly concerned with differences in intuitional method due to difference of generality in the intuitive beliefs recognised as ultimately valid. There is, however, another class of differences arising from a variation of view as to the precise quality immediately apprehended in the moral intuition. These are peculiarly subtle and difficult to fix in clear and precise language, and I therefore reserve them for a separate chapter.

NOTE.—Intuitional moralists have not always taken sufficient care in expounding their system to make clear whether they regard as ultimately valid, moral judgments on single acts, or general rules prescribing particular kinds of acts, or more universal and fundamental principles. For example, Dugald Stewart uses the term "perception" to denote the immediate operation of the moral faculty ; at the same time, in describing what is thus perceived, he always seems to have in view general rules.

Still we can tolerably well distinguish among English ethical writers those who have confined themselves mainly to the definition and arrangement of the Morality of Common Sense, from those who have aimed at a more philosophical treatment of the content of moral intuition. And we find that the distinction corresponds in the main to a difference of periods : and that—what perhaps we should hardly have expected—the more philosophical school is the earlier. The explanation of this may be partly found by referring to the doctrines in antagonism to which, in the respective periods, the Intuitional method asserted and developed itself. In the first period all orthodox moralists were occupied in refuting Hobbism. But this system, though based on Materialism and Egoism, was yet intended as ethically constructive. Accepting in the main the commonly received rules of social morality, it explained them as the conditions of peaceful existence which enlightened self-interest directed each individual to obey ; provided only the social order to which they belonged was not merely ideal, but made actual by a strong government. Now no doubt this view renders the theoretical basis of duty seriously unstable ; still, assuming a decently good government, Hobbism may claim to at once explain and establish, instead of undermining, the morality of Common Sense. And therefore, though some of Hobbes' antagonists (as Cudworth) contented themselves with simply reaffirming the absoluteness of morality, the more thoughtful felt that system must be met by system and explanation by explanation, and that they must penetrate beyond the dogmas of common sense to some more irrefragable certainty. And so, while Cumberland found this deeper basis in the notion of " the common good of all Rationals" as an ultimate end, Clarke sought to exhibit the more fundamental of the received rules as axioms of perfect self-evidence, necessarily forced upon the mind in contemplating human beings and their relations. Clarke's results, however, were not found satisfactory : and by degrees the attempt to exhibit morality as a body of scientific truth fell into discredit, and the disposition to dwell on the emotional side of the moral consciousness became prevalent. But when ethical discussion thus passed over into psychological analysis and classification, the conception of the objectivity of duty, on which the authority of moral sentiment depends, fell gradually out of view : for example, we find Hutcheson asking why the moral sense should not vary in different human beings, as the palate does, without dreaming that there is any peril to morality in admitting such variations as legitimate. When, however, the new doctrine was endorsed by the dreaded name of Hume, its dangerous nature, and the need of bringing again into prominence the cognitive element of moral consciousness, were clearly seen : and this work was undertaken as a part of the general philosophic protest of the Scottish School against the Empiricism that had culminated in Hume. But this school claimed as its characteristic merit that it met Empiricism on its own ground, and showed among the facts of psychological experience which the Empiricist professed to observe, the assumptions which he repudiated. And thus in Ethics it was led rather to expound and reaffirm the morality of Common Sense, than to offer any profounder principles which could not be so easily supported by an appeal to common experience.

CHAPTER IX

GOOD

§ 1. WE have hitherto spoken of the quality of conduct discerned by our moral faculty as 'rightness,' which is the term commonly used by English moralists. We have regarded this term, and its equivalents in ordinary use, as implying the existence of a dictate or imperative of reason, which prescribes certain actions either unconditionally, or with reference to some ulterior end.

It is, however, possible to take a view of virtuous action in which, though the validity of moral intuitions is not disputed, this notion of rule or dictate is at any rate only latent or implicit, the moral ideal being presented as attractive rather than imperative. Such a view seems to be taken when the action to which we are morally prompted, or the quality of character manifested in it, is judged to be 'good' in itself (and not merely as a means to some ulterior Good). This, as was before noticed, was the fundamental ethical conception in the Greek schools of Moral Philosophy generally; including even the Stoics, though their system, from the prominence that it gives to the conception of Natural Law, forms a transitional link between ancient and modern ethics. And this historical illustration may serve to exhibit one important result of substituting the idea of 'goodness' for that of 'rightness' of conduct, which at first sight might be thought a merely verbal change. For the chief characteristics of ancient ethical controversy as distinguished from modern may be traced to the employment of a generic notion instead of a specific one in expressing the common moral judgments on actions. Virtue or Right action is commonly regarded as only a species of the Good : and so, on this view of the moral intuition, the first question that offers itself, when we endeavour to systematise conduct, is how to determine the relation of this species of good to the rest of the genus.   It was on this question that the Greek thinkers argued, from first to last.   Their speculations can scarcely be understood by us unless with a certain effort we throw the quasi-jural notions of modern ethics aside, and ask (as they did) not " What is Duty and what is its ground?" but " Which of the objects that men think good is truly Good or the Highest Good ? " or, in the more specialised form of the question which the moral intuition introduces, " What is the relation of the kind of Good we call Virtue, the qualities of conduct and character which men commend and admire, to other good things ? "

This, then, is the first difference to be noticed between the two forms of the intuitive judgment.   In the recognition of conduct as ' right ' is involved an authoritative prescription to do it : but when we have judged conduct to be good, it is not yet clear that we ought to prefer this kind of good to all other good things : some standard for estimating the relative values of different ' goods ' has still to be sought.

I propose, then, to examine the import of the notion 'Good' in the whole range of its application ;—premising that, as it is for the constituents of Ultimate Good that we require a standard of comparison, we are not directly concerned with anything that is clearly only good as a means to the attainment of some ulterior end.   If, indeed, we had only this latter case to consider, it would be plausible to interpret ' good ' without reference to human desire or choice, as meaning merely ' fit ' or ' adapted ' for the production of certain effects—a good horse for riding, a good gun for shooting, etc. But as we apply the notion also to ultimate ends, we must seek a meaning for it which will cover both applications.

§ 2. There is, however, a simple interpretation of the term—which is widely maintained to be the true one—according to which everything which we judge to be good is implicitly conceived as a means to the end of pleasure, even when we do not make in our judgment any explicit reference to this or any other ulterior end.   On this view, any comparison of things in respect of their 'goodness' would seem to be really a comparison of them as sources of pleasure; so that any attempt to systematise our intuitions of goodness, whether in conduct and character or in other things, must reasonably lead us straight to Hedonism. And no doubt, if we consider the application of the term, outside the sphere of character and conduct, to things that are not definitely regarded as means to the attainment of some ulterior object of desire, we find a close correspondence between our apprehension of pleasure derived from an object, and our recognition that the object is in itself 'good.' The good things of life are things which give pleasure, whether sensual or emotional: as good dinners, wines, poems, pictures, music: and this gives a *prima facie* support to the interpretation of 'good' as equivalent to 'pleasant.' I think, however, that if we reflect on the application of the term to the cases most analogous to that of conduct—*i.e.* to what we may call 'objects of taste'—we shall find that this interpretation of it has not clearly the support of common sense. In the first place, allowing that the judgment that any object is good of its kind is closely connected with the apprehension of pleasure derived from it, we must observe that it is generally to a specific kind of pleasure that the affirmation of goodness corresponds; and that if the object happens to give us pleasure of a different kind, we do not therefore call it good—at least without qualification. For instance, we should not call a wine good solely because it was very wholesome; nor a poem on account of its moral lessons. And hence when we come to consider the meaning of the term 'good' as applied to conduct, there is no reason, so far, to suppose that it has any reference or correspondence to *all* the pleasures that may result from the conduct. Rather the perception of goodness or virtue in actions would seem to be analogous to the perception of beauty[1] in material things:

[1] It is, however, necessary to distinguish between the ideas of *Moral Goodness* and *Beauty* as applied to human actions: although there is much affinity between them, and they have frequently been identified, especially by the Greek thinkers. No doubt both the ideas themselves and the corresponding pleasurable emotions, arising on the contemplation of conduct, are often indistinguishable: a noble action affects us like a scene, a picture, or a strain of music: and the delineation of human virtue is an important part of the means which the artist has at his disposal for producing his peculiar effects. Still, on looking

which is normally accompanied with a specific pleasure which we call 'æsthetic,' but has often no discoverable relation to the general usefulness or agreeableness of the thing discerned to be beautiful: indeed, we often recognise this kind of excellence in things hurtful and dangerous.

But further: as regards æsthetic pleasures, and the sources of such pleasures that we commonly judge to be good, it is the received opinion that some persons have more and others less 'good taste': and it is only the judgment of persons of good taste that we recognise as valid in respect of the real goodness of the things enjoyed. We think that of his own pleasure each individual is the final judge, and there is no appeal from his decision,—at least so far as he is comparing pleasures within his actual experience; but the affirmation of goodness in any object involves the assumption of a universally valid standard, which, as we believe, the judgment of persons to whom we attribute good taste approximately represents. And it seems clear that the term 'good' as applied to 'taste' does not mean 'pleasant'; it merely imports the conformity of the æsthetic judgment so characterised to the supposed ideal, deviation from which implies error and defect. Nor does it appear to be always the person of best taste who derives the greatest enjoyment from any kind of good and pleasant things. We are familiar with the fact that connoisseurs of wines, pictures, etc., often retain their intellectual faculty of appraising the merits of the objects which they criticise, and deciding on their respective places in the scale of excellence, even when their susceptibilities to pleasure from these objects are comparatively blunted and exhausted. And more generally we see that freshness and fulness of feeling by no means go along with taste and judgment: and that a person who possesses the

---

closer, we see not only that there is much good conduct which is not beautiful, or at least does not sensibly impress us as such ; but even that certain kinds of crime and wickedness have a splendour and sublimity of their own. For example, such a career as Cæsar Borgia's, as Renan says, is "beau comme une tempête, comme un abîme." It is true, I think, that in all such cases the beauty depends upon the exhibition in the criminal's conduct of striking gifts and excellences mingled with the wickedness : but it does not seem that we can abstract the latter without impairing the æsthetic effect. And hence I conceive, we have to distinguish the sense of beauty in conduct from the sense of moral goodness.

former may derive more pleasure from inferior objects than another may from the best.

To sum up: the general admission that things which are called 'good' are productive of pleasure, and that the former quality is inseparable in thought from the latter, does not involve the inference that the common estimates of the goodness of conduct may be fairly taken as estimates of the amount of pleasure resulting from it. For (1) analogy would lead us to conclude that the attribution of goodness, in the case of conduct as of objects of taste generally, may correspond not to all the pleasure that is caused by the conduct, but to a specific pleasure, in this case the contemplative satisfaction which the conduct causes to a disinterested spectator : and (2) it may not excite even this specific pleasure generally in proportion to its goodness, but only (at most) in persons of good moral taste : and even in their case we can distinguish the intellectual apprehension of goodness—which involves the conception of an ideal objective standard—from the pleasurable emotion which commonly accompanies it ; and may suppose the latter element of consciousness diminished almost indefinitely.

Finally, when we pass from the *adjective* to the *substantive* 'good,' it is at once evident that this latter cannot be understood as equivalent to 'pleasure' or 'happiness' by any persons who affirm—as a significant proposition and not as a mere tautology—that the Pleasure or Happiness of human beings is their Good or Ultimate Good. Such affirmation, which would, I think, be ordinarily made by Hedonists, obviously implies that the *meaning* of the two terms is different, however closely their denotation may coincide. And it does not seem that any fundamental difference of meaning is implied by the grammatical variation from adjective to substantive.

§ 3. What then can we state as the general meaning of the term 'good' ? Shall we say—with Hobbes, and many since Hobbes—that ' whatsoever is the object of any man's Desire, that it is which he for his part calleth Good, and the object of his aversion, Evil ' ? To simplify the discussion, we will consider only what a man desires for itself—not as a means to an ulterior result,—and for himself—not benevolently for others : his own Good [1] and ultimate Good. We have first to meet the

---

[1] It would seem that, according to the common view of 'good,' there are

obvious objection that a man often desires what he knows is on the whole bad for him: the pleasure of drinking champagne which is sure to disagree with him, the gratification of revenge when he knows that his true interest lies in reconciliation. The answer is that in such cases the desired result is accompanied or followed by other effects which when they come excite aversion stronger than the desire for the desired effect: but that these bad effects, though fore-*seen* are not fore-*felt*: the representation of them does not adequately modify the predominant direction of desire as a present fact. But, granting this, and fixing attention solely on the result desired, apart from its concomitants and consequences—it would still seem that what is desired at any time is, as such, merely apparent Good, which may not be found good when fruition comes, or at any rate not so good as it appeared. It may turn out a 'Dead Sea apple,' mere dust and ashes in the eating: more often, fruition will partly correspond to expectation, but may still fall short of it in a marked degree. And sometimes—even while yielding to the desire—we are aware of the illusoriness of this expectation of 'good' which the desire carries with it. I conclude, therefore, that if we are to conceive of the elements of ultimate Good as capable of quantitative comparison—as we do when we speak of preferring a 'greater' good to a 'lesser,' —we cannot identify the object of desire with 'good' simply, or 'true good,' but only with 'apparent good.'

But further: a prudent man is accustomed to suppress, with more or less success, desires for what he regards as out of his power to attain by voluntary action—as fine weather, perfect health, great wealth or fame, etc.; but any success he may have in diminishing the actual intensity of such desires has no effect in leading him to judge the objects desired less 'good.'

It would seem then, that if we interpret the notion 'good' in relation to 'desire,' we must identify it not with the actually

occasions in which an individual's sacrifice of his own good on the whole, according to the most rational conception of it that he can form, would apparently realise greater good for others. Whether, indeed, such a sacrifice is ever really required, and whether, if so, it is truly reasonable for the individual to sacrifice his own good on the whole, are among the profoundest questions of ethics: and I shall carefully consider them in subsequent chapters (especially Book iii. chap. xiv.). I here only desire to avoid any prejudgment of these questions in my definition of 'my own good.'

desired, but rather with the *desirable* :—meaning by ' desirable ' not necessarily ' what *ought* to be desired ' but what would be desired, with strength proportioned to the degree of desirability, if it were judged attainable by voluntary action, supposing the desirer to possess a perfect forecast, emotional as well as intellectual, of the state of attainment or fruition.

It still remains possible that the choice of any particular good, thus defined as an object of pursuit, may be on the whole bad, on account of its concomitants and consequences; even though the particular result when attained is not found other than it was imagined in the condition of previous desire. If, therefore, in seeking a definition of ' ultimate Good ' we mean ' good on the whole,' we have—following the line of thought of the preceding paragraph—to express its relation to Desire differently. In the first place we have to limit our view to desire which becomes practical in volition; as I may still regard as desirable results which I judge it on the whole imprudent to aim at. But, even with this limitation, the relation of my ' good on the whole ' to my desire is very complicated. For it is not even sufficient to say that my Good on the whole is what I should actually desire and seek if all the consequences of seeking it could be foreknown and adequately realised by me in imagination at the time of making my choice. No doubt an equal regard for all the moments of our conscious experience—so far, at least, as the mere difference of their position in time is concerned—is an essential characteristic of rational conduct. But the mere fact, that a man does not afterwards feel for the consequences of an action aversion strong enough to cause him to regret it, cannot be accepted as a complete proof that he has acted for his ' good on the whole.' Indeed, we commonly reckon it among the worst consequences of some kinds of conduct that they alter men's tendencies to desire, and make them desire their lesser good more than their greater : and we think it all the worse for a man—even in this world—if he is never roused out of such a condition and lives till death the life of a contented pig, when he might have been something better. To avoid this objection, it would have to be said that a man's future good on the whole is what he would now desire and seek on the whole if all the consequences of all the different lines of conduct open to him were accurately foreseen and adequately realised in imagination at the present point of time.

This hypothetical composition of impulsive forces involves so elaborate and complex a conception, that it is somewhat paradoxical to say that this is what we commonly *mean* when we talk of a man's 'good on the whole.' Still, I cannot deny that this hypothetical object of a resultant desire supplies an intelligible and admissible interpretation of the terms 'good' (substantive) and 'desirable,' as giving philosophical precision to the vaguer meaning with which they are used in ordinary discourse : and it would seem that a calm comprehensive desire for 'good' conceived somewhat in this way, though more vaguely, is normally produced by intellectual comparison and experience in a reflective mind. The notion of 'Good' thus attained has an ideal element : it is something that *is* not always actually desired and aimed at by human beings : but the ideal element is entirely interpretable in terms of *fact*, actual or hypothetical, and does not introduce any judgment of value, fundamentally distinct from judgments relating to existence ;—still less any 'dictate of Reason.'[1]

It seems to me, however, more in accordance with common sense to recognise—as Butler does—that the calm desire for my 'good on the whole' is *authoritative*; and therefore carries with it implicitly a rational dictate to aim at this end, if in any case a conflicting desire urges the will in an opposite direction. Still we may keep the notion of 'dictate' or 'imperative' merely implicit and latent,—as it seems to be in ordinary judgments as to 'my good' and its opposite—by interpreting 'ultimate good on the whole for me' to mean what I should practically desire if my desires were in harmony with reason, assuming my own existence alone to be considered. On this view, "ultimate good on the whole," unqualified by reference to a particular subject, must be taken to mean what as a rational being I should desire and seek to realise, assuming myself to have an equal concern for *all* existence. When conduct is judged to be 'good' or 'desirable' in itself,

[1] As before said (chap. iii. § 4), so far as my 'good on the whole' is adopted as an end of action, the notion of 'ought'—implying a dictate or imperative of Reason—becomes applicable to the necessary or fittest means to the attainment of the adopted end.

independently of its consequences, it is, I conceive, this latter point of view that is taken. Such a judgment differs, as I have said, from the judgment that conduct is 'right,' in so far as it does not involve a definite precept to perform it; since it still leaves it an open question whether this particular kind of good is the greatest good that we can under the circumstances obtain. It differs further, as we may now observe, in so far as good or excellent actions are not implied to be in our power in the same strict sense as 'right' actions—any more than any other good things : and in fact there are many excellences of behaviour which we cannot attain by any effort of will, at least directly and at the moment : hence we often feel that the recognition of goodness in the conduct of others does not carry with it a clear precept to do likewise, but rather

> the vague desire
> That stirs an imitative will.

In so far as this is the case Goodness of Conduct becomes an ulterior end, the attainment of which lies outside and beyond the range of immediate volition.

§ 4. It remains to consider by what standard the value of conduct or character,[1] thus intuitively judged to be good in itself, is to be co-ordinated and compared with that of other good things. I shall not now attempt to establish such a standard ; but a little reflection may enable us to limit considerably the range of comparison for which it is required. For I think that if we consider carefully such permanent results as are commonly judged to be good, other than qualities of human beings, we can find nothing that, on reflection, appears to possess this quality of goodness out of relation to human existence, or at least to some consciousness or feeling.[2]

---

[1] Character is only known to us through its manifestation in conduct ; and I conceive that in our common recognition of Virtue as having value in itself, we do not ordinarily distinguish character from conduct : we do not raise the question whether character is to be valued for the sake of the conduct in which it is manifested, or conduct for the sake of the character that it exhibits and develops. How this question should be answered when it is raised will be more conveniently considered at a later stage of the discussion. See Book iii. chap. ii. § 2, and chap. xiv. § 1.

[2] No doubt there is a point of view, sometimes adopted with great earnestness, from which the whole universe and not merely a certain condition of rational or sentient beings is contemplated as 'very good' : just as the Creator in Genesis

For example, we commonly judge some inanimate objects, scenes, etc. to be good as possessing beauty, and others bad from ugliness: still no one would consider it rational to aim at the production of beauty in external nature, apart from any possible contemplation of it by human beings. In fact when beauty is maintained to be objective, it is not commonly meant that it exists as beauty out of relation to any mind whatsoever: but only that there is some standard of beauty valid for all minds.

It may, however, be said that beauty and other results commonly judged to be good, though we do not conceive them to exist out of relation to human beings (or at least minds of some kind), are yet so far separable as ends from the human beings on whom their existence depends, that their realisation may conceivably come into competition with the perfection or happiness of these beings. Thus, though beautiful things cannot be thought worth producing except as possible objects of contemplation, still a man may devote himself to their production without any consideration of the persons who are to contemplate them. Similarly knowledge is a good which cannot exist except in minds; and yet one may be more interested in the development of knowledge than in its possession by any particular minds; and may take the former as an ultimate end without regarding the latter.

Still, as soon as the alternatives are clearly apprehended, it will, I think, be generally held that beauty, knowledge, and other ideal goods, as well as all external material things, are only reasonably to be sought by men in so far as they conduce either (1) to Happiness or (2) to the Perfection or Excellence of human existence. I say "human," for though most utilitarians consider the pleasure (and freedom from pain) of the inferior animals to be included in the Happiness which they take as the right and proper end of conduct, no one seems to contend that we ought to aim at perfecting brutes, except as a means to our ends, or at least as objects of scientific or

is described as contemplating it. But such a view can scarcely be developed into a method of Ethics. For practical purposes, we require to conceive some parts of the universe as at least less good than they might be. And we do not seem to have any ground for drawing such a distinction between different portions of the non-sentient universe, considered in themselves and out of relation to conscious or sentient beings.

æsthetic contemplation for us. Nor, again, can we include, as a practical end, the existence of beings above the human. We certainly apply the idea of Good to the Divine Existence, just as we do to His work, and indeed in a pre-eminent manner : and when it is said that " we should do all things to the glory of God," it may seem to be implied that the existence of God is made better by our glorifying Him. Still this inference when explicitly drawn appears somewhat impious ; and theologians generally recoil from it, and refrain from using the notion of a possible addition to the Goodness of the Divine Existence as a ground of human duty. Nor can the influence of our actions on other extra-human intelligences besides the Divine be at present made matter of scientific discussion.

I shall therefore confidently lay down, that if there be any Good other than Happiness to be sought by man, as an ultimate practical end, it can only be the Goodness, Perfection, or Excellence of Human Existence. How far this notion includes more than Virtue, what its precise relation to Pleasure is, and to what method we shall be logically led if we accept it as fundamental, are questions which we shall more conveniently discuss after the detailed examination of these two other notions, Pleasure and Virtue, in which we shall be engaged in the two following Books.

BOOK II

EGOISTIC HEDONISM

BOOK II

CHAPTER I

THE PRINCIPLE AND METHOD OF EGOISM

§ 1. THE object of the present Book is to examine the method of determining reasonable conduct which has been already defined in outline under the name of Egoism: taking this term as equivalent to Egoistic Hedonism, and as implying the adoption of his own greatest happiness as the ultimate end of each individual's actions. It may be doubted whether this ought to be included among received "methods of *Ethics*"; since there are strong grounds for holding that a system of morality, satisfactory to the moral consciousness of mankind in general, cannot be constructed on the basis of simple Egoism. In subsequent chapters [1] I shall carefully discuss these reasons: at present it seems sufficient to point to the wide acceptance of the principle that it is reasonable for a man to act in the manner most conducive to his own happiness. We find it expressly admitted by leading representatives both of Intuitionism and of that Universalistic Hedonism to which I propose to restrict the name of Utilitarianism. I have already noticed that Bentham, although he puts forward the greatest happiness of the greatest number as the "true standard of right and wrong," yet regards it as "right and proper" that each individual should aim at his own greatest happiness. And Butler is equally prepared to grant "that our ideas of happiness and misery are of all our ideas the nearest and most important to us . . . that, though virtue or moral rectitude does indeed

[1] See chap. iii. § 2, and chap. v. of this Book.

consist in affection to and pursuit of what is right and good as such ; yet, when we sit down in a cool hour, we can neither justify to ourselves this or any other pursuit till we are convinced that it will be for our happiness, or at least not contrary to it." [1]

And even Clarke [2]—notwithstanding the emphatic terms in which he has maintained that "Virtue truly deserves to be chosen for its own sake and Vice to be avoided"—yet admits that it is "not truly reasonable that men by adhering to Virtue should part with their lives, if thereby they eternally deprived themselves of all possibility of receiving any advantage from that adherence."

And, generally, in the ages of Christian faith, it has been obvious and natural to hold that the realisation of virtue is essentially an enlightened and far-seeing pursuit of Happiness for the agent. Nor has this doctrine been held only by persons of a cold and calculating turn of mind : we find it urged with emphasis by so chivalrous and high-minded a preacher as Bishop Berkeley. No doubt this is only one side or element of the Christian view : the opposite doctrine, that an action done from motives of self-interest is not properly virtuous, has continually asserted itself as either openly conflicting or in some manner reconciled with the former. Still the former, though less refined and elevated, seems to have been the commoner view. Indeed, it is hardly going too far to say that common sense assumes that ' interested ' actions, tending to promote the agent's happiness, are *prima facie* reasonable : and that the *onus probandi* lies with those who maintain that disinterested conduct, as such, is reasonable.

But, as has been before said, in the common notions of ' interest,' ' happiness,' etc., there is a certain amount of vagueness and ambiguity : so that in order to fit these terms for the purposes of scientific discussion, we must, while retaining the main part of their signification, endeavour to make it more precise. In my judgment this result is attained if by ' greatest possible Happiness ' we understand the greatest attainable surplus of pleasure over pain ; the two terms being used, with equally comprehensive meanings, to include respectively all

<hr>

[1] Butler, Serm. xi.
[2] *Boyle Lectures* (1705). Prop. i. p. 116.

kinds of agreeable and disagreeable feelings.   Further, if this
quantitative definition of the end be accepted, consistency
requires that pleasures should be sought in proportion to their
pleasantness ; and therefore the less pleasant consciousness must
not be preferred to the more pleasant, on the ground of any other
qualities that it may possess.   The distinctions of *quality* that
Mill and others urge may still be admitted as grounds of
preference, but only in so far as they can be resolved into
distinctions of quantity.   This is the type to which the
practical reasoning that is commonly called 'Egoistic' tends
to conform, when we rigorously exclude all ambiguities and
inconsistencies : and it is only in this more precise form that
it seems worth while to subject such reasoning to a detailed
examination.   We must therefore understand by an Egoist a
man who when two or more courses of action are open to him,
ascertains as accurately as he can the amounts of pleasure and
pain that are likely to result from each, and chooses the one
which he thinks will yield him the greatest surplus of pleasure
over pain.

§ 2. It must, however, be pointed out that the adoption of
the fundamental *principle* of Egoism, as just explained, by no
means necessarily implies the ordinary empirical method of
seeking one's own pleasure or happiness.   A man may aim at
the greatest happiness within his reach, and yet not attempt to
ascertain empirically what amount of pleasure and pain is likely
to attend any given course of action ; believing that he has
some surer, deductive method for determining the conduct
which will make him most happy in the long-run.   He may
believe this on grounds of Positive Religion, because God has
promised happiness as a reward for obedience to certain definite
commands : or on grounds of Natural Religion, because God
being just and benevolent must have so ordered the world that
Happiness will in the long-run be distributed in proportion to
Virtue.   It is (*e.g.*) by a combination of both these arguments
that Paley connects the Universalistic Hedonism that he adopts
as a method for determining duties, with the Egoism which seems
to him self-evident as a fundamental principle of rational conduct.   Or again, a man may connect virtue with happiness by a
process of *a priori* reasoning, purely ethical ; as Aristotle seems
to do by the assumption that the 'best' activity will be always

attended by the greatest pleasure as its inseparable concomitant; 'best' being determined by a reference to moral intuition, or to the common moral opinions of men generally, or of well-bred and well-educated men. Or the deduction by which Maximum Pleasure is inferred to be the result of a particular kind of action may be psychological or physiological: we may have some general theory as to the connexion of pleasure with some other physical or psychical fact, according to which we can deduce the amount of pleasure that will attend any particular kind of behaviour: as (*e.g.*) it is widely held that a perfectly healthy and harmonious exercise of our different bodily and mental functions is the course of life most conducive to pleasure in the long-run. In this latter case, though accepting unreservedly the Hedonistic principle, we shall not be called upon to estimate and compare particular pleasures, but rather to define the notions of 'perfect health' and 'harmony of functions' and consider how these ends may be attained. Still those who advocate such deductive methods commonly appeal to ordinary experience, at least as supplying confirmation or verification; and admit that the pleasantness and painfulness of pleasures and pains are only directly known to the individual who experiences them. It would seem, therefore, that—at any rate—the obvious method of Egoistic Hedonism is that which we may call Empirical-reflective: and it is this I conceive that is commonly used in egoistic deliberation. It will be well, therefore, to examine this method in the first instance; to ascertain clearly the assumptions which it involves, and estimate the exactness of its results.

CHAPTER II

EMPIRICAL HEDONISM

§ 1. THE first and most fundamental assumption, involved not only in the empirical method of Egoistic Hedonism, but in the very conception of 'Greatest Happiness' as an end of action, is the commensurability of Pleasures and Pains. By this I mean that we must assume the pleasures sought and the pains shunned to have determinate quantitative relations to each other; for otherwise they cannot be conceived as possible elements of a total which we are to seek to make as great as possible. It is not absolutely necessary to exclude the supposition that there are some kinds of pleasure so much more pleasant than others, that the smallest conceivable amount of the former would outweigh the greatest conceivable amount of the latter; since, if this were ascertained to be the case, the only result would be that any hedonistic calculation involving pleasures of the former class might be simplified by treating those of the latter class as practically non-existent.[1] I think,

---

[1] We find it sometimes asserted by persons of enthusiastic and passionate temperament, that there are feelings so exquisitely delightful, that one moment of their rapture is preferable to an eternity of agreeable consciousness of an inferior kind. These assertions, however, are perhaps consciously hyperbolical, and not intended to be taken as scientific statements : but in the case of pain, it has been deliberately maintained by a thoughtful and subtle writer, with a view to important practical conclusions, that "torture" so extreme as to be "incommensurable with moderate pain" is an actual fact of experience. (See "A Chapter in the Ethics of Pain," by the late Edmund Gurney, in a volume of essays entitled *Tertium Quid.*) This doctrine, however, does not correspond to my own experience; nor does it appear to me to be supported by the common sense of mankind :—at least I do not find, in the practical forethought of persons noted for caution, any recognition of the danger of agony such that, in order to avoid the smallest extra

however, that in all ordinary prudential reasoning, at any rate, the assumption is implicitly made that all the pleasures and pains that man can experience bear a finite ratio to each other in respect of pleasantness and its opposite.   So far as this ratio can be made definite the Intensity of a pleasure (or pain) can be balanced against its Duration:[1] for if we conceive one pleasure (or pain), finite in duration, to be intensively greater than another in some definite ratio, it seems to be implied in this conception that the latter if continuously increased in extent—without change in its intensity—would at a certain point just balance the former in amount.

If pleasures, then, can be arranged in a scale, as greater or less in some finite degree; we are led to the assumption of a hedonistic zero, or perfectly neutral feeling, as a point from which the positive quantity of pleasures may be measured. And this latter assumption emerges still more clearly when we consider the comparison and balancing of pleasures with pains, which Hedonism necessarily involves.   For pain must be reckoned as the negative quantity of pleasure, to be balanced against and subtracted from the positive in estimating happiness on the whole; we must therefore conceive, as at least ideally possible, a point of transition in consciousness at which we pass from the positive to the negative.   It is not absolutely necessary to assume that this strictly indifferent or neutral feeling ever actually occurs.   Still experience seems to show that a state at any rate very nearly approximating to it is even common: and we certainly experience continual transi-

risk of it, the greatest conceivable amount of moderate pain should reasonably be incurred.

[1] Bentham gives four qualities of any pleasure or pain (taken singly) as important for purposes of Hedonistic calculation : (1) Intensity, (2) Duration, (3) Certainty, (4) Proximity.   If we assume (as above argued) that Intensity must be commensurable with Duration, the influence of the other qualities on the comparative value of pleasures and pains is not difficult to determine : for we are accustomed to estimate the value of chances numerically, and by this method we can tell exactly (in so far as the degree of uncertainty can be exactly determined) how much the doubtfulness of a pleasure detracts from its value : and *proximity* is a property which it is reasonable to disregard except in so far as it diminishes uncertainty.   For my feelings a year hence should be just as important to me as my feelings next minute, if only I could make an equally sure forecast of them.   Indeed this equal and impartial concern for all parts of one's conscious life is perhaps the most prominent element in the common notion of the *rational*—as opposed to the merely *impulsive*—pursuit of pleasure.

tions from pleasure to pain and *vice versâ*, and thus (unless we conceive all such transitions to be abrupt) we must exist at least momentarily in this neutral state.

In what I have just said, I have by implication denied the paradox of Epicurus [1] that the state of painlessness is equivalent to the highest possible pleasure; so that if we can obtain absolute freedom from pain, the goal of Hedonism is reached, after which we may vary, but cannot increase, our pleasure. This doctrine is opposed to common sense and common experience. But it would, I think, be equally erroneous, on the other hand, to regard this neutral feeling—hedonistic zero, as I have called it—as the normal condition of our consciousness, out of which we occasionally sink into pain, and occasionally rise into pleasure. Nature has not been so niggardly to man as this: so long as health is retained, and pain and irksome toil banished, the mere performance of the ordinary habitual functions of life is, according to my experience, a frequent source of moderate pleasures, alternating rapidly with states nearly or quite indifferent. Thus we may venture to say that the 'apathy' which so large a proportion of Greek moralists in the post-Aristotelian period regarded as the ideal state of existence, was not really conceived by them as "without one pleasure and without one pain"; but rather as a state of placid intellectual contemplation, which in philosophic minds might easily reach a high degree of pleasure.

§ 2. We have yet to give to the notions of pleasure and pain the precision required for quantitative comparison. In dealing with this point, and in the rest of the hedonistic discussion, it will be convenient for the most part to speak of pleasure only, assuming that pain may be regarded as the negative quantity of pleasure, and that accordingly any statements made with respect to pleasure may be at once applied, by obvious changes of phrase, to pain.

The equivalent phrase for Pleasure, according to Mr. Spencer,[2] is "a feeling which we seek to bring into consciousness and retain there"; and similarly, Mr. Bain says that "pleasure and pain, in the actual or real experience, are to be held as identical with motive power." But—granting that

---

[1] Cf. Cic. *de Fin.* Book i. chap. xi. § 38.
[2] *Principles of Psychology*, Part ii. chap. ix. § 125.

pleasures normally excite desire—it still does not seem to me that I judge pleasures to be greater and less exactly in proportion as they stimulate the will to actions tending to sustain them.   Of course neither Mr. Bain nor Mr. Spencer must be understood to lay down that all pleasures when actually felt actually stimulate to exertion of some kind; since this is obviously not true of the pleasures of repose, a warm bath, etc. The stimulus must in such cases be understood to be latent and potential; only becoming actual when action is required to prevent the cessation or diminution of the pleasure.   Thus a man enjoying rest after fatigue is vaguely conscious of a strong clinging to his actual condition, and of a latent readiness to resist any impulse to change it.   Further, the stimulus of moderate pleasures and pains may become unfelt through habitual repression.   For instance, in a habitually temperate man the stimulus to prolong the pleasure of eating or drinking usually ceases before the pleasure ceases : it is only occasionally that he feels the need of controlling an impulse to eat or drink up to the point of satiety.   So again, a protracted pain of moderate intensity and free from alarm—such as a dull prolonged toothache—seems sometimes to lose its felt stimulus to action without losing its character as pain.   Here again the stimulus may be properly conceived as latent : since if asked whether we should like to get rid of even a mild toothache, we should certainly answer yes.

But even if we confine our attention to cases where the stimulus is palpable and strong, Mr. Bain's identification of " pleasure and pain " with motive power does not appear to me to accord exactly with our common empirical judgments.   He himself contrasts the " disproportionate strain of active powers in one direction," to which " any sudden and great delight may give rise," with the " proper frame of mind under delight," which is " to inspire no endeavours except what the charm of the moment justifies." [1]   And he elsewhere explains that " our pleasurable emotions are all liable to detain the mind unduly," through the " atmosphere of excitement " with which they are surrounded, carrying the mind " beyond the estimate of pleasure and pain, to the state named ' passion,' " in which a man is not " moved solely by the strict

[1] *The Emotions and the Will*, 3rd Edition, p. 392.

value of the pleasure," but also by "the engrossing power of the excitement."[1]   It is true that in such cases Mr. Bain seems to hold that these "disturbances and anomalies of the will *scarcely* begin to tell in the actual feeling,"[2] but it seems to me clear that exciting pleasures are liable to exercise, even when actually felt, a volitional stimulus out of proportion to their intensity as pleasures; and Mr. Bain himself seems to recognise this in a passage where he says that " acute pleasures and pains stimulate the will perhaps more strongly than an equivalent stimulation of the massive kind." [3]   I also find that some feelings which stimulate strongly to their own removal are either not painful at all or only slightly painful:—*e.g.* ordinarily the sensation of being tickled.   If this be so, it is obviously inexact to define pleasure, *for purposes of measurement,* as the kind of feeling that we seek to retain in consciousness.   Shall we then say that there is a measurable quality of feeling expressed by the word " pleasure," which is independent of its relation to volition, and strictly undefinable from its simplicity ?—like the quality of feeling expressed by " sweet," of which also we are conscious in varying degrees of intensity. This seems to be the view of some writers : but, for my own part, when I reflect on the notion of pleasure,—using the term in the comprehensive sense which I have adopted, to include the most refined and subtle intellectual and emotional grati- fications, no less than the coarser and more definite sensual enjoyments,—the only common quality that I can find in the feelings so designated seems to be that relation to desire and volition expressed by the general term " desirable," in the sense previously explained.   I propose therefore to define Pleasure —when we are considering its " strict value " for purposes of quantitative comparison—as a feeling which, when experienced by intelligent beings, is at least implicitly apprehended as desirable or—in cases of comparison—preferable.

Here, however, a new question comes into view.   When I stated in the preceding chapter, as a fundamental assumption of Hedonism, that it is reasonable to prefer pleasures in propor- tion to their intensity, and not to allow this ground of preference

---

[1] *Mental and Moral Science*, Book iv. chap. iv. § 4.
[2] *Ibid.* Book iv. chap. v. § 4.
[3] *Ibid.* Book iii. chap. i. § 8.

to be outweighed by any merely qualitative difference, I implied that the preference of pleasures on grounds of quality as opposed to quantity—as 'higher' or 'nobler'—is actually possible : and indeed such non-hedonistic preference is commonly thought to be of frequent occurrence. But if we take the definition of pleasure just given—that it is the kind of feeling which we apprehend to be desirable or preferable—it seems to be a contradiction in terms to say that the less pleasant feeling can ever be thought preferable to the more pleasant.

This contradiction may be avoided as follows. It will be generally admitted that the pleasantness of a feeling is only directly cognisable by the individual who feels it at the time of feeling it. Thus, though (as I shall presently argue), in so far as any estimate of pleasantness involves comparison with feelings only represented in idea, it is liable to be erroneous through imperfections in the representation—still, no one is in a position to controvert the preference of the sentient individual, so far as the quality of the present feeling alone is concerned. When, however, we judge of the preferable quality (as 'elevation' or 'refinement') of a state of consciousness as distinct from its pleasantness,[1] we seem to appeal to some common standard which others can apply as well as the sentient individual. Hence I should conclude that when one kind of pleasure is judged to be qualitatively superior to another, although less pleasant, it is not really the feeling itself that is preferred, but something in the mental or physical conditions or relations under which it arises, regarded as cognisable objects of our common thought. For certainly if I in thought distinguish any feeling from all its conditions and concomitants—and also from all its effects on the subsequent feelings of the same individual or of others—and contemplate it merely as the transient feeling of a single subject ; it seems to me impossible to find in it any other preferable quality than that which we call its pleasantness, the degree of which is only cognisable directly by the sentient individual.

[1] It was before observed that by saying that one pleasure is superior in *quality* to another we may mean that it is preferable when considered merely as pleasant : in which case difference in kind resolves itself into difference in degree.

It should be observed that if this definition of pleasure be accepted, and if, as before proposed, ' Ultimate Good ' be taken as equivalent to 'what is ultimately desirable,' the fundamental proposition of ethical Hedonism has chiefly a negative significance ; for the statement that ' Pleasure is the Ultimate Good ' will only mean that nothing is ultimately desirable except desirable feeling, apprehended as desirable by the sentient individual at the time of feeling it. This being so, it may be urged against the definition that it could not be accepted by a moralist of stoical turn, who while recognising pleasure as a fact refused to recognise it as in any degree ultimately desirable. But I think such a moralist ought to admit an implied judgment that a feeling is *per se* desirable to be inseparably connected with its recognition as pleasure ; while holding that sound philosophy shows the illusoriness of such judgments. This, in fact, seems to have been substantially the view of the Stoic school.

However this may be, I conceive that the preference which pure Hedonism regards as ultimately rational, should be defined as the preference of feeling valued merely as feeling, according to the estimate implicitly or explicitly made by the sentient individual at the time of feeling it ; without any regard to the conditions and relations under which it arises. Accordingly we may state as the fundamental assumption of what I have called Quantitative Hedonism,—implied in the adoption of " greatest surplus of pleasure over pain " as the ultimate end, —that all pleasures and pains, estimated merely as feelings, have for the sentient individual cognisable degrees of desirability, positive or negative ; observing further, that the empirical method of Hedonism can only be applied so far as we assume that these degrees of desirability are definitely given in experience.

There is one more assumption of a fundamental kind, which is not perhaps involved in the acceptance of the Hedonistic calculus considered as purely theoretical, but is certainly implied if it be put forward as a practical method for determining right conduct : the assumption, namely, that we can by foresight and calculation increase our pleasures and decrease our pains. It may perhaps be thought pedantic to state it formally : and in fact no one will deny that the conditions upon which our pleasures and pains depend are to some extent cognisable by us and within our own control.   But, as we shall see, it has been maintained that the practice of Hedonistic observation and calculation has an inevitable tendency to decrease our pleasures generally, or the most important of them : so that it becomes a question whether we can gain our greatest happiness by seeking it, or at any rate by trying to seek it with scientific exactness.

NOTE.—It is sometimes thought to be a necessary assumption of Hedonists that a surplus of pleasure over pain is actually attainable by human beings : a proposition which an extreme pessimist would deny.   But the conclusion that life is always on the whole painful would not prove it to be unreasonable for a man to aim ultimately at minimising pain, if this is still admitted to be possible ; though it would, no doubt, render immediate suicide, by some painless process, the only reasonable course for a perfect egoist—unless he looked forward to another life.

CHAPTER III

EMPIRICAL HEDONISM—*Continued*

§ 1. LET, then, pleasure be defined as feeling which the sentient individual at the time of feeling it implicitly or explicitly apprehends to be desirable;—desirable, that is, when considered merely as feeling, and not in respect of its objective conditions or consequences, or of any facts that come directly within the cognisance and judgment of others besides the sentient individual. And let it be provisionally assumed that feelings generally can be compared from this point of view, with sufficient definiteness for practical purposes, and empirically known to be more or less pleasant in some definite degree. Then the empirical-reflective method of Egoistic Hedonism will be, to represent beforehand the different series of feelings that our knowledge of physical and psychical causes leads us to expect from the different lines of conduct that lie open to us; judge which series, as thus represented, appears on the whole preferable, taking all probabilities into account; and adopt the corresponding line of conduct. It may be objected that the calculation is too complex for practice; since any complete forecast of the future would involve a vast number of contingencies of varying degrees of probability, and to calculate the Hedonistic value of each of these chances of feeling would be interminable. Still we may perhaps reduce the calculation within manageable limits, without serious loss of accuracy, by discarding all manifestly imprudent conduct, and neglecting the less probable and less important contingencies; as we do in some of the arts that have more definite ends, such as strategy and medicine. For if the general in ordering a march, or the

131

physician in recommending a change of abode, took into consideration all the circumstances that were at all relevant to the end sought, their calculations would become impracticable; accordingly they confine themselves to the most important; and we may deal similarly with the Hedonistic art of life.

There are, however, objections urged against the Hedonistic method which go much deeper; and by some writers are pressed to the extreme of rejecting the method altogether. A careful examination of these objections seems to be the most convenient way of obtaining a clear view, both of the method itself and of the results that may reasonably be expected from it.

I should, however, point out that we are now only concerned with what may be called *intrinsic* objections to Egoistic Hedonism; arguments, that is, against the possibility of obtaining by it the results at which it aims. We are not now to consider whether it is reasonable for an individual to take his own happiness as his ultimate end; or how far the rules of action deduced from the adoption of this end, and from the actual conditions of the individual's existence, will coincide with current opinions as to what is right. These questions, according to the plan of my work, are postponed for future consideration:[1] our sole concern at present is with objections tending to show the intrinsic impracticability of Hedonism as a rational method.

We are met, in the first place, by an objection which, if valid at all, must be admitted to be decisive. It has been affirmed[2] by Green that "pleasure as feeling, in distinction "from its conditions that are not feelings, cannot be con-"ceived." If so, Rational Hedonism would certainly be impossible : but the proposition seems equally opposed to common sense, and to the universal assumption of empirical psychologists; who, in investigating elaborately and systematically the conditions, mental and physical, of pleasure and pain, necessarily assume that these feelings can be distinguished in thought from their "conditions which are not

---

[1] See chap. v. of this Book, chap. xiv. of Book iii., and the concluding chapter of the treatise.

[2] See Green's Introduction to vol. ii. of Hume's *Treatise on Human Nature*, § 7. The statement is substantially repeated in the same writer's *Prolegomena to Ethics.*

feelings." I also find that the writer himself from whom I have quoted, in a later treatise,[1] conducts long arguments respecting pleasure which are only intelligible if the distinction between pleasure and its conditions is thoroughly grasped and steadily contemplated. Indeed he carries a distinction of this kind to an extreme point of subtlety; as he requires us to distinguish the "self-satisfaction sought in all desire "that amounts to will" from the "pleasure" that "there is "in all self-satisfaction if attained": whereas other moralists regard self-satisfaction as a species of pleasure.[2] To maintain that we can distinguish pleasure from self-satisfaction, and cannot distinguish it from its conditions, seems to me too violent a paradox to need refutation. It is possible that Green may only mean that pleasure cannot be thought to exist apart from conditions which are not feelings, and that it necessarily varies with any variation in its conditions. The statement thus interpreted I do not deny: but it is quite irrelevant to the question whether pleasure can be *estimated* separately from its conditions, or whether pleasures received under different conditions can be quantitatively compared. I cannot have the pleasure of witnessing a tragedy or the pleasure of witnessing a farce, without having along with either a complex of innumerable thoughts and images, very diverse in quality in the two cases: but this does not prevent me from deciding confidently whether the tragedy or the farce will afford me most pleasure on the whole.

I pass to another objection made by the same writer to the Hedonistic conception of the supreme end of action as "the greatest possible sum of pleasures." (It should be "the "greatest possible surplus of pleasure over pain": but the difference is unimportant for the present argument.) The phrase, he says, is "intrinsically unmeaning": but his justification for this statement appears to be different in different treatises. At first he boldly affirmed that "pleasant feelings "are not quantities that can be added,"[3] apparently because "each is over before the other begins." The latter statement,

---

[1] *Prolegomena to Ethics*, § 158.
[2] *E.g.* Butler, *Sermon* xi. says, "Every man hath a desire for his own happiness . . . the object [desired] is our own happiness, enjoyment, satisfaction."
[3] Introduction to Hume, *l.c.*

however, is equally true of the parts of time : but it would be obviously absurd to say that hours, days, years are "not "quantities that can be added." Possibly this consideration occurred to Green before writing the *Prolegomena to Ethics* : at any rate in the latter treatise he admits that states " of " pleasant feeling " can be added together in " thought," only denying that they can be added " in enjoyment or imagina- " tion of enjoyment." [1] But this concedes all that is required for the Hedonistic valuation of future feelings ; no Hedonist ever supposed that the happiness he aims at making as great as possible was something to be enjoyed all at once, or ever wanted to imagine it as so enjoyed. And unless the transi- ency of pleasure diminishes its pleasantness—a point which I will presently consider—I cannot see that the possibility of realising the Hedonistic end is at all affected by the necessity of realising it in successive parts. Green, in an- other passage,[2] appears to lay down that " an end " which is " to serve the purpose of a criterion " must " enable us to " distinguish actions that bring men nearer to it from those " which do not." This, however, would only be the case if by an " end " is necessarily meant a goal or consummation, which, after gradually drawing nearer to it, we reach all at once : but this is not, I conceive, the sense in which the word is ordinarily understood by ethical writers : and certainly all that I mean by it is an object of rational aim—whether attained in successive parts or not—which is not sought as a means to the attainment of any ulterior object, but for itself. And so long as any one's prospective balance of pleasure over pain admits of being made greater or less by immediate action in one way or another,[3] there seems no reason why ' Maximum Happiness ' should not provide as serviceable a criterion of conduct as any ' chief good ' capable of being possessed all at once, or in some way independent of the condition of time.

§ 2. If, however, it be maintained, that the consciousness

---

[1] *Prolegomena to Ethics*, § 221.

[2] *Ibid.* § 359.

[3] This Green in several passages seems expressly to admit—*e.g.* (§ 332) he says that certain measures " needed in order to supply conditions favourable to good character, tend also to make life more pleasant on the whole " : and, else- where, that " it is easy to show that an overbalance of pain would result to those capable of being affected by it " from the neglect of certain duties.

of the transiency of pleasure either makes it less pleasant at the time or causes a subsequent pain, and that the deliberate and systematic pursuit of pleasure tends to intensify this consciousness; the proposition, if borne out by experience, would certainly constitute a relevant objection to the method of Egoistic Hedonism. And this view would seem to be in the mind of the writer above quoted (though it is nowhere clearly put forward): since he affirms that it is " impossible that self- " satisfaction should be found in any succession of pleasures ";[1] as self-satisfaction being " satisfaction for a self that abides and " contemplates itself as abiding " must be at least relatively permanent:[2] and it is, I suppose, implied that the disappointment of the Hedonist, who fails to find self-satisfaction where he seeks for it, is attended with pain or loss of pleasure.[3] If this be so, and if the self-satisfaction thus missed can be obtained by the resolute adoption of some other principle of action, it would certainly seem that the systematic pursuit of pleasure is in some danger of defeating itself: it is therefore important to consider carefully how far this is really the case.

So far as my own experience goes, it does not appear to me that the mere transiency of pleasures is a serious source of discontent, so long as one has a fair prospect of having as valuable pleasures in the future as in the past—or even so long as the life before one has any substantial amount of pleasure to offer. But I do not doubt that an important element of happiness, for all or most men, is derived from the consciousness of possessing " relatively permanent " sources of pleasure—whether external, as wealth, social position, family, friends ; or internal, as knowledge, culture, strong and lively interest in the wellbeing of fairly prosperous persons or institutions. This, however, does not, in my opinion, constitute an objection to Hedonism : it rather seems obvious, from the hedonistic point of view, that " as soon " as intelligence discovers that there are fixed objects, permanent " sources of pleasure, and large groups of enduring interests, " which yield a variety of recurring enjoyments, the rational " will, preferring the greater to the less, will unfailingly devote

---

[1] *Prolegomena to Ethics*, § 176.   [2] *Op. cit.* § 232.

[3] I cannot state this positively, because—as I have said—Green expressly distinguishes self-satisfaction from pleasure, and does not expressly affirm that its absence is attended by pain.

"its energies to the pursuit of these."[1]   It may be replied that
if these permanent sources of pleasure are consciously sought
merely as a means to the hedonistic end, they will not afford
the happiness for which they are sought.   With this I to
some extent agree; but I think that if the normal complexity
of our impulses be duly taken into account, this statement will
be found not to militate against the adoption of Hedonism, but
merely to signalise a danger against which the Hedonist has to
guard.   In a previous chapter [2] I have, after Butler, laid stress
on the difference between impulses that are, strictly speaking,
directed towards pleasure, and 'extra-regarding' impulses which
do not aim at pleasure,—though much, perhaps most, of our
pleasure consists in the gratification of these latter, and therefore depends upon their existence.   I there argued that in
many cases the two kinds of impulse are so far incompatible
that they do not easily coexist in the same moment of consciousness.   I added, however, that in the ordinary condition of our
activity the incompatibility is only momentary, and does not
prevent a real harmony from being attained by a sort of alternating rhythm of the two impulses in consciousness.   Still it
seems undeniable that this harmony is liable to be disturbed;
and that while on the one hand individuals may and do sacrifice
their greatest apparent happiness to the gratification of some
imperious particular desire, so, on the other hand, self-love is
liable to engross the mind to a degree incompatible with a
healthy and vigorous outflow of those 'disinterested' impulses
towards particular objects, the pre-existence of which is
necessary to the attainment, in any high degree, of the happiness at which self-love aims.   I should not, however, infer from
this that the pursuit of pleasure is necessarily self-defeating
and futile; but merely that the principle of Egoistic Hedonism,
when applied with a due knowledge of the laws of human
nature, is practically self-limiting; i.e. that a rational method
of attaining the end at which it aims requires that we should
to some extent put it out of sight and not directly aim at it.
I have before spoken of this conclusion as the 'Fundamental
Paradox of Egoistic Hedonism'; but though it presents itself
as a paradox, there does not seem to be any difficulty in its
practical realisation, when once the danger indicated is clearly

---

[1] Sully, *Pessimism*, chap. xi. p. 282.   [2] Book i. chap. iv.

seen. For it is an experience only too common among men, in whatever pursuit they may be engaged, that they let the original object and goal of their efforts pass out of view, and come to regard the means to this end as ends in themselves : so that they at last even sacrifice the original end to the attainment of what is only secondarily and derivatively desirable. And if it be thus easy and common to forget the end in the means overmuch, there seems no reason why it should be difficult to do it to the extent that Rational Egoism prescribes : and, in fact, it seems to be continually done by ordinary persons in the case of amusements and pastimes of all kinds.

It is true that, as our desires cannot ordinarily be produced by an effort of will—though they can to some extent be repressed by it—if we started with no impulse except the desire of pleasure, it might seem difficult to execute the practical paradox of attaining pleasure by aiming at something else. Yet even in this hypothetical case the difficulty is less than it appears. For the reaction of our activities upon our emotional nature is such that we may commonly bring ourselves to take an interest in any end by concentrating our efforts upon its attainment. So that, even supposing a man to begin with absolute indifference to everything except his own pleasure, it does not follow that if he were convinced that the possession of other desires and impulses were necessary to the attainment of the greatest possible pleasure, he could not succeed in producing these. But this supposition is never actually realised. Every man, when he commences the task of systematising his conduct, whether on egoistic principles or any other, is conscious of a number of different impulses and tendencies within him, other than the mere desire for pleasure, which urge his will in particular directions, to the attainment of particular results : so that he has only to place himself under certain external influences, and these desires and impulses will begin to operate without any effort of will.

It is sometimes thought, however, that there is an important class of refined and elevated impulses with which the supremacy of self-love is in a peculiar way incompatible, such as the love of virtue, or personal affection, or the religious impulse to love and obey God. But at any rate in the common view of these impulses, this difficulty does not seem to be recognised. None of the school of moralists that followed Shaftesbury in contending that it is a man's true interest to foster in himself strictly disinterested social affections, has noted any inherent incompatibility between the existence of these affections and the supremacy of rational self-love. And similarly Christian preachers who have commended the religious life as really the happiest, have not thought genuine religion irreconcilable with the conviction that each man's own happiness is his most near and intimate concern.

Other persons, however, seem to carry the religious consciousness and the feeling of human affection to a higher stage of refinement, at which a stricter disinterestedness is exacted. They maintain that the essence of either feeling, in its best form, is absolute self-renunciation and self-sacrifice. And certainly these seem incompatible with self-love, however cautiously self-limiting. A man cannot both wish to secure his own happiness and be willing to lose it. And yet how if willingness to lose it is the true means of securing it? Can self-love not merely reduce indirectly its prominence in consciousness, but directly and unreservedly annihilate itself?

This emotional feat does not seem to me possible: and therefore I must admit that a man who embraces the principle of Rational Egoism cuts himself off from the special pleasure that attends this absolute sacrifice and abnegation of self. But however exquisite this may be, the pitch of emotional exaltation and refinement necessary to attain it is comparatively so rare, that it is scarcely included in men's common estimate of happiness. I do not therefore think that an important objection to Rational Egoism can be based upon its incompatibility with this particular consciousness: nor that the common experience of mankind really sustains the view that the desire of one's own happiness, if accepted as supreme and regulative, inevitably defeats its own aim through the consequent diminution and desiccation of the impulses and emotional capacities necessary to the attainment of happiness in a high degree; though it certainly shows a serious and subtle danger in this direction.

§ 3. There is, however, another way in which the habit of mind necessarily resulting from the continual practice of hedonistic comparison is sometimes thought to be unfavourable to the attainment of the hedonistic end : from a supposed incompatibility between the habit of reflectively observing and examining pleasure, and the capacity for experiencing pleasure in normal fulness and intensity. And it certainly seems important to consider what effect the continual attention to our pleasures, in order to observe their different degrees, is likely to have on these feelings themselves. The inquiry at first sight seems to lead to irreconcilable contradiction in our view of pleasure. For if pleasure only exists as it is felt, the more conscious we are of it, the more pleasure we have : and it would seem that the more our attention is directed towards it, the more fully we shall be conscious of it. On the other hand Hamilton's statement that " knowledge and feeling " (cognition and pleasure or pain) are always " in a certain inverse proportion to each other," corresponds *prima facie* to our common experience : for the purely cognitive element of consciousness seems to be neither pleasurable nor painful, so that the more our consciousness is occupied with cognition, the less room there seems to be for feeling.

This view, however, rests on the assumption that the total intensity of our consciousness is a constant quantity ; so that when one element of it positively increases, the rest must positively—as well as relatively—diminish. And it does not appear to me that experience gives us any valid ground for making this general assumption : it rather seems that at certain times in our life intellect and feeling are simultaneously feeble ; so that the same mental excitement may intensify both simultaneously.

Still it seems to be a fact that any very powerful feeling, reaching to the full intensity of which our consciousness is normally capable, is commonly diminished by a contemporaneous stroke of cognitive effort : hence it is a general difficulty in the way of exact observation of our emotions that the object cognised seems to shrink and dwindle in proportion as the cognitive regard grows keen and eager. How then are we to reconcile this with the proposition first laid down, that pleasure only exists as we are conscious of it ? The answer seems to be that the mere consciousness of a present feeling—apart from any distinct representative elements—cannot diminish the feeling of which it is an indispensable and inseparable condition :

but in introspective cognition we go beyond the present feeling, comparing and classifying it with remembered or imagined feelings; and the effort of representing and comparing these other feelings tends to decrease the mere presentative consciousness of the actual pleasure.

I conclude, then, that there is a real danger of diminishing pleasure by the attempt to observe and estimate it. But the danger seems only to arise in the case of very intense pleasures, and only if the attempt is made at the moment of actual enjoyment; and since the most delightful periods of life have frequently recurring intervals of nearly neutral feeling, in which the pleasures immediately past may be compared and estimated without any such detriment, I do not regard the objection founded on this danger as particularly important.

§ 4. More serious, in my opinion, are the objections urged against the possibility of performing, with definite and trustworthy results, the comprehensive and methodical comparison of pleasures and pains which the adoption of the Hedonistic standard involves. I cannot indeed doubt that men habitually compare pleasures and pains in respect of their intensity: that (*e.g.*) when we pass from one state of consciousness to another, or when in any way we are led to recall a state long past, we often unhesitatingly declare the present state to be more or less pleasant than the past: or that we declare some pleasant experiences to have been 'worth,' and others 'not worth,' the trouble it took to obtain them, or the pain that followed them. But, granting this, it may still be maintained (1) that this comparison as ordinarily made is both occasional and very rough, and that it can never be extended as. systematic Hedonism requires, nor applied, with any accuracy, to all possible states however differing in quality; and (2) that as commonly practised it is liable to illusion, of which we can never measure the precise amount, while we are continually forced to recognise its existence. This illusion was even urged by Plato as a ground for distrusting the apparent affirmation of consciousness in respect of *present* pleasure. Plato thought that the apparent intensity of the coarser bodily pleasures was illusory; because these states of consciousness, being preceded by pain, were really only states of relief from pain, and so properly neutral, neither pleasant nor painful—examples of what I have called the hedonistic zero—only appearing pleasant from contrast with the preceding pain.

To this, however, it has been answered, that in estimating pleasure there is no conceivable appeal from the immediate decision of consciousness : that here the Phenomenal is the Real—there is no other real that we can distinguish from it. And this seems to me true, in so far as we are concerned only with the present state.   But then—apart from the difficulty just noticed of observing a pleasure while it is felt without thereby diminishing it—it is obvious that in any estimate of its intensity we are necessarily comparing it with some other state.   And this latter must generally be a representation, not an actual feeling : for though we can sometimes experience two or perhaps more pleasures at once, we are rarely in such cases able to compare them satisfactorily : for either the causes of the two mutually interfere, so that neither reaches its normal degree of intensity ; or, more often, the two blend into one state of pleasant consciousness the elements of which we cannot estimate separately.   But if it is therefore inevitable that one term at least in our comparison should be an imagined pleasure, we see that there is a possibility of error in any such comparison ; for the imagined feeling may not adequately represent the pleasantness of the corresponding actual feeling. And in the egoistic comparison, the validity of which we are now discussing, the objects primarily to be compared are all represented elements of consciousness : for we are desiring to choose between two or more possible courses of conduct, and therefore to forecast future feelings.

Let us then examine more closely the manner in which this comparison is ordinarily performed, that we may see what positive grounds we have for mistrusting it.

In estimating for practical purposes the value of different pleasures open to us, we commonly trust most to our prospective imagination : we project ourselves into the future, and imagine what such and such a pleasure will amount to under hypothetical conditions.   This imagination, so far as it involves conscious inference, seems to be chiefly determined by our own experience of past pleasures, which are usually recalled generically, or in large aggregates, though sometimes particular instances of important single pleasures occur to us as definitely remembered :

but partly, too, we are influenced by the experience of others sympathetically appropriated: and here again we sometimes definitely refer to particular experiences which have been communicated to us by individuals, and sometimes to the traditional generalisations which are thought to represent the common experience of mankind.

Now it does not seem that such a process as this is likely to be free from error: and, indeed, no one pretends that it is. In fact there is scarcely any point upon which moralisers have dwelt with more emphasis than this, that man's forecast of pleasure is continually erroneous. Each of us frequently recognises his own mistakes: and each still more often attributes to others errors unseen by themselves, arising either from misinterpretation of their own experience, or from ignorance or neglect of that of others.

How then are these errors to be eliminated? The obvious answer is that we must substitute for the instinctive, largely implicit, inference just described a more scientific process of reasoning: by deducing the probable degree of our future pleasure or pain in any given circumstances from inductive generalisations based on a sufficient, number of careful observations of our own and others' experience. We have then to ask, first, how far can each of us estimate accurately his own past experience of pleasures and pains? secondly, how far can this knowledge of the past enable him to forecast, with any certainty, the greatest happiness within his reach in the future? thirdly, how far can he appropriate, for the purposes of such forecasts, the past experience of others?

As regards the first of these questions, it must be remembered that it is not sufficient to know generally that we derive pleasures and pains from such and such sources; we require to know approximately the positive or negative degree of each feeling; unless we can form some quantitative estimate of them, it is futile to try to attain our *greatest possible* happiness—at least by an empirical method. We have therefore to compare quantitatively each pleasure as it occurs, or as recalled in imagination, with other imagined pleasures: and the question is, how far such comparisons can be regarded as trustworthy.

Now for my own part, when I reflect on my pleasures and pains, and endeavour to compare them in respect of intensity,

it is only to a very limited extent that I can obtain clear and
definite results from such comparisons, even taking each separately in its simplest form:—whether the comparison is made at
the moment of experiencing one of the pleasures, or between
two states of consciousness recalled in imagination.   This is
true even when I compare feelings of the same kind : and the
vagueness and uncertainty increases, in proportion as the feelings differ in kind.   Let us begin with sensual gratifications,
which are thought to be especially definite and palpable.
Suppose I am enjoying a good dinner : if I ask myself whether
one kind of dish or wine gives me more pleasure than another,
sometimes I can decide, but very often not.   So if I reflect
upon two modes of bodily exercise that I may have taken : if
one has been in a marked degree agreeable or tedious, I take
note of it naturally ; but it is not natural to me to go further
than this in judging of their pleasurableness or painfulness,
and the attempt to do so does not seem to lead to any clear
affirmation.   And similarly of intellectual exercises and states
of consciousness predominantly emotional: even when the
causes and quality of the feelings compared are similar, it is
only when the differences in pleasantness are great, that
hedonistic comparison seems to yield any definite result.   But
when I try to arrange in a scale pleasures differing in kind ; to
compare (e.g.) labour with rest, excitement with tranquillity,
intellectual exercise with emotional effusion, the pleasure of
scientific apprehension with that of beneficent action, the
delight of social expansion with the delight of æsthetic recep-
tion ; my judgment wavers and fluctuates far more, and in
the majority of cases I cannot give any confident decision.   And
if this is the case with what Bentham calls ' pure '—i.e. painless
—pleasures, it is still more true of those even commoner states
of consciousness, where a certain amount of pain or discomfort
is mixed with pleasure, although the latter preponderates.   If it
is hard to say which of two different states of contentment was
the greater pleasure, it seems still harder to compare a state of
placid satisfaction with one of eager but hopeful suspense, or
with triumphant conquest of painful obstacles.   And perhaps it
is still more difficult to compare pure pleasures with pure pains,
and to say how much of the one kind of feeling we consider to
be exactly balanced by a given amount of the other when they

do not occur simultaneously : while an estimate of simultaneous feelings is, as we have seen, generally unsatisfactory from the mutual interference of their respective causes.

§ 5. But again, if these judgments are not clear and definite, still less are they consistent. I do not now mean that one man's estimate of the value of any kind of pleasures differs from another's : for we have assumed each sentient individual to be the final judge of the pleasantness and painfulness of his own feelings, and therefore this kind of discrepancy does not affect the validity of the judgments, and creates no difficulty until any one tries to appropriate the experience of others. But I mean that each individual's judgment of the comparative value of his own pleasures is apt to be different at different times, though it relates to the same past experiences ; and that this variation is a legitimate ground for distrusting the validity of any particular comparison.

The causes of this variation seem to be partly due to the nature of the represented feeling, and partly to the general state of the mind at the time of making the representation. To begin with the former : we find that different kinds of past pleasures and pains do not equally admit of being revived in imagination. Thus, generally speaking, our more emotional and more representative pains are more easily revived than the more sensational and presentative : for example, it is at this moment much more easy for me to imagine the discomfort of expectancy which preceded a past sea-sickness than the pain of the actual nausea : although I infer—from the recollection of judgments passed at the time—that the former pain was trifling compared with the latter. To this cause it seems due that past hardships, toils, and anxieties often appear pleasurable when we look back upon them, after some interval ; for the excitement, the heightened sense of life that accompanied the painful struggle, would have been pleasurable if taken by itself ; and it is this that we recall rather than the pain. In estimating pleasures the other cause of variation is more conspicuous ; we are conscious of changes occasional or periodic in our estimate of them, depending upon changes in our mental or bodily condition. E.g. it is a matter of common remark with respect to the gratifications of appetite that we cannot estimate them adequately in the state of satiety, and that we are apt to exaggerate them in the state of desire. (I do not deny that intensity of antecedent desire intensifies the pleasure of fruition ; so that this pleasure not only *appears*, as Plato thought, but actually *is* greater owing to the strength of the desire that has preceded. Still it is a matter of common experience that pleasures which have been intensely desired are often found to disappoint expectation.)

There seem to be no special states of aversion, determined by bodily causes, and related to certain pains as our appetites to their correspondent pleasures ; but most persons are liable to be thrown by the prospect of certain pains into the state of passionate aversion which we call fear, and to be thereby led to estimate such pains as worse than they would be judged to be in a calmer mood.

Further, when feeling any kind of pain or uneasiness we seem liable to underrate pain of a very dissimilar kind : thus in danger we value repose, overlooking its *ennui*, while the tedium of security makes us imagine the mingled excitement of past danger as almost purely pleasurable. And again when we are absorbed in any particular pleasant activity, the pleasures attending dissimilar activities are apt to be contemned : they appear coarse or thin, as the case may be : and this constitutes a fundamental objection to noting the exact degree of a pleasure at the time of experiencing it. The eager desire, which often seems an indispensable element of the whole state of pleasurable activity, generally involves a similar bias : indeed any strong excitement, in which our thought is concentrated on a single result or group of results—whether it be the excitement of aversion, fear, hope, or suspense—tends to make us inappreciative of alien pleasures and pains alike. And, speaking more generally, we cannot imagine as very intense a pleasure of a kind that at the time of imagining it we are incapable of experiencing : as (*e.g.*) the pleasures of intellectual or bodily exercise at the close of a wearying day ; or any emotional pleasure when our susceptibility to the special emotion is temporarily exhausted. On the other hand, it is not easy to guard against error, as philosophers have often thought, by making our estimate in a cool and passionless state. For there are many pleasures which require precedent desire, and even enthusiasm and highly wrought excitement, in order to be experienced in their full intensity; and it is not likely that we should appreciate these adequately in a state of perfect tranquillity.

§ 6. These considerations make clearer the extent of the assumptions of Empirical Quantitative Hedonism, stated in the preceding chapter : viz. (1) that our pleasures and pains have each a definite degree, and (2) that this degree is empirically cognisable. Firstly, if pleasure only exists as it is felt, the belief that every pleasure and pain has a definite intensive quantity or degree must remain an *a priori* assumption, incapable of positive empirical verification. For the pleasure can only have the degree as compared with other feelings, of the same or some different kind ; but, generally speaking, since this comparison can only be made in imagination, it can only yield the hypothetical result that if certain feelings could be felt together, precisely as they have been felt separately, one would be found more desirable than the other in some definite ratio. If, then, we are asked what ground we have for regarding this imaginary result as a valid representation of reality, we cannot say more than that the belief in its general validity is irresistibly suggested in reflection on experience, and remains at any rate uncontradicted by experience.

But secondly, granting that each of our pleasures and pains has really a definite degree of pleasantness or painfulness, the question still remains whether we have any means of accurately measuring these degrees. Is there any reason to suppose that the mind is ever in such a state as to be a perfectly neutral and colourless medium for imagining all kinds of pleasures ? Experience certainly shows us the frequent occurrence of moods in which we have an apparent bias for or against a particular kind of feeling. Is it not probable that there is always some bias of this kind ? that we are always more in tune for some pleasures, more sensitive to some pains, than we are to others ? It must, I think, be admitted that the exact cognition of the place of each kind of feeling in a scale of desirability, measured positively and negatively from a zero of perfect indifference, is at best an ideal to which we can never tell how closely we approximate. Still in the variations of our judgment and the disappointment of our expectations we have experience of errors of which we can trace the causes and allow for them, at least roughly ; correcting in thought the defects of imagination. And since what we require for practical guidance is to estimate not individual past experiences, but the value of a kind of pleasure or pain, as obtained under certain circumstances or conditions; we can to some extent diminish the chance of error in this estimate by making a number of observations and imaginative comparisons, at different times and in different moods. In so far as these agree we may legitimately feel an increased confidence in the result: and in so far as they differ, we can at least reduce our possible error by striking an average of the different estimates. It will be evident, however, that such a method as this cannot be expected to yield more than a rough approximation to the supposed truth.

§ 7. We must conclude then that our estimate of the hedonistic value of any past pleasure or pain, is liable to an amount of error which we cannot calculate exactly; because the represented pleasantness of different feelings fluctuates and varies indefinitely with changes in the actual condition of the representing mind. We have now to observe that, for similar reasons, even supposing we could adequately allow for, and so exclude, this source of error in our comparison of past pleasures, it is liable to intrude again in arguing from the past to the future. For our capacity for particular pleasures may be about to change, or may have actually changed since the experiences that form the data of our calculation. We may have reached the point of satiety in respect of some of our past pleasures, or otherwise lost our susceptibility to them, owing to latent changes in our constitution: or we may have increased our susceptibility to pains inevitably connected with them: or altered conditions of life may have generated in us new desires and aversions, and given relative importance to new sources of happiness. Or any or all of these changes may be expected to occur, before the completion of the course of conduct upon which we are now deciding. The most careful estimate of a girl's pleasures (supposing a girl gifted with the abnormal habit of reflection that would be necessary) would not much profit a young woman: and the hedonistic calculations of youth require modification as we advance in years.

It may be said, however, that no one, in making such a forecast, can or does rely entirely on his own experience: when endeavouring to estimate the probable effect upon his happiness of new circumstances and influences, untried rules of conduct and fashions of life, he always argues partly from the experience of others. This is, I think, generally true: but by including inferences from other men's experience we inevitably introduce a new possibility of error; for such inference proceeds on the assumption of a similarity of nature among human beings, which is never exactly true, while we can never exactly know how much it falls short of the truth; though we have sufficient evidence of the striking differences between the feelings produced in different men by similar causes, to convince us that the assumption would in many cases be wholly misleading. On this ground Plato's reason for claiming that the life of the Philosopher has more pleasure than that of the Sensualist is palpably inadequate. The philosopher, he argues, has tried both kinds of pleasure, sensual as well as intellectual, and prefers the delights of philosophic life; the sensualist ought therefore to trust his decision and follow his example. But who can tell that the philosopher's constitution is not such as to render the enjoyments of the senses, in his case, comparatively feeble? while on the other hand the sensualist's mind may not be able to attain more than a thin shadow of the philosopher's delight. And so, generally speaking, if we are to be guided by another's experience, we require to be convinced not only that he is generally accurate in observing, analysing, and comparing his sensations, but also that his relative susceptibility to the different kinds of pleasure and pain in question coincides with our own. If he is unpractised in introspective observation, it is possible that he may mistake even the external conditions of his own happiness; and so the communication of his experience may be altogether misleading. But however accurately he has analysed and determined the causes of his feelings, that similar causes would produce similar effects in us must always be uncertain. And the uncertainty is increased indefinitely if our adviser has to recall in memory out of a distant past some of the pleasures or pains to be compared. Thus in the ever-renewed controversy between Age and Youth, wisdom is not after all so clearly on the side of maturer counsels as it seems to be at first sight. When a youth is warned by his senior to abstain from some pleasure, on the ground of prudence, because it is not worth the possible pleasures that must be sacrificed for it and the future pains that it will entail; it is difficult for him to know how far the elder man can recall—even if he could once feel—the full rapture of the delight that he is asking the younger to renounce.

And further, this source of error besets us in a more extended and more subtle manner than has yet been noticed. For our sympathetic apprehension of alien experiences of pleasure and pain has been so continually exercised, in so many ways, during the whole of our life, both by actual observation and oral communication with other human beings, and through books and other modes of symbolic suggestion; that it is impossible to say how far it has unconsciously blended with our own experience, so as to colour and modify it when represented in memory. Thus we may easily overlook the discrepancy between our own experience and that of others, in respect of the importance of certain sources of pleasure and pain, if no sudden and striking disappointment of expectations forces it on our notice. Only with considerable care and attention can sympathetic persons separate their own real likes and dislikes from those of their associates: and we can never tell whether this separation has been completely effected.

But again: the practical inference from the past to the future is further complicated by the fact that we can alter ourselves. For it may be that our past experience has been greatly affected by our being not properly attuned to certain pleasures, as (*e.g.*) those of art, or study, or muscular exercise, or society, or beneficent action; or not duly hardened against certain sources of pain, such as toil, or anxiety, or abstinence from luxuries: and there may be within our power some process of training or hardening ourselves which may profoundly modify our susceptibilities. And this consideration is especially important,—and at the same time especially difficult to deal with,—when we attempt to appropriate the experience of another. For we may find that he estimates highly pleasures which we not only have never experienced at all, but cannot possibly experience without a considerable alteration of our nature. For example, the pleasures of the religious life, the raptures of prayer and praise and the devotion of the soul to God, are commonly thought to require Conversion or complete change of nature before they can be experienced. And in the same way the sacrifice of sensual inclination to duty is disagreeable to the non-moral man when he at first attempts it, but affords to the truly virtuous man a deep and strong delight.   And similarly almost all the more refined intellectual and emotional pleasures require training and culture in order to be enjoyed : and since this training does not always succeed in producing any considerable degree of susceptibility, it may always be a matter of doubt for one from whom it would require the sacrifice of other pleasures, whether such sacrifice is worth making.

The foregoing considerations must, I think, seriously reduce our confidence in what I have called the Empirical-reflective method of Egoistic Hedonism.   I do not conclude that we should reject it altogether : I am conscious that, in spite of all the difficulties that I have urged, I continue to make comparisons between pleasures and pains with practical reliance on their results.   But I conclude that it would be at least highly desirable, with a view to the systematic direction of conduct, to control and supplement the results of such comparisons by the assistance of some other method : if we can find any on which we see reason to rely.

CHAPTER IV

OBJECTIVE HEDONISM AND COMMON SENSE

§ 1. BEFORE we examine those methods of seeking one's own happiness which are more remote from the empirical, it will be well to consider how far we may reasonably avoid the difficulties and uncertainties of the method of reflective comparison, by relying on the current opinions and accepted estimates of the value of different objects commonly sought as sources of pleasure.

It certainly seems more natural to men, at least in the main plan and ordering of their lives, to seek and consciously estimate the objective conditions and sources of happiness, rather than happiness itself; and it may plausibly be said that by relying on such estimates of objects we avoid the difficulties that beset the introspective method of comparing feelings: and that the common opinions as to the value of different sources of pleasure express the net result of the combined experience of mankind from generation to generation: in which the divergences due to the limitations of each individual's experience, and to the differently tinged moods in which different estimates have been taken, have balanced and neutralised each other and so disappeared.

I do not wish to undervalue the guidance of common sense in our pursuit of happiness. I think, however, that when we consider these common opinions as premises for the deductions of systematic egoism, they must be admitted to be open to the following grave objections.

In the first place, Common Sense gives us only, at the best, an estimate true for an average or typical human being: and,

151

as we have already seen, it is probable that any particular individual will be more or less divergent from this type.   In any case, therefore, each person will have to correct the estimate of common opinion by the results of his own experience in order to obtain from it trustworthy guidance for his own conduct : and this process of correction, it would seem, must be involved in all the difficulties from which we are trying to escape.   But, secondly, the experience of the mass of mankind is confined within limits too narrow for its results to be of much avail in the present inquiry.   The majority of human beings spend most of their time in labouring to avert starvation and severe bodily discomfort : and the brief leisure that remains to them, after supplying the bodily needs of food, sleep, etc., is spent in ways determined rather by impulse, routine, and habit, than by a deliberate estimate of probable pleasure.   It would seem, then, that the common sense to which we have here to refer can only be that of a minority of comparatively rich and leisured persons.

But again, we cannot tell that the mass of mankind, or any section of the mass, is not generally and normally under the influence of some of the causes of mal-observation previously noticed.   We avoid the " idols of the cave " by trusting Common Sense, but what is to guard us against the " idols of the tribe " ?   Moreover, the common estimate of different sources of happiness seems to involve all the confusion of ideas and points of view, which in defining the empirical method of Hedonism we have taken some pains to eliminate.   In the first place it does not distinguish between objects of natural desire and sources of experienced pleasure.   Now we have seen (Book i. chap. iv.) that these two are not exactly coincident—indeed we find numerous examples of men who continue not only to feel but to indulge desires, the gratification of which they know by ample experience to be attended with more pain than pleasure. And therefore the current estimate of the desirability of objects of pursuit cannot be taken to express simply men's experience of pleasure and pain : for men are apt to think desirable what they strongly desire, whether or not they have found it conducive to happiness on the whole : and so the common opinion will tend to represent a compromise between the average force of desires and the average experience of the consequences of gratifying them.

We must allow again for the intermingling of moral with purely hedonistic preferences in the estimate of common sense. For even when men definitely expect greater happiness from the course of conduct which they choose than from any other, it is often because they think it the right, or more excellent, or more noble course; making, more or less unconsciously, the assumption (which we shall presently have to consider) that the morally best action will prove to be also the most conducive to the agent's happiness. And a similar assumption seems to be made—without adequate warrant—as regards merely æsthetic preferences.

Again, the introduction of the moral and æsthetic points of view suggests the following doubt :—Are we to be guided by the preferences which men avow, or by those which their actions would lead us to infer ? On the one hand, we cannot doubt that men often, from weakness of character, fail to seek what they sincerely believe will give them most pleasure in the long-run : on the other hand, as a genuine preference for virtuous or refined pleasure is a mark of genuine virtue or refined taste, men who do not really feel such preference are unconsciously or consciously influenced by a desire to gain credit for it, and their express estimate of pleasures is thus modified and coloured.

§ 2. But, even if we had no doubt on general grounds that Common Sense would prove our best guide in the pursuit of happiness, we should still be perplexed by finding its utterances on this topic very deficient in clearness and consistency. I do not merely mean that they are different in different ages and countries—that we might explain as due to variations in the general conditions of human life—: but that serious conflicts and ambiguities are found if we consider only the current common sense of our own age and country. We can make a list of sources of happiness apparently recommended by an overwhelming *consensus* of current opinion : as health, wealth, friendship and family affections, fame and social position, power, interesting and congenial occupation and amusement,—including the gratification, in some form, of the love of knowledge, and of those refined, partly sensual, partly emotional, susceptibilities which we call æsthetic.[1] But if we

---

[1] The consideration of the importance of Morality as a source of happiness is reserved for the next chapter.

inquire into the relative value of these objects of common pursuit, we seem to get no clear answer from Common Sense— unless, perhaps, it would be generally agreed that health ought to be paramount to all other secondary ends : though even on this point we could not infer general agreement from observation of the actual conduct of mankind.   Nay, even as regards the positive estimate of these sources of happiness, we find on closer examination that the supposed *consensus* is much less clear than it seemed at first.   Not only are there numerous and important bodies of dissidents from the current opinions : but the very same majority, the same Common Sense of Mankind that maintains these opinions, is found in a singular and unexpected manner to welcome and approve the paradoxes of these dissidents.   Men show a really startling readiness to admit that the estimates of happiness which guide them in their ordinary habits and pursuits are erroneous and illusory ; and that from time to time the veil is, as it were, lifted, and the error and illusion made manifest.

For, first, men seem to attach great value to the ample gratification of bodily appetites and needs : the wealthier part of mankind spend a considerable amount of money and fore- thought upon the means of satisfying these in a luxurious manner : and though they do not often deliberately sacrifice health to this gratification—common sense condemns that as irrational—still one may say that they are habitually courageous in pressing forward to the very verge of this imprudence.

And yet the same people are fond of saying that " hunger is the best sauce," and that " temperance and labour will make plain food more delightful than the most exquisite products of the culinary art."   And they often argue with perfect sin- cerity that the rich have really no advantage, or scarcely any advantage, over the comparatively poor, in respect of these pleasures ; for habit soon renders the more luxurious provision for the satisfaction of their acquired needs no more pleasant to the rich than the appeasing of his more primitive appe- tites is to the poor man.   And the same argument is often extended to all the material comforts that wealth can purchase. It is often contended that habit at once renders us indifferent to these while they are enjoyed, and yet unable to dispense with them without annoyance : so that the pleasures of the merely animal life are no greater to the rich than to the poor, but only more insecure. And from this there is but a short step to the conclusion, that wealth, in the pursuit of which most men agree in concentrating their efforts, and on the attainment of which all congratulate each other,—wealth, for which so many risk their health, shorten their lives, reduce their enjoyments of domestic life, and sacrifice the more refined pleasures of curiosity and art,—is really a very doubtful gain, in the majority of cases; because the cares and anxieties which it entails balance, for most men, the slight advantage of the luxuries which it purchases.[1]

And similarly, although social rank and status is, in England, an object of passionate pursuit, yet it is continually said, with general approval, that it is of no intrinsic value as a means of happiness; that though the process of ascending from a lower grade to a higher is perhaps generally agreeable, and the process of descending from a higher to a lower certainly painful, yet permanent existence on the loftier level is no more pleasant than on the humbler; that happiness is to be found as easily in a cottage as in a palace (if not, indeed, more easily in the cottage): and so forth.

Still more trite are the commonplaces as to the emptiness and vanity of the satisfaction to be derived from Fame and Reputation. The case of posthumous fame, indeed, is a striking instance of the general proposition before laid down, that the commonly accepted ends of action are determined partly by the average force of desires that are not directed towards pleasure, nor conformed to experiences of pleasure. For posthumous fame seems to rank pretty high among the objects that common opinion regards as good or desirable for the individual: and the pursuit of it is not ordinarily stigmatised as contrary to prudence, even if it leads a man to sacrifice other important sources of happiness to a result of which he never expects to be actually conscious. Yet the slightest reflection

---

[1] It is striking to find the author of the *Wealth of Nations*, the founder of a long line of plutologists who are commonly believed to exalt the material means of happiness above all other, declaring that "wealth and greatness are mere trinkets of frivolous utility," and that "in ease of body and peace of mind, all the different ranks of life are nearly upon a level, and the beggar who suns himself by the side of the highway possesses that security which kings are fighting for." Adam Smith, *Moral Sentiments*, Part iv. chap. i.

shows such a pursuit to be *prima facie* irrational,[1] from an egoistic point of view ; and every moraliser has found this an obvious and popular topic.   The actual consciousness of present fame is no doubt very delightful to most persons : still the moraliser does not find it difficult to maintain that even this is attended with such counterbalancing disadvantages as render its hedonistic value very doubtful.

Again, the current estimate of the desirability of Power is tolerably high, and perhaps the more closely and analytically we examine the actual motives of men, the more widespread and predominant its pursuit will appear : for many men seem to seek wealth, knowledge, even reputation, as a means to the attainment of power, rather than for their own sakes or with a view to other pleasures.   And yet men assent willingly when they are told that the pursuit of power, as of fame, is prompted by a vain ambition, never satisfied, but only rendered more uneasy by such success as is possible for it : that the anxieties which attend not only the pursuit but the possession of power, and the jealousies and dangers inseparable from the latter, far outweigh its pleasures.

Society of some sort no one can deny to be necessary to human happiness : but still the kind and degree of social intercourse which is actually sought by the more wealthy and leisured portion of the community, with no little expenditure of time, trouble, and means, is often declared to yield a most thin and meagre result of pleasure.

We find, no doubt, great agreement among modern moralisers as to the importance of the exercise of the domestic affections as a means of happiness : and this certainly seems to have a prominent place in the plan of life of the majority of mankind.   And yet it may fairly be doubted whether men in general do value domestic life very highly, apart from the gratification of sexual passion.   Certainly whenever any part of civilised society is in such a state that men can freely indulge this passion and at the same time avoid the burden of

---

[1] No doubt such a pursuit may be justified to self-love by dwelling on the pleasures of hope and anticipation which attend it.   But this is obviously an after-thought.   It is not for the sake of these originally that posthumous fame is sought by him whom it spurs

"To scorn delights and live laborious days."

a family, without any serious fear of social disapprobation, celibacy tends to become common : it has even become so common as to excite the grave anxiety of legislators. And though such conduct has always been disapproved by common sense, it seems to be rather condemned as anti-social than as imprudent.

Thus our examination shows great instability and uncertainty in the most decisive judgments of common sense ; since, as I have said, bodily comfort and luxury, wealth, fame, power, society are the objects which common opinion seems most clearly and confidently to recommend as sources of pleasure. For though the pleasures derived from Art and the contemplation of the beautiful in Nature, and those of curiosity and the exercise of the intellect generally, are highly praised, it is difficult to formulate a " common opinion " in respect of them, since the high estimates often set upon them seem to express the real experience of only small minorities. And though these have persuaded the mass of mankind, or that portion of it which is possessed of leisure, to let Culture be regarded as an important source of happiness ; they can scarcely be said to have produced any generally accepted opinion as to its importance in comparison with the other sources before mentioned, the pleasures of which are more genuinely appreciated by the majority ; still less as to the relative value of different elements of this culture.

But even supposing the *consensus*, in respect of sources of happiness, were far more complete and clear than impartial reflection seems to show, its value would still be considerably impaired by the dissent of important minorities, which we have not yet noticed. For example, many religious persons regard all mundane pleasures as mean and trifling ; so full of vanity and emptiness that the eager pursuit of them is only possible through ever-renewed illusion, leading to ever-repeated disappointment. And this view is shared by not a few reflective persons who have no religious bias : as is evident from the numerous adherents that Pessimism has won in recent times. Indeed a somewhat similar judgment, on the value of the ordinary objects of human pursuit, has been passed by many philosophers who have not been pessimists : and when we consider that it is the philosopher's especial business to reflect with care and precision on the facts of consciousness, we shall hesitate, in any dispute between philosophers and the mass of mankind, to let our conclusion be determined by merely counting heads. On the other hand, as has been already observed, the philosopher's susceptibilities and capacities of feeling do not fairly represent those of humanity in general : and hence if he ventures to erect the results of his individual experience into a universal standard, he is likely to overrate some pleasures and underrate others. Perhaps the most convincing illustrations of this are furnished by thinkers not of the idealist or transcendental type, but professed Hedonists, such as Epicurus and Hobbes. We cannot accept as fair expressions of the ordinary experience of the human race either Epicurus's identification of painlessness with the highest degree of pleasure, or Hobbes's asseveration that the gratifications of curiosity " far exceed in intensity all carnal delights." Thus we seem to be in this dilemma : the mass of mankind, to whose common opinion we are naturally referred for catholically authoritative beliefs respecting the conditions of happiness, are deficient in the faculty or the habit of observing and recording their experience : and usually, in proportion as a man is, by nature and practice, a better observer, the phenomena that he has to observe are more and more divergent from the ordinary type.

§ 3. On the whole, it must, I think, be admitted that the Hedonistic method cannot be freed from inexactness and uncertainty by appealing to the judgments of common sense respecting the sources of happiness. At the same time I would not exaggerate the difficulty of combining these into a tolerably coherent body of probable doctrine, not useless for practical guidance. For first, it must be observed, that it is only occasionally and to a limited extent that these commonly commended sources of happiness come into competition with one another and are presented as alternatives. For example, the pursuit of wealth often leads also to power (besides the power that lies in wealth) and to reputation : and again, these objects of desire can usually be best attained—as far as it is in our power to attain them at all—by employment which in itself gives the pleasure that normally attends energetic exercise of one's best faculties : and this congenial employment is not incompatible with adequate exercise of the affections, social and domestic; nor with cultivated amusement (which must always be carefully limited in amount if it is to be really amusing). And no one doubts that to carry either employment or amusement to a degree that injures health involves generally a sacrifice of happiness, no less than over-indulgence in sensual gratifications.

And as for the philosophical or quasi-philosophical paradoxes as to the illusoriness of sensual enjoyments, wealth, power, fame, etc., we may explain the widespread acceptance which these find by admitting a certain general tendency to exaggeration in the common estimates of such objects of desire, which from time to time causes a reaction and an equally excessive temporary depreciation of them. As we saw (chap. iii.) it is natural for men to value too highly the absent pleasures for which they hope and long: power and fame, for example, are certainly attended with anxieties and disgusts which are not foreseen when they are represented in longing imagination: yet it may still be true that they bring to most men a clear balance of happiness on the whole. It seems clear, again, that luxury adds *less* to the ordinary enjoyment of life than most men struggling with penury suppose: there are special delights attending the hard-earned meal, and the rarely-recurring amusement, which must be weighed against the profuser pleasures that the rich can command: so that we may fairly conclude that increase of happiness is very far from keeping pace with increase of wealth. On the other hand, when we take into account all the pleasures of Culture, Power, Fame, and Beneficence, and still more the security that wealth gives against the pains of privation and the anxieties of penury—for the owner himself and those whom he loves—we can hardly doubt that increase of wealth brings on the average *some* increase of happiness: at least until a man reaches an income beyond that of the great majority in any actual community. Thus on the whole it would seem to be a reasonable conclusion that, while it is extravagant to affirm that happiness is "equally distributed through all ranks and callings," it is yet *more* equally distributed than the aspect of men's external circumstances would lead us to infer: especially considering the importance of the pleasures that attend the exercise of the

affections.   Again, common sense is quite prepared to recognise that there are persons of peculiar temperament to whom
the ordinary pleasures of life are really quite trifling in comparison with more refined enjoyments : and also that men
generally are liable to fall, for certain periods, under the sway
of absorbing impulses, which take them out of the range
within which the judgments of common sense are even
broadly and generally valid.   No one (*e.g.*) expects a lover
to care much for anything except the enjoyments of love ; nor
considers that an enthusiast sacrifices happiness in making
everything give way to his hobby.

In fact we may say that common sense scarcely claims to
provide more than rather indefinite general rules, which no
prudent man should neglect without giving himself a reason
for doing so.   Such reasons may either be drawn from one's
knowledge of some peculiarities in one's nature, or from the experience of others whom one has ground for believing to be more
like oneself than the average of mankind are.   Still, as we saw,
there is considerable risk of error in thus appropriating the
special experience of other individuals : and, in short, it does not
appear that by any process of this kind,—either by appealing
to the common opinion of the many, or to that of cultivated
persons, or to that of those whom we judge most to resemble
ourselves,—we can hope to solve with precision or certainty
the problems of egoistic conduct.

The question then remains, whether any general theory
can be attained of the causes of pleasure and pain so certain
and practically applicable that we may by its aid rise above
the ambiguities and inconsistencies of common or sectarian
opinion, no less than the shortcomings of the empirical-reflective
method, and establish the Hedonistic art of life on a thoroughly
scientific basis.   To the consideration of this question I shall
proceed in the last chapter of this book : but before entering
upon it, I wish to examine carefully a common belief as to
the means of attaining happiness which—though it hardly
claims to rest upon a scientific basis—is yet generally conceived by those who hold it to have a higher degree of
certainty than most of the current opinions that we have
been examining.   This is the belief that a man will attain
the greatest happiness open to him by the performance of his

Duty as commonly recognised and prescribed—except so far
as he may deviate from this standard in obedience to a truer
conception of the conduct by which universal good is to be
realised or promoted.[1] The special importance of this opinion
to a writer on Morals renders it desirable to reserve our discussion of it for a separate chapter.

[1] In the following chapter I have not entered into any particular consideration of the case in which the individual's conscience is definitely in conflict with
the general moral consciousness of his age and country : because, though it is
commonly held to be a man's duty always to obey the dictates of his own conscience, even at the risk of error, it can hardly be said to be a current opinion
that he will always attain the greatest happiness open to him by conforming
to the dictates of his conscience even when it conflicts with received morality.

CHAPTER V

HAPPINESS AND DUTY

§ 1. THE belief in the connexion of Happiness with Duty is one to which we find a general tendency among civilised men, at least after a certain stage in civilisation has been reached. But it is doubtful whether it would be affirmed, among ourselves, as a generalisation from experience, and not rather as a matter of direct Divine Revelation, or an inevitable inference from the belief that the world is governed by a perfectly Good and Omnipotent Being. To examine thoroughly the validity of the latter belief is one of the most important tasks that human reason can attempt: but involving as it does an exhaustive inquiry into the evidences of Natural and Revealed Religion, it could hardly be included within the scope of the present treatise.[1] Here, then, I shall only consider the coincidence of Duty and Happiness in so far as it is maintained by arguments drawn from experience and supposed to be realised in our present earthly life. Perhaps, so restricted, the coincidence can hardly be said to be "currently believed": indeed it may be suggested that the opposite belief is implied in the general admission of the necessity of rewards and punishments in a future state, in order to exhibit and realise completely the moral government of the world. But reflection will show that this implication is not necessary; for it is possible to hold that even here virtue is always rewarded and vice punished, so far as to make the virtuous course of action always the most prudent; while yet the rewards

---

[1] Such discussion of the question as seemed desirable in a work like this will be found in the concluding chapter of the treatise.

and punishments are not sufficient to satisfy our sense of justice. Admitting that the virtuous man is often placed on earth in circumstances so adverse that his life is not as happy as that of many less virtuous; it is still possible to maintain that by virtue he will gain the maximum of happiness that can be gained under these circumstances, all appearances to the contrary notwithstanding. And this view has certainly been held by moralists of reputation on grounds drawn from actual experience of human life ; and seems often to be confidently put forward on similar grounds by popular preachers and moralisers. It appears therefore desirable to subject this opinion to a careful and impartial examination. In conducting this examination, at the present stage of our inquiry, we shall have to use the received notions of Duty without further definition or analysis: but it is commonly assumed by those whose view we are to examine that these conceptions—as they are found in the moral consciousness of ordinary well-meaning persons—are at least approximately valid and trustworthy; and the preceding chapters will have fully shown that the generalisations of Hedonism must be established, if at all, by large considerations and decisive preponderances, and that it would be idle in considering a question of this kind to take account of slight differences, and to pretend to weigh in our mental scales comparatively small portions of happiness.[1]

§ 2. Accepting, then, the common division[2] of duties into self-regarding and social, it may be conceded that as far as the first are concerned the view that we are examining is not likely to provoke any controversy: for by ' duties towards oneself ' are commonly meant acts that tend directly or indirectly to promote one's happiness. We may therefore confine our attention to the social department of Duty, and consider whether by observing the moral rules that prescribe certain modes of behaviour towards others we shall always tend to secure the greatest balance of happiness to ourselves.

[1] For a similar reason I shall here treat the notions of ' Duty ' and ' Virtuous action ' as practically coincident ; reserving for future discussion the divergences between the two which reflection on the common usage of the terms appears to indicate. See Book iii. chap. ii.

[2] Whatever modifications of this division may afterwards appear to be necessary (cf. Book iii. chap. ii. § 1, and chap. vii. § 1) will not, I think, tend to invalidate the conclusions of the present chapter.

Here it will be convenient to adopt with some modification the terminology of Bentham; and to regard the pleasures consequent on conformity to moral rules, and the pains consequent on their violation, as the 'sanctions' of these rules. These 'sanctions' we may classify as External and Internal. The former class will include both 'Legal Sanctions,' or penalties inflicted by the authority, direct or indirect, of the sovereign; and 'Social Sanctions,' which are either the pleasures that may be expected from the approval and goodwill of our fellow-men generally, and the services that they will be prompted to render both by this goodwill and by their appreciation of the usefulness of good conduct, or the annoyance and losses that are to be feared from their distrust and dislike. The internal sanctions of duty—so far as it diverges from the conduct which self-interest apart from morality would dictate—will lie in the pleasurable emotion attending virtuous action, or in the absence of remorse, or will result more indirectly from some effect on the mental constitution of the agent produced by the maintenance of virtuous dispositions and habits. This classification is important for our present purpose, chiefly because the systems of rules to which these different sanctions are respectively attached may be mutually conflicting. The Positive Morality of any community undergoes development, and is thus subject to changes which affect the consciences of the few before they are accepted by the many; so that the rules at any time sustained by the strongest social sanctions may not only fall short of, but even clash with, the intuitions of those members of the community who have most moral insight. For similar reasons Law and Positive Morality may be at variance, in details. For though a law could not long exist, which it was universally thought wrong to obey; there may easily be laws commanding conduct that is considered immoral by some more or less enlightened fraction of the community, especially by some sect or party that has a public opinion of its own: and any individual may be so much more closely connected with this fraction than with the rest of the community, that the social sanction may in his case practically operate against the legal.

This conflict of sanctions is of great importance in considering whether these sanctions, as at present capable of being foreseen, are sufficient in all cases to determine a rational egoist to the performance of social duty : for the more stress we lay on either the legal or the social sanctions of moral conduct, the greater difficulty we shall have in proving the coincidence of duty and self-interest in the exceptional cases in which we find these sanctions arrayed against what we conceive to be duty.

But even if we put these cases out of sight, it still seems clear that the external sanctions of morality alone are not always sufficient to render immoral conduct also imprudent. We must indeed admit that in an even tolerably well-ordered society—*i.e.* in an ordinary civilised community in its normal condition—all serious open violation of law is contrary to prudence, unless it is an incident in a successful process of violent revolution : and further, that violent revolutions would very rarely—perhaps never—be made by a combination of persons, all perfectly under the control of enlightened self-love; on account of the general and widespread destruction of security and of other means of happiness which such disturbances inevitably involve. Still, so long as actual human beings are not all rational egoists, such times of disorder will be liable to occur : and we cannot say that *under existing circumstances* it is a clear universal precept of Rational Self-love that a man should "seek peace and ensue it"; since the disturbance of political order may offer to a cool and skilful person, who has the art of fishing in troubled waters, opportunities of gaining wealth, fame, and power, far beyond what he could hope for in peaceful times. In short, though we may admit that a society composed entirely of rational egoists would, when once organised, tend to remain in a stable and orderly condition, it does not follow that any individual rational egoist will always be on the side of order in any existing community.[1]

But at any rate, in the most orderly societies with which we are acquainted, the administration of law and justice is never in so perfect a state as to render *secret* crimes always

---

[1] I do not here consider the case of revolutionists aiming sincerely at the general wellbeing ; since the morality of such revolutions will generally be so dubious, that these cases cannot furnish any clear argument on either side of the question here discussed.

acts of folly, on the score of the legal penalties attached to them.   For however much these may outweigh the advantages of crime, cases must inevitably occur in which the risk of discovery is so small, that on a sober calculation the almost certain gain will more than compensate for the slight chance of the penalty.   And finally, in no community is the law actually in so perfect a state that there are not certain kinds of flagrantly anti-social conduct which slip through its meshes and escape legal penalties altogether, or incur only such legal penalties as are outweighed by the profit of law-breaking.

§ 3.   Let us proceed, then, to consider how far the social sanction in such cases supplies the defects of the legal.   No doubt the hope of praise and liking and services from one's fellow-men, and the fear of forfeiting these and incurring instead aversion, refusal of aid, and social exclusion, are considerations often important enough to determine the rational egoist to law-observance, even in default of adequate legal penalties. Still these sanctions are liable to fail just where the legal penalties are defective; social no less than legal penalties are evaded by secret crimes; and in cases of criminal revolutionary violence, the efficacy of the social sanction is apt to be seriously impaired by the party spirit enlisted on the side of the criminal. For it has to be observed that the force of the social sanction diminishes very rapidly, in proportion to the number of dissidents from the common opinion that awards it.   Disapprobation that is at once intense and quite universal would be so severe a penalty as perhaps to outweigh any imaginable advantages; since it seems impossible for a human being to live happily, whatever other goods he may enjoy, without the kindly regards of some of his fellows : and so, in contemplating the conventional portrait of the tyrant, who is represented as necessarily suspicious of those nearest him, even of the members of his own family, we feel prepared to admit that such a life must involve the extreme of unhappiness.   But when we turn to contemplate the actual tyrannical usurpers, wicked statesmen, successful leaders of unwarranted rebellion, and, speaking generally, the great criminals whose position raises them out of the reach of legal penalties, it does not appear that the moral odium under which they lie must necessarily count for much in an egoistic calculation of the gain and loss resulting from their conduct.   For this disesteem is only expressed by a portion of the community: and its utterance is often drowned in the loud-voiced applause of the multitude whose admiration is largely independent of moral considerations. Nor are there wanting philosophers and historians whose judgment manifests a similar independence.

It seems, then, impossible to affirm that the external sanctions of men's legal duties will always be sufficient to identify duty with interest. And a corresponding assertion would be still more unwarranted in respect of moral duties not included within the sphere of Law. In saying this, I am fully sensible of the force of what may be called the Principle of Reciprocity, by which certain utilitarians have endeavoured to prove the coincidence of any individual's interest with his social duties. Virtues (they say) are qualities either useful or directly agreeable to others: thus they either increase the market value of the virtuous man's services, and cause others to purchase them at a higher rate and to allot to him more dignified and interesting functions; or they dispose men to please him, both out of gratitude and in order to enjoy the pleasures of his society in return: and again—since man is an imitative animal—the exhibition of these qualities is naturally rewarded by a reciprocal manifestation of them on the part of others, through the mere influence of example. I do not doubt that the prospect of these advantages is an adequate motive for cultivating many virtues and avoiding much vice. Thus on such grounds a rational egoist will generally be strict and punctual in the fulfilment of all his engagements, and truthful in his assertions, in order to win the confidence of other men; and he will be zealous and industrious in his work, in order to obtain gradually more important and therefore more honourable and lucrative employment; and he will control such of his passions and appetites as are likely to interfere with his efficiency; and will not exhibit violent anger or use unnecessary harshness even towards servants and subordinates; and towards his equals and superiors in rank he will be generally polite and complaisant and good-humoured, and prompt to show them all such kindness as costs but little in proportion to the pleasure it gives. Still, reflection seems to show that the conduct recommended by this line of reasoning does not really coincide with moral duty. For, first, what one requires for social success is

that one should *appear*, rather than *be*, useful to others : and
hence this motive will not restrain one from doing secret harm
to others, or even from acting openly in a way that is really
harmful, though not perceived to be so.   And again, a man is
not useful to others by his virtue only, but sometimes rather by
his vice ; or more often by a certain admixture of unscrupulous-
ness with his good and useful qualities.   And further, morality
prescribes the performance of duties equally towards all, and
that we should abstain as far as possible from harming any
but on the principle of Reciprocity we should exhibit our useful
qualities chiefly towards the rich and powerful, and abstain
from injuring those who can retaliate ; while we may reasonably
omit our duties to the poor and feeble, if we find a material
advantage in so doing, unless they are able to excite the sympathy of persons who can harm us.   Moreover, some vices (as
for example, many kinds of sensuality and extravagant luxury)
do not inflict any immediate or obvious injury on any individual, though they tend in the long-run to impair the general
happiness : hence few persons find themselves strongly moved
to check or punish this kind of mischief.

Doubtless in the last-mentioned cases the mere disrepute
inevitably attaching to open immorality is an important consideration.   But I do not think that this will be seriously
maintained to be sufficient always to turn the scales of prudence
against vice—at least by any one who has duly analysed the
turbid and fluctuating streams of social opinion upon which the
good or ill repute of individuals mainly depends, and considered
the conflicting and divergent elements that they contain.   Many
moralists have noticed the discrepancy in modern Europe
between the Law of Honour (or the more important rules
maintained by the social sanction of polite persons) and the
morality professed in society at large.   This is, however, by
no means the only instance of a special code, divergent in
certain points from the moral rules generally accepted in the
community where it exists.   Most religious sects and parties,
and probably the majority of trades and professions, exhibit
this phenomenon in some degree.   I do not mean merely
that special rules of behaviour are imposed upon members
of each profession, corresponding to their special social
functions and relations : I mean that a peculiar moral opinion

is apt to grow up, conflicting to a certain extent with the
opinion of the general public. The most striking part of this
divergence consists generally in the approval or excusal of
practices disapproved by the current morality : as (*e.g.*) licence
among soldiers, bribery among politicians in certain ages and
countries, unveracity of various degrees among priests and
advocates, fraud in different forms among tradesmen.   In such
cases there are generally strong natural inducements to disobey
the stricter rule (in fact it would seem to be to the continual
pressure of these inducements that the relaxation of the rule
has been due): while at the same time the social sanction is
weakened to such an extent that it is sometimes hard to say
whether it outweighs a similar force on the other side.   For a
man who, under these circumstances, conforms to the stricter
rule, if he does not actually meet with contempt and aversion
from those of his calling, is at least liable to be called eccentric
and fantastic : and this is still more the case if by such conformity he foregoes advantages not only to himself but to his
relatives or friends or party.   Very often this professional or
sectarian excusal of immorality of which we are speaking is not
so clear and explicit as to amount to the establishment of a rule,
conflicting with the generally received rule: but is still sufficient
to weaken indefinitely the social sanction in favour of the latter.
And, apart from these special divergences, we may say generally
that in most civilised societies there are two different degrees
of positive morality, both maintained in some sort by common
consent; a stricter code being publicly taught and avowed, while
a laxer set of rules is privately admitted as the only code which
can be supported by social sanctions of any great force.   By
refusing to conform to the stricter code a man is often not liable
to incur exclusion from social intercourse, or any material
hindrance to professional advancement, or even serious dislike
on the part of any of the persons whose society he will most
naturally seek ; and under such circumstances the mere loss of
a certain amount of reputation is not likely to be felt as a very
grave evil, except by persons peculiarly sensitive to the pleasures
and pains of reputation.   And there would seem to be many
men whose happiness does not depend on the approbation or
disapprobation of the moralist—and of mankind in general in
so far as they support the moralist—to such an extent as to

make it prudent for them to purchase this praise by any great sacrifice of other goods.

§ 4. We must conclude, then, that if the conduct prescribed to the individual by the avowedly accepted morality of the community of which he is a member, can be shown to coincide with that to which Rational Self-love would prompt, it must be, in many cases, solely or chiefly on the score of the internal sanctions. In considering the force of these sanctions, I shall eliminate those pleasures and pains which lie in the anticipation of rewards and punishments in a future life : for as we are now supposing the calculations of Rational Egoism to be performed without taking into account any feelings that are beyond the range of experience, it will be more consistent to exclude also the pleasurable or painful anticipations of such feelings.

Let us, then, contemplate by itself the satisfaction that attends the performance of duty as such (without taking into consideration any ulterior consequences), and the pain that follows on its violation. After the discussions of the two preceding chapters I shall not of course attempt to weigh exactly these pleasures and pains against others ; but I see no empirical grounds for believing that such feelings are always sufficiently intense to turn the balance of prospective happiness in favour of morality. This will hardly be denied if the question is raised in respect of isolated acts of duty. Let us take an extreme case, which is yet quite within the limits of experience. The call of duty has often impelled a soldier or other public servant, or the adherent of a persecuted religion, to face certain and painful death, under circumstances where it might be avoided with little or no loss even of reputation. To prove such conduct always reasonable from an egoistic point of view, we have to assume that, in all cases where such a duty could exist and be recognised, the mere pain [1] that would follow on

---

[1] Under the notion of 'moral pain' (or pleasure) I intend to include, in this argument, all pain (or pleasure) that is due to sympathy with the feelings of others. It is not convenient to enter, at this stage of the discussion, into a full discussion of the relation of Sympathy to Moral Sensibility ; but I may say that it seems to me certain, on the one hand, that these two emotional susceptibilities are actually distinct in most minds, whatever they may have been originally ; and on the other hand that sympathetic and strictly moral feelings are almost inextricably blended in the ordinary moral consciousness : so that, for the purposes of the present argument it is not of fundamental importance to draw a distinction between them. I have, however, thought it desirable to undertake a

evasion of duty would be so great as to render the whole remainder of life hedonistically worthless. Surely such an assumption would be paradoxical and extravagant. Nothing that we know of the majority of persons in any society would lead us to conclude that their moral feelings taken alone form so preponderant an element of their happiness. And a similar conclusion seems irresistible even in more ordinary cases, where a man is called on to give up, for virtue's sake, not life, but a considerable share of the ordinary sources of human happiness. Can we say that all, or even most, men are so constituted that the satisfactions of a good conscience are certain to repay them for such sacrifices, or that the pain and loss involved in them would certainly be outweighed by the remorse that would follow the refusal to make them ? [1]

Perhaps, however, so much as this has scarcely ever been expressly maintained. What Plato in his *Republic* and other writers on the same side have rather tried to prove, is not that at any particular moment duty will be, to every one on whom it may devolve, productive of more happiness than any other course of conduct ; but rather that it is every one's interest on the whole to choose the life of the virtuous man. But even this it is very difficult even to render probable : as will appear, I think, if we examine the lines of reasoning by which it is commonly supported.

To begin with Plato's argument. He represents the soul of the virtuous man as a well-ordered polity of impulses, in which every passion and appetite is duly obedient to the rightful sovereignty of reason, and operates only within the limits laid down by the latter. He then contrasts the tranquil peace

---

further examination of sympathy—as the internal sanction on which Utilitarians specially lay stress—in the concluding chapter of this treatise : to which, accordingly, the reader may refer.

[1] A striking confirmation of this is furnished by those Christian writers of the last century who treat the *moral* unbeliever as a fool who sacrifices his happiness both here and hereafter. These men were, for the most part, earnestly engaged in the practice of virtue, and yet this practice had not made them love virtue so much as to prefer it, even under ordinary circumstances, to the sensual and other enjoyments that it excludes. It seems then absurd to suppose that, in the case of persons who have not developed and strengthened by habit their virtuous impulses, the pain that might afterwards result from resisting the call of duty would always be sufficient to neutralise all other sources of pleasure.

of such a mind with the disorder of one where a succession of
baser impulses, or some ruling passion, lords it over reason : and
asks which is the happiest, even apart from external rewards
and punishments. But we may grant all that Plato claims,
and yet be no further advanced towards the solution of the
question before us. For here the issue does not lie between
Reason and Passion, but rather—in Butler's language—between
Rational Self-love and Conscience. We are supposing the
Egoist to have all his impulses under control, and are only
asking how this control is to be exercised. Now we have seen
that the regulation and organisation of life best calculated to
attain the end of self-interest appears *prima facie* divergent at
certain points from that to which men in general are prompted
by a sense of duty. In order to maintain Plato's position it has
to be shown that this appearance is false ; and that a system
of self-government, which under certain circumstances leads us
to pain, loss, and death, is still that which self-interest requires.
It can scarcely be said that our nature is such that only this
anti-egoistic kind of regulation is possible ; that the choice lies
between this and none at all. It is easy to imagine a rational
egoist, strictly controlling each of his passions and impulses—
including his social sentiments—within such limits that its
indulgence should not involve the sacrifice of some greater
gratification : and experience seems to show us many examples
of persons who at least approximate as closely to this type as
any one else does to the ideal of the orthodox moralist. Hence
if the regulation of Conscience be demonstrably the best means
to the individual's happiness, it must be because the order kept
by Self-love involves a sacrifice of pleasure on the whole, as
compared with the order kept by Conscience. And if this is
the case, it would seem that it can only be on account of the
special emotional pleasure attending the satisfaction of the
moral sentiments, or special pain or loss of happiness consequent on their repression and violation.

Before, however, we proceed further, a fundamental difficulty
must be removed which has probably some time since suggested
itself to the reader. If a man thinks it reasonable to seek his
own interest, it is clear that he cannot himself disapprove of
any conduct that comes under this principle or approve of the
opposite. And hence it may appear that the pleasures and

pains of conscience cannot enter into the calculation whether
a certain course of conduct is ˷or is not in accordance with
Rational Egoism, because they cannot attach themselves in the
egoist's mind to any modes of action which have not been
already decided, on other grounds, to be reasonable or the reverse.
And this is to a certain extent true; but we must here recur
to the distinction (indicated in Book i. chap. iii. § 1) between
the general impulse to do what we believe to be reasonable,
and special sentiments of liking or aversion for special kinds of
conduct, independent of their reasonableness. In the moral
sentiments as they exist in ordinary men, these two kinds of
feeling are indistinguishably blended; because it is commonly
believed that the rules of conduct to which the common moral
sentiments are attached are in some way or other reasonable.
We can, however, conceive the two separated: and in fact, as was
before said, we have experience of such separation whenever a
man is led by a process of thought to adopt a different view of
morality from that in which he has been trained; for in such a
case there will always remain in his mind some quasi-moral
likings and aversions, no longer sustained by his deliberate
judgment of right and wrong. And thus there is every reason
to believe that most men, however firmly they might adopt the
principles of Egoistic Hedonism, would still feel sentiments
prompting to the performance of social duty, as commonly
recognised in their society, independently of any conclusion that
the actions prompted by such sentiments were reasonable and
right. For such sentiments would always be powerfully supported by the sympathy of others, and their expressions of
praise and blame, liking and aversion: and since it is agreed
that the conduct commonly recognised as virtuous is *generally*
coincident with that which enlightened self-love would dictate,
a rational egoist's habits of conduct will be such as naturally to
foster these (for him) 'quasi-moral' feelings. The question
therefore arises—not whether the egoist should cherish and
indulge these sentiments up to a certain point, which all would
admit—but whether he can consistently encourage them to
grow to such a pitch that they will always prevail over the
strongest opposing considerations; or, to put it otherwise,
whether prudence requires him to give them the rein and let
them carry him whither they will. We have already seen

ground for believing that Rational Self-love will best attain its end by limiting its conscious operation and allowing free play to disinterested impulses : can we accept the further paradox that it is reasonable for it to abdicate altogether its supremacy over some of these impulses ?

On a careful consideration of the matter, it will appear, I think, that this abdication of self-love is not really a possible occurrence in the mind of a sane person, who still regards his own interest as the reasonable ultimate end of his actions. Such a man may, no doubt, resolve that he will devote himself unreservedly to the practice of virtue, without any particular consideration of what appears to him to be his interest : he may perform a series of acts in accordance with this resolution, and these may gradually form in him strong habitual tendencies to acts of a similar kind. But it does not seem that these habits of virtue can ever become so strong as to gain irresistible control over a sane and reasonable will. When the occasion comes on which virtue demands from such a man an extreme sacrifice —the imprudence of which must force itself upon his notice, however little he may be in the habit of weighing his own pleasures and pains—he must always be able to deliberate afresh, and to act (as far as the control of his will extends) without reference to his past actions. It may, however, be said that, though an egoist retaining his belief in rational egoism cannot thus abandon his will to the sway of moral enthusiasm, still, supposing it possible for him to change his conviction and prefer duty to interest,—or supposing we compare him with another man who makes this choice,—we shall find that a gain in happiness on the whole results from this preference. It may be held that the pleasurable emotions attendant upon such virtuous or quasi-virtuous habits as are compatible with adhesion to egoistic principles are so inferior to the raptures that attend the unreserved and passionate surrender of the soul to virtue, that it is really a man's interest—even with a view to the present life only—to obtain, if he can, the convictions that render this surrender possible ; although under certain circumstances it must necessarily lead him to act in a manner which, considered by itself, would be undoubtedly imprudent. This is certainly a tenable proposition, and I am quite disposed to think it true of persons with specially refined moral sensibilities. But—though from the imperfections of the hedonistic calculus the proposition cannot in any case be conclusively disproved—it seems, as I have said, to be opposed to the broad results of experience, so far as the great majority of mankind are concerned. Observation would lead me to suppose that most men are so constituted as to feel far more keenly pleasures (and pains) arising from some other source than the conscience; either from the gratifications of sense, or from the possession of power and fame, or from strong human affections, or from the pursuit of science, art, etc.; so that in many cases perhaps not even early training could have succeeded in giving to the moral feelings the requisite predominance: and certainly where this training has been wanting, it seems highly improbable that a mere change of ethical conviction could develop their moral susceptibilities so far as to make it clearly their earthly interest to resolve on facing all sacrifices for the fulfilment of duty.

To sum up: although the performance of duties towards others and the exercise of social virtue seem to be *generally* the best means to the attainment of the individual's happiness, and it is easy to exhibit this coincidence between Virtue and Happiness rhetorically and popularly; still, when we carefully analyse and estimate the consequences of Virtue to the virtuous agent, it appears improbable that this coincidence is complete and universal. We may conceive the coincidence becoming perfect in a Utopia where men were as much in accord on moral as they are now on mathematical questions, where Law was in perfect harmony with Moral Opinion, and all offences were discovered and duly punished: or we may conceive the same result attained by intensifying the moral sentiments of all members of the community, without any external changes (which indeed would then be unnecessary). But just in proportion as existing societies and existing men fall short of this ideal, rules of conduct based on the principles of Egoistic Hedonism seem liable to diverge from those which most men are accustomed to recognise as prescribed by Duty and Virtue.

CHAPTER VI

DEDUCTIVE HEDONISM

§ 1. In the preceding chapter we have seen reason to conclude that, while obedience to recognised rules of duty tends, under ordinary circumstances, to promote the happiness of the agent, there are yet no adequate empirical grounds for regarding the performance of duty as a universal or infallible means to the attainment of this end. Even, however, if it were otherwise, even if it were demonstrably reasonable for the egoist to choose duty at all costs under all circumstances, the systematic endeavour to realise this principle would not—according to common notions of morality—solve or supersede the problem of determining the right method for seeking happiness. For the received moral code allows within limits the pursuit of our own happiness, and even seems to regard it as morally prescribed;[1] and still more emphatically inculcates the promotion of the happiness of other individuals, with whom we are in various ways specially connected: so that, under either head, the questions that we have before considered as to the determination and measurement of the elements of happiness would still require some kind of answer.

It remains to ask how far a scientific investigation of the causes of pleasure and pain can assist us in dealing with this practical problem.

Now it is obvious that for deciding which of two courses of action is preferable on hedonistic grounds, we require not

---

[1] "It should seem that a due concern about our own interest or happiness, and a reasonable endeavour to secure and promote it, . . . is virtue, and the contrary behaviour faulty and blamable." Butler (in the Dissertation *Of the Nature of Virtue* appended to the *Analogy*).

only to measure pains and pleasures of different kinds, but also to ascertain how they may be produced or averted. In most important prudential decisions, complex chains of consequences are foreseen as intervening between the volition we are immediately to initiate and the feelings which constitute the ultimate end of our efforts; and the degree of accuracy with which we forecast each link of these chains obviously depends upon our knowledge, implicit or explicit, of the relations of cause and effect among various natural phenomena. But if we suppose the different elements and immediate sources of happiness to have been duly ascertained and valued, the investigation of the conditions of production of each hardly belongs to a general treatise on the method of ethics; but rather to some one or other of the special arts subordinate to the general art of conduct. Of these subordinate arts some have a more or less scientific basis, while others are in a merely empirical stage; thus if we have decided how far health is to be sought, it belongs to the systematic art of hygiene, based on physiological science, to furnish a detailed plan of seeking it; so far, on the other hand, as we aim at power or wealth or domestic happiness, such instruction as the experience of others can give will be chiefly obtained in an unsystematic form, either from advice relative to our own special circumstances, or from accounts of success and failure in analogous situations. In either case the exposition of such special arts does not appear to come within the scope of the present treatise; nor could it help us in dealing with the difficulties of measuring pleasures and pains which we have considered in the previous chapters.

It may, however, be thought that a knowledge of the causes of pleasure and pain may carry us beyond the determination of the means of gaining particular kinds of pleasure and avoiding particular kinds of pain; and enable us to substitute some deductive method of evaluing the elements of happiness for the empirical-reflective method of which we have seen the defects.[1]

---

[1] This view is suggested by Mr. Herbert Spencer's statement—in a letter to J.S. Mill, published in Mr. Bain's *Mental and Moral Science*; and partially reprinted in Mr. Spencer's *Data of Ethics*, chap. iv. § 21—that "it is the business of moral science to deduce, from the laws of life and the conditions of existence, what

A hedonistic method, indeed, that would dispense altogether with direct estimates of the pleasurable and painful consequences of actions is almost as inconceivable as a method of astronomy that would dispense with observations of the stars. It is, however, conceivable that by induction from cases in which empirical measurement is easy we may obtain generalisations that will give us more trustworthy guidance than such measurement can do in complicated cases; we may be able to ascertain some general psychical or physical concomitant or antecedent of pleasure and pain, more easy to recognise, foresee, measure, and produce or avert in such cases, than pleasure and pain themselves. I am willing to hope that this refuge from the difficulties of Empirical Hedonism may some time or other be open to us: but I cannot perceive that it is at present available. There is at present, so far as I can judge, no satisfactorily established general theory of the causes of pleasure and pain; and such theories as have gained a certain degree of acceptance, as partially true or probable, are manifestly not adapted for the practical application that we here require.

The chief difficulty of finding a universally applicable theory of the causes of pleasures and pains is easily explained. Pleasures and pains may be assumed to have universally—like other psychical facts—certain cerebral nerve-processes, specific-

---

kinds of actions necessarily tend to produce happiness, and what kinds to produce unhappiness," and that when it has done this, "its deductions are to be recognised as laws of conduct; and are to be conformed to irrespective of a direct estimate of happiness or misery." I ought, however, to say that Mr. Spencer has made it clear in his latest treatise that the only cogent deductions of this kind which he conceives to be possible relate to the behaviour not of men here and now, but of ideal men living in an ideal society, and living under conditions so unlike those of actual humanity that all their actions produce "pleasure unalloyed with pain anywhere" (*Data of Ethics*, § 101). The laws of conduct in this Utopia constitute, in Mr. Spencer's view, the subject-matter of "Absolute Ethics"; which he distinguishes from the "Relative Ethics" that concerns itself with the conduct of the imperfect men who live under the present imperfect social conditions, and of which the method is, as he admits, to a great extent "necessarily empirical" (*Data of Ethics*, § 108). How far such a system as Mr. Spencer calls Absolute Ethics can be rationally constructed, and how far its construction would be practically useful, I shall consider in a later part of this treatise (Book iv. chap. iv.), when I come to deal with the method of Universalistic Hedonism: at present I am only concerned with the question how far any deductive Ethics is capable of furnishing practical guidance to an individual seeking his own greatest happiness here and now.

ally unknown, as their inseparable concomitants: accordingly, we may seek their causes either in antecedent physical or antecedent psychical facts. But in one important class of cases the chief cognisable antecedents are obviously of the former kind, while in another important class they are obviously of the latter kind: the difficulty is to establish any theory equally applicable to both classes, or to bring the results of the two lines of inquiry under a single generalisation without palpably unsupported hypotheses. In the case of pleasures and pains — especially pains — connected with sensation the most important cognisable antecedents are clearly physical. I do not deny that, when the pain is foreseen, the attitude of mind in which it is met may materially influence its magnitude: indeed, in the hypnotic condition of the brain, the feeling of pain may be apparently altogether prevented by an antecedent belief that it will not be felt. Still in the main, under ordinary conditions, the pains of sensation—probably the intensest in the experience of most persons—invade and interrupt our psychical life from without; and it would be idle to look for the chief causes of their intensity or quality among antecedent psychical facts. This is not equally true of the most prominent pleasures of sense: since antecedent desire, if not an absolutely indispensable condition of such pleasures, seems at any rate necessary to their attaining a high degree of intensity. Still the chief causes of these desires themselves are clearly physical states and processes—not merely neural—in the organism of the sentient individual: and this is also true of a more indefinite kind of pleasure, which is an important element of ordinary human happiness,—the "well-feeling" that accompanies and is a sign of physical well-being.

On the other hand, when we investigate the causes of the pleasures and pains that belong to intellectual exercises or the play of personal affections,—or of the pleasures (and to some extent pains) that belong to the contemplation of beauty (or its opposite) in art or nature,—no physiological theory can carry us far, owing to our ignorance of the neural processes that accompany or antecede these feelings.

This is my general conclusion: the grounds for which I propose to illustrate and explain further in the present

chapter. It would, however, seem to be quite beyond my
limits to attempt anything like an exhaustive discussion of
either psychological or physiological theories of the causes of
pleasure and pain. I shall confine myself to certain leading
generalisations, which seem to have a special interest for
students of ethics; either because ethical motives have had
a share in causing their acceptance; or because—though
inadequately grounded as general theories—they appear to
have a partial and limited value for practical guidance.

§ 2. Let us begin by considering a theory, primarily
psychological, which has at least the merit of antiquity—as it
is admittedly derived from Aristotle,[1]—and is, in some form
or other, still current.[2] It is that expressed by Sir W.
Hamilton[3] in the following propositions: " Pleasure is the
" reflex of the spontaneous and unimpeded exertion of a power
" of whose energy we are conscious: pain, a reflex of the over-
" strained or repressed exertion of such a power." The phrases
suggest *active* as ordinarily distinguished from *passive* states;
but Hamilton explains that "energy" and similar terms
" are to be understood to denote indifferently all the processes
" of our higher and lower life of which we are conscious,"—on
the ground that consciousness itself implies more than a mere
passivity of the subject. I think, however, that the theory is
evidently framed primarily to suit the pleasures and pains that
belong to the intellectual life as such, and is only applied by a
somewhat violent straining to an important class among the
pleasures and pains that belong to man's animal life. For
Hamilton explains his terms (*a*) "spontaneous" and (*b*)
"unimpeded" to imply respectively (*a*) absence of "forcible
repression" or "forcible stimulation" of the power exercised,
and (*b*) absence of checks or hindrances on the part of the

---

[1] Aristotle's theory is, briefly, that every normal sense-perception or rational
activity has its correspondent pleasure, and that the most perfect is the most
pleasant : the most perfect in the case of any faculty being the exercise of the
faculty in good condition on the best object. The pleasure follows the activity
immediately, giving it a kind of finish, "like the bloom of youth." Pleasures
vary in kind, as the activities that constitute life vary : the best pleasures are
those of the philosophic life.

[2] See Bouillier, *Du plaisir et de la douleur*, chap. iii. ; L. Dumont, *Théorie
scientifique de la sensibilité*, chap. iii. ; as well as Stout, *Analytic Psychology*,
chap. xii.—to which I refer later.

[3] *Lectures on Metaphysics*, vol. ii. Lect. xlii.

object about which it is conversant. But these terms seem to
have no clear psychical import in application to organic
sensations of the kind ordinarily called passive. *E.g.* the
feelings and vague representations of bodily processes which
constitute the consciousness of a toothache are as free from
conscious repression or stimulation as those which constitute
the consciousness that accompanies a warm bath :—except so
far as the mere presence of pain implies constraint, since we
experience it unwillingly, and the mere presence of pleasure
implies the opposite : but in this sense constraint and its
opposite are characteristics of the effects to be explained, and
cannot therefore be regarded as their causes.

Indeed, the ethical interest and value of the theory appears
to me to lie in its very one-sidedness. It tends to correct a
vulgar error in the estimate of pleasure, by directing attention
strongly to the importance of a class of pleasures which
ordinary pleasure-seeking probably undervalues,—the pleasures
that specially belong to a life filled with strenuous activity,
whether purely intellectual, or practical and partly physical.[1]
In the same way it effectively dispels the popular inadvertence of regarding labour as normally painful because some
labour is so, and because the pleasures connected with relief
from toil—the pleasures of repose and play—are in the
experience of most persons more striking than the pleasures of
strenuous activity. At the same time, even if we limit the
theory to the pleasures and pains immediately connected
with voluntary activity—intellectual or physical—it seems to
me devoid not only of definite guidance, but also of adequate
theoretical precision. For it seems to imply that the exercise
of our powers is always made less pleasant by the presence of
impediments ; but this is obviously not true either of mainly
intellectual or mainly physical activities. Some obstacles
undeniably increase pleasure by drawing out force and skill to
overcome them, as is clearly shown in the case of games and
sports : and even if we understand pain-causing impediments
to be only such hindrances as repress and diminish action, I
do not find that the theory is supported by experience, except

---

[1] In Aristotle's exposition of this theory—which with him is only a theory of
pleasure—the ethical motive of exhibiting the philosophic life as preferable to
that of the sensualist, in respect of the pleasures it affords, is quite unmistakable.

so far as the repression causes the specific discomfort of unsatisfied desire. *E.g.* I find entertainment rather than discomfort
in trying to make out objects in a dim light, or the meaning
of a speech in a strange language, provided that failure does
not interfere with the attainment of any end to which I attach
importance.   It is a fundamental defect in Hamilton's theory,
even in its more limited application, that it ignores the teleo-
logical character of normal human activity.

This defect is avoided in a modification of the theory that
a recent writer has adopted.   "The antithesis," says Mr.
Stout,[1] "between pleasure and pain is coincident with the
"antithesis between free and impeded progress towards an end.
"Unimpeded progress is pleasant in proportion to the intensity
"and complexity of mental excitement.   An activity which is
". . . thwarted and retarded . . . is painful in proportion to its
"intensity and complexity and to the degree of the hindrance."
Mr. Stout admits the difficulty of applying this principle of
explanation to the pleasures and pains of sense:[2] and—unlike Hamilton—he expressly recognises that "a struggle with
"difficulties which is not too prolonged or too intense may
"enhance the pleasure of success out of all proportion to its
"own painfulness."   But this qualification seems to render the
propositions first laid down unimportant from our present
practical point of view, whatever may be their theoretical
value.   I think, too, that the importance of antecedent desire,
as a condition of the pleasures and pains attendant on voluntary
activities, should be more expressly recognised.   When desire
is strong, hopeful effort to overcome difficulties in the way of
fruition tends to be proportionally pleasurable—apart from
actual success—while disappointment or the fear of disappointment similarly tends to be painful: but when desire
is not strong, the shock of thwarted activity and unfulfilled
expectation may be rather agreeable than otherwise.   Thus,
suppose I take a walk for pleasure, intending to reach a neigh-
bouring village, and find an unexpected flood crossing my road;
if I have no strong motive for arriving at the village, the

[1] *Analytic Psychology*, chap. xii. § 2.
[2] The physiological theory which Mr. Stout puts forward, as at once correspondent and supplementary to his psychological generalisation, will be noticed
later.

surprise and consequent change in the plan of my walk will probably be on the whole a pleasurable incident.

The importance of eager desire as a condition of pleasure is noteworthy from an ethical point of view: as it gives the psychological basis for the familiar precept to repress—with a view to private happiness—desires for ends that are either unattainable or incompatible with the course of life which prudence marks out; and for the somewhat less trite maxim of encouraging and developing desires that prompt in the same direction as rational choice.

Suppose now we drop the dubious term "unimpeded"—retaining Hamilton's idea of "overstrained or repressed exertion" as the condition of pain—and at the same time passing to a physical point of view, mean by "activity" the activity of an *organ*. We thus reach what is substantially Mr. Spencer's doctrine, that pains are the psychical concomitants of excessive or deficient actions of organs, while pleasures are the concomitants of medium activities.[1] In considering this theory it will be convenient to take pains and pleasures separately: as it is obviously based primarily on experiences of pain rather than of pleasure,—especially of the pains of sense to which Hamilton's theory seemed palpably inapplicable. Instances are abundant in which pain is obviously caused by excessive stimulation of nerves. Thus when we gradually increase the intensity of sensible heat, pressure, muscular effort, we encounter pain at a certain point of the increase; "deafening" sounds are highly disagreeable; and to confront a tropical sun with unprotected eyeballs would soon become torture. Some pains, again, as Spencer points out, arise from the excessive actions of organs whose normal actions yield no feelings: as when the digestive apparatus is overtaxed. Still in none of these cases does it seem clear that pain supervenes through a mere intensification *in degree* of the action of the organ in question; and not rather through some change in the kind of action—some inchoate disintegration or disorganisation. And this latter cause—rather than mere quantity of stimulation—is strongly suggested by a consideration of the pains due to wounds and diseases, and even of the transient digestive discomforts which arise from an improper kind rather than an

[1] *Psychology*, chap. ix. § 128.

improper quantity of food. And a similar explanation seems
to me most probable in the case of pains which, according to
Mr. Spencer, arise from "deficient" action. He speaks of
these as "discomforts or cravings"; but, as I have before
pointed out,[1] bodily appetites and other desires may be strongly-
felt impulses to action without being appreciably painful : and,
in my experience, when they become decidedly painful, some
disturbance tending to derangement may be presumed either
in the organ primarily concerned or in the organism as a
whole. Thus hunger, in my experience, may be extremely
keen without being appreciably painful : and when I find it
painful, experience leads me to expect a temporarily reduced
power of assimilation, indicating some disorganisation in the
digestive apparatus.[2]

In any case, empirical evidence supports "excessive
action" of an organ as a cause of pain far more clearly than
"deficient action." Indeed a consideration of this evidence has
led some psychologists to adopt the generalisation [3] that there
is no quality of sensation absolutely pleasant or unpleasant, but
that every kind of sensation as it grows in intensity begins at
a certain point to be pleasurable, and continues such up to a
certain further point at which it passes rapidly through indifference into pain. My own experience, however, fails to
support this generalisation. I agree with Gurney [4] that "of
many tastes and odours the faintest possible suggestion is disagreeable"; while other feelings resulting from stimulation of
sense-organs appear to remain highly pleasurable at the highest
degree of stimulation which the actual conditions of physical
life appear to allow.

However this may be, whether we conceive the nervous
action of which pain is an immediate consequent or concomitant as merely excessive in quantity, or in some way dis-

---

[1] Book i. chap. iv.

[2] It may be added that in the case of emotional pains and pleasures, the
notion of *quantitative* difference between the cerebral nerve-processes, antecedent
respectively to the one and the other, seems altogether unwarrantable : the pains
of shame, disappointed ambition, wounded love, do not appear to be distinguishable from the pleasures of fame, success, reciprocated affection, by any difference
of intensity in the impressions or ideas accompanied by the pleasures and pains
respectively.

[3] See Wundt, *Grundzüge der physiologischen Psychologie*, chap. x.

[4] *Power of Sound*, chap. i. § 2.

cordant or disorganised in quality, it is obvious that neither
explanation can furnish us with any important practical
guidance: since we have no general means of ascertaining,
independently of our experience of pain itself, what nervous
actions are excessive or disorganised: and the cases where we
have such means do not present any practical problems which
the theory enables us to solve.   No one doubts that wounds
and diseases are to be avoided under all ordinary circumstances: and in the exceptional circumstances in which we
may be moved to choose them as the least of several evils,
the exactest knowledge of their precise operation in causing
pain is not likely to assist our choice.

It may be said, however,—turning from pain to pleasure,
—that the generalisation which we have been considering at
any rate gives us a psychophysical basis for the ancient
maxim of "avoiding excess" in the pursuit of pleasure.   But
we have to observe that the practical need of this maxim is
largely due to the qualifications which the psychophysical
generalisation requires to make it true.   Thus it is especially
needed in the important cases in which over-stimulation
is followed by pain not at once but after an interval of
varying length.   *E.g.* alcoholic drinking, to many, remains
pleasurable at the time up to the point of excess at which
the brain can no longer perform its functions: it is "next
morning" that the pain comes, or perhaps—in the case of
"well-seasoned" topers—not till after many years of habitual
excess.   It should be noted also that it is not always the
organ of which the exercise gives pleasure that also, through
over-exercise, causes the pain of excess.   Thus when we are
tempted to eat too much, the seductive pleasure is mainly
due to the nerves of taste which are not overtaxed; the pains
come from the organs of digestion, whose faint, vague pleasures
alone would hardly tempt the voluptuary to excess.   In the
case of dangerous mental excitements the penalty on excess
is usually still more indirect.

On the whole, granting that pleasure like virtue resides
somewhere in the mean, it must be admitted that this proposition gives no practical directions for attaining it.   For
first, granting that both excessive and deficient activities of
organs cause pain, the question still remains—as Spencer him-

self says—What determines in any case the lower and the higher limits within which action is pleasurable? Spencer's answer to this question I will consider presently. But there is a question no less obvious to which he does not expressly advert, viz. why among the normal activities of our physical organs, that have counterparts in consciousness, some only are pleasurable in any appreciable degree, while many if not most are nearly or quite indifferent. It seems undeniable (*e.g.*) that while tastes and smells are mostly either agreeable or disagreeable, most sensations of touch and many of sight and sound are not appreciably[1] either; and that, in the daily routine of healthy life, eating and drinking are ordinarily pleasant, while dressing and undressing, walking and muscular movements generally are practically indifferent.

It does not seem that an adequate explanation can be found in the operation of habit.[2] It is no doubt true that actions through frequent uniform repetition tend to become automatic and lose their conscious counterparts, and hedonic indifference certainly seems in some cases to be a stage through which such actions pass on the way to unconsciousness. Thus even a business walk in a strange town is normally pleasant through the novelty of the sights: but a similar walk in the town where one lives is ordinarily indifferent, or nearly so; while if one's attention is strongly absorbed by the business, it may be performed to a great extent unconsciously. On the other hand, the operations of habit often have the opposite effect of making activities pleasant which were at first indifferent or even disagreeable: as in the case of acquired tastes, physical or intellectual. Indeed such experiences have long been—I think, quite legitimately—used by moralists as an encouragement to irksome duties, on the ground that their irksomeness will be transient, through the operation of habit, while the gain of their performance will be permanent. Mr. Spencer, indeed, regards such experiences as so important that he ventures to base on them the prediction that " pleasure will eventually accompany

---

[1] I say "appreciably" because the controverted psychological question whether there are any *strictly* neutral or indifferent modifications of consciousness seems to me unimportant from a practical point of view. See Sully, *Human Mind,* chap. xiii. § 2.   [2] See Stout, *Analytic Psychology, l.c.*

every mode of action demanded by social conditions." This, however, seems unduly optimistic, in view not only of the first-
mentioned tendency of habit to hedonic indifference, but also of
a third tendency to render actions, at first indifferent or even
pleasant, gradually more irksome.   Thus our intellect gradually
wearies of monotonous activities, and the *ennui* may sometimes become intense : so again the relish of a kind of diet
at first agreeable may turn through monotony into disgust.

Some quite different explanation must therefore be sought
for the varying degrees in which pleasure accompanies normal
activities.   Can we find this in a suggestion of Mr. Spencer's,
developed by Mr. Grant Allen,[1] that the pleasurableness of
normal organic activities depends on their *intermittence,* and
that "the amount of pleasure is probably . . . in the inverse
ratio of the natural frequency of excitation" of the nerve-
fibres involved ?   This theory certainly finds some support
in the fact that the sensual pleasures generally recognised
as greatest are those attending the activities of organs which
are normally left unexercised for considerable intervals.   Still,
there are many facts that it does not explain—*e.g.* the great
differences in the pleasures obtainable at any given time by
different stimulations of the same sense ;   the phenomenon
expressed in the proverbial phrase "L'appétit vient en
mangeant" ;   and the fact that the exercise of the visual
organs after apparently dreamless sleep does not give
appreciably keener pleasure than it does at ordinary times.
It would seem that we must seek for some special cause
of the pleasurable effect of intermittence in certain cases.
And this cannot be merely the greater intensity of the
nervous action that takes place when long-unexercised and
well-nourished nerve-centres are stimulated : for why, if that
were the explanation, should the normal consciousness of full
nervous activity, gradually attained—as when we are in full
swing of energetic unwearied work of a routine kind—be
often nearly or quite indifferent ?

Among the various competing hypotheses offered at this
point of our inquiry—no one of which, I believe, has attained
anything like general acceptance as covering the whole ground
—I select for discussion one that has special ethical interest.

[1] *Physiological Æsthetics,* chap. ii.

According to this hypothesis,[1] the organic process accompanied by pleasure is to be conceived as a "restoration of equilibrium" after "disturbance": so that the absence of appreciable pleasure in the case of certain normal activities is explained by the absence of antecedent disturbance. This view is obviously applicable to certain classes of pleasures which, though by no means rare are incidental in a normal life :—the pleasure of relief after physical pain, or after the strain of great anxiety, and the pleasure of repose after unusual exertions, intellectual or muscular. But when we attempt to apply it to sensational pleasures generally, the indefiniteness of the notion of "equilibrium," as applied to the processes of a living organism, becomes manifest. For our physical life consists of a series of changes, for the most part periodically recurrent with slight modification after short intervals : and it is difficult to see why we should attach the idea of "disturbance" or "restoration of equilibrium" to any one among these normal processes rather than any other :— e.g. it is difficult to see why the condition of having expended energy should be regarded as a departure from equilibrium any more than the condition of having just taken in nutriment. In fact, to render the hypothesis we are considering at all applicable to normal pleasures of sense, we have to pass from the physiological to the psychological point of view, and take note of the psychical state of *desire*, as a consciously *unrestful* condition, of which the essence is a felt impulse to pass out of this state towards the attainment of the desired object. Our hypothesis, then, may take this unrestful consciousness as a sign of what, from a physiological point of view, is "disturbance of equilibrium," and similarly, the satisfaction of desire may be taken to be, physiologically, a restoration of equilibrium. On this assumption, the theory becomes undeniably applicable to those gratifications of sensual appetite which form the most prominent element of the pleasures of sense, as popularly conceived.

Now we have already noted that by a wide-spread confusion of thought, desire has often been regarded as a species of pain. Accordingly, the theory that we are considering was originally prompted by the ethical motive of depreciating the

---

[1] See Stout, *Analytic Psychology*, chap. xii. § 4.

vulgarly overvalued pleasures of satisfied bodily appetite, by laying stress on their inseparable connexion with antecedent pain. The depreciation, however, fails so far as the appetite which is a necessary antecedent condition of the pleasure is—though an unrestful state—not appreciably painful.[1]

In any case, admitting the physical counterpart of conscious desire to be a 'disturbance of equilibrium,' or an effect and sign of such disturbance, the theory seems open to obvious objections, if it is extended to cover the whole range of the pleasures of sense. For conscious desire is certainly not a necessary condition of experiencing the simple pleasures of the special senses: normally no sense of want has preceded the experience of pleasant sights, sounds, odours, flavours, or of the more important pleasures, more complex in their psychical conditions, which we call æsthetic. No doubt in special cases antecedent privation may produce a conscious want of these latter pleasures which may increase their intensity when they are at length attained : or even without any felt privation, the prospect of enjoying such pleasures may produce a keen desire for the enjoyment, which may be regarded as a " disturbance of equilibrium " no less plausibly than a bodily appetite. But it would be quite unwarrantable therefore to suppose a similar disturbance, though unfelt, in the ordinary cases where pleasures of this kind are experienced without any antecedent consciousness of desire or want.

I have perhaps said enough to support my general conclusion that psychophysical speculation as to the causes of pleasure and pain does not at present afford a basis for a deductive method of practical Hedonism. But, before passing from this topic, I may remark that the difficulties in the way of any such theory seem especially great in the case of the complex pleasures which we distinguish as " æsthetic." All would agree that æsthetic gratification, when at all high, depends on a subtle harmony of different elements in a complex state of consciousness ; and that the pleasure resulting from such harmonious combination is indefinitely greater than the sum of the simpler pleasures which the uncombined elements would yield. But even those who estimate most

---

[1] See Book i. chap. iv. *Note.*

highly the success that has so far been attained in discovering the conditions of this harmony, in the case of any particular art, would admit that mere conformity to the conditions thus ascertained cannot secure the production of æsthetic pleasure in any considerable degree.   However subtly we state in general terms the objective relations of elements in a delightful work of art, on which its delight seems to depend, we must always feel that it would be possible to produce out of similar elements a work corresponding to our general description which would give no delight at all; the touch that gives delight depends upon an instinct for which no deductive reasoning can supply a substitute.   This is true, even without taking into account the wide divergences that we actually find in the æsthetic sensibilities of individuals: still less, therefore, is it needful to argue that, from the point of view of an individual seeking his own greatest happiness, none but a mainly inductive and empirical method of estimating æsthetic pleasures can be made available.

§ 3. I now pass to consider a theory which may be distinguished from those discussed in the preceding section as being biological rather than psychophysical : since it directs attention not to the actual present characteristics of the organic states or changes of which pleasures and pains are the concomitants or immediate consequents, but to their relations to the life of the organism as a whole.   I mean the theory that " pains are the correlatives of actions injurious to the organism, while pleasures are the correlatives of acts conducive to its welfare."   Mr. Spencer, from whom the above propositions are quoted,[1] subsequently explains " injurious " and " conducive to welfare " to mean respectively " tending to decrease or loss of life," and " tending to continuance or increase of life ": but in his deduction by which the above conclusion is summarily established, " injurious " and " beneficial " are used as equivalent simply to " destructive " and "preservative" of organic life: and it will be more convenient to take the terms first in this simpler signification.

Mr. Spencer's argument is as follows :—

" If we substitute for the word Pleasure the equivalent phrase—a feeling which we seek to bring into consciousness and retain there ; and if

[1] *Principles of Psychology*, § 125, and *Data of Ethics*, § 33.

we substitute for the word Pain the equivalent phrase—a feeling which we seek to get out of consciousness and to keep out ; we see at once that, if the states of consciousness which a creature endeavours to maintain are the correlatives of injurious actions, and if the states of consciousness which it endeavours to expel are the correlatives of beneficial actions, it must quickly disappear through persistence in the injurious and avoidance of the beneficial.   In other words, those races of beings only can have survived in which, on the average, agreeable or desired feelings went along with activities conducive to the maintenance of life, while disagreeable and habitually-avoided feelings went along with activities directly or indirectly destructive of life ; and there must ever have been, other things equal, the most numerous and long-continued survivals among races in which these adjustments of feelings to actions were the best, tending ever to bring about perfect adjustment."

Now I am not concerned to deny the value of this summary deduction for certain purposes.   But it can easily be shown to be inadequate to afford a basis for a deductive method of seeking maximum happiness for the individual, by substituting Preservation for Pleasure as the end directly aimed at.   In the first place, Mr. Spencer only affirms the conclusion to be true, as he rather vaguely says, " on the average " : and it is obvious that though the tendency to find injurious acts pleasant or preservative acts painful must be a disadvantage to any species of animal in the struggle for existence, it may—if existing only to a limited extent—be outweighed by other advantages, so that the organism in which it exists may survive in spite of it. This, I say, is obvious *a priori* : and common experience, as Mr. Spencer admits, shows " in many conspicuous ways " that this has been actually the case with civilised man during the whole period of history that we know : owing to the changes caused by the course of civilisation, " there has arisen and must long continue a deep and involved derangement of the natural connexions between pleasures and beneficial actions and between pains and detrimental actions."   This seems to be in itself a sufficient objection to founding a deductive method of Hedonism on Mr. Spencer's general conclusion.   It is, indeed, notorious that civilised men take pleasure in various forms of unhealthy conduct and find conformity to the rules of health irksome ; and it is also important to note that they may be, and actually are, susceptible of keen pleasure from acts and processes that have no material tendency to preserve life.   Nor is there any difficulty in explaining this on the "evolution hypothesis"; since we cannot argue *a priori* from this hypothesis that the development of the nervous system in human beings may not bring with it intense susceptibilities to pleasure from non-preservative processes, if only the preservation of the individuals in whom such susceptibilities are developed is otherwise adequately provided for.   Now this latter supposition is obviously realised in the case of persons of leisure in civilised society; whose needs of food, clothing, shelter, etc., are abundantly supplied through the complex social habit which we call the institution of private property: and I know no empirical ground for supposing that a cultivated man tends, in consequence of the keen and varied pleasure which he seeks and enjoys, to live longer than a man who goes through a comparatively dull round of monotonous routine activity, interspersed by slightly pleasurable intervals of repose and play.

§ 4. If, however, the individual is not likely to obtain a maximum of Pleasure by aiming merely at Preservation, it remains to consider whether "quantity of life" will serve any better.   Now it is of course true that so far as nervous action is attended by consciousness pleasurable in quality, the more there is of it, the happier we shall be.   But even if we assume that the more intense and full life is "on the average" the happier, it by no means follows that we shall gain *maximum* pleasure by aiming merely at intensity of consciousness: for we experience intense pains even more indubitably than intense pleasures, and in those "full tides of soul," in which we seem to be most alive, painful consciousness may be mixed in almost any proportion.   And further we often experience excitement nearly or quite neutral in quality (*i.e.* not distinctly pleasurable or painful), which reaches a great pitch of intensity, as in the case of laborious struggles with difficulties, and perplexing conflicts of which the issue is doubtful.

It may, however, be replied that "quantity of life" must be taken to imply not merely intensity of consciousness, but multiplicity and variety — a harmonious and many-sided development of human nature.   And experience certainly seems to support the view that men lose happiness by allowing some of their faculties or capacities to be withered and dwarfed for want of exercise, and thus not leaving themselves sufficient

variety of feelings or activities : especially as regards the bodily
organs, it will be agreed that the due exercise of most, if not
all, is indispensable to the health of the organism ; and further,
that the health maintained by this balance of functions is a
more important source of the individual's happiness than the
unhealthy over-exercise of any one organ can be. Still, it
would appear that the harmony of functions necessary to
health is a very elastic one, and admits of a very wide margin
of variation, as far as the organs under voluntary control are
concerned. A man (*e.g.*) who exercises his brain alone will
probably be ill in consequence : but he may exercise his brain
much and his legs little, or *vice versa*, without any morbid
results. And, in the same way, we cannot lay down the
proposition, that a varied and many-sided life is the happiest,
with as much precision as would be necessary if it were to
be accepted as a basis for deductive Hedonism. For it seems
to be also largely true, on the other side, that the more we
come to exercise any faculty with sustained and prolonged
concentration, the more pleasure we derive from such exercise,
up to the point at which it becomes wearisome, or turns into
a semi-mechanical routine which renders consciousness dull
and languid. It is, no doubt, important for our happiness
that we should keep within this limit : but we cannot fix it
precisely in any particular case without special experience :
especially as there seems always to be a certain amount of
weariness and tedium which must be resisted and overcome,
if we would bring our faculties into full play, and obtain the
full enjoyment of our labour. And similarly in respect of
passive emotional consciousness : if too much sameness of
feeling results in languor, too much variety inevitably involves
shallowness. The point where concentration ought to stop,
and where dissipation begins, varies from man to man, and
must, it would seem, be decided by the specific experience of
individuals.

There is, however, another and simpler way in which the
maxim of 'giving free development to one's nature' may be
understood : *i.e.* in the sense of yielding to spontaneous
impulses, instead of endeavouring to govern these by elaborate
forecasts of consequences : a scientific justification for this
course being found in the theory that spontaneous or instinc-

tive impulses really represent the effects of previous experiences
of pleasure and pain on the organism in which they appear,
or its ancestors. On this ground, it has been maintained that
in complicated problems of conduct, experience will "enable
the constitution to estimate the respective amounts of pleasure
and pain consequent upon each alternative," where it is
"impossible for the intellect" to do this: and "will further
cause the organism instinctively to shun that course which
produces on the whole most suffering."[1] That there is an
important element of truth in this contention I would not
deny. But any broad conclusion that non-rational inclination
is a better guide than reason to the individual's happiness
would be quite unwarranted by anything that we know or
can plausibly conjecture respecting biological evolution. For—
overlooking the effect of natural selection to foster impulses
tending to the preservation of the race rather than the pleasure
of the individual, and granting that every sentient organism
tends to adapt itself to its environment, in such a manner as
to acquire instincts of some value in guiding it to pleasure and
away from pain—it by no means follows that in the human
organism one particular kind of adaptation, that which proceeds
by unconscious modification of instinct, is to be preferred to
that other kind of adaptation which is brought about by
conscious comparison and inference. It rather seems clear,
that this proposition can only be justified by a comparison of
the consequences of yielding to instinctive impulses with the
consequences of controlling them by calculations of resulting
pleasure and pain. But it will hardly be maintained that
in the majority of clear instances where non-rational impulse
conflicts with rational forecast, a subsequent calculation of
consequences appears to justify the former; the assertion
would be in too flagrant conflict with the common sense and
common experience of mankind. Hence, however true it may
be that in certain cases instinct is on the whole a safer guide
than prudential calculation, it would still seem that we can
only ascertain these cases by careful reflection on experience:
we cannot determine the limits to which prudential calculation

---

[1] The quotations are from Mr. Spencer's *Social Statics*, chap. iv. : but I should
explain that in the passage quoted Mr. Spencer is not writing from the point of
view of Egoistic Hedonism.

may prudently be carried, except by this very calculation itself.

We seem, then, forced to conclude that there is no scientific short-cut to the ascertainment of the right means to the individual's happiness: every attempt to find a 'high priori road' to this goal brings us back inevitably to the empirical method. For instead of a clear principle universally valid, we only get at best a vague and general rule, based on considerations which it is important not to overlook, but the relative value of which we can only estimate by careful observation and comparison of individual experience. Whatever uncertainty besets these processes must necessarily extend to all our reasonings about happiness. I have no wish to exaggerate these uncertainties, feeling that we must all continue to seek happiness for ourselves and for others, in whatever obscurity we may have to grope after it: but there is nothing gained by underrating them, and it is idle to argue as if they did not exist.

BOOK III

INTUITIONISM

BOOK III

CHAPTER I

INTUITIONISM

§ 1. THE effort to examine, closely but quite neutrally, the system of Egoistic Hedonism, with which we have been engaged in the last Book, may not improbably have produced on the reader's mind a certain aversion to the principle and method examined, even though (like myself) he may find it difficult not to admit the 'authority' of self-love, or the 'rationality' of seeking one's own individual happiness. In considering 'enlightened self-interest' as supplying a *prima facie* tenable principle for the systematisation of conduct, I have given no expression to this sentiment of aversion, being anxious to ascertain with scientific impartiality the results to which this principle logically leads. When, however, we seem to find on careful examination of Egoism (as worked out on a strictly empirical basis) that the common precepts of duty, which we are trained to regard as sacred, must be to the egoist rules to which it is only generally speaking and for the most part reasonable to conform, but which under special circumstances must be decisively ignored and broken,—the offence which Egoism in the abstract gives to our sympathetic and social nature adds force to the recoil from it caused by the perception of its occasional practical conflict with common notions of duty. But further, we are accustomed to expect from Morality clear and decisive precepts or counsels: and such rules as can be laid down for seeking the individual's greatest happiness cannot but appear wanting in these qualities.

199

A dubious guidance to an ignoble end appears to be all that the calculus of Egoistic Hedonism has to offer. And it is by appealing to the superior certainty with which the dictates of Conscience or the Moral Faculty are issued, that Butler maintains the practical supremacy of Conscience over Self-love, in spite of his admission (in the passage before quoted[1]) of theoretical priority in the claims of the latter.[2] A man knows certainly, he says, what he ought to do: but he does not certainly know what will lead to his happiness.

In saying this, Butler appears to me fairly to represent the common moral sense of ordinary mankind, in our own age no less than in his. The moral judgments that men habitually pass on one another in ordinary discourse imply for the most part that duty is usually not a difficult thing for an ordinary man to *know*, though various seductive impulses may make it difficult for him to *do* it. And in such maxims as that duty should be performed ' advienne que pourra,' that truth should be spoken without regard to consequences, that justice should be done ' though the sky should fall,' it is implied that we have the power of seeing clearly that certain kinds of actions are right and reasonable in themselves, apart from their consequences;—or rather with a merely partial consideration of consequences, from which other consequences admitted to be possibly good or bad are definitely excluded.[3] And such a power is claimed for the human mind by most of the writers who have maintained the existence of moral intuitions ; I have therefore thought myself justified in treating this claim as characteristic of the method which I distinguish as Intuitional.

---

[1] See p. 119.

[2] It may seem, he admits, that "since interest, one's own happiness, is a manifest obligation," in any case in which virtuous action appears to be not conducive to the agent's interest, he would be "under two contrary obligations, *i.e.* under none at all. But," he urges, "the obligation on the side of interest really does not remain. For the natural authority of the principle of reflection or conscience is an obligation . . . the most certain and known : whereas the contrary obligation can at the utmost appear no more than probable : since no man can be *certain* in any circumstances that vice is his interest in the present world, much less can he be certain against another : and thus the certain obligation would entirely supersede and destroy the uncertain one."—(Preface to Butler's *Sermons*.)

[3] I have before observed (Book i. chap. viii. § 1) that in the common notion of an act we include a certain portion of the whole series of changes partly caused by the volition which initiated the so-called act.

At the same time, as I have before observed, there is a wider sense in which the term 'intuitional' might be legitimately applied to either Egoistic or Universalistic Hedonism; so far as either system lays down as a first principle—which if known at all must be intuitively known—that happiness is the only rational ultimate end of action. To this meaning I shall recur in the concluding chapters (xiii. and xiv.) of this Book; in which I shall discuss more fully the intuitive character of these hedonistic principles. But since the adoption of this wider meaning would not lead us to a distinct ethical method, I have thought it best, in the detailed discussion of Intuitionism which occupies the first eleven chapters of this Book, to confine myself as far as possible to Moral Intuition understood in the narrower sense above defined.

§ 2. Here, perhaps, it may be said that in thus defining Intuitionism I have omitted its most fundamental characteristic; that the Intuitionist properly speaking—in contrast with the Utilitarian—does not judge actions by an external standard at all; that true morality, in his view, is not concerned with outward actions as such, but with the state of mind in which acts are done—in short with "intentions" and "motives."[1] I think, however, that this objection is partly due to a misunderstanding. Moralists of all schools, I conceive, would agree that the moral judgments which we pass on actions relate primarily to intentional actions regarded as intentional. In other words, what we judge to be 'wrong'—in the strictest ethical sense—is not any part of the actual effects, as such, of the muscular movements immediately caused by the agent's volition, but the effects which he foresaw in willing the act; or, more strictly, his volition or choice of realising the effects as foreseen.[2] When I speak therefore of acts, I must be understood to mean—unless the contrary is stated—acts

---

[1] Some would add "character" and "disposition." But since characters and disposition not only cannot be known directly but can only be definitely conceived by reference to the volitions and feelings in which they are manifested, it does not seem to me possible to regard them as the primary objects of intuitive moral judgments. See chap. ii. § 2 of this Book.

[2] No doubt we hold a man responsible for unintended bad consequences of his acts or omissions, when they are such as he might with ordinary care have foreseen ; still, as I have before said (p. 60), we admit on reflection that moral blame only attaches to such careless acts or omissions indirectly, in so far as the carelessness is the result of some previous wilful neglect of duty.

presumed to be intentional and judged as such: on this point I do not think that any dispute need arise.

The case of motives is different and requires careful discussion. In the first place the distinction between "motive" and "intention" in ordinary language is not very precise: since we apply the term "motive" to foreseen consequences of an act, so far as they are conceived to be objects of desire to the agent, or to the desire of such consequences: and when we speak of the intention of an act we usually, no doubt, have desired consequences in view. I think, however, that for purposes of exact moral or jural discussion, it is best to include under the term 'intention' all the consequences of an act that are foreseen as certain or probable; since it will be admitted that we cannot evade responsibility for any foreseen bad consequences of our acts by the plea that we felt no desire for them, either for their own sake or as means to ulterior ends:[1] such undesired accompaniments of the desired results of our volitions are clearly chosen or willed by us. Hence the intention of an act may be judged to be wrong, while the motive is recognised as good; as when a man commits perjury to save a parent's or a benefactor's life. Such judgments are, in fact, continually passed in common moral discourse. It may, however, be said that an act cannot be right, even when the intention is such as duty would prescribe, if it be done from a bad motive: that—to take a case suggested by Bentham—a man who prosecutes from malice a person whom he believes to be guilty, does not really act rightly; for, though it may be his duty to prosecute, he ought not to do it from malice. It is doubtless true that it is our duty to get rid of bad motives if we can; so that a man's intention cannot be *wholly* right, unless it includes the repression, so far as possible, of a motive known to be bad. But no one, I think, will contend that we can always suppress entirely a strong emotion; and such suppression will be especially difficult if we are to do the

---

[1] I think that common usage, when carefully considered, will be found to admit this definition. Suppose a nihilist blows up a railway train containing an emperor and other persons: it will no doubt be held correct to say simply that his intention was to kill the emperor; but it would be thought absurd to say that he 'did not intend' to kill the other persons, though he may have had no desire to kill them and may have regarded their death as a lamentable incident in the execution of his revolutionary plans.

act to which the wrong impulse prompts; while yet, if that act be clearly a duty which no one else can so properly perform, it would be absurd to say that we ought to omit it because we cannot altogether exclude an objectionable motive. It is sometimes said that, though we may not be able in doing our duty to exclude a bad motive altogether from our minds, it is still possible to refuse to act from it. But I think that this is only possible so far as the details of action to which a right motive would prompt differ to some extent from those to which a wrong motive would prompt. No doubt this is often the case :—thus, in Bentham's example, a malevolent prosecutor may be prompted to take unfair advantage of his enemy, or cause him needless pain by studied insults; and it is obviously possible for him—and his duty—to resist such promptings. But so far as precisely the same action is prompted by two different motives, both present in my consciousness, I am not conscious of any power to cause this action to be determined by one of the two motives to the exclusion of the other. In other words, while a man can resolve to aim at any end which he conceives as a possible result of his voluntary action, he cannot simultaneously resolve *not* to aim at any other end which he believes will be promoted by the same action; and if that other end be an object of desire to him, he cannot, while aiming at it, refuse to act from this desire.[1]

[1] A further source of confusion between "intention" and "motive" arises from the different points of view from which either may be judged. Thus an act may be one of a series which the agent purposes to do for the attainment of a certain end : and our moral judgment of it may be very different, according as we judge the intention of the particular act, or the general intention of the series regarded as a whole. Either point of view is legitimate, and both are often required; for we commonly recognise that, of the series of acts which a man does to attain (*e.g.*) any end of ambition, some may be right or allowable, while others are wrong; while the general intention to attain the end by wrong means, if necessary, as well as right—

> "Get place and wealth, if possible with grace ;
> If not, by any means get wealth and place "—

is clearly a wrong intention. So again, in judging a motive to be good or bad, we may either consider it simply in itself, or in connexion with other balancing and controlling motives—either actually present along with it, or absent when they ought to be present. Thus in the above case we do not commonly think the desire for wealth or rank bad in itself; but we think it bad as the sole motive of a statesman's public career. It is easy to see that one or other of these different distinctions is apt to blend with and confuse the simple distinction between intention and motive.

On the whole, then, I conclude (1) that while many actions are commonly judged to be made *better* or *worse* by the presence or absence of certain motives, our judgments of *right* and *wrong* strictly speaking relate to intentions, as distinguished from motives ;[1] and (2) that while intentions affecting the agent's own feelings and character are morally prescribed no less than intentions to produce certain external effects, still, the latter form the primary—though not the sole—content of the main prescriptions of duty, as commonly affirmed and understood : but the extent to which this is the case, will become more clear as we proceed.

It has indeed been maintained by moralists of influence that the moral value of our conduct depends upon the degree to which we are actuated by the one motive which they regard as truly moral : viz. the desire or free choice[2] of doing what is right as such, realising duty or virtue for duty or virtue's sake :[3] and that a perfectly good act must be done entirely from this motive.   I think, however, that it is difficult to combine this view—which I may conveniently distinguish as Stoical—with the belief, which modern orthodox moralists have usually been concerned to maintain, that it is always a man's true interest to act virtuously.   I do not mean that a man who holds this belief must necessarily be an egoist : but it seems to me impossible for him to exclude from his motives a regard for his own interest, while yet believing that it will be promoted by the act which he is willing.   If, therefore, we hold that this self-regard impairs the moral value of an act otherwise virtuous, and at the same time hold that virtue is always conducive to the virtuous agent's interest, we seem driven to the conclusion that knowledge of the true relation between virtue and happiness is an insuperable obstacle to the attainment of moral

---

[1] The view that moral judgments relate primarily or most properly to motives will be more fully discussed in chap. xii. of this Book.

[2] I use these alternative terms in order to avoid the Free Will Controversy.

[3] Many religious persons would probably say that the motive of obedience or love to God was the highest.   But those who take this view would generally say that obedience and love are due to God as a Moral Being, possessing the attributes of Infinite Wisdom and Goodness, and not otherwise : and if so, these religious motives would seem to be substantially identical with regard for duty and love of virtue, though modified and complicated by the addition of emotions belonging to relations between persons.

perfection.   I cannot accept this paradox : and in subsequent chapters I shall try to show that the Stoical view of moral goodness is not on the whole sustained by a comprehensive survey and comparison of common moral judgments : since in some cases acts appear to have the quality of virtue even more strikingly when performed from some motive other than the love of virtue as such.   For the present I wish rather to point out that the doctrine above stated is diametrically opposed to the view that the universal or normal motives of human action are either particular desires of pleasure or aversions to pain for the agent himself, or the more general regard to his happiness on the whole which I term Self-love ; that it also excludes the less extreme doctrine that duties may be to some extent properly done from such self-regarding motives ; and that one or other of these positions has frequently been held by writers who have expressly adopted an Intuitional method of Ethics.   For instance, we find Locke laying down, without reserve or qualification, that " good and evil are nothing but pleasure and pain, or that which occasions or procures pleasure or pain to us : " [1] so that " it would be utterly in vain to suppose a rule set to the free actions of man, without annexing it to some reward or punishment to determine his will."   On the other hand, he expresses, with no less emphasis, the conviction that " from self-evident propositions, by necessary consequences, as incontestable as those in mathematics, the measures of right and wrong might be made out," [2] so that " morality might be placed among the sciences capable of demonstration."   The combination of these two doctrines gives us the view that moral rules are essentially laws of God, which men are impelled to obey, solely or mainly, from fear or hope of divine punishments or rewards ; and some such view as this seems to be widely accepted, by plain men without very refined moral sensibilities.

As an example, again, of thinkers who, while recognising in human nature a disinterested regard for duty or virtue as such, still consider that self-love is a proper and legitimate motive to right conduct, we may refer to Butler and his disciples.   Butler regards " reasonable self-love " as not

---

[1] Locke's *Essay*, II. c. 28, §§ 5, 6.   [2] *Ibid.* IV. c. 3, § 18.

merely a normal motive to human action, but as being—no less than conscience—a " chief or superior principle in the nature of man "; so that an action " becomes unsuitable " to this nature, if the principle of self-love be violated.   Accordingly the aim of his teaching is not to induce men to choose duty rather than interest, but to convince them that there is no inconsistency between the two; that self-love and conscience lead " to one and the same course of life."

This intermediate doctrine appears to me to be more in harmony with the common sense of mankind on the whole than either of the extreme views before contrasted.   But I do not conceive that any one of the three positions is inconsistent with fundamental assumptions of the Intuitional method. Even those who hold that human beings cannot reasonably be expected to conform to moral rules disinterestedly, or from any other motive than that supplied by the sanctions divinely attached to them, still commonly conceive God as supreme Reason, whose laws must be essentially reasonable : and so far as such laws are held to be cognisable by the ' light of nature '—so that morality, as Locke says, may be placed among demonstrative sciences—the method of determining them will be none the less intuitional because it is combined with the belief that God will reward their observance and punish their violation.   On the other hand those who hold that regard for duty as duty is an indispensable condition of acting rightly, would generally admit that acting rightly is not adequately defined as acting from a pure desire to act rightly; that though, in a certain sense, a man who sincerely desires and intends to act rightly does all he can, and completely fulfils duty, still such a man may have a wrong judgment as to the particulars of his duty, and therefore, in another sense, may act wrongly.   If this be admitted, it is evident that, even on the view that the desire or resolution to fulfil duty as such is essential to right action, a distinction between two kinds of rightness is required; which we may express by saying that an act is—on this view—" formally " [1]

---

[1] I do not myself usually employ the antithesis of Form and Matter in philosophical exposition, as it appears to me open to the charge of obscurity and ambiguity.   In the present case we may interpret " formal rightness " as denoting at once a *universal* and *essential*, and a *subjective* or *internal* condition of the rightness of actions.

right, if the agent in willing is moved by pure desire to fulfil duty or chooses duty for duty's sake; "materially" right, if he intends the right particular effects. This distinction being taken, it becomes plain that there is no reason why the same principles and method for determining material rightness, or rightness of particular effects, should not be adopted by thinkers who differ most widely on the question of formal rightness; and it is, obviously, with material rightness that the work of the systematic moralist is mainly concerned.

§ 3. The term 'formal rightness,' as above used, implying a *desire* or choice of the act as right, implies also a *belief* that it is so. But the latter condition may exist without the former : I cannot perform an act from pure love of duty without believing it to be right : but I can believe it to be right and yet do it from some other motive. And there seems to be more agreement among moralists who adopt the Intuitional Method as to the moral indispensability of such a belief, than we have found with respect to the question of motive : at least, it would, I conceive, be universally held that no act can be absolutely right, whatever its external aspect and relations, which is believed by the agent to be wrong.[1] Such an act we may call " subjectively " wrong, even though " objectively " right. It may still be asked whether it is better in any particular case that a man should do what he mistakenly believes to be his duty, or what really is his duty in the particular circumstances—considered apart from his mistaken belief—and would be completely right if he could only think so. The question is rather subtle and perplexing to Common Sense : it is therefore worth while to point out that it can have only a limited and subordinate practical application. For no one, in considering what he ought himself to do in any particular case, can distinguish what he believes to be right from what really is so : the necessity for a practical choice between 'subjective' and 'objective' rightness can only present itself in respect of the conduct of another person whom it is in our power to influence. If

---

[1] It is not, I conceive, commonly held to be indispensable, in order to constitute an act completely right, that a belief that it is right should be actually present in the agent's mind : it might be completely right, although the agent never actually raised the question of its rightness or wrongness. See p. 225.

another is about to do what we think wrong while he thinks
it right, and we cannot alter his belief but can bring other
motives to bear on him that may overbalance his sense of duty,
it becomes necessary to decide whether we ought thus to tempt
him to realise what we believe to be objectively right against
his own convictions. I think that the moral sense of mankind
would pronounce against such temptation,—thus regarding the
Subjective rightness of an action as more important than the
Objective,—unless the evil of the act prompted by a mistaken
sense of duty appeared to be very grave.[1] But however
essential it may be that a moral agent should do what he
believes to be right, this condition of right conduct is too
simple to admit of systematic development: it is, therefore,
clear that the details of our investigation must relate mainly
to ' objective ' rightness.

There is, however, one practical rule of some value, to be
obtained by merely reflecting on the general notion of rightness,[2] as commonly conceived. In a previous chapter [3] I endeavoured to make this notion clearer by saying that ' what
I judge to be right must, unless I am in error, be judged to be
so by all rational beings who judge truly of the matter.' This
statement does not imply that what is judged to be right for
one man must necessarily be judged so for another: ' objective '
rightness may vary from A to B no less than the ' objective '
facts of their nature and circumstances vary. There seems,
however, to be this difference between our conceptions of
ethical and physical objectivity respectively : that we commonly
refuse to admit in the case of the former—what experience
compels us to admit as regards the latter—variations for which

---

[1] The decision would, I think, usually be reached by weighing bad consequences to the agent's character against bad consequences of a different kind.
In extreme cases the latter consideration would certainly prevail in the view
of common sense. Thus we should generally approve a statesman who crushed
a dangerous rebellion by working on the fear or cupidity of a leading rebel who
was rebelling on conscientious grounds. Cf. *post*, Book iv. chap. iii. § 3.

[2] The antithesis of ' subjective ' and ' objective ' cannot be applied to the condition of right conduct considered in this paragraph : for this formal condition
is at once subjective and objective ; being, as I argue, involved in our common
notion of right conduct, it is, therefore, necessarily judged by us to be of really
universal application : and, though it does not secure complete objective rightness, it is an important protection against objective wrongness.

[3] Cf. Book i. chap. iii. § 3.

we can discover no rational explanation. In the variety of
coexistent physical facts we find an accidental or arbitrary
element in which we have to acquiesce, as we cannot conceive
it to be excluded by any extension of our knowledge of physical
causation. If we ask, for example, why any portion of space
empirically known to us contains more matter than any
similar adjacent portion, physical science can only answer by
stating (along with certain laws of change) some antecedent
position of the parts of matter which needs explanation no less
than the present; and however far back we carry our ascertainment of such antecedent positions, the one with which we leave
off seems as arbitrary as that with which we started. But
within the range of our cognitions of right and wrong, it will be
generally agreed that we cannot admit a similar unexplained
variation. We cannot judge an action to be right for A and
wrong for B, unless we can find in the natures or circumstances
of the two some difference which we can regard as a reasonable
ground for difference in their duties. If therefore I judge any
action to be right for myself, I implicitly judge it to be right
for any other person whose nature and circumstances do not
differ from my own in some important respects. Now by
making this latter judgment explicit, we may protect ourselves against the danger which besets the conscience, of
being warped and perverted by strong desire, so that we too
easily think that we ought to do what we very much wish to
do. For if we ask ourselves whether we believe that any
similar person in similar circumstances ought to perform the
contemplated action, the question will often disperse the false
appearance of rightness which our strong inclination has given
to it. We see that we should not think it right for another,
and therefore that it cannot be right for us. Indeed this
test of the rightness of our volitions is so generally effective,
that Kant seems to have held that all particular rules of
duty can be deduced from the one fundamental rule " Act as if
the maxim of thy action were to become by thy will a universal
law of nature." [1] But this appears to me an error analogous to

---

[1] See the *Grundlegung zur Metaphysik der Sitten* (pp. 269-273, Hartenstein ; Abbott's transl. [1879] pp. 54-61). Here Kant first says, "There is
therefore but one categorical imperative, namely, this : *Act only on that maxim
whereby thou canst at the same time will that it should become a universal*

that of supposing that Formal Logic supplies a complete criterion of truth. I should agree that a volition which does not stand this test [1] is to be condemned; but I hold that a volition which does stand it may after all be wrong. For I conceive that all (or almost all) persons who act conscientiously could sincerely will the maxims on which they act to be universally adopted: while at the same time we continually find such persons in thoroughly conscientious disagreement as to what each ought to do in a given set of circumstances. Under these circumstances, to say that all such persons act rightly—in the objective sense—because their maxims all conform to Kant's fundamental rule, would obliterate altogether the distinction between subjective and objective rightness; it would amount to affirming that whatever any one thinks right is so, unless he is in error as to the facts of the case to which his judgment applies. But such an affirmation is in flagrant conflict with common sense; and would render the construction of a scientific code of morality futile: as the very object of such a code is to supply a standard for rectifying men's divergent opinions.

We may conclude then that the moral judgments which the present method attempts to systematise are primarily and for the most part intuitions of the rightness or goodness (or the reverse) of particular kinds of external effects of human volition, presumed to be intended by the agent, but considered independently of the agent's own view as to the rightness or wrongness of his intention; though the quality of motives, as distinct from intentions, has also to be taken into account.

§ 4. But the question may be raised, whether it is

---

law. Now, if all imperatives of duty can be deduced from this one imperative as from their principle . . . we shall at least be able to show what we understand by [duty] and what this notion means." He then demonstrates the application of the principle to four cases, selected as representative of "the many actual duties"; and continues: "if now we attend to ourselves on occasion of *any* transgression of duty, we shall find that we in fact do not will that our maxim should be a universal law, for that is impossible for us " . . . : then, summing up the conclusion of this part of his argument, he says, " we have exhibited clearly and definitely for *every practical application* the content of the categorical imperative which must contain the principle of all duty, if there is such a thing at all."

[1] I do not mean that I am prepared to accept Kant's fundamental maxim, in the precise form in which he has stated it : but the qualifications which it seems to me to require will be more conveniently explained later.

legitimate to take for granted (as I have hitherto been doing) the existence of such intuitions? And, no doubt, there are persons who deliberately deny that reflection enables them to discover any such phenomenon in their conscious experience as the judgment or apparent perception that an act is in itself right or good, in any other sense than that of being the right or fit means to the attainment of some ulterior end. I think, however, that such denials are commonly recognised as paradoxical, and opposed to the common experience of civilised men :—at any rate if the psychological question, as to the *existence* of such moral judgments or apparent perceptions of moral qualities, is carefully distinguished from the ethical question as to their *validity*, and from what we may call the 'psychogonical' question as to their *origin*. The first and second of these questions are sometimes confounded, owing to an ambiguity in the use of the term "intuition"; which has sometimes been understood to imply that the judgment or apparent perception so designated is *true*. I wish therefore to say expressly, that by calling any affirmation as to the rightness or wrongness of actions "intuitive," I do not mean to prejudge the question as to its ultimate validity, when philosophically considered: I only mean that its truth is apparently known immediately, and not as the result of reasoning. I admit the possibility that any such "intuition" may turn out to have an element of error, which subsequent reflection and comparison may enable us to correct; just as many apparent perceptions through the organ of vision are found to be partially illusory and misleading: indeed the sequel will show that I hold this to be to an important extent the case with moral intuitions commonly so called.

The question as to the validity of moral intuitions being thus separated from the simple question ' whether they actually exist,' it becomes obvious that the latter can only be decided for each person by direct introspection or reflection. It must not therefore be supposed that its decision is a simple matter, introspection being always infallible: on the contrary, experience leads me to regard men as often liable to confound with moral intuitions other states or acts of mind essentially different from them,—blind impulses to certain kinds of action or vague sentiments of preference for them, or conclusions from rapid and half-unconscious processes of reasoning, or current opinions to which familiarity has given an illusory air of self-evidence. But any errors of this kind, due to careless or superficial reflection, can only be cured by more careful reflection. This may indeed be much aided by communication with other minds; it may also be aided, in a subordinate way, by an inquiry into the antecedents of the apparent intuition, which may suggest to the reflective mind sources of error to which a superficial view of it is liable. Still the question whether a certain judgment presents itself to the reflective mind as intuitively known cannot be decided by any inquiry into its antecedents or causes.[1]

It is, however, still possible to hold that an inquiry into the Origin of moral intuitions must be decisive in determining their Validity. And in fact it has been often assumed, both by Intuitionists and their opponents, that if our moral faculty can be shown to be 'derived' or 'developed' out of other pre-existent elements of mind or consciousness, a reason is thereby given for distrusting it; while if, on the other hand, it can be shown to have existed in the human mind from its origin, its trustworthiness is thereby established. Either assumption appears to me devoid of foundation. On the one hand, I can see no ground for supposing that a faculty thus derived, is, as such, more liable to error than if its existence in the individual possessing it had been differently caused:[2] to put it otherwise, I cannot see how the mere ascertainment that certain apparently self-evident judgments have been caused in known and determinate ways, can be in itself a valid ground for distrusting this class of apparent cognitions. I cannot even admit that those who affirm the truth of such judgments are bound

---

[1] See Book i. chap. iii. p. 32.

[2] I cannot doubt that every one of our cognitive faculties,—in short the human mind as a whole,—has been derived and developed, through a gradual process of physical change, out of some lower life in which cognition, properly speaking, had no place. On this view, the distinction between 'original' and 'derived' reduces itself to that between 'prior' and 'posterior' in development: and the fact that the moral faculty appears somewhat later in the process of evolution than other faculties can hardly be regarded as an argument against the validity of moral intuition; especially since this process is commonly conceived to be homogeneous throughout. Indeed such a line of reasoning would be suicidal; as the cognition that the moral faculty is developed is certainly later in development than moral cognition, and would therefore, by this reasoning, be less trustworthy.

to show in their causes a tendency to make them true : indeed
the acceptance of any such *onus probandi* would seem to me
to render the attainment of philosophical certitude impossible.
For the premises of the required demonstration must consist of
caused beliefs, which as having been caused will equally stand
in need of being proved true, and so on *ad infinitum* : unless
it be held that we can find among the premises of our reasonings certain apparently self-evident judgments which have had
no antecedent causes, and that these are therefore to be accepted
as valid without proof.   But such an assertion would be an
extravagant paradox : and, if it be admitted that all beliefs are
equally in the position of being effects of antecedent causes, it
seems evident that this characteristic alone cannot serve to
invalidate any of them.

I hold, therefore, that the *onus probandi* must be thrown
the other way : those who dispute the validity of moral or other
intuitions on the ground of their derivation must be required
to show, not merely that they are the effects of certain causes,
but that these causes are of a kind that tend to produce invalid
beliefs.   Now it is not, I conceive, possible to prove by any
theory of the derivation of the moral faculty that the fundamental ethical conceptions 'right' or 'what ought to be done,'
'good' or 'what it is reasonable to desire and seek,' are invalid,
and that consequently *all* propositions of the form '*X* is right'
or 'good' are untrustworthy : for such ethical propositions, relating as they do to matter fundamentally different from that
with which physical science or psychology deals, cannot be
inconsistent with any physical or psychological conclusions.
They can only be shown to involve error by being shown to
contradict each other : and such a demonstration cannot lead
us cogently to the sweeping conclusion that all are false.   It
may, however, be possible to prove that some ethical beliefs
have been caused in such a way as to make it probable that
they are wholly or partially erroneous : and it will hereafter be
important to consider how far any Ethical intuitions, which we
find ourselves disposed to accept as valid, are open to attack on
such psychogonical grounds.   At present I am only concerned
to maintain that no general demonstration of the derivedness
or developedness of our moral faculty can supply an adequate
reason for distrusting it.

On the other hand, if we have been once led to distrust our moral faculty on other grounds—as (*e.g.*) from the want of clearness and consistency in the moral judgments of the same individual, and the discrepancies between the judgments of different individuals—it seems to me equally clear that our confidence in such judgments cannot properly be re-established by a demonstration of their 'originality.' I see no reason to believe that the 'original' element of our moral cognition can be ascertained; but if it could, I see no reason to hold that it would be especially free from error.

§ 5. How then can we hope to eliminate error from our moral intuitions? One answer to this question was briefly suggested in a previous chapter where the different phases of the Intuitional Method were discussed. It was there said that in order to settle the doubts arising from the uncertainties and discrepancies that are found when we compare our judgments on particular cases, reflective persons naturally appeal to general rules or formulæ: and it is to such general formulæ that Intuitional Moralists commonly attribute ultimate certainty and validity. And certainly there are obvious sources of error in our judgments respecting concrete duty which seem to be absent when we consider the abstract notions of different kinds of conduct; since in any concrete case the complexity of circumstances necessarily increases the difficulty of judging, and our personal interests or habitual sympathies are liable to disturb the clearness of our moral discernment. Further, we must observe that most of us feel the need of such formulæ not only to correct, but also to supplement, our intuitions respecting particular concrete duties. Only exceptionally confident persons find that they always seem to see clearly what ought to be done in any case that comes before them. Most of us, however unhesitatingly we may affirm rightness and wrongness in ordinary matters of conduct, yet not unfrequently meet with cases where our unreasoned judgment fails us; and where we could no more decide the moral issue raised without appealing to some general formula, than we could decide a disputed legal claim without reference to the positive law that deals with the matter.

And such formulæ are not difficult to find: it only requires a little reflection and observation of men's moral discourse to make a collection of such general rules, as to the validity of which there would be apparent agreement at least among moral persons of our own age and civilisation, and which would cover with approximate completeness the whole of human conduct. Such a collection, regarded as a code imposed on an individual by the public opinion of the community to which he belongs, we have called the Positive Morality of the community : but when regarded as a body of moral truth, warranted to be such by the *consensus* of mankind,—or at least of that portion of mankind which combines adequate intellectual enlightenment with a serious concern for morality—it is more significantly termed the morality of Common Sense.

When, however, we try to apply these currently accepted principles, we find that the notions composing them are often deficient in clearness and precision. For instance, we should all agree in recognising Justice and Veracity as important virtues ; and we shall probably all accept the general maxims, that ' we ought to give every man his own ' and that ' we ought to speak the truth ' : but when we ask (1) whether primogeniture is just, or the disendowment of corporations, or the determination of the value of services by competition, or (2) whether and how far false statements may be allowed in speeches of advocates, or in religious ceremonials, or when made to enemies or robbers, or in defence of lawful secrets, we do not find that these or any other current maxims enable us to give clear and unhesitating decisions. And yet such particular questions are, after all, those to which we naturally expect answers from the moralist. For we study Ethics, as Aristotle says, for the sake of Practice : and in practice we are concerned with particulars.

Hence it seems that if the formulæ of Intuitive Morality are really to serve as scientific axioms, and to be available in clear and cogent demonstrations, they must first be raised—by an effort of reflection which ordinary persons will not make—to a higher degree of precision than attaches to them in the common thought and discourse of mankind in general. We have, in fact, to take up the attempt that Socrates initiated, and endeavour to define satisfactorily the general notions of duty and virtue which we all in common use for awarding approbation or disapprobation to conduct. This is the task upon which we shall be engaged in the nine chapters that follow. I must beg the reader to bear in mind that throughout these chapters I am not trying to prove or disprove Intuitionism, but merely by reflection on the common morality which I and my reader share, and to which appeal is so often made in moral disputes, to obtain as explicit, exact, and coherent a statement as possible of its fundamental rules.

CHAPTER II

§ 1. BEFORE, however, we attempt to define particular virtues or departments of duty, it will be well to examine further the notions of Duty and Virtue in general, and the relations between the two, as we find them implicitly conceived by the common sense of mankind, which we are endeavouring to express. Hitherto I have taken Duty to be broadly convertible with Right conduct: I have noticed, however, that the former term—like "ought" and "moral obligation"—implies at least the *potential* presence of motives prompting to wrong conduct; and is therefore not applicable to beings to whom no such conflict of motives can be attributed. Thus God is not conceived as performing duties, though He is conceived as realising Justice and other kinds of Rightness in action. For a similar reason, we do not commonly apply the term 'duty' to right actions—however necessary and important—when we are so strongly impelled to them by non-moral inclinations that no moral impulse is conceived to be necessary for their performance. Thus we do not say generally that it is a duty to eat and drink enough: though we do often say this to invalids who have lost their appetite. We should therefore perhaps keep most close to usage if we defined Duties as 'those Right actions or abstinences, for the adequate accomplishment of which a moral impulse is conceived to be at least occasionally necessary.' But as this line of distinction is vague, and continually varying, I shall not think it necessary to draw attention to it in the detailed discussion of duties: it seems sufficient to point out that we shall be chiefly concerned with such right conduct as comes within the definition just suggested.

It may be said, however, that there is another implication in the term " duty " which I have so far overlooked, but which its derivation—and that of the equivalent term ' obligation '—plainly indicates: viz. that it is " due " or owed *to* some one. But I think that here the derivation does not govern the established usage: rather, it is commonly recognised that duties owed *to* persons, or " relative " duties, are only one species, and that some duties—as (*e.g.*) Truth-speaking—have no such relativity. No doubt it is possible to view any duty as relative to the person or persons immediately affected by its performance; but it is not usual to do this where the immediate effects are harmful—as where truth-speaking causes a physically injurious shock to the person addressed— : and though it may still be conceived to be ultimately good for society, and so " due " to the community or to humanity at large, that truth should even in this case be spoken, this conception hardly belongs to the intuitional view that ' truth should be spoken regardless of consequences.' Again, it may be thought by religious persons that the performance of duties is owed not to the human or other living beings affected by them, but to God as the author of the moral law. And I certainly would not deny that our common conception of duty involves an implied relation of an individual will to a universal will conceived as perfectly rational: but I am not prepared to affirm that this implication is necessary, and an adequate discussion of the difficulties involved in it would lead to metaphysical controversies which I am desirous of avoiding. I propose, therefore, in this exposition of the Intuitional method, to abstract from this relation of Duty generally to a Divine Will: and, for reasons partly similar, to leave out of consideration the particular " duties to God " which Intuitionists have often distinguished and classified. Our view of the general rules of " duty to man " (or to other animals)—so far as such rules are held to be cognisable by moral intuition—will, I conceive, remain the same, whether or not we regard such rules as imposed by a Supreme Rational Will: since in any case they will be such as we hold it rational for all men to obey, and therefore such as a Supreme Reason would impose. I shall not therefore treat the term " Duty " as implying necessarily a relation either to a universal Imponent or to the individuals primarily affected by the performance of duties : but shall use it as equivalent generally to Right conduct, while practically concentrating attention on acts and abstinences for which a moral impulse is thought to be more or less required.

The notion of Virtue presents more complexity and difficulty, and requires to be discussed from different points of view. We may begin by noticing that there seem to be some particular virtues (such as Generosity) which may be realised in acts objectively—though not subjectively—wrong, from want of insight into their consequences : and even some (such as Courage) which may be exhibited in wrong acts that are known by the agent to be such. But though the contemplation of such acts excites in us a quasi-moral admiration, in the latter case we certainly should not call them virtuous, and it is doubtful whether we should do so in the former case, if we were using the term strictly. It will therefore involve no material deviation from usage, if we limit the term " Virtue " to qualities exhibited in right conduct :[1] accordingly I propose to adopt this limitation in subsequent discussions.

How far, then, are we to regard the spheres of Duty and Virtue (thus defined) as co-extensive ? To a great extent they undoubtedly are so, in the common application of the terms, but not altogether : since in its common use each term seems to include something excluded from the other. We should scarcely say that it was virtuous—under ordinary circumstances—to pay one's debts, or give one's children a decent education, or keep one's aged parents from starving ; these being duties which most men perform, and only bad men neglect. On the other hand, there are acts of high and noble virtue which we commonly regard as going beyond the strict duty of the agent ; since, while we praise their performance, we do not condemn their non-performance. Here, however, a difficulty seems to arise ; for we should not deny that it is, in some sense, a man's strict duty to do whatever action he judges most excellent, so far as it is in his power.

---

[1] It is more convenient, for the purpose of expounding the morality of common sense, to understand by Virtue a quality exhibited in right conduct ; for then we can use the common notions of the particular virtues as heads for the classification of the most important kinds or aspects of right conduct as generally recognised. And I think that this employment of the term is as much in accordance with ordinary usage as any other equally precise use would be.

But can we say that it is as much in a man's power to realise Virtue as it is to fulfil Duty ?[1] To some extent, no doubt, we should say this : no quality of conduct is ever called a virtue unless it is thought to be *to some extent* immediately attainable at will by all ordinary persons, when circumstances give opportunity for its manifestation. In fact the line between virtues and other excellences of behaviour is commonly drawn by this characteristic of voluntariness ;—an excellence which we think no effort of will could at once enable us to exhibit in any appreciable degree is called a gift, grace, or talent, but not properly a virtue. Writers like Hume,[2] who obliterate this line, diverge manifestly from common sense. Still I regard it as manifestly paradoxical to maintain that it is in the power of any one at any time to realise virtue in the highest form or degree ; (*e.g.*) no one would affirm that any ordinary man can at will exhibit the highest degree of courage—in the sense in which courage is a virtue—when occasion arises. It would seem, therefore, that we can distinguish a margin of virtuous conduct, which may be beyond the strict duty of any individual as being beyond his power.

Can we then, excluding this margin, say that virtuous conduct, so far as it is in a man's power, coincides completely with his duty ? Certainly we should agree that a truly moral man cannot say to himself, " This is the best thing on the whole for me to do, but yet it is not my duty to do it though it is in my power " : this would certainly seem to common sense an immoral paradox.[3] And yet there seem to be acts and abstinences which we praise as virtuous, without imposing them as duties upon all who are able to do them ; as for a rich man to live very plainly and devote his income to works of public beneficence.

---

[1] In Book i. chap. v. § 3 I have explained the sense in which Determinists no less than Libertarians hold that it is in a man's power to do his duty.

[2] Cf. *Inquiry concerning the Principles of Morals*, Appendix iv.

[3] If the phrase in the text were used by a moral person, with a sincere and predominant desire to do his duty, it must, I conceive, be used in one of two senses : either (1) half-ironically, in recognition of a customary standard of virtuous conduct which the speaker is not prepared expressly to dispute, but which he does not really adopt as valid—as when we say that it would be virtuous to read a new book, hear a sermon, pay a visit, etc. ; or (2) it might be used loosely to mean that such and such conduct *would* be best if the speaker were differently constituted.

Perhaps we may harmonise these inconsistent views by distinguishing between the questions 'what a man ought to do or forbear' and 'what other men ought to blame him for not doing or forbearing': and recognising that the standard normally applied in dealing with the latter question is laxer than would be right in dealing with the former. But how is this double standard to be explained? We may partly explain it by the different degrees of our knowledge in the two cases: there are many acts and forbearances of which we cannot lay down definitely that they ought to be done or forborne, unless we have the complete knowledge of circumstances which a man commonly possesses only in his own case, and not in that of other men. Thus I may easily assure myself that I ought to subscribe to a given hospital: but I cannot judge whether my neighbour ought to subscribe, as I do not know the details of his income and the claims which he is bound to satisfy. I do not, however, think that this explanation is always applicable: I think that there are not a few cases in which we refrain from blaming others for the omission of acts which we do not doubt that we in their place should have thought it our duty to perform. In such cases the line seems drawn by a more or less conscious consideration of what men ordinarily do, and by a social instinct as to the practical effects of expressed moral approbation and disapprobation: we think that moral progress will on the whole be best promoted by our praising acts that are above the level of ordinary practice, and confining our censure—at least if precise and particular—to acts that fall clearly below this standard. But a standard so determined must be inevitably vague, and tending to vary as the average level of morality varies in any community, or section of a community: indeed it is the aim of preachers and teachers of morality to raise it continually. Hence it is not convenient to use it in drawing a theoretical line between Virtue and Duty: and I have therefore thought it best to employ the terms so that virtuous conduct may include the performance of duty as well as whatever good actions may be commonly thought to go beyond duty; though recognising that Virtue in its ordinary use is most conspicuously manifested in the latter.

§ 2. So far I have been considering the term 'Virtuous'

as applied to conduct.   But both this general term, and the names connoting particular virtues—" just," " liberal," " brave," etc.—are applied to persons as well as to their acts : and the question may be raised which application is most appropriate or primary.   Here reflection, I think, shows that these attributes are not thought by us to belong to acts considered apart from their agents : so that Virtue seems to be primarily a quality of the soul or mind, conceived as permanent in comparison with the transient acts and feelings in which it is manifested.   As so conceived it is widely held to be a possession worth aiming at for its own sake ; to be, in fact, a part of that Perfection of man which is by some regarded as the sole Ultimate Good.   This view I shall consider in a subsequent chapter.[1]   Meanwhile it may be observed that Virtues, like other habits and dispositions, though regarded as comparatively permanent attributes of the mind, are yet attributes of which we can only form definite notions by conceiving the particular transient phenomena in which they are manifested. If then we ask in what phenomena Virtuous character is manifested, the obvious answer is that it is manifested in voluntary actions, so far as intentional ; or, more briefly, in volitions.   And many, perhaps most, moralists would give this as a complete answer.   If they are not prepared to affirm with Kant that a good will is the only absolute and unconditional Good, they will at any rate agree with Butler that " the object of the moral faculty is actions, comprehending under that name active or practical principles : those principles from which men would act if occasions and circumstances gave them power." And if it be urged that more than this is included (e.g.) in the Christian conception of the Virtue of Charity, the " love of our neighbour," they will explain with Kant that by this love we must not understand the emotion of affection, but merely the resolution to benefit, which alone has " true moral worth."

I do not, however, think that the complete exclusion of an emotional element from the conception of Virtue would be really in harmony with the common sense of mankind.   I think that in our common moral judgments certain kinds of virtuous actions are held to be at any rate adorned and made better by the presence of certain emotions in the virtuous agent : though

[1] Chap. xiv. of this Book.

no doubt the element of volition is the more important and indispensable. Thus the Virtue of Chastity or Purity, in its highest form, seems to include more than a mere settled resolution to abstain from unlawful lust; it includes some sentiment of repugnance to impurity. Again, we recognise that benefits which spring from affection and are lovingly bestowed are more acceptable to the recipients than those conferred without affection, in the taste of which there is admittedly something harsh and dry: hence, in a certain way, the affection, if practical and steady, seems a higher excellence than the mere beneficent disposition of the will, as resulting in more excellent acts. In the case of Gratitude even the rigidity of Kant [1] seems to relax, and to admit an element of emotion as indispensable to the virtue: and there are various other notions, such as Loyalty and Patriotism, which it is difficult—without paradox—either to exclude from a list of virtues or to introduce stripped bare of all emotional elements.

A consideration of the cases last mentioned will lead us to conclude that, in the view of Common Sense, the question (raised in the preceding chapter), whether an act is virtuous in proportion as it was done from regard for duty or virtue, must be answered in the negative: for the degree in which an act deserves praise as courageous, loyal, or patriotic does not seem to be reduced by its being shown that the predominant motive to the act was natural affection and not love of virtue as such. Indeed in some cases I think it clear that we commonly attribute virtue to conduct where regard for duty or virtue is not consciously present at all: as in the case of a heroic act of courage—let us say, in saving a fellow-creature from death—under an impulse of spontaneous sympathy. So again, when we praise a man as "genuinely humble" we certainly do not imply that he is conscious of fulfilling a duty—still less that he is conscious of exhibiting a virtue—by being humble.

It further appears to me that in the case of many important virtues we do not commonly consider the ultimate spring of action—whether it be some emotional impulse or the rational choice of duty as duty—in attributing a particular virtue to particular persons: what we regard as indispensable is merely a

---

[1] Cf. *Met. Anf. d. Tugendlehre*, § 33 : "diese Tugend, welche mit Innigkeit der wohlwollenden Gesinnung zugleich Zärtlichkeit des Wohlwollens verbindet."

settled resolve to will a certain kind of external effects. Thus
we call a man veracious if his speech exhibits, in a noteworthy
degree, a settled endeavour to produce in the minds of others
impressions exactly correspondent to the facts, whatever his
motive may be for so doing : whether he is moved, solely or
mainly, by a regard for virtue, or a sense of the degradation of
falsehood, or a conviction that truth-speaking is in the long run
the best policy, or a sympathetic aversion to the inconveniences
which misleading statements cause to other people.   I do not
mean that we regard these motives as of equal moral value : but
that the presence or absence of any one or other of them is not
implied in our attribution of the virtue of veracity.   Similarly
we attribute Justice, if a man has a settled habit of weighing
diverse claims and fulfilling them in the ratio of their importance ; Good Faith if he has a settled habit of strictly keeping
express or tacit engagements : and so forth.   Even where we
clearly take motives into account, in judging of the degree of
virtue it is often rather the force of seductive motives resisted
than the particular nature of the prevailing springs of action
which we consider.   Thus we certainly think virtue has been
manifested in a higher degree in just or veracious conduct,
when the agent had strong temptations to be unjust or unvera-
cious ; and in the same way there are certain dispositions or
habits tending to good conduct which are called virtues when
there are powerful seductive motives operating and not otherwise ; e.g. when we attribute the virtue of temperance to a man
who eats and drinks a proper amount, it is because we also
attribute to him appetites prompting to excess.

At the same time I admit that Common Sense seems liable
to some perplexity as to the relation of virtue to the moral
effort required for resisting unvirtuous impulses.   On the one
hand a general assent would be given to the proposition that
virtue is especially drawn out and exhibited in a successful conflict with natural inclination : and perhaps even to the more
extreme statement that there is no virtue [1] in doing what one
likes.   On the other hand we should surely agree with Aristotle
that Virtue is imperfect so long as the agent cannot do the virtuous action without a conflict of impulses ; since it is from a

---

[1] Or no " merit " :—but so far as this latter notion is precisely applied, it will
be more appropriately considered in ch. v. of this Book (on Justice).

wrong bent of natural impulse that we find it hard to do what
is best, and it seems absurd to say that the more we cure ourselves of this wrong bent, the less virtuous we grow.   Perhaps we
may solve the difficulty by recognising that our common idea of
Virtue includes two distinct elements, the one being the most
perfect ideal of moral excellence that we are able to conceive for
human beings, while the other is manifested in the effort of
imperfect men to attain this ideal.   Thus in proportion as a
man comes to like any particular kind of good conduct and to
do it without moral effort, we shall not say that his conduct
becomes less virtuous but rather more in conformity with a
true moral ideal ; while at the same time we shall recognise
that in this department of his life he has less room to exhibit
that other kind of virtue which is manifested in resistance to
seductive impulses, and in the energetic striving of the will to
get nearer to ideal perfection.

So far I have been considering the manifestation of virtue
in emotions and volitions, and have not expressly adverted to
the intellectual conditions of virtuous acts : though in speaking
of such acts it is of course implied that the volition is accompanied with an intellectual representation of the particular
effects willed.   It is not, however, implied that in willing such
effects we must necessarily think of them as right or good :
and I do not myself think that, in the view of common sense,
this is an indispensable condition of the virtuousness of an act ;
for it seems that some kinds of virtuous acts may be done so
entirely without deliberation that no moral judgment was
passed on them by the agent.   This might be the case, for
instance, with an act of heroic courage, prompted by an
impulse of sympathy with a fellow-creature in sudden peril.
But it is, I conceive, clearly necessary that such an act should
not be even vaguely thought to be bad.   As I have already
said, it is more doubtful how far an act which is conceived by
the agent to be good, but which is really bad, is ever judged
by common sense to be virtuous [1] : but if we agree to restrict
the term to acts which we regard as right, it is again obvious

---

[1] I have before said that decidedly wrong acts are frequently considered to
exhibit in a high degree the tendencies which, when exhibited in right acts, we
call particular virtues—generosity, courage, patriotism, etc. : and this is especially true of acts bad through ignorance.

that the realisation of virtue may not be in the power of any given person at any given time, through lack of the requisite intellectual conditions.[1]

To sum up the results of a rather complicated discussion: I consider Virtue as a quality manifested in the performance of duty (or good acts going beyond strict duty): it is indeed primarily attributed to the mind or character of the agent; but it is only known to us through its manifestations in feelings and acts. Accordingly, in endeavouring to make precise our conceptions of the particular virtues, we have to examine the states of consciousness in which they are manifested. Examining these, we find that the element of volition is primarily important, and in some cases almost of sole importance, but yet that the element of emotion cannot be altogether discarded without palpable divergence from common sense. Again, concentrating our attention on the volitional element, we find that in most cases what we regard as manifestations of virtue are the volitions to produce certain particular effects; the general determination to do right as right, duty for duty's sake, is indeed thought to be of fundamental importance as a generally necessary spring of virtuous action; but it is not thought to be an indispensable condition of the existence of virtue in any particular case. Similarly in considering the emotional element, though an ardent love of virtue or aversion to vice generally is a valuable stimulus to virtuous conduct, it is not a universally necessary condition of it: and in the case of some acts the presence of other emotions—such as kind affection—makes the acts better than if they were done from a purely moral motive. Such emotions, however, cannot be commanded at will: and this is also true of the knowledge of what ought to be done in any particular case,—which, if we restrict the term 'virtuous' to right acts, is obviously required

---

[1] This, I think, is a conclusion which common sense on the whole accepts: though I note a considerable reluctance to accept it; which, however, is not shown in the attribution of virtue to persons who do clearly wrong acts, but rather in an effort to explain their ignorance as caused by some previous wilful wrongdoing. We try to persuade ourselves that if (e.g.) Torquemada did not know that it was wrong to torture heretics, he might have known if he had not wilfully neglected means of enlightenment: but there are many cases in which this kind of explanation is unsupported by facts, and I see no ground for accepting it as generally true.

to render conduct perfectly virtuous. For these and other reasons I consider that though Virtue is distinguished by us from other excellences by the characteristic of voluntariness—it must be *to some extent* capable of being realised at will when occasion arises—this voluntariness attaches to it only in a certain degree ; and that, though a man can always do his Duty if he knows it, he cannot always realise virtue in the highest degree.

It should, however, be observed that even when it is beyond our power to realise virtue immediately at will, we recognise a duty of cultivating it and seeking to develop it : and this duty of cultivation extends to all virtuous habits or dispositions in which we are found to be deficient, so far as we can thus increase our tendency to do the corresponding acts in future ; however completely such acts may on each occasion be within the control of the will. It is true that for acts of this latter kind, so far as they are perfectly deliberate, we do not seem to need any special virtuous habits ; if only we have knowledge of what is right and best to be done, together with a sufficiently strong wish to do it.[1] But, in order to fulfil our duties thoroughly, we are obliged to act during part of our lives suddenly and without deliberation : on such occasions there is no room for moral reasoning, and sometimes not even for explicit moral judgment ; so that in order to act virtuously, we require such particular habits and dispositions as are denoted by the names of the special virtues : and it is a duty to foster and develop these in whatever way experience shows this to be possible.

The complicated relation of virtue to duty, as above determined, must be borne in mind throughout the discussion of the particular virtues, to which I shall proceed in the following chapters. But, as we have seen, the main part of the manifestation of virtue in conduct consists in voluntary actions, which it is within the power of any individual to do—so far as they are recognised by him as right,—and which therefore come within our definition of Duty, as above laid down ; it will not therefore be necessary, during the greater part of the ensuing discussion, to distinguish between principles of virtuous

---

[1] Hence the Socratic doctrine that ' all virtue is knowledge ' ; on the assumption that a rational being must necessarily wish for what is good.

conduct and principles of duty ; since the definitions of the two will coincide.

§ 3. Here, however, a remark is necessary, which to some extent qualifies what was said in the preceding chapter, where I characterised the common notions of particular virtues— justice, etc.—as too vague to furnish exact determinations of the actions enjoined under them. I there assumed that rules of duty ought to admit of precise definition in a universal form : and this assumption naturally belongs to the ordinary or jural view of Ethics as concerned with a moral code : since we should agree that if obligations are imposed on any one he ought at least to know what they are, and that a law indefinitely drawn must be a bad law. But so far as we contemplate virtue as something that goes beyond strict duty and is not always capable of being realised at will, this assumption is not so clearly appropriate : since from this point of view we naturally compare excellence of conduct with beauty in the products of the Fine Arts. Of such products we commonly say, that though rules and definite prescriptions may do much, they can never do all; that the highest excellence is always due to an instinct or tact that cannot be reduced to definite formulæ. We can describe the beautiful products when they are produced, and to some extent classify their beauties, giving names to each ; but we cannot prescribe any certain method for producing each kind of beauty. So, it may be said, stands the case with virtues : and hence the attempt to state an explicit maxim, by applying which we may be sure of producing virtuous acts of any kind, must fail : we can only give a general account of the virtue—a description, not a definition—and leave it to trained insight to find in any particular circumstances the act that will best realise it. On this view, which I may distinguish as Æsthetic Intuitionism, I shall have something to say hereafter.[1] But I conceive that our primary business is to examine the larger claims of those Rational or Jural Intuitionists, who maintain that Ethics admits of exact and scientific treatment, having for its first principles the general rules of which we have spoken, or the most fundamental of them : and who thus hold out to us a hope of getting rid of the fluctuations and discrepancies of opinion, in which we

---

[1] See chap. xiv. § 1 of this Book.

acquiesce in æsthetic discussions, but which tend to endanger seriously the authority of ethical beliefs. And we cannot, I think, decide on the validity of such claims without examining in detail the propositions which have been put forward as ethical axioms, and seeing how far they prove to be clear and explicit, or how far others may be suggested presenting these qualities. For it would not be maintained, at least by the more judicious thinkers of this school, that such axioms are always to be found with proper exactness of form by mere observation of the common moral reasonings of men; but rather that they are at least implied in these reasonings, and that when made explicit their truth is self-evident, and must be accepted at once by an intelligent and unbiassed mind. Just as some mathematical axioms are not and cannot be known to the multitude, as their certainty cannot be seen except by minds carefully prepared,—but yet, when their terms are properly understood, the perception of their absolute truth is immediate and irresistible. Similarly, if we are not able to claim for a proposed moral axiom, in its precise form, an explicit and actual assent of " *orbis terrarum*," it may still be a truth which men before vaguely apprehended, and which they will now unhesitatingly admit.

In this inquiry it is not of great importance in what order we take the virtues. We are not to examine the system of any particular moralist, but the Morality (as it was called) of Common Sense; and the discussion of the general notions of Duty and Virtue, in which we have been engaged in the present chapter, will have shown incidentally the great difficulty of eliciting from Common Sense any clear principle of classification of the particular duties and virtues. Hence I have thought it best to reserve what I have to say on the subject of classification till a later period of the discussion; and in the first place to take the matter to be investigated quite empirically, as we find it in the common thought expressed in the common language of mankind. The systems of moralists commonly attempt to give some definite arrangement to this crude material: but in so far as they are systematic they generally seem forced to transcend Common Sense, and define what it has left doubtful; as I shall hereafter try to show.

For the present, then, it seems best, in this empirical

investigation, to take the virtues rather in the order of their importance ; and, as there are some that seem to have a special comprehensiveness of range, and to include under them, in a manner, all or most of the others, it will be convenient to begin with these. Of these Wisdom is perhaps the most obvious : in the next chapter, therefore, I propose to examine our common conceptions of Wisdom, and certain other cognate or connected virtues or excellences.

CHAPTER III

WISDOM AND SELF-CONTROL

§ 1. WISDOM was always placed by the Greek philosophers first in the list of virtues, and regarded as in a manner comprehending all the others: in fact in the post-Aristotelian schools the notion of the Sage or ideally Wise man (σοφός) was regularly employed to exhibit in a concrete form the rules of life laid down by each system. In common Greek usage, however, the term just mentioned would signify excellence in purely speculative science, no less than practical wisdom[1]: and the English term Wisdom has, to some extent, the same ambiguity. It is, however, chiefly used in reference to practice: and even when applied to the region of pure speculation suggests especially such intellectual gifts and habits as lead to sound practical conclusions: namely, comprehensiveness of view, the habit of attending impartially to a number of diverse considerations difficult to estimate exactly, and good judgment as to the relative importance of each. At any rate, it is only Practical Wisdom which we commonly class among Virtues, as distinguished from purely intellectual excellences. How then shall we define Practical Wisdom? The most obvious part of its meaning is a tendency to discern, in the conduct of life generally, the best means to the attainment of any ends that the natural play of human motives may lead us to seek: as contrasted with technical skill, or the faculty of selecting the best means to given ends in a certain limited and special department of human action. Such skill in the special arts

[1] Indeed Aristotle, who stood alone among the schools sprung from Socrates in distinguishing sharply 'theoretic' from 'practical' wisdom, restricts the term σοφία to the former, and uses another word (φρόνησις) to denote the latter.

is partly communicable by means of definite rules, and partly a matter of tact or instinct, depending somewhat on natural gifts and predispositions, but to a great extent acquired by exercise and imitation; and similarly practical Wisdom, if understood to be Skill in the Art of Life, would involve a certain amount of scientific knowledge, the portions of different sciences bearing directly on human action, together with empirical rules relating to the same subject-matter; and also the tact or trained instinct just mentioned, which would even be more prominent here, on account of the extreme complexity of the subject-matter. But it does not appear from this analysis why this skill should be regarded as a virtue: and reflection will show that we do not ordinarily mean by wisdom merely the faculty of finding the best means to any ends: for we should not call the most accomplished swindler wise; whereas we should not hesitate to attribute to him cleverness, ingenuity, and other purely intellectual excellences. So again we apply the term " worldly-wise " to a man who skilfully chooses the best means to the end of ambition; but we should not call such a man ' wise ' without qualification. Wisdom, in short, appears to me to imply right judgment in respect of ends as well as means.

Here, however, a subtle question arises. For the assumption on which this treatise proceeds is that there are several ultimate ends of action, which all claim to be rational ends, such as every man ought to adopt. Hence, if Wisdom implies right judgment as to ends, it is clear that a person who regards some one end as the sole right or rational ultimate end will not consider a man wise who adopts any other ultimate end. Can we say then that in the common use of the word Wisdom any one ultimate end is distinctly implied to the exclusion of others? It may be suggested, perhaps, that in the moral view of Common Sense which we are now trying to make clear, since Wisdom itself is prescribed or commended as a quality of conduct intuitively discerned to be right or good, the ultimate end which the wise man prefers must be just this attainment of rightness or goodness in conduct generally; rather than pleasure for himself or others, or any other ulterior end. I think, however, that in the case of this notion it is impossible to carry out that analysis of ordinary practical reasoning into several distinct methods, each admitting and needing separate development, upon which the plan of this treatise is founded. For, as we saw, it is characteristic of Common Sense to assume coincidence or harmony among these different competing methods. And hence, while as regards most particular virtues and duties, the exercise of moral judgment in ordinary men is *prima facie* independent of hedonistic calculations, and occasionally in apparent conflict with their results,—so that the reconciliation of the different procedures presents itself as a problem to be solved—in the comprehensive notion of Wisdom the antagonism is latent. Common Sense seems to mean by a Wise man, a man who attains at once all the different rational ends ; who by conduct in perfect conformity with the true moral code attains the greatest happiness possible both for himself and for mankind (or that portion of mankind to which his efforts are necessarily restricted). But if we find this harmony unattainable,—if, for example, Rational Egoism seems to lead to conduct opposed to the true interests of mankind in general, and we ask whether we are to call Wise the man who seeks, or him who sacrifices, his private interests,—Common Sense gives no clear reply.

§ 2. Let us now return to the question whether Wisdom, as exhibited in right judgment as to ends, is in any degree attainable at will, and so, according to our definition, a Virtue. At first sight, the perception of the right end may seem not to be voluntary any more than the cognition of any other kind of truth ; and though in most cases the attainment of truth requires voluntary effort, still we do not generally think it possible for any man, by this alone, to attain even approximately the right solution of a difficult intellectual problem. It is often said, however, that the cognition of Moral truth depends largely upon the ' heart,' that is, upon a certain condition of our desires and other emotions : and it would seem to be on this view that Wisdom is regarded as a Virtue ; and we may admit it as such, according to the definition before given, so far as this condition of feeling is attainable at will. Still, on closer scrutiny, there hardly seems to be agreement as to the right emotional conditions of the cognition of ends : as some would say that prayer or ardent aspiration produced the most favourable state, while others would urge that emotional excitement is likely to perturb the judgment, and would say that we need for right apprehension rather tranquillity of feeling : and some would contend that a complete suppression of selfish impulses was the essential condition, while others would regard this as chimerical and impossible, or, if possible, a plain misdirection of effort. On these points we cannot decide in the name of Common Sense : but it would be generally agreed that there are certain violent passions and sensual appetites which are known to be liable to pervert moral apprehensions, and that these are to some extent under the control of the Will; so that a man who exercises moral effort to resist their influence, when he wishes to decide on ends of action, may be said to be so far voluntarily wise.

And this applies to some extent even to that other function of Wisdom, first discussed, which consists in the selection of the best means to the attainment of given ends. For experience seems to show that our insight in practical matters is liable to be perverted by desire and fear, and that this perversion may be prevented by an effort of self-control: so that unwisdom, even here, is at least not altogether involuntary. Thus in a dispute which may lead to a quarrel, I may be entirely unable to show foresight and skill in maintaining my right in such a manner as to avoid needless exasperation, and so far may be unable to conduct the dispute wisely: but it is always in my power, before taking each important step, to reduce the influence of anger or wounded *amour propre* on my decisions, and I may avoid much unwisdom in this way. And it is to be observed that volition has a more important part to play in developing or protecting our insight into the right conduct of life, than it has in respect of the technical skill to which we compared Practical Wisdom ; in proportion as the reasonings in which Practical Wisdom is exhibited are less clear and exact, and the con- clusions inevitably more uncertain. For desire and fear could hardly make one go wrong in an arithmetical calculation ; but in estimating a balance of complicated practical probabilities it is more difficult to resist the influence of strong inclination : and it would seem to be a more or less definite consciousness of the continual need of such resistance, which leads us to regard Wisdom as a Virtue.

We may say then that Practical Wisdom, so far as it is a

virtue, involves a habit of resistance to desires and fears which is commonly distinguished as Self-control. But suppose a man has determined with full insight the course of conduct that it is reasonable for him to adopt under any given circumstances, the question still remains whether he will certainly adopt it. Now I hardly think that Common Sense considers the *choice*, as distinct from the *cognition*, of right ends to belong to Wisdom; and yet we should scarcely call a man wise who deliberately chose to do what he knew to be contrary to reason. The truth seems to be that the notion of such a choice, though the modern mind admits it as possible,[1] is somewhat unfamiliar in comparison with either (1) impulsive irrationality, or (2) mistaken choice of bad for good. In the last case, if the mistake is entirely involuntary, the choice has, of course, no subjective wrongness: often, however, the mistaken conclusion is caused by a perverting influence of desire or fear of which the agent is obscurely conscious, and which might be resisted and dispelled by an effort of will. As so caused, the mistake falls under the head of culpable unwisdom, due to want of self-control similar in kind—though not in degree—to that which is exhibited in the rarer phenomenon of a man deliberately choosing to do what he knows to be bad for him.

The case of impulsive wrongdoing is somewhat different. It is clear that a resolution made after deliberation, in accordance with our view of what is right, should not be abandoned or modified except deliberately—at least if time for fresh deliberation be allowed—: and the self-control required to resist impulses prompting to such abandonment or modification— which we may perhaps call Firmness,—is an indispensable auxiliary to Wisdom. But the gusts of impulse that the varying occasions of life arouse sometimes take effect so rapidly that the resolution to which they run counter is not actually recalled at the time: and in this case the self-control or firmness required to prevent unreasonable action seems to be not attainable at will, when it is most wanted. We can, however, cultivate this important habit by graving our resolves deeper in the moments of deliberation that

---

[1] I have already adverted to the difference between ancient and modern thought in this respect. Cf. *ante*, Book i. chap. v. § 1, p. 59, note.

continually intervene among the moments of impulsive action.

§ 3. In examining the functions of Wisdom, other subordinate excellences come into view, which are partly included in our ideal conception of Wisdom, and partly auxiliary or supplementary. Some of these, however, no one would exactly call virtues: such as Sagacity in selecting the really important points amid a crowd of others, Acuteness in seeing aids or obstacles that lie somewhat hidden, Ingenuity in devising subtle or complicated means to our ends, and other cognate qualities more or less vaguely defined and named. We cannot be acute, or ingenious, or sagacious when we please, though we may become more so by practice. The same may be said of Caution, so far as Caution implies taking into due account *material* circumstances unfavourable to our wishes and aims: for by no effort of will can we certainly see what circumstances are material; we can only look steadily and comprehensively. The term 'Caution,' however, may also be legitimately applied to a species of Self-control which we shall properly regard as a Virtue: viz. the tendency to deliberate whenever and so long as deliberation is judged to be required, even though powerful impulses urge us to immediate action.[1]

And, in antithesis to Caution, we may notice as another minor virtue the quality called Decision, so far as we mean by Decision the habit of resisting an irrational impulse to which men are liable, of continuing to some extent in the deliberative attitude when they know that deliberation is no longer expedient, and that they ought to be acting. 'Decision,' however, is often applied (like 'Caution') to denote solely or chiefly a merely intellectual excellence; viz. the tendency to judge rightly as to the time for closing deliberation.

---

[1] It may be observed that there is another meaning again in which the term 'Caution' is sometimes used. Since of the various means which we may use to gain any end, some are more and some less certain; and some are dangerous—that is, involve a chance of consequences either antagonistic to our pursuit, or on different grounds to be avoided—while others are free from such danger; 'Caution' is often used to denote the temper of mind which inclines to the more certain and less dangerous means. In this sense, in so far as the chance in each case of winning the end, and the value of the end as compared with other ends, and as weighed against the detriment which its pursuit may entail, can be precisely estimated, the limits of the duty of Caution may obviously be determined without difficulty.

I conclude then that so far as such qualities as those which I have distinguished as Caution, and Decision, are recognised as Virtues and not merely as intellectual excellences, it is because they are, in fact. species of Self-control; *i.e.* because they involve voluntary adoption of and adhesion to rational judgments as to conduct, in spite of certain irrational motives prompting in an opposite direction. Now it may seem at first sight that if we suppose perfect correctness of judgment combined with perfect self-control, the result will be a perfect performance of duty in all departments; and the realisation of perfect Virtue, except so far as this involves the presence of certain special emotions not to be commanded at will.[1] And no doubt a perfectly wise and self-controlled man cannot be conceived as breaking or neglecting any moral rule. But it is important to observe that even sincere and single-minded efforts to realise what we see to be right may vary in intensity; and that therefore the tendency to manifest a high degree of intensity in such efforts is properly praised as Energy, if the quality be purely volitional; or under some such name as Zeal or Moral Ardour, if the volitional energy be referred to intensity of emotion, and yet not connected with any emotion more special than the general love of what is Right or Good.

NOTE.—It is to be observed that in the discussions of this chapter the question at issue between Intuitional and Utilitarian Ethics is not yet reached. For, granting that we can elicit by reflection clear rules of duty under the heads of Wisdom, Caution and Decision, the rules are obviously not independent; they presuppose an intellectual judgment otherwise obtained, or capable of being obtained, as to what is right or expedient to do.

[1] See p. 223, and § 2 of the next chapter.

CHAPTER IV

BENEVOLENCE

§ 1. WE have seen that the virtue of Practical Wisdom comprehends all others, so far as virtuous conduct in each department necessarily results from a clear knowledge and choice of the true ultimate end or ends of action, and of the best means to the attainment of such end or ends.[1] From this point of view, we may consider the names of the special virtues as denoting special departments of this knowledge; which it is now our business to examine more closely.

When, however, we contemplate these, we discern that there are other virtues, which, in different ways, may be regarded as no less comprehensive than Wisdom. Especially in modern times, since the revival of independent ethical speculation, there have always been thinkers who have maintained, in some form, the view that Benevolence is a supreme and architectonic virtue, comprehending and summing up all the others, and fitted to regulate them and determine their proper limits and mutual relations.[2] This widely supported claim to supremacy seems an adequate reason for giving to Benevolence the first place after Wisdom, in our examination of the commonly received maxims of Duty and Virtue.

The general maxim of Benevolence would be commonly

[1] The qualifications which this proposition requires have been already noticed, and will be further illustrated as we proceed.

[2] The phase of this view most current at present would seem to be Utilitarianism, the principles and method of which will be more fully discussed hereafter : but in some form or degree it has been held by many whose affinities are rather with the Intuitional school.

238

said to be, " that we ought to love all our fellow-men,' or " all our fellow-creatures ": but, as we have already seen, there is some doubt among moralists as to the precise meaning of the term " love," in this connexion : since, according to Kant and others, what is morally prescribed as the Duty of Benevolence is not strictly the affection of love or kindness, so far as this contains an emotional element, but only the determination of the will to seek the good or happiness of others.   And I agree that it cannot be a strict duty to feel an emotion, so far as it is not directly within the power of the Will to produce it at any given time.   Still (as I have said) it seems to me that this emotional element is included in our common notion of Charity or Philanthropy, regarded as a Virtue : and I think it paradoxical [1] to deny that it raises the mere beneficent dis- position of the will to a higher degree of excellence, and renders its effects better.   If this be so, it will be a duty to cultivate the affection so far as it is possible to do so : and indeed this would seem (no less than the permanent disposi- tion to do good) to be a normal effect of repeated beneficent resolves and actions : since, as has often been observed, a benefit tends to excite love in the agent towards the recipient of the benefit, no less than in the recipient towards the agent. It must be admitted, however, that this effect is less certain than the production of the benevolent disposition ; and that some men are naturally so unattractive to others that the latter can feel no affection, though they may entertain bene- volent dispositions, towards the former.   At any rate, it would seem to be a duty generally, and till we find the effort fruit- less, to cultivate kind affections towards those whom we ought to benefit ; not only by doing kind actions, but by placing our- selves under any natural influences which experience shows to have a tendency to produce affection.

But we have still to ascertain more particularly the nature of the actions in which this affection or disposition of will is shown.   They are described popularly as ' doing good.'   Now we have before [2] noticed that the notion ' good,' in ordinary thought, includes, undistinguished and therefore unharmonised, the different conceptions that men form of the ultimate end of rational action.   It follows that there is a corresponding

---

[1] See note at end of chapter.   [2] Cf. Book i. chaps. vii. ix.

ambiguity in the phrase 'doing good': since, though many would unhesitatingly take it to mean the promotion of Happiness, there are others who, holding that Perfection and not Happiness is the true ultimate Good, consistently maintain that the real way to 'do good' to people is to increase their virtue or aid their progress towards Perfection. There are, however, even among anti-Epicurean moralists, some—such as Kant—who take an opposite view, and argue that my neighbour's Virtue or Perfection cannot be an end to me, because it depends upon the free exercise of his own volition, which I cannot help or hinder. But on the same grounds it might equally well be argued that I cannot *cultivate* Virtue in myself, but only practise it from moment to moment: whereas even Kant does not deny that we can cultivate virtuous dispositions in ourselves, and that in other ways than by the performance of virtuous acts: and Common Sense always assumes this to be possible and prescribes it as a duty. And surely it is equally undeniable that we can cultivate virtue in others: and indeed such cultivation is clearly the object not only of education, but of a large part of social action, especially of our expression of praise and blame. And if Virtue is an ultimate end for ourselves, to be sought for its own sake, benevolence must lead us to do what is possible to obtain it for our neighbour. And indeed we see that in the case of intense individual affection, the friend or lover generally longs that the beloved should be excellent and admirable as well as happy: perhaps, however, this is because love involves preference, and the lover desires that the beloved should be really worthy of preference as well as actually preferred by him, as otherwise there is a conflict between Love and Reason.

On the whole then, I do not find, in the common view of what Benevolence bids us promote for others, any clear selection indicated between the different and possibly conflicting elements of Good as commonly conceived. But we may say, I think, that the promotion of Happiness is practically the chief part of what Common Sense considers to be prescribed as the external duty of Benevolence: and for clearness' sake we will confine our attention to this in the remainder of the discussion.[1] It should be observed that by happiness we are not to

---

[1] A further reason for so doing will appear in the sequel; when we come to

understand simply the gratification of the actual desires of others, for men too often desire what would tend to their unhappiness in the long run : but the greatest possible amount of pleasure or satisfaction for them on the whole—in short, such happiness as was taken to be the rational end for each individual in the system of Egoistic Hedonism.   It is this that Rational Benevolence bids us provide for others ; and if one who loves is led from affectionate sympathy with the longings of the beloved to gratify those longings believing that the gratification will be attended with an overplus of painful consequences, we commonly say that such affection is weak and foolish.

§ 2. It remains to ask towards whom this disposition or affection is to be maintained, and to what extent.   And, firstly, it is not quite clear whether we owe benevolence to men alone, or to other animals also.   That is, there is a general agreement that we ought to treat all animals with kindness, so far as to avoid causing them unnecessary pain ; but it is questioned whether this is directly due to sentient beings as such, or merely prescribed as a means of cultivating kindly dispositions towards men.   Intuitional moralists of repute have maintained this latter view : I think, however, that Common Sense is disposed to regard this as a hard-hearted paradox, and to hold with Bentham that the pain of animals is *per se* to be avoided.   Passing to consider how our benevolence ought to be distributed among our fellow-men, we may conveniently make clear the Intuitional view by contrasting it with that of Utilitarianism.   For Utilitarianism is sometimes said to resolve all virtue into universal and impartial Benevolence : it does not, however, prescribe that we should love all men equally, but that we should aim at Happiness generally as our ultimate end, and so consider the happiness of any one individual as equally important with the equal happiness of any other, as an element of this total ; and should distribute our kindness so as to make this total as great as possible, in whatever way this result may be attained. Practically of course the distribution of any individual's ser-

survey the general relation of Virtue to Happiness, as the result of that detailed examination of the particular virtues which forms the main subject of the present book.   Cf. *post*, chap. xiv. of this Book.

vices will, even on this view, be unequal: as each man will obviously promote the general happiness best by rendering services to a limited number, and to some more than others: but the inequality, on the Utilitarian theory, is secondary and derivative. Common Sense, however, seems rather to regard it as immediately certain without any such deduction that we owe special dues of kindness to those who stand in special relations to us. The question then is, on what principles, when any case of doubt or apparent conflict of duties arises, we are to determine the nature and extent of the special claims to affection and kind services which arise out of these particular relations of human beings. Are problems of this kind to be solved by considering which course of conduct is on the whole most conducive to the general happiness, or can we find independent and self-evident principles sufficiently clear and precise to furnish practical guidance in such cases? The different answers given to this fundamental question will obviously constitute the main difference between the Intuitional and Utilitarian methods; so far as the 'good' which the benevolent man desires and seeks to confer on others is understood to be Happiness.

When, however, we come to investigate this question we are met with a difficulty in the arrangement of the subject, which, like most difficulties of classification, deserves attentive consideration, as it depends upon important characteristics of the matter that has to be arranged. In a narrower sense of the term, Benevolence is not unfrequently distinguished from— and even contrasted with—Justice; we may of course exercise both towards the same persons, but we commonly assume that the special function of Benevolence begins where Justice ends; and it is rather with this special function that we are concerned in considering claims to affection, and to kind services normally prompted by affection. At the same time, if we consider these services as strictly due to persons in certain relations, the moral notion under which these duties are presented to us is not easily distinguishable from that of Justice; while yet these duties can hardly be withdrawn from the sphere of Benevolence in the narrowest sense. It is sometimes given as a distinction between Justice and Benevolence, that the services which Justice prescribes can be claimed as a right by their recipient, while Benevolence is essentially unconstrained: but we certainly think (*e.g.*) that parents have a right to filial affection and to the services that naturally spring from it.   It is further said that the duties of Affection are essentially indefinite, while those we classify under the head of Justice are precisely defined: and no doubt this is partly true.   We not only find it hard to say exactly how much a son owes his parents, but we are even reluctant[1] to investigate this: we do not think that he ought to ask for a precise measure of his duty, in order that he may do just so much and no more; while a great part of Justice consists in the observance of stated agreements and precise rules.   At the same time it is difficult to maintain this distinction as a ground of classification; for the duties of Affection are admittedly liable to come into competition with each other, and with other duties; and when this apparent conflict of duties occurs, we manifestly need as precise a definition as possible of the conflicting obligations, in order to make a reasonable choice among the alternatives of conduct presented to us.   Accordingly in the following chapter (§ 2) I shall show how this competition of claims renders our common notion of Justice applicable to these no less than to other duties: meanwhile, it seems proper to treat here separately of all duties that arise out of relations where affection normally exists, and where it ought to be cultivated, and where its absence is deplored if not blamed. For all are agreed that there are such duties, the non-performance of which is a ground for censure, beyond the obligations imposed by law, or arising out of specific contract, which will come under a different head.

Beyond these duties, again, there seems to be a region of performance where the services rendered cannot properly be claimed as of debt, and blame is not felt to be due for non-performance: and with regard to this region, too,—which clearly belongs to Benevolence as contrasted with Justice— there is some difficulty in stating the view of Common Sense morality.   There are two questions to be considered.   We have to ask, firstly, whether services rendered from affection,

---

[1] This reluctance, however, seems largely due to the fact that this precise measure of duty is most frequently demanded when the issue lies between Duty and Self-interest.

over and above what strict Duty is thought to require, are to be deemed Virtuous; and secondly, whether the affection itself is to be considered worthy of admiration as a moral excellence, and therefore a mental condition that we should strive to attain. I think that Common Sense clearly regards as virtuous the disposition to render substantial positive services to men at large, and promote their well-being,—whether such a disposition springs out of natural kindliness of feeling towards human beings generally, or whether it is merely the result of moral effort and resolve—provided it is accompanied by an adequate degree of intellectual enlightenment.[1] And the same may be said of the less comprehensive affection that impels men to promote the well-being of the community of which they are members; and again of the affection that normally tends to accompany the recognition of rightful rule or leadership in others. In some ages and countries Patriotism and Loyalty have been regarded as almost supreme among the virtues; and even now Common Sense gives them a high place.

But when we pass to more restricted, and, ordinarily more intense, affections, such as those which we feel for relations and friends, it becomes more difficult to determine whether they are to be considered as moral excellences and cultivated as such.

First, to avoid confusion, we must remark that Love is not merely a desire to do good to the object beloved, although it always involves such a desire. It is primarily a pleasurable emotion, which seems to depend upon a certain sense of union with another person, and it includes besides the benevolent impulse, a desire of the society of the beloved: and this element may predominate over the former, and even conflict with it, so that the true interests of the beloved may be

---

[1] It must be admitted that the more the benevolent impulse is combined with the habit of considering the complex consequences of different courses of action that may be presented as alternatives, and comparing the amounts of happiness to others respectively resulting from them, the more good, *ceteris paribus*, is likely to be caused by it on the whole. And so far as there seems to be a certain natural incompatibility between this habit of calculation and comparison and the spontaneous fervour of kindly impulse, Common Sense is somewhat puzzled which to prefer; and takes refuge in an ideal that transcends this incompatibility and includes the two.

sacrificed. In this case we call the affection selfish, and do not praise it at all, but rather blame. If now we ask whether intense Love for an individual, considered merely as a benevolent impulse, is in itself a moral excellence, it is difficult to extract a very definite answer from Common Sense: but I think it inclines on the whole to the negative. We are no doubt generally inclined to admire any kind of conspicuously 'altruistic' conduct and any form of intense love, however restricted in its scope; yet it hardly seems that the susceptibility to such individualised benevolent emotions is exactly regarded as an essential element of moral Perfection, which we ought to strive after and cultivate like other moral excellences; we seem, in fact, to doubt whether such effort is desirable in this case, at least beyond the point up to which such affection is thought to be required for the performance of recognised duties. Again, we think it natural and desirable that—as generally speaking each person feels strong affection for only a few individuals,—in his efforts to promote directly the well-being of others he should, to a great extent, follow the promptings of such restricted affection: but we are hardly prepared to recommend that he should render services to special individuals beyond what he is bound to render, and such as are the natural expression of an eager and overflowing affection, without having any such affection to express: although, as was before said, in certain intimate relations we do not approve of the limits of duty being too exactly measured.

On the whole, then, I conclude that—while we praise and admire enthusiastic Benevolence and Patriotism, and are touched and charmed by the spontaneous lavish outflow of Gratitude, Friendship, and the domestic affections—still what chiefly concerns us as moralists, under the present head, is the ascertainment of the right rules of distribution of services and kind acts, in so far as we consider the rendering of these to be morally obligatory. For provided a man fulfils these duties (and observes the other recognised rules of morality) Common Sense is not prepared to say how far it is right or good that he should sacrifice any other noble and worthy aim—such as the cultivation of knowledge or any of the fine arts—to the claims of philanthropy or personal affection: there seem to be no generally accepted "intuitional" principles for determining such a choice of alternatives.[1]

§ 3. What then are the duties that we owe to our fellow-men—so far as they do not seem to come under the head of Justice more properly than Benevolence? Perhaps the mere enumeration of them is not difficult. We should all agree that each of us is bound to show kindness to his parents and spouse and children, and to other kinsmen in a less degree: and to those who have rendered services to him, and any others whom he may have admitted to his intimacy and called friends: and to neighbours and to fellow-countrymen more than others: and perhaps we may say to those of our own race more than to black or yellow men, and generally to human beings in proportion to their affinity to ourselves. And to our country as a corporate whole we believe ourselves to owe the greatest sacrifices when occasion calls (but in a lower stage of civilisation this debt is thought to be due rather to one's king or chief): and a similar obligation seems to be recognised, though less definitely and in a less degree, as regards minor corporations of which we are members. And to all men with whom we may be brought into relation we are held to owe slight services, and such as may be rendered without inconvenience: but those who are in distress or urgent need have a claim on us for special kindness. These are generally recognised claims: but we find considerable difficulty and divergence, when we attempt to determine more precisely their extent and relative obligation: and the divergence becomes indefinitely greater when we compare the customs and common opinions now existing among ourselves in respect of such claims, with those of other ages and countries. For example, in earlier ages of society a peculiar sacredness was attached to the tie of hospitality, and claims arising out of it were considered peculiarly stringent: but this has changed as hospitality in the progress of civilisation has become a luxury rather than a necessary, and we do not think that we owe much to a man because we have asked him to dinner. Or again we may take an instance where the alteration is perhaps actually going on—the claims of kindred

---

[1] This question will be further discussed in the concluding chapter of this Book (chap. xiv.).

in respect of bequest. We should now commonly think that a man ought usually to leave his property to his children : but that if he has no children we think he may do what he likes with it, unless any of his brothers or sisters are in poverty, in which case compassion seems to blend with and invigorate the evanescent claim of consanguinity. But in an age not long past a childless man was held to be morally bound to leave his money to his collateral relatives : and thus we are naturally led to conjecture that in the not distant future, any similar obligation to children—unless they are in want or unless their education is not completed—may have vanished out of men's minds. A similar change might be traced in the commonly recognised duty of children to parents.

It may however be urged that this variation of custom is no obstacle to the definition of duty, because we may lay down that the customs of any society ought to be obeyed so long as they are established, just as the laws ought, although both customs and laws may be changed from time to time. And no doubt it is generally expedient to conform to established customs : still, on reflection, we see that it cannot be laid down as an absolute duty. For the cases of Custom and Law are not similar : as in every progressive community there is a regular and settled mode of abrogating laws that are found bad : but customs cannot be thus formally abolished, and we only get rid of them through the refusal of private individuals to obey them ; and therefore it must be sometimes right to do this, if some customs are vexatious and pernicious, as we frequently judge those of antique and alien communities to be. And if we say that customs should generally be obeyed, but that they may be disobeyed when they reach a certain degree of inexpediency, our method seems to resolve itself into Utilitarianism : for we cannot reasonably rest the general obligation upon one principle, and determine its limits and exceptions by another. If the duties above enumerated can be referred to independent and self-evident principles, the limits of each must be implicitly given in the intuition that reveals the principle.

§ 4. In order then to ascertain how far we possess such principles, let us examine in more detail what Common Sense seems to affirm in respect of these duties.

They seem to range themselves under four heads. There are (1) duties arising out of comparatively permanent relationships not voluntarily chosen, such as Kindred and in most cases Citizenship and Neighbourhood: (2) those of similar relationships voluntarily contracted, such as Friendship: (3) those that spring from special services received, or Duties of Gratitude: and (4) those that seem due to special need, or Duties of Pity. This classification is, I think, convenient for discussion: but I cannot profess that it clearly and completely avoids cross divisions; since, for example, the principle of Gratitude is often appealed to as supplying the *rationale* for the duties owed by children to parents. Here, however, we come upon a material disagreement and difficulty in determining the maxim of this species of duty. It would be agreed that children owe to their parents respect and kindness generally, and assistance in case of infirmity or any special need: but it seems doubtful how far this is held by Common Sense to be due on account of the relationship alone, or on account of services rendered during infancy, and how far it is due to cruel or neglectful parents. Most perhaps would say, here and in other cases, that mere nearness of blood constituted a certain claim: but they would find it hard to agree upon its exact force.[1]

But, apart from this, there seems great difference of opinion as to what is due from children to parents who have performed their duty; as, for example, how far obedience is due from a child who is no longer in its parents' guardianship or dependent on them for support:—whether (*e.g.*) a son or a daughter is bound not to oppose a parent's wishes in marrying or choosing a profession. Practically we find that parental control is greater in the case of persons who can enrich their children by testament: still we can hardly take this into consideration in determining the ideal of filial duty: for to this, whatever it may be, the child is thought to be absolutely bound, and not as a *quidproquo* in anticipation of future benefits: and many would hold that a parent had no moral right to

---

[1] It may be said that a child owes gratitude to the authors of its existence. But life alone, apart from any provision for making life happy, seems a boon of doubtful value, and one that scarcely excites gratitude when it was not conferred from any regard for the recipient.

disinherit a child, except as a penalty for a transgression of duty.

And this leads to what we may conveniently examine next, the duty of parents to children. This too we might partly classify under a different head, viz. that of duties arising out of special needs: for no doubt children are naturally objects of compassion, on account of their helplessness, to others besides their parents. But on the latter they have a claim of a different kind, springing from the universally recognised duty of not causing pain or any harm to other human beings, directly or indirectly, except in the way of deserved punishment: for the parent, being the cause of the child's existing in a helpless condition, would be indirectly the cause of the suffering and death that would result to it if neglected. Still this does not seem an adequate explanation of parental duty, as recognised by Common Sense. For we commonly blame a parent who leaves his children entirely to the care of others, even if he makes ample provision for their being nourished and trained up to the time at which they can support themselves by their own labour. We think that he owes them affection (as far as this can be said to be a duty) and the tender and watchful care that naturally springs from affection : and, if he can afford it, somewhat more than the necessary minimum of food, clothing, and education. Still it does not seem clear how far beyond this he is bound to go. It is easy to say broadly that he ought to promote his children's happiness by all means in his power: and no doubt it is natural for a good parent to find his own best happiness in his children's, and we are disposed to blame any one who markedly prefers his own interest to theirs : still it seems unreasonable that he should purchase a small increase of their happiness by a great sacrifice of his own : and moreover there are other worthy and noble ends which may (and do) come into competition with this. To take instances of actual occurrence: one parent is led to give up some important and valuable work, which perhaps no one else can or will do, in order to leave his children a little more wealth : another brings them to the verge of starvation in order to perfect an invention or prosecute scientific researches. We seem to condemn either extreme : yet what clear and accepted principle can be stated for determining the true mean ?

Again, as we have seen, some think that a parent has no right to bequeath his inheritance away from his children, unless they have been undutiful: and in some states this is even forbidden by law.   Others, however, hold that children as such have no claims to their parents' wealth : but only if there is a tacit understanding that they will succeed to it, or, at any rate, if they have been reared in such habits of life and social relations as will render it difficult and painful for them to live without inherited wealth.

It would be tedious to go in detail through all the degrees of consanguinity, as it is clear that our conception of the mutual duties of kinsmen becomes vaguer as the kinship becomes more remote.   Among children of the same parents, brought up together, affection of more or less strength grows up so naturally and commonly, that we regard those who feel no affection for their brothers and sisters with a certain aversion and moral contempt, as somewhat inhuman : and we think that in any case the services and kind acts which naturally spring from affection ought to be rendered to some extent; but the extent seems quite undefined.   And even towards remoter kinsmen we think that a certain flow of kindly feeling will attend the representation of consanguinity in men of good dispositions.   Some indeed still think that cousins have a moral right to a man's inheritance in default of nearer heirs, and to assistance in any need · but it seems equally common to hold that they can at most claim to be selected *ceteris paribus* as the recipients of bounty, and that an unpromising cousin should not be preferred to a promising stranger.

§ 5. I have placed Neighbourhood along with Kindred among the relations out of which a certain claim for mutual services is thought to spring.   However, no one perhaps would say that mere local juxtaposition is in itself a ground of duties: it seems rather that neighbours naturally feel more sympathy with one another than with strangers, as the tie of common humanity is strengthened even by such conjunction and mutual association as mere neighbourhood (without co-operation or friendship) may involve, and a man in whom this effect is not produced is thought more or less inhuman.   And so in large towns where this mutual sympathy does not so naturally grow up (for all the townsmen are in a sense neighbours, and one cannot easily sympathise with each individual in a multitude), the tie of neighbourhood is felt to be relaxed, and neighbour only claims from neighbour, as the nearest man, what one man may claim from another. For there are some services, slight in ordinary times but greater in the case of exceptional need, which any man is thought to have a right to ask from any other : so that a comparatively trifling circumstance may easily give a special direction to this general claim, and make it seem reasonable that the service should be asked from one person rather than another. Thus any degree of kinship seems to have this effect (since the representation of this tends to produce a feeling of union and consequent sympathy), and so even the fact of belonging to the same province, as creating a slight probability of community of origin ; and again similarities of various kinds, as one sympathises more easily with one's like, and so persons naturally seek aid in distress from those of the same age, or sex, or rank, or profession. The duty of neighbourhood seems therefore only a particular application of the duty of general benevolence or humanity. And the claim of fellow-countrymen is of the same kind : that is, if they are taken as individuals ; for one's relation to one's country as a whole is thought to be of a different kind, and to involve much more stringent obligations.

Still the duties of Patriotism are difficult to formulate. For the mere obedience to the laws of a country which morality requires from all its inhabitants seems to come under another head : and aliens are equally bound to this. And in the case of most social functions which men undertake, patriotism is at least not a prominent nor indispensable motive : for they undertake them primarily for the sake of payment ; and having undertaken them, are bound by Justice and Good Faith to perform them adequately. However, if any of the functions of Government are unpaid, we consider that men exhibit patriotism in performing them : for though it is plausible to say that they get their payment in social distinction, still on reflection this view does not appear to be quite appropriate ; since social distinction is intended to express feelings of honour and respect, and we cannot properly render these as part of a bargain, but only as a tribute paid to virtue or excellence of some kind. But how far any individual is bound to undertake such functions is not quite clear : and the question seems generally decided by considerations of expediency,—except in so far as duties of this kind devolve, legally or constitutionally, upon all the citizens in a free country, as is ordinarily the case to some extent. Among these the duty of fighting the national enemies is prominent in many countries : and even where this function has become a salaried and voluntarily adopted profession, it is often felt to be in a special sense the ' service of one's country,' and we think it at least desirable and best that it should be performed with feelings of patriotism : as we find it somewhat degrading and repulsive that a man should slaughter his fellow-men for hire. And in great crises of national existence the affection of Patriotism is naturally intensified : and even in ordinary times we praise a man who renders services to his country over and above the common duties of citizenship. But whether a citizen is at any time morally bound to more than certain legally or constitutionally determined duties, does not seem to be clear : nor, again, is there general agreement on the question whether by voluntary expatriation [1] he can rightfully relieve himself of all moral obligations to the community in which he was born.

Nor, finally, does there seem to be any *consensus* as to what each man owes to his fellow-men, as such. The Utilitarian doctrine, as we have seen, is that each man ought to consider the happiness of any other as *theoretically* of equal importance with his own, and only of less importance *practically*, in so far as he is better able to realise the latter. And it seems to me difficult to say decidedly that this is *not* the principle of general Benevolence, as recognised by the common sense of mankind. But it must be admitted that there is also current a lower and narrower estimate of the services that we are held to be strictly bound to render to our fellow-

---

[1] In 1868 it was affirmed, in an Act passed by the Congress of the United States, that "the right of expatriation is a natural and inherent right of all people." I do not know how far this would be taken to imply that a man has a moral right to leave his country whenever he finds it convenient—provided no claims except those of Patriotism retain him there. But if it was intended to imply this, I think the statement would not be accepted in Europe without important limitations : though I cannot state any generally accepted principle from which such limitations could be clearly deduced.

men generally. This lower view seems to recognise (1)—as was before noticed—a negative duty to abstain from causing pain or harm to any of our fellow-men, except in the way of deserved punishment; to which we may add, as an immediate corollary, the duty of making reparation for any harm that we may have done them:[1] and (2) a positive duty to render, when occasion offers, such services as require either no sacrifice on our part, or at least one very much less in importance than the service rendered. Further, a general obligation of being 'useful to society' by some kind of systematic work is vaguely recognised; rich persons who are manifest drones incur some degree of censure from the majority of thoughtful persons. Beyond this somewhat indefinite limit of Duty extends the Virtue of Benevolence without limit: for excess is not thought to be possible in doing good to others, nor in the disposition to do it, unless it leads us to neglect definite duties.

Under the notion of Benevolence as just defined, the minor rules of Gentleness, Politeness, Courtesy, etc. may be brought, in so far as they prescribe the expression of general goodwill and abstinence from anything that may cause pain to others in conversation and social demeanour. There is, however, an important part of Politeness which it may be well to notice and discuss separately; the duty, namely, of showing marks of Reverence to those to whom they are properly due.

Reverence we may define as the feeling which accompanies the recognition of Superiority or Worth in others. It does not seem to be necessarily in itself benevolent, though often accompanied by some degree of love. But its ethical characteristics seem analogous to those of benevolent affection, in so far as, while it is not a feeling directly under the control of the will, we yet expect it under certain circumstances and morally dislike its absence, and perhaps commonly consider the expression of it to be sometimes a duty, even when the feeling itself is absent.

Still, as to this latter duty of expressing reverence, there

---

[1] How far we are bound to make reparation when the harm is involuntary, and such as could not have been prevented by ordinary care on our part, is not clear: but it will be convenient to defer the consideration of this till the next chapter (§ 5): as the whole of this department of duty is more commonly placed under the head of Justice.

seems to be great divergence of opinion.   For the feeling seems
to be naturally excited by all kinds of superiority,—not merely
moral and intellectual excellences, but also superiorities of
rank and position : and indeed in the common behaviour
of men it is to the latter that it is more regularly and
formally rendered.   And yet, again, it is commonly said
that Reverence is more properly due to the former, as being
more real and intrinsic superiorities : and many think that
to show any reverence to men of rank and position rather
than to others is servile and degrading : and some even
dislike the marks of respect which in most countries are
exacted by official superiors from their subordinates, saying
that obedience legally defined is all that is properly owed in
this relation.

A more serious difficulty of a somewhat similar kind arises
when we consider how far it is a duty to cultivate the affection
of Loyalty : meaning by this term—which is used in various
senses—the affection that is normally felt by a well-disposed
servant or official subordinate towards a good master or official
superior.   On the one hand it is widely thought that the duties
of obedience which belong to these relations will be better
performed if affection enters into the motive, no less than the
duties of the family relations : but in the former case it seems
to be a tenable view that the habits of orderliness and good
faith—ungrudging obedience to law and ungrudging fulfilment
of contract—will ordinarily suffice, without personal affection;
and, on the other hand, a disposition to obey superiors, beyond
the limits of their legal or contractual rights to issue commands,
may easily be mischievous in its effects, if the superiors are
ill-disposed.   In the case of a wise and good superior it is,
indeed, clearly advantageous that inferiors should be disposed
to obey beyond these limits ; but it is not therefore clear that
this disposition is one which it should be made a duty to
cultivate beyond the degree in which it results spontaneously
from a sense of the superior's goodness and wisdom.   Nor do
I think that any decided enunciation of duty on this point
can be extracted from Common Sense.

§ 6. We have next to consider the duties of Affection that
arise out of relationships voluntarily assumed.   Of these the
most important is the Conjugal Relation.   And here we may

begin by asking whether it be the duty of human beings generally to enter into this relation. It is no doubt normal to do so, and most persons are prompted to it by strong desires : but in so far as it can be said to be prescribed by Common Sense, it does not seem an independent duty, but derivative from and subordinate to the general maxims of Prudence and Benevolence.[1] And in all modern civilised societies, law and custom leave the conjugal union perfectly optional : but the conditions under which it may be formed, and to a certain extent the mutual rights and duties arising out of it, are carefully laid down by law ; and it is widely thought that this department of law more than others ought to be governed by independent moral principles, and to protect, as it were, by an outer barrier, the kind of relation which morality prescribes. If we ask what these principles are, Common Sense—in modern European communities—seems to answer that the marriage union ought to be (1) exclusively monogamic, (2) at least designed to be permanent, and (3) not within certain degrees of consanguinity. I do not, however, think that any of these propositions can on reflection be maintained to be self-evident. Even against incest we seem to have rather an intense sentiment than a clear intuition ; and it is generally recognised that the prohibition of all but monogamic unions can only be rationally maintained on utilitarian grounds.[2] As regards the permanence of the marriage-contract all would no doubt agree that fidelity is admirable in all affections, and especially in so close and intimate a relation as the conjugal : but we cannot tell *a priori* how far it is possible to prevent decay of love in all cases : and it is certainly not self-evident that the conjugal

---

[1] I raise this question, because if the rule of 'living according to Nature' were really adopted as a first principle, in any ordinary meaning of the term 'nature,' it would certainly seem to be the duty of all normal human beings to enter into conjugal relations : but just this instance seems to show that the principle is not accepted by Common Sense. See Book i. chap. vi. § 2.

[2] The moral necessity of prohibiting polygamy is sometimes put forward as an immediate inference from the equality of the numbers of the two sexes. This argument, however, seems to require the assumption that all men and women ought to marry : but this scarcely any one will expressly affirm : and actually considerable numbers remain unmarried, and there is no reason to believe that in countries where polygamy is allowed, paucity of supply has ever made it practically difficult for any man to find a mate.

relation ought to be maintained when love has ceased ; nor that if the parties have separated by mutual consent they ought to be prohibited from forming fresh unions.   In so far as we are convinced of the rightness of this regulation, it is always, I think, from a consideration of the generally mischievous consequences that would ensue if it were relaxed.

Further, in considering the evils on the opposite side we are led to see that there is no little difference of opinion among moral persons as to the kind of feeling which is morally indispensable to this relation.   For some would say that marriage without intense and exclusive affection is degrading even though sanctioned by law : while others would consider this a mere matter of taste, or at least of prudence, provided there was no mutual deception : and between these two views we might insert several different shades of opinion.

Nor, again, is there agreement as to the external duties arising out of the relationship.   For all would lay down conjugal fidelity, and mutual assistance (according to the customary division of labour between men and women—unless this should be modified by mutual agreement).   But beyond this we find divergence : for some state that " the marriage contract binds each party, whenever individual gratification is concerned, to prefer the happiness of the other party to its own [1] ": while others would say that this degree of unselfishness is certainly admirable, but as a mere matter of duty it is enough if each considers the other's happiness equally with his (or her) own.   And as to the powers and liberties that ought to be allowed to the wife, and the obedience due from her to the husband—I need scarcely at the present time (1874) waste space in proving that there is no *consensus* of moral opinion.

§ 7. The conjugal relation is, in its origin, of free choice, but when it has once been formed, the duties of affection that arise out of it are commonly thought to be analogous to those arising out of relations of consanguinity.   It therefore holds an intermediate position between these latter, and ordinary friendships, partnerships, and associations, which men are equally free to make and to dissolve.   Now most associations

---

[1] Cf. Wayland, *Elements of Moral Science*, Book ii. part ii. class 2, § 2.

that men form are for certain definite ends, determined by express contract or tacit understanding: accordingly the duty arising out of them is merely that of fidelity to such contract or understanding, which will be considered later under the heads of Justice and Good Faith. But this does not seem to be the case with what in a strict sense of the term are called Friendships [1]: for although Friendship frequently arises among persons associated for other ends, yet the relation is always conceived to have its end in itself, and to be formed primarily for the development of mutual affection between the friends, and the pleasure which attends this. Still, it is thought that when such an affection has once been formed it creates mutual duties which did not previously exist: we have therefore to inquire how far this is the case, and on what principles these can be determined.

Now here a new kind of difficulty has to be added to those which we have already found in attempting to formulate Common Sense. For we find some who say that, as it is essential to Friendship that the mutual kindly feeling, and the services springing from it, should be spontaneous and unforced, neither the one nor the other should be imposed as a duty ; and, in short, that this department of life should be fenced from the intrusion of moral precepts, and left to the free play of natural instinct. And this doctrine all would perhaps admit to a certain extent : as, indeed, we have accepted it with regard to all the deeper flow and finer expression of feeling even in the domestic relations : for it seemed pedantic and futile to prescribe rules for this, or even (though we naturally admire and praise any not ungraceful exhibition of intense and genuine affection) to delineate an ideal of excellence for all to aim at. Still, there seemed to be an important sphere of strict duty—however hard to define—in the relations of children to parents, etc., and even in the case of friendship it seems contrary to common sense to recognise no such sphere ; as it not unfrequently occurs to us to judge that one friend has behaved wrongly to another, and to speak as if there were a clearly cognisable code of behaviour in such relations.

---

[1] I use the term here to imply a mutual affection more intense than the kindly feeling which a moral man desires to feel towards all persons with whom he is brought into continual social relations, through business or otherwise.

Perhaps, however, we may say that all clear cases of wrong conduct towards friends come under the general formula of breach of understanding. Friends not unfrequently make definite promises of service, but we need not consider these, as their violation is prohibited by a different and clearer moral rule. But further, as all love is understood to include [1] a desire for the happiness of its object, the profession of friendship seems to bind one to seek this happiness to an extent proportionate to such profession. Now common benevolence (cf. *ante*, § 5) prescribes at least that we should render to other men such services as we can render without any sacrifice, or with a sacrifice so trifling as to be quite out of proportion to the service rendered. And since the profession of friendship— though the term is used to include affections of various degree— must imply a greater interest in one's friend's happiness than in that of men in general, it must announce a willingness to make more or less considerable sacrifices for him, if occasion offers. If then we decline to make such sacrifices, we do wrong by failing to fulfil natural and legitimate expectations. So far there seems no source of difficulty except the indefiniteness inevitably arising from the wide range of meanings covered by the term Friendship. But further questions arise in consequence of the changes of feeling to which human nature is liable: first, whether it is our duty to resist such changes as much as we can; and secondly, whether if this effort fails, and love diminishes or departs, we ought still to maintain a disposition to render services corresponding to our past affection. And on these points there does not seem to be agreement among moral and refined persons. For, on the one hand, it is natural to us to admire fidelity in friendship and stability of affections, and we commonly regard these as most important excellences of character: and so it seems strange if we are not to aim at these as at all other excellences, as none more naturally stir us to imitation. And hence many would be prepared to lay down that we ought not to withdraw affection once given, unless the friend behaves ill: while some would say that even in this case we ought not to break the friendship unless the crime is very great. Yet, on the other hand, we

---

[1] It was before observed that this is only one—and not always the most prominent—element of the whole emotional state which we call love.

feel that such affection as is produced by deliberate effort of will is but a poor substitute for that which springs spontaneously, and most refined persons would reject such a boon: while, again, to conceal the change of feeling seems insincere and hypocritical.

But as for services, a refined person would not accept such from a former friend who no longer loves him: unless in extreme need, when any kind of tie is, as it were, invigorated by the already strong claim which common humanity gives each man upon all others. Perhaps, therefore, there cannot be a duty to offer such services in any case, when the need is not extreme. Though this inference is not quite clear: for in relations of affection we often praise one party for offering what we rather blame the other for accepting. But it seems that delicate questions of this kind are more naturally referred to canons of good taste and refined feeling than of morality proper: or at least only included in the scope of morality in so far as we have a general duty to cultivate good taste and refinement of feeling, like other excellences.

On the whole, then, we may say that the chief difficulties in determining the moral obligations of friendship arise (1) from the indefiniteness of the tacit understanding implied in the relation, and (2) from the disagreement which we find as to the extent to which Fidelity is a positive duty. It may be observed that the latter difficulty is especially prominent in respect of those intimacies between persons of different sex which precede and prepare the way for marriage.

§ 8. I pass now to the third head, Gratitude. It has been already observed that the obligation of children to parents is sometimes based upon this: and in other affectionate relationships it commonly blends with and much strengthens the claims that are thought to arise out of the relations themselves; though none of the duties that we have discussed seem referable entirely to gratitude. But where gratitude is due, the obligation is especially clear and simple. Indeed the duty of requiting benefits seems to be recognised wherever morality extends; and Intuitionists have justly pointed to this recognition as an instance of a truly universal intuition. Still, though the general force of the obligation is not open to doubt (except of the sweeping and abstract kind with which we have not here to deal), its nature and extent are by no means equally clear.

In the first place, it may be asked whether we are only bound to repay services, or whether we owe the special affection called Gratitude; which seems generally to combine kindly feeling and eagerness to requite with some sort of emotional recognition of superiority, as the giver of benefits is in a position of superiority to the receiver. On the one hand we seem to think that, in so far as any affection can possibly be a duty, kindly feeling towards benefactors must be such: and yet to persons of a certain temperament this feeling is often peculiarly hard to attain, owing to their dislike of the position of inferiority; and this again we consider a right feeling to a certain extent, and call it 'independence' or 'proper pride'; but this feeling and the effusion of gratitude do not easily mix, and the moralist finds it difficult to recommend a proper combination of the two. Perhaps it makes a great difference whether the service be lovingly done: as in this case it seems inhuman that there should be no response of affection: whereas if the benefit be coldly given, the mere recognition of the obligation and settled disposition to repay it seem to suffice. And 'independence' alone would prompt a man to repay the benefit in order to escape from the burden of obligation. But it seems doubtful whether in any case we are morally satisfied with this as the sole motive.

It is partly this impatience of obligation which makes a man desirous of giving as requital more than he has received; for otherwise his benefactor has still the superiority of having taken the initiative. But also the worthier motive of affection urges us in the same direction: and here, as in other affectionate services, we do not like too exact a measure of duty; a certain excess falling short of extravagance seems to be what we admire and praise. In so far, however, as conflict of claims makes it needful to be exact, we think perhaps that an equal return is what the duty of gratitude requires, or rather willingness to make such a return, if it be required, and if it is in our power to make it without neglecting prior claims. For we do not think it obligatory to requite services in all cases, even if it be in our power to do so, if the benefactor appear to be sufficiently supplied with the means of happiness: but if he either demand it or obviously stand in need of it, we think it ungrateful not to make an equal return. But when we try to define this notion of 'equal return,' obscurity and divergence begin. For (apart from the difficulty of comparing different kinds of services where we cannot make repayment in kind) Equality has two distinct meanings, according as we consider the effort made by the benefactor, or the service rendered to the benefited. Now perhaps if either of these be great, the gratitude is naturally strong: for the apprehension of great earnestness in another to serve us tends to draw from us a proportionate response of affection : and any great pleasure or relief from pain naturally produces a corresponding emotion of thankfulness to the man who has voluntarily caused this, even though his effort may have been slight. And hence it has been suggested, that in proportioning the dues of gratitude we ought to take whichever of the two considerations will give the highest estimate. But this does not seem in accordance with Common Sense : for the benefit may be altogether unacceptable, and it is hard to bind us to repay in full every well-meant blundering effort to serve us ; though we feel vaguely that some return should be made even for this. And though it is more plausible to say that we ought to requite an accepted service without weighing the amount of our benefactor's sacrifice, still when we take extreme cases the rule seems not to be valid : *e.g.* if a poor man sees a rich one drowning and pulls him out of the water, we do not think that the latter is bound to give as a reward what he would have been willing to give for his life. Still, we should think him niggardly if he only gave his preserver half-a-crown : which might, however, be profuse repayment for the cost of the exertion. Something between the two seems to suit our moral taste : but I find no clear accepted principle upon which the amount can be decided.

The last claim to be considered is that of Special Need. This has been substantially stated already, in investigating the obligation of General Benevolence or Common Humanity. For it was said that we owe to all men such services as we can render by a sacrifice or effort small in comparison with the service : and hence, in proportion as the needs of other men present themselves as urgent, we recognise the duty of relieving them out of our superfluity. But I have thought it right to notice the duty separately, because we are commonly prompted to fulfil it by the specific emotion of Pity or Compassion. Here, again, there seems a doubt how far it is good to foster and encourage this emotion—as distinct from the practical habit of rendering prompt aid and succour in distress, whenever such succour is judged to be right. On the one hand, the emotional impulse tends to make the action of relieving need not only easier to the agent, but more graceful and pleasing: on the other hand, it is generally recognised that mistaken pity is more likely to lead us astray than—*e.g.*—mistaken gratitude : as it is more liable to interfere dangerously with the infliction of penalties required for the maintenance of social order, or with the operation of motives to industry and thrift, necessary for economic well-being.

And when—to guard against the last-mentioned danger— we try to define the external duty of relieving want, we find ourselves face to face with what is no mere problem of the closet, but a serious practical perplexity to most moral persons at the present day. For many ask whether it is not our duty to refrain from all superfluous indulgences, until we have removed the misery and want that exist around us, as far as they are removable by money. And in answering this question Common Sense seems to be inevitably led to a consideration of the economic consequences of attempting—either by taxation and public expenditure, or by the voluntary gifts of private persons—to provide a sufficient income for all needy members of the community ; and is thus gradually brought to substitute for the Intuitional method of dealing with problems of this kind a different procedure, having at least much affinity with the Utilitarian method.[1]

In conclusion, then, we must admit that while we find a number of broad and more or less indefinite rules unhesitatingly laid down by Common Sense in this department of duty, it is difficult or impossible to extract from them, so far as they are commonly accepted, any clear and precise principles for determining the extent of the duty in any case. And yet, as we saw, such particular principles of distribution of the services to which good-will prompts seem to be required for

[1] See Book iv. chap. iii. § 3.

the perfection of practice no less than for theoretical completeness; in so far as the duties which we have been considering
are liable to come into apparent conflict with each other and
with other prescriptions of the moral code.

In reply it may perhaps be contended that if we are
seeking exactness in the determination of duty, we have begun
by examining the wrong notion: that, in short, we ought to
have examined Justice rather than Benevolence.   It may be
admitted that we cannot find as much exactness as we sometimes practically need, by merely considering the common
conceptions of the duties to which men are prompted by
natural affections; but it may still be maintained that we shall
at any rate find such exactness adequately provided for under
the head of Justice.   This contention I will proceed to examine
in the next chapter.

NOTE.—It should be borne in mind throughout the discussion carried
on in this and the next six chapters that what we are primarily endeavouring to ascertain is not true morality but the morality of Common Sense:
so that if any moral proposition is admitted to be paradoxical, the admission excludes it,—not as being necessarily false, but as being not what
Common Sense holds.

CHAPTER V

JUSTICE

§ 1. WE have seen that in delineating the outline of duty, as intuitively recognised, we have to attempt to give to common terms a definite and precise meaning. This process of definition always requires some reflection and care, and is sometimes one of considerable difficulty. But there is no case where the difficulty is greater, or the result more disputed, than when we try to define Justice.

Before making the attempt, it may be as well to remind the reader what it is that we have to do. We have not to inquire into the derivation of the notion of Justice, as we are not now studying the history of our ethical thought, but its actual condition. Nor can we profess to furnish a definition which will correspond to every part of the common usage of the term; for many persons are undoubtedly vague and loose in their application of current moral notions. But it is an assumption of the Intuitional method [1] that the term 'justice' denotes a quality which it is ultimately desirable to realise in the conduct and social relations of men; and that a definition may be given of this which will be accepted by all competent judges as presenting, in a clear and explicit form, what they have always meant by the term, though perhaps implicitly and vaguely. In seeking such a definition we may, so to speak, clip the ragged edge of common usage, but we must not make excision of any considerable portion.[2]

---

[1] How far an independent principle of Justice is required for the Utilitarian method will be hereafter considered. (Book iv. chap. i.)

[2] Aristotle, in expounding the virtue of Δικαιοσύνη, which corresponds to our Justice, notices that the word has two meanings; in the wider of which it

Perhaps the first point that strikes us when we reflect upon our notion of Justice is its connexion with Law. There is no doubt that just conduct is to a great extent determined by Law, and in certain applications the two terms seem interchangeable. Thus we speak indifferently of 'Law Courts' and 'Courts of Justice,' and when a private citizen demands Justice, or his just rights, he commonly means to demand that Law should be carried into effect. Still reflection shows that we do not mean by Justice merely conformity to Law. For, first, we do not always call the violators of law unjust, but only of some Laws: not, for example, duellists or gamblers. And secondly, we often judge that Law as it exists does not completely realise Justice; our notion of Justice furnishes a standard with which we compare actual laws, and pronounce them just or unjust. And, thirdly, there is a part of just conduct which lies outside the sphere even of Law as it ought to be; for example, we think that a father may be just or unjust to his children in matters where the law leaves (and ought to leave) him free.

We must then distinguish Justice from what has been called the virtue or duty of Order, or Law-observance: and perhaps, if we examine the points of divergence just mentioned, we shall be led to the true definition of Justice.

Let us therefore first ask, Of what kind of laws is the observance generally thought to be a realisation of Justice? In most cases they might be described as laws which define and secure the interests of assignable individuals. But this description is not complete, as Justice is admittedly concerned in the apportionment of adequate punishment to each offender; though we should not say that a man had an interest in the adequacy of his punishment. Let us say, then, that the laws in which Justice is or ought to be realised, are laws which distribute and allot to individuals either objects of desire,

---

includes in a manner all Virtue, or at any rate the social side or aspect of Virtue generally. The word 'Justice' does not appear to be used in English in this comprehensive manner (except occasionally in religious writings, from the influence of the Greek word as used in the New Testament): although the verb "to justify" seems to have this width of meaning; for when I say that one is "justified" in doing so and so, I mean no more than that such conduct is right for him. In the present discussion, at any rate, I have confined myself to the more precise signification of the term.

liberties and privileges, or burdens and restraints, or even pains as such. These latter, however, are only allotted by law to persons who have broken other laws. And as all law is enforced by penalties, we see how the administration of law generally may be viewed as the administration of Justice, in accordance with this definition: not because all laws are primarily and in their first intention distributive, but because the execution of law generally involves the due allotment of pains and losses and restraints to the persons who violate it. Or, more precisely, we should say that this legal distribution *ought* to realise Justice, for we have seen that it may fail to do so. We have next to ask, therefore, What conditions must laws fulfil in order that they may be just in their distributive effects?

Here, however, it may seem that we are transgressing the limit which divides Ethics from Politics: for Ethics is primarily concerned with the rules which ought to govern the private conduct of individuals; and it is commonly thought that private persons ought to obey even laws that they regard as unjust, if established by lawful authority. Still, this is doubted in the case of laws that seem extremely unjust: as (*e.g.*) the Fugitive Slave law in the United States before the rebellion. At any rate it seems desirable that we should here digress somewhat into political discussion; partly in order to elucidate the notion of Justice, which seems to be essentially the same in both regions, and partly because it is of great practical importance to individuals, in regulating private conduct beyond the range of Law-observance, to know whether the laws and established order of the society in which they live are just or unjust.

Now perhaps the most obvious and commonly recognised characteristic of just laws is that they are Equal: and in some departments of legislation, at least, the common notion of Justice seems to be exhaustively expressed by that of Equality. It is commonly thought, for example, that a system of taxation would be perfectly just if it imposed exactly equal burdens upon all:[1] and though this notion of 'equal burden' is itself somewhat difficult to define with the precision required for

---

[1] I ought to say that, in my view, this only applies to taxes in the narrower sense in which they are distinguished from payments for services received by individuals from Government. In the case of these latter, I conceive that Justice

practical application, still we may say that Justice here is thought to resolve itself into a kind of equality. However, we cannot affirm generally that all laws ought to affect all persons equally, for this would leave no place for any laws allotting special privileges and burdens to special classes of the community; but we do not think all such laws necessarily unjust: *e.g.* we think it not unjust that only persons appointed in a certain way should share in legislation, and that men should be forced to fight for their country but not women. Hence some have said that the only sense in which justice requires a law to be equal is that its execution must affect equally all the individuals belonging to any of the classes specified in the law. And no doubt this rule excludes a very real kind of injustice: it is of the highest importance that judges and administrators should never be persuaded by money or otherwise to show 'respect of persons.' So much equality, however, is involved in the very notion of a law, if it be couched in general terms : and it is plain that laws may be equally executed and yet unjust: for example, we should consider a law unjust which compelled only red-haired men to serve in the army, even though it were applied with the strictest impartiality to all red-haired men. We must therefore conclude, that, in laying down the law no less than in carrying it out, all inequality [1] affecting the interests of individuals which appears arbitrary, and for which no sufficient

is rather held to lie in duly proportioning payment to amount of service received. Some persons have held that all payments made to Government ought to be determined on this principle : and this view seems to me to be consistent with the individualistic ideal of political order, which I shall presently examine : but, as I have elsewhere tried to show (*Princ. of Pol. Econ.* Book iii. chap. viii.), there is an important department of Governmental expenditure to which this principle is not applicable.

[1] It may be well to notice a case in which the very equality of application, which is, as has been said, implied in the mere idea of a law couched in general terms, is felt to be unjust. This is the case where the words of a statute, either from being carelessly drawn, or on account of the inevitable defects of even the most precise terminology, include (or exclude) persons and circumstances which are clearly not included in (or excluded from) the real intent and purpose of the law. In this case a particular decision, strictly in accordance with a law which generally considered is just, may cause extreme injustice : and so the difference between actual Law and Justice is sharply brought out. Still we cannot in this way obtain principles for judging generally of the justice of laws.

reason can be given, is held to be unjust. But we have still to ask, what kind of reasons for inequality Justice admits and from what general principle (or principles) all such reasons are to be deduced?

§ 2. Perhaps we shall find it easier to answer this question, if we examine the notion of Justice as applied to that part of private conduct which lies beyond the sphere of law. Here, again, we may observe that the notion of Justice always involves allotment of something considered as advantageous or disadvantageous: whether it be money or other material means of happiness; or praise, or affection, or other immaterial good, or some merited pain or loss. Hence I should answer the question raised in the preceding chapter (§ 3), as to the classification of the duties there discussed under the heads of Justice and Benevolence respectively, by saying that the fulfilment of any duty of the affections, considered by itself, does not exemplify Justice: but that when we come to compare the obligations arising out of different affectionate relations, and to consider the right allotment of love and kind services, the notion of Justice becomes applicable. In order to arrange this allotment properly we have to inquire what is Just. What then do we mean by a just man in matters where law-observance does not enter? It is natural to reply that we mean an impartial man, one who seeks with equal care to satisfy all claims which he recognises as valid and does not let himself be unduly influenced by personal preferences. And this seems an adequate account of the virtue of justice so far as we consider it merely subjectively, and independently of the intellectual insight required for the realisation of objective justice in action: if we neglect to give due consideration to any claim which we regard as reasonable, our action cannot be just in intention. This definition suffices to exclude wilful injustice: but it is obvious that it does not give us a sufficient criterion of just acts, any more than the absence of arbitrary inequality was found to be a sufficient criterion of just laws.[1] We want to know what are reasonable claims.

[1] It should be observed that we cannot even say, in treating of the private conduct of individuals, that *all* arbitrary inequality is recognised as unjust: it would not be commonly thought unjust in a rich bachelor with no near relatives to leave the bulk of his property in providing pensions exclusively for indigent red-haired men, however unreasonable and capricious the choice might appear.

Well, of these the most important—apart from the claims discussed in the preceding chapter—seems to be that resulting from contract. This is to a certain extent enforced by law : but it is clear to us that a just man will keep engagements generally, even when there may be no legal penalty attached to their violation. The exact definition of this duty, and its commonly admitted qualifications, will be discussed in the next chapter : but of its general bindingness Common Sense has no doubt.

Further, we include under the idea of binding engagements not merely verbal promises, but also what are called ' implied contracts ' or ' tacit understandings.' But this latter term is a difficult one to keep precise : and, in fact, is often used to include not only the case where A has in some way positively implied a pledge to B, but also the case where B has certain expectations of which A is aware. Here, however, the obligation is not so clear : for it would hardly be said that a man is bound to dispel all erroneous expectations that he may know to be formed respecting his conduct, at the risk of being required to fulfil them. Still, if the expectation was such as most persons would form under the circumstances, there seems to be some sort of moral obligation to fulfil it, if it does not conflict with other duties, though the obligation seems less definite and stringent than that arising out of contract. Indeed I think we may say that Justice is generally, though somewhat vaguely, held to prescribe the fulfilment of all such expectations (of services, etc.) as arise naturally and normally out of the relations, voluntary or involuntary, in which we stand towards other human beings. But the discussions in the preceding chapter have shown the difficulty of defining even those duties of this kind which, in an indefinite form, seemed certain and indisputable : while others are only defined by customs which to reflection appear arbitrary. And though while these customs persist, the expectations springing from them are in a certain sense natural, so that a just man seems to be under a kind of obligation to fulfil them, this obligation cannot be regarded as clear or complete, for two reasons that were given in the last chapter ; first, because customs are continually varying, and as long as any one is in a state of variation, growing or decaying, the validity of the customary claim is obviously doubtful ; and secondly, because it does not seem right that an irrational and inexpedient custom should last for ever, and yet it can only be abolished by being " more honoured in the breach than in the observance."

This line of reflection therefore has landed us in a real perplexity respecting the department of duty which we are at present examining. Justice is something that we conceive to be intrinsically capable of perfectly definite determination : a scrupulously just man, we think, must be very exact and precise in his conduct. But when we consider that part of Justice which consists in satisfying such natural and customary claims as arise independently of contract, it seems impossible to estimate these claims with any exactness. The attempt to map out the region of Justice reveals to us a sort of margin or dim borderland, tenanted by expectations which are not quite claims and with regard to which we do not feel sure whether Justice does or does not require us to satisfy them. For the ordinary actions of men proceed on the expectation that the future will resemble the past : hence it seems natural to expect that any particular man will do as others do in similar circumstances, and, still more, that he will continue to do whatever he has hitherto been in the habit of doing ; accordingly his fellow-men are inclined to think themselves wronged by his suddenly omitting any customary or habitual act, if the omission causes them loss or inconvenience.[1] On the other hand, if a man has given no pledge to maintain a custom or habit, it seems hard that he should be bound by the unwarranted expectations of others. In this perplexity, common sense often appears to decide differently cases similar in all respects, except in the quantity of disappointment caused by the change. For instance, if a poor man were to leave one tradesman and deal with another because the first had turned Quaker, we should hardly call it an act of injustice, however unreasonable we might think it : but if a rich country gentleman were to act similarly towards a poor neighbour, many persons would say that it was unjust persecution.

The difficulty just pointed out extends equally to the duties of kindness—even to the specially stringent and sacred duties

[1] It may be observed that sometimes claims generated in this way have legal validity ; as when a right of way is established without express permission of the landowner, merely by his continued indulgence.

of the domestic affections and gratitude—discussed in the previous chapter. We cannot get any new principle for settling any conflict that may present itself among such duties, by asking 'what Justice requires of us': the application of the notion of Justice only leads us to view the problem in a new aspect—as a question of the right *distribution* of kind services—it does not help us to solve it. Had we clear and precise intuitive principles for determining the claims (*e.g.*) of parents on children, children on parents, benefactors on the recipients of their benefits, we might say exactly at what point or to what extent the satisfaction of one of these claims ought in justice to be postponed to the satisfaction of another, or to any worthy aim of a different kind: but I know no method of determining a problem of this kind which is not either implicitly utilitarian, or arbitrarily dogmatic, and unsupported by Common Sense.

§ 3. If now we turn again to the political question, from which we diverged, we see that we have obtained from the preceding discussion one of the criteria of the justice of laws which we were seeking—viz. that they must avoid running counter to natural and normal expectations—: but we see at the same time that the criterion cannot be made definite in its application to private conduct, and it is easy to show that there is the same indefiniteness and consequent difficulty in applying it to legislation. For Law itself is a main source of natural expectations; and, since in ordinary times the alterations in law are very small in proportion to the amount unaltered, there is always a natural expectation that the existing laws will be maintained: and although this is, of course, an indefinite and uncertain expectation in a society like ours, where laws are continually being altered by lawful authority, it is sufficient for people in general to rely upon in arranging their concerns, investing their money, choosing their place of abode, their trade and profession, etc. Hence when such expectations are disappointed by a change in the law, the disappointed persons complain of injustice, and it is to some extent admitted that justice requires that they should be compensated for the loss thus incurred. But such expectations are of all degrees of definiteness and importance, and generally extend more widely as they decrease in value, like the ripples made by throwing a stone into a pond, so that it is practically impossible to compensate them all: at the same time, I know no intuitive principle by which we could separate valid claims from invalid, and distinguish injustice from simple hardship.[1]

But even if this difficulty were overcome further reflection must, I think, show that the criterion above given is incomplete or imperfectly stated: otherwise it would appear that no old law could be unjust, since laws that have existed for a long time must create corresponding expectations.   But this is contrary to Common Sense: as we are continually becoming convinced that old laws are unjust (*e.g.* laws establishing slavery): indeed, this continually recurring conviction seems to be one of the great sources of change in the laws of a progressive society.

Perhaps we may say that there are natural expectations which grow up from other elements of the social order, independent of and so possibly conflicting with laws: and that we call rules unjust which go counter to these.   Thus *e.g.* primogeniture appears to many unjust, because all the land-owner's children are brought up in equally luxurious habits, and share equally the paternal care and expenditure, and so the inequality of inheritance seems paradoxical and harsh.   Still, we cannot explain every case in this way: for example, the conviction that slavery is unjust can hardly be traced to anything in the established order of the slave-holding society, but seems to arise in a different way.

The truth is, this notion of ' natural expectations' is worse than indefinite: the ambiguity of the term conceals a fundamental conflict of ideas, which appears more profound and far-reaching in its consequences the more we examine it.   For the word 'natural,' as used in this connexion, covers and conceals the whole chasm between the actual and the ideal— what is and what ought to be.   As we before noticed,[2] the term seems, as ordinarily used, to contain the distinct ideas of (1) the common as opposed to the exceptional, and (2) the original or primitive as contrasted with the result of later

---

[1] This is the case even, as I say, when laws are altered lawfully: still more after any exceptional crisis at which there has occurred a rupture of political order: for then the legal claims arising out of the new order which is thus rooted in disorder conflict with those previously established in a manner which admits of no theoretical solution: it can only be settled by a rough practical compromise.   See next chapter, § 3.

[2] Book i. chap. vi. § 2

conventions and institutions. But it is also used to signify, in more or less indefinite combination with one or other of these meanings, 'what would exist in an ideal state of society.' And it is easy to see how these different meanings have been blended and confounded. For since by 'Nature' men have really meant God, or God viewed in a particular aspect—God, we may say, as known to us in experience—when they have come to conceive a better state of things than that which actually exists, they have not only regarded this ideal state as really exhibiting the Divine purposes more than the actual, and as being so far more 'natural': but they have gone further, and supposed more or less definitely that this ideal state of things must be what God originally created, and that the defects recognisable in what now exists must be due to the deteriorating action of men. But if we dismiss this latter view, as unsupported by historical evidence, we recognise more plainly the contrast and conflict between the other two meanings of 'natural,' and the corresponding discrepancy between the two elements of the common notion of Justice. For, from one point of view, we are disposed to think that the *customary* distribution of rights, goods, and privileges, as well as burdens and pains, is natural and just, and that this ought to be maintained by law, as it usually is: while, from another point of view, we seem to recognise an ideal system of rules of distribution which ought to exist, but perhaps have never yet existed, and we consider laws to be just in proportion as they conform to this ideal. It is the reconciliation between these two views which is the chief problem of political Justice.[1]

On what principles, then, is the ideal to be determined? This is, in fact, the question which has been chiefly in view from the outset of the chapter; but we could not satisfactorily discuss it until we had distinguished the two elements of Justice, as commonly conceived—one conservative of law and custom, and the other tending to reform them. It is on this latter that we shall now concentrate our attention.

When, however, we examine this ideal, as it seems to show

---

[1] It is characteristic of an unprogressive society that in it these two points of view are indistinguishable ; the Jural Ideal absolutely coincides with the Customary, and social perfection is imagined to consist in the perfect observance of a traditional system of rules.

itself in the minds of different men in different ages and countries, we observe various forms of it, which it is important to distinguish.

In the first place, it must be noticed that an ideal constitution of society may be conceived and sought with many other ends in view besides the right distribution of good and evil among the individuals that compose it: as (*e.g.*) with a view to conquest and success in war, or to the development of industry and commerce, or to the highest possible cultivation of the arts and sciences. But any such political ideal as this is beyond the range of our present consideration, as it is not constructed on the basis of our common notion of Justice. Our present question is, Are there any clear principles from which we may work out an ideally just distribution of rights and privileges, burdens and pains, among human beings as such ? There is a wide-spread view, that in order to make society just certain Natural Rights should be conceded to all members of the community, and that positive law should at least embody and protect these, whatever other regulations it may contain : but it is difficult to find in Common Sense any definite agreement in the enumeration of these Natural Rights, still less any clear principles from which they can be systematically deduced.

§ 4. There is, however, one mode of systematising these Rights and bringing them under one principle, which has been maintained by influential thinkers ; and which, though now perhaps somewhat antiquated, is still sufficiently current to deserve careful examination. It has been held that Freedom from interference is really the whole of what human beings, originally and apart from contracts, can be strictly said to *owe* to each other : at any rate, that the protection of this Freedom (including the enforcement of Free Contract) is the sole proper aim of Law, *i.e.* of those rules of mutual behaviour which are maintained by penalties inflicted under the authority of Government. All natural Rights, on this view, may be summed up in the Right to Freedom ; so that the complete and universal establishment of this Right would be the complete realisation of Justice,— the Equality at which Justice is thought to aim being interpreted as Equality of Freedom.

Now when I contemplate this as an abstract formula, though I cannot say that it is self-evident to me as the true fundamental principle of Ideal Law, I admit that it commends itself much to my mind; and I might perhaps persuade myself that it is owing to the defect of my faculty of moral (or jural) intuition that I fail to see its self-evidence. But when I endeavour to bring it into closer relation to the actual circumstances of human society, it soon comes to wear a different aspect.

In the first place, it seems obviously needful to limit the extent of its application. For it involves the negative principle that no one should be coerced for his own good alone; but no one would gravely argue that this ought to be applied to the case of children, or of idiots, or insane persons. But if so, can we know *a priori* that it ought to be applied to all sane adults? since the above-mentioned exceptions are commonly justified on the ground that children, etc., will manifestly be better off if they are forced to do and abstain as others think best for them; and it is, at least, not intuitively certain that the same argument does not apply to the majority of mankind in the present state of their intellectual progress. Indeed, it is often conceded by the advocates of this principle that it does not hold even in respect of adults in a low state of civilisation. But if so, what criterion can be given for its application, except that it must be applied wherever human beings are sufficiently intelligent to provide for themselves better than others would provide for them? and thus the principle would present itself not as absolute, but merely a subordinate application of the wider principle of aiming at the general happiness or wellbeing of mankind.

But, again, the term Freedom is ambiguous. If we interpret it strictly, as meaning Freedom of Action alone, the principle seems to allow any amount of mutual annoyance except constraint. But obviously no one would be satisfied with such Freedom as this. If, however, we include in the idea absence of pain and annoyance inflicted by others, it becomes at once evident that we cannot prohibit all such annoyances without restraining freedom of action to a degree that would be intolerable; since there is scarcely any gratification of a man's natural impulses which may not cause some annoyance to others. Hence in distinguishing the mutual annoyances that ought to be allowed from those that must be prohibited we seem forced to balance the evils of constraint against pain and loss of a different kind: while if we admit the Utilitarian criterion so far, it is difficult to maintain that annoyance to individuals is never to be permitted in order to attain any positive good result, but only to prevent more serious annoyance.

Thirdly, in order to render a social construction possible on this basis, we must assume that the right to Freedom includes the right to limit one's freedom by contract; and that such contracts, if they are really voluntary and not obtained by fraud or force, and if they do not violate the freedom of others, are to be enforced by legal penalties. But I cannot see that enforcement of Contracts is strictly included in the notion of realising Freedom; for a man seems to be most completely free when no one of his volitions is allowed to have any effect in causing the *external* coercion of any other. If, again, this right of limiting Freedom is itself unlimited, a man might thus freely contract himself out of freedom into slavery, so that the principle of freedom would turn out suicidal; and yet to deduce from this principle a limited right of limiting freedom by contract seems clearly impossible.[1]

But if it be difficult to define freedom as an ideal to be realised in the merely personal relations of human beings, the difficulty is increased when we consider the relation of men to the material means of life and happiness.

For it is commonly thought that the individual's right to Freedom includes the right of appropriating material things. But, if Freedom be understood strictly, I do not see that it implies more than his right to non-interference while actually using such things as can only be used by one person at once: the right to prevent others from using at any future time anything that an individual has once seized seems an interference with the free action of others beyond what is needed to secure the freedom, strictly speaking, of the appropriator. It may perhaps be said that a man, in appropriating a particular thing, does not interfere with the freedom of others, because the rest

---

[1] This question, how far the conception of Freedom involves unlimited right to limit Freedom by free contract, will meet us again in the next chapter, when we consider the general duty of obedience to Law.

of the world is still open to them. But others may want just what he has appropriated : and they may not be able to find anything so good at all, or at least without much labour and search ; for many of the instruments and materials of comfortable living are limited in quantity. This argument applies especially to property in land : and it is to be observed that, in this case, there is a further difficulty in determining how much a man is to be allowed to appropriate by 'first occupation.' If it be said that a man is to be understood to occupy what he is able to use, the answer is obvious that the use of land by any individual may vary almost indefinitely in extent, while diminishing proportionally in intensity. For instance, it would surely be a paradoxical deduction from the principle of Freedom to maintain that an individual had a right to exclude others from pasturing sheep on any part of the land over which his hunting expeditions could extend.[1] But if so can it be clear that a shepherd has such a right against one who wishes to till the land, or that one who is using the surface has a right to exclude a would-be miner ? I do not see how the deduction is to be made out. Again, it may be disputed whether the right of Property, as thus derived, is to include the right of controlling the disposal of one's possessions after death. For this to most persons seems naturally bound up with ownership : yet it is paradoxical to say that we interfere with a man's freedom of action by anything that we may do after his death to what he owned during his life : and jurists have often treated this right as purely conventional and not therefore included in 'natural law.'

Other difficulties might be raised : but we need not pursue them, for if Freedom be taken simply to mean that one man's actions are to be as little as possible restrained by others, it is obviously more fully realised without appropriation. And if it be said that it includes, beside this, facility and security in the gratification of desires, and that it is Freedom in this sense that we think should be equally distributed, and that this cannot be realised without appropriation ; then it may be replied, that in a society where nearly all material things are already appro-

---

[1] It has often been urged as a justification for expropriating savages from the land of new colonies that tribes of hunters have really no moral right to property in the soil over which they hunt.

priated, this kind of Freedom is not and cannot be equally distributed. A man born into such a society, without inheritance, is not only far less free than those who possess property, but he is less free than if there had been no appropriation. It may be said [1] that, having freedom of contract, he will give his services in exchange for the means of satisfying his wants; and that this exchange must necessarily give him more than he could have got if he had been placed in the world by himself; that, in fact, any human society always renders the part of the earth that it inhabits more capable of affording gratification of desires to each and all of its later-born members than it would otherwise be. But however true this may be as a general rule, it is obviously not so in all cases : as men are sometimes unable to sell their services at all, and often can only obtain in exchange for them an insufficient subsistence. And, even granting it to be true, it does not prove that society, by appropriation, has not interfered with the natural freedom of its poorer members : but only that it compensates them for such interference, and that the compensation is adequate : and it must be evident that if compensation in the form of material commodities can be justly given for an encroachment on Freedom, the realisation of Freedom cannot be the one ultimate end of distributive Justice.

§ 5. It seems, then, that though Freedom is an object of keen and general desire, and an important source of happiness, both in itself and indirectly from the satisfaction of natural impulses which it allows, the attempt to make it the fundamental notion of theoretical Jurisprudence is attended with insuperable difficulties : and that even the Natural Rights which it claims to cover cannot be brought under it except in a very forced and arbitrary manner.[2] But further, even if this were otherwise, an equal distribution of Freedom does not seem to exhaust our notion of Justice. Ideal Justice, as we commonly conceive it, seems to demand that not only Freedom but all other benefits and burdens should be distributed, if not

---

[1] This is the argument used by optimistic political economists such as Bastiat.

[2] The further consideration of Political Freedom, with which we shall be occupied in the next chapter, will afford additional illustrations of the difficulties involved in the notion.

equally, at any rate justly,—Justice in distribution being regarded as not identical with Equality, but merely exclusive of arbitrary inequality.

How, then, shall we find the principle of this highest and most comprehensive ideal ?

We shall be led to it, I think, by referring again to one of the grounds of obligation to render services, which was noticed in the last chapter : the claim of Gratitude.   It there appeared that we have not only a natural impulse to requite benefits, but also a conviction that such requital is a duty, and its omission blameworthy, to some extent at least ; though we find it difficult to define the extent.   Now it seems that when we, so to say, *universalise* this impulse and conviction, we get the element in the common view of Justice, which we are now trying to define.   For if we take the proposition ' that good done to any individual ought to be requited by him,' and leave out the relation to the individual in either term of the proposition, we seem to have an equally strong conviction of the truth of the more general statement ' that good deeds ought to be requited.' [1]   And if we take into consideration all the different kinds and degrees of services, upon the mutual exchange of which society is based, we get the proposition ' that men ought to be rewarded in proportion to their deserts.'   And this would be commonly held to be the true and simple principle of distribution in any case where there are no claims arising from Contract or Custom to modify its operation.

For example, it would be admitted that—if there has been no previous arrangement—the profits of any work or enterprise should be divided among those who have contributed to its success in proportion to the worth of their services.   And it may be observed, that some thinkers maintain the proposition discussed in the previous section—that Law ought to aim at securing the greatest possible Freedom for each individual— not as absolute and axiomatic, but as derivative from the

---

[1] If the view given in the text be sound, it illustrates very strikingly the difference between natural instincts and moral intuitions.   For the impulse to requite a service is, on its emotional side, quite different from that which prompts us to claim the fruits of our labour, or "a fair day's wages for a fair day's work."   Still, our apprehension of the *duty* of Gratitude seems capable of being subsumed under the more general intuition ' that desert ought to be requited.'

principle that Desert ought to be requited; on the ground that the best way of providing for the requital of Desert is to leave men as free as possible to exert themselves for the satisfaction of their own desires, and so to win each his own requital. And this seems to be really the principle upon which the Right of Property is rested, when it is justified by the proposition that ' every one has an exclusive right to the produce of his labour.' For on reflection it is seen that no labour really 'produces' any material thing, but only adds to its value : and we do not think that a man can acquire a right to a material thing belonging to another, by spending his labour on it—even if he does so in the *bona fide* belief that it is his own property—but only to adequate *compensation* for his labour ; this, therefore, is what the proposition just quoted must mean. The principle is, indeed, sometimes stretched to explain the original right of property in materials, as being in a sense ' produced ' (*i.e.* found) by their first discoverer ;[1] but here again, reflection shows that Common Sense does not grant this (as a *moral* right) absolutely. but only in so far as it appears to be not more than adequate compensation for the discoverer's trouble. For example, we should not consider that the first finder of a large uninhabited region had a moral right to appropriate the whole of it. Hence this justification of the right of property refers us ultimately to the principle ' that every man ought to receive adequate requital for his labour.' So, again, when we speak of the world as justly governed by God, we seem to mean that, if we could know the whole of human existence, we should find that happiness is distributed among men according to their deserts. And Divine Justice is thought to be a pattern which Human Justice is to imitate as far as the conditions of human society allow.

This kind of Justice, as has been said, seems like Gratitude universalised : and the same principle applied to punishment

---

[1] It certainly requires a considerable strain to bring the 'right of First Discovery' under the notion of 'right to the produce of one's labour.' Hence Locke and others have found it necessary to suppose, as the ultimate justification of the former right, 'a tacit consent' of mankind in general that all things previously unappropriated shall belong to the first appropriator. But this must be admitted to be a rather desperate device of ethico-political construction : on account of the fatal facility with which it may be used to justify almost any arbitrariness in positive law.

may similarly be regarded as Resentment universalised ; though the parallel is incomplete, if we are considering the present state of our moral conceptions.   History shows us a time in which it was thought not only as natural, but as clearly right and incumbent on a man, to requite injuries as to repay benefits : but as moral reflection developed in Europe this notion was repudiated, so that Plato taught that it could never be right really to harm any one, however he may have harmed us. And this is the accepted doctrine in Christian societies, as regards requital by individuals of personal wrongs.   But in its universalised form the old conviction still lingers in the popular view of Criminal Justice : it seems still to be widely held that Justice requires pain to be inflicted on a man who has done wrong, even if no benefit result either to him or to others from the pain.   Personally, I am so far from holding this view that I have an instinctive and strong moral aversion to it : and I hesitate to attribute it to Common Sense, since I think that it is gradually passing away from the moral consciousness of educated persons in the most advanced communities : but I think it is still perhaps the more ordinary view.

This, then, is one element of what Aristotle calls Corrective Justice, which is embodied in criminal law.   It must not be confounded with the principle of Reparation, on which legal awards of damages are based.   We have already noticed this as a simple deduction from the maxim of general Benevolence, which forbids us to do harm to our fellow-creatures : for if we have harmed them, we can yet approximately obey the maxim by giving compensation for the harm.   Though here the question arises whether we are bound to make reparation for harm that has been quite blamelessly caused : and it is not easy to answer it decisively.[1]   On the whole, I

---

[1] The reader will find an interesting illustration of the perplexity of Common Sense on this point in Mr. O. W. Holmes, Junior's, book on *The Common Law*, chap. iii., where the author gives a penetrating discussion of the struggle, in the development of the doctrine of torts in English Law, between two opposing views : (1) that "the risk of a man's conduct is thrown upon him as the result of some moral short-coming," and (2) that "a man acts at his peril always, and wholly irrespective of the state of his consciousness upon the matter."   The former is the view that has in the main prevailed in English Law ; and this seems to me certainly in harmony with the Common Sense of mankind, so far

think we should condemn a man who did not offer some reparation for any serious injury caused by him to another— even if quite involuntarily caused, and without negligence: but perhaps we regard this rather as a duty of Benevolence— arising out of the general sympathy that each ought to have for others, intensified by this special occasion—than as a duty of strict Justice. If, however, we limit the requirement of Reparation, under the head of strict Justice, to cases in which the mischief repaired is due to acts or omissions in some degree culpable, a difficulty arises from the divergence between the moral view of culpability, and that which social security requires. Of this I will speak presently.[1] In any case there is now[2] no danger of confusion or collision between the principle of Reparative and that of Retributive Justice, as the one is manifestly concerned with the claims of the injured party, and the other with the deserts of the wrongdoer: though in the actual administration of Law the obligation of paying compensation for wrong may sometimes be treated as a sufficient punishment for the wrongdoer.

When, however, we turn again to the other branch of Retributive Justice, which is concerned with the reward of services, we find another notion, which I will call Fitness, often blended indistinguishably[3] with the notion of Desert, and so needing to be carefully separated from it; and when the distinction has been made, we see that the two are liable to come into collision. I do not feel sure that the principle of ' distribution according to Fitness' is found, strictly speaking, in the analysis of the ordinary notion of Justice: but it certainly enters into our common conception of the ideal or

---

as legal liability is concerned; but I do not think that the case is equally clear as regards moral obligation.

[1] Cf. *post*, pp. 292-3. It may be added that there is often a further difficulty in ascertaining the amount of compensation due: for this frequently involves a comparison of things essentially disparate, and there are some kinds of harm which it seems impossible to compensate.

[2] In the earlier stage of moral development, referred to in the preceding paragraph, retribution inflicted on the wrongdoer was regarded as the normal mode of reparation to the person injured. But this view is contrary to the moral Common Sense of Christian Societies.

[3] I think the term "merit" often blends the two notions, as when we speak of "promotion by merit." By moralists, however, "merit" is generally used as exactly equivalent to what I have called "desert."

perfectly rational order of society, as regards the distribution both of instruments and functions, and (to some extent at least) of other sources of happiness.   We certainly think it reasonable that instruments should be given to those who can use them best, and functions allotted to those who are most competent to perform them : but these may not be those who have rendered most services in the past.   And again, we think it reasonable that particular material means of enjoyment should fall to the lot of those who are susceptible of the respective kinds of pleasure; as no one would think of allotting pictures to a blind man, or rare wines to one who had no taste : hence we should probably think it fitting that artists should have larger shares than mechanics in the social distribution of wealth, though they may be by no means more deserving.   Thus the notions of Desert and Fitness appear at least occasionally conflicting; but perhaps, as I have suggested, Fitness should rather be regarded as a utilitarian principle of distribution, inevitably limiting the realisation of what is abstractly just, than as a part of the interpretation of Justice proper: and it is with the latter that we are at present concerned.   At any rate it is the Requital of Desert that constitutes the chief element of Ideal Justice, in so far as this imports something more than mere Equality and Impartiality.   Let us then examine more closely wherein Desert consists; and we will begin with Good Desert or Merit, as being of the most fundamental and permanent importance; for we may hope that crime and its punishment will decrease and gradually disappear as the world improves, but the right or best distribution of the means of wellbeing is an object that we must always be striving to realise.

§ 6. And first, the question which we had to consider in defining Gratitude again recurs : whether, namely, we are to apportion the reward to the effort made, or to the results attained.   For it may be said that the actual utility of any service must depend much upon favourable circumstances and fortunate accidents, not due to any desert of the agent : or again, may be due to powers and skills which were connate, or have been developed by favourable conditions of life, or by good education, and why should we reward him for these ? (for the last-mentioned we ought rather to reward those who have educated him). And certainly it is only in so far as *moral* excellences are exhibited in human achievements that they are commonly thought to be such as God will reward. But by drawing this line we do not yet get rid of the difficulty. For it may still be said that good actions are due entirely, or to a great extent, to good dispositions and habits, and that these are partly inherited and partly due to the care of parents and teachers; so that in rewarding these we are rewarding the results of natural and accidental advantages, and it is unreasonable to distinguish these from others, such as skill and knowledge, and to say that it is even ideally just to reward the one and not the other. Shall we say, then, that the reward should be proportionate to the amount of voluntary effort for a good end? But Determinists will say that even this is ultimately the effect of causes extraneous to the man's self. On the Determinist view, then, it would seem to be ideally just (if anything is so) that all men should enjoy equal amounts of happiness: for there seems to be no justice in making *A* happier than *B*, merely because circumstances beyond his own control have first made him better. But why should we not, instead of ' all men,' say ' all sentient beings ' ? for why should men have more happiness than any other animal? But thus the pursuit of ideal justice seems to conduct us to such a precipice of paradox that Common Sense is likely to abandon it. At any rate the ordinary idea of Desert has thus altogether vanished.[1] And thus we seem to be led to the conclusion which I anticipated in Book i. chap. v.: that in this one department of our moral consciousness the idea of Free Will seems involved in a peculiar way in the moral ideas of Common Sense, since if it is eliminated the important notions of Desert or Merit and Justice require material modification.[2]

---

[1] The only tenable Determinist interpretation of Desert is, in my opinion, the Utilitarian : according to which, when a man is said to deserve reward for any services to society, the meaning is that it is expedient to reward him, in order that he and others may be induced to render similar services by the expectation of similar rewards. Cf. *post*, Book iv. chap. iii. § 4.

[2] Perhaps we may partly attribute to the difficulties above discussed, that the notion of Desert has sometimes dropped out of the ideal of Utopian reconstructors of society, and 'Equality of Happiness' has seemed to be the only end. Justice, it has been thought, prescribes simply that each should have an equal share of happiness, as far as happiness depends on the action of others. But there seems to be much difficulty in working this out: for (apart

At the same time, the difference between Determinist and Libertarian Justice can hardly have any practical effect. For in any case it does not seem possible to separate in practice that part of a man's achievement which is due strictly to his free choice from that part which is due to the original gift of nature and to favouring circumstances:[1] so that we must necessarily leave to providence the realisation of what we conceive as the theoretical ideal of Justice, and content ourselves with trying to reward voluntary actions in proportion to the worth of the services intentionally rendered by them.

If, then, we take as the principle of ideal justice, so far as this can be practically aimed at in human society, the requital of voluntary services in proportion to their worth, it remains to consider on what principle or principles the comparative worth of different services is to be rationally estimated. There is no doubt that we commonly assume such an estimate to be possible; for we continually speak of the 'fair' or 'proper' price of any kind of services as something generally known, and condemn the demand for more than this as extortionate. It may be said that the notion of Fairness or Equity which we ordinarily apply in such judgments is to be distinguished from that of Justice; Equity being in fact often contrasted with strict Justice, and conceived as capable of coming into collision with it. And this is partly true: but I think the wider and no less usual sense of the term Justice, in which it includes Equity or Fairness, is the only one that can be conveniently

from the considerations of Fitness above mentioned) equal happiness is not to be attained by equal distribution of objects of desire. For some require more and some less to be equally happy. Hence, it seems, we must take differences of *needs* into consideration. But if merely mental needs are included (as seems reasonable) we should have to give less to cheerful, contented, self-sacrificing people than to those who are naturally moody and *exigeant*, as the former can be made happy with less. And this is too paradoxical to recommend itself to Common Sense.

[1] No doubt, it would be possible to remove, to some extent, the inequalities that are attributable to circumstances, by bringing the best education within the reach of all classes, so that all children might have an equal opportunity of being selected and trained for any functions for which they seemed to be fit: and this seems to be prescribed by ideal justice, in so far as it removes or mitigates arbitrary inequality. Accordingly in those ideal reconstructions of society, in which we may expect to find men's notions of abstract justice exhibited, such an institution as this has generally found a place. Still, there will be much natural inequality which we cannot remove or even estimate.

adopted in an ethical treatise : for in any case where Equity comes into conflict with strict justice, its dictates are held to be in a higher sense just, and what ought to be ultimately carried into effect in the case considered—though not, perhaps, by the administrators of law.   I treat Equity, therefore, as a species of Justice; though noting that the former term is more ordinarily used in cases where the definiteness attainable is recognised as somewhat less than in ordinary cases of rightful claims arising out of law or contract.   On what principle, then, can we determine the " fair " or " equitable " price of services ? When we examine the common judgments of practical persons in which this judgment occurs, we find, I think, that the ' fair ' in such cases is ascertained by a reference to analogy and custom, and that any service is considered to be ' fairly worth ' what is usually given for services of the kind.   Hence this element of the notion of Justice may seem, after all, to resolve itself into that discussed in § 2 : and in some states of society it certainly appears that the payment to be given for services is as completely fixed by usage as any other customary duty, so that it would be a clear disappointment of normal expectation to deviate from this usage.   But probably no one in a modern civilised community would maintain in its full breadth this identification of the Just with the Usual price of services : and so far as the judgments of practical persons may seem to imply this, I think it must be admitted that they are superficial or merely inadvertent, and ignore the established mode of determining the market prices of commodities by free competition of producers and traders.   For where such competition operates the market value rises and falls, and is different at different places and times; so that no properly instructed person can expect any fixity in it, or complain of injustice merely on account of the variations in it.

Can we then say that ' market value ' (as determined by free competition) corresponds to our notion of what is ideally just ?

This is a question of much interest, because this is obviously the mode of determining the remuneration of services that would be universal in a society constructed on the principle previously discussed, of securing the greatest possible Freedom to all members of the community.   It should be observed that this, which we may call the Individualistic Ideal, is the type to which modern civilised communities have, until lately, been tending to approximate : and it is therefore very important to know whether it is one which completely satisfies the demands of morality ; and whether Freedom, if not an absolute end or First Principle of abstract Justice, is still to be sought as the best means to the realisation of a just social order by the general requital of Desert.

At first sight it seems plausible to urge that the ' market value' represents the estimate set upon anything by mankind generally, and therefore gives us exactly that ' common sense ' judgment respecting value which we are now trying to find. But on examination it seems likely that the majority of men are not properly qualified to decide on the value of many important kinds of services, from imperfect knowledge of their nature and effects ; so that, as far as these are concerned, the true judgment will not be represented in the market-place.   Even in the case of things which a man is generally able to estimate, it may be manifest in a particular case that he is ignorant of the real utility of what he exchanges ; and in this case the ' free ' contract hardly seems to be fair : though if the ignorance was not caused by the other party to the exchange, Common Sense is hardly prepared to condemn the latter as unjust for taking advantage of it.   For instance, if a man has discovered by a legitimate use of geological knowledge and skill that there is probably a valuable mine on land owned by a stranger, reasonable persons would not blame him for concealing his discovery until he had bought the mine at its market value : yet it could not be said that the seller got what it was really worth.   In fact Common Sense is rather perplexed on this point : and the *rationale* of the conclusion at which it arrives, must, I conceive, be sought in economic considerations, which take us quite beyond the analysis of the common notion of Justice.[1]

Again, there are social services recognised as highly important which generally speaking have no price in any market, on account of the indirectness and uncertainty of their practical utility : as, for instance, scientific discoveries.   The extent to which any given discovery will aid industrial invention is so

---

[1] Cf. *post*, Book iv. chap. iii. § 4.

uncertain, that even if the secret of it could be conveniently kept, it would not usually be profitable to buy it.

But even if we confine our attention to products and services generally marketable, and to bargains thoroughly understood on both sides, there are still serious difficulties in the way of identifying the notions of 'free' and 'fair' exchange. Thus, where an individual, or combination of individuals, has the monopoly of a certain kind of services, the market-price of the aggregate of such services can under certain conditions be increased by diminishing their total amount; but it would seem absurd to say that the social Desert of those rendering the services is thereby increased, and a plain man has grave doubts whether the price thus attained is fair. Still less is it thought fair to take advantage of the transient monopoly produced by emergency: thus, if I saw Crœsus drowning and no one near, it would not be held fair in me to refuse to save him except at the price of half his wealth. But if so, can it be fair for any class of persons to gain competitively by the unfavourable economic situation of another class with which they deal? And if we admit that it would be unfair, where are we to draw the line? For any increase of the numbers of a class renders its situation for bargaining less favourable : since the market price of different services depends partly upon the ease or difficulty of procuring them—as Political Economists say, ' on the relation between the supply of services and the demand for them '—and it does not seem that any individual's social Desert can properly be lessened merely by the increased number or willingness of others rendering the same services. Nor, indeed, does it seem that it can be decreased by his own willingness, for it is strange to reward a man less because he is zealous and eager in the performance of his function; yet in bargaining the less willing always has the advantage. And, finally, it hardly appears that the social worth of a man's service is necessarily increased by the fact that his service is rendered to those who can pay lavishly; but his reward is certainly likely to be greater from this cause.

Such considerations as these have led some political thinkers to hold that Justice requires a mode of distributing payment for services, entirely different from that at present effected by free competition : and that all labourers ought to be paid according to the intrinsic value of their labour as estimated by enlightened and competent judges. If the Socialistic Ideal—as we may perhaps call it—could be realised without counter-balancing evils, it would certainly seem to give a nearer approximation to what we conceive as Divine Justice than the present state of society affords. But this supposes that we have found the rational method of determining value : which, however, is still to seek. Shall we say that these judges are to take the value of a service as proportionate to the amount of happiness produced by it ? If so, the calculation is, of course, exposed to all the difficulties of the hedonistic method discussed in Book ii. : but supposing these can be overcome, it is still hard to say how we are to compare the value of different services that must necessarily be combined to produce happy life. For example, how shall we compare the respective values of necessaries and luxuries ? for we may be more sensible of the enjoyment derived from the latter, but we could not have this at all without the former. And, again, when different kinds of labour co-operate in the same production, how are we to estimate their relative values ? for even if all mere unskilled labour may be brought to a common standard, this seems almost impossible in the case of different kinds of skill. For how shall we compare the labour of design with that of achievement ? or the super-vision of the whole with the execution of details ? or the labour of actually producing with that of educating producers ? or the service of the *savant* who discovers a new principle, with that of the inventor who applies it ?

I do not see how these questions, or the difficulties noticed in the preceding paragraph, can be met by any analysis of our common notion of Justice. To deal with such points at all satisfactorily we have, I conceive, to adopt quite a different line of reasoning : we have to ask, not what services of a certain kind are intrinsically worth, but what reward can procure them and whether the rest of society gain by the services more than the equivalent reward. We have, in short, to give up as impracticable the construction of an ideally just social order,[1] in which all services are rewarded in exact pro-

[1] It is not perhaps necessary that I should here enlarge on the *practical* obstacles in the way of any attempt to realise such an ideal system.

portion to their intrinsic value.   And, for similar reasons, we
seem forced to conclude, more generally, that it is impossible
to obtain clear premises for a reasoned method of determining
exactly different amounts of Good Desert.   Indeed, perhaps,
Common Sense scarcely holds such a method to be possible :
for though it considers Ideal Justice to consist in rewarding
Desert, it regards as Utopian any general attempt to realise
this ideal in the social distribution of the means of happiness.
In the actual state of society it is only within a very limited
range that any endeavour is made to reward Good Desert.
Parents attempt this to some extent in dealing with their
children, and the State in rewarding remarkable public services
rendered by statesmen, soldiers, etc. : but reflection on these
cases will show how very rough and imperfect are the
standards used in deciding the amount due.   And ordinarily
the only kind of Justice which we try to realise is that
which consists in the fulfilment of contracts and definite
expectations ; leaving the general fairness of Distribution by
Bargaining to take care of itself.

§ 7. When we pass to consider the case of Criminal
Justice, we find, in the first place, difficulties corresponding
to those which we have already noticed.   We find, to begin,
a similar implication and partial confusion of the ideas of
Law and Justice.   For, as was said, by ' bringing a man to
Justice ' we commonly mean ' inflicting legal punishment ' on
him : and we think it right that neither more nor less than
the penalty prescribed by law should be executed, even though
we may regard the legal scale of punishment as unjust.   At
the same time, we have no such perplexity in respect of
changes in the law as occurs in the case of Civil Justice ; for
we do not think that a man can acquire, by custom, pre-
scriptive rights to over-lenient punishment, as he is thought
to do to an unequal distribution of liberties and privileges.
If now we investigate the ideal of Criminal Justice, as
intuitively determined, we certainly find that in so far as
punishment is not regarded as merely preventive,[1] it is
commonly thought that it ought to be proportioned to the

---

[1] I have already expressed my opinion that this Utilitarian view of punishment is gradually tending to prevail ; but I do not think that it has yet
prevailed.

gravity of crime.[1] Still, when we endeavour to make the
method of apportionment perfectly rational and precise, the
difficulties seem at least as great as in the case of Good
Desert. For, first, the assumption of Free Will seems
necessarily to come in here also; since if a man's bad deeds
are entirely caused by nature and circumstances, it certainly
appears, as Robert Owen urged, that he does not properly
deserve to be punished for them; Justice would rather seem
to require us to try to alter the conditions under which he
acts. And we actually do punish deliberate offences more
than impulsive, perhaps as implying a more free choice of
evil. Again, we think that offences committed by persons
who have had no moral training, or a perverted training, are
really less criminal; at the same time it is commonly agreed
that men can hardly remit punishment on this account.
Again the gravity—from a moral point of view—of a crime
seems to be at least much reduced, if the motive be laudable,
as when a man kills a villain whose crimes elude legal punishment, or heads a hopeless rebellion for the good of his
country: still it would be paradoxical to affirm that we
ought to reduce punishment proportionally: Common Sense
would hold that—whatever God may do—men must, generally speaking, inflict severe punishment for any gravely
mischievous act forbidden by law which has been intentionally
done, even though it may have been prompted by a good
motive.

But even if we neglect the motive, and take the intention
only into account, it is not easy to state clear principles for
determining the gravity of crimes. For sometimes, as in the
case of the patriotic rebel, the intention of the criminal is to
do what is right and good: and in many cases, though he
knows that he is doing wrong, he does not intend to cause
any actual harm to any sentient being; as when a thief
takes what he thinks will not be missed. Again, we do not
commonly think that a crime is rendered less grave by being

---

[1] Of course those who hold that the essence of Justice consists in securing
external Freedom among the members of a community, and that punishment
is only justified as a means to this end, naturally think that in awarding
punishment we ought to consider merely its efficacy as such means. But this
can scarcely be put forward as an interpretation of the common notion of Just
Punishment.

kept perfectly secret; and yet a great part of the harm done
by a crime is the 'secondary evil' (as Bentham calls it) of
the alarm and insecurity which it causes; and this part is
cut off by complete secrecy. It may be replied that this
latter difficulty is not a practical one; because we are not
called upon to punish a crime until it has been discovered,
and then the secondary evil has been caused, and is all the
greater because of the previous secrecy. But it remains true
that it was not designed for discovery; and therefore that
this part of the evil caused by the crime was not intended by
the criminal. And if we say that the heinousness of the
crime depends on the loss of happiness that would generally
be caused by such acts if they were allowed to go unpunished, and that we must suppose the criminal to be
aware of this; we seem to be endeavouring to force a utilitarian theory into an intuitional form by means of a legal
fiction.

We have hitherto spoken of intentional wrong-doing: but
positive law awards punishment also for harm that is due to
rashness or negligence; and the justification of this involves
us in further difficulties. Some jurists seem to regard rashness and negligence as positive states of mind, in which the
agent consciously refuses the attention or reflection which he
knows he ought to give; and no doubt this sort of wilful
recklessness does sometimes occur, and seems as properly
punishable as if the resulting harm had been positively
intended. But the law as actually administered does not
require evidence that this was the agent's state of mind
(which indeed in most cases it would be impossible to give):
but is content with proof that the harm might have been
prevented by such care as an average man would have shown
under the circumstances. And most commonly by 'carelessness' we simply mean a purely negative psychological fact, i.e.
that the agent did not perform certain processes of observation
or reflection; it is therefore at the time strictly involuntary,
and so scarcely seems to involve ill-desert. It may be said
perhaps that though the present carelessness is not blameworthy, the past neglect to cultivate habits of care is so. But
in many individual instances we cannot reasonably infer even
this past neglect; and in such cases the utilitarian theory of

punishment, which regards it as a means of preventing similar harmful acts in the future, seems alone applicable. Similar difficulties arise, as was before hinted (p. 282), in determining the limits within which Reparation is due; that is, on the view that it is not incumbent on us to make compensation for all harm caused by our muscular actions, but only for harm which—if not intentional—was due to our rashness or negligence.

The results of this examination of Justice may be summed up as follows. The prominent element in Justice as ordinarily conceived is a kind of Equality: that is, Impartiality in the observance or enforcement of certain general rules allotting good or evil to individuals. But when we have clearly distinguished this element, we see that the definition of the virtue required for practical guidance is left obviously incomplete. Inquiring further for the right general principles of distribution, we find that our common notion of Justice includes—besides the principle of Reparation for injury—two quite distinct and divergent elements. The one, which we may call Conservative Justice, is realised (1) in the observance of Law and Contracts and definite understandings, and in the enforcement of such penalties for the violation of these as have been legally determined and announced; and (2) in the fulfilment of natural and normal expectations. This latter obligation, however, is of a somewhat indefinite kind. But the other element, which we have called Ideal Justice, is still more difficult to define; for there seem to be two quite distinct conceptions of it, embodied respectively in what we have called the Individualistic and the Socialistic Ideals of a political community. The first of these takes the realisation of Freedom as the ultimate end and standard of right social relations: but on examining it closer we find that the notion of Freedom will not give a practicable basis for social construction without certain arbitrary[1] definitions and limitations: and even if we admit these, still a society in which Freedom is realised as far as is feasible does not completely suit our sense of Justice. *Prima facie*, this is more satisfied

---

[1] By 'arbitrary' I mean such definitions and limitations as destroy the self-evidence of the principle; and, when closely examined, lead us to regard it as subordinate.

by the Socialistic Ideal of Distribution, founded on the principle of requiting Desert: but when we try to make this principle precise, we find ourselves again involved in grave difficulties; and similar perplexities beset the working out of rules of Criminal Justice on the same principle.

CHAPTER VI

LAWS AND PROMISES

§ 1. In the discussion of Justice the moral obligations of obedience to Law and observance of Contract have been included, and have, indeed, appeared to be the most definite part of the complex system of private duties commonly included under that term. At the same time, as we have seen, there are some laws, the violation of which does not interfere with the rights of others, and therefore has not the characteristics of an act of Injustice. While again, the duty of Fidelity to promises is also commonly conceived as independent of any injury that might be done to the promisee by breaking it: for (*e.g.*) men ordinarily judge that promises to the dead, though they are beyond the reach of injury, ought to be kept: indeed, some would regard them as even more sacred than promises made to the living. It seems therefore desirable to examine the propositions 'that Law ought to be obeyed' and 'that promises ought to be kept,' considered as independent principles.

To begin with the former: how are we to ascertain what the Law is which, as is commonly thought, we are morally bound to obey, as such? It is plain that we cannot here distinguish Legal from other rules by considering the sanctions actually attached to them, as we had occasion to do in a previous chapter.[1] For commands issued by rebels and usurpers are held to have as such no general binding-ness, though they may be enforced by judicial penalties; it would be generally agreed that so far as it is our duty to obey such commands this is solely in order to avoid the

---

[1] Cf. *ante*, Book ii. chap. v. § 2.

greater evils which might result to ourselves and others from our disobedience; and that the extent of such a duty must be determined by considerations of expediency. Nor, again, can we say that all commands even of a legitimate sovereign are to be regarded as Laws in the sense in which the term must be taken in the proposition that 'laws ought to be obeyed': since we all recognise that a rightful sovereign may command his subjects to do what is wrong, and that it is then their duty to disobey him. It seems therefore that for our present purpose we must define Laws to be Rules of Conduct laid down by a Rightful Authority, commanding within the limits of its authority.

There are therefore two questions to be settled, if the proposition that laws ought to be obeyed is to furnish practical guidance: (1) how we are to distinguish the Rightful Lawmaker—whether individual or body, and (2) how we are to ascertain the limits of this lawmaker's authority. The questions should be distinguished; but, as we shall see, they can only be partially separated. Beginning with the first question, we may assume that the authority to make laws resides in some living man or men. No doubt in some societies, at some stages of their development, the whole or a part of the code of laws habitually observed, or at least recognised as binding, has been believed to be of divine or semi-divine institution; or perhaps from mere antiquity to possess a sanctity superior to that of any living authority, so as to be not legitimately alterable. But we hardly find this view in the Common Sense of civilised Europe, upon which we are now reflecting: at any rate in our societies there is not thought to be any portion of the definite prescriptions of positive law which, in virtue of its origin, is beyond the reach of alteration by any living authority.

Where then is this authority to be found?

In the answers commonly given to this question, the conflict between the Ideal and the Traditional or Customary, which has perplexed us in seeking the definition of Justice, meets us again in an even more complicated form. For not only do some say that obedience is always due to the traditionally legitimate authority in any country, while others maintain that an authority constituted in accordance with

certain abstract principles is essentially legitimate, and that
a nation has a right to claim that such an authority shall
be established, even at the risk of civil strife and bloodshed :
but often, too, the authority actually established is not even
traditionally legitimate.   So that we have to distinguish
three claims to authority, each of which may come into
conflict with either of the other two: (1) that of the
Government held to be ideally or abstractly right, and such
as ought to be established: (2) that of the Government *de
jure*, according to the constitutional traditions in any given
country : and (3) that of the *de facto* Government.

§ 2. Let us begin by considering the Ideal. Here I do not
propose to consider all views as to the right constitution of
supreme authority which speculative thinkers have put forward;
but only such as have a *prima facie* claim to express the
Common Sense of mankind on the subject. Of these the most
important, and the most widely urged and admitted, is the
principle that the Sovereign in any community can only be
rightly constituted by the Consent of the Subjects. This, as
was noticed in the preceding chapter, is involved in the
adoption of Freedom as the ultimate end of political order :
if no one originally owes anything to another except non-
interference, he clearly ought only to be placed in the relation
of Subject to Sovereign by his own consent. And thus, in
order to reconcile the original right of Freedom with the
actual duty of Law-observance, some supposition of a social
compact appears necessary ; by means of which Obedience to
Law becomes merely a special application of the duty of
keeping compacts.

In what way, then, are the terms of this fundamental
compact to be known ? No one now maintains the old view
that the transition from the 'natural' to the 'political' state
actually took place by means of an " original contract," which
conferred indelible legitimacy on some particular form of social
organisation. Shall we say, then, that a man by remaining
a member of a community enters into a 'tacit undertaking'
to obey the laws and other commands imposed by the authority
generally recognised as lawful in that community ? In this
way however the Ideal lapses into the Customary : and the
most unlimited despotism, if established and traditional, might

claim to rest on free consent as well as any other form of government: so that the principle of abstract Freedom would lead to the justification of the most unqualified concrete tyranny and servitude; and thus our theory would end by riveting men's chains under pretence of exalting their freedom. If to avoid this result, we suppose that certain 'Natural Rights' are inalienable—or tacitly reserved in the tacit compact— and that laws are not strictly legitimate which deprive a man of these, we are again met by the difficulty of deducing these inalienable rights from any clear and generally accepted principles. For instance, as we have seen, a widely accepted opinion is that all such rights may be summed up in the notion of Freedom; but we have also seen that this principle is ambiguous, and especially that the right of private property as commonly recognised cannot be clearly deduced from it; and if so it would certainly be most paradoxical to maintain that no government can legitimately claim obedience for any commands except such as carry out the principle of protecting from interference the Freedom of the individuals governed. It has been thought that we can avoid this difficulty by constituting the supreme organ of government so that any law laid down by it will always be a law to which every person called on to obey it will have consented personally or by his representatives: and that a government so constituted, in which—to adopt Rousseau's phrase—every one " obeys himself alone," will completely reconcile freedom and order. But how is this result to be attained? Rousseau held that it could be attained by pure direct democracy, each individual subordinating his private will to the " general will " of the sovereign people of which all are equally members. But this " general will " must be practically the will of the majority: and it is paradoxical to affirm that the freedom and natural rights of a dissentient minority are effectively protected by establishing the condition that the oppressors must exceed the oppressed in number. Again, if the principle be absolute it ought to apply to all human beings alike: and if to avoid this absurdity we exclude children, an arbitrary line has to be drawn: and the exclusion of women, which even those who regard the suffrage as a natural right are often disposed to maintain, seems altogether indefensible. And to suppose—as some have done—that the ideal of "obeying oneself alone" can be even approximately realised by Representative Democracy, is even more patently absurd. For a Representative assembly is normally chosen only by a part of the nation, and each law is approved only by a part of the assembly : and it would be ridiculous to say that a man has assented to a law passed by a mere majority of an assembly against one member of which he has voted.

But, again, to lay down absolutely that the laws of any community ought to express the will of the majority of its members seems incompatible with the view so vigorously maintained by Socrates and his most famous disciples, that laws ought to be made by people who understand law-making. For though the majority of a representative assembly in a particular country at a particular time may be more fit to make laws for their country than any set of experts otherwise selected, it is certainly not self-evident that this will be universally the case. Yet surely the Socratic proposition (which is merely a special application of the principle noticed in the latter part of the preceding chapter, 'that function should be allotted to the fittest') has as much claim to be considered a primary intuition as the one that we have been discussing. Indeed, the secular controversy between Aristocracy and Democracy seems ultimately reducible to a conflict between those two principles : a conflict of which it is impossible to find a solution, so long as the argument remains in the *a priori* region.

§ 3. However, to discuss this exhaustively would carry us too far beyond the range of Ethics proper: but we may perhaps conclude that it is impossible to elicit from Common Sense any clear and certain intuitions as to the principles on which an ideal constitution should be constructed. And there is an equal want of agreement as to the intrinsic lawfulness of introducing such a constitution in violation of the traditional and established order in any community. For some think that a nation has a natural right to a government approximately conformed to the ideal, and that this right may be maintained by force in the last resort. Others, however, hold that, though the ideal polity may rightly be put forward and commended, and every means used to promote its realisation which the established government in any country permits,—still, rebellion can never be justifiable for this purpose alone. While others, —perhaps the majority,— would decide the question on grounds of expediency, balancing the advantages of improvement against the evils of disorder.

But further, as we saw, it is not so easy to say what the established government is. For sometimes an authority declared by law to be illegitimate issues ordinances and controls the administration of justice. The question then arises, how far obedience is due to such an authority. All are agreed that usurpation ought to be resisted; but as to the right behaviour towards an established government which has sprung from a successful usurpation, there is a great difference of opinion. Some think that it should be regarded as legitimate, as soon as it is firmly established: others that it ought to be obeyed at once, but under protest, with the purpose of renewing the conflict on a favourable opportunity: others think that this latter is the right attitude at first, but that a usurping government, when firmly established, loses its illegitimacy gradually, and that it becomes, after a while, as criminal to rebel against it as it was originally to establish it. And this last seems, on the whole, the view of Common Sense; but the point at which the metamorphosis is thought to take place can hardly be determined otherwise than by considerations of expediency.

But again, it is only in the case of an absolute government, where customary obedience is unconditionally due to one or more persons, that the fundamental difficulties of ascertaining the legitimacy of authority are of the simple kind just discussed. In a constitutionally governed state numerous other moral disagreements arise. For, in such a state, while it is of course held that the sovereign is morally bound to conform to the constitution,[1] it is still disputed whether the

---

[1] It is perhaps hardly necessary that I should here notice the Hobbist doctrine, revived in a modified form by Austin, that "the power of the sovereign is incapable of [legal] limitation." For no one now maintains pure Hobbism: and Austin is as far as possible from meaning that there cannot be an express or tacit understanding between Sovereign and Subjects, the violation of which by the former may make it morally right for the latter to rebel. In fact, as used by him, Hobbes' doctrine reduces itself to the rather unimportant proposition that a sovereign will not be punished for unconstitutional conduct through the agency of his own law-courts, so long as he remains sovereign. I

subjects' obligation to obedience is properly conceived as conditional upon this conformity : and whether they have the moral right (1) to refuse obedience to an unconstitutional command; and (2) even to inflict on the sovereign the penalty of rebellion for violating the constitution. Again, in determining what the constitutional obligations really are we find much perplexity and disagreement, not merely as to the exact ascertainment of the relevant historical facts but as to the principles on which these facts ought to be treated. For the various limitations of sovereign authority comprised in the constitution have often been originally concessions extorted by fear from a sovereign previously absolute; and it is doubted how far such concessions are morally binding on the sovereign from whom they were wrested, and still more how far they are binding on succeeding sovereigns. Or, *vice versâ*, a people may have allowed liberties once exercised to fall into disuse; and it is doubted whether it retains the right of reclaiming them. And, generally, when a constitutional rule has to be elicited from a comparison of precedents, it is open to dispute whether a particular act of either party should be regarded as a constitutive precedent or as an illegitimate encroachment. And hence we find that, in constitutional countries, men's view of what their constitution traditionally is has often been greatly influenced by their view of what it ideally ought to be: in fact, the two questions have rarely been kept quite distinct.

§ 4. But even in cases where we can ascertain clearly to what authority obedience is properly due, further difficulties are liable to arise when we attempt to define the limits of such obedience. For in modern society, as we have seen, all admit that any authority ought to be disobeyed which commands immoral acts; but this is one of those tautological propositions, so common in popular morality, which convey no real information; the question is, what acts there are which do not cease to be immoral when they have been commanded by a rightful authority. There seems to be no clear principle upon which these can be determined. It has sometimes been said that the

may take this opportunity of observing that Austin's definition of Law is manifestly unsuited for our present purpose : since a law, in his view, is not a command that ought to be obeyed, but a command for the violation of which we may expect a particular kind of punishment.

Law cannot override definite duties; but the obligation of fidelity to contract is peculiarly definite, and yet we do not consider it right to fulfil a contract of which a law, passed subsequently to the making of the contract, has forbidden the execution. And, in fact, we do not find any practical agreement on this question, among persons who would not consciously accept the utilitarian method of deciding it by a balance of conflicting expediences. For some would say that the duties of the domestic relations must yield to the duty of law-observance, and that (*e.g.*) a son ought not to aid a parent actively or passively in escaping the punishment of crime : while others would consider this rule too inhuman to be laid down, and others would draw the line between assistance and connivance. And similarly, when a rightly constituted government commands acts unjust and oppressive to others; Common Sense recoils from saying either that all such commands ought to be obeyed or that all ought to be disobeyed; but—apart from utilitarian considerations—I can find no clear accepted principle for distinguishing those unjust commands of a legitimate government which ought to be obeyed from those which ought not to be obeyed. Again, some jurists hold that we are not strictly bound to obey laws, when they command what is not otherwise a duty, or forbid what is not otherwise a sin ; on the ground that in the case of duties prescribed only by positive laws, the alternatives of obeying or submitting to the penalty are morally open to us.[1] Others, however, think this principle too lax ; and certainly if a widespread preference of penalty to obedience were shown in the case of any particular law, the legislation in question would be thought to have failed. Nor, on the other hand, does there seem to be any agreement as to whether one is bound to submit to unjust penalties.

Since, then, on all these points there is found to be so much difference of opinion, it seems idle to maintain that there is any clear and precise axiom or first principle of Order, in-

---

[1] Cf. Blackstone, *Introduction*, § 2. " In relation to those laws which enjoin only positive duties, and forbid only such things as are not *mala in se*, but *mala prohibita* merely, without any intermixture of moral guilt, annexing a penalty to non-compliance, here I apprehend conscience is no further concerned, than by directing a submission to the penalty in case of our breach of those laws . . . the alternative is offered to every man, ' either abstain from this or submit to such a penalty.' "

tuitively seen to be true by the common reason and conscience of mankind.   There is, no doubt, a vague general habit of obedience to laws as such (even if bad laws), which may fairly claim the universal *consensus* of civilised society : but when we try to state any explicit principle corresponding to this general habit, the *consensus* seems to abandon us, and we are inevitably drawn into controversies which seem to admit of no solution except that offered by the utilitarian method.[1]

§ 5. We have next to treat of Good Faith, or Fidelity to Promises ; which it is natural to consider in this place, because, as has been seen, the Duty of Law-observance has by some thinkers been based upon a prior duty of fulfilling a contract. The Social Contract however, as above examined, seems at best merely a convenient fiction, a logical artifice, by which the mutual jural relations of the members of a civilised community may be neatly expressed : and in stating the ethical principles of Common Sense, such a fiction would seem to be out of place.   It must, however, be allowed that there has frequently been a close historical connection between the Duty of Law-observance and the duty of Good Faith.   In the first place, a considerable amount of Constitutional Law at least, in certain ages and countries, has been established or confirmed by compacts expressly made between different sections of the community ; who agree that for the future government shall be carried on according to certain rules.   The duty of observing these rules thus presents itself as a Duty of Fidelity to compact.   Yet more is this the case, when the question is one of imposing not a law, but a law-giver ; whose authority is strengthened by the exaction of an oath of allegiance from his subjects generally or a representative portion of them.   Still, even in such cases, it can only be by a palpable fiction that the mass of the citizens can be regarded as bound by an engagement which only a few of them have actually taken.

We may begin our examination of the duty of Keeping Promises by noticing that some moralists have classified or even identified it with Veracity.   From one point of view there certainly seems to be an analogy between the two ; as we fulfil the obligations of Veracity and Good Faith alike by effecting a

---

[1] Into the ethical difficulties peculiar to International Law, I have not thought it worth while to enter.

correspondence between words and facts—in the one case by making fact correspond with statement, and in the other by making statement correspond with fact. But the analogy is obviously superficial and imperfect; for we are not bound to make our actions correspond with our assertions generally, but only with our promises. If I merely assert my intention of abstaining from alcohol for a year, and then after a week take some, I am (at worst) ridiculed as inconsistent: but if I have pledged myself to abstain, I am blamed as untrustworthy. Thus the essential element of the Duty of Good Faith seems to be not conformity to my own statement, but to expectations that I have intentionally raised in others.

On this view, however, the question arises whether, when a promise has been understood in a sense not intended by the promiser, he is bound to satisfy expectations which he did not voluntarily create. It is, I think, clear to Common Sense that he is so bound in some cases, if the expectation was natural and such as most men would form under the circumstances: but this would seem to be one of the more or less indefinite duties of Justice, and not properly of Good Faith, as there has not been, strictly speaking, any promise at all. The normal effect of language is to convey the speaker's meaning to the person addressed (here the promiser's to the promisee), and we always suppose this to have taken place when we speak of a promise. If through any accident this normal effect is missed, we may say that there is no promise, or not a perfect promise.

The moral obligation, then, of a promise is perfectly constituted when it is understood by both parties in the same sense. And by the term 'promise' we include not words only, but all signs and even tacit understandings not expressly signified in any way, if such clearly form a part of the engagement. The promiser is bound to perform what both he and the promisee understood to be undertaken.

§ 6. Is, then, this obligation intuitively seen to be independent and certain ?

It is often said to be so: and perhaps we may say that it seems so to unreflective common sense. But reflection seems at least to disclose a considerable number of qualifications of the principle; some clear and precise, while others are more or less indefinite.

In the first place, thoughtful persons would commonly admit that the obligation of a promise is relative to the promisee, and may be annulled by him.   And therefore if the promisee be dead, or otherwise inaccessible and incapable of granting release, there is constituted an exceptional case, of which the solution presents some difficulty.[1]

Secondly, a promise to do an immoral act is held not to be binding, because the prior obligation not to do the act is paramount; just as in law a contract to do what a man is not legally free to do, is invalid: otherwise one could evade any moral obligation by promising not to fulfil it, which is clearly absurd.[2]   And the same principle is of course applicable to immoral omissions or forbearances to act: here however, a certain difficulty arises from the necessity of distinguishing between different kinds or degrees of obligatoriness in duties; since it is clear that a promise may sometimes make it obligatory to abstain from doing what it would otherwise have been a duty to do.   Thus it becomes my duty not to give money to a meritorious hospital if I have promised all I can spare to an undeserving friend; though apart from the promise it might have been my duty to prefer the hospital to the friend.   We have, however, already seen the difficulty of defining the limits of strict duty in many cases: thus (e.g.) it might be doubted how far the promise of aid to a friend ought to override the duty of giving one's children a good education.   The extent, therefore, to which the obligation of a promise overrides prior obligations becomes practically somewhat obscure.

§ 7.   Further qualifications of the duty of fidelity to promises, the consideration of which is involved in more difficulty and dispute, are suggested when we examine more closely the conditions under which promises are made, and the consequences of executing them.   In the first place, it is much disputed how far promises obtained by 'fraud or force' are binding.   As regards fraud, if the promise was understood

---

[1] Vows to God constitute another exception : and it is thought by many that if these are binding, there must be some way in which God can be understood to grant release from them.   But this it is beyond my province to discuss.

[2] The case is somewhat different when the act has become immoral after the promise was made : still, here also, the prior duty of abstaining from it would be universally held to prevail.

to be conditional on the truth of a statement which is found
to be false, it is of course not binding, according to the
principle I originally laid down. But a promise may be
made in consequence of such a fraudulent statement, and yet
made quite unconditionally. Even so, if it were clearly
understood that it would not have been made but for the
false statement,[1] probably most persons would regard it as not
binding. But the false statement may be only one consideration among others, and it may be of any degree of weight;
and it seems doubtful whether we should feel justified in
breaking a promise, because a single fraudulent statement had
been a part of the inducement to make it: still more if there
has been no explicit assertion, but only a suggestion of what
is false: or no falsehood at all, stated or suggested, but only
a concealment of material circumstances. We may observe
that certain kinds of concealment are treated as legitimate by
our law: in most contracts of sale, for example, the law adopts
the principle of 'caveat emptor,' and does not refuse to enforce
the contract because the seller did not disclose defects in the
article sold, unless by some words or acts he produced the
belief that it was free from such defects. Still, this does not
settle the moral question how far a promise is binding if any
material concealment is shown to have been used to obtain it.
We have also to consider the case in which an erroneous impression has not been wilfully produced, but was either shared
by the promisee or produced in some way unintentionally.
Perhaps in this last case most would say that the bindingness
of the promise is not affected, unless it was expressly conditional. But on all these points Common Sense seems
doubtful: and somewhat similar difficulties present themselves
when we endeavour to define the obligation of promises partly
obtained by some degree of illegal violence and intimidation.

§ 8. But, secondly, even if a promise has been made quite
freely and fairly, circumstances may alter so much before the
time comes to fulfil it, that the effects of keeping it may be
quite other than those which were foreseen when it was made.
In such a case probably all would agree that the promisee
ought to release the promiser. But if he declines to do this,

---

[1] What is here said of a 'statement' may be extended to any mode of
producing a false impression.

it seems difficult to decide how far the latter is bound.   Some would say that he is in all cases: while others would consider that a considerable alteration of circumstances removed the obligation—perhaps adding that all engagements must be understood to be taken subject to a general understanding that they are only binding if material circumstances remain substantially the same.   But such a principle very much impairs the theoretical definiteness of the duty.

This difficulty assumes a new aspect when we consider the case already noticed, of promises made to those who are now dead or temporarily out of the reach of communications.   For then there is no means of obtaining release from the promise, while at the same time its performance may be really opposed to the wishes—or what would have been the wishes—of both parties.   The difficulty is sometimes concealed by saying that it is our duty to carry out the 'intention' of the promise.   For as so used the word Intention is, in common parlance, ambiguous: it may either mean the signification which the promisee attached to the terms employed, as distinct from any other signification which the common usage of words might admit: or it may include ulterior consequences of the performance of the promise, which he had in view in exacting it.   Now we do not commonly think that the promiser is concerned with the latter.   He certainly has not pledged himself to aim generally at the end which the promisee has in view, but only so far as some particular means are concerned : and if he considers these means not conducive to the end, he is not thereby absolved from his promise, under ordinary circumstances.   But in the case supposed, when circumstances have materially changed, and the promise does not admit of revision, probably most persons would say that we ought to take into consideration the ulterior wishes of the promisee, and carry out what we sincerely think *would* have been his intention.   But the obligation thus becomes very vague : since it is difficult to tell from a man's wishes under one set of circumstances what he would have desired under circumstances varying from these in a complex manner : and practically this view of the obligation of a promise generally leads to great divergence of opinion.   Hence it is not surprising that some hold that even in such a case the obligation ought to be interpreted strictly : while others go to the other extreme, and maintain that it ceases altogether.

But again, it was said that a promise cannot abrogate a prior obligation; and, as a particular application of this rule, it would be generally agreed that no promise can make it right to inflict harm on any one. On further consideration, however, it appears doubtful how far the persons between whom the promise passed are included in the scope of this restriction. For, first, it does not seem to be commonly held that a man is as strictly bound not to injure himself as he is to avoid harming others; and so it is scarcely thought that a promise is not binding because it was a foolish one, and will entail an amount of pain or burden on the promiser out of proportion to the good done to the promisee. Still, if we take an extreme case, where the sacrifice is very disproportionate to the gain, many conscientious persons would think that the promise ought rather to be broken than kept. And, secondly, a different question arises when we consider the possibility of injuring the promisee by fulfilling the promise. For when it is said to be wrong to do harm to any one, we do not commonly mean only what he thinks harm, but what really is so, though he may think it a benefit; for it seems clearly a crime for me to give any one what I know to be poison, even though he may be stubbornly convinced that it is wholesome food. But now suppose that I have promised A to do something, which, before I fulfil the promise, I see reason to regard as likely to injure him. The circumstances may be precisely the same, and only my view of them have changed. If A takes a different view and calls on me to fulfil the promise, is it right to obey him? Surely no one would say this in an extreme case, such as that of the poison. But if the rule does not hold for an extreme case, where can we draw the line? at what point ought I to give up my judgment to A, unless my own conviction is weakened? Common Sense seems to give no clear answer.

§ 9. I have laid down that a promise is binding in so far as it is understood on both sides similarly: and such an understanding is ordinarily attained with sufficient clearness, as far as the apprehension of express words or signs is concerned. Still, even here obscurity and misapprehension

sometimes occur; and in the case of the tacit understandings
with which promises are often complicated, a lack of definite
agreement is not improbable.   It becomes, therefore, of
practical importance to decide the question previously raised :
What duty rests on the promiser of satisfying expectations
which he did not intend to create ?   I called this a duty not
so much of Good Faith as of Justice, which prescribes the
fulfilment of normal expectations.   How then shall we determine what these are ?   The method by which we commonly
ascertain them seems to be the following.   We form the
conception of an average or normal man, and consider what
expectations he would form under the circumstances, inferring
this from the beliefs and expectations which men generally
entertain under similar circumstances.   We refer, therefore,
to the customary use of language, and customary tacit understandings current among persons in the particular relations
in which promiser and promisee stand.   Such customary
interpretations and understandings are of course not obligatory
upon persons entering into an engagement : but they constitute
a standard which we think we may presume to be known to
all men, and to be accepted by them, except in so for as it is
explicitly rejected.   If one of the parties to an engagement
has deviated from this common standard without giving express
notice, we think it right that he should suffer any loss that
may result from the misunderstanding.   This criterion then
is generally applicable : but if custom is ambiguous or shifting
it cannot be applied ; and then the just claims of the parties
become a problem, the solution of which is very difficult, if
not strictly indeterminate.

So far we have supposed that the promiser can choose his
own words, and that if the promisee finds them ambiguous he
can get them modified, or (what comes to the same thing)
explained, by the promiser.   But we have now to observe
that in the case of promises made to the community, as a
condition of obtaining some office or emolument, a certain unalterable form of words has to be used if the promise is made
at all.   Here the difficulties of moral interpretation are much
increased.   It may be said, indeed, that the promise ought to
be interpreted in the sense in which its terms are understood
by the community : and, no doubt, if their usage is quite

uniform and unambiguous, this rule of interpretation is sufficiently obvious and simple. But since words are often used in different ways by different members of the same society, and especially with different degrees of strictness and laxity, it often happens that a promise to the community cannot strictly be said to be understood in any one sense: the question therefore arises, whether the promiser is bound to keep it in the sense in which it will be most commonly interpreted, or whether he may select any of its possible meanings. And if the formula is one of some antiquity, it is further questioned, whether it ought to be interpreted in the sense which its words would now generally bear, or in that which they bore when it was drawn up; or, if they were then ambiguous, in the sense which appears to have been attached to them by the government that imposed the promise. On all these points it is difficult to elicit any clear view from Common Sense. And the difficulty is increased by the fact that there are usually strong inducements to make these formal engagements, which cause even tolerably conscientious persons to take them in a strained and unnatural sense. When this has been done continually by many persons, a new general understanding grows up as to the meaning of the engagements: sometimes they come to be regarded as 'mere forms,' or, if they do not reach this point of degradation, they are at least understood in a sense differing indefinitely from their original one. The question then arises, how far this process of gradual illegitimate relaxation or perversion can modify the moral obligation of the promise for a thoroughly conscientious person. It seems clear that when the process is complete, we are right in adopting the new understanding as far as Good Faith is concerned, even if it palpably conflicts with the natural meaning of language; although it is always desirable in such cases that the form of the promise should be changed to correspond with the changed substance. But when, as is ordinarily the case, the process is incomplete, since a portion of the community understands the engagement in the original strict sense, the obligation becomes difficult to determine, and the judgments of conscientious persons respecting it become divergent and perplexed.

To sum up the results of the discussion : it appears that a

clear *consensus* can only be claimed for the principle that a promise, express or tacit, is binding, if a number of conditions are fulfilled : viz. if the promiser has a clear belief as to the sense in which it was understood by the promisee, and if the latter is still in a position to grant release from it, but unwilling to do so, if it was not obtained by force or fraud, if it does not conflict with definite prior obligations, if we do not believe that its fulfilment will be harmful to the promisee, or will inflict a disproportionate sacrifice on the promiser, and if circumstances have not materially changed since it was made. If any of these conditions fails, the *consensus* seems to become evanescent, and the common moral perceptions of thoughtful persons fall into obscurity and disagreement.

CHAPTER VII

THE CLASSIFICATION OF DUTIES—VERACITY

§ 1. It may easily seem that when we have discussed Benevolence, Justice, and the observance of Law and Contract, we have included in our view the whole sphere of social duty, and that whatever other maxims we find accepted by Common Sense must be subordinate to the principles which we have been trying to define.

For whatever we owe definitely to our fellow-men, besides the observance of special contracts, and of positive laws, seems —at least by a slight extension of common usage—to be naturally included under Justice: while the more indefinite obligations which we recognise seem to correspond to the goodwill which we think ought to exist among all members of the human family, together with the stronger affections appropriate to special relations and circumstances. And hence it may be thought that the best way of treating the subject would have been to divide Duty generally into Social and Self-regarding, and again to subdivide the former branch into the heads which I have discussed one by one; afterwards adding such minor details of duty as have obtained special names and distinct recognition. And this is perhaps the proper place to explain why I did not adopt this course. The division of duties into Social and Self-regarding, though obvious, and acceptable enough as a rough *prima facie* classification, does not on closer examination seem exactly appropriate to the Intuitional Method. For these titles naturally suggest that the happiness or well-being, of the agent or of others, is always the end and final determinant of right action: whereas the Intuitional doctrine is, that at least certain kinds of

312

conduct are prescribed absolutely, without reference to their ulterior consequences. And if a more general meaning be given to the terms, and by Social duties we understand those which consist in the production of certain effects upon others, while in the Self-regarding we aim at producing certain effects upon ourselves, the division is still an unsuitable one. For these consequences are not clearly recognised in the enunciation of common rules of morality : and in many cases we produce marked effects both on ourselves and on others, and it is not easy to say which (in the view of Common Sense) are most important: and again, this principle of division would sometimes make it necessary to cut in two the class of duties prescribed under some common notion ; as the same rule may govern both our social and our solitary conduct. Take, for example, the acts morally prescribed under the head of Courage. It seems clear that the prominence given to this Virtue in historic systems of morality has been due to the great social importance that must always attach to it, so long as communities of men are continually called upon to fight for their existence and well-being : but still the quality of bravery is the same essentially, whether it be exhibited for selfish or social ends.

It is no doubt true that when we examine with a view to definition the kinds of conduct commended or prescribed in any list of Virtues commonly recognised, we find, to a great extent, that the maxims we obtain are clearly not absolute and independent: that the quality denoted by our term is admittedly only praiseworthy in so far as it promotes individual or general welfare, and becomes blameworthy— though remaining in other respects the same—when it operates adversely to these ends. We have already noticed this result in one or two instances, and it will be illustrated at length in the following chapters. But though this is the case to a great extent, it is, for our present purpose, of special importance to note the—real or apparent—exceptions to the rule ; because they are specially characteristic of the method that we call Intuitionism.

One of the most important of these exceptions is Veracity: and the affinity in certain respects of this duty—in spite of fundamental differences—to the duty of Good Faith or

Fidelity to Promises renders it convenient to examine the two in immediate succession. Under either head a certain correspondence between words and facts is prescribed: and hence the questions that arise when we try to make the maxims precise are somewhat similar in both cases. For example, just as the duty of Good Faith did not lie in conforming our acts to the *admissible* meaning of certain words,[1] but to the meaning which we knew to be put on them by the promisee; so the duty of Truthspeaking is not to utter words which *might*, according to common usage, produce in other minds beliefs corresponding to our own, but words which we believe will have this effect on the persons whom we address. And this is usually a very simple matter, as the natural effect of language is to convey our beliefs to other men, and we commonly know quite well whether we are doing this or not. A certain difficulty arises, as in the case of promises, from the use of set forms imposed either by law or by custom; to which most of the discussion of the similar difficulty in the preceding chapter applies with obvious modifications. In the case of formulæ imposed by law—such (*e.g.*) as declarations of religious belief—it is doubtful whether we may understand the terms in any sense which they commonly bear, or are to take them in the sense intended by the Legislature that imposed them; and again, a difficulty is created by the gradual degradation or perversion of their meaning, which results from the strong inducements offered for their general acceptance; for thus they are continually strained and stretched until a new general understanding seems gradually to grow up as to the meaning of certain phrases; and it is continually disputed whether we may veraciously use the phrases in this new signification. A similar process continually alters the meaning of conventional expressions current in polite society. When a man declares that he 'has great pleasure in accepting' a vexatious invitation, or is 'the obedient servant' of one whom he regards as an inferior, he uses phrases which were probably once deceptive. If they are so no longer, Common Sense condemns as over-scrupulous the refusal to use them where it is customary to do so. But Common

---

[1] The case where set forms are used being the *exceptio probans regulam*.

Sense seems doubtful and perplexed where the process of degradation is incomplete, and there are still persons who may be deceived: as in the use of the reply that one is 'not at home' to an inconvenient visitor from the country.

However, apart from the use of conventional phrases, the rule 'to speak the truth' is not generally difficult of application in conduct.   And many moralists have regarded this, from its simplicity and definiteness, as a quite unexceptionable instance of an ethical axiom.   I think, however, that patient reflection will show that this view is not really confirmed by the Common Sense of mankind.

§ 2. In the first place, it does not seem clearly agreed whether Veracity is an absolute and independent duty, or a special application of some higher principle.   We find (*e.g.*) that Kant regards it as a duty owed to oneself to speak the truth, because 'a lie is an abandonment or, as it were, annihilation of the dignity of man.'   And this seems to be the view in which lying is prohibited by the code of honour, except that it is not thought (by men of honour as such) that the dignity of man is impaired by *any* lying: but only that lying for selfish ends, especially under the influence of fear, is mean and base.   In fact there seems to be circumstances under which the code of honour prescribes lying. Here, however, it may be said to be plainly divergent from the morality of Common Sense.   Still, the latter does not seem to decide clearly whether truth-speaking is absolutely a duty, needing no further justification: or whether it is merely a general right of each man to have truth spoken to him by his fellows, which right however may be forfeited or suspended under certain circumstances.   Just as each man is thought to have a natural right to personal security generally, but not if he is himself attempting to injure others in life and property: so if we may even kill in defence of ourselves and others, it seems strange if we may not lie, if lying will defend us better against a palpable invasion of our rights: and Common Sense does not seem to prohibit this decisively.   And again, just as the orderly and systematic slaughter which we call war is thought perfectly right under certain circumstances, though painful and revolting: so in the word-contests of the law-courts, the lawyer is commonly held to be justified in untruthfulness within strict rules and limits: for an advocate is thought to be over-scrupulous who refuses to say what he knows to be false, if he is instructed to say it.[1]   Again, where deception is designed to benefit the person deceived, Common Sense seems to concede that it may sometimes be right: for example, most persons would not hesitate to speak falsely to an invalid, if this seemed the only way of concealing facts that might produce a dangerous shock: nor do I perceive that any one shrinks from telling fictions to children, on matters upon which it is thought well that they should not know the truth.   But if the lawfulness of benevolent deception in any case be admitted, I do not see how we can decide when and how far it is admissible, except by considerations of expediency; that is, by weighing the gain of any particular deception against the imperilment of mutual confidence involved in all violation of truth.

The much argued question of religious deception (' pious fraud') naturally suggests itself here.   It seems clear, however, that Common Sense now pronounces against the broad rule, that falsehoods may rightly be told in the interests of religion.   But there is a subtler form in which the same principle is still maintained by moral persons.   It is sometimes said that the most important truths of religion cannot be conveyed into the minds of ordinary men, except by being enclosed, as it were, in a shell of fiction; so that by relating such fictions as if they were facts, we are really performing an act of substantial veracity.[2]   Reflecting upon this argument, we see that it is not after all so clear wherein Veracity consists.   For from the beliefs immediately communicated by any set of affirmations inferences are naturally drawn, and we may clearly foresee that they will be drawn.   And though commonly we intend that both the beliefs immediately com-

---

[1] It can hardly be said that the advocate merely *reports* the false affirmations of others : since the whole force of his pleading depends upon his adopting them and working them up into a view of the case which, for the time at least, he appears to hold.

[2] *E.g.* certain religious persons hold—or held in 1873—that it is right solemnly to affirm a belief that God created the world in 6 days and rested on the 7th, meaning that 1 : 6 is the divinely ordered proportion between rest and labour.

municated and the inferences drawn from them should be true, and a person who always aims at this is praised as candid and sincere : still we find relaxation of the rule prescribing this intention claimed in two different ways by at least respectable sections of opinion. For first, as was just now observed, it is sometimes held that if a conclusion is true and important, and cannot be satisfactorily communicated otherwise, we may lead the mind of the hearer to it by means of fictitious premises. But the exact reverse of this is perhaps a commoner view : viz. that it is only an absolute duty to make our actual affirmations true : for it is said that though the ideal condition of human converse involves perfect sincerity and candour, and we ought to rejoice in exhibiting these virtues where we can, still in our actual world concealment is frequently necessary to the well-being of society, and may be legitimately effected by any means short of actual falsehood. Thus it is not uncommonly said that in defence of a secret we may not indeed *lie*,[1] *i.e.* produce directly beliefs contrary to fact ; but we may " turn a question aside," *i.e.* produce indirectly, by natural inference from our answer, a negatively false belief ; or " throw the inquirer on a wrong scent," *i.e.* produce similarly a positively false belief. These two methods of concealment are known respectively as *suppressio veri* and *suggestio falsi*, and many think them legitimate under certain circumstances : while others say that if deception is to be practised at all, it is mere formalism to object to any one mode of effecting it more than another.

On the whole, then, reflection seems to show that the rule of Veracity, as commonly accepted, cannot be elevated into a definite moral axiom : for there is no real agreement as to how far we are bound to impart true beliefs to others : and while it is contrary to Common Sense to exact absolute candour under all circumstances, we yet find no self-evident secondary principle, clearly defining when it is not to be exacted.

§ 3. There is, however, one method of exhibiting *a priori* the absolute duty of Truth, which we must not overlook ; as, if it be valid, it would seem that the exceptions and qualifications above mentioned have been only admitted by Common Sense from inadvertence and shallowness of thought.

---

[1] Cf. Whewell, *Elements of Morality*, Book ii. chap. xv. § 299.

It is said that if it were once generally understood that lies were justifiable under certain circumstances, it would immediately become quite useless to tell the lies, because no one would believe them; and that the moralist cannot lay down a rule which, if generally accepted, would be suicidal. To this there seem to be three answers. In the first place it is not necessarily an evil that men's confidence in each other's assertions should, *under certain peculiar circumstances*, be impaired or destroyed: it may even be the very result which we should most desire to produce: *e.g.* it is obviously a most effective protection for legitimate secrets that it should be universally understood and expected that those who ask questions which they have no right to ask will have lies told them: nor, again, should we be restrained from pronouncing it lawful to meet deceit with deceit, merely by the fear of impairing the security which rogues now derive from the veracity of honest men. No doubt the ultimate result of general unveracity under the circumstances would be a state of things in which such falsehoods would no longer be told: but unless this ultimate result is undesirable, the prospect of it does not constitute a reason why the falsehoods should not be told so long as they are useful. But, secondly, since the beliefs of men in general are not formed purely on rational grounds, experience shows that unveracity may long remain partially effective under circumstances where it is generally understood to be legitimate. We see this in the case of the law-courts. For though jurymen are perfectly aware that it is considered the duty of an advocate to state as plausibly as possible whatever he has been instructed to say on behalf of any criminal he may defend, still a skilful pleader may often produce an impression that he sincerely believes his client to be innocent: and it remains a question of casuistry how far this kind of hypocrisy is justifiable. But, finally, it cannot be assumed as certain that it is never right to act upon a maxim of which the universal application would be an undoubted evil. This assumption may seem to be involved in what was previously admitted as an ethical axiom, that what is right for me must be right for 'all persons under similar conditions.'[1] But reflection will show that there is a special case within the range of the axiom in which its

---

[1] Cf. chap i. § 3 of this Book.

application is necessarily self-limiting, and excludes the practical universality which the axiom appears to suggest: *i.e.* where the agent's conditions include (1) the knowledge that his maxim is not universally accepted, and (2) a reasoned conviction that his act will not tend to make it so, to any important extent. For in this case the axiom will practically only mean that it will be right for all persons to do as the agent does, if they are sincerely convinced that the act will not be widely imitated; and this conviction must vanish if it *is* widely imitated. It can hardly be said that these conditions are impossible: and if they are possible, the axiom that we are discussing can only serve, in its present application, to direct our attention to an important danger of unveracity, which constitutes a strong—but not formally conclusive— utilitarian ground for speaking the truth.[1]

NOTE.—Mr. Stephen (*Science of Ethics*, chap. v. § 33) explains the exceptions to the rule of truth-speaking as follows:—

"The rule, 'Lie not,' is the external rule, and corresponds approximately to the internal rule, 'Be trustworthy.' Cases occur where the rules diverge, and in such cases it is the internal rule which is morally approved. Truthfulness is the rule because in the vast majority of cases we trust a man in so far as he speaks the truth; in the exceptional cases, the mutual confidence would be violated when the truth, not when the lie, is spoken."

This explanation seems to me for several reasons inadequate. (1) If we may sometimes lie to defend the life or secrets of others, it is paradoxical to say that we may not do so to defend our own; but a falsehood in self-defence obviously cannot be justified as an application of the maxim "be trustworthy." (2) Even when the falsehood is in legitimate defence of others against attacks, we cannot say that the speaker manifests "trustworthiness" without qualification; for the deceived assailant trusts his veracity, otherwise he would not be deceived: the question therefore is under what circumstances the confidence of *A* that I shall speak the truth may legitimately be disappointed in order not to disappoint the confidence of *B* that I shall defend his life and honour. This question Mr. Stephen's explanation does not in any way aid us to answer.

The general question raised by Mr. Stephen, as to the value of "internal rules," expressed in the form "Be this," in contrast to external rules, expressed in the form "Do this," will be dealt with in a subsequent chapter (xiv. § 1).

[1] See Book iv. chap. v. § 3 for a further discussion of this axiom.

CHAPTER VIII

OTHER SOCIAL DUTIES AND VIRTUES

§ 1. When we proceed to inquire how far the minor social duties and virtues recognised by Common Sense appear on examination to be anything more than special applications of the Benevolence—general or particular—discussed in chap. iv., the department of duty which most prominently claims our attention, is that which deals with the existence, and determines the legitimacy, of feelings antithetical to the benevolent.

For it seems that malevolent affections are as natural to man as the benevolent: not indeed in the same sense—for man tends to have normally some kindly feeling for any fellow-man, when there is no special cause operating to make him love or hate, (though this tendency is obscured in the lower stages of social development by the habitual hostility between strange tribes and races); but still such special causes of malevolent feeling continually occur, and, in the main, exemplify a psychological law analogous to that by which the growth of benevolent feelings is explained. For just as we are apt to love those who are the cause of pleasure to us whether by voluntary benefits or otherwise: so by strict analogy we naturally dislike those who have done us harm, either consciously from malevolence or mere selfishness, or even unconsciously, as when another man is an obstacle to our attainment of a much-desired end. Thus we naturally feel ill-will to a rival who deprives us of an object of competition: and so in persons in whom the desire of superiority is strong, a certain dislike of any one who is more successful or prosperous than themselves is easily aroused: and this envy, however repulsive to our moral sense, seems as natural as any other malevolent emotion.   And it is to be observed that each of the elements into which we can analyse malevolent affection finds its exact counterpart in the analysis of the benevolent : as the former includes a dislike of the presence of its object and a desire to inflict pain on it, and also a capacity of deriving pleasure from the pain thus inflicted.[1]

If now we ask how far indulgence of malevolent emotions is right and proper, the answer of Common Sense is not easy to formulate.   For some would say broadly that they ought to be repressed altogether or as far as possible.   And no doubt we blame all envy (though sometimes to exclude it altogether requires a magnanimity which we praise): and we regard as virtues or natural excellences the *good-humour* which prevents one from feeling even pain to a material extent—not to say resentment—from trifling annoyances inflicted by others, the *meekness* which does not resent even graver injuries, the *mildness* and *gentleness* which refrain from retaliating them, and the *placability* which accords forgiveness rapidly and easily.   We are even accustomed to praise the *mercy* which spares even deserved punishment : because though we never exactly disapprove of the infliction of deserved punishment, and hold it to be generally a duty of government—and in certain cases of private persons—to inflict it, we do not think that this duty admits of no exceptions ; we think that in exceptional cases considerations not strictly relevant to the question of justice may be properly regarded as reasons for remitting punishment, and we admire the sympathetic nature that eagerly avails itself of these legitimate occasions for remission.

On the other hand Common Sense admits instinctive resent-

---

[1] It is to be observed that men derive pleasure from the pains and losses of others, in various ways, without the specific emotion which I distinguish as malevolent affection : either (1) from the sense of power exercised—which explains much of the wanton cruelty of schoolboys, despots, etc.—or (2) from a sense of their own superiority or security in contrast with the failures and struggles of others, or (3) even merely from the excitement sympathetically caused by the manifestation or representation of any strong feeling in others ; a real tragedy is interesting in the same way as a fictitious one.   But these facts, though psychologically interesting, present no important ethical problems ; since no one doubts that pain ought not to be inflicted from such motives as these.

ment for wrong to be legitimate and proper: and even a more
sustained and deliberate malevolence is commonly approved as
virtuous indignation.   The problem, then, is how to reconcile
these diverse approvals.   Even as regards external duty, there
is some difficulty ; since, though it is clear to common sense that
in a well-ordered society punishment of adults ought generally
to be inflicted by government, and that a private individual
wronged ought not to "take the law into his own hands,"—
still there are in all societies injuries to individuals which the
law does not punish at all or not adequately, and for which
effective requital is often possible without transgressing the
limits of legality ; and there seems to be no clear agreement
as to the right manner of dealing with these.   For the Christian
code is widely thought to prescribe a complete and absolute
forgiveness of such offences, and many Christians have endeavoured to carry out this rule by dismissing the offences
as far as possible from their minds, or at least allowing the
memory of them to have no effect on their outward conduct.
Few, however, would deny that, so far as a wrong done to me
gives ground for expecting future mischief from the offender
to myself or to others, I am bound as a rational being to
take due precautions against this future mischief ; and probably
most would admit that such precautions for the future, in the
case we are considering, may include the infliction of punishment for the past, where impunity would give a dangerous
temptation to a repetition of the unpunished offence.   If we
ask, therefore, how far forgiveness is practically possible, the
answer seems admittedly to depend on two considerations :
(1) how far the punishment to which resentment prompts is
really required in the interests of society, and (2) how far, if so,
it will be adequately inflicted if the person wronged refrains
from inflicting it.   But, obviously, so far as we allow the
question to be settled by these considerations we are introducing a method difficult to distinguish from the Utilitarian.

And we seem led to a similar result in discussing the
legitimacy of malevolent feeling.   Here again we find much
disagreement among thoughtful persons : for many would say
that though the emotion of anger is legitimate, it ought to
be directed always against wrong acts as such, and not against
the agent : for even where the anger may legitimately prompt

us to punish him, it ought never to overcome our kindly feeling towards him.   And certainly if this state of mind is possible, it seems the simplest reconciliation of the general maxim of Benevolence with the admitted duty of inflicting punishment. On the other hand, it is urged, with some reason, that to retain a genuine kindly feeling towards a man, while we are gratifying a strong impulse of aversion to his acts by inflicting pain on him, requires a subtle complexity of emotion too far out of the reach of ordinary men to be prescribed as a duty : and that we must allow as right and proper a temporary suspension of benevolence towards wrong-doers until they have been punished. Some, again, make a distinction between Instinctive and Deliberate Resentment : saying that the former is legitimate in so far as it is required for the self-defence of individuals and the repression of mutual violence, but that deliberate resentment is not similarly needed, for if we act deliberately we can act from a better motive.   Others, however, think that a deliberate and sustained desire to punish wrong-doers is required in the interests of society, since the mere desire to realise Justice will not practically be strong enough to repress offences : and that it is as serious a mistake to attempt to substitute the desire of Justice for natural resentment as it would be to substitute prudence for natural appetite in eating and drinking, or mere dutifulness for filial affection.[1]

Again, a distinction may be taken between the impulse to inflict pain and the desire of the antipathetic pleasure which the agent will reap from this infliction ; so that, while we approve the former under certain circumstances, we may still regard the latter as altogether inadmissible.   It would seem, however, that a man under the influence of a strong passion of resentment can hardly exclude from his mind altogether an anticipation of the pleasure that he will feel when the passion is gratified; and if so, he can hardly exclude altogether the desire of this gratification. If, therefore, it is important for the well-being of society that men should derive hearty satisfaction from the punishment of a nefarious criminal, it is perhaps going too far to prohibit absolutely the desire of this satisfaction ; though we may say

---

[1] Butler (Sermon VIII., *Upon Resentment*) recognises that deliberate resentment "has in fact a good influence upon the affairs of the world" ; though "it were much to be wished that men would act from a better principle."

that a man ought not to cherish this desire, and gloat over the anticipated pleasure.

On the whole we may perhaps sum up by saying that a superficial view of the matter naturally leads us to condemn sweepingly all malevolent feelings and the acts to which they prompt, as contrary to the general duty of benevolence: but that the common sense of reflective persons recognises the necessity of relaxing this rule in the interests of society: only it is not clear as to the limits or principles of this relaxation, though inclined to let it be determined by considerations of expediency.

§ 2. The remaining virtues that are clearly and exclusively social, will be easily seen to have no independent maxims; the conduct in which they are respectively realised being merely the fulfilment, under special conditions, of the rules already discussed. We need not, then, enter upon an exhaustive examination of these minor virtues—for it is not our object to frame a complete glossary of ethical terms—: but for illustration's sake it may be well to discuss one or two of them; and I will select for examination Liberality with its cognate notions, partly on account of the prominence that it has had in the earlier ages of thought, and partly because of a certain complexity in the feelings with which it is usually regarded. Considered as a Virtue, Liberality seems to be merely Benevolence, as exhibited in the particular service of giving money, beyond the limits of strict duty as commonly recognised:—for in so far as it can be called a duty to be liberal, it is because in the performance of the more or less indefinite duties enumerated in chap. iv. we do not like exactness to be sought; a certain excess is needful if the duty is to be well done. And perhaps in the case of the poor this graceful excess is excluded by prudence: for though a poor man might make a great sacrifice in a small gift we should call this generous but scarcely liberal; Liberality appears to require an external abundance in the gift even more than a self-sacrificing disposition. It seems therefore to be possible only to the rich: and, as I have hinted, in the admiration commonly accorded to it there seems to be mingled an element rather æsthetic than moral. For we are all apt to admire power, and we recognise the latent power of wealth gracefully exhibited in a certain degree of careless profusion when the object is to give happiness to others. Indeed the vulgar admire the same carelessness as manifested even in selfish luxury.

The sphere of Liberality, then, lies generally in the fulfilment of the indefinite duties of Benevolence. But there is a certain borderground between Justice and Benevolence where it is especially shown; namely, in the full satisfaction of all customary expectations, even when indefinite and uncertain; as (*e.g.*) in the remuneration of services, in so far as this is governed by custom; and even where it is left entirely to free contract, and therefore naturally determined by haggling and bargaining (as market value generally), it is characteristic of a liberal man to avoid this haggling and to give somewhat higher remuneration than the other party might be induced to take, and similarly to take for his own services a somewhat lower payment than he might persuade the other to give. And again, since laws and promises and especially tacit understandings are sometimes doubtful and ambiguous, a liberal man will in such cases unhesitatingly adopt the interpretation which is least in his own favour, and pay the most that he can by any fairminded person be thought to owe, and exact the least that reasonably can be thought to be due to himself: that is, if the margin be, relatively to his resources, not considerable.[1] And of a man who does the opposite of all this we predicate Meanness; this being the vice antithetical to Liberality. Here again there seems no place for this particular vice if the amount at stake be considerable; for then we think it not mean to exact one's own rights to the full, and worse than mean to refuse another what he ought to have; in fact in such cases we think that any indefiniteness as to rights should be practically removed by the decision of a judge or arbitrator. The vice of meanness then is, we may say, bounded on the side of vice by injustice: the mean man is blamed not for violation of Justice, but, because he chooses a trifling gain to himself rather than the avoidance of disappointment to others. And here, again, it should be observed, an element not strictly moral is included in the common disapprobation of meanness. For, as we have seen,

---

[1] If the amount at stake is such as to constitute a real sacrifice, the conduct seems to be more than liberal, and (unless blamed as extravagant) is rather praised as generous or highminded.

a certain carelessness of money is admired as a sign of power and superiority : and the opposite habit is a symbol of inferiority. The mean man then is apt to be despised as having the bad taste to show this symbol needlessly, preferring a little gain to the respect of his fellow-men.

Meanness, however, has a wider sphere than Liberality, and refers not merely to the taking or refusing of money, but to taking advantages generally : in this wider sense the opposite virtue is Generosity.

In so far as the sphere of Generosity coincides with that of Liberality, the former seems partly to transcend the latter, partly to refer more to feelings than to outward acts, and to imply a completer triumph of unselfish over selfish impulses. In the wider sense it is strikingly exhibited in conflict and competition of all kinds. Here it is sometimes called Chivalry. Reflection shows us that the essence of this beautiful virtue is the realisation of Benevolence under circumstances which make it peculiarly difficult and therefore peculiarly admirable. For Generosity or Chivalry towards adversaries or competitors seems to consist in showing as much kindness and regard for their well-being as is compatible with the ends and conditions of conflict : one prominent form of this being the endeavour to realise ideal justice in these conditions, not merely by observing all the rules and tacit understandings under which the conflict is conducted, but by resigning even accidental advantages. Such resignation, however, is not considered a strict duty : nor is there any agreement as to how far it is right and virtuous ; for what some would praise and approve, others would regard as quixotic and extravagant.

To sum up, we may say that the terms Liberality and Generosity, so far as they are strictly ethical, denote the virtue of Benevolence (perhaps including Justice to some extent) as exhibited in special ways and under special conditions. And the examination of the other minor social virtues would evidently lead to similar general results : though it might not always be easy to agree on their definitions.

CHAPTER IX

SELF-REGARDING VIRTUES

§ 1. I CONCEIVE that according to the morality of Common Sense, an ultimate harmony between (1) Self-interest and (2) Virtue is assumed or postulated; so that the performance of duty and cultivation of Virtue generally may be regarded as a " duty to self," as being always conducive to the agent's true interest and well-being. But further, Common Sense (in modern Europe) recognises a strict duty of preserving one's own life, even when the prospect life offers is one in which pain préponderates over pleasure; it is, indeed, held to be right and praiseworthy to encounter certain death in the performance of strict duty, or for the preservation of the life of another, or for any very important gain to society; but not merely in order to avoid pain to the agent. At the same time, within the limits fixed by this and other duties, Common Sense considers, I think,[1] that it is a duty to seek our own happiness, except in so far as we can promote the welfare of others by sacrificing it. This " due concern about our own interest or happiness " may be called the Duty of Prudence. It should, however, be observed that—since it is less evident that men do not adequately desire their own greatest good, than

---

[1] Kant argues (*Met. Anfangsgr. d. Tugendlehre*, Th. I., § iv.) that as every one "inevitably wills" means to promote his own happiness this cannot be regarded as a duty. But, as I have before urged (Book i. chap. iv. § 1), a man does not "inevitably will" to do what he believes will be most conducive to his own *greatest* happiness.

The view in the text is that of Butler (Dissertation *Of the nature of Virtue*); who admits that "nature has not given us so sensible a disapprobation of imprudence and folly as of falsehood, injustice, and cruelty"; but points out that such sensible disapprobation is for various reasons less needed in the former case.

that their efforts are not sufficiently well directed to its attainment—in conceiving Prudence as a Virtue or Excellence, attention is often fixed almost exclusively on its intellectual side. Thus regarded, Prudence may be said to be merely Wisdom made more definite by the acceptance of Self-interest as its sole ultimate end : the habit of calculating carefully the best means to the attainment of our own interest, and resisting all irrational impulses which may tend to perturb our calculations or prevent us from acting on them.

§ 2. There are, however, current notions of particular virtues, which might be called Self-regarding; but yet with respect to which it is not quite clear whether they are merely particular applications of Prudence, or whether they have independent maxims. Of these Temperance, one of the four cardinal virtues anciently recognised, seems the most prominent. In its ordinary use, Temperance is the habit of controlling the principal appetites (or desires which have an immediate corporeal cause). The habit of moderating and controlling our desires generally is recognised by Common Sense as useful and desirable, but with less distinctness and emphasis.

All are agreed that our appetites need control: but in order to establish a maxim of Temperance, we have to determine within what limits, on what principle, and to what end they ought to be controlled. Now in the case of the appetites for food, drink, sleep, stimulants, etc., no one doubts that bodily health and vigour is the end naturally subserved by their gratification, and that the latter ought to be checked whenever it tends to defeat this end (including in the notion of health the most perfect condition of the mental faculties, so far as this appears to depend upon the general state of the body). And, further, the indulgence of a bodily appetite is manifestly imprudent, if it involves the loss of any greater gratification of whatever kind : and otherwise wrong if it interferes with the performance of duties; though it is perhaps doubtful how far this latter indulgence would commonly be condemned as ' intemperance.'

Some, however, deduce from the obvious truth, that the maintenance of bodily health is the chief natural end of the appetites, a more rigid rule of restraint, and one that goes beyond prudence. They say that this end ought to fix not only the negative but the positive limit of indulgence; that the pleasure derived from the gratification of appetite should never be sought *per se* (even when it does not impair health, or interfere with duty, or with a greater pleasure of a different kind); but only in so far as such gratification is positively conducive to health. When we consider to what a marked divergence from the usual habits of the moral rich this principle would lead, we might be disposed to say that it is clearly at variance with Common Sense: but it often meets with verbal assent.

There is, again, a third and intermediate view which accepts the principle that the gratification of appetite is not to be sought for its own sake, but admits other ends as legitimate besides the mere maintenance of health and strength :—*e.g.* "cheerfulness, and the cultivation of the social affections." [1] Some such principle seems to be more or less consciously held by many persons: hence we find that solitary indulgence in the pleasures of the table is very frequently regarded with something like moral aversion: and that the banquets which are given and enjoyed by moral persons, are vaguely supposed to have for their end not the common indulgence of sensual appetites, but the promotion of conviviality and conversational entertainment. For it is generally believed that the enjoyment in common of a luxurious meal develops social emotions, and also stimulates the faculties of wit and humour and lively colloquy in general; and feasts which are obviously not contrived with a view to such convivial and colloquial gratifications seem to be condemned by refined persons. Still it would be going too far to state, as a maxim supported by Common Sense in respect of sensual pleasures generally, that they are never to be sought except they positively promote those of a higher kind.

§ 3. In the last section we have spoken chiefly of the appetites for food and drink. It is, however, in the case of the appetite of sex that the regulation morally prescribed most clearly and definitely transcends that of mere prudence : which is indicated by the special notion of Purity or Chastity.[2]

---

[1] See Whewell's *Elements of Morality*, Book ii. chap. x.

[2] The notion of Chastity is nearly equivalent to that of Purity, only somewhat more external and superficial.

At first sight it may perhaps appear that the regulation of the sexual appetite prescribed by the received moral code merely confines its indulgence within the limits of the union sanctioned by law : only that here, as the natural impulse is peculiarly powerful and easily excited, it is especially necessary to prohibit any acts, internal as well as external, that tend even indirectly to the transgression of these limits. And this is to a great extent true : still on reflection it will appear, I think, that our common notion of purity implies a standard independent of law ; for, first, conformity to this does not necessarily secure purity : and secondly, all illegitimate sexual intercourse is not thought to be impure,[1] and it is only by inadvertence that the two notions are sometimes confounded. But it is not very clear what this standard is. For when we interrogate the moral consciousness of mankind, we seem to find two views, a stricter and a laxer, analogous to the two interpretations of Temperance last noticed. It is agreed that the sexual appetite ought never to be indulged for the sake of the sensual gratification merely, but as a means to some higher end : but some say that the propagation of the species is the only legitimate, as it is obviously the primary natural, end : while others regard the development of mutual affection in a union designed to be permanent as an end perfectly admissible and right. I need not point out that the practical difference between the two views is considerable ; so that this question is one which it is necessary to raise and decide. But it may be observed that any attempt to lay down minute and detailed rules on this subject seems to be condemned by Common Sense as tending to defeat the end of purity ; as such minuteness of moral legislation invites men in general to exercise their thoughts on this subject to an extent which is practically dangerous.[2]

I ought to point out that the Virtue of Purity is certainly not merely self-regarding, and is therefore properly out of place in this chapter : but the convenience of discussing it

---

[1] In so far as mere illegitimacy of union is conceived to be directly and specially prohibited, and not merely from considerations of Prudence and Benevolence, it is regarded as a violation of Order rather than of Purity.

[2] It was partly owing to the serious oversight of not perceiving that Purity itself forbids too minute a system of rules for the observance of purity that the mediæval Casuistry fell into disrepute.

along with Temperance has led me to take it out of its natural order. Some, however, would go further, and say that it ought to be treated as a distinctly social virtue: for the propagation and rearing of children is one of the most important of social interests: and they would maintain that Purity merely connotes a sentiment protective of these important functions, supporting the rules which we consider necessary to secure their proper performance. But it seems clear that, though Common Sense undoubtedly recognises this tendency of the sentiment of Purity to maintain the best possible provision for the continuance of the human race, it still does not regard that as the fundamental point in the definition of this rule of duty, and the sole criterion in deciding whether acts do or do not violate the rule.

There seem to be no similar special questions with respect to most other desires. We recognise, no doubt, a general duty of self-control: but this is merely as a means to the end of acting rationally (whatever our interpretation of rational action may be); it only prescribes that we should yield to no impulse which prompts us to act in antagonism to ends or rules deliberately accepted. Further, there is a certain tendency among moral persons to the ascetic opinion that the gratification of merely sensual impulse is in itself somewhat objectionable: but this view does not seem to be taken by Common Sense in particular cases;—we do not (*e.g.*) commonly condemn the most intense enjoyment of muscular exercise, or warmth, or bathing. The only other case, besides that of the appetites above discussed, in which the Common Sense of our age and country seems to regard as right or admirable the repression of natural impulses, beyond what Prudence and Benevolence would dictate, is that of the promptings of pain and fear. An important instance of this is to be found in the before-mentioned rule prohibiting suicide absolutely, even in face of the strongest probability that the rest of a man's life will be both miserable and burdensome to others. But in other cases also praise is apparently bestowed on endurance of pain and danger, beyond what is conducive to happiness; as we shall have occasion to observe in the next chapter.

CHAPTER X

COURAGE, HUMILITY, ETC.

§ 1. BESIDES the Virtue of Purity, which we found it convenient to discuss in the last chapter, there remain one or two prominent excellences of character which do not seem to be commonly admired and inculcated with any distinct reference either to private or to general happiness; and which, though in most cases obviously conducive to one or other of these ends, sometimes seem to influence conduct in a direction at variance with them.

For example, Courage is a quality which excites general admiration, whether it is shown in self-defence, or in aiding others, or even when we do not see any benefit resulting from the particular exhibition of it. Again, in Christian societies, Humility (if believed sincere) often obtains unqualified praise, in spite of the loss that may evidently result from a man's underrating his own abilities. It will be well, therefore, to examine how far in either case we can elicit a clear and independent maxim defining the conduct commended under each of these notions.

To begin with Courage. We generally denote by this term a disposition to face danger of any kind without shrinking. We sometimes also call those who bear pain unflinchingly courageous: but this quality of character we more commonly distinguish as Fortitude. Now it seems plain that if we seek for a definition of *strict duty*, as commonly recognised, under the head either of Courage or of Fortitude, we can find none that does not involve a reference to other maxims and ends. For no one would say that it is our *duty* to face danger or to bear avoidable pain generally, but only

if it meets us in the course of duty.[1] And even this needs
further qualification : for as regards such duties as those (*e.g.*) of
general Benevolence, it would be commonly allowed that the
agent's pain and danger are to be taken into account in
practically determining their extent :—it would be held that
we are not bound to endure any pain except for the prevention
of manifestly greater pain to another, or the attainment of a
more important amount of positive good : nor to run any risk,
unless the chance of additional benefit to be gained for another
outweighs the cost and chance of loss to ourselves if we fail.
Indeed it is doubtful whether the common estimate of the
duty of Benevolence could be said to amount quite to this.[2]

When, however, we consider Courage as an Excellence
rather than a duty, it seems to hold a more independent
position in our moral estimation. And this view corresponds
more completely than the other to the common application
of the notion ; as there are many acts of courage, which are not
altogether within the control of the Will, and therefore cannot
be regarded as strict duties. For (1) danger is frequently
sudden and needs to be met without deliberation, so that our
manner of meeting it can only be semi-voluntary. And (2)
though naturally timid persons can perhaps with effort control
fear as they can anger or appetite, if time be allowed for
deliberation, and can prevent it from taking effect in dereliction
of duty : still this result is not all that is required for the
performance of such courageous acts as need more than ordinary
energy—for the energy of the timid virtuous man is liable to be
exhausted in the effort to control his fear : *e.g.* in battle he can
perhaps stand still to be killed as well as the courageous man,
but not charge with the same impetuosity or strike with the
same vigour and precision.[3]

So far then as Courage is not completely voluntary, we
have to consider whether it is a desirable quality rather

---

[1] In the case of pain which cannot be avoided we consider that Fortitude will
suppress outcries and lamentations : though in so far as these relieve the sufferer
without annoying others, the duty seems doubtful.

[2] Cf. *ante*, chap. iv. § 5 of this Book.

[3] The above remarks apply in a less degree to the "moral courage" by
which men face the pains and dangers of social disapproval in the performance
of what they believe to be duty : for the adequate accomplishment of such acts
depends less on qualities not within the control of the will at any given time.

than whether we are strictly bound to exhibit it. And here there seems no doubt that we commonly find it morally admirable without reference to any end served by it, and when the dangers which call it forth might be avoided without any dereliction of duty. At the same time we call a man foolhardy who runs unnecessarily into danger beyond a certain degree. Where then is the limit to be fixed? On utilitarian principles we should endeavour to strike as exact a balance as possible between the amount of danger incurred in any case and the probable benefit of cultivating and developing by practice a habit so frequently necessary for the due performance of important duties. This will obviously give a different result for different states of society and different callings and professions; as most people need this instinctive courage less in civilised societies than in semi-barbarous ones, and civilians less than soldiers. Perhaps the instinctive admiration of mankind for acts of daring does not altogether observe this limit: but we may say, I think, that in so far as it attempts to justify itself on reflection, it is commonly in some such way as this; and Common Sense does not seem to point to any limit depending on a different principle.

§ 2. As the Virtue of Courage is prominent in Pagan ethics, and in the Code of Honour which may be regarded as a sort of survival of the pagan view of morality, so Humility especially belongs to the ideal set before mankind by Christianity. The common account, however, of this virtue is somewhat paradoxical. For it is generally said that Humility prescribes a low opinion of our own merits: but if our merits are comparatively high, it seems strange to direct us to have a low opinion of them. It may be replied, that though our merits may be high when compared with those of ordinary men, there are always some to be found superior, and we can compare ourselves with these, and in the extreme case with ideal excellence, of which all fall far short; and that we ought to make this kind of comparison and not the other kind, and contemplate our faults—of which we shall assuredly find a sufficiency—and not our merits. But surely in the most important deliberations which human life offers, in determining what kind of work we shall undertake and to what social functions we shall aspire, it is often necessary that we should compare our qualifications carefully with those of average men, if we are to decide rightly. And it would seem just as irrational to underrate ourselves as to overrate; and though most men are more prone to the latter mistake, there are certainly some rather inclined to the former.

I think that if we reflect carefully on the common judgments in which the notion of Humility is used, we shall find that the quality commonly *praised* under this name (which is not always used eulogistically), is not properly regulative of the opinions we form of ourselves—for here as in other opinions we ought to aim at nothing but Truth—but tends to the repression of two different seductive emotions, one entirely self-regarding, the other relating to others and partly taking effect in social behaviour.   Partly, the Virtue of Humility is manifested in repressing the emotion of self-admiration, which springs naturally from the contemplation of our own merits, and as it is highly agreeable, prompts to such contemplation.   This admiring self-complacency is generally condemned: but not, I think, by an intuition that claims to be ultimate, as it is commonly justified by the reason that such self-admiration, even if well-grounded, tends to check our progress towards higher virtue.   The mere fact of our feeling this admiration is thought to be evidence that we have not sufficiently compared ourselves with our ideal, or that our ideal is not sufficiently high: and it is thought to be indispensable to moral progress that we should have a high ideal and should continually contemplate it.   At the same time, we obviously need some care in the application of this maxim. For all admit that self-respect is an important auxiliary to right conduct: and moralists continually point to the satisfactions of a good conscience as part of the natural reward which Providence has attached to virtue: yet it is difficult to separate the glow of self-approbation which attends the performance of a virtuous action from the complacent self-consciousness which Humility seems to exclude.   Perhaps we may say that the feeling of self-approbation itself is natural and a legitimate pleasure, but that if prolonged and fostered it is liable to impede moral progress: and that what Humility prescribes is such repression of self-satisfaction as will tend on the whole to promote this end.   On this view the maxim of Humility is clearly a dependent one: the end to which it is subordinate is

progress in Virtue generally.   As for such pride and self-satisfaction as are based not on our own conduct and its results,
but on external and accidental advantages, these are condemned as involving a false and absurd view as to the nature
of real merit.

But we not only take pleasure in our own respect and
admiration, but still more, generally speaking, in the respect
and admiration of others.   The desire for this, again, is held
to be to some extent legitimate, and even a valuable aid to
morality : but as it is a dangerously seductive impulse, and
frequently acts in opposition to duty, it is felt to stand in
special need of self-control.   Humility, however, does not so
much consist in controlling this desire, as in repressing the
claim for its satisfaction which we are naturally disposed to
make upon others.   We are inclined to demand from others
' tokens of respect,' some external symbol of their recognition of
our elevated place in the scale of human beings ; and to complain
if our demands are not granted.   Such claims and demands
Humility bids us repress.   It is thought to be our duty not
to exact, in many cases, even the expression of reverence which
others are strictly bound to pay.   And yet here, again, there is
a limit, in the view of Common Sense, at which this quality of
behaviour passes over into a fault : for the omission of marks of
respect [1] is sometimes an insult which impulses commonly
regarded as legitimate and even virtuous (sense of Dignity, Self-
respect, Proper Pride, etc.) prompt us to repel.   I do not,
however, think it possible to claim a *consensus* for any formula
for determining this limit.

[1] I do not refer to customary marks of respect for officials, the omission of
which would be a breach of established order ; since the special political reason
for requiring these obviously takes the question beyond the sphere of application
of the Virtue of Humility.

CHAPTER XI

REVIEW OF THE MORALITY OF COMMON SENSE

§ 1. WE have now concluded such detailed examination of the morality of Common Sense as, on the plan laid down in chap. i. of this Book, it seemed desirable to undertake. We have not discussed all the terms of our common moral vocabulary : but I believe that we have omitted none that are important either in themselves or relatively to our present inquiry. For of those that remain we may fairly say, that they manifestly will not furnish independent maxims : for reflection will show that the conduct designated by them is either prescribed merely as a means to the performance of duties already discussed ; or is really identical with the whole or part of some of these, viewed in some special aspect, or perhaps specialised by the addition of some peculiar circumstance or condition.

Let us now pause and survey briefly the process in which we have been engaged, and the results which we have elicited.

We started with admitting the point upon the proof of which moralists have often concentrated their efforts, the existence of apparently independent moral intuitions. It seemed undeniable that men judge some acts to be right and wrong in themselves, without consideration of their tendency to produce happiness to the agent or to others : and indeed without taking their consequences into account at all, except in so far as these are included in the common notion of the act. We saw, however, that in so far as these judgments are passed in particular cases, they seem to involve (at least for the more reflective part of mankind) a reference of the case to some general rule of duty : and that in the frequent cases of doubt or conflict of judgments as to the rightness of any action, appeal is commonly made to such rules or maxims, as the ultimately valid principles of moral cognition. In order, therefore, to throw the Morality of Common Sense into a scientific form, it seemed necessary to obtain as exact a statement as possible of these generally recognised principles. I did not think that I could dispense myself from this task by any summary general argument, based on the unscientific character of common morality. There is no doubt that the moral opinions of ordinary men are in many points loose, shifting, and mutually contradictory, but it does not follow that we may not obtain from this fluid mass of opinion, a deposit of clear and precise principles commanding universal acceptance. The question, whether we can do this or not, seemed to me one which should not be decided *a priori* without a fair trial: and it is partly in order to prepare materials for this trial that the survey in the preceding eight chapters has been conducted. I have endeavoured to ascertain impartially, by mere reflection on our common moral discourse, what are the general principles or maxims, according to which different kinds of conduct are judged to be right and reasonable in different departments of life. I wish it to be particularly observed, that I have in no case introduced my own views, in so far as I am conscious of their being at all peculiar to myself: my sole object has been to make explicit the implied premises of our common moral reasoning. I now wish to subject the results of this survey to a final examination, in order to decide whether these general formulæ possess the characteristics by which self-evident truths are distinguished from mere opinions.

§ 2. There seem to be four conditions, the complete fulfilment of which would establish a significant proposition, apparently self-evident, in the highest degree of certainty attainable: and which must be approximately realised by the premises of our reasoning in any inquiry, if that reasoning is to lead us cogently to trustworthy conclusions.

I. The terms of the proposition must be clear and precise. The rival originators of modern Methodology, Descartes and Bacon, vie with each other in the stress that they lay on this point: and the latter's warning against the " notiones male terminatæ " of ordinary thought is peculiarly needed in ethical

discussion.   In fact my chief business in the preceding survey
has been to free the common terms of Ethics, as far as possible,
from objection on this score.

II. The self-evidence of the proposition must be ascertained by careful reflection.   It is needful to insist on this,
because most persons are liable to confound intuitions, on the
one hand with mere impressions or impulses, which to careful
observation do not present themselves as claiming to be
dictates of Reason ; and on the other hand, with mere opinions,
to which the familiarity that comes from frequent hearing
and repetition often gives a false appearance of self-evidence
which attentive reflection disperses.   In such cases the
Cartesian method of testing the ultimate premises of our
reasonings, by asking ourselves if we clearly and distinctly
apprehend them to be true, may be of real use ; though it
does not, as Descartes supposed, afford a complete protection
against error.   A rigorous demand for self-evidence in our
premises is a valuable protection against the misleading influence of our own irrational impulses on our judgments : while
at the same time it not only distinguishes as inadequate the
mere external support of authority and tradition, but also
excludes the more subtle and latent effect of these in fashion-
ing our minds to a facile and unquestioning admission of
common but unwarranted assumptions.

And we may observe that the application of this test is
especially needed in Ethics.   For, on the one hand, it cannot
be denied that any strong sentiment, however purely subjective,
is apt to transform itself into the semblance of an intuition ;
and it requires careful contemplation to detect the illusion.
Whatever we desire we are apt to pronounce desirable : and we
are strongly tempted to approve of whatever conduct gives us
keen pleasure.[1]   And on the other hand, among the rules of
conduct to which we customarily conform, there are many
which reflection shows to be really derived from some external
authority : so that even if their obligation be unquestionable,
they cannot be intuitively ascertained. This is of course the case
with the Positive Law of the community to which we belong.
There is no doubt that we ought,—at least generally speaking,

---

[1] Hence the practical importance of the Formal test of Rightness, on which
Kant insists : cf. *ante*, chap. i. § 3 of this Book.

—to obey this : but what it is we cannot of course ascertain by any process of abstract reflection, but only by consulting Reports and Statutes. Here, however, the sources of knowledge are so definite and conspicuous, that we are in no danger of confounding the knowledge gained from studying them with the results of abstract contemplation. The case is somewhat different with the traditional and customary rules of behaviour which exist in every society, supplementing the regulative operation of Law proper : here it is much more difficult to distinguish the rules which a moral man is called upon to define for himself, by the application of intuitively known principles, from those as to which some authority external to the individual is recognised as the final arbiter.[1]

We may illustrate this by referring to two systems of rules which we have before[2] compared with Morality ; the Law of Honour, and the Law of Fashion or Etiquette. I noticed that there is an ambiguity in the common terms ' honourable ' and ' dishonourable '; which are no doubt sometimes used, like ethical terms, as implying an absolute standard. Still, when we speak of the Code of Honour we seem to mean rules of which the exact nature is to be finally determined by an appeal to the general opinion of well-bred persons : we admit that a man is in a sense ' dishonoured ' when this opinion condemns him, even though we may think his conduct unobjectionable or even intrinsically admirable.[3] Similarly, when we consider from the point of view of reason the rules of Fashion or Etiquette, some may seem useful and commendable, some indifferent and arbitrary, some perhaps absurd and burdensome : but nevertheless we recognise that the final authority on matters of Etiquette is the custom of polite society ; which feels itself under no obligation of reducing its rules to rational principles. Yet it must be observed that each individual in any society commonly finds in himself a knowledge not obviously incomplete of the rules of Honour and Etiquette, and an impulse to conform to them without requiring any further reason for doing so. Each often seems to see at a glance what

---

[1] The final arbiter, that is, on the question what the rule is : of course the moral obligation to conform to any rule laid down by an external authority must rest on some principle which the individual's reason has to apply.

[2] Cf. Book i. chap. iii. § 2.   [3] Cf. Book i. chap. iii. § 2.

is honourable and polite just as clearly as he sees what is right : and it requires some consideration to discover that in the former cases custom and opinion are generally the final authority from which there is no appeal.   And even in the case of rules regarded as distinctly moral, we can generally find an element that seems to us as clearly conventional as the codes just mentioned, when we contemplate the morality of other men, even in our own age and country.   Hence we may reasonably suspect a similar element in our own moral code : and must admit the great importance of testing rigorously any rule which we find that we have a habitual impulse to obey ; to see whether it really expresses or can be referred to a clear intuition of rightness.

III. The propositions accepted as self-evident must be mutually consistent.   Here, again, it is obvious that any collision between two intuitions is a proof that there is error in one or the other, or in both.   Still, we frequently find ethical writers treating this point very lightly.   They appear to regard a conflict of ultimate rules as a difficulty that may be ignored or put aside for future solution, without any slur being thrown on the scientific character of the conflicting formulæ.   Whereas such a collision is absolute proof that at least one of the formulæ needs qualification : and suggests a doubt whether the correctly qualified proposition will present itself with the same self-evidence as the simpler but inadequate one ; and whether we have not mistaken for an ultimate and independent axiom one that is really derivative and subordinate.

IV. Since it is implied in the very notion of Truth that it is essentially the same for all minds, the denial by another of a proposition that I have affirmed has a tendency to impair my confidence in its validity.   And in fact ' universal ' or ' general ' consent has often been held to constitute by itself a sufficient evidence of the truth of the most important beliefs ; and is practically the only evidence upon which the greater part of mankind can rely.   A proposition accepted as true upon this ground alone has, of course, neither self-evidence nor demonstrative evidence for the mind that so accepts it ; still, the secure acceptance that we commonly give to the generalisations of the empirical sciences rests—

even in the case of experts—largely on the belief that other experts have seen for themselves the evidence for these generalisations, and do not materially disagree as to its adequacy. And it will be easily seen that the absence of such disagreement must remain an indispensable negative condition of the certainty of our beliefs. For if I find any of my judgments, intuitive or inferential, in direct conflict with a judgment of some other mind, there must be error somewhere: and if I have no more reason to suspect error in the other mind than in my own, reflective comparison between the two judgments necessarily reduces me temporarily to a state of neutrality. And though the total result in my mind is not exactly suspense of judgment, but an alternation and conflict between positive affirmation by one act of thought and the neutrality that is the result of another, it is obviously something very different from scientific certitude.

Now if the account given of the Morality of Common Sense in the preceding chapters be in the main correct, it seems clear that, generally speaking, its maxims do not fulfil the conditions just laid down. So long as they are left in the state of somewhat vague generalities, as we meet them in ordinary discourse, we are disposed to yield them unquestioning assent, and it may be fairly claimed that the assent is approximately universal—in the sense that any expression of dissent is eccentric and paradoxical. But as soon as we attempt to give them the definiteness which science requires, we find that we cannot do this without abandoning the universality of acceptance. We find, in some cases, that alternatives present themselves, between which it is necessary that we should decide; but between which we cannot pretend that Common Sense does decide, and which often seem equally or nearly equally plausible. In other cases the moral notion seems to resist all efforts to obtain from it a definite rule: in others it is found to comprehend elements which we have no means of reducing to a common standard, except by the application of the Utilitarian —or some similar—method. Even where we seem able to educe from Common Sense a more or less clear reply to the questions raised in the process of definition, the principle that results is qualified in so complicated a way that its self-evidence becomes dubious or vanishes altogether. And thus in each case what at first seemed like an intuition turns out to be either the mere expression of a vague impulse, needing regulation and limitation which it cannot itself supply, but which must be drawn from some other source: or a current opinion, the reasonableness of which has still to be shown by a reference to some other principle.

In order that this result may be adequately exhibited, I must ask the reader to travel with me again through the series of principles elicited from Common Sense in the previous chapters, and to examine them from a somewhat different point of view. Before, our primary aim was to ascertain impartially what the deliverances of Common Sense actually are: we have now to ask how far these enunciations can claim to be classed as Intuitive Truths.

The reader should observe that throughout this examination a double appeal is made; on the one hand to his individual moral consciousness, and, on the other hand, to the Common Sense of mankind, as expressed generally by the body of persons on whose moral judgment he is prepared to rely. I ask him (1) whether he can state a clear, precise, self-evident first principle, according to which he is prepared to judge conduct under each head: and (2) if so, whether this principle is really that commonly applied in practice, by those whom he takes to represent Common Sense.[1]

§ 3. If we begin by considering the duty of acting wisely, discussed in chap. iii., we may seem perhaps to have before us an axiom of undoubted self-evidence. For acting wisely appeared to mean taking the right means to the best ends; *i.e.* taking the means which Reason indicates to the ends which Reason prescribes. And it is evident that it must be right to act reasonably. Equally undeniable is the immediate

---

[1] It has been fairly urged that I leave the determinations of Common Sense very loose and indefinite : and if I were endeavouring to bring out a more positive result from this examination, I ought certainly to have discussed further how we are to ascertain the 'experts' on whose 'consensus' we are to rely, in this or any other subject. But my scientific conclusions are to so great an extent negative, that I thought it hardly necessary to enter upon this discussion. I have been careful not to *exaggerate* the doubtfulness and inconsistency of Common Sense : should it turn out to be *more* doubtful and inconsistent than I have represented it, my argument will only be strengthened.

inference from, or negative aspect of, this principle; that it is wrong to act in opposition to rational judgment. This, taken in connexion with the empirical fact of impulses in our minds conflicting with Reason, gives—as another self-evident principle—the maxim of Temperance or Self-control in its widest interpretation; *i.e.* 'That reason should never give way to Appetite or Passion.'[1] And these principles have sometimes been enounced with no little solemnity as answering the fundamental question of Ethics and supplying the basis or summary of a doctrine of Practice.

But this statement of principles turns out to be one of those stages, so provokingly frequent in the course of ethical reflection, which, as far as practical guidance is concerned, are really brief circuits, leading us back to the point from which we started. Or rather, to prevent misapprehension, it should be observed that the maxims just given may be understood in two senses: in one sense they are certainly self-evident, but they are also insignificant: in another sense they include more or less distinctly a direction to an important practical duty, but as so understood they lose their self-evidence. For if the rules of Wisdom and Self-control mean (1) that we ought always to do what we see to be reasonable, and (2) that we are not to yield to any impulse urging us in an opposite direction; they simply affirm that it is our duty (1) generally, and (2) under special temptations, to do what we judge to be our duty:[2] and convey no information as to the method and principles by which duty is to be determined.

But if these rules are further understood (as they sometimes are understood) to prescribe the cultivation of a habit of acting rationally; that is, of referring each act to definitely conceived principles and ends, instead of allowing it to be determined by instinctive impulses; then I cannot see that the affirmation of

---

[1] In chap. ix. Temperance was regarded as subordinate to, or a special application of, Prudence or Self-love moralised: because this seemed to be on the whole the view of Common Sense, which in the preceding chapters I have been endeavouring to follow as closely as possible, both in stating the principles educed and in the order of their exposition.

[2] The admission that these maxims are self-evident must be taken subject to the distinction before established between "subjective" and "objective" rightness. It is a necessary condition of my acting rightly that I should not do what I judge to be wrong: but if my judgment is mistaken, my action in accordance with it will not be "objectively" right.

this as an universal and absolute rule of duty is self-evidently true. For when Reason is considered not in the present as actually commanding, but as an End of which a fuller realisation has to be sought in the future ; the point of view from which its sovereignty has to be judged is entirely changed. The question is no longer whether the dictates of Reason ought always to be obeyed, but whether the dictation of Reason is always a Good ; whether any degree of predominance of Reason over mere Impulse must necessarily tend to the perfection of the conscious self of which both are elements. And it is surely not self-evident that this predominance cannot be carried too far ; and that Reason is not rather self-limiting, in the knowledge that rational ends are sometimes better attained by those who do not directly aim at them as rational. Certainly Common Sense is inclined to hold that in many matters instinct is a better spring of action than reason : thus it is commonly said that a healthy appetite is a better guide to diet than a doctor's prescription : and, again, that marriage is better undertaken as a consequence of falling in love than in execution of a tranquil and deliberate design : and we before observed (chap. iv.) that there is a certain excellence in services springing from spontaneous affection which does not attach to similar acts done from pure sense of duty. And in the same way experience seems to show that many acts requiring promptitude and vigour are likely to be more energetic and effective, and that many acts requiring tact and delicacy are likely to be more graceful and pleasant to others, if they are done not in conscious obedience to the dictates of Reason but from other motives. It is not necessary here to decide how far this view is true : it suffices to say that we do not know intuitively that it is not true to some extent; we do not know that there may not be—to use Plato's analogy— *over-government* in the individual soul no less than in the state. The residuum, then, of clear intuition which we have so far obtained, is the insignificant proposition that it is our duty to do what we judge to be our duty.

§ 4. Let us pass now to what I have called the duties of the Affections, the rules that prescribe either love itself in some degree, or the services that naturally spring from it in those relations where it is expected and desired. Here, in the first place, the question how far we are bound to render these services when we do not feel the affection is answered differently in many cases by different persons, and no determination of the limit seems self-evident. And similarly if we ask whether affection itself is a duty ; for on the one hand it is at least only partially within the control of the will, and in so far as it can be produced by voluntary effort, there is thought to be something unsatisfactory and unattractive in the result; and on the other hand, in certain relations it seems to be commonly regarded as a duty. On those points the doctrine of Common Sense is rather a rough compromise between conflicting lines of thought than capable of being deduced from a clear and universally accepted principle. And if we confine ourselves to the special relations where Common Sense admits no doubt as to the broad moral obligation of at least rendering such services as affection naturally prompts, still the recognised rules of external duty in these relations are, in the first place, wanting in definiteness and precision : and secondly, they do not, when rigorously examined, appear to be, or to be referable to, independent intuitions so far as the *particularity* of the duties is concerned. Let us take, for example, the duty of parents to children. We have no doubt about this duty as a part of the present order of society, by which the due growth and training of the rising generation is distributed among the adults. But when we reflect on this arrangement itself, we cannot see *intuitively* that it is the best possible. It may be plausibly maintained that children would be better trained, physically and mentally, if they were brought up under the supervision of physicians and philosophers, in large institutions maintained out of the general taxes. We cannot decide *a priori* which of these alternatives is preferable ; we have to refer to psychological and sociological generalisations, obtained by empirical study of human nature in actual societies. If, however, we consider the duty of parents by itself, out of connexion with this social order, it is certainly not self-evident that we owe more to our own children than to others whose happiness equally depends on our exertions. To get the question clear, let us suppose that I am thrown with my family upon a desert island, where I find an abandoned orphan. Is it evident that I am less bound to provide this child, as far as lies in my power, with the means of subsistence, than I am to provide for my own children? According to some, my special duty to the latter would arise from the fact that I have brought them into being: but, if so, it would seem that on this principle I have a right to diminish their happiness, provided I do not turn it into a negative quantity; since, as without me they would not have existed at all, they can, as my children, have no claim upon me for more than an existence on the whole above zero in respect of happiness. We might even deduce a parental right (so far as this special claim is concerned) to extinguish children painlessly at any point of their existence, if only their life up to that point has been on the whole worth having; for how can persons who would have had no life at all but for me fairly complain that they are not allowed more than a certain quantity?[1] I do not mean to assert that these doctrines are even implicitly held by Common Sense: but merely to show that here, as elsewhere, the pursuit of an irrefragable intuition may lead us unaware into a nest of paradoxes.

It seems, then, that we cannot, after all, say that the special duty of parents to children, considered by itself, possesses clear self-evidence: and it was easy to show (cf. chap. iv.) that as recognised by Common Sense its limits are indeterminate.

The rule prescribing the duty of children to parents need not detain us; for to Common Sense it certainly seems doubtful whether this is not merely a particular case of gratitude; and we certainly have no clear intuition of what is due to parents who do not deserve gratitude. Again, the moral relation of husband and wife seems to depend chiefly upon contract and definite understanding. It is, no doubt, usually thought that Morality, as well as law prescribes certain conditions for all connubial contracts: and in our own age and country it is held that they should be (1) monogamic and (2) permanent. But it seems clear that neither of these opinions would be maintained to be a primary intuition. Whether these or any other legal regulations of the union of the sexes

---

[1] It may be noticed that a view very similar to this has often been maintained in considering what God is in justice bound to do for human beings in consequence of the quasi-parental relation in which He stands to them.

can be deduced from some intuitive principle of Purity, we will presently consider: but as for such conjugal duties as are not prescribed by Law, probably no one at the present day would maintain that there is any such general agreement as to what these are, as would support the theory that they may be known *a priori*.[1]

If, then, in these domestic relations—where the duties of affection are commonly recognised as so imperative and important—we can find no really independent and self-evident principles for determining them, I need not perhaps spend time in showing that the same is the case in respect of the less intimate ties (of kindred, neighbourhood, etc.) that bind us to other human beings. Indeed, this was made sufficiently manifest in our previous discussion of those other duties.

No doubt there are certain obligations towards human beings generally which are, speaking broadly, unquestionable: as, for example, the negative duty of abstaining from causing pain to others against their will, except by way of deserved punishment (whether this is to be placed under the head of Justice or Benevolence); and of making reparation for any pain which we may have caused. Still, when we consider the extent of these duties and try to define their limits,—when we ask how far we may legitimately cause pain to other men (or other sentient beings) in order to obtain happiness for ourselves or third persons, or even to confer a greater good on the sufferer himself, if the pain be inflicted against his will,—we do not seem able to obtain any clear and generally accepted principle for deciding this point, unless the Utilitarian formula be admitted as such. Again, as regards Reparation, there is, as we have seen, a fundamental doubt how far this is due for harm that has been involuntarily caused.

Similarly, all admit that we have a general duty of rendering services to our fellow-men and especially to those who are in special need, and that we are bound to make sacrifices for them, when the benefit that we thereby confer very decidedly

---

[1] It is not irrelevant to notice the remarkable divergence of suggestions for the better regulation of marriage, to which reflective minds seem to be led when they are once set loose from the trammels of tradition and custom ; as exhibited in the speculations of philosophers in all ages—especially of those (as *e.g.* Plato) to whom we cannot attribute any sensual or licentious bias.

outweighs the loss to ourselves; but when we ask how far we are bound to give up our own happiness in order to promote that of our fellows, while it can hardly be said that Common Sense distinctly accepts the Utilitarian principle, it yet does not definitely affirm any other.

And even the common principle of Gratitude, though its stringency is immediately and universally felt, seems yet essentially indeterminate: owing to the unsolved question whether the requital of a benefit ought to be proportionate to what it cost the benefactor, or to what it is worth to the recipient.

§ 5. When we pass to consider that element of Justice which presented itself as Gratitude universalised, the same difficulty recurs in a more complicated form. For here, too, we have to ask whether the Requital of Good Desert ought to be proportioned to the benefit rendered, or to the effort made to render it. And if we scrutinise closely the common moral notion of Retributive Justice, it appears, strictly taken, to imply the metaphysical doctrine of Free Will; since, according to this conception, the reasonableness of rewarding merit is considered solely in relation to the past, without regard to the future bad consequences to be expected from leaving merit without encouragement: and if every excellence in any one's actions or productions seems referable ultimately to causes other than himself, the individual's claim to requital, from this point of view, appears to vanish. On the other hand it is obviously paradoxical in estimating Desert to omit the moral excellences due to hereditary transmission and education: or even intellectual excellences, since good intention without foresight is commonly held to constitute a very imperfect merit. Even if we cut through this speculative difficulty by leaving the ultimate reward of real Desert to Divine Justice, we still seem unable to find any clear principles for framing a scale of merit. And much the same may be said, *mutatis mutandis*, of the scale of Demerit which Criminal Justice seems to require.

And even if these difficulties were overcome, we should still be only at the commencement of the perplexities in which the practical determination of Justice on self-evident principles is involved. For the examination of the contents

of this notion, which we conducted in chap. v., furnished us not
with a single definite principle, but with a whole swarm of
principles, which are unfortunately liable to come into conflict
with each other; and of which even those that when singly
contemplated have the air of being self-evident truths, do not
certainly carry with them any intuitively ascertainable definition of their mutual boundaries and relations. Thus, for
example, in constructing an ideally perfect distribution of the
means of happiness, it seems necessary to take into account
the notion (as I called it) of Fitness, which, though often
confounded with Desert, seems essentially distinct from it.
For the social ‘distribuend’ includes not merely the means of
obtaining pleasurable passive feelings, but also functions and
instruments, which are important sources of happiness, but
which it is obviously reasonable to give to those who can
perform and use them. And even as regards the material
means of comfort and luxury—wealth, in short—we do not
find that the same amount produces the same result of
happiness in every case: and it seems reasonable that the
means of refined and varied pleasure should be allotted to
those who have the corresponding capacities for enjoyment.[1]
And yet these may not be the most deserving, so that this
principle may clearly conflict with that of requiting Desert.

And either principle, as we saw, is liable to come into
collision with the widely-accepted doctrine that the proper
ultimate end of Law is to secure the greatest possible Freedom
of action to all members of the community : and that all that
any individual, strictly speaking, owes to any other is non-
interference, except so far as he has further bound himself by
free contract. But further, when we come to examine this
principle in its turn, we find that, in order to be capable at
all of affording a practical basis for social construction, it needs
limitations and qualifications which make it look less like an
independent principle than a “middle axiom” of Utilitarianism;
and that it cannot without a palpable strain be made to cover
the most important rights which Positive Law secures. For

---

[1] For example, many seem to hold that wealth is, roughly speaking, rightly
distributed when cultivated persons have abundance and the uncultivated a bare
subsistence, since the former are far more capable of deriving happiness from
wealth than the latter.

example, the justification of permanent appropriation is surely rather that it supplies the only adequate motive for labour than that it, strictly speaking, realises Freedom : nor can the questions that arise in determining the limits of the right of property—such as whether it includes the right of bequest—be settled by any deductions from this supposed fundamental principle.   Nor again, can even the enforcement of contracts be fairly said to be a realisation of Freedom ; for a man seems, strictly speaking, freer when no one of his volitions is allowed to cause an external control of any other.   And if we disregard this as a paradoxical subtlety, we are met on the opposite side by the perplexity that if abstract Freedom is consistent with any engagement of future services, it must on the same grounds be consistent with such as are perpetual and unqualified, and so even with actual slavery.   And this question becomes especially important when we consider that the duty of obeying positive laws has by many been reconciled with the abstract right of Freedom, by supposing a 'tacit compact' or understanding between each individual and the rest of his community.   This Compact, however, seems on examination too clearly fictitious to be put forward as a basis of moral duty : as is further evident from the indefinitely various qualifications and reservations with which the 'understanding' has by different thinkers been supposed to be 'understood.'   Hence many who maintain the 'Birthright of Freedom' consider that the only abstractedly justifiable social order is one in which no laws are imposed without the *express* consent of those who are to obey them.   But we found it impossible really to construct society upon this basis : and such Representative Governments as have actually been established only appear to realise this idea by means of sweeping limitations and transparent fictions.   It was manifest, too, that the maximum of what may be called Constitutional Freedom—*i.e.* the most perfect conformity between the action of a government and the wishes of the majority of its subjects —need by no means result in the realisation of the maximum of Civil Freedom in the society so governed.

But even if we could delineate to our satisfaction an ideal social order, including an ideal form of government, we have still to reconcile the duty of realising this with the conformity due to the actual order of society. For we have a strong conviction that positive laws ought, generally speaking, to be obeyed: and, again, our notion of Justice seemed to include a general duty of satisfying the expectations generated by custom and precedent. Yet if the actual order of society deviates very much from what we think ought to exist, the duty of conforming to it seems to become obscure and doubtful. And apart from this we cannot say that Common Sense regards it as an axiom that Laws ought to be obeyed. Indeed, all are agreed that they ought to be disobeyed when they command what is wrong: though we do not seem able to elicit any clear general view as to what remains wrong after it has been commanded by the sovereign. And, again, the positive laws that ought to be obeyed as such must be the commands issued by a (morally) rightful authority: and though these will ordinarily coincide with the commands legally enforced, we cannot say that this is always the case; for the courts may be temporarily subservient to a usurper; or, again, the sovereign hitherto habitually obeyed may be one against whom it has become right to rebel (since it is generally admitted that this is sometimes right). We require, then, principles for determining when usurpation becomes legitimate and when rebellion is justifiable: and we do not seem able to elicit these from Common Sense—except so far as it may be fairly said that on this whole subject Common Sense inclines more to the Utilitarian method than it does in matters of private morality.

Still less can we state the general duty of satisfying ' natural expectations '—*i.e.* such expectations as an average man would form under given circumstances—in the form of a clear and precise moral axiom. No doubt a just man will generally satisfy customary claims: but it can hardly be maintained that the mere existence of a custom renders it clearly obligatory that any one should conform to it who has not already promised to do so; especially since bad customs can only be abolished by individuals venturing to disregard them.

§ 6. We have still to examine (whether as a branch of Justice or under a separate head) the duty of fulfilling express promises and distinct understandings. The peculiar confidence

which moralists have generally felt in this principle is strikingly illustrated by those endeavours to extend its scope which
we have just had occasion to notice : and it certainly seems to
surpass in simplicity, certainty, and definiteness the moral
rules that we have hitherto discussed.   Here, then, if anywhere, we seem likely to find one of those ethical axioms of
which we are in search.   Now we saw that the notion of a
Promise requires several qualifications not commonly noticed
to make it precise : but this alone is no reason why it may
not be fitly used in framing a maxim, which when enunciated
and understood will properly claim universal acceptance as
self-evident.   For similarly the uninstructed majority of mankind could not define a circle as a figure bounded by a line
of which every point is equidistant from the centre : but
nevertheless, when the definition is explained to them, they
will accept it as expressing the perfect type of that notion of
roundness which they have long had in their minds.   And the
same potential universality of acceptance may, I think, be
fairly claimed for the propositions that the promise which the
Common Sense of mankind recognises as binding must be
understood by promiser and promisee in the same sense at the
time of promising, and that it is relative to the promisee and
capable of being annulled by him, and that it cannot override
determinate [1] prior obligations.

But the case is different with the other qualifications which
we had to discuss.   When once the question of introducing
these has been raised, we see that Common Sense is clearly
divided as to the answer.   If we ask (*e.g.*) how far our promise
is binding if it was made in consequence of false statements, on
which, however, it was not understood to be conditional ; or if
important circumstances were concealed, or we were in any way
led to believe that the consequences of keeping the promise
would be different from what they turn out to be ; or if the
promise was given under compulsion ; or if circumstances have
materially altered since it was given, and we find that the
results of fulfilling it will be different from what we foresaw
when we promised ; or even if it be only our knowledge of
consequences which has altered, and we now see that fulfil-

---

[1] I refer later (p. 360) to the difficulty before noticed in respect of such prior
obligations as are not strictly determinate.

ment will entail on us a sacrifice out of proportion to the benefit received by the promisee; or perhaps see that it will even be injurious to him though he may not think so;— different conscientious persons would answer these and other [1] questions (both generally and in particular cases) in different ways: and though we could perhaps obtain a decided majority for some of these qualifications and against others, there would not in any case be a clear *consensus* either way. And, moreover, the mere discussion of these points seems to make it plain that the confidence with which the " unsophisticated conscience " asserts unreservedly " that promises ought to be kept," is due to inadvertence ; and that when the qualifications to which we referred are fairly considered, this confidence inevitably changes into hesitation and perplexity. It should be added, that some of these qualifications themselves suggest a reference to the more comprehensive principle of Utilitarianism, as one to which this particular rule is naturally subordinate.

Again, reflection upon the place of this duty in a classified system of moral obligations tends to confirm our distrust of the ordinary enunciations of Common Sense in respect of it. For, as was seen, Fidelity to promises is very commonly ranked with Veracity ; as though the mere fact of my having said that I would do a thing were the ground of my duty to do it. But on reflection we perceive that the obligation must be regarded as contingent on the reliance that another has placed on my assertion : that, in fact, the breach of duty is constituted by the disappointment of expectations voluntarily raised. And when we see this we become less disposed to maintain the absoluteness of the duty : it seems now to depend upon the amount of harm done by disappointing expectations ; and we shrink from saying that the promise ought to be kept, if the keeping it would involve an amount of harm that seems decidedly to outweigh this.

The case of Veracity we may dismiss somewhat more briefly, as here it was still more easy to show that the common enunciation of the unqualified duty of Truth-speaking is made without full consideration, and cannot approve itself to the

---

[1] I have omitted as less important the special questions connected with promises to the dead or to the absent, or where a form of words is prescribed.

reflective mind as an absolute first principle. For, in the first place, we found no clear agreement as to the fundamental nature of the obligation; or as to its exact scope, *i.e.* whether it is our actual affirmation as understood by the recipient which we are bound to make correspondent to fact (as far as we can), or whatever inferences we foresee that he is likely to draw from this, or both. To realise perfect Candour and Sincerity, we must aim at both: and we no doubt admire the exhibition of these virtues: but few will maintain that they ought to be exhibited under all circumstances. And, secondly, it seems to be admitted by Common Sense, though vaguely and reluctantly, that the principle, however defined, is not of universal application; at any rate it is not thought to be clearly wrong that untruths should be told to children, or madmen, or invalids, or by advocates, or to enemies or robbers, or even to persons who ask questions which they have no right to ask (if a mere refusal to answer would practically reveal an important secret). And when we consider the limitations generally admitted, it seems still more plain than in the last case, that they are very commonly determined by utilitarian reasonings, implicit or explicit.

§ 7. If, then, the prescriptions of Justice, Good Faith, and Veracity, as laid down by Common Sense, appear so little capable of being converted into first principles of scientific Ethics, it seems scarcely necessary to inquire whether such axioms can be extracted from the minor maxims of social behaviour, such as the maxim of Liberality or the rules restraining the Malevolent Affections: or, again, from such virtues as Courage and Humility, which we found it difficult to class as either social or self-regarding. Indeed, it was made plain in chap. viii. that as regards the proper regulation of resentment, Common Sense can only be saved from inconsistency or hopeless vagueness by adopting the 'interest of society' as the ultimate standard: and in the same way we cannot definitely distinguish Courage from Foolhardiness except by a reference to the probable tendency of the daring act to promote the wellbeing of the agent or of others, or to some definite rule of duty prescribed under some other notion.

It is true that among what are commonly called " duties to self" we find the duty of self-preservation prescribed with apparent absoluteness,—at least so far as the sacrifice of one's life is not imperatively required for the preservation of the lives of others, or for the attainment of some result conceived to be very important to society. I think, however, that when confronted with the question of preserving a life which we can foresee will be both miserable and burdensome to others —*e.g.* the life of a man stricken with a fatal disease which precludes the possibility of work of any kind, during the weeks or months of agony that remain to him,—though Common Sense would still deny the legitimacy of suicide, even under these conditions, it would also admit the necessity of finding reasons for the denial. This admission would imply that the universal wrongness of suicide is at any rate not self-evident. And the reasons that would be found— so far as they did not ultimately depend upon premises drawn from Revelational Theology—would, I think, turn out to be utilitarian, in a broad sense of the term: it would be urged that if any exceptions to the rule prohibiting suicide were allowed, dangerous encouragement would be given to the suicidal impulse in other cases in which suicide would really be a weak and cowardly dereliction of social duty: it would also probably be urged that the toleration of suicide would facilitate secret murders. In short, the independent axiom of which we are in search seems to disappear on close examination in this case no less than in others.

So again, reflection seems to show that the duties of Temperance, Self-control, and other cognate virtues, are only clear and definite in so far as they are conceived as subordinate either to Prudence (as is ordinarily the case), or to Benevolence or some definite rule of social duty, or at least to some end— such as 'furtherance of moral progress'[1]—of which the conception involves the notion of duty supposed to be already determinate. Certainly the authority of Common Sense cannot be fairly claimed for any restriction even of the bodily appetites for food and drink, that is not thus subordinated.

In the case, however, of the sexual appetite, a special regulation seems to be prescribed on some independent principle under the notion of Purity or Chastity. In chap. ix.

---

[1] It was this conception that seemed to give the true standard of Humility, considered as a purely internal duty.

of this Book, where we examined this notion, it appeared that Common Sense is not only not explicit, but actually averse to explicitness, on this subject. As my aim in the preceding chapters was to give, above all things, a faithful exposition of the morality of Common Sense, I allowed my inquiry to be checked by this (as it seemed) clearly recognisable sentiment. But when it becomes our primary object to test the intuitive evidence of the moral principles commonly accepted, it seems necessary to override this aversion : for we can hardly ascertain whether rational conviction is attainable as to the acts allowed and forbidden under this notion and its opposite, without subjecting it to the same close scrutiny that we have endeavoured to give to the other leading notions of Ethics. Here the briefest account of such a scrutiny will be sufficient. I am aware that in giving even this I cannot but cause a certain offence to minds trained in good moral habits : but I trust I may claim the same indulgence as is commonly granted to the physiologist, who also has to direct the student's attention to objects which a healthy mind is naturally disinclined to contemplate.

§ 8. What, then, is the conduct which Purity forbids (for the principle is more easily discussed in its negative aspect) ? As the normal and obvious end of sexual intercourse is the propagation of the species, some have thought that all indulgence of appetite, except as a means to this end, should be prohibited. But this doctrine would lead to a restriction of conjugal intercourse far too severe for Common Sense. Shall we say, then, that Purity forbids such indulgence except under the conditions of conjugal union defined by Law ? But this answer, again, further reflection shows to be unsatisfactory. For, first, we should not, on consideration, call a conjugal union impure, *merely* because the parties had wilfully omitted to fulfil legal conditions, and had made a contract which the law declined to enforce. We might condemn their conduct, but we should not apply to it this notion. And, secondly, we feel that positive law may be unfavourable to Purity, and that in fact Purity, like Justice, is something which the law ought to maintain, but does not always. We have to ask, then, what kind of sexual relations we are to call essentially impure, whether countenanced or not by Law and Custom ? There appear to be no distinct principles, having any claim to self-evidence, upon which the question can be answered so as to command general assent. It would be difficult even to state such a principle for determining the degree of consanguinity between husband and wife which constitutes a union incestuous; although the aversion with which such unions are commonly regarded is a peculiarly intense moral sentiment; and the difficulty becomes indefinitely greater when we consider the *rationale* of prohibited degrees of affinity. Again, probably few would stigmatise a legal polygynous connexion as impure, however they might disapprove of the law and of the state of society in which such a law was established: but if legal Polygyny is not impure, is Polyandry, when legal and customary—as is not unfrequently the case among the lower races of man—to be so characterised? and if not, on what rational principle can the notion be applied to institutions and conduct? Again, where divorce by mutual consent, with subsequent marriage, is legalised, we do not call this an offence against Purity: and yet if the principle of free change be once admitted, it seems paradoxical to distinguish purity from impurity merely by less rapidity of transition;[1] and to condemn as impure even 'Free Love,' in so far as it is earnestly advocated as a means to a completer harmony of sentiment between men and women, and not to mere sensual license.

Shall we, then, fall back upon the presence of mutual affection (as distinguished from mere appetite) as constituting the essence of pure sexual relations? But this, again, while too lax from one point of view, seems from another too severe for Common Sense: as we do not condemn marriages without affection as impure, although we disapprove of them as productive of unhappiness. Such marriages, indeed, are sometimes stigmatised as "legalised prostitution," but the phrase is felt to be extravagant and paradoxical; and it is even doubtful whether we do disapprove of them under all circumstances; as (*e.g.*) in the case of royal alliances.

Again, how shall we judge of such institutions as those of Plato's Commonwealth, establishing community of women and children, but at the same time regulating sexual indulgence

---

[1] It should be observed that I am not asking for an exact quantitative decision, but whether we can really think that the decision depends upon considerations of this kind

with the strictest reference to social ends? Our habitual standards seem inapplicable to such novel circumstances.

The truth seems to be, that reflection on the current sexual morality discovers to us two distinct grounds for it: first and chiefly, the maintenance of a certain social order, believed to be most conducive to the prosperous continuance of the human race: and, secondly, the protection of habits of feeling in individuals believed to be generally most important to their perfection or their happiness. We commonly conceive that both these ends are to be attained by the same regulations: and in an ideal state of society this would perhaps be the case: but in actual life there is frequently a partial separation and incompatibility between them. But further, if the repression of sexual license is prescribed merely as a means to these ends, it does not seem that we can affirm as self-evident that it is always a necessary means in either case: on the contrary, it seems clear that such an affirmation would be unreliable apart from empirical confirmation. We cannot reasonably be sure, without induction from sociological observations, that a certain amount of sexual license will be incompatible with the maintenance of population in sufficient numbers and good condition. And if we consider the matter in its relation to the individual's perfection, it is certainly clear that he misses the highest and best development of his emotional nature, if his sexual relations are of a merely sensual kind: but we can hardly know *a priori* that this lower kind of relation interferes with the development of the higher (nor indeed does experience seem to show that this is universally the case). And this latter line of argument has a further difficulty. For the common opinion that we have to justify does not merely condemn the lower kind of development in comparison with the higher, but in comparison with none at all. Since we do not positively blame a man for remaining celibate (though we perhaps despise him somewhat unless the celibacy is adopted as a means to a noble end): it is difficult to show why we should condemn —in its bearing on the individual's emotional perfection solely—the imperfect development afforded by merely sensual relations.

§ 9. Much more might be said to exhibit the perplexities in which the attempt to define the rule of Purity or Chastity involves us. But I do not desire to extend the discussion beyond what is necessary for the completion of my argument. It seems to me that the conclusion announced in § 2 of this chapter has now been sufficiently justified. We have examined the moral notions that present themselves with a *prima facie* claim to furnish independent and self-evident rules of morality : and we have in each case found that from such regulation of conduct as the Common Sense of mankind really supports, no proposition can be elicited which, when fairly contemplated, even appears to have the characteristic of a scientific axiom. It is therefore scarcely needful to proceed to a systematic examination of the manner in which Common Sense provides for the co-ordination of these principles. In fact, this question seems to have been already discussed as far as is profitable : for the attempt to define each principle singly has inevitably led us to consider their mutual relations : and it was in the cases where two moral principles came into collision that we most clearly saw the vagueness and inconsistency with which the boundaries of each are determined by Common Sense. For example, the distinction between perfectly stringent moral obligations, and such laxer duties as may be modified by a man's own act, is often taken : and it is one which, as we saw, is certainly required in formulating the Common-Sense view of the effect of a promise in creating new obligations : but it is one which we cannot apply with any practical precision, because of the high degree of indeterminateness which we find in the common notions of duties to which the highest degree of stringency is yet commonly attributed.

It only remains to guard my argument from being understood in a more sweeping sense than it has been intended or is properly able to bear. Nothing that I have said even tends to show that we have not distinct moral impulses, claiming authority over all others, and prescribing or forbidding kinds of conduct as to which there is a rough general agreement, at least among educated persons of the same age and country. It is only maintained that the objects of these impulses do not admit of being scientifically determined by any reflective analysis of common sense. The notions of Benevolence, Justice, Good Faith, Veracity, Purity, etc., are not necessarily emptied of significance for us, because we have found it impossible to define

them with precision.   The main part of the conduct prescribed
under each notion is sufficiently clear : and the general rule
prescribing it does not necessarily lose its force because there
is in each case a margin of conduct involved in obscurity and
perplexity, or because the rule does not on examination appear
to be absolute and independent.   In short, the Morality of
Common Sense may still be perfectly adequate to give practical
guidance to common people in common circumstances : but the
attempt to elevate it into a system of Intuitional Ethics brings
its inevitable imperfections into prominence without helping us
to remove them.[1]

[1] It should be observed that the more positive treatment of Common-sense
Morality, in its relation to Utilitarianism, to which we shall proceed in chap. iii. of
the following Book, is intended as an indispensable supplement of the negative
criticism which has just been completed.

CHAPTER XII

MOTIVES OR SPRINGS OF ACTION CONSIDERED AS SUBJECTS OF
MORAL JUDGMENT

§ 1. IN the first chapter of this third Book I was careful
to point out that motives, as well as intentions, form part of
the subject-matter of our common moral judgments : and indeed
in our notion of ' conscientiousness ' the habit of reflecting on
motives, and judging them to be good or bad, is a prominent
element. It is necessary, therefore, in order to complete our
examination of the Intuitional Method, to consider this comparison of motives, and ascertain how far it can be made
systematic, and pursued to conclusions of scientific value.
And this seems a convenient place for treating of this part
of the subject : since it has been maintained by an important
school of English moralists that Desires and Affections rather
than Acts are the proper subjects of the ethical judgment :
and it is natural to fall back upon this view when systematic
reflection on the morality of Common Sense has shown us the
difficulty of obtaining a precise and satisfactory determination
of rightness and wrongness in external conduct.

To avoid confusion, it should be observed that the term
' motive ' is commonly used in two ways. It is sometimes
applied to those among the foreseen consequences of any act
which the agent desired in willing : and sometimes to the
desire, or conscious impulse itself. The two meanings are in a
manner correspondent, as, where impulses are different, there
must always be some sort of difference in their respective
objects. But for our present purpose it is more convenient to
take the latter meaning : as it is our own impulsive nature
that we have practically to deal with, in the way of control-

362

ling, resisting, indulging the different impulses; and therefore it is the ethical value of these that we are primarily concerned to estimate: and we often find that two impulses, which would be placed very far apart in any psychological list, are directed towards an end materially identical, though regarded from a different point of view in each case. As (*e.g.*) both appetite and Rational self-love may impel a man to seek a particular sensual gratification ; though in the latter case it is regarded under the general notion of pleasure, and as forming part of a sum called Happiness. In this chapter, then, I shall use the term Motive to denote the desires of particular results, believed to be attainable as consequences of our voluntary acts, by which desires we are stimulated to will those acts.[1]

The first point to notice in considering the ethical result of a comprehensive comparison of motives is, that the issue in any internal conflict is not usually thought to be between

[1] In Green's *Prolegomena to Ethics*, Book ii. chaps. i. and ii. a peculiar view is taken of "motives, of that kind by which it is the characteristic of moral or human action, to be determined." Such motives, it is maintained, must be distinguished from desires in the sense of "mere solicitations of which a man is conscious" ; they are "constituted by the reaction of the man's self upon these, and its identification of itself with one of them." In fact the "direction of the self-conscious self to the realisation of an object" which I should call an act of will, is the phenomenon to which Green would restrict the term "desire in that sense in which desire is the principle and notion of an imputable human action."

The use of terms here suggested appears to me inconvenient, and the psychological analysis implied in it to a great extent erroneous. I admit that in certain simple cases of choice, where the alternatives suggested are each prompted by a single definite desire, there is no psychological inaccuracy in saying that in willing the act to which he is stimulated by any such desire the agent "identifies himself with the desire." But in more complex cases the phrase appears to me incorrect, as obliterating important distinctions between the two kinds of psychical phenomena which are usually and conveniently distinguished as "desires" and volitions. In the first place, as I have before pointed out (chap. i. § 2 of this Book), it often happens that certain foreseen consequences of volition, which as foreseen are undoubtedly *willed* and—in a sense—*chosen* by the agents, are not objects of desire to him at all, but even possibly of aversion—aversion, of course, overcome by his desire of other consequences of the same act. In the second place, it is specially important, from an ethical point of view, to notice that, among the various desires or aversions aroused in us by the complex foreseen consequences of a contemplated act, there are often impulses with which we do not identify ourselves, but which we even try to suppress as far as possible : though as it is not possible to suppress them completely—especially if we do the act to which they prompt—we cannot say that they do not operate as motives.

positively good and bad, but between better and less good, more or less estimable or elevated motives.   The only kind of motive which (if any) we commonly judge to be *intrinsically* bad, apart from the circumstances under which it operates, is malevolent affection ; that is, the desire, however aroused, to inflict pain or harm on some other sentient being.   And reflection shows (as we saw in chap. viii. of this Book) that Common Sense does not pronounce even this kind of impulse absolutely bad : since we commonly recognise the existence of 'legitimate resentment' and 'righteous indignation' ; and though moralists try to distinguish between anger directed 'against the act' and 'against the agent,' and between the impulse to inflict pain and the desire of the antipathetic pleasure that the agent will reap from this infliction, it may be fairly doubted whether it is within the capacity of ordinary human nature to maintain these distinctions in practice.   At any rate there is no other motive except deliberate malevolence which Common Sense condemns as absolutely bad.   The other motives that are commonly spoken of in 'dyslogistic' terms seem to be most properly called (in Bentham's language) 'Seductive' rather than bad.   That is, they prompt to forbidden conduct with conspicuous force and frequency : but when we consider them carefully we find that there are certain limits, however narrow, within which their operation is legitimate.

The question, then, is how far the intuitive knowledge that our common judgments seem to imply of the relative goodness of different kinds of motives is found on reflection to satisfy the conditions laid down in the preceding chapter. I have before [1] argued that it is incorrect to regard this comparison of *motives* as the normal form of our common moral judgments, nor do I see any ground for holding it to be the original form.   I think that in the normal development of man's moral consciousness, both in the individual and in the race, moral judgments are first passed on outward acts, and that motives do not come to be definitely considered till later ; just as external perception of physical objects precedes introspection.   At the same time, in my view, it does not therefore follow that the comparison of motives is not the final and most perfect form of the moral judgment.   It might

---

[1] Cf. *ante*, chap. i. § 2 of this Book.

approve itself as such by the systematic clearness and mutual consistency of the results to which it led, when pursued by different thinkers independently : and by its freedom from the puzzles and difficulties to which other developments of the Intuitional Method seem to be exposed.

It appears, however, on examination that, on the one hand, many (if not all) of the difficulties which have emerged in the preceding discussion of the commonly received principles of conduct are reproduced in a different form when we try to arrange Motives in order of excellence : and on the other hand, such a construction presents difficulties peculiar to itself, and the attempt to solve these exhibits greater and more fundamental differences among Intuitive moralists, as regards Rank of Motive, than we found to exist as regards Rightness of outward acts.

§ 2. In the first place, it has to be decided whether we are to include in our list of motives the Moral Sentiments, or impulses towards particular kinds of virtuous conduct as such, *e.g.* Candour, Veracity, Fortitude. It seems unwarrantable to exclude them, as such sentiments are observable as distinct and independent impulses in most well-trained minds, and we sometimes recognise their existence in considerable intensity, as when we speak of a man being ' enthusiastically brave,' or ' intensely veracious,' or as ' having a passion for justice.' At the same time their admission places us in the following dilemma. Either the objects of these impulses are represented by the very notions that we have been examining—in which case, after we have decided that any impulse is better than its rival, all the perplexities set forth in the previous chapters will recur, before we can act on our decision ; for what avails it to recognise the superiority of the impulse to do justice, if we do not know what it is just to do ?—or if in any case the object which a moral sentiment prompts us to realise is conceived more simply, without the qualifications which a complete reflection on Common Sense forced us to recognise ; then, as the previous investigation shows, we shall certainly not find agreement as to the relation between this and other impulses. For example, a dispute, whether the impulse to speak the truth ought or ought not to be followed, will inevitably arise when Veracity seems opposed either to the

general good, or to the interests of some particular person;
that is, when it conflicts with 'particular' or 'universal'
benevolence. Hutcheson expressly places these latter impulses
in a higher rank than "candour, veracity, fortitude"; reserving the highest moral approbation for "the most extensive
benevolence" or "calm, stable, universal goodwill to all."[1]
But this view, which coincides practically with Utilitarianism,
would certainly be disputed by most Intuitional moralists.
Again, some of these moralists (as Kant) regard all actions
as bad—or not good—which are not done from pure regard
for duty or choice of Right as Right: while Hutcheson, who
represents the opposite pole of Intuitional Ethics, equally
distinguishes the love of Virtue as a separate impulse; but
treats it as at once co-ordinate in rank and coincident in its
effects with universal Benevolence.

So, again, moralists diverge widely in estimating the
ethical value of Self-love. For Butler seems to regard it
as one of two superior and naturally authoritative impulses,
the other being Conscience: nay, in a passage before quoted,
he even concedes that it would be reasonable for Conscience
to yield to it, if the two could possibly conflict. Other
moralists (and Butler elsewhere)[2] appear to place Self-love
among virtuous impulses under the name of Prudence:
though among these they often rank it rather low, and would
have it yield in case of conflict, to nobler virtues. Others,
again, exclude it from Virtue altogether: e.g. Kant, in one
of his treatises,[3] says that the end of Self-love, one's own
happiness, cannot be an end for the Moral Reason; that the
force of the reasonable will, in which Virtue consists, is
always exhibited in resistance to natural egoistic impulses.

Dr. Martineau, whose system is framed on the basis that
I am now examining, attempts to avoid some of the difficulties
just pointed out by refusing to admit the existence of any
virtuous impulses except the "preference for the superior of
the competing springs of action in each case" of a conflict

---

[1] Hutcheson, *System of Moral Philosophy*, Book i. chap. iv. § 10.

[2] See the Dissertation *Of the Nature of Virtue* appended to the *Analogy*.

[3] The *Metaphysische Anfangsgründe der Tugendlehre*: but it ought to be
observed that the ethical view briefly expounded in the *Kritik der reinen
Vernunft* appears to have much more affinity with Butler's.

of motives. "I cannot admit," he says, "either the *loves of Virtues*—of candour, veracity, fortitude—or the virtues themselves, as so many additional impulses over and above those from the conflict of which they are formed. I do not confess my fault *in order to be candid* . . . unless I am a prig, I never think of candour, as predicable, or going to be predicable, of me at all."[1] I am not, however, sure whether Dr. Martineau really means to *deny* the existence of persons who act from a conscious desire to realise an ideal of Candour or Fortitude, or whether he merely means to express *disapproval* of such persons : in the former sense his statement seems to me a psychological paradox, in conflict with ordinary experience : in the latter sense it seems an ethical paradox, affording a striking example of that diversity of judgments as to the rank of motives, to which I am now drawing attention.

§ 3. But even if we put out of sight the Moral sentiments and Self-love, it is still scarcely possible to frame a scale of motives arranged in order of merit, for which we could claim anything like a clear consent, even of cultivated and thoughtful persons. On one or two points, indeed, we seem to be generally agreed ; *e.g.* that the bodily appetites are inferior to the benevolent affections and the intellectual desires ; and perhaps that impulses tending primarily to the well-being of the individual are lower in rank than those which we class as extra-regarding or disinterested. But beyond a few vague statements of this kind, it is very difficult to proceed. For example, when we compare personal affections with the love of knowledge or of beauty, or the passion for the ideal in any form, much doubt and divergence of opinion become manifest. Indeed, we should hardly agree on the relative rank of the benevolent affections taken by themselves ; for some would prefer the more intense, though narrower, while others would place the calmer and wider feelings in the highest rank. Or again, since Love, as we saw,[2] is a complex emotion, and commonly includes, besides the desire of the good or happiness of the beloved, a desire for union or intimacy of some kind ; some would consider an affection more elevated in proportion as

---

[1] *Types of Ethical Theory*, Vol. ii. p. 284, 2nd edition.
[2] Cf. *ante*, chap. iv. § 2 of this Book.

the former element predominated, while others would regard the latter as at least equally essential to the highest kind of affection.

Again, we may notice the love of Fame as an important and widely operative motive, which would be ranked very differently by different persons: for some would place the former "spur that the clear spirit doth raise" among the most elevated impulses after the moral sentiments; while others think it degrading to depend for one's happiness on the breath of popular favour.

Further, the more we contemplate the actual promptings that precede any volition, the more we seem to find complexity of motive the rule rather than the exception, at least in the case of educated persons: and from this composition of impulses there results a fundamental perplexity as to the principles on which our decision is to be made, even supposing that we have a clear view of the relative worth of the elementary impulses. For the compound will generally contain nobler and baser elements, and we can hardly get rid of the latter; since—as I have before said—though we may frequently suppress and expel a motive by firmly resisting it, it does not seem possible to exclude it if we do the act to which it prompts. Suppose, then, that we are impelled in one direction by a combination of high and low motives, and in another by an impulse that ranks between the two in the scale, how shall we decide which course to follow? Such a case is by no means uncommon: *e.g.* an injured man may be moved by an impulse of pity to spare his injurer, while a regard for justice and a desire of revenge combined impel him to inflict punishment. Or, again, a Jew of liberal views might be restrained from eating pork by a desire not to shock the feelings of his friends, and might be moved to eat it by the desire to vindicate true religious liberty combined with a liking for pork. How are we to deal with such a case as this? For it will hardly be suggested that we should estimate the relative proportions of the different motives and decide accordingly;—qualitative analysis of our motives is to some extent possible to us, but the quantitative analysis that this would require is not in our power.

But even apart from this difficulty arising from complexity

of motives, I think it impossible to assign a definite and constant ethical value to each different kind of motive, without reference to the particular circumstances under which it has arisen, the extent of indulgence that it demands, and the consequences to which this indulgence would lead in any particular case. I may conveniently illustrate this by reference to the table, drawn up by Dr. Martineau,[1] of springs of action arranged in order of merit.

.LOWEST.

1. Secondary Passions :—Censoriousness, Vindictiveness, Suspiciousness.
2. Secondary Organic Propensions :—Love of Ease and Sensual Pleasure.
3. Primary Organic Propensions :—Appetites.
4. Primary Animal Propension :—Spontaneous Activity (unselective).
5. Love of Gain (reflective derivative from Appetite).
6. Secondary Affections (sentimental indulgence of sympathetic feelings).
7. Primary Passions :—Antipathy, Fear, Resentment.
8. Causal energy :—Love of Power, or Ambition ; Love of Liberty.
9. Secondary Sentiments :—Love of Culture.
10. Primary Sentiments of Wonder and Admiration.
11. Primary Affections, Parental and Social; with (approximately) Generosity and Gratitude.
12. Primary Affection of Compassion.
13. Primary Sentiment of Reverence.

HIGHEST.

This scale seems to me open to much criticism, both from a psychological and from an ethical point of view :[2] but, granting that it corresponds broadly to the judgments that men commonly pass as to the different elevation of different motives, it seems to me in the highest degree paradoxical to lay down that each class of motives is always to be preferred to the class below it, without regard to circumstances and consequences. So far as it is true that " the conscience says to every one, ' Do not eat till you are hungry and stop when you are hungry no more,' " it is not, I venture to think, because a " regulative right is clearly vested in primary instinctive needs, relatively to their secondaries," but because

---

[1] *Types of Ethical Theory*, vol. ii. p. 266. Dr. Martineau explains that the chief composite springs are inserted in their approximate place, subject to the variations of which their composition renders them susceptible.

[2] Thus we might ask why the class of " passions " is so strangely restricted, why conjugal affection is omitted, whether wonder can properly be regarded as a definite motive, whether " censoriousness " is properly ranked with " vindictiveness " as one of the " lowest passions," etc.

experience has shown that to seek the gratification of the palate apart from the satisfaction of hunger is generally dangerous to physical well-being; and it is in view of this danger that the conscience operates. If we condemn "a ship captain," who, "caught in a fog off a lee shore, neglects, through indolence and love of ease, to slacken speed and take cautious soundings and open his steam-whistle," it is not because we intuitively discern Fear to be a higher motive than Love of Ease, but because the consequences disregarded are judged to be indefinitely more important than the gratification obtained : if we took a case in which fear was not similarly sustained by prudence, our judgment would certainly be different.

The view of Common Sense appears rather to be that most natural impulses have their proper spheres, within which they should be normally operative, and therefore the question whether in any case a higher motive should yield to a lower one cannot be answered decisively in the general way in which Dr. Martineau answers it : the answer must depend on the particular conditions and circumstances of the conflict. We recognise it as possible that a motive which we commonly rank as higher may wrongly intrude into the proper sphere of one which we rank as lower, just as the lower is liable to encroach on the higher ; only since there is very much less danger of the former intrusion, it naturally falls into the background in ethical discussions and exhortations that have a practical aim. The matter is complicated by the further consideration that as the character of a moral agent becomes better, the motives that we rank as "higher" tend to be developed, so that their normal sphere of operation is enlarged at the expense of the lower. Hence there are two distinct aims in moral regulation and culture, so far as they relate to motives : (1) to keep the "lower" motive within the limits within which its operation is considered to be legitimate and good on the whole, so long as we cannot substitute for it the equally effective operation of a higher motive ; and at the same time (2) to effect this substitution of "higher" for "lower" gradually, as far as can be done without danger,— up to a limit which we cannot definitely fix, but which we certainly conceive, for the most part, as falling short of complete exclusion of the lower motive.

I may illustrate by reference to the passion of resentment of which I before spoke. The view of reflective common sense is, I think, that the malevolent impulse so designated, as long as it is strictly limited to resentment against wrong and operates in aid of justice, has a legitimate sphere of action in the social life of human beings as actually constituted: that, indeed, its suppression would be gravely mischievous, unless we could at the same time intensify the ordinary man's regard for justice or for social well-being so that the total strength of motives prompting to the punishment of crime should not be diminished. It is, no doubt, "to be wished," as Butler says, that men would repress wrong from these higher motives rather than from passionate resentment; but we cannot hope to effect this change in human beings generally except by a slow and gradual process of elevation of character: therefore supposing a conflict between "Compassion," which is highest but one in Dr. Martineau's scale, and "Resentment," which he places about the middle, it is by no means to be laid down as a general rule that compassion ought to prevail. We ought rather—with Butler—to regard resentment as a salutary "balance to the weakness of pity," which would be liable to prevent the execution of justice if resentment were excluded.

Or we might similarly take the impulse which comes lowest (among those not condemned altogether) in Dr. Martineau's scale—the "Love of Ease and Sensual Pleasure." No doubt this impulse, or group of impulses, is continually leading men to shirk or scamp their strict duty, or to fall in some less definite way below their own ideal of conduct; hence the attitude habitually maintained towards it by preachers and practical moralists is that of repression. Still, common sense surely recognises that there are cases in which even this impulse ought to prevail over impulses ranked above it in Dr. Martineau's scale; we often find men prompted—say by "love of gain"—to shorten unduly their hours of recreation; and in the case of a conflict of motives under such circumstances we should judge it best that victory should remain on the side of the "love of ease and pleasure," and that the encroachment of "love of gain" should be repelled.

I do not, however, think that in either of these instances

the conflict of motives would remain such as I have just described: I think that though the struggle might begin as a duel between resentment and compassion, or between love of ease and love of gain, it would not be fought out in the lists so drawn ; since higher motives would inevitably be called in as the conflict went on, regard for justice and social well-being on the side of resentment, regard for health and ultimate efficiency for work on the side of love of ease ; and it would be the intervention of these higher motives that would decide the struggle, so far as it was decided rightly and as we should approve.   This certainly is what would happen in my own case, if the supposed conflict were at all serious and its decision deliberate ; and this constitutes my final reason for holding that such a scale as Dr. Martineau has drawn up, of motives arranged according to their moral rank, can never have more than a very subordinate ethical importance.   I admit that it may serve to indicate in a rough and general way the kinds of desires which it is ordinarily best to encourage and indulge, in comparison with other kinds which are ordinarily likely to compete and collide with them ; and we might thus settle summarily some of the comparatively trifling conflicts of motive which the varying and complex play of needs, habits, interests, and their accompanying emotions, continually stirs in our daily life.   But if a serious question of conduct is raised, I cannot conceive myself deciding it morally by any comparison of motives below the highest : it seems to me that the question must inevitably be carried up for decision into the court of whatever motive we regard as supremely regulative : so that the comparison ultimately decisive would be not between the lower motives primarily conflicting, but between the effects of the different lines of conduct to which these lower motives respectively prompt, considered in relation to whatever we regard as the ultimate end or ends of reasonable action.   And this, I conceive, will be the course naturally taken by the moral reflection not only of utilitarians, but of all who follow Butler in regarding our passions and propensions as forming naturally a " system or constitution," in which the ends of lower impulses are subordinate as means to the ends of certain governing motives, or are comprehended as parts in these larger ends.

CHAPTER XIII

PHILOSOPHICAL INTUITIONISM

§ 1. Is there, then, no possibility of attaining, by a more profound and discriminating examination of our common moral thought, to real ethical axioms—intuitive propositions of real clearness and certainty?

This question leads us to the examination of that third phase of the intuitive method, which was called Philosophical Intuitionism.[1] For we conceive it as the aim of a philosopher, as such, to do somewhat more than define and formulate the common moral opinions of mankind. His function is to tell men what they ought to think, rather than what they do think: he is expected to transcend Common Sense in his premises, and is allowed a certain divergence from Common Sense in his conclusions. It is true that the limits of this deviation are firmly, though indefinitely, fixed: the truth of a philosopher's premises will always be tested by the acceptability of his conclusions: if in any important point he be found in flagrant conflict with common opinion, his method is likely to be declared invalid. Still, though he is expected to establish and concatenate at least the main part of the commonly accepted moral rules, he is not necessarily bound to take them as the basis on which his own system is constructed. Rather, we should expect that the history of Moral Philosophy—so far at least as those whom we may call orthodox thinkers are concerned—would be a history of attempts to enunciate, in full breadth and clearness, those primary intuitions of Reason, by the scientific application of

---

[1] Cf. *ante*, Book i. chap. viii. § 4.

which the common moral thought of mankind may be at once systematised and corrected.

And this is to some extent the case. But Moral Philosophy, or philosophy as applied to Morality, has had other tasks to occupy it, even more profoundly difficult than that of penetrating to the fundamental principles of Duty. In modern times especially, it has admitted the necessity of demonstrating the harmony of Duty with Interest; that is, with the Happiness or Welfare of the agent on whom the duty in each case is imposed. It has also undertaken to determine the relation of Right or Good generally to the world of actual existence: a task which could hardly be satisfactorily accomplished without an adequate explanation of the existence of Evil. It has further been distracted by questions which, in my view, are of psychological rather than ethical importance, as to the 'innateness' of our notions of Duty, and the origin of the faculty that furnishes them. With their attention concentrated on these difficult subjects, each of which has been mixed up in various ways with the discussion of fundamental moral intuitions, philosophers have too easily been led to satisfy themselves with ethical formulæ which implicitly accept the morality of Common Sense *en bloc*, ignoring its defects; and merely express a certain view of the relation of this morality to the individual mind or to the universe of actual existence. Perhaps also they have been hampered by the fear (not, as we have seen, unfounded) of losing the support given by 'general assent' if they set before themselves and their readers too rigid a standard of scientific precision. Still, in spite of all these drawbacks, we find that philosophers have provided us with a considerable number of comprehensive moral propositions, put forward as certain and self-evident, and such as at first sight may seem well adapted to serve as the first principles of scientific morality.

§ 2. But here a word of caution seems required, which has been somewhat anticipated in earlier chapters, but on which it is particularly needful to lay stress at this point of our discussion: against a certain class of sham-axioms, which are very apt to offer themselves to the mind that is earnestly seeking for a philosophical synthesis of practical rules, and to delude the unwary with a tempting aspect of clear self-

evidence.   These are principles which appear certain and
self-evident because they are substantially tautological : because, when examined, they are found to affirm no more than
that it is right to do that which is—in a certain department
of life, under certain circumstances and conditions—right to
be done.   One important lesson which the history of moral
philosophy teaches is that, in this region, even powerful
intellects are liable to acquiesce in tautologies of this kind ;
sometimes expanded into circular reasonings, sometimes hidden
in the recesses of an obscure notion, often lying so near the
surface that, when once they have been exposed, it is hard to
understand how they could ever have presented themselves as
important.

Let us turn, for illustration's sake, to the time-honoured
Cardinal Virtues.   If we are told that the dictates of Wisdom
and Temperance may be summed up in clear and certain
principles, and that these are respectively,

(1) It is right to act rationally,
(2) It is right that the Lower parts of our nature should
be governed by the Higher,

we do not at first feel that we are not obtaining valuable
information.   But when we find (cf. *ante*, chap. xi. § 3) that
" acting rationally " is merely another phrase for " doing what
we see to be right," and, again, that the " higher part " of our
nature to which the rest are to submit is explained to be
Reason, so that " acting temperately " is only " acting rationally " under the condition of special non-rational impulses
needing to be resisted, the tautology of our " principles " is
obvious.   Similarly when we are asked to accept as the
principle of Justice " that we ought to give every man his
own," the definition seems plausible—until it appears that we
cannot define " his own " except as equivalent to " that which
it is right he should have."

The definitions quoted may be found in modern writers :
but it seems worthy of remark that throughout the ethical
speculation of Greece,[1] such universal affirmations as are

_____

[1] I am fully sensible of the peculiar interest and value of the ethical thought
of ancient Greece.   Indeed through a large part of the present work the influence
of Plato and Aristotle on my treatment of this subject has been greater than that

presented to us concerning Virtue or Good conduct seem almost always to be propositions which can only be defended from the charge of tautology, if they are understood as definitions of the problem to be solved, and not as attempts at its solution. For example, Plato and Aristotle appear to offer as constructive moralists the scientific knowledge on ethical matters of which Socrates proclaimed the absence; knowledge, that is, of the Good and Bad in human life. And they seem to be agreed that such Good as can be realised in the concrete life of men and communities is chiefly Virtue,—or (as Aristotle more precisely puts it) the *exercise* of Virtue: so that the practical part of ethical science must consist mainly in the knowledge of Virtue. If, however, we ask how we are to ascertain the kind of conduct which is properly to be called Virtuous, it does not seem that Plato can tell us more of each virtue in turn than that it consists in (1) the knowledge of what is Good in certain circumstances and relations, and (2) such a harmony of the different elements of man's appetitive nature, that their resultant impulse may be always in accordance with this knowledge. But it is just this knowledge (or at least its principles and method) that we are expecting him to give us: and to explain to us instead the different exigencies under which we need it, in no way satisfies our expectation. Nor, again, does Aristotle bring us much nearer such knowledge by telling us that the Good in conduct is to be found somewhere between different kinds of Bad. This at best only indicates the *whereabouts* of Virtue: it does not give us a method for finding it.

On the Stoic system,[1] as constructed by Zeno and Chrysippus, it is perhaps unfair to pronounce decisively, from the accounts given of it by adversaries like Plutarch, and such semi-intelligent expositors as Cicero, Diogenes Laertius, and Stobæus. But, as far as we can judge of it, we must pronounce the exposition of its general principles a

of any modern writer. But I am here only considering the value of the general principles for determining what ought to be done, which the ancient systems profess to supply.

[1] The following remarks apply less to *later* Stoicism—especially the Roman Stoicism which we know at first hand in the writings of Seneca and Marcus Aurelius ; in which the relation of the individual man to Humanity generally is more prominent than it is in the earlier form of the system.

complicated enchainment of circular reasonings, by which the inquirer is continually deluded with an apparent approach to practical conclusions, and continually led back to the point from which he set out.

The most characteristic formula of Stoicism seems to have been that declaring 'Life according to Nature' to be the ultimate end of action. The spring of the motion that sustained this life was in the vegetable creation a mere unfelt impulse : in animals it was impulse accompanied with sensation : in man it was the direction of Reason, which in him was naturally supreme over all merely blind irrational impulses. What then does Reason direct ? 'To live according to Nature' is one answer: and thus we get the circular exposition of ethical doctrine in its simplest form. Sometimes, however, we are told that it is 'Life according to Virtue': which leads us into the circle already noticed in the Platonic-Aristotelian philosophy ; as Virtue, by the Stoics also, is only defined as knowledge of Good and Bad in different circumstances and relations. Indeed, this latter circle is given by the Stoics more neatly and perfectly : for with Plato and Aristotle Virtue was not the *sole*, but only the *chief* content of the notion Good, in its application to human life : but in the view of Stoicism the two notions are absolutely coincident. The result, then, is that Virtue is knowledge of what is good and ought to be sought or chosen, and of what is bad and ought to be shunned or rejected: while at the same time there is nothing good or properly choice-worthy, nothing bad or truly formidable, except Virtue and Vice respectively. But if Virtue is thus declared to be a science that has no object except itself, the notion is inevitably emptied of all practical content. In order, therefore, to avoid this result and to reconcile their system with common sense, the Stoics explained that there were other things in human life which were in a manner preferable, though not strictly good, including in this class the primary objects of men's normal impulses. On what principle then are we to select these objects when our impulses are conflicting or ambiguous ? If we can get an answer to this question, we shall at length have come to something practical. But here again the Stoic could find no other general answer except either that we were to choose what was Reasonable, or that we were to act in accordance with Nature : each of which answers obviously brings us back into the original circle at a different point.[1]

In Butler's use of the Stoic formula, this circular reasoning seems to be avoided : but it is so only so long as the intrinsic reasonableness of right conduct is ignored or suppressed. Butler assumes with his opponents that it is reasonable to live according to Nature, and argues that Conscience or the faculty that imposes moral rules is naturally supreme in man. It is therefore reasonable to obey Conscience. But are the rules that Conscience lays down merely known to us as the dictates of arbitrary authority, and not as in themselves reasonable ? This would give a surely dangerous absoluteness of authority to the possibly unenlightened conscience of any individual : and Butler is much too cautious to do this : in fact, in more than one passage of the *Analogy* [2] he expressly adopts the doctrine of Clarke, that the true rules of morality are essentially reasonable. But if Conscience is, after all, Reason applied to Practice, then Butler's argument seems to bend itself into the old circle : ' it is reasonable to live according to Nature, and it is natural to live according to Reason.'

In the next chapter I shall have to call attention to another logical circle into which we are liable to slide, if we refer to the Good or Perfection, whether of the agent or of others, in giving an account of any special virtue ; if we allow ourselves, in explaining Good or Perfection, to use the general notion of virtue (which is commonly regarded as an important element of either). Meanwhile I have already given, perhaps, more than sufficient illustration of one of the most important dangers that beset the students of Ethics. In the laudable attempt to escape from the doubtfulness, disputableness, and

---

[1] It should be observed that in determining the particulars of external duty the Stoics to some extent used the notion ' nature ' in a different way : they tried to derive guidance from the complex adaptation of means to ends exhibited in the organic world. But since in their view the whole course of the Universe was both perfect and completely predetermined, it was impossible for them to obtain from any observation of actual existence a clear and consistent principle for preferring and rejecting alternatives of conduct : and in fact their most characteristic practical precepts show a curious conflict between the tendency to accept what was customary as ' natural,' and the tendency to reject what seemed arbitrary as unreasonable.

[2] Cf. *Analogy*, Part ii. chap. i. and chap. viii.

apparent arbitrariness of current moral opinions, he is liable to take refuge in principles that are incontrovertible but tautological and insignificant.

§ 3. Can we then, between this Scylla and Charybdis of ethical inquiry, avoiding on the one hand doctrines that merely bring us back to common opinion with all its imperfections, and on the other hand doctrines that lead us round in a circle, find any way of obtaining self-evident moral principles of real significance ?   It would be disheartening to have to regard as altogether illusory the strong instinct of Common Sense that points to the existence of such principles, and the deliberate convictions of the long line of moralists who have enunciated them.   At the same time, the more we extend our knowledge of man and his environment, the more we realise the vast variety of human natures and circumstances that have existed in different ages and countries, the less disposed we are to believe that there is any definite code of absolute rules, applicable to all human beings without exception.   And we shall find, I think, that the truth lies between these two conclusions. There are certain absolute practical principles, the truth of which, when they are explicitly stated, is manifest ; but they are of too abstract a nature, and too universal in their scope, to enable us to ascertain by immediate application of them what we ought to do in any particular case ; particular duties have still to be determined by some other method.

One such principle was given in chap. i. § 3 of this Book ; where I pointed out that whatever action any of us judges to be right for himself, he implicitly judges to be right for all similar persons in similar circumstances.   Or, as we may otherwise put it, ' if a kind of conduct that is right (or wrong) for me is not right (or wrong) for some one else, it must be on the ground of some difference between the two cases, other than the fact that I and he are different persons.'   A corresponding proposition may be stated with equal truth in respect of what ought to be done *to*—not *by*—different individuals.   These principles have been most widely recognised, not in their most abstract and universal form, but in their special application to the situation of two (or more) individuals similarly related to each other : as so applied, they appear in what is popularly known as the Golden Rule, ' Do to others as you would have

them do to you.' This formula is obviously unprecise in statement; for one might wish for another's co-operation in sin,
and be willing to reciprocate it. Nor is it even true to say
that we ought to do to others only what we think it right
for them to do to us; for no one will deny that there may be
differences in the circumstances—and even in the natures—
of two individuals, *A* and *B*, which would make it wrong for
A to treat *B* in the way in which it is right for *B* to treat *A*.
In short the self-evident principle strictly stated must take
some such negative form as this; 'it cannot be right for *A* to
treat *B* in a manner in which it would be wrong for *B* to
treat *A*, merely on the ground that they are two different
individuals, and without there being any difference between
the natures or circumstances of the two which can be stated as
a reasonable ground for difference of treatment.' Such a principle manifestly does not give complete guidance—indeed its
effect, strictly speaking, is merely to throw a definite *onus probandi* on the man who applies to another a treatment of which
he would complain if applied to himself; but Common Sense
has amply recognised the practical importance of the maxim:
and its truth, so far as it goes, appears to me self-evident.

A somewhat different application of the same fundamental
principle that individuals in similar conditions should be
treated similarly finds its sphere in the ordinary administration of Law, or (as we say) of 'Justice.' Accordingly in § 1
of chap. v. of this Book I drew attention to 'impartiality in the
application of general rules,' as an important element in the
common notion of Justice; indeed, there ultimately appeared
to be no other element which could be intuitively known with
perfect clearness and certainty. Here again it must be plain
that this precept of impartiality is insufficient for the complete
determination of just conduct, as it does not help us to decide
what kind of rules should be thus impartially applied; though
all admit the importance of excluding from government, and
human conduct generally, all conscious partiality and 'respect
of persons.'

The principle just discussed, which seems to be more
or less clearly implied in the common notion of 'fairness'
or 'equity,' is obtained by considering the similarity of the
individuals that make up a Logical Whole or Genus. There

are others, no less important, which emerge in the consideration of the similar parts of a Mathematical or Quantitative
Whole.   Such a Whole is presented in the common notion of
the Good—or, as is sometimes said, ' good on the whole '—of any
individual human being.   The proposition ' that one ought to
aim at one's own good' is sometimes given as the maxim of
Rational Self-love or Prudence : but as so stated it does not
clearly avoid tautology; since we may define 'good' as 'what one
ought to aim at.'   If, however, we say 'one's good on the whole,'
the addition suggests a principle which, when explicitly stated,
is, at any rate, not tautological.   I have already referred to this
principle [1] as that ' of impartial concern for all parts of our
conscious life ':—we might express it concisely by saying ' that
Hereafter *as such* is to be regarded neither less nor more than
Now.'   It is not, of course, meant that the good of the present
may not reasonably be preferred to that of the future on account
of its greater certainty : or again, that a week ten years hence
may not be more important to us than a week now, through
an increase in our means or capacities of happiness.   All that
the principle affirms is that the mere difference of priority and
posteriority in time is not a reasonable ground for having more
regard to the consciousness of one moment that to that of
another.   The form in which it practically presents itself to
most men is ' that a smaller present good is not to be preferred
to a greater future good' (allowing for difference of certainty):
since Prudence is generally exercised in restraining a present
desire (the object or satisfaction of which we commonly regard
as *pro tanto* ' a good '), on account of the remoter consequences
of gratifying it.   The commonest view of the principle would
no doubt be that the present *pleasure* or *happiness* is reasonably
to be foregone with the view of obtaining greater pleasure or
happiness hereafter : but the principle need not be restricted
to a hedonistic application ; it is equally applicable to any other
interpretation of ' one's own good,' in which good is conceived
as a mathematical whole, of which the integrant parts are
realised in different parts or moments of a lifetime.   And
therefore it is perhaps better to distinguish it here from the
principle ' that Pleasure is the sole Ultimate Good,' which does
not seem to have any logical connexion with it.

[1] Cf. *ante*, note to p. 124.

So far we have only been considering the 'Good on the Whole' of a single individual: but just as this notion is constructed by comparison and integration of the different 'goods' that succeed one another in the series of our conscious states, so we have formed the notion of Universal Good by comparison and integration of the goods of all individual human—or sentient—existences. And here again, just as in the former case, by considering the relation of the integrant parts to the whole and to each other, I obtain the self-evident principle that the good of any one individual is of no more importance, from the point of view (if I may say so) of the Universe, than the good of any other; unless, that is, there are special grounds for believing that more good is likely to be realised in the one case than in the other. And it is evident to me that as a rational being I am bound to aim at good generally,—so far as it is attainable by my efforts,—not merely at a particular part of it.

From these two rational intuitions we may deduce, as a necessary inference, the maxim of Benevolence in an abstract form: viz. that each one is morally bound to regard the good of any other individual as much as his own, except in so far as he judges it to be less, when impartially viewed, or less certainly knowable or attainable by him. I before observed that the duty of Benevolence as recognised by common sense seems to fall somewhat short of this. But I think it may be fairly urged in explanation of this that *practically* each man, even with a view to universal Good, ought chiefly to concern himself with promoting the good of a limited number of human beings, and that generally in proportion to the closeness of their connexion with him. I think that a 'plain man,' in a modern civilised society, if his conscience were fairly brought to consider the hypothetical question, whether it would be morally right for him to seek his own happiness on any occasion if it involved a certain sacrifice of the greater happiness of some other human being,—without any counterbalancing gain to any one else,— would answer unhesitatingly in the negative.

I have tried to show how in the principles of Justice, Prudence, and Rational Benevolence as commonly recognised there is at least a self-evident element, immediately cognisable by abstract intuition; depending in each case on the relation which individuals and their particular ends bear as parts to their wholes, and to other parts of these wholes. I regard the apprehension, with more or less distinctness, of these abstract truths, as the permanent basis of the common conviction that the fundamental precepts of morality are essentially reasonable. No doubt these principles are often placed side by side with other precepts to which custom and general consent have given a merely illusory air of self-evidence : but the distinction between the two kinds of maxims appears to me to become manifest by merely reflecting upon them. I know by direct reflection that the propositions, ' I ought to speak the truth,' ' I ought to keep my promises '—however true they may be— are not self-evident to me ; they present themselves as propositions requiring rational justification of some kind. On the other hand, the propositions, ' I ought not to prefer a present lesser good to a future greater good,' and ' I ought not to prefer my own lesser good to the greater good of another,' [1] do present themselves as self-evident ; as much (e.g.) as the mathematical axiom that ' if equals be added to equals the wholes are equal.'

It is on account of the fundamental and manifest importance, in my view, of the distinction above drawn between (1) the moral maxims which reflection shows not to possess ultimate validity, and (2) the moral maxims which are or involve genuine ethical axioms, that I refrained at the outset of this investigation from entering at length into the psychogonical question as to the origin of apparent moral intuitions. For no psychogonical theory has ever been put forward professing to discredit the propositions that I regard as really axiomatic, by showing that the causes which produced them were such as had a tendency to make them false : while as regards the former class of maxims, a psychogonical proof that they are untrustworthy when taken as absolutely and without qualification true is in my view, superfluous : since direct reflection shows me they have no claim to be so taken. On the other hand, so far as psychogonical theory represents moral rules as, speaking broadly and generally, means to the ends of individual and social good or well-being, it obviously tends to give a general

---

[1] To avoid misapprehension I should state that in these propositions the consideration of the different degrees of *certainty* of Present and Future Good, Own and Others' Good respectively, is supposed to have been fully taken into account *before* the future or alien Good is judged to be greater.

support to the conclusions to which the preceding discussion has brought us by a different method : since it leads us to regard other moral rules as subordinate to the principles of Prudence and Benevolence.[1]

§ 4. I should, however, rely less confidently on the conclusions set forth in the preceding section, if they did not appear to me to be in substantial agreement—in spite of superficial differences—with the doctrines of those moralists who have been most in earnest in seeking among commonly received moral rules for genuine intuitions of the Practical Reason. I have already pointed out[2] that in the history of English Ethics the earlier intuitional school show, in this respect, a turn of thought on the whole more philosophical than that which the reaction against Hume rendered prevalent. Among the writers of this school there is no one who shows more earnestness in the effort to penetrate to really self-evident principles than Clarke.[3] Accordingly, I find that Clarke lays down, in respect of our behaviour towards our fellow-men, two fundamental "rules of righteousness" :[4] the first of which he terms Equity, and the second Love or Benevolence. The Rule of Equity he states thus : "Whatever I judge reasonable or unreasonable that another should do for me : that by the same judgment I declare

---

[1] It may, however, be thought that in exhibiting this aspect of the morality of Common Sense, psychogonical theory leads us to define in a particular way the general notion of 'good' or 'well-being,' regarded as a result which morality has a demonstrable natural tendency to produce. This point will be considered subsequently (chap. xiv. § 1 of this Book : and Book iv. chap. iv.).

[2] Cf. ante, Book i. chap. viii. Note, pp. 103, 104.

[3] In drawing attention to Clarke's system, I ought perhaps to remark that his anxiety to exhibit the parallelism between ethical and mathematical truth (on which Locke before him had insisted) renders his general terminology inappropriate, and occasionally leads him into downright extravagances. *E.g.* it is patently absurd to say that "a man who wilfully acts contrary to Justice wills things to be what they are not and cannot be" : nor are "Relations and Proportions" or "fitnesses and unfitnesses of things" very suitable designations for the matter of moral intuition. But for the present purpose there is no reason to dwell on these defects.

[4] Clarke's statement of the "Rule of Righteousness with respect to ourselves" I pass over, because it is, as he states it, a derivative and subordinate rule. It is that we should preserve our being, be temperate, industrious, etc., *with a view to the performance of Duty :* which of course supposes Duty (*i.e.* the ultimate and absolute rules of Duty) already determined. I may observe that the reasonableness of Prudence or Self-love is only recognised by Clarke indirectly ; in a passage which I quoted before (p. 120).

reasonable or unreasonable that I should *in the like case* do for
him " [1]—which is of course, the 'Golden Rule' precisely stated.
The obligation to " Universal Love or Benevolence " he exhibits
as follows :—

" If there be a natural and necessary difference between
Good and Evil : and that which is Good is fit and reasonable,
and that which is Evil is unreasonable, to be done : and that
which is the Greatest Good is always the most fit and reasonable to be chosen : then . . . every rational creature ought in
its sphere and station, according to its respective powers and
faculties, to do all the Good it can to its fellow-creatures : to
which end, universal Love and Benevolence is plainly the most
certain, direct, and effectual means." [2]

Here the mere statement that a rational agent is bound
to aim at universal good is open to the charge of tautology,
since Clarke defines ' Good ' as ' that which is fit and reasonable to be done.' But Clarke obviously holds that each
individual ' rational creature ' is capable of receiving good in
a greater or less degree, such good being an integrant part
of universal good. This indeed is implied in the common
notion, which he uses, of ' doing Good to one's fellow-creatures,'
or, as he otherwise expresses it, ' promoting their welfare and
happiness.' And thus his principle is implicitly what was
stated above, that the good or welfare of any one individual
must as such be an object of rational aim to any other
reasonable individual no less than his own similar good or
welfare.

(It should be observed, however, that the proposition that
Universal Benevolence is the right means to the attainment
of universal good, is not quite self-evident ; since the end may
not always be best attained by directly aiming at it. Thus
Rational Benevolence, like Rational Self-Love, may be self-
limiting ; may direct its own partial suppression in favour of
other impulses.)

Among later moralists, Kant is especially noted for his
rigour in separating the purely rational element of the
moral code : and his ethical view also appears to me to
coincide to a considerable extent, if not completely, with
that set forth in the preceding section. I have already

---

[1] *Boyle Lectures* (1705), etc., pp. 86, 87.   [2] *l.c.* p. 92.

noticed that his fundamental principle of duty is the ' formal ' rule of " acting on a maxim that one can will to be law universal "; which, duly restricted,[1] is an immediate practical corollary from the principle that I first noticed in the preceding section. And we find that when he comes to consider the ends at which virtuous action is aimed, the only really ultimate end which he lays down is the object of Rational Benevolence as commonly conceived—the happiness of other men.[2] He regards it as evident *a priori* that each man as a rational agent is bound to aim at the happiness of other men : indeed, in his view, it can only be stated as a *duty* for me to seek my own happiness so far as I consider it as a part of the happiness of mankind in general. I disagree with the negative side of this statement, as I hold with Butler that " one's own happiness is a manifest obligation " independently of one's relation to other men ; but, regarded on its positive side, Kant's conclusion appears to agree to a great extent with the view of the duty of Rational Benevolence that I have given :—though I am not altogether able to assent to the arguments by which Kant arrives at his conclusion.[3]

§ 5. I must now point out—if it has not long been apparent to the reader—that the self-evident principles laid down in § 3 do not specially belong to Intuitionism in the restricted sense which, for clear distinction of methods, I gave to this term at the outset of our investigation. The axiom of Prudence, as I have given it, is a self-evident principle, implied in Rational Egoism as commonly accepted.[4] Again, the axiom of Justice or Equity as above stated—' that similar

---

[1] I think that Kant, in applying this axiom, does not take due account of certain restrictive considerations. Cf. chap. vii. § 3 of this Book, and also Book iv. chap. v. § 3.

[2] Kant no doubt gives the agent's own Perfection as another absolute end ; but when we come to examine his notion of perfection, we find that it is not really determinate without the statement of other ends of reason, for the accomplishment of which we are to perfect ourselves. See *Met. Anfangsgr. d. Tugendlehre*, I. Theil, § v. " The perfection that belongs to men generally . . . " can be nothing else than the cultivation of one's power, and also of one's will, " to satisfy the requirements of duty in general."

[3] See note at the end of the chapter.

[4] On the relation of Rational Egoism to Rational Benevolence—which I regard as the profoundest problem of Ethics—my final view is given in the last chapter of this treatise.

cases ought to be treated similarly'—belongs in all its applications to Utilitarianism as much as to any system commonly called Intuitional: while the axiom of Rational Benevolence is, in my view, required as a rational basis for the Utilitarian system.

Accordingly, I find that I arrive, in my search for really clear and certain ethical intuitions, at the fundamental principle of Utilitarianism. I must, however, admit that the thinkers who in recent times have taught this latter system, have not, for the most part, expressly tried to exhibit the truth of their first principle by means of any such procedure as that above given. Still, when I examine the "proof" of the "principle of Utility" presented by the most persuasive and probably the most influential among English expositors of Utilitarianism,—J. S. Mill,—I find the need of some such procedure to complete the argument very plain and palpable.

Mill begins by explaining[1] that though "questions of ultimate ends are not amenable" to "proof in the ordinary and popular meaning of the term," there is a "larger meaning of the word proof" in which they are amenable to it. "The subject," he says, is "within the cognisance of the rational faculty. . . . Considerations may be presented capable of determining the intellect to" accept "the Utilitarian formula." He subsequently makes clear that by "acceptance of the Utilitarian formula" he means the acceptance, not of the agent's own greatest happiness, but of "the greatest amount of happiness altogether" as the ultimate "end of human action" and "standard of morality": to promote which is, in the Utilitarian view, the supreme "directive rule of human conduct." Then when he comes to give the "proof"—in the larger sense before explained—of this rule or formula, he offers the following argument. "The sole evidence it is possible to produce that anything is desirable, is that people do actually desire it. . . . No reason can be given why the general happiness is desirable, except that each person, so far as he believes it to be attainable, desires his own happiness. This, however, being a fact, we have not only all the proof which the case admits of, but all which it is possible to require, that happiness is a good:

[1] *Utilitarianism*, chap. i. pp. 6, 7, and chap. ii. pp. 16, 17.

that each person's happiness is a good to that person, and the general happiness, therefore, a good to the aggregate of persons."[1] He then goes on to argue that pleasure, and pleasure alone, is what all men actually do desire.

Now, as we have seen, it is as a "standard of right and wrong," or "directive rule of conduct," that the utilitarian principle is put forward by Mill: hence, in giving as a statement of this principle that "the general happiness is *desirable*," he must be understood to mean (and his whole treatise shows that he does mean) that it is what each individual *ought* to desire, or at least—in the stricter sense of ' ought '—to aim at realising in action.[2] But this proposition is not established by Mill's reasoning, even if we grant that what is actually desired may be legitimately inferred to be in this sense desirable. For an aggregate of actual desires, each directed towards a different part of the general happiness, does not constitute an actual desire for the general happiness, existing in any individual; and Mill would certainly not contend that a desire which does not exist in any individual can possibly exist in an aggregate of individuals. There being therefore no actual desire—so far as this reasoning goes—for the general happiness, the proposition that the general happiness is desirable cannot be in this way established: so that there is a gap in the expressed argument, which can, I think, only be filled by some such proposition as that which I have above tried to exhibit as the intuition of Rational Benevolence.

Utilitarianism is thus presented as the final form into which Intuitionism tends to pass, when the demand for really self-evident first principles is rigorously pressed. In order, however, to make this transition logically complete, we require to interpret ' Universal Good ' as ' Universal Happiness.' And this interpretation cannot, in my view, be justified by arguing, as Mill does, from the psychological fact that Happiness is the sole object of men's actual desires, to the ethical conclusion

---

[1] *l.c.* chap. iv. pp. 52, 53.

[2] It has been suggested that I have overlooked a confusion in Mill's mind between two possible meanings of the term ' desirable,' (1) what can be desired and (2) what ought to be desired. I intended to show by the two first sentences of this paragraph that I was aware of this confusion, but thought it unnecessary for my present purpose to discuss it.

that it alone is desirable or good; because in Book i. chap. iv. of this treatise I have attempted to show that Happiness or Pleasure is not the only object that each for himself actually desires. The identification of Ultimate Good with Happiness is properly to be reached, I think, by a more indirect mode of reasoning; which I will endeavour to explain in the next Chapter.

NOTE.—The great influence at present exercised by Kant's teaching makes it worth while to state briefly the arguments by which he attempts to establish the duty of promoting the happiness of others, and the reasons why I am unable to regard these arguments as cogent. In some passages he attempts to exhibit this duty as an immediate deduction from his fundamental formula—" act from a maxim that thou canst will to be universal law"—when considered in combination with the desire for the kind services of others which (as he assumes) the exigencies of life must arouse in every man. The maxim, he says, "that each should be left to take care of himself without either aid or interference," is one that we might indeed *conceive* existing as a universal law : but it would be impossible for us to *will* it to be such. "A will that resolved this would be inconsistent with itself, for many cases may arise in which the individual thus willing needs the benevolence and sympathy of others" (*Grundlegung*, p. 50 [Rosenkrantz]). Similarly elsewhere (*Metaph. Anfangsgr. d. Tugendlehre*, Einleit. § 8 and § 30) he explains at more length that the Self-love which necessarily exists in every one involves the desire of being loved by others and receiving aid from them in case of need. We thus necessarily constitute ourselves an end for others, and claim that they shall contribute to our happiness : and so, according to Kant's fundamental principle, we must recognise the duty of making *their* happiness *our* end.

Now I cannot regard this reasoning as strictly cogent. In the first place, that every man in need wishes for the aid of others is an empirical proposition which Kant cannot know *a priori*. We can certainly conceive a man in whom the spirit of independence and the distaste for incurring obligations would be so strong that he would choose to endure any privations rather than receive aid from others. But even granting that every one, in the actual moment of distress, must necessarily wish for the assistance of others ; still a strong man, after balancing the chances of life, may easily think that he and such as he have more to gain, on the whole, by the general adoption of the egoistic maxim ; benevolence being likely to bring them more trouble than profit.

In other passages, however, Kant reaches the same conclusion by an apparently different line of argument. He lays down that, as all action of rational beings is done for some end, there must be some absolute end, corresponding to the absolute rule before given, that imposes on our maxims the form of universal law. This absolute end, prescribed by Reason necessarily and *a priori* for all rational beings as such, can be nothing but Reason itself, or the Universe of Rationals; for what the rule inculcates is, in fact, that we should act as rational units in a universe of rational beings (and therefore on principles conceived and embraced as universally applicable). Or again, we may reach the same result negatively. For all particular ends at which men aim are constituted such by the existence of impulses directed towards some particular objects. Now we cannot tell *a priori* that any one of these special impulses forms part of the constitution of all men: and therefore we cannot state it as an absolute dictate of Reason that we should aim at any such special object. If, then, we thus exclude all particular empirical ends, there remains only the principle that "all Rational beings as such are ends to each": or, as Kant sometimes puts it, that "humanity exists as an end in itself."

Now, says Kant, so long as I confine myself to mere non-interference with others, I do not positively make Humanity my end; my aims remain selfish, though restricted by this condition of non-interference with others. My action, therefore, is not truly virtuous; for Virtue is exhibited and consists in the effort to realise the end of Reason in opposition to mere selfish impulses. Therefore "the ends of the subject, which is itself an end, must of necessity be my ends, if the representation of Humanity as an end in itself is to have its full weight with me" (*Grundlegung*, p. 59), and my action is to be truly rational and virtuous.

Here, again, I cannot accept the form of Kant's argument. The conception of "humanity as an end in itself" is perplexing: because by an End we commonly mean something to be realised, whereas "humanity" is, as Kant says, "a self-subsistent end": moreover, there seems to be a sort of paralogism in the deduction of the principle of Benevolence by means of this conception. For the humanity which Kant maintains to be an end in itself is Man (or the aggregate of men) *in so far as rational*. But the subjective ends of other men, which Benevolence directs us to take as our own ends, would seem, according to Kant's own view, to depend upon and correspond to their *non-rational* impulses —their empirical desires and aversions. It is hard to see why, if man *as a rational being* is an absolute end to other rational beings, they must therefore adopt his subjective aims as determined by his non-rational impulses.

CHAPTER XIV

ULTIMATE GOOD

§ 1. At the outset of this treatise [1] I noticed that there are two forms in which the object of ethical inquiry is considered; it is sometimes regarded as a Rule or Rules of Conduct, 'the Right,' sometimes as an end or ends, 'the Good.' I pointed out that in the moral consciousness of modern Europe the two notions are *prima facie* distinct; since while it is commonly thought that the obligation to obey moral rules is absolute, it is not commonly held that the whole Good of man lies in such obedience; this view, we may say, is—vaguely and respectfully but unmistakably—repudiated as a Stoical paradox. The ultimate Good or Wellbeing of man is rather regarded as an ulterior result, the connexion of which with his Right Conduct is indeed commonly held to be certain, but is frequently conceived as supernatural, and so beyond the range of independent ethical speculation. But now, if the conclusions of the preceding chapters are to be trusted, it would seem that the practical determination of Right Conduct depends on the determination of Ultimate Good. For we have seen (*a*) that most of the commonly received maxims of Duty—even of those which at first sight appear absolute and independent—are found when closely examined to contain an implicit subordination to the more general principles of Prudence and Benevolence: and (*b*) that no principles except these, and the formal principle of Justice or Equity can be admitted as at once intuitively clear and certain; while, again, these principles themselves, so far as they are self-evident, may be stated as precepts to seek (1) one's own good on the whole, repressing all seductive impulses

---

[1] See Book i. chap. i. § 2.

prompting to undue preference of particular goods, and (2) others' good no less than one's own, repressing any undue preference for one individual over another.   Thus we are brought round again to the old question with which ethical speculation in Europe began, 'What is the Ultimate Good for man ?'—though not in the egoistic form in which the old question was raised.   When, however, we examine the controversies to which this question originally led, we see that the investigation which has brought us round to it has tended definitely to exclude one of the answers which early moral reflection was disposed to give to it.   For to say that 'General Good' consists solely in general Virtue,—if we mean by Virtue conformity to such prescriptions and prohibitions as make up the main part of the morality of Common Sense—would obviously involve us in a logical circle; since we have seen that the exact determination of these prescriptions and prohibitions must depend on the definition of this General Good.

Nor, I conceive, can this argument be evaded by adopting the view of what I have called ' Æsthetic Intuitionism ' and regarding Virtues as excellences of conduct clearly discernible by trained insight, although their nature does not admit of being stated in definite formulæ.   For our notions of special virtues do not really become more independent by becoming more indefinite: they still contain, though perhaps more latently, the same reference to ' Good ' or ' Wellbeing ' as an ultimate standard.   This appears clearly when we consider any virtue in relation to the cognate vice—or at least *non-virtue* —into which it tends to pass over when pushed to an extreme, or exhibited under inappropriate conditions.   For example, Common Sense may seem to regard Liberality, Frugality, Courage, Placability, as intrinsically desirable : but when we consider their relation respectively to Profusion, Meanness, Foolhardiness, Weakness, we find that Common Sense draws the line in each case not by immediate intuition, but by reference either to some definite maxim of duty, or to the general notion of ' Good ' or Wellbeing: and similarly when we ask at what point Candour, Generosity, Humility cease to be virtues by becoming 'excessive.'   Other qualities commonly admired, such as Energy, Zeal, Self-control, Thoughtfulness, are obviously regarded as virtues only when they are directed to

good ends. In short, the only so-called Virtues which can be
thought to be essentially and always such, and incapable of
excess, are such qualities as Wisdom, Universal Benevolence,
and (in a sense) Justice; of which the notions manifestly involve
this notion of Good, supposed already determinate. Wisdom
is insight into Good and the means to Good; Benevolence
is exhibited in the purposive actions called "doing Good":
Justice (when regarded as essentially and always a Virtue)
lies in distributing Good (or evil) impartially according to
right rules. If then we are asked what is this Good which it
is excellent to know, to bestow on others, to distribute impartially, it would be obviously absurd to reply that it is just this
knowledge, these beneficent purposes, this impartial distribution.

Nor, again, can I perceive that this difficulty is in any
way met by regarding Virtue as a quality of "character"
rather than of "conduct," and expressing the moral law in
the form, "Be this," instead of the form "Do this." [1] From
a practical point of view, indeed, I fully recognise the importance of urging that men should aim at an ideal of
character, and consider action in its effects on character. But
I cannot infer from this that character and its elements—
faculties, habits, or dispositions of any kind—are the constituents of Ultimate Good. It seems to me that the opposite
is implied in the very conception of a faculty or disposition;
it can only be defined as a tendency to act or feel in a certain
way under certain conditions; and such a tendency appears
to me clearly not valuable in itself but for the acts and feelings in which it takes effect, or for the ulterior consequences
of these,—which consequences, again, cannot be regarded as
Ultimate Good, so long as they are merely conceived as modifications of faculties, dispositions, etc. When, therefore, I say
that effects on character are important, it is a summary way
of saying that by the laws of our mental constitution the
present act or feeling is a cause tending to modify importantly
our acts and feelings in the indefinite future: the comparatively permanent result supposed to be produced in the mind
or soul, being a tendency that will show itself in an indefinite
number of particular acts and feelings, may easily be more
important, in relation to the ultimate end, than a single act

---

[1] Cf. Stephen, *Science of Ethics*, chap. iv. § 16.

or the transient feeling of a single moment: but its comparative permanence appears to me no ground for regarding it as itself a constituent of ultimate good.

§ 2. So far, however, I have been speaking only of particular virtues, as exhibited in conduct judged to be objectively right: and it may be argued that this is too external a view of the Virtue that claims to constitute Ultimate Good. It may be said that the difficulty that I have been urging vanishes if we penetrate beyond the particular virtues to the root and essence of virtue in general, —the determination of the will to do whatever is judged to be right and to aim at realising whatever is judged to be best—; since this subjective rightness or goodness of will, being independent of knowledge of what is objectively right or good, is independent of that presupposition of Good as already known and determined, which we have seen to be implied in the common conceptions of virtue as manifested in outward acts. I admit that if subjective rightness or goodness of Will is affirmed to be the Ultimate Good, the affirmation does not exactly involve the logical difficulty that I have been urging. None the less is it fundamentally opposed to Common Sense; since the very notion of subjective rightness or goodness of will implies an objective standard, which it directs us to seek, but does not profess to supply. It would be a palpable and violent paradox to set before the right-seeking mind no end except this right-seeking itself, and to affirm this to be the sole Ultimate Good, denying that any effects of right volition can be in themselves good, except the subjective rightness of future volitions, whether of self or of others. It is true that no rule can be recognised, by any reasonable individual, as more authoritative than the rule of doing what he judges to be right; for, in deliberating with a view to my own immediate action, I cannot distinguish between doing what is objectively right, and realising my own subjective conception of rightness. But we are continually forced to make the distinction as regards the actions of others and to judge that conduct may be objectively wrong though subjectively right: and we continually judge conduct to be objectively wrong because it tends to cause pain and loss of happiness to others,—apart from any effect on the subjective

rightness of their volitions. It is as so judging that we
commonly recognise the mischief and danger of fanaticism :—
meaning by a fanatic a man who resolutely and unswervingly
carries out his own conception of rightness, when it is a
plainly mistaken conception.

The same result may be reached even without supposing
so palpable a divorce between subjective and objective rightness of volition as is implied in the notion of fanaticism.   As
I have already pointed out,[1] though the 'dictates of Reason'
are always to be obeyed, it does not follow that 'the dictation
of Reason'—the predominance of consciously moral over non-
moral motives—is to be promoted without limits ; and indeed
Common Sense appears to hold that some things are likely
to be better done, if they are done from other motives than
conscious obedience to practical Reason or Conscience.   It
thus becomes a practical question how far the dictation of
Reason, the predominance of moral choice and moral effort in
human life, is a result to be aimed at : and the admission of
this question implies that conscious rightness of volition is not
the sole ultimate good.   On the whole, then, we may conclude
that neither (1) subjective rightness or goodness of volition,
as distinct from objective, nor (2) virtuous character, except as
manifested or realised in virtuous conduct, can be regarded as
constituting Ultimate Good : while, again, we are precluded
from identifying Ultimate Good with virtuous conduct, because our conceptions of virtuous conduct, under the different
heads or aspects denoted by the names of the particular
virtues, have been found to presuppose the prior determination
of the notion of Good—that Good which virtuous conduct is
conceived as producing or promoting or rightly distributing.

And what has been said of Virtue, seems to me still more
manifestly true of the other talents, gifts, and graces which
make up the common notion of human excellence or Perfection.
However immediately the excellent quality of such gifts and
skills may be recognised and admired, reflection shows that
they are only valuable on account of the good or desirable
conscious life in which they are or will be actualised, or which
will be somehow promoted by their exercise.

§ 3. Shall we then say that Ultimate Good is Good

---

[1] Chap. xi. § 3 ; see also chap. xii. § 3.

or Desirable conscious or sentient Life—of which Virtuous action is one element, but not the sole constituent? This seems in harmony with Common Sense; and the fact that particular virtues and talents and gifts are largely valued as means to ulterior good does not necessarily prevent us from regarding their exercise as also an element of Ultimate Good: just as the fact that physical action, nutrition, and repose, duly proportioned and combined, are means to the maintenance of our animal life, does not prevent us from regarding them as indispensable elements of such life. Still it seems difficult to conceive any kind of activity or process as both means and end, from precisely the same point of view and in respect of precisely the same quality: and in both the cases above mentioned it is, I think, easy to distinguish the aspect in which the activities or processes in question are to be regarded as means from that in which they are to be regarded as in themselves good or desirable. Let us examine this first in the case of the physical processes. It is in their purely physical aspect, as complex processes of corporeal change, that they are means to the maintenance of life: but so long as we confine our attention to their corporeal aspect,—regarding them merely as complex movements of certain particles of organised matter—it seems impossible to attribute to these movements, considered in themselves, either goodness or badness. I cannot conceive it to be an ultimate end of rational action to secure that these complex movements should be of one kind rather than another, or that they should be continued for a longer rather than a shorter period. In short, if a certain quality of human Life is that which is ultimately desirable, it must belong to human Life regarded on its psychical side, or, briefly, Consciousness.

But again: it is not all life regarded on its psychical side which we can judge to be ultimately desirable: since psychical life as known to us includes pain as well as pleasure, and so far as it is painful it is not desirable. I cannot therefore accept a view of the wellbeing or welfare of human beings—as of other living things—which is suggested by current zoological conceptions and apparently maintained with more or less definiteness by influential writers; according to which, when we attribute goodness or badness to the manner of existence of any living organism, we should be understood to attribute to it a tendency either (1) to self-preservation, or (2) to the preservation of the community or race to which it belongs—so that what " Wellbeing " adds to mere " Being " is just promise of future being. It appears to me that this doctrine needs only to be distinctly contemplated in order to be rejected. If all life were as little desirable as some portions of it have been, in my own experience and in that (I believe) of all or most men, I should judge all tendency to the preservation of it to be unmitigatedly bad. Actually, no doubt, as we generally hold that human life, even as now lived, has on the average, a balance of happiness, we regard what is preservative of life as generally good, and what is destructive of life as bad : and I quite admit that a most fundamentally important part of the function of morality consists in maintaining such habits and sentiments as are necessary to the continued existence, in full numbers, of a society of human beings under their actual conditions of life. But this is not because the mere existence of human organisms, even if prolonged to eternity, appears to me in any way desirable ; it is only assumed to be so because it is supposed to be accompanied by Consciousness on the whole desirable ; it is therefore this Desirable Consciousness which we must regard as ultimate Good.

In the same way, so far as we judge virtuous activity to be a part of Ultimate Good, it is, I conceive, because the consciousness attending it is judged to be in itself desirable for the virtuous agent ; though at the same time this consideration does not adequately represent the importance of Virtue to human wellbeing, since we have to consider its value as a means as well as its value as an end. We may make the distinction clearer by considering whether Virtuous life would remain on the whole good for the virtuous agent, if we suppose it combined with extreme pain. The affirmative answer to this question was strongly supported in Greek philosophical discussion : but it is a paradox from which a modern thinker would recoil : he would hardly venture to assert that the portion of life spent by a martyr in tortures was in itself desirable,—though it might be his duty to suffer the pain with a view to the good of others, and even his interest to suffer it with a view to his own ultimate happiness.

§ 4. If then Ultimate Good can only be conceived as
Desirable Consciousness—including the Consciousness of Virtue
as a part but only as a part—are we to identify this notion
with Happiness or Pleasure, and say with the Utilitarians that
General Good is general happiness?   Many would at this point
of the discussion regard this conclusion as inevitable: to say
that all other things called good are only means to the end of
making conscious life better or more desirable, seems to them
the same as saying that they are means to the end of happiness.   But very important distinctions remain to be considered.
According to the view taken in a previous chapter,[1] in affirming Ultimate Good to be Happiness or Pleasure, we imply (1)
that nothing is desirable except desirable feelings, and (2) that
the desirability of each feeling is only directly cognisable by
the sentient individual at the time of feeling it, and that therefore this particular judgment of the sentient individual must be
taken as final [2] on the question how far each element of feeling
has the quality of Ultimate Good.   Now no one, I conceive,
would estimate in any other way the desirability of feeling
considered merely as feeling: but it may be urged that our
conscious experience includes besides Feelings, Cognitions and
Volitions, and that the desirability of these must be taken into
account, and is not to be estimated by the standard above
stated.   I think, however, that when we reflect on a cognition
as a transient fact of an individual's psychical experience,—
distinguishing it on the one hand from the feeling that
normally accompanies it, and on the other hand from that
relation of the knowing mind to the object known which is
implied in the term " true " or " valid cognition " [3]—it is seen
to be an element of consciousness quite neutral in respect of
desirability: and the same may be said of Volitions, when we
abstract from their concomitant feelings, and their relation to
an objective norm or ideal, as well as from all their conse-

---

[1] Book ii. chap. ii.

[2] Final, that is, so far as the quality of the present feeling is concerned.   I
have pointed out that so far as any estimate of the desirability or pleasantness
of a feeling involves comparison with feelings only represented in idea, it is
liable to be erroneous through imperfections in the representation.

[3] The term "cognition" without qualification more often implies what is
signified by "true" or "valid": but for the present purpose it is necessary to
eliminate this implication.

quences. It is no doubt true that in ordinary thought certain states of consciousness—such as Cognition of Truth, Contemplation of Beauty, Volition to realise Freedom or Virtue—are sometimes judged to be preferable on other grounds than their pleasantness : but the general explanation of this seems to be (as was suggested in Book ii. chap. ii. § 2) that what in such cases we really prefer is not the present consciousness itself, but either effects on future consciousness more or less distinctly foreseen, or else something in the objective relations of the conscious being, not strictly included in his present consciousness.

The second of these alternatives may perhaps be made clearer by some illustrations. A man may prefer the mental state of apprehending truth to the state of half-reliance on generally accredited fictions,[1] while recognising that the former state may be more painful than the latter, and independently of any effect which he expects either state to have upon his subsequent consciousness. Here, on my view, the real object of preference is not the consciousness of knowing truth, considered merely as consciousness,—the element of pleasure or satisfaction in this being more than outweighed by the concomitant pain,—but the relation between the mind and something else, which, as the very notion of 'truth' implies, is whatever it is independently of our cognition of it, and which I therefore call objective. This may become more clear if we imagine ourselves learning afterwards that what we took for truth is not really such : for in this case we should certainly feel that our preference had been mistaken ; whereas if our choice had really been between two elements of transient consciousness, its reasonableness could not be affected by any subsequent discovery.

Similarly, a man may prefer freedom and penury to a life of luxurious servitude, not because the pleasant consciousness of being free outweighs in prospect all the comforts and securities that the other life would afford, but because he has a predominant aversion to that relation between his will and the will of another which we call slavery : or, again, a philosopher may choose what he conceives as 'inner freedom' —the consistent self-determination of the will—rather than

---

[1] Cf. Lecky, *History of European Morals*, pp. 52 *seqq.*

the gratifications of appetite; though recognising that the latter are more desirable, considered merely as transient feelings. In either case, he will be led to regard his preference as mistaken, if he be afterwards persuaded that his conception of Freedom or self-determination was illusory; that we are all slaves of circumstances, destiny, etc.

So again, the preference of conformity to Virtue, or contemplation of Beauty, to a state of consciousness recognised as more pleasant seems to depend on a belief that one's conception of Virtue or Beauty corresponds to an ideal to some extent objective and valid for all minds. Apart from any consideration of future consequences, we should generally agree that a man who sacrificed happiness to an erroneous conception of Virtue or Beauty made a mistaken choice.

Still, it may be said that this is merely a question of definition: that we may take 'conscious life' in a wide sense, so as to include the objective relations of the conscious being implied in our notions of Virtue, Truth, Beauty, Freedom; and that from this point of view we may regard cognition of Truth, contemplation of Beauty, Free or Virtuous action, as in some measure preferable alternatives to Pleasure or Happiness—even though we admit that Happiness must be included as a part of Ultimate Good. In this case the principle of Rational Benevolence, which was stated in the last chapter as an indubitable intuition of the practical Reason, would not direct us to the pursuit of universal happiness alone, but of these "ideal goods" as well, as ends ultimately desirable for mankind generally.

§ 5. I think, however, that this view ought not to commend itself to the sober judgment of reflective persons. In order to show this, I must ask the reader to use the same twofold procedure that I before requested him to employ in considering the absolute and independent validity of common moral precepts. I appeal firstly to his intuitive judgment after due consideration of the question when fairly placed before it: and secondly to a comprehensive comparison of the ordinary judgments of mankind. As regards the first argument, to me at least it seems clear after reflection that these objective relations of the conscious subject, when distinguished from the consciousness accompanying and resulting from them, are not ultimately and intrinsically desirable; any more than material or other objects are, when considered apart from any relation to conscious existence. Admitting that we have actual experience of such preferences as have just been described, of which the ultimate object is something that is not merely consciousness: it still seems to me that when (to use Butler's phrase) we "sit down in a cool hour," we can only justify to ourselves the importance that we attach to any of these objects by considering its conduciveness, in one way or another, to the happiness of sentient beings.

The second argument, that refers to the common sense of mankind, obviously cannot be made completely cogent; since, as above stated, several cultivated persons do habitually judge that knowledge, art, etc.—not to speak of Virtue—are ends independently of the pleasure derived from them. But we may urge not only that all these elements of "ideal good" are productive of pleasure in various ways; but also that they seem to obtain the commendation of Common Sense, roughly speaking, in proportion to the degree of this productiveness. This seems obviously true of Beauty; and will hardly be denied in respect of any kind of social ideal: it is paradoxical to maintain that any degree of Freedom, or any form of social order, would still be commonly regarded as desirable even if we were certain that it had no tendency to promote the general happiness. The case of Knowledge is rather more complex; but certainly Common Sense is most impressed with the value of knowledge, when its 'fruitfulness' has been demonstrated. It is, however, aware that experience has frequently shown how knowledge, long fruitless, may become unexpectedly fruitful, and how light may be shed on one part of the field of knowledge from another apparently remote: and even if any particular branch of scientific pursuit could be shown to be devoid of even this indirect utility, it would still deserve some respect on utilitarian grounds; both as furnishing to the inquirer the refined and innocent pleasures of curiosity, and because the intellectual disposition which it exhibits and sustains is likely on the whole to produce fruitful knowledge. Still in cases approximating to this last, Common Sense is somewhat disposed to complain of the misdirection of valuable effort; so that the meed of honour commonly paid to Science seems to be graduated, though perhaps unconsciously, by a tolerably exact utilitarian scale. Certainly the moment the legitimacy of any branch of scientific inquiry is seriously disputed, as in the recent case of vivisection, the controversy on both sides is generally conducted on an avowedly utilitarian basis.

The case of Virtue requires special consideration : since the encouragement in each other of virtuous impulses and dispositions is a main aim of men's ordinary moral discourse ; so that even to raise the question whether this encouragement can go too far has a paradoxical air. Still, our experience includes rare and exceptional cases in which the concentration of effort on the cultivation of virtue has seemed to have effects adverse to general happiness, through being intensified to the point of moral fanaticism, and so involving a neglect of other conditions of happiness. If, then, we admit as actual or possible such 'infelicific' effects of the cultivation of Virtue, I think we shall also generally admit that, in the case supposed, conduciveness to general happiness should be the criterion for deciding how far the cultivation of Virtue should be carried.

At the same time it must be allowed that we find in Common Sense an aversion to admit Happiness (when explained to mean a sum of pleasures) to be the sole ultimate end and standard of right conduct. But this, I think, can be fully accounted for by the following considerations.

I. The term Pleasure is not commonly used so as to include clearly *all* kinds of consciousness which we desire to retain or reproduce : in ordinary usage it suggests too prominently the coarser and commoner kinds of such feelings ; and it is difficult even for those who are trying to use it scientifically to free their minds altogether from the associations of ordinary usage, and to mean by Pleasure only Desirable Consciousness or Feeling of whatever kind. Again, our knowledge of human life continually suggests to us instances of pleasures which will inevitably involve as concomitant or consequent either a greater amount of pain or a loss of more important pleasures : and we naturally shrink from including even hypothetically in our conception of ultimate good these — in Bentham's phrase — " impure " pleasures ; especially since we have, in many cases, moral or æsthetic instincts warning us against such pleasures.

II. We have seen [1] that many important pleasures can only be felt on condition of our experiencing desires for other things than pleasure. Thus the very acceptance of Pleasure as the ultimate end of conduct involves the practical rule that it is not always to be made the conscious end. Hence, even if we are considering merely the good of one human being taken alone, excluding from our view all effects of his conduct on others, still the reluctance of Common Sense to regard pleasure as the sole thing ultimately desirable may be justified by the consideration that human beings tend to be less happy if they are exclusively occupied with the desire of personal happiness. *E.g.* (as was before shown) we shall miss the valuable pleasures which attend the exercise of the benevolent affections if we do not experience genuinely disinterested impulses to procure happiness for others (which are, in fact, implied in the notion of ' benevolent affections ').

III. But again, I hold, as was expounded in the preceding chapter, that disinterested benevolence is not only thus generally in harmony with rational Self-love, but also in another sense and independently rational : that is, Reason shows me that if my happiness is desirable and a good, the equal happiness of any other person must be equally desirable. Now, when Happiness is spoken of as the sole ultimate good of man, the idea most commonly suggested is that each individual is to seek his own happiness at the expense (if necessary) or, at any rate, to the neglect of that of others : and this offends both our sympathetic and our rational regard for others' happiness. It is, in fact, rather the end of Egoistic than of Universalistic Hedonism, to which Common Sense feels an aversion. And certainly one's individual happiness is, in many respects, an unsatisfactory mark for one's supreme aim, apart from any direct collision into which the exclusive pursuit of it may bring us with rational or sympathetic Benevolence. It does not possess the characteristics which, as Aristotle says, we " divine " to belong to Ultimate Good : being (so far, at least, as it can be empirically foreseen) so narrow and limited, of such necessarily brief duration, and so shifting and insecure

[1] Book i. chap. iv. ; cf. Book ii. chap. iii.

while it lasts. But Universal Happiness, desirable consciousness or feeling for the innumerable multitude of sentient
beings, present and to come, seems an End that satisfies our
imagination by its vastness, and sustains our resolution by its
comparative security.

It may, however, be said that if we require the individual
to sacrifice his own happiness to the greater happiness of
others on the ground that it is reasonable to do so, we really
assign to the individual a different ultimate end from that
which we lay down as the ultimate Good of the universe of
sentient beings : since we direct him to take, as ultimate,
Happiness for the Universe, but Conformity to Reason for
himself. I admit the substantial truth of this statement,
though I should avoid the language as tending to obscure
the distinction before explained between " obeying the dictates "
and " promoting the dictation " of reason. But granting the
alleged difference, I do not see that it constitutes an argument
against the view here maintained, since the individual is
essentially and fundamentally different from the larger whole
—the universe of sentient beings—of which he is conscious
of being a part ; just because he has a known relation to
similar parts of the same whole, while the whole itself has no
such relation. I accordingly see no inconsistency in holding
that while it *would* be reasonable for the aggregate of sentient
beings, if it could act collectively, to aim at its own happiness
only as an ultimate end—and would be reasonable for any
individual to do the same, if he were the only sentient being
in the universe—it may yet be *actually* reasonable for an
individual to sacrifice his own Good or happiness for the
greater happiness of others.[1]

At the same time I admit that, in the earlier age of ethical
thought which Greek philosophy represents, men sometimes
judged an act to be ' good ' *for the agent*, even while recognising
that its consequences would be on the whole painful to him,
—as (*e.g.*) a heroic exchange of a life full of happiness for a
painful death at the call of duty. I attribute this partly to a

---

[1] I ought at the same time to say that I hold it no less reasonable for an
individual to take his own happiness as his ultimate end. This "Dualism of
the Practical Reason" will be further discussed in the concluding chapter of
the treatise.

confusion of thought between what it is reasonable for an individual to desire, when he considers his own existence alone, and what he must recognise as reasonably to be desired, when he takes the point of view of a larger whole : partly, again, to a faith deeply rooted in the moral consciousness of mankind, that there cannot be really and ultimately any conflict between the two kinds of reasonableness.[1] But when ' Reasonable Self-love ' has been clearly distinguished from Conscience, as it is by Butler and his followers, we find it is naturally understood to mean desire for one's own Happiness : so that in fact the interpretation of ' one's own good,' which was almost peculiar in ancient thought to the Cyrenaic and Epicurean heresies, is adopted by some of the most orthodox of modern moralists. Indeed it often does not seem to have occurred to these latter that this notion can have any other interpretation.[2] If, then, when any one hypothetically concentrates his attention on himself, Good is naturally and almost inevitably conceived to be Pleasure, we may reasonably conclude that the Good of any number of similar beings, whatever their mutual relations may be, cannot be essentially different in quality.

IV. But lastly, from the universal point of view no less than from that of the individual, it seems true that Happiness is likely to be better attained if the extent to which we set ourselves consciously to aim at it be carefully restricted. And this not only because action is likely to be more effective if our effort is temporarily concentrated on the realisation of more limited ends—though this is no doubt an important reason :—but also because the fullest development of happy life for each individual seems to require that he should have other external objects of interest besides the happiness of other conscious beings. And thus we may conclude that the pursuit of the ideal objects before mentioned, Virtue, Truth, Freedom, Beauty, etc., *for their own sakes*, is indirectly and

----

[1] We may illustrate this double explanation by a reference to some of Plato's Dialogues, such as the *Gorgias*, where the ethical argument has a singularly mixed effect on the mind. Partly, it seems to us more or less dexterous sophistry, playing on a confusion of thought latent in the common notion of good : partly a noble and stirring expression of a profound moral faith.

[2] Cf. Stewart, *Philosophy of the Active and Moral Powers*, Book ii. chap. i.

secondarily, though not primarily and absolutely, rational; on account not only of the happiness that will result from their attainment, but also of that which springs from their disinterested pursuit. While yet if we ask for a final criterion of the comparative value of the different objects of men's enthusiastic pursuit, and of the limits within which each may legitimately engross the attention of mankind, we shall none the less conceive it to depend upon the degree in which they respectively conduce to Happiness.

If, however, this view be rejected, it remains to consider whether we can frame any other coherent account of Ultimate Good. If we are not to systematise human activities by taking Universal Happiness as their common end, on what other principles are we to systematise them? It should be observed that these principles must not only enable us to compare among themselves the values of the different non-hedonistic ends which we have been considering, but must also provide a common standard for comparing these values with that of Happiness; unless we are prepared to adopt the paradoxical position of rejecting happiness as absolutely valueless. For we have a practical need of determining not only whether we should pursue Truth rather than Beauty, or Freedom or some ideal constitution of society rather than either, or perhaps desert all of these for the life of worship and religious contemplation; but also how far we should follow any of these lines of endeavour, when we foresee among its consequences the pains of human or other sentient beings, or even the loss of pleasures that might otherwise have been enjoyed by them.[1]

I have failed to find—and am unable to construct—any systematic answer to this question that appears to me deserving of serious consideration: and hence I am finally led to the conclusion (which at the close of the last chapter seemed to be premature) that the Intuitional method rigorously applied yields as its final result the doctrine of

---

[1] The controversy on vivisection, to which I referred just now, affords a good illustration of the need that I am pointing out. I do not observe that any one in this controversy has ventured on the paradox that the pain of sentient beings is not *per se* to be avoided.

pure Universalistic Hedonism,[1]—which it is convenient to denote by the single word, Utilitarianism.

[1] I have before noticed (Book ii. chap. iii. p. 134) the metaphysical objection taken by certain writers to the view that Happiness is Ultimate Good ; on the ground that Happiness (= sum of pleasures) can only be realised in successive parts, whereas a "Chief Good" must be "something of which some being can be conceived in possession"—something, that is, which he can have all at once. On considering this objection it seemed to me that, in so far as it is even plausible, its plausibility depends on the exact form of the notion 'a Chief Good' (or 'Summum Bonum'), which is perhaps inappropriate as applied to Happiness. I have therefore in this chapter used the notion of 'Ultimate Good': as I can see no shadow of reason for affirming that that which is Good or Desirable *per se*, and not as a means to some further end, must *necessarily* be capable of being possessed all at once. I can understand that a man may aspire after a Good of this latter kind : but so long as Time is a necessary form of human existence, it can hardly be surprising that human good should be subject to the condition of being realised in successive parts.

BOOK IV

UTILITARIANISM

BOOK IV

CHAPTER I

THE MEANING OF UTILITARIANISM

§ 1. THE term Utilitarianism is, at the present day, in common use, and is supposed to designate a doctrine or method with which we are all familiar. But on closer examination, it appears to be applied to several distinct theories, having no necessary connexion with one another, and not even referring to the same subject-matter. It will be well, therefore, to define, as carefully as possible, the doctrine that is to be denoted by the term in the present Book : at the same time distinguishing this from other doctrines to which usage would allow the name to be applied, and indicating, so far as seems necessary, its relation to these.

By Utilitarianism is here meant the ethical theory, that the conduct which, under any given circumstances, is objectively right, is that which will produce the greatest amount of happiness on the whole ; that is, taking into account all whose happiness is affected by the conduct. It would tend to clearness if we might call this principle, and the method based upon it, by some such name as " Universalistic Hedonism " : and I have therefore sometimes ventured to use this term, in spite of its cumbrousness.

The first doctrine from which it seems necessary to distinguish this, is the Egoistic Hedonism expounded and discussed in Book ii. of this treatise. The difference, however, between the propositions (1) that each ought to seek his own happiness, and (2) that each ought to seek the happiness of all, is so obvious and glaring, that instead of dwelling upon it we seem rather called upon to explain how the two ever came to be confounded, or in any way included under one notion. This question and the general relation between the two doctrines were briefly discussed in a former chapter.[1] Among other points it was there noticed that the confusion between these two ethical theories was partly assisted by the confusion with both of the psychological theory that in voluntary actions every agent does, universally or normally, seek his own individual happiness or pleasure. Now there seems to be no *necessary* connexion between this latter proposition and any ethical theory : but in so far as there is a natural tendency to pass from psychological to ethical Hedonism, the transition must be—at least primarily— to the Egoistic phase of the latter. For clearly, from the fact that every one actually does seek his own happiness we cannot conclude, as an immediate and obvious inference, that he ought to seek the happiness of other people.[2]

Nor, again, is Utilitarianism, as an ethical doctrine, necessarily connected with the psychological theory that the moral sentiments are derived, by "association of ideas" or otherwise, from experiences of the non-moral pleasures and pains resulting to the agent or to others from different kinds of conduct. An Intuitionist might accept this theory, so far as it is capable of scientific proof, and still hold that these moral sentiments, being found in our present consciousness as independent impulses, ought to possess the authority that they seem to claim over the more primary desires and aversions from which they have sprung : and an Egoist on the other hand might fully admit the altruistic element of the derivation, and still hold that these and all other impulses (including even Universal Benevolence) are properly under the rule of Rational Self-love : and that it is really only reasonable to gratify them in so far as we may expect to find our private happiness in such gratification. In short, what is often called the "utilitarian" theory of the origin of the moral sentiments cannot by itself

---

[1] Book i. chap. vi. It may be worth while to notice, that in Mill's well-known treatise on Utilitarianism this confusion, though expressly deprecated, is to some extent encouraged by the author's treatment of the subject.

[2] I have already criticised (Book iii. chap. xiii.) the mode in which Mill attempts to exhibit this inference.

provide a proof of the ethical doctrine to which I in this treatise restrict the term Utilitarianism. I shall, however, hereafter try to show that this psychological theory has an important though subordinate place in the establishment of Ethical Utilitarianism.[1]

Finally, the doctrine that Universal Happiness is the ultimate *standard* must not be understood to imply that Universal Benevolence is the only right or always best *motive* of action. For, as we have before observed, it is not necessary that the end which gives the criterion of rightness should always be the end at which we consciously aim : and if experience shows that the general happiness will be more satisfactorily attained if men frequently act from other motives than pure universal philanthropy, it is obvious that these other motives are reasonably to be preferred on Utilitarian principles.

§ 2. Let us now examine the principle itself somewhat closer. I have already attempted (Book ii. chap. i.) to render the notion of Greatest Happiness as clear and definite as possible ; and the results there obtained are of course as applicable to the discussion of Universalistic as to that of Egoistic Hedonism. We shall understand, then, that by Greatest Happiness is meant the greatest possible surplus of pleasure over pain, the pain being conceived as balanced against an equal amount of pleasure, so that the two contrasted amounts annihilate each other for purposes of ethical calculation. And of course, here as before, the assumption is involved that all pleasures included in our calculation are capable of being compared quantitatively with one another and with all pains ; that every such feeling has a certain intensive quantity, positive or negative (or, perhaps, zero), in respect of its desirableness, and that this quantity may be to some extent known : so that each may be at least roughly weighed in ideal scales against any other. This assumption is involved in the very notion of Maximum Happiness ; as the attempt to make ' as great as possible ' a sum of elements not quantitatively commensurable would be a mathematical absurdity. Therefore whatever weight is to be attached to the objections brought against this assumption (which was discussed in chap. iii. of Book ii.) must of course tell against the present method.

[1] Cf. *post*, chap. iv.

We have next to consider who the "all" are, whose happiness is to be taken into account. Are we to extend our concern to all the beings capable of pleasure and pain whose feelings are affected by our conduct? or are we to confine our view to human happiness? The former view is the one adopted by Bentham and Mill, and (I believe) by the Utilitarian school generally: and is obviously most in accordance with the universality that is characteristic of their principle. It is the Good *Universal*, interpreted and defined as 'happiness' or 'pleasure,' at which a Utilitarian considers it his duty to aim: and it seems arbitrary and unreasonable to exclude from the end, as so conceived, any pleasure of any sentient being.

It may be said that by giving this extension to the notion, we considerably increase the scientific difficulties of the hedonistic comparison, which have already been pointed out (Book ii. chap. iii.): for if it be difficult to compare the pleasures and pains of other men accurately with our own, a comparison of either with the pleasures and pains of brutes is obviously still more obscure. Still, the difficulty is at least not greater for Utilitarians than it is for any other moralists who recoil from the paradox of disregarding altogether the pleasures and pains of brutes. But even if we limit our attention to human beings, the extent of the subjects of happiness is not yet quite determinate. In the first place, it may be asked, How far we are to consider the interests of posterity when they seem to conflict with those of existing human beings? It seems, however, clear that the time at which a man exists cannot affect the value of his happiness from a universal point of view; and that the interests of posterity must concern a Utilitarian as much as those of his contemporaries, except in so far as the effect of his actions on posterity—and even the existence of human beings to be affected—must necessarily be more uncertain. But a further question arises when we consider that we can to some extent influence the number of future human (or sentient) beings. We have to ask how, on Utilitarian principles, this influence is to be exercised. Here I shall assume that, for human beings generally, life on the average yields a positive balance of pleasure over pain. This has been denied by thoughtful persons: but the denial seems to me clearly opposed to the common experience of mankind, as expressed in their commonly accepted principles of action.   The great majority of men, in the great majority of conditions under which human life is lived, certainly act as if death were one of the worst of evils, for themselves and for those whom they love: and the administration of criminal justice proceeds on a similar assumption.[1]

Assuming, then, that the average happiness of human beings is a positive quantity, it seems clear that, supposing the average happiness enjoyed remains undiminished, Utilitarianism directs us to make the number enjoying it as great as possible.   But if we foresee as possible that an increase in numbers will be accompanied by a decrease in average happiness or *vice versa,* a point arises which has not only never been formally noticed, but which seems to have been substantially overlooked by many Utilitarians.   For if we take Utilitarianism to prescribe, as the ultimate end of action, happiness on the whole, and not any individual's happiness, unless considered as an element of the whole, it would follow that, if the additional population enjoy on the whole positive happiness, we ought to weigh the amount of happiness gained by the extra number against the amount lost by the remainder. So that, strictly conceived, the point up to which, on Utilitarian principles, population ought to be encouraged to increase, is not that at which average happiness is the greatest possible,— as appears to be often assumed by political economists of the school of Malthus—but that at which the product formed by

---

[1] Those who held the opposite opinion appear generally to assume that the appetites and desires which are the mainspring of ordinary human action are in themselves painful : a view entirely contrary to my own experience, and, I believe, to the common experience of mankind.   See chap. iv. § 2 of Book i.   So far as their argument is not a development of this psychological error, any plausibility it has seems to me to be obtained by dwelling onesidedly on the annoyances and disappointments undoubtedly incident to normal human life, and on the exceptional sufferings of small minorities of the human race, or perhaps of most men during small portions of their lives.

The reader who wishes to see the paradoxical results of pessimistic utilitarianism seriously worked out by a thoughtful and suggestive writer, may refer to Professor Macmillan's book on the *Promotion of General Happiness* (Swan Sonnenschein and Co. 1890).   The author considers that "the philosophical world is pretty equally divided between optimists and pessimists," and his own judgment on the question at issue between the two schools appear to be held in suspense.

multiplying the number of persons living into the amount of average happiness reaches its maximum.

It may be well here to make a remark which has a wide application in Utilitarian discussion. The conclusion just given wears a certain air of absurdity to the view of Common Sense ; because its show of exactness is grotesquely incongruous with our consciousness of the inevitable inexactness of all such calculations in actual practice. But, that our practical Utilitarian reasonings must necessarily be rough, is no reason for not making them as accurate as the case admits ; and we shall be more likely to succeed in this if we keep before our mind as distinctly as possible the strict type of the calculation that we should have to make, if all the relevant considerations could be estimated with mathematical precision.

There is one more point that remains to be noticed. It is evident that there may be many different ways of distributing the same quantum of happiness among the same number of persons ; in order, therefore, that the Utilitarian criterion of right conduct may be as complete as possible, we ought to know which of these ways is to be preferred. This question is often ignored in expositions of Utilitarianism. It has perhaps seemed somewhat idle, as suggesting a purely abstract and theoretical perplexity, that could have no practical exemplification ; and no doubt, if all the consequences of actions were capable of being estimated and summed up with mathematical precision, we should probably never find the excess of pleasure over pain exactly equal in the case of two competing alternatives of conduct. But the very indefiniteness of all hedonistic calculations, which was sufficiently shown in Book ii., renders it by no means unlikely that there may be no *cognisable* difference between the quantities of happiness involved in two sets of consequences respectively ; the more rough our estimates necessarily are, the less likely we shall be to come to any clear decision between two apparently balanced alternatives. In all such cases, therefore, it becomes practically important to ask whether any mode of distributing a given quantum of happiness is better than any other. Now the Utilitarian formula seems to supply no answer to this question : at least we have to supplement the principle of seeking the greatest happiness on the whole by some principle of Just or

Right distribution of this happiness. The principle which most Utilitarians have either tacitly or expressly adopted is that of pure equality—as given in Bentham's formula, " everybody to count for one, and nobody for more than one." And this principle seems the only one which does not need a special justification; for, as we saw, it must be reasonable to treat any one man in the same way as any other, if there be no reason apparent for treating him differently.[1]

[1] It should be observed that the question here is as to the distribution of *Happiness*, not the *means of happiness*. If more happiness on the whole is produced by giving the same means of happiness to B rather than to A, it is an obvious and incontrovertible deduction from the Utilitarian principle that it ought to be given to B, whatever inequality in the distribution of the *means* of happiness this may involve.

CHAPTER II

THE PROOF OF UTILITARIANISM

In Book ii., where we discussed the method of Egoistic
Hedonism, we did not take occasion to examine any proof of
its first principle: and in the case of Universalistic Hedonism
also, what primarily concerns us is not how its principle is to
be proved to those who do not accept it, but what consequences
are logically involved in its acceptance. At the same time it
is important to observe that the principle of aiming at universal
happiness is more generally felt to require some proof, or at
least (as Mill puts it) some "considerations determining the
mind to accept it," than the principle of aiming at one's own
happiness. From the point of view, indeed, of abstract
philosophy, I do not see why the Egoistic principle should
pass unchallenged any more than the Universalistic. I do
not see why the axiom of Prudence should not be questioned,
when it conflicts with present inclination, on a ground similar
to that on which Egoists refuse to admit the axiom of Rational
Benevolence. If the Utilitarian has to answer the question,
'Why should I sacrifice my own happiness for the greater
happiness of another?' it must surely be admissible to ask the
Egoist, 'Why should I sacrifice a present pleasure for a greater
one in the future? Why should I concern myself about my
own future feelings any more than about the feelings of other
persons?' It undoubtedly seems to Common Sense paradoxical
to ask for a reason why one should seek one's own happiness on
the whole; but I do not see how the demand can be repudiated
as absurd by those who adopt the views of the extreme
empirical school of psychologists, although those views are

commonly supposed to have a close affinity with Egoistic Hedonism. Grant that the Ego is merely a system of coherent phenomena, that the permanent identical ' I ' is not a fact but a fiction, as Hume and his followers maintain; why, then, should one part of the series of feelings into which the Ego is resolved be concerned with another part of the same series, any more than with any other series ?

However, I will not press this question now ; since I admit that Common Sense does not think it worth while to supply the individual with reasons for seeking his own interest.[1] Reasons for doing his duty—according to the commonly accepted standard of duty—are not held to be equally super-fluous : indeed we find that utilitarian reasons are continually given for one or other of the commonly received rules of morality.   Still the fact that certain rules are commonly received as binding, though it does not establish their self-evidence, renders it generally unnecessary to prove their authority to the Common Sense that receives them : while for the same reason a Utilitarian who claims to supersede them by a higher principle is naturally challenged, by Intuitionists no less than by Egoists, to demonstrate the legitimacy of his claim.   To this challenge some Utilitarians would reply by saying that it is impossible to " prove " a first principle ; and this is of course true, if by proof we mean a process which ex-hibits the principle in question as an inference from premises upon which it remains dependent for its certainty ; for these premises, and not the inference drawn from them, would then be the real first principles.   Nay, if Utilitarianism is to be *proved* to a man who already holds some other moral principles, —whether he be an Intuitional moralist, who regards as final the principles of Truth, Justice, Obedience to authority, Purity, etc., or an Egoist who regards his own interest as the ultimately reasonable end of his conduct,—it would seem that the process must be one which establishes a conclusion actually *superior* in validity to the premises from which it starts.   For the Utili-tarian prescriptions of duty are *prima facie* in conflict, at certain points and under certain circumstances, both with rules which the Intuitionist regards as self-evident, and with the

---

[1] The relation of Egoistic to Universalistic Hedonism is further examined in the concluding chapter.

dictates of Rational Egoism; so that Utilitarianism, if accepted at all, must be accepted as overruling Intuitionism and Egoism. At the same time, if the other principles are not throughout taken as valid, the so-called proof does not seem to be addressed to the Intuitionist or Egoist at all.   How shall we deal with this dilemma?   How is such a process—clearly different from ordinary proof—possible or conceivable?   Yet there certainly seems to be a general demand for it.   Perhaps we may say that what is needed is a line of argument which on the one hand allows the validity, to a certain extent, of the maxims already accepted, and on the other hand shows them to be not absolutely valid, but needing to be controlled and completed by some more comprehensive principle.

Such a line of argument, addressed to Egoism, was given in chap. xiii. of the foregoing book.   It should be observed that the applicability of this argument depends on the manner in which the Egoistic first principle is formulated.   If the Egoist strictly confines himself to stating his conviction that he ought to take his own happiness or pleasure as his ultimate end, there seems no opening for any line of reasoning to lead him to Universalistic Hedonism as a first principle;[1] it cannot be proved that the difference between his own happiness and another's happiness is not *for him* all-important.   In this case all that the Utilitarian can do is to effect as far as possible a reconciliation between the two principles, by expounding to the Egoist the *sanctions* of rules deduced from the Universalistic principle,—*i.e.* by pointing out the pleasures and pains that may be expected to accrue to the Egoist himself from the observation and violation respectively of such rules.   It is obvious that such an exposition has no tendency to make him accept the greatest happiness of the greatest number as his ultimate end; but only as a means to the end of his own happiness.   It is therefore totally different from a *proof* (as above explained) of Universalistic Hedonism.   When, however, the Egoist puts forward, implicitly or explicitly, the proposition that his happiness or pleasure is Good, not only *for him* but from the point of view of the Universe,—as (*e.g.*)

---

[1] It is to be observed that he may be led to it in other ways than that of argument: *i.e.* by appeals to his sympathies, or to his moral or quasi-moral sentiments.

by saying that 'nature designed him to seek his own happiness,'—it then becomes relevant to point out to him that *his* happiness cannot be a more important part of Good, taken universally, than the equal happiness of any other person. And thus, starting with his own principle, he may be brought to accept Universal happiness or pleasure as that which is absolutely and without qualification Good or Desirable: as an end, therefore, to which the action of a reasonable agent as such ought to be directed.

This, it will be remembered, is the reasoning [1] that I used in chap. xiii. of the preceding book in exhibiting the principle of Rational Benevolence as one of the few Intuitions which stand the test of rigorous criticism. It should be observed, however, that as addressed to the Intuitionist, this reasoning only shows the Utilitarian first principle to be *one* moral axiom: it does not prove that it is *sole* or *supreme*. The premises with which the Intuitionist starts commonly include other formulæ held as independent and self-evident. Utilitarianism has therefore to exhibit itself in the twofold relation above described, at once negative and positive, to these formulæ. The Utilitarian must, in the first place, endeavour to show to the Intuitionist that the principles of Truth, Justice,[2] etc. have only a dependent and subordinate validity: arguing either that the principle is really only affirmed by Common Sense as a general rule admitting of exceptions and qualifications, as in the case of Truth, and that we require some further principle for systematising these exceptions and qualifications; or that the fundamental notion is vague and needs further determination, as in the case of Justice;[2] and further, that the different rules are liable to conflict with each other, and that we require some higher principle to decide the issue thus raised; and again, that the rules are differently formulated by different persons, and that these differences admit of no Intuitional solution, while they show the vague-

---

[1] I ought to remind the reader that the argument in chap. xiii. only leads to the first principle of Utilitarianism, if it be admitted that Happiness is the only thing ultimately and intrinsically Good or Desirable. I afterwards in chap. xiv. endeavoured to bring Common Sense to this admission.

[2] That is, so far as we mean by Justice anything more than the simple negation of arbitrary inequality.

ness and ambiguity of the common moral notions to which the Intuitionist appeals.

This part of the argument I have perhaps sufficiently developed in the preceding book. It remains to supplement this line of reasoning by developing the positive relation that exists between Utilitarianism and the Morality of Common Sense: by showing how Utilitarianism sustains the general validity of the current moral judgments, and thus supplements the defects which reflection finds in the intuitive recognition of their stringency; and at the same time affords a principle of synthesis, and a method for binding the unconnected and occasionally conflicting principles of common moral reasoning into a complete and harmonious system. If systematic reflection upon the morality of Common Sense thus exhibits the Utilitarian principle as that to which Common Sense naturally appeals for that further development of its system which this same reflection shows to be necessary, the proof of Utilitarianism seems as complete as it can be made. And since, further—apart from the question of proof—it is important in considering the method of Utilitarianism to determine exactly its relation to the commonly received rules of morality, it will be proper to examine this relation at some length in the following chapter.

CHAPTER III

RELATION OF UTILITARIANISM TO THE MORALITY OF COMMON SENSE

§ 1. It has been before observed (Book i. chap. vi.) that the two sides of the double relation in which Utilitarianism stands to the Morality of Common Sense have been respectively prominent at two different periods in the history of English ethical thought. Since Bentham we have been chiefly familiar with the negative or aggressive aspect of the Utilitarian doctrine. But when Cumberland, replying to Hobbes, put forward the general tendency of the received moral rules to promote the "common Good[1] of all Rationals" his aim was simply Conservative: it never occurs to him to consider whether these rules as commonly formulated are in any way imperfect, and whether there are any discrepancies between such common moral opinions and the conclusions of Rational Benevolence. So in Shaftesbury's system the "Moral" or "Reflex Sense" is supposed to be always pleased with that "balance" of the affections which tends to the good or happiness of the whole, and displeased with the opposite. In Hume's treatise this coincidence is drawn out more in detail, and with a more definite assertion that the perception of utility[2] (or the re-

---

[1] It ought to be observed that Cumberland does not adopt a hedonistic interpretation of Good. Still, I have followed Hallam in regarding him as the founder of English Utilitarianism : since it seems to have been by a gradual and half-unconscious process that 'Good' came to have the definitely hedonistic meaning which it has implicitly in Shaftesbury's system, and explicitly in that of Hume.

[2] I should point out that Hume uses "utility" in a narrower sense than that which Bentham gave it, and one more in accordance with the usage of ordinary language. He distinguishes the "useful" from the "immediately agreeable" :

verse) is in each case the source of the moral likings (or
aversions) which are excited in us by different qualities of
human character and conduct. And we may observe that
the most penetrating among Hume's contemporary critics,
Adam Smith, admits unreservedly the objective coincidence of
Rightness or Approvedness and Utility : though he maintains,
in opposition to Hume, that "it is not the view of this utility
or hurtfulness, which is either the first or the principal source
of our approbation or disapprobation." After stating Hume's
theory that "no qualities of the mind are approved of as
virtuous, but such as are useful or agreeable either to the
person himself or to others, and no qualities are disapproved
of as vicious but such as have a contrary tendency"; he
remarks that "Nature seems indeed to have so happily
adjusted our sentiments of approbation and disapprobation
to the conveniency both of the individual and of the society,
that after the strictest examination it will be found, I believe,
that this is universally the case."

And no one can read Hume's *Inquiry into the First
Principles of Morals* without being convinced of this at least,
that if a list were drawn up of the qualities of character and
conduct that are directly or indirectly productive of pleasure to
ourselves or to others, it would include all that are commonly
known as virtues. Whatever be the origin of our notion of
moral goodness or excellence, there is no doubt that "Utility"
is a general characteristic of the dispositions to which we apply
it : and that, so far, the Morality of Common Sense may be
truly represented as at least unconsciously Utilitarian. But it
may still be objected, that this coincidence is merely general and
qualitative, and that it breaks down when we attempt to draw
it out in detail, with the quantitative precision which Bentham
introduced into the discussion. And no doubt there is a great
difference between the assertion that virtue is always productive
of happiness, and the assertion that the right action is under
all circumstances that which will produce the greatest possible

so that while recognising "utility" as the main ground of our moral approbation
of the more important virtues, he holds that there are other elements of personal merit which we approve because they are "immediately agreeable," either
to the person possessed of them or to others. It appears, however, more convenient to use the word in the wider sense in which it has been current since
Bentham.

happiness on the whole.   But it must be borne in mind that Utilitarianism is not concerned to prove the absolute coincidence in results of the Intuitional and Utilitarian methods. Indeed, if it could succeed in proving as much as this, its success would be almost fatal to its practical claims; as the adoption of the Utilitarian principle would then become a matter of complete indifference.   Utilitarians are rather called upon to show a natural transition from the Morality of Common Sense to Utilitarianism, somewhat like the transition in special branches of practice from trained instinct and empirical rules to the technical method that embodies and applies the conclusions of science: so that Utilitarianism may be presented as the scientifically complete and systematically reflective form of that regulation of conduct, which through the whole course of human history has always tended substantially in the same direction. For this purpose it is not necessary to prove that existing moral rules are *more* conducive to the general happiness than any others: but only to point out in each case some manifest felicific tendency which they possess.

Hume's dissertation, however, incidentally exhibits much more than a simple and general harmony between the moral sentiments with which we commonly regard actions and their foreseen pleasurable and painful consequences.   And, in fact, the Utilitarian argument cannot be fairly judged unless we take fully into account the cumulative force which it derives from the complex character of the coincidence between Utilitarianism and Common Sense.

It may be shown, I think, that the Utilitarian estimate of consequences not only supports broadly the current moral rules, but also sustains their generally received limitations and qualifications: that, again, it explains anomalies in the Morality of Common Sense, which from any other point of view must seem unsatisfactory to the reflective intellect; and moreover, where the current formula is not sufficiently precise for the guidance of conduct, while at the same time difficulties and perplexities arise in the attempt to give it additional precision, the Utilitarian method solves these difficulties and perplexities in general accordance with the vague instincts of Common Sense, and is naturally appealed to for such solution in ordinary moral discussions.   It may be shown further, that it not only

supports the generally received view of the relative importance
of different duties, but is also naturally called in as arbiter,
where rules commonly regarded as co-ordinate come into conflict : that, again, when the same rule is interpreted somewhat
differently by different persons, each naturally supports his view
by urging its Utility, however strongly he may maintain the rule
to be self-evident and known *a priori* : that where we meet
with marked diversity of moral opinion on any point, in the
same age and country, we commonly find manifest and impressive utilitarian reasons on both sides : and that finally the
remarkable discrepancies found in comparing the moral codes
of different ages and countries are for the most part strikingly
correlated to differences in the effects of actions on happiness,
or in men's foresight of, or concern for, such effects.   Most of
these points are noticed by Hume, though in a somewhat casual
and fragmentary way : and many of them have been incidentally illustrated in the course of the examination of Common
Sense Morality, with which we were occupied in the preceding
Book.   But considering the importance of the present question,
it may be well to exhibit in systematic detail the cumulative
argument which has just been summed up, even at the risk
of repeating to some extent the results previously given.

§ 2. We may begin by replying to an objection which is
frequently urged against Utilitarianism.   How, it is asked, if
the true ground of the moral goodness or badness of actions lies
in their utility or the reverse, can we explain the broad distinction drawn by Common Sense between the moral and other
parts of our nature ?   Why is the excellence of Virtue so
strongly felt to be different in kind, not merely from the
excellence of a machine, or a fertile field, but also from the
physical beauties and aptitudes, the intellectual gifts and
talents of human beings.   I should answer that—as was argued
in an earlier chapter (Book iii. chap. ii.)—qualities that are, in
the strictest sense of the term, Virtuous, are always such as we
conceive capable of being immediately realised by voluntary
effort, at least to some extent ; so that the prominent obstacle
to virtuous action is absence of adequate motive.   Hence we
expect that the judgments of moral goodness or badness,
passed either by the agent himself or by others, will—by the
fresh motive which they supply on the side of virtue—have

an immediate practical effect in causing actions to be at least
externally virtuous: and the habitual consciousness of this
will account for almost any degree of difference between moral
sentiments and the pleasure and pain that we derive from the
contemplation of either extra-human or non-voluntary utilities
and inutilities.   To this, however, it is replied, that among
the tendencies to strictly voluntary actions there are many not
commonly regarded as virtuous, which are yet not only useful
but on the whole *more* useful than many virtues.   " The selfish
instinct that leads men to accumulate confers ultimately more
advantage on the world than the generous instinct that leads
men to give. . . . It is scarcely doubtful that a modest,
diffident, and retiring nature, distrustful of its own abilities,
and shrinking with humility from conflict, produces on the
whole less benefit to the world than the self-assertion of an
audacious and arrogant nature, which is impelled to every
struggle, and develops every capacity.   Gratitude has no
doubt done much to soften and sweeten the intercourse of life,
but the corresponding feeling of revenge was for centuries the
one bulwark against social anarchy, and is even now one of the
chief restraints to crime.   On the great theatre of public life,
especially in periods of great convulsions where passions are
fiercely roused, it is neither the man of delicate scrupulosity
and sincere impartiality, nor yet the single-minded religious
enthusiast, incapable of dissimulation or procrastination, who
confers most benefit on the world.   It is much rather the
astute statesman, earnest about his ends, but unscrupulous
about his means, equally free from the trammels of conscience and from the blindness of zeal, who governs because
he partly yields to the passions and the prejudices of his
time.   But . . . it has scarcely yet been contended that the
delicate conscience which in these cases impairs utility constitutes vice."[1]

These objections are forcibly urged ; but they appear to
me not very difficult to answer, it being always borne in mind
that the present argument does not aim at proving an exact
coincidence between Utilitarian inferences and the intuitions
of Common Sense, but rather seeks to represent the latter as
inchoately and imperfectly Utilitarian.

[1] Lecky, *Hist. of Eur. Mor.* chap. i. pp. 37, 40 *seqq.* (13th impression).

In the first place, we must carefully distinguish between the recognition of goodness in dispositions, and the recognition of rightness in conduct. An act that a Utilitarian must condemn as likely to do more harm than good may yet show a disposition or tendency that will on the whole produce more good than harm. This is eminently the case with scrupulously conscientious acts. However true it may be that unenlightened conscientiousness has impelled men to fanatical cruelty, mistaken asceticism, and other infelicific conduct, I suppose no Intuitionist would maintain that carefulness in conforming to accepted moral rules has not, on the whole, a tendency to promote happiness. It may be observed, however, that when we perceive the effects of a disposition generally felicific to be in any particular case adverse to happiness, we often apply to it, as so operating, some term of condemnation : thus we speak, in the case above noticed, of ' over-scrupulousness ' or ' fanaticism.' But in so far as we perceive that the same disposition would generally produce good results, it is not inconsistent still to regard it, abstracting from the particular case, as a good element of character. Secondly, although, in the view of a Utilitarian, only the useful is praiseworthy, he is not bound to maintain that it is necessarily worthy of praise in proportion as it is useful. From a Utilitarian point of view, as has been before said, we must mean by calling a quality ' deserving of praise,' that it is expedient to praise it, with a view to its future production : accordingly, in distributing our praise of human qualities, on utilitarian principles, we have to consider primarily not the usefulness of the quality, but the usefulness of the praise : and it is obviously not expedient to encourage by praise qualities which are likely to be found in excess rather than in defect. Hence (*e.g.*) however necessary self-love or resentment may be to society, it is quite in harmony with Utilitarianism that they should not be recognised as virtues by Common Sense, in so far as it is reasonably thought that they will always be found operating with at least sufficient intensity. We find, however, that when self-love comes into conflict with impulses seen to be on the whole pernicious, it is praised as Prudence : and that when a man seems clearly deficient in resentment, he is censured for tameness : though as malevolent impulses are much more

obviously productive of pain than pleasure, it is not unnatural
that their occasional utility should be somewhat overlooked.
The case of Humility and Diffidence may be treated in a somewhat similar way.   As we saw,[1] it is only inadvertently that
Common Sense praises the tendency to underrate one's own
powers: on reflection it is generally admitted that it cannot
be good to be in error on this or any other point.   But the
desires of Superiority and Esteem are so strong in most men,
that arrogance and self-assertion are both much commoner than
the opposite defects, and at the same time are faults peculiarly
disagreeable to others: so that humility gives us an agreeable
surprise, and hence Common Sense is easily led to overlook the
more latent and remote bad consequences of undue self-distrust.

We may observe further that the perplexity which we
seemed to find in the Morality of Common Sense, as to the
relation of moral excellence to moral effort, is satisfactorily
explained and removed when we adopt a Utilitarian point of
view : for on the one hand it is easy to see how certain acts—
such as kind services—are likely to be more felicific when performed without effort, and from other motives than regard for
duty : while on the other hand a person who in doing similar
acts achieves a triumph of duty over strong seductive inclinations, exhibits thereby a character which we recognise as felicific
in a more general way, as tending to a general performance of
duty in all departments.   So again, there is a simple and obvious
utilitarian solution of another difficulty which I noticed, as to
the choice between Subjective and Objective rightness in the
exceptional case in which alone the two can be presented as
alternatives,—*i.e.* when we are considering whether we shall
influence another to act contrary to his conviction as to what
is right.   A utilitarian would decide the question by weighing
the felicific consequences of the particular right act against the
infelicific results to be apprehended hereafter from the moral
deterioration of the person whose conscientious convictions were
overborne by other motives : unless the former effects were very
important he would reasonably regard the danger to character
as the greater : but if the other's mistaken sense of duty
threatened to cause a grave disaster, he would not hesitate to
overbear it by any motives which it was in his power to apply.

[1] Book iii. chap. x.

And in practice I think that the Common Sense of mankind would come to similar conclusions by more vague and semi-conscious reasoning of the same kind.

In order, however, to form a precise estimate of the extent to which Utilitarianism agrees or disagrees with Common Sense, it seems best to examine the more definite judgments of right and wrong in conduct, under the particular heads represented by our common notions of virtues and duties. I may begin by pointing out once more that so far as any adequately precise definitions of these notions are found to involve, implicitly or explicitly, the notion of 'good' or of 'right' supposed already determinate, they can afford no ground for opposing a Utilitarian interpretation of these fundamental conceptions. For example, we saw this to be the case with the chief of the intellectual excellences discussed in Book iii. chap. iii. Wisdom, as commonly conceived, is not exactly the faculty of choosing the right means to the end of universal happiness ; rather, as we saw, its notion involves an uncritical synthesis of the different ends and principles that are distinguished and separately examined in the present treatise. But if its import is not distinctly Utilitarian, it is certainly not anything else as distinct from Utilitarian : if we can only define it as the faculty or habit of choosing the right or best means to the right or best end, for that very reason our definition leaves it quite open to us to give the notions 'good' and 'right' a Utilitarian import.

§ 3. Let us then examine first the group of virtues and duties discussed in Book iii. chap. iv., under the head of Benevolence. As regards the general conception of the duty, there is, I think, no divergence that we need consider between the Intuitional and Utilitarian systems. For though Benevolence would perhaps be more commonly defined as a disposition to promote the Good of one's fellow-creatures, rather than their Happiness (as definitely understood by Utilitarians); still, as the chief element in the common notion of good (besides happiness) is moral good or Virtue,[1] if we can show that the other virtues are—speaking broadly—all qualities conducive to the happiness of the agent himself or of others, it is evident that Benevolence, whether it prompts us to promote the virtue

---

[1] Book iii. chap. iv. § 1.

of others or their happiness, will aim directly or indirectly at the Utilitarian end.[1]

Nor, further, does the comprehensive range which Utilitarians give to Benevolence, in stating as their ultimate end the greatest happiness of all sentient beings, seem to be really opposed to Common Sense ; for in so far as certain Intuitional moralists restrict the scope of the direct duty of Benevolence to human beings, and regard our duties to brute animals as merely indirect and derived " from the duty of Self-culture," they rather than their Utilitarian opponents appear paradoxical. And if, in laying down that each agent is to consider all other happiness as equally important with his own, Utilitarianism seems to go beyond the standard of duty commonly prescribed under the head of Benevolence, it yet can scarcely be said to conflict with Common Sense on this point.   For the practical application of this theoretical impartiality of Utilitarianism is limited by several important considerations.   In the first place, generally speaking, each man is better able to provide for his own happiness than for that of other persons, from his more intimate knowledge of his own desires and needs, and his greater opportunities of gratifying them.   And besides, it is under the stimulus of self-interest that the active energies of most men are most easily and thoroughly drawn out : and if this were removed, general happiness would be diminished by a serious loss of those means of happiness which are obtained by labour ; and also, to some extent, by the diminution of the labour itself.   For these reasons it would not under actual circumstances promote the universal happiness if each man were to concern himself with the happiness of others as much as with his own.   While if I consider the duty abstractly and ideally, even Common Sense morality seems to bid me " love my neighbour as myself."

It might indeed be plausibly objected, on the other hand, that under the notions of Generosity, Self-sacrifice, etc., Common Sense praises (though it does not prescribe as obligatory) a suppression of egoism beyond what Utilitarianism approves : for we perhaps admire as virtuous a man who gives up his own happiness for another's sake, even when the happiness that he

---

[1] It will be seen that I do not here assume in their full breadth the conclusions of chap. xiv. of the preceding Book.

confers is clearly less than that which he resigns, so that there is a diminution of happiness on the whole. But (1) it seems very doubtful whether we do altogether approve such conduct when the disproportion between the sacrifice and the benefit is obvious and striking : and (2) a spectator is often unable to judge whether happiness is lost on the whole, as (*a*) he cannot tell how far he who makes the sacrifice is compensated by sympathetic and moral pleasure, and (*b*) the remoter felicific consequences flowing from the moral effects of such a sacrifice on the agent and on others have to be taken into account : while (3) even if there be a loss in the particular case, still our admiration of self-sacrifice will admit of a certain Utilitarian justification, because such conduct shows a disposition far above the average in its general tendency to promote happiness, and it is perhaps this disposition that we admire rather than the particular act.

It has been said,[1] however, that the special claims and duties belonging to special relations, by which each man is connected with a few out of the whole number of human beings, are expressly ignored by the rigid impartiality of the Utilitarian formula : and hence that, though Utilitarianism and Common Sense may agree in the proposition that all right action is conducive to the happiness of some one or other, and so far beneficent, still they are irreconcileably divergent on the radical question of the *distribution* of beneficence.

Here, however, it seems that even fair-minded opponents have scarcely understood the Utilitarian position. They have attacked Bentham's well-known formula, "every man to count for one, nobody for more than one," on the ground that the general happiness will be best attained by inequality in the distribution of each one's services. But so far as it is clear that it will be best attained in this way, Utilitarianism will necessarily prescribe this way of aiming at it ; and Bentham's dictum must be understood merely as making the conception of the ultimate end precise—laying down that one person's happiness is to be counted for as much as another's (supposed equal in degree) as an element of the general happiness—not as directly prescribing the rules of conduct by which this end will be best attained. And the reasons why it is, generally speak-

---

[1] Cf. J. Grote, *An Examination of the Utilitarian Philosophy*, chap. v.

ing, conducive to the general happiness that each individual should distribute his beneficence in the channels marked out by commonly recognised ties and claims, are tolerably obvious.

For first, in the chief relations discussed in chap. iv. of Book iii.—the domestic, and those constituted by consanguinity, friendship, previous kindnesses, and special needs,—the services which Common Sense prescribes as duties are commonly prompted by natural affection, while at the same time they tend to develop and sustain such affection. Now the subsistence of benevolent affections among human beings is itself an important means to the Utilitarian end, because (as Shaftesbury and his followers forcibly urged) the most intense and highly valued of our pleasures are derived from such affections; for both the emotion itself is highly pleasurable, and it imparts this quality to the activities which it prompts and sustains, and the happiness thus produced is continually enhanced by the sympathetic echo of the pleasures conferred on others. And again, where genuine affection subsists, the practical objections to spontaneous beneficence, which were before noticed, are much diminished in force. For such affection tends to be reciprocated, and the kindnesses which are its outcome and expression commonly win a requital of affection: and in so far as this is the case, they have less tendency to weaken the springs of activity in the person benefited; and may even strengthen them by exciting other sources of energy than the egoistic—personal affection, and gratitude, and the desire to deserve love, and the desire to imitate beneficence. And hence it has been often observed that the injurious effects of almsgiving are at least much diminished if the alms are bestowed with unaffected sympathy and kindliness, and in such a way as to elicit a genuine response of gratitude. And further, the beneficence that springs from affection is less likely to be frustrated from defect of knowledge: for not only are we powerfully stimulated to study the real conditions of the happiness of those whom we love, but also such study is rendered more effective from the sympathy which naturally accompanies affection.

On these grounds the Utilitarian will evidently approve of the cultivation of affection and the performance of affectionate services. It may be said, however, that what we ought to approve is not so much affection for special individuals, but rather a feeling more universal in its scope—charity, philanthropy, or (as it has been called) the 'Enthusiasm of Humanity.' And certainly all special affections tend occasionally to come into conflict with the principle of promoting the general happiness : and Utilitarianism must therefore prescribe such a culture of the feelings as will, so far as possible, counteract this tendency. But it seems that most persons are only capable of strong affections towards a few human beings in certain close relations, especially the domestic : and that if these were suppressed, what they would feel towards their fellow-creatures generally would be, as Aristotle says, " but a watery kindness " and a very feeble counterpoise to self-love : so that such specialised affections as the present organisation of society normally produces afford the best means of developing in most persons a more extended benevolence, to the degree to which they are capable of feeling it. Besides, each person is for the most part, from limitation either of power or knowledge, not in a position to do much good to more than a very small number of persons ; it therefore seems, on this ground alone, desirable that his chief benevolent impulses should be correspondingly limited.

And this leads us to consider, secondly, the reasons why, affection apart, it is conducive to the general happiness that special claims to services should be commonly recognised as attaching to special relations ; so as to modify that impartiality in the distribution of beneficence which Utilitarianism *prima facie* inculcates. For clearness' sake it seems best to take this argument separately, though it cannot easily be divided from the former one, because the services in question are often such as cannot so well be rendered without affection. In such cases, as we saw,[1] Common Sense regards the affection itself as a duty, in so far as it is capable of being cultivated : but still prescribes the performance of the services even if the affection be unhappily absent. Indeed we may properly consider the services to which we are commonly prompted by the domestic affections, and also those to which we are moved by gratitude and pity, as an integral part of the system of mutual aid by which the normal life and happiness of society is maintained, under existing circumstances ; being an indispensable supplement to the still more essential services which are definitely

---

[1] Book iii. chap. iv. § 1.

prescribed by Law, or rendered on commercial terms as a part of an express bargain. As political economists have explained, the means of happiness are immensely increased by that complex system of co-operation which has been gradually organised among civilised men : and while it is thought that under such a system it will be generally best on the whole to let each individual exchange such services as he is disposed to render for such return as he can obtain for them by free contract, still there are many large exceptions to this general principle. Of these the most important is constituted by the case of children. It is necessary for the well-being of mankind that in each generation children should be produced in adequate numbers, neither too many nor too few ; and that, as they cannot be left to provide for themselves, they should be adequately nourished and protected during the period of infancy ; and further, that they should be carefully trained in good habits, intellectual, moral, and physical : and it is commonly believed that the best or even the only known means of attaining these ends in even a tolerable degree is afforded by the existing institution of the Family, resting as it does on a basis of legal and moral rules combined. For Law fixes a minimum of mutual services and draws the broad outlines of behaviour for the different members of the family, imposing[1] on the parents lifelong union and complete mutual fidelity and the duty of providing for their children the necessaries of life up to a certain age ; in return for which it gives them the control of their children for the same period, and sometimes lays on the latter the burden of supporting their parents when aged and destitute : so that Morality, in inculcating a completer harmony of interests and an ampler interchange of kindnesses, is merely filling in the outlines drawn by Law. We found, however, in attempting to formulate the different domestic duties as recognised by Common Sense, that there seemed to be in most cases a large vague margin with respect to which general agreement could not be affirmed, and which, in fact, forms an arena for continual disputes. But we have now to observe that it is just this margin which reveals most clearly the latent Utilitarianism

---

[1] Strictly speaking, of course, the Law of modern states does not enforce this, but only refuses to recognise connubial contracts of any other kind : but the social effect is substantially the same.

of common moral opinion: for when the question is once raised as to the precise mutual duties (*e.g.*) of husbands and wives, or of parents and children, each disputant commonly supports his view by a forecast of the effects on human happiness to be expected from the general establishment of any proposed rule; this seems to be the standard to which the matter is, by common consent, referred.

Similarly the claim to services that arises out of special need (which natural sympathy moves us to recognise) may obviously be rested on an utilitarian basis: indeed the proper fulfilment of this duty seems so important to the well-being of society, that it has in modern civilised communities generally been brought to some extent within the sphere of Governmental action. We noticed that the main utilitarian reason why it is not right for every rich man to distribute his superfluous wealth among the poor, is that the happiness of all is on the whole most promoted by maintaining in adults generally (except married women), the expectation that each will be thrown on his own resources for the supply of his own wants. But if I am made aware that, owing to a sudden calamity that could not have been foreseen, another's resources are manifestly inadequate to protect him from pain or serious discomfort, the case is altered; my theoretical obligation to consider his happiness as much as my own becomes at once practical; and I am bound to make as much effort to relieve him as will not entail a greater loss of happiness to myself or others. If, however, the calamity is one which might have been foreseen and averted by proper care, my duty becomes more doubtful: for then by relieving him I seem to be in danger of encouraging improvidence in others. In such a case a Utilitarian has to weigh this indirect evil against the direct good of removing pain and distress: and it is now more and more generally recognised that the question of providing for the destitute has to be treated as a utilitarian problem of which these are the elements,—whether we are considering the minimum that should be secured to them by law, or the proper supplementary action of private charity.

Poverty, however, is not the only case in which it is conducive to the general happiness that one man should render unbought services to another. In any condition or calling a man may find himself unable to ward off some evil, or to realise some legitimate or worthy end, without assistance of such kind as he cannot purchase on the ordinary commercial terms;— assistance which, on the one hand, will have no bad effect on the receiver, from the exceptional nature of the emergency, while at the same time it may not be burdensome to the giver. Here, again, some jurists have thought that where the service to be rendered is great, and the burden of rendering it very slight, it might properly be made matter of legal obligation: so that (*e.g.*) if I could save a man from drowning by merely holding out a hand, I should be legally punishable if I omitted the act. But, however this may be, the moral rule condemning the refusal of aid in such emergencies is obviously conducive to the general happiness.

Further, besides these—so to say—*accidentally* unbought services, there are some for which there is normally no market-price; such as counsel and assistance in the intimate perplexities of life, which one is only willing to receive from genuine friends. It much promotes the general happiness that such services should be generally rendered. On this ground, as well as through the emotional pleasures which directly spring from it, we perceive Friendship to be an important means to the Utilitarian end. At the same time we feel that the charm of Friendship is lost if the flow of emotion is not spontaneous and unforced. The combination of these two views seems to be exactly represented by the sympathy that is not quite admiration with which Common Sense regards all close and strong affections; and the regret that is not quite disapproval with which it contemplates their decay.

In all cases where it is conducive to the general happiness that unbought services should be rendered, Gratitude (if we mean by this a settled disposition to repay the benefit in whatever way one can on a fitting opportunity) is enjoined by Utilitarianism no less than by Common Sense; for experience would lead us to expect that no kind of onerous services will be adequately rendered unless there is a general disposition to requite them. In fact we may say that a general understanding that all services which it is expedient that A should render to B will be in some way repaid by B, is a natural supplement of the more definite contracts by which the main part of the great social interchange of services is arranged.   Indeed the one kind of requital merges in the other, and no sharp line can be drawn between the two : we cannot always say distinctly whether the requital of a benefit is a pure act of gratitude or the fulfilment of a tacit understanding.[1] There is, however, a certain difficulty in this view of gratitude as analogous to the fulfilment of a bargain. For it may be said that of the services peculiar to friendship disinterestedness is an indispensable characteristic ; and that in all cases benefits conferred without expectation of reward have a peculiar excellence, and are indeed peculiarly adapted to arouse gratitude ; but if they are conferred in expectation of such gratitude, they lose this excellence ; and yet, again, it would be very difficult to treat as a friend one from whom gratitude was not expected.   This seems, at first sight, an inextricable entanglement : but here, as in other cases, an apparent ethical contradiction is found to reduce itself to a psychological complexity.   For most of our actions are done from several different motives, either coexisting or succeeding one another in rapid alternation : thus a man may have a perfectly disinterested desire to benefit another, and one which might possibly prevail over all conflicting motives if all hope of requital were cut off, and yet it may be well that this generous impulse should be sustained by a vague trust that requital will not be withheld. And in fact the apparent puzzle really affords another illustration of the latent Utilitarianism of Common Sense.   For, on the one hand, Utilitarianism prescribes that we should render services whenever it is conducive to the general happiness to do so, which may often be the case without taking into account the gain to oneself which would result from their requital: and on the other hand, since we may infer from the actual selfishness of average men that such services would not be adequately rendered without expectation of requital, it is also conducive to the general happiness that men should recognise a moral obligation to repay them.

We have discussed only the most conspicuous of the duties of affection : but it is probably obvious that similar reasonings would apply in the case of the others.

---

[1] Sometimes such unbargained requital is even legally obligatory : as when children are bound to repay the care spent on them by supporting their parents in decrepitude.

In all such cases there are three distinct lines of argument which tend to show that the commonly received view of special claims and duties arising out of special relations, though *prima facie* opposed to the impartial universality of the Utilitarian principle, is really maintained by a well-considered application of that principle. First, morality is here in a manner protecting the normal channels and courses of natural benevolent affections ; and the development of such affections is of the highest importance to human happiness, both as a direct source of pleasure, and as an indispensable preparation for a more enlarged "altruism." And again, the mere fact that such affections are normal, causes an expectation of the services that are their natural expression ; and the disappointment of such expectations is inevitably painful. While finally, apart from these considerations, we can show in each case strong utilitarian reasons why, generally speaking, services should be rendered to the persons commonly recognised as having such claims rather than to others.

We have to observe, in conclusion, that the difficulties which we found in the way of determining by the Intuitional method the limits and the relative importance of these duties are reduced in the Utilitarian system, to difficulties of hedonistic comparison.[1] For each of the preceding arguments has shown us different kinds of pleasures gained and pains averted by the fulfilment of the claims in question. There are, first, those which the service claimed would directly promote or avert : secondly, there is the pain and secondary harm of disappointed expectation, if the service be not rendered : thirdly, we have to reckon the various pleasures connected with the exercise of natural benevolent affections, especially when reciprocated, including the indirect effects on the agent's character of maintaining such affections. All these different pleasures and pains combine differently, and with almost infinite variation as circumstances vary, into utilitarian reasons for each of the claims in question ; none of these reasons being absolute and conclusive, but each having its own weight, while liable to be outweighed by others.

§ 4. I pass to consider another group of duties, often

---

[1] Further discussion of the method of dealing with these difficulties, in their utilitarian form, will be found in the two following chapters.

contrasted with those of Benevolence, under the comprehensive notion of Justice.

"That Justice is useful to society," says Hume, "it would be a superfluous undertaking to prove ": what he endeavours to show at some length is "that public utility is the *sole* origin of Justice ": and the same question of origin has occupied the chief attention of J. S. Mill.[1] Here, however, we are not so much concerned with the growth of the sentiment of Justice from experiences of utility, as with the Utilitarian basis of the mature notion ; while at the same time if the analysis previously given be correct, the Justice that is commonly demanded and inculcated is something more complex than these writers have recognised.   What Hume (*e.g.*) means by Justice is rather what I should call Order, understood in its widest sense : the observance of the actual system of rules, whether strictly legal or customary, which bind together the different members of any society into an organic whole, checking malevolent or otherwise injurious impulses, distributing the different objects of men's clashing desires, and exacting such positive services, customary or contractual, as are commonly recognised as matters of debt.   And though there have rarely been wanting plausible empirical arguments for the revolutionary paradox quoted by Plato, that "laws are imposed in the interest of rulers," it remains true that the general conduciveness to social happiness of the habit of Order or Law-observance, is, as Hume says, too obvious to need proof ; indeed it is of such paramount importance to a community, that even where particular laws are clearly injurious it is usually expedient to observe them, apart from any penalty which their breach might entail on the individual.   We saw, however, that Common Sense sometimes bids us refuse obedience to bad laws, because "we ought to obey God rather than men " (though there seems to be no clear intuition as to the kind or degree of badness that justifies resistance); and further allows us, in special emergencies, to violate rules generally good, for "necessity has no law," and "salus populi suprema lex."

These and similar common opinions seem at least to suggest that the limits of the duty of Law-observance are to be determined by utilitarian considerations.   While, again, the

---

[1] *Utilitarianism,* chap. v.

Utilitarian view gets rid of the difficulties in which the attempt to define intuitively the truly legitimate source of legislative authority involved us;[1] at the same time that it justifies to some extent each of the different views current as to the intrinsic legitimacy of governments.   For, on the one hand, it finds the moral basis of any established political order primarily in its effects rather than its causes; so that, generally speaking, obedience will seem due to any *de facto* government that is not governing very badly.   On the other hand, in so far as laws originating in a particular way are likely to be (1) better, or (2) more readily observed, it is a Utilitarian duty to aim at introducing this mode of origination: and thus in a certain stage of social development it may be right that (*e.g.*) a 'representative system' should be popularly demanded, or possibly (in extreme cases) even introduced by force: while, again, there is expediency in maintaining an ancient mode of legislation, because men readily obey such: and loyalty to a dispossessed government may be on the whole expedient, even at the cost of some temporary suffering and disorder, in order that ambitious men may not find usurpation too easy.   Here, as elsewhere, Utilitarianism at once supports the different reasons commonly put forward as absolute, and also brings them theoretically to a common measure, so that in any particular case we have a principle of decision between conflicting political arguments.

As was before said, this Law-observance, in so far at least as it affects the interests of other individuals, is what we frequently mean by Justice.   It seems, however,[2] that the notion of Justice, exhaustively analysed, includes several distinct elements combined in a somewhat complex manner: we have to inquire, therefore, what latent utilities are represented by each of these elements.

Now, first, a constant part of the notion, which appears in it even when the Just is not distinguished from the Legal, is impartiality or the negation of arbitrary inequality.   This impartiality, as we saw[3] (whether exhibited in the establishment or in the administration of laws), is merely a special application of the wider maxim that it cannot be right to

---

[1] Cf. Book iii. chap. vi. §§ 2, 3.
[2] Cf. Book iii. chap. v.   [3] Book iii. chap. xiii. § 3.

treat two persons differently if their cases are similar in all material circumstances. And Utilitarianism, as we saw, admits this maxim no less than other systems of Ethics. At the same time, this negative criterion is clearly inadequate for the complete determination of what is just in laws, or in conduct generally; when we have admitted this, it still remains to ask, "What are the inequalities in laws, and in the distribution of pleasures and pains outside the sphere of law, which are not arbitrary and unreasonable? and to what general principles can they be reduced?"

Here in the first place we may explain, on utilitarian principles, why apparently arbitrary inequality in a certain part of the conduct of individuals [1] is not regarded as injustice or even —in some cases—as in any way censurable. For freedom of action is an important source of happiness to the agents, and a socially useful stimulus to their energies: hence it is obviously expedient that a man's free choice in the distribution of wealth or kind services should not be restrained by the fear of legal penalties, or even of social disapprobation, beyond what the interests of others clearly require; and therefore, when distinctly recognised claims are satisfied, it is *pro tanto* expedient that the mere preferences of an individual should be treated by others as legitimate grounds for inequality in the distribution of his property or services. Nay, as we have before seen, it is within certain limits expedient that each individual should practically regard his own unreasoned impulses as reasonable grounds of action: as in the rendering of services prompted by such affections as are normally and properly spontaneous and unforced.

Passing to consider the general principles upon which 'just claims' as commonly recognised appear to be based, we notice that the grounds of a number of such claims may be brought under the general head of 'normal expectations'; but that the stringency of such obligations varies much in degree, according as the expectations are based upon definite engagements, or on some vague mutual understanding, or are merely such as an average man would form from past experience of the conduct of other men. In these latter cases Common Sense appeared to be somewhat perplexed as to the validity of the claims. But for the Utilitarian the difficulty has ceased to exist. He will

---

[1] Cf. *ante*, p. 268 note.

hold any disappointment of expectations to be *pro tanto* an evil, but a greater evil in proportion to the previous security of the expectant individual, from the greater shock thus given to his reliance on the conduct of his fellow-men generally : and many times greater in proportion as the expectation is generally recognised as normal and reasonable, as in this case the shock extends to all who are in any way cognisant of his disappointment.   The importance to mankind of being able to rely on each other's actions is so great, that in ordinary cases of absolutely definite engagements there is scarcely any advantage that can counterbalance the harm done by violating them. Still, we found [1] that several exceptions and qualifications to the rule of Good Faith were more or less distinctly recognised by Common Sense : and most of these have a utilitarian basis, which it does not need much penetration to discern.   To begin, we may notice that the superficial view of the obligation of a promise which makes it depend on the assertion of the promiser, and not, as Utilitarians hold, on the expectations produced in the promisee, cannot fairly be attributed to Common Sense : which certainly condemns a breach of promise much more strongly when others have acted in reliance on it, than when its observance did not directly concern others, so that its breach involves for them only the indirect evil of a bad precedent,— as when a man breaks a pledge of total abstinence.   We see, again, how the utilitarian reasons for keeping a promise are diminished by a material change of circumstances,[2] for in that case the expectations disappointed by breaking it are at least not those which the promise originally created.   It is obvious, too, that it is a disadvantage to the community that men should be able to rely on the performance of promises procured by fraud or unlawful force, so far as encouragement is thereby given to the use of fraud or force for this end.[3]   We saw, again,[4] that when the performance would be injurious to the promisee, Common Sense is disposed to admit that its obligation is superseded ; and is at least doubtful whether the promise

---

[1] Book iii. chap. vi.   [2] Cf. *ante*, Book iii. chap. vi. § 8.

[3] In the case of force, however, there is the counterbalancing consideration that the unlawful aggressor may be led to inflict worse injury on his victim, if he is unable to rely on the latter's promise.

[4] Cf. Book iii. chap. vi. § 8.

should be kept, even when it is only the promiser who would be injured, if the harm be extreme ;—both which qualifications are in harmony with Utilitarianism. And similarly for the other qualifications and exceptions : they all turn out to be as clearly utilitarian, as the general utility of keeping one's word is plain and manifest.

But further, the expediency of satisfying normal expectations, even when they are not based upon a definite contract, is undeniable ; it will clearly conduce to the tranquillity of social existence, and to the settled and well-adjusted activity on which social happiness greatly depends, that such expectations should be as little as possible baulked. And here Utilitarianism relieves us of the difficulties which beset the common view of just conduct as something absolutely precise and definite. For in this vaguer region we cannot draw a sharp line between valid and invalid claims ; ' injustice ' shades gradually off into mere ' hardship.' Hence the Utilitarian view that the disappointment of natural expectations is an evil, but an evil which must sometimes be incurred for the sake of a greater good, is that to which Common Sense is practically forced, though it is difficult to reconcile it with the theoretical absoluteness of Justice in the Intuitional view of Morality.

The gain of recognising the relativity of this obligation will be still more felt, when we consider what I distinguished as Ideal Justice, and examine the general conceptions of this which we find expressed or latent in current criticisms of the existing order of Society.

We have seen that there are two competing views of an ideally just social order—or perhaps we may say two extreme types between which the looser notions of ordinary men seem to fluctuate—which I called respectively Individualistic and Socialistic. According to the former view an ideal system of Law ought to aim at Freedom, or perfect mutual non-interference of all the members of the community, as an absolute end. Now the general utilitarian reasons for leaving each rational adult free to seek happiness in his own way are obvious and striking : for, generally speaking, each is best qualified to provide for his own interests, since even when he does not know best what they are and how to attain them, he is at any rate most keenly concerned for them : and again, the consciousness of freedom and concomitant responsibility increases the average effective activity of men : and besides, the discomfort of constraint is directly an evil and *pro tanto* to be avoided.   Still, we saw [1] that the attempt to construct a consistent code of laws, taking Maximum Freedom (instead of Happiness) as an absolute end, must lead to startling paradoxes and insoluble puzzles : and in fact the practical interpretation of the notion ' Freedom,' and the limits within which its realisation has been actually sought, have always—even in the freest societies—been more or less consciously determined by considerations of expediency.   So that we may fairly say that in so far as Common Sense has adopted the Individualistic ideal in politics, it has always been as subordinate to and limited by the Utilitarian first principle.[2]

It seems, however, that what we commonly demand or long for, under the name of Ideal Justice, is not so much the realisation of Freedom, as the distribution of good and evil according to Desert : indeed it is as a means to this latter end that Freedom is often advocated ; for it is said that if we protect men completely from mutual interference, each will reap the good and bad consequences of his own conduct, and so be happy or unhappy in proportion to his deserts.   In particular, it has been widely held that if a free exchange of wealth and services is allowed, each individual will obtain from society, in money or other advantages, what his services are really worth.   We saw, however, that the price which an individual obtains under a system of perfect free trade, for wealth or services exchanged by him, may for several reasons be not proportioned to the social utility of what he exchanges : and reflective Common Sense seems to admit this disproportion as to some extent legitimate, under the influence of utilitarian considerations correcting the unreflective utterances of moral sentiments.

To take a particular case : if a moral man were asked how far it is right to take advantage in bargaining of another's ignorance, probably his first impulse would be to condemn such a procedure altogether.   But reflection, I think, would show

---

[1] Book iii. chap. v. § 4.

[2] In another work (*Principles of Political Economy*, Book iii. chap. ii.) I have tried to show that complete *laisser faire*, in the organisation of industry, tends in various ways to fall short of the most economic production of wealth.

him that such a censure would be too sweeping : that it would
be contrary to Common Sense to "blame A for having, in
negotiating with a stranger B, taken advantage of B's ignorance of facts known to himself, provided that A's superior
knowledge had been obtained by a legitimate use of diligence
and foresight, which B might have used with equal success . . .
What prevents us from censuring in this and similar cases is, I
conceive, a more or less conscious apprehension of the indefinite
loss to the wealth of the community that is likely to result
from any effective social restrictions on the free pursuit and
exercise " of economic knowledge.   And for somewhat similar
reasons of general expediency, if the question be raised whether
it is fair for a class of persons to gain by the unfavourable
economic situation of any class with which they deal, Common
Sense at least hesitates to censure such gains—at any rate
when such unfavourable situation is due "to the gradual action
of general causes, for the existence of which the persons who
gain are not specially responsible." [1]

The general principle of ' requiting good desert,' so far as
Common Sense really accepts it as practically applicable to the
relations of men in society, is broadly in harmony with Utilitarianism ; since we obviously encourage the production of
general happiness by rewarding men for felicific conduct ; only
the Utilitarian scale of rewards will not be determined entirely
by the magnitude of the services performed, but partly also by
the difficulty of inducing men to perform them.   But this
latter element seems to be always taken into account (though
perhaps unconsciously) by Common Sense : for, as we have
been led to notice,[2] we do not commonly recognise merit in
right actions, if they are such as men are naturally inclined
to perform rather too much than too little.   Again, in cases
where the Intuitional principle that ill-desert lies in wrong
intention conflicts with the Utilitarian view of punishment as
purely preventive, we find that in the actual administration
of criminal justice. Common Sense is forced, however reluctantly, into practical agreement with Utilitarianism.   Thus
after a civil war it demands the execution of the most purely

[1] The quotations are from my *Principles of Political Economy*, Book iii. chap.
ix. ; where these questions are discussed at somewhat greater length.

[2] Cf. *ante*, § 2, and Book iii. chap. ii. § 1.

patriotic rebels ; and after a railway accident it clamours for the severe punishment of unintentional neglects, which, except for their consequences, would have been regarded as very venial.

If, however, in any distribution of pleasures and privileges, or of pains and burdens, considerations of desert do not properly come in (*i.e.* if the good or evil to be distributed have no relation to any conduct on the part of the persons who are to receive either)—or if it is practically impossible to take such considerations into account—then Common Sense seems to fall back on simple equality as the principle of just apportionment.[1] And we have seen that the Utilitarian, in the case supposed, will reasonably accept Equality as the only mode of distribution that is not arbitrary ; and it may be observed that this mode of apportioning the means of happiness is likely to produce more happiness on the whole, not only because men have a disinterested aversion to unreason, but still more because they have an aversion to any kind of inferiority to others (which is much intensified when the inferiority seems unreasonable). This latter feeling is so strong that it often prevails in spite of obvious claims of desert ; and it may even be sometimes expedient that it should so prevail.

For, finally, it must be observed that Utilitarianism furnishes us with a common standard to which the different elements included in the notion of Justice may be reduced. Such a standard is imperatively required : as these different elements are continually liable to conflict with each other. The issue, for example, in practical politics between Conservatives and Reformers often represents such a conflict : the question is, whether we ought to do a certain violence to expectations arising naturally out of the existing social order, with the view of bringing about a distribution of the means of happiness more in accordance with ideal justice. Here, if my analysis of the common notion of Justice be sound, the attempt to extract from it a clear decision of such an issue must necessarily fail : as the conflict is, so to say, permanently latent in the very core of Common Sense. But the Utilitarian will

---

[1] I have before observed that it is quite in harmony with Utilitarian principles to recognise a sphere of private conduct within which each individual may distribute his wealth and kind services as unequally as he chooses, without incurring censure as unjust.

merely use this notion of Justice as a guide to different kinds of utilities; and in so far as these are incompatible, he will balance one set of advantages against the other, and decide according to the preponderance.

§ 5. The duty of Truth-speaking is sometimes taken as a striking instance of a moral rule not resting on a Utilitarian basis. But a careful study of the qualifications with which the common opinion of mankind actually inculcates this duty seems to lead us to an opposite result: for not only is the general utility of truth-speaking so manifest as to need no proof, but wherever this utility seems to be absent, or outweighed by particular bad consequences, we find that Common Sense at least hesitates to enforce the rule. For example, if a man be pursuing criminal ends, it is *prima facie* injurious to the community that he should be aided in his pursuit by being able to rely on the assertions of others. Here, then, deception is *prima facie* legitimate as a protection against crime: though when we consider the bad effects on habit, and through example, of even a single act of unveracity, the case is seen to be, on Utilitarian principles, doubtful: and this is just the view of Common Sense. Again, though it is generally a man's interest to know the truth, there are exceptional cases in which it is injurious to him—as when an invalid hears bad news—and here, too, Common Sense is disposed to suspend the rule. Again, we found it difficult to define exactly wherein Veracity consists; for we may either require truth in the spoken words, or in the inferences which the speaker foresees will be drawn from them, or in both. Perfect Candour, no doubt, would require it in both: but in the various circumstances where this seems inexpedient, we often find Common Sense at least half-willing to dispense with one or other part of the double obligation. Thus we found a respectable school of thinkers maintaining that a religious truth may properly be communicated by means of a historical fiction: and, on the other hand, the unsuitability of perfect frankness to our existing social relations is recognised in the common rules of politeness, which impose on us not unfrequently the necessity of suppressing truths and suggesting falsehoods. I would not say that in any of these cases Common Sense pronounces quite decidedly in favour of unveracity: but then neither is

Utilitarianism decided, as the utility of maintaining a general habit of truth-speaking is so great, that it is not easy to prove it to be clearly outweighed by even strong special reasons for violating the rule.

Yet it may be worth while to point out how the different views as to the legitimacy of Malevolent impulses, out of which we found it hard to frame a consistent doctrine for Common Sense, exactly correspond to different forecasts of the consequences of gratifying such impulses. *Prima facie*, the desire to injure any one in particular is inconsistent with a deliberate purpose of benefiting as much as possible people in general; accordingly, we find that what I may call Superficial Common Sense passes a sweeping condemnation on such desires.   But a study of the actual facts of society shows that resentment plays an important part in that repression of injuries which is necessary to social wellbeing; accordingly, the reflective moralist shrinks from excluding it altogether.   It is evident, however, that personal ill-will is a very dangerous means to the general happiness : for its direct end is the exact opposite of happiness ; and though the realisation of this end may in certain cases be the least of two evils, still the impulse if encouraged is likely to prompt to the infliction of pain beyond the limits of just punishment, and to have an injurious reaction on the character of the angry person.   Accordingly, the moralist is disposed to prescribe that indignation be directed always against acts, and not against persons ; and if indignation so restricted would be efficient in repressing injuries, this would seem to be the state of mind most conducive to the general happiness.   But it is doubtful whether average human nature is capable of maintaining this distinction, and whether, if it could be maintained, the more refined aversion would by itself be sufficiently efficacious : accordingly, Common Sense hesitates to condemn personal ill-will against wrong-doers—even if it includes a desire of malevolent satisfaction.

Finally, it is easy to show that Temperance, Self-control, and what are called the Self-regarding virtues generally, are ' useful ' to the individual who possesses them : and if it is not quite clear, in the view of Common Sense, to what end that regulation and government of appetites and passions, which moralists have so much inculcated and admired, is to be directed; at least there seems no obstacle in the way of our defining this end as Happiness.   And even in the ascetic extreme of Self-control, which has sometimes led to the repudiation of sensual pleasures as radically bad, we may trace an unconscious Utilitarianism.   For the ascetic condemnation has always been chiefly directed against those pleasures, in respect of which men are especially liable to commit excesses dangerous to health; and free indulgence in which, even when it keeps clear of injury to health, is thought to interfere with the development of other faculties and susceptibilities which are important sources of happiness.

§ 6. An apparent exception to this statement may seem to be constituted in the case of the sexual appetite, by the regulation prescribed under the notion of Purity or Chastity. And there is no doubt that under this head we find condemned, with special vehemence and severity, acts of which the immediate effect is pleasure not obviously outweighed by subsequent pain.   But a closer examination of this exception transforms it into an important contribution to the present argument: as it shows a specially complex and delicate correspondence between moral sentiments and social utilities.

In the first place, the peculiar intensity and delicacy of the moral sentiments that govern the relations of the sexes are thoroughly justified by the vast importance to society of the end to which they are obviously a means,—the maintenance, namely, of the permanent unions which are held to be necessary for the proper rearing and training of children.   Hence the first and fundamental rule in this department is that which directly secures conjugal fidelity: and the utilitarian grounds for protecting marriage indirectly, by condemning all extra-nuptial intercourse of the sexes, are obvious: for to remove the moral censure that rests on such intercourse would seriously diminish men's motives for incurring the restraints and burdens which marriage entails; and the youth of both sexes would form habits of feeling and conduct tending to unfit them for marriage; and, if such intercourse were fertile, it would be attended with that imperfect care of the succeeding generation, which it seems the object of permanent unions to prevent; while if it were sterile, the future of the human race would, as far as we can see, be still more profoundly imperilled.

But, further, it is only on Utilitarian principles that we can account for the anomalous difference which the morality of Common Sense has always made between the two sexes as regards the simple offence of unchastity. For the offence is commonly more deliberate in the man, who has the additional guilt of soliciting and persuading the woman; in the latter, again, it is far more often prompted by some motive that we rank higher than mere lust: so that, according to the ordinary canons of intuitional morality, it ought to be more severely condemned in the man. The actual inversion of this result can only be justified by taking into account the greater interest that society has in maintaining a high standard of female chastity. For the degradation of this standard must strike at the root of family life, by impairing men's security in the exercise of their parental affections: but there is no corresponding consequence of male unchastity, which may therefore prevail to a considerable extent without imperilling the very existence of the family, though it impairs its wellbeing.

At the same time, the condemnation of unchastity in men by the common moral sense of Christian countries at the present day, is sufficiently clear and explicit: though we recognise the existence of a laxer code—the morality, as it is called, of 'the world'—which treats it as indifferent, or very venial. But the very difference between the two codes gives a kind of support to the present argument; as it corresponds to easily explained differences of insight into the consequences of maintaining certain moral sanctions. For partly, it is thought by 'men of the world' that men cannot practically be restrained from sexual indulgence, at least at the period of life when the passions are strongest: and hence that it is expedient to tolerate such kind and degree of illicit sexual intercourse as is not directly dangerous to the wellbeing of families. Partly, again, it is maintained by some, in bolder antagonism to Common Sense, that the existence of a certain limited amount of such intercourse (with a special class of women, carefully separated, as at present, from the rest of society) is scarcely a real evil, and may even be a positive gain in respect of general happiness; for continence is perhaps somewhat dangerous to health, and in any case involves a loss of pleasure considerable in intensity; while at the same time the maintenance of as numerous a population as is desirable in an old society does not require that more than a certain proportion of the women in each generation should become mothers of families ; and if some of the surplus make it their profession to enter into casual and temporary sexual relations with men, there is no necessity that their lives should compare disadvantageously in respect of happiness with those of other women in the less favoured classes of society.

This view has perhaps a superficial plausibility : but it ignores the essential fact that it is only by the present severe enforcement against unchaste women of the penalties of social contempt and exclusion, resting on moral disapprobation, that the class of courtesans is kept sufficiently separate from the rest of female society to prevent the contagion of unchastity from spreading; and that the illicit intercourse of the sexes is restrained within such limits as not to interfere materially with the due development of the race. This consideration is sufficient to decide a Utilitarian to support generally the established rule against this kind of conduct, and therefore to condemn violations of the rule as on the whole infelicific, even though they may perhaps appear to have this quality only in consequence of the moral censure attached to them.[1] Further, the ' man of the world ' ignores the vast importance to the human race of maintaining that higher type of sexual relations which is not, generally speaking, possible, except where a high value is set upon chastity in both sexes. From this point of view the Virtue of Purity may be regarded as providing a necessary shelter under which that intense and elevated affection between the sexes, which is most conducive both to the happiness of the individual and to the wellbeing of the family, may grow and flourish.

And in this way we are able to explain what must have perplexed many reflective minds in contemplating the common-sense regulation of conduct under the head of Purity : viz. that on the one hand the sentiment that supports these rules is very intense, so that the subjective difference between right and wrong in this department is marked with peculiar strength :

---

[1] It is obvious that so long as the social sanction is enforced, the lives of the women against whom society thus issues its ban must tend to be unhappy from disorder and shame, and the source of unhappiness to others ; and also that the breach by men of a recognised and necessary moral rule must tend to have injurious effects on their moral habits generally.

while on the other hand it is found impossible to give a clear definition of the conduct condemned under this notion. For the impulse to be restrained is so powerful and so sensitive to stimulants of all kinds, that, in order that the sentiment of purity may adequately perform its protective function, it is required to be very keen and vivid ; and the aversion to impurity must extend far beyond the acts that primarily need to be prohibited, and include in its scope everything (in dress, language, social customs, etc.) which may tend to excite lascivious ideas. At the same time it is not necessary that the line between right and wrong in such matters should be drawn with theoretical precision : it is sufficient for practical purposes if the main central portion of the region of duty be strongly illuminated, while the margin is left somewhat obscure. And, in fact, the detailed regulations which it is important to society to maintain depend so much upon habit and association of ideas, that they must vary to a great extent from age to age and from country to country.

§ 7. The preceding survey has supplied us with several illustrations of the manner in which Utilitarianism is normally introduced as a method for deciding between different conflicting claims, in cases where common sense leaves their relative importance obscure,—as (*e.g.*) between the different duties of the affections, and the different principles which analysis shows to be involved in our common conception of Justice—: and we have also noticed how, when a dispute is raised as to the precise scope and definition of any current moral rule, the effects of different acceptations of the rule on general happiness or social wellbeing are commonly regarded as the ultimate grounds on which the dispute is to be decided. In fact these two arguments practically run into one ; for it is generally a conflict between maxims that impresses men with the need of giving each a precise definition. It may be urged that the consequences to which reference is commonly made in such cases are rather effects on ' social wellbeing ' than on ' general happiness ' as understood by Utilitarians ; and that the two notions ought not to be identified. I grant this : but in the last chapter of the preceding Book I have tried to show that Common Sense is unconsciously utilitarian in its practical determination of those very elements in the notion of Ultimate

Good or Wellbeing which at first sight least admit of a hedonistic interpretation. We may now observe that this hypothesis of ' Unconscious Utilitarianism' explains the different relative importance attached to particular virtues by different classes of human beings, and the different emphasis with which the same virtue is inculcated on these different classes by mankind generally. For such differences ordinarily correspond to variations—real or apparent—in the Utilitarian importance of the virtues under different circumstances. Thus we have noticed the greater stress laid on chastity in women than in men : courage, on the other hand, is more valued in the latter, as they are more called upon to cope energetically with sudden and severe dangers. And for similar reasons a soldier is expected to show a higher degree of courage than (e.g.) a priest. Again, though we esteem candour and scrupulous sincerity in most persons, we scarcely look for them in a diplomatist who has to conceal secrets, nor do we expect that a tradesman in describing his goods should frankly point out their defects to his customers.

Finally, when we compare the different moral codes of different ages and countries, we see that the discrepancies among them correspond, at least to a great extent, to differences either in the actual effects of actions on happiness, or in the extent to which such effects are generally foreseen—or regarded as important—by the men among whom the codes are maintained. Several instances of this have already been noticed : and the general fact, which has been much dwelt upon by Utilitarian writers, is also admitted and even emphasised by their opponents. Thus Dugald Stewart [1] lays stress on the extent to which the moral judgments of mankind have been modified by "the diversity in their physical circumstances," the "unequal degrees of civilisation which they have attained," and " their unequal measures of knowledge or of capacity." He points out, for instance, that theft is regarded as a very venial offence in the South Sea Islanders, because little or no labour is there required to support life ; that the lending of money for interest is commonly reprehended in societies where commerce is imperfectly developed, because the ' usurer ' in such communities is commonly in the odious position of wringing a gain out of

---

[1] *Active and Moral Powers*, Book ii. chap. iii.

the hard necessities of his fellows; and that where the legal arrangements for punishing crime are imperfect, private murder is either justified or regarded very leniently. Many other examples might be added to these if it were needful. But I conceive that few persons who have studied the subject will deny that there is a certain degree of correlation between the variations in the moral code from age to age, and the variations in the real or perceived effects on general happiness of actions prescribed or forbidden by the code. And in proportion as the apprehension of consequences becomes more comprehensive and exact, we may trace not only change in the moral code handed down from age to age, but progress in the direction of a closer approximation to a perfectly enlightened Utilitarianism. Only we must distinctly notice another important factor in the progress, which Stewart has not mentioned: the extension, namely, of the capacity for sympathy in an average member of the community. The imperfection of earlier moral codes is at least as much due to defectiveness of sympathy as of intelligence; often, no doubt, the ruder man did not perceive the effects of his conduct on others; but often, again, he perceived them more or less, but felt little or no concern about them. Thus it happens that changes in the conscience of a community often correspond to changes in the extent and degree of the sensitiveness of an average member of it to the feelings of others. Of this the moral development historically worked out under the influence of Christianity affords familiar illustrations.[1]

I am not maintaining that this correlation between the development of current morality and the changes in the consequences of conduct as sympathetically forecast, is perfect and exact. On the contrary,—as I shall have occasion to point out in the next chapter—the history of morality shows us many evidences of what, from the Utilitarian point of view, appear to be partial aberrations of the moral sense. But even in these instances

---

[1] Among definite changes in the current morality of the Græco-Roman civilised world, which are to be attributed mainly if not entirely to the extension and intensification of sympathy due to Christianity, the following may be especially noted : (1) the severe condemnation and final suppression of the practice of exposing infants ; (2) effective abhorrence of the barbarism of gladiatorial combats ; (3) immediate moral mitigation of slavery, and a strong encouragement of emancipation ; (4) great extension of the eleemosynary provision made for the sick and poor.

we can often discover a germ of unconscious Utilitarianism; the aberration is often only an exaggeration of an obviously useful sentiment, or the extension of it by mistaken analogy to cases to which it does not properly apply, or perhaps the survival of a sentiment which once was useful but has now ceased to be so.

Further, it must be observed that I have carefully abstained from asserting that the perception of the rightness of any kind of conduct has always—or even ordinarily—been derived by conscious inference from a perception of consequent advantages. This hypothesis is naturally suggested by such a survey as the preceding; but the evidence of history hardly seems to me to support it: since, as we retrace the development of ethical thought, the Utilitarian basis of current morality, which I have endeavoured to exhibit in the present chapter, seems to be rather less than more distinctly apprehended by the common moral consciousness. Thus (*e.g.*) Aristotle sees that the sphere of the Virtue of Courage (ἀνδρεία), as recognised by the Common Sense of Greece, is restricted to dangers in war: and we can now explain this limitation by a reference to the utilitarian importance of this kind of courage, at a period of history when the individual's happiness was bound up more completely than it now is with the welfare of his state, while the very existence of the latter was more frequently imperilled by hostile invasions: but this explanation lies quite beyond the range of Aristotle's own reflection. The origin of our moral notions and sentiments lies hid in those obscure regions of hypothetical history where conjecture has free scope: but we do not find that, as our retrospect approaches the borders of this realm, the conscious connexion in men's minds between accepted moral rules and foreseen effects on general happiness becomes more clearly traceable. The admiration felt by early man for beauties or excellences of character seems to have been as direct and unreflective as his admiration of any other beauty: and the stringency of law and custom in primitive times presents itself as sanctioned by the evils which divine displeasure will supernaturally inflict on their violators, rather than by even a rude and vague forecast of the natural bad consequences of non-observance. It is therefore not as the mode of regulating conduct with which mankind began, but rather as that to which we can now see that human development has been always tending, as the adult and not the germinal form of Morality, that Utilitarianism may most reasonably claim the acceptance of Common Sense.

---

[1] If we consider the relation of Ethics to Politics from a Utilitarian point of view, the question, what rules of conduct for the governed should be fixed by legislators and applied by judges, will be determined by the same kind of forecast of consequences as will be used in settling all questions of private morality : we shall endeavour to estimate and balance against each other the effects of such rules on the general happiness. In so far, however, as we divide the Utilitarian theory of private conduct from that of legislation, and ask which is prior, the answer would seem to be different in respect of different parts of the legal code.

1. To a great extent the rules laid down in a utilitarian code of law will be such as any man sincerely desirous of promoting the general happiness would generally endeavour to observe, even if they were not legally binding. Of this kind is the rule of not inflicting any bodily harm or gratuitous annoyance on any one, except in self-defence or as retribution for wrong; the rule of not interfering with another's pursuit of the means of happiness, or with his enjoyment of wealth acquired by his own labour or the free consent of others; the rule of fulfilling all engagements freely entered into with any one,—at any rate unless the fulfilment were harmful to others, or much more harmful to oneself than beneficial to him, or unless there were good grounds for supposing that the other party would not perform his share of a bilateral contract—; and the rule of supporting one's children while helpless, and one's parents if decrepit, and of educating one's children suitably to their future life. As regards such rules as these, Utilitarian Ethics seems independent of Politics, and naturally prior to it; we first consider what conduct is right for private individuals, and then to how much of this they can advantageously be compelled by legal penalties.

---

[1] This passage, which in the second and subsequent editions occurred in chap. ii. of Book i., was omitted by Professor Sidgwick from that chapter in the sixth edition, with the intention of incorporating it in Book iv., which he did not live to revise.

2. There are other rules again which it is clearly for the general happiness to observe, if only their observance is enforced on others ; *e.g.* abstinence from personal retaliation of injuries, and a more general and unhesitating fulfilment of contracts than would perhaps be expedient if they were not legally enforced.

3. But again, in the complete determination of the mutual claims of members of society to services and forbearances, there are many points on which the utilitarian theory of right private conduct apart from law would lead to a considerable variety of conclusions, from the great difference in the force of the relevant considerations under different circumstances ; while at the same time uniformity is either indispensable, to prevent disputes and disappointments, or at least highly desirable, in order to maintain effectively such rules of conduct as are *generally* — though not *universally* — expedient. Under this head would come the exacter definition of the limits of appropriation, — *e.g.* as regards property in literary compositions and technical inventions, — and a large part of the law of inheritance, and of the law regulating the family relations. In such cases, in so far as they are capable of being theoretically determined, Utilitarian Ethics seems to blend with Utilitarian Politics in a rather complicated way; since we cannot determine the right conduct for a private individual in any particular case, without first considering what rule (if any) it would be on the whole expedient to maintain, in the society of which he is a member, by legal penalties, as well as by the weaker and less definite sanctions of moral opinion. This problem, moreover, in any concrete case is necessarily further complicated by the consideration of the delicate mutual relations of Positive Law and Positive Morality — as we may call the actual moral opinions generally held in a given society at a given time. For on the one hand it is dangerous in legislation to advance beyond Positive Morality, by prohibiting actions (or inactions) that are generally approved or tolerated ; on the other hand, up to the point at which this danger becomes serious, legislation is a most effective instrument for modifying or intensifying public opinion, in the direction in which it is desirable that it should progress. Leaving this difficult question of social dynamics, we may say that normally

in a well-organised society the most important and indispensable rules of social behaviour will be legally enforced and the less important left to be maintained by Positive Morality. Law will constitute, as it were, the skeleton of social order, clothed upon by the flesh and blood of Morality.

CHAPTER IV

THE METHOD OF UTILITARIANISM

§ 1. IF the view maintained in the preceding chapter as to the general Utilitarian basis of the Morality of Common Sense may be regarded as sufficiently established, we are now in a position to consider more closely to what method of determining right conduct the acceptance of Utilitarianism will practically lead. The most obvious method, of course, is that of Empirical Hedonism, discussed in Book ii. chap. iii.; according to which we have in each case to compare all the pleasures and pains that can be foreseen as probable results of the different alternatives of conduct presented to us, and to adopt the alternative which seems likely to lead to the greatest happiness on the whole.

In Book ii., however, it appeared that even the more restricted application of this method, which we there had to consider, was involved in much perplexity and uncertainty. Even when an individual is only occupied in forecasting his own pleasures, it seems difficult or impossible for him to avoid errors of considerable magnitude; whether in accurately comparing the pleasantness of his own past feelings, as represented in memory, or in appropriating the experience of others, or in arguing from the past to the future. And these difficulties are obviously much increased when we have to take into account all the effects of our actions on all the sentient beings who may be affected by them. At the same time, in Book ii. we could not find any satisfactory substitute for this method of empirical comparison. It did not appear reasonable to take refuge in the uncriticised beliefs of men in general as to the sources of happiness: indeed, it seemed impossible to extract any adequately clear and definite *consensus* of opinion from the confused and varying utterances of Common Sense on this subject. Nor again could it be shown that the individual would be more likely to attain the greatest happiness open to him by practically confining his efforts to the realisation of any scientifically ascertainable physical or psychical conditions of happiness : nor did it seem possible to infer on empirical grounds that the desired result would be secured by conformity to the accepted principles of morality.   But when we consider these latter in relation, not to the happiness of the individual, but to that of human (or sentient) beings generally, it is clear from the preceding chapter that the question of harmony between Hedonism and Intuitionism presents *prima facie* an entirely different aspect.   Indeed from the considerations that we have just surveyed it is but a short and easy step to the conclusion that in the Morality of Common Sense we have ready to hand a body of Utilitarian doctrine ; that the " rules of morality for the multitude " are to be regarded as " positive beliefs of mankind as to the effects of actions on their happiness," [1] so that the apparent first principles of Common Sense may be accepted as the " middle axioms " of Utilitarian method ; direct reference being only made to utilitarian considerations, in order to settle points upon which the verdict of Common Sense is found to be obscure and conflicting.   On this view the traditional controversy between the advocates of Virtue and the advocates of Happiness would seem to be at length harmoniously settled.

And the arguments for this view which have been already put forward certainly receive support from the hypothesis, now widely accepted, that the moral sentiments are ultimately derived, by a complex and gradual process, from experiences of pleasure and pain.   The hypothesis, in a summary form, would seem to be this ; (1) in the experience of each member of the human community the pain or alarm caused to him by actions of himself and of others tends by association to excite in him a dislike of such actions, and a similar though feebler effect is produced by his perception of pain or danger caused

---

[1] Cf. J. S. Mill, *Utilitarianism*, chap. ii.   Mill, however, only affirms that the "rules of morality for the multitude " are to be accepted by the philosopher provisionally, until he has got something better.

to others with whom he is connected by blood, or by community
of interest, or any special tie of sympathy : (2) experience
also tends more indirectly to produce in him sentiments restraining him from actions painful or alarming to others,
through his dread of their resentment and its consequences,
—especially dread of his chief's anger, and, where religious
influence has become strong, of the anger of supernatural
beings : (3) with these latter feelings blends a sympathetic
aversion to the pain of other men generally, which—at first
comparatively feeble—tends to grow in force as morality develops.   In the same way experiences of pleasure and gratitude,
and desire of the goodwill of others and its consequences, tend
to produce liking for actions that are perceived to cause
pleasure to self or to others.   The similar aversions and likings
that are thus produced in the majority of the members of any
society, through the general similarity of their natures and
conditions, tend to become more similar through communication and imitation,—the desire of each to retain the goodwill
of others operating to repress individual divergencies.   Thus
common likings for conduct that affects pleasurably the community generally or some part of it, and common dislikes
for conduct causing pain and alarm, come to be gradually
developed ; they are transmitted from generation to generation, partly perhaps by physical inheritance, but chiefly by
tradition from parents to children, and imitation of adults
by the young ; in this way their origin becomes obscured,
and they finally appear as what are called the moral
sentiments.   This theory does not, in my view, account
adequately for the actual results of the faculty of moral judgment and reasoning, so far as I can examine them by reflection
on my own moral consciousness : for this, as I have before said,
does not yield any apparent intuitions that stand the test of
rigorous examination except such as, from their abstract and
general character, have no cognisable relation to particular
experiences of any kind.[1]   But that the theory gives a partially
true explanation of the historical origin of particular moral
sentiments and habits and commonly accepted rules, I see no
reason to doubt ; and thus regarded it seems to supplement

---

[1] I refer to the abstract principles of Prudence, Justice, and Rational
Benevolence as defined in chap. xiii. of the preceding Book.

the arguments of the preceding chapter that tend to exhibit the morality of common sense as unconsciously or 'instinctively' utilitarian.

But it is one thing to hold that the current morality expresses, partly consciously but to a larger extent unconsciously, the results of human experience as to the effects of actions : it is quite another thing to accept this morality *en bloc,* so far as it is clear and definite, as the best guidance we can get to the attainment of maximum general happiness. However attractive this simple reconciliation of Intuitional and Utilitarian methods may be, it is not, I think, really warranted by the evidence. In the first place, I hold that in a complete view of the development of the moral sense a more prominent place should be given to the effect of sympathy with the impulses that prompt to actions, as well as with the feelings that result from them. It may be observed that Adam Smith [1] assigns to this operation of sympathy,—the echo (as it were) of each agent's passion in the breast of unconcerned spectators,—the first place in determining our approval and disapproval of actions [2]; sympathy with the effect of conduct on others he treats as a merely secondary factor, correcting and qualifying the former. Without going so far as this, I think that there are certainly many cases where the resulting moral consciousness would seem to indicate a balance or compromise between the two kinds of sympathy ; and the compromise may easily be many degrees removed from the rule which Utilitarianism would prescribe. For though the passions and other active impulses are doubtless themselves influenced, no less than the moral sentiments, by experiences of pleasure and pain ; still

---

[1] *Theory of Moral Sentiments,* Book i.

[2] This operation of sympathy is strikingly illustrated in the penal codes of primitive communities, both by the mildness of the punishments inflicted for homicide, and by the startling differences between the penalties allotted to the same crime according as the criminal was taken in the act or not. "It is curious to observe," says Sir H. Maine (*Ancient Law,* chap. x.), "how completely the men of primitive times were persuaded that the impulses of the injured person were the proper measure of the vengeance he was entitled to exact, and how literally they imitated the probable rise and fall of his passions in fixing the scale of punishment." And even in more civilised societies there is a very common feeling of uncertainty as to the propriety of inflicting punishment for crimes committed long ago, which seems traceable to the same source.

this influence is not sufficient to make them at all trustworthy
guides to general, any more than to individual, happiness—as
some of our moral sentiments themselves emphatically announce.
But even if we consider our common moral sentiments as
entirely due—directly or indirectly—to the accumulated and
transmitted experiences of primary and sympathetic pains and
pleasures; it is obvious that the degree of accuracy with
which sentiments thus produced will guide us to the promotion of general happiness must largely depend upon the
degree of accuracy with which the whole sum of pleasurable and
painful consequences, resulting from any course of action, has
been represented in the consciousness of an average member of
the community.   And it is seen at a glance that this representation has always been liable to errors of great magnitude, from
causes that were partly noticed in the previous chapter, when
we were considering the progress of morality.   We have to
allow, first, for limitation of sympathy ; since in every age and
country the sympathy of an average man with other sentient
beings, and even his egoistic regard for their likings and aversions, has been much more limited than the influence of his
actions on the feelings of others.   We must allow further for
limitation of intelligence : for in all ages ordinary men have
had a very inadequate knowledge of natural sequences ; so that
such indirect consequences of conduct as have been felt have
been frequently traced to wrong causes, and been met by wrong
moral remedies, owing to imperfect apprehension of the relation
of means to ends.   Again, where the habit of obedience to
authority and respect for rank has become strong, we must
allow for the possibly perverting influence of a desire to win
the favour or avert the anger of superiors.   And similarly we
must allow again for the influences of false religions ; and also
for the possibility that the sensibilities of religious teachers
have influenced the code of duty accepted by their followers,
in points where these sensibilities were not normal and representative, but exceptional and idiosyncratic.[1]

---

[1] No doubt this influence is confined within strict limits : no authority can
permanently impose on men regulations flagrantly infelicific : and the most
practically originative of religious teachers have produced their effect chiefly by
giving new force and vividness to sentiments already existing (and recognised
as properly authoritive) in the society upon which they acted.   Still, it might

On the other hand, we must suppose that these deflecting influences have been more or less limited and counteracted by the struggle for existence in past ages among different human races and communities; since, so far as any moral habit or sentiment was unfavourable to the preservation of the social organism, it would be a disadvantage in the struggle for existence, and would therefore tend to perish with the community that adhered to it. But we have no reason to suppose that this force would be adequate to keep positive morality always in conformity with a Utilitarian ideal. For (1) imperfect morality would be only one disadvantage among many, and not, I conceive, the most important, unless the imperfection were extreme,—especially in the earlier stages of social and moral development, in which the struggle for existence was most operative: and (2) a morality perfectly preservative of a human community might still be imperfectly felicific, and so require considerable improvement from a Utilitarian point of view.[1] Further, analogy would lead us to expect that however completely adapted the moral instincts of a community may be at some particular time to its conditions of existence, any rapid change of circumstances would tend to derange the adaptation, from survival of instincts formerly useful, which through this change become useless or pernicious. And indeed, apart from any apparent changes in external circumstances, it might result from the operation of some law of human development, that the most completely organised experience of human happiness in the past would guide us but imperfectly to the right means of making it a maximum in the future. For example, a slight decrease in the average strength of some common impulse might render the traditional rules and sentiments, that regulate this impulse, infelicific on the whole. And if, when we turn from these abstract considerations to history, and examine the actual morality of other ages and countries, we undoubtedly find that, considered as an instrument for producing general happiness, it continually seems to exhibit palpable imperfections,—there is surely a strong presumption that there are similar imperfections to be discovered in our own moral

have made a great difference to the human race if (*e.g.*) Mohammed had been fond of wine, and indifferent to women.

[1] On this point I shall have occasion to speak further in the next section.

code, though habit and familiarity prevent them from being obvious.

Finally, we must not overlook the fact that the divergences which we find when we compare the moralities of different ages and countries, exist to some extent side by side in the morality of any one society at any given time. It has already been observed that whenever divergent opinions are entertained by a minority so large, that we cannot fairly regard the dogma of the majority as the plain utterance of Common Sense, an appeal is necessarily made to some higher principle, and very commonly to Utilitarianism. But a smaller minority than this, particularly if composed of persons of enlightenment and special acquaintance with the effects of the conduct judged, may reasonably inspire us with distrust of Common Sense : just as in the more technical parts of practice we prefer the judgment of a few trained experts to the instincts of the vulgar. Yet again, a contemplation of these divergent codes and their relation to the different circumstances in which men live, suggests that Common-Sense morality is really only adapted for ordinary men in ordinary circumstances—although it may still be expedient that these ordinary persons should regard it as absolutely and universally prescribed, since any other view of it may dangerously weaken its hold over their minds. So far as this is the case we must use the Utilitarian method to ascertain how far persons in special circumstances require a morality more specially adapted to them than Common Sense is willing to concede : and also how far men of peculiar physical or mental constitution ought to be exempted from ordinary rules, as has sometimes been claimed for men of genius, or men of intensely emotional nature, or men gifted with more than usual prudence and self-control.

Further, it is important to notice, that besides the large amount of divergence that exists between the moral instincts of different classes and individuals, there is often a palpable discrepancy between the moral instincts of any class or individual, and such Utilitarian reasonings as their untrained intellects are in the habit of conducting. There are many things in conduct which many people think right but not expedient, or at least which they would not think expedient if they had not first judged them to be right ; in so far as they reason from experience only, their conclusions as to what conduces to the general happiness are opposed to their moral intuitions.   It may be said that this results generally from a hasty and superficial consideration of expediency ; and that the discrepancy would disappear after a deeper and completer examination of the consequences of actions.   And I do not deny that this would often turn out to be the case : but as we cannot tell *a priori* how far it would be so, this only constitutes a further argument for a comprehensive and systematic application of a purely Utilitarian method.

We must conclude, then, that we cannot take the moral rules of Common Sense as expressing the *consensus* of competent judges, up to the present time, as to the kind of conduct which is likely to produce the greatest amount of happiness on the whole.   It would rather seem that it is the unavoidable duty of a systematic Utilitarianism to make a thorough revision of these rules, in order to ascertain how far the causes previously enumerated (and perhaps others) have actually operated to produce a divergence between Common Sense and a perfectly Utilitarian code of morality.

§ 2. But in thus stating the problem we are assuming that the latter term of this comparison can be satisfactorily defined and sufficiently developed ; that we can frame with adequate precision a system of rules, constituting the true moral code for human beings as deduced from Utilitarian principles.   And this seems to have been commonly assumed by the school whose method we are now examining.   But when we set ourselves in earnest to the construction of such a system, we find it beset with serious difficulties.   For, passing over the uncertainties involved in hedonistic comparison generally, let us suppose that the *quantum* of happiness that will result from the establishment of any plan of behaviour among human beings can be ascertained with sufficient exactness for practical purposes— even when the plan is as yet constructed in imagination alone. It still has to be asked, What is the nature of the human being for whom we are to construct this hypothetical scheme of conduct ?   For humanity is not something that exhibits the same properties always and everywhere : whether we consider the intellect of man or his feelings, or his physical condition and circumstances, we find them so different in different ages

and countries, that it seems *prima facie* absurd to lay down a
set of ideal Utilitarian rules for mankind generally.   It may be
said that these differences after all relate chiefly to details ; and
that there is in any case sufficient uniformity in the nature and
circumstances of human life always and everywhere to render
possible an outline scheme of ideal behaviour for mankind at
large.   But it must be answered, that it is with details that we
are now principally concerned ; for the previous discussion has
sufficiently shown that the conduct approved by Common Sense
has a *general* resemblance to that which Utilitarianism would
prescribe ; but we wish to ascertain more exactly how far the
resemblance extends, and with what delicacy and precision the
current moral rules are adapted to the actual needs and conditions of human life.

Suppose, then, that we contract the scope of investigation, and only endeavour to ascertain the rules appropriate to
men as we know them, in our own age and country.   We are
immediately met with a dilemma : the men whom we know are
beings who accept more or less definitely a certain moral code :
if we take them as they are in this respect, we can hardly at the
same time conceive them as beings for whom a code is yet to
be constructed *de novo :* if, on the other hand, we take an
actual man—let us say, an average Englishman—and abstract
his morality, what remains is an entity so purely hypothetical,
that it is not clear what practical purpose can be served by
constructing a system of moral rules for the community of such
beings.   Could we indeed assume that the scientific deduction
of such a system would ensure its general acceptance ; could
we reasonably expect to convert all mankind at once to Utilitarian principles, or even all educated and reflective mankind,
so that all preachers and teachers should take universal happiness as the goal of their efforts as unquestioningly as physicians
take the health of the individual body ; and could we be sure
that men's moral habits and sentiments would adjust themselves
at once and without any waste of force to these changed rules :—
then perhaps in framing the Utilitarian code we might fairly
leave existing morality out of account.   But I cannot think
that we are warranted in making these suppositions ; I think
we have to take the moral habits, impulses, and tastes of men
as a material given us to work upon no less than the rest of

their nature, and as something which, as it only partly results
from reasoning in the past, so can only be partially modified by
any reasoning which we can now apply to it.   It seems therefore
clear that the solution of the hypothetical Utilitarian problem of
constructing an ideal morality for men conceived to be in other
respects as experience shows them to be, but with their actual
morality abstracted, will not give us the result which we
practically require.

It will perhaps be said, "No doubt such an ideal Utilitarian
morality can only be gradually, and perhaps after all imperfectly, introduced; but still it will be useful to work it out as a
pattern to which we may approximate."   But, in the first place,
it may not be really possible to approximate to it: since any
particular existing moral rule, though not the ideally best even
for such beings as existing men under the existing circumstances, may yet be the best that they can be got to obey: so
that it would be futile to propose any other, or even harmful,
as it might tend to impair old moral habits without effectively
replacing them by new ones.   And secondly, the endeavour
gradually to approximate to a morality constructed on the
supposition that the non-moral part of existing human nature
remains unchanged, may lead us wrong: because the state
of men's knowledge and intellectual faculties, and the range of
their sympathies, and the direction and strength of their prevailing impulses, and their relations to the external world and
to each other, are continually being altered, and such alteration
is to some extent under our control and may be felicific in a
high degree: and any material modifications in important
elements and conditions of human life may require corresponding changes in established moral rules and sentiments, in order
that the greatest possible happiness may be attained by the
human being whose life is thus modified.   In short, the construction of a Utilitarian code, regarded as an ideal towards
which we are to progress, is met by a second dilemma:—The
nature of man and the conditions of his life cannot usefully be
assumed to be constant, unless we are confining our attention
to the present or proximate future; while again, if we are considering them in the present or proximate future, we must take
into account men's actual moral habits and sentiments, as a part
of their nature not materially more modifiable than the rest.

Nor, again, can I agree with Mr. Spencer [1] in thinking that it is possible to solve the problems of practical ethics by constructing the final perfect form of society, towards which the process of human history is tending; and determining the rules of mutual behaviour which ought to be, and will be, observed by the members of this perfect society. For, firstly, granting that we can conceive as possible a human community which is from a utilitarian point of view perfect; and granting also Mr. Spencer's definition of this perfection—viz. that the voluntary actions of all the members cause " pleasure unalloyed by pain anywhere " to all who are affected by them [2]—; it still seems to me quite impossible to forecast the natures and relations of the persons composing such a community, with sufficient clearness and certainty to enable us to define even in outline their moral code. And secondly, even if it were otherwise, even if we could construct scientifically Mr. Spencer's ideal morality, I do not think such a construction would be of much avail in solving the practical problems of actual humanity. For a society in which—to take one point only—there is no such thing as punishment, is necessarily a society with its essential structure so unlike our own, that it would be idle to attempt any close imitation of its rules of behaviour. It might possibly be best for us to conform approximately to some of these rules; but this we could only know by examining each particular rule in detail; we could have no general grounds for concluding that it would be best for us to conform to them as far as possible. For even supposing that this ideal society is ultimately to be realised, it must at any rate be separated from us by a considerable interval of evolution; hence it is not unlikely that the best way of progressing towards it will be some other than the apparently directest way, and that we shall reach it more easily if we begin by moving away from it. Whether this is so or not, and to what extent, can only be known by carefully examining the effects of con-

---

[1] I refer especially to the views put forward by Mr. Spencer in the concluding chapters of his *Data of Ethics*.

[2] This definition, however, does not seem to me admissible, from a utilitarian point of view : since a society in this sense perfect might not realise the maximum of possible happiness ; it might still be capable of a material increase of happiness through pleasures involving a slight alloy of pain, such as Mr. Spencer's view of perfection would exclude.

duct on actual human beings, and inferring its probable effects on the human beings whom we may expect to exist in the proximate future.

§ 3. Other thinkers of the evolutionist school suggest that the difficulties of Utilitarian method might be avoided, in a way more simple than Mr. Spencer's, by adopting, as the *practically* ultimate end and criterion of morality, " health " or " efficiency " of the social organism, instead of happiness.   This view is maintained, for instance, in Mr. Leslie Stephen's *Science of Ethics* ;[1] and deserves careful examination.   As I understand Mr. Stephen, he means by " health " that state of the social organism which tends to its preservation under the conditions of its existence, as they are known or capable of being predicted ; and he means the same by " efficiency " ;— since the work for which, in his view, the social organism has to be " efficient " is simply the work of living, the function of " going on."   I say this because " efficiency " might be understood to imply some ' task of humanity ' which the social organism has to execute, beyond the task of merely living ; and similarly " health " might be taken to mean a state tending to the preservation not of existence merely, but of *desirable* existence—desirability being interpreted in some non-hedonistic manner : and in this case an examination of either term would lead us again over the ground traversed in the discussion on Ultimate Good (in chap. xiv. of the preceding Book).[2]   But I do not understand that any such implications were in Mr. Stephen's mind ; and they certainly would not be in harmony with the general drift of his argument.   The question, therefore, is whether, if General Happiness be admitted to be the really ultimate end in a system of morality, it is nevertheless reasonable to take Preservation of the social organism as the practically ultimate " scientific criterion " of moral rules.

---

[1] See especially chap. ix. Pars. 12-15.

[2] It is obvious that if ' desirability,' in the above definition, were interpreted hedonistically, the term "health" would merely give us a new name for the general problem of utilitarian morality ; not a new suggestion for its solution. I ought to say that the notions of " social welfare " or " wellbeing " are elsewhere used by Mr. Stephen, in the place of those here quoted, but I do not think that he means by them any more than what I understand him to mean by "health" or "efficiency"—*i.e.* that state of the social organism which tends to its preservation under the conditions of its existence.

My reasons for answering this question in the negative are two-fold. In the first place I know no adequate grounds for supposing that if we aim exclusively at the preservation of the social organism we shall secure the maximum attainable happiness of its individual members: indeed, so far as I know, of two social states which equally tend to be preserved one may be indefinitely happier than the other. As has been before observed,[1] a large part of the pleasures which cultivated persons value most highly—æsthetic pleasures—are derived from acts and processes that have no material tendency to preserve the individual's life:[2] and the statement remains true if we substitute the social organism for the individual. And I may add that much refined morality is concerned with the prevention of pains which have no demonstrable tendency to the destruction of the individual or of society. Hence, while I quite admit that the maintenance of preservative habits and sentiments is the most indispensable function of utilitarian morality—and perhaps almost its sole function in the earlier stages of moral development, when to live at all was a difficult task for human communities—I do not therefore think it reasonable that we should be content with the mere securing of existence for humanity generally, and should confine our efforts to promoting the increase of this security, instead of seeking to make the secured existence more desirable.

But, secondly, I do not see on what grounds Mr. Stephen holds that the criterion of ' tendency to the preservation of the social organism' is necessarily capable of being applied with greater precision than that of 'tendency to general happiness,' even so far as the two ends are coincident: and that the former "satisfies the conditions of a scientific criterion." I should admit that this would probably be the case, if the Sociology that we know were a science actually constructed, and not merely the sketch of a possible future science: but Mr. Stephen has himself told us that sociology at present "consists of nothing more than a collection of unverified guesses and vague

---

[1] Book ii. chap. vi. § 3.

[2] I do not mean to assert that 'play' in some form is not necessary for physical health : but there is a long step from the encouragement of play, so far as salutary, to the promotion of social culture.

generalisations, disguised under a more or less pretentious apparatus of quasi-scientific terminology." This language is stronger than I should have ventured to use; but I agree generally with the view that it expresses ; and it appears to me difficult for a writer who holds this view to maintain that the conception of " social health," regarded as a criterion and standard of right conduct, is in any important degree more " scientific " than the conception of " general happiness."

Holding this estimate of the present condition of Sociology, I consider that, from the utilitarian point of view, there are equally decisive reasons against the adoption of any such notion as " development" of the social organism—instead of mere preservation—as the practically ultimate end and criterion of morality. On the one hand, if by " development " is meant an increase in " efficiency " or preservative qualities, this notion is only an optimistic specialisation of that just discussed (involving the—I fear—unwarranted assumption that the social organism tends to become continually more efficient); so that no fresh arguments need be urged against it. If, however, something different is meant by development—as (e.g.) a disciple of Mr. Spencer might mean an increase in " definite coherent heterogeneity," whether or not such increase was preservative—then I know no scientific grounds for concluding that we shall best promote general happiness by concentrating our efforts on the attainment of this increase. I do not affirm it to be impossible that every increase in the definite coherent heterogeneity of a society of human beings may be accompanied or followed by an increase in the aggregate happiness of the members of the society : but I do not perceive that Mr. Spencer, or any one else, has even attempted to furnish the kind of proof which this proposition requires.[1]

To sum up : I hold that the utilitarian, in the existing state of our knowledge, cannot possibly construct a morality *de novo*

---

[1] It may be observed that the increased heterogeneity which the development of modern industry has brought with it, in the form of a specialisation of industrial functions which tends to render the lives of individual workers narrow and monotonous, has usually been regarded by philanthropists as seriously infelicific ; and as needing to be counteracted by a general diffusion of the intellectual culture now enjoyed by the few—which, if realised, would tend *pro tanto* to make the lives of different classes in the community *less* heterogeneous.

either for man as he is (abstracting his morality), or for man as he ought to be and will be. He must start, speaking broadly, with the existing social order, and the existing morality as a part of that order: and in deciding the question whether any divergence from this code is to be recommended, must consider chiefly the immediate consequences of such divergence, upon a society in which such a code is conceived generally to subsist. No doubt a thoughtful and well-instructed Utilitarian may see dimly a certain way ahead, and his attitude towards existing morality may be to some extent modified by what he sees. He may discern in the future certain evils impending, which can only be effectually warded off by the adoption of new and more stringent views of duty in certain departments: while, on the other hand, he may see a prospect of social changes which will render a relaxation of other parts of the moral code expedient or inevitable. But if he keeps within the limits that separate scientific prevision from fanciful Utopian conjecture, the form of society to which his practical conclusions relate will be one varying but little from the actual, with its actually established code of moral rules and customary judgments concerning virtue and vice.

CHAPTER V

THE METHOD OF UTILITARIANISM—*Continued*

§ 1. IF, then, we are to regard the morality of Common Sense as a machinery of rules, habits, and sentiments, roughly and generally but not precisely or completely adapted to the production of the greatest possible happiness for sentient beings generally; and if, on the other hand, we have to accept it as the actually established machinery for attaining this end, which we cannot replace at once by any other, but can only gradually modify; it remains to consider the practical effects of the complex and balanced relation in which a scientific Utilitarian thus seems to stand to the Positive Morality of his age and country.

Generally speaking, he will clearly conform to it, and endeavour to promote its development in others. For, though the imperfection that we find in all the actual conditions of human existence—we may even say in the universe at large as judged from a human point of view—is ultimately found even in Morality itself, in so far as this is contemplated as Positive; still, practically, we are much less concerned with correcting and improving than we are with realising and enforcing it. The Utilitarian must repudiate altogether that temper of rebellion against the established morality, as something purely external and conventional, into which the reflective mind is always apt to fall when it is first convinced that the established rules are not intrinsically reasonable. He must, of course, also repudiate as superstitious that awe of it as an absolute or Divine Code which Intuitional moralists inculcate.[1] Still, he will naturally

---

[1] I do not mean that this sentiment is in my view incompatible with Utili-

contemplate it with reverence and wonder, as a marvellous product of nature, the result of long centuries of growth, showing in many parts the same fine adaptation of means to complex exigencies as the most elaborate structures of physical organisms exhibit : he will handle it with respectful delicacy as a mechanism, constructed of the fluid element of opinions and dispositions, by the indispensable aid of which the actual *quantum* of human happiness is continually being produced ; a mechanism which no 'politicians or philosophers' could create, yet without which the harder and coarser machinery of Positive Law could not be permanently maintained, and the life of man would become— as Hobbes forcibly expresses it—" solitary, poor, nasty, brutish, and short."

Still, as this actual moral order is admittedly imperfect, it will be the Utilitarian's duty to aid in improving it ; just as the most orderly, law-abiding member of a modern civilised society includes the reform of laws in his conception of political duty. We have therefore to consider by what method he will ascertain the particular modifications of positive morality which it would be practically expedient to attempt to introduce, at any given time and place. Here our investigation seems, after all, to leave Empirical Hedonism as the only method ordinarily applicable for the ultimate decision of such problems—at least until the science of Sociology shall have been really constructed. I do not mean that the rudiments of Sociological knowledge which we now possess are of no practical value : for certainly changes in morality might be suggested—and have actually been proposed by persons seriously concerned to benefit their fellow-creatures—which even our present imperfect knowledge would lead us to regard as dangerous to the very existence of the social organism. But such changes for the most part involve changes in positive law as well : since most of the rules of which the observance is fundamentally important for the preservation of an organised community are either directly or indirectly maintained by legal sanctions : and it would be going too far beyond the line which, in my view, separates ethics from politics, to discuss changes of this kind in the present book. The rules

---

tarianism ; I mean that it must not attach itself to any subordinate rules of conduct, but only to the supreme principle of acting with impartial concern for all elements of general happiness.

with which we have primarily to deal, in considering the utilitarian method of determining private duty, are rules supported by merely moral sanctions; and the question of maintaining or modifying such rules concerns, for the most part, the well-being rather than the very existence of human society. The consideration of this question, therefore, from a utilitarian point of view, resolves itself into a comparison between the total amounts of pleasure and pain that may be expected to result respectively from maintaining any given rule as at present established, and from endeavouring to introduce that which is proposed in its stead. That this comparison must generally be of a rough and uncertain kind, we have already seen; and it is highly important to bear this in mind; but yet we seem unable to find any substitute for it. It is not meant, of course, that each individual is left to his own unassisted judgment in dealing with such questions: there is a mass of traditional experience, which each individual imbibes orally or from books, as to the effects of conduct upon happiness; but the great formulæ in which this experience is transmitted are, for the most part, so indefinite, the proper range of their application so uncertain, and the observation and induction on which they are founded so uncritical, that they stand in continual need of further empirical verification; especially as regards their applicability to any particular case.

It is perhaps not surprising that some thinkers [1] of the Utilitarian school should consider that the task of hedonistic calculation which is thus set before the utilitarian moralist is too extensive: and should propose to simplify it by marking off a "large sphere of individual option and self-guidance," to which "ethical dictation" does not apply. I should quite admit that it is clearly expedient to draw a dividing line of this kind: but it appears to me that there is no simple general method of drawing it; that it can only be drawn by careful utilitarian calculation applied with varying results to the various relations and circumstances of human life. To attempt the required division by means of any such general formula as that 'the individual is not responsible to society for that part of his conduct which concerns himself alone and others only

---

[1] For example, Mr. Bain in *Mind* (Jan. 1883, pp. 48, 49).

with their free and undeceived consent'[1] seems to me practically futile : since, owing to the complex enlacements of interest and sympathy that connect the members of a civilised community, almost any material loss of happiness by any one individual is likely to affect some others without their consent to some not inconsiderable extent.   And I do not see how it is from a utilitarian point of view justifiable to say broadly with J. S. Mill that such secondary injury to others, if merely " constructive or presumptive," is to be disregarded in view of the advantages of allowing free development to individuality ; for if the injury feared is great, and the presumption that it will occur is shown by experience to be strong, the definite risk of evil from the withdrawal of the moral sanction must, I conceive, outweigh the indefinite possibility of loss through the repression of individuality in one particular direction.[2]   But further : even supposing that we could mark off the " sphere of individual option and self-guidance " by some simple and sweeping formula, still within this sphere the individual, if he wishes to guide himself reasonably on utilitarian principles, must take some account of all important effects of his actions on the happiness of others ; and if he does this methodically, he must, I conceive, use the empirical method which we have examined in Book ii.   And— to prevent any undue alarm at this prospect—we may observe that every sensible man is commonly supposed to determine at least a large part of his conduct by what is substantially this method ; it is assumed that, within the limits which morality lays down, he will try to get as much happiness as he can for himself and for other human beings, according to the relations in which they stand to him, by combining in some way his own experience with that of other men as to the felicific and infelicific effects of actions.   And it is actually in this way that each man usually deliberates (*e.g.*) what profession to choose for himself, or what mode of education for his children, whether to aim at marriage or remain single, whether to settle in town or country, in England or abroad, etc.   No doubt there are, as we saw,[3]

---

[1] This sentence is not an exact quotation, but a summary of the doctrine set forth by J. S. Mill in his treatise *On Liberty* (Introduction).

[2] See Mill *On Liberty*, chap. iv.   It may be observed that Mill's doctrine is certainly opposed to common sense : since (*e.g.*) it would exclude from censure almost all forms of sexual immorality committed by unmarried and independent adults.   [3] Cf. Book iii. chap. xiv.

other ends besides Happiness, such as Knowledge, Beauty, etc., commonly recognised as unquestionably desirable, and therefore largely pursued without consideration of ulterior consequences: but when the pursuit of any of these ends involves an apparent sacrifice of happiness in other ways, the practical question whether under these circumstances such pursuit ought to be maintained or abandoned seems always decided by an application, however rough, of the method of pure empirical Hedonism.

And in saying that this must be the method of the Utilitarian moralist, I only mean that no other can normally be applied in reducing to a common measure the diverse elements of the problems with which he has to deal. Of course, in determining the nature and importance of each of these diverse considerations, the utilitarian art of morality will lay various sciences under contribution. Thus, for example, it will learn from Political Economy what effects a general censure of usurers, or the ordinary commendation of liberality in almsgiving, is likely to have on the wealth of the community; it will learn from the physiologist the probable consequences to health of a general abstinence from alcoholic liquors or any other restraint on appetite proposed in the name of Temperance; it will learn from the experts in any science how far knowledge is likely to be promoted by investigations offensive to any prevalent moral or religious sentiment. But how far the increase of wealth or of knowledge, or even the improvement of health, should under any circumstances be subordinated to other considerations, I know no scientific method of determining other than that of empirical Hedonism. Nor, as I have said, does it seem to me that any other method has ever been applied or sought by the common sense of mankind, for regulating the pursuit of what our older moralists called ' Natural Good,'— i.e. of all that is intrinsically desirable except Virtue or Morality, within the limits fixed by the latter; the Utilitarian here only performs somewhat more consistently and systematically than ordinary men the reasoning processes which are commonly admitted to be appropriate to the questions that this pursuit raises. His distinctive characteristic, as a Utilitarian, is that he has to apply the same method to the criticism and correction of the limiting morality itself. The particulars of this criticism will obviously vary almost indefinitely with the variations in

human nature and circumstances: I here only propose to
discuss the general points of view which a Utilitarian critic
must take, in order that no important class of relevant considerations may be omitted.

§ 2. Let us first recall the distinction previously noticed [1]
between duty as commonly conceived,—that to which a man
is bound or obliged—, and praiseworthy or excellent conduct;
since, in considering the relation of Utilitarianism to the moral
judgments of Common Sense, it will be convenient to begin
with the former element of current morality, as the more
important and indispensable; *i.e.* with the *ensemble* of rules imposed by common opinion in any society, which form a kind of
unwritten legislation, supplementary to Law proper, and enforced by the penalties of social disfavour and contempt. This
legislation, as it does not emanate from a definite body of
persons acting in a corporate capacity, cannot be altered by
any formal deliberations and resolutions of the persons on
whose *consensus* it rests; any change in it must therefore
result from the private action of individuals, whether determined by Utilitarian considerations or otherwise. As we
shall presently see, the practical Utilitarian problem is liable
to be complicated by the conflict and divergence which is
found to some extent in all societies between the moral
opinions of different sections of the community: but it will
be convenient to confine our attention in the first instance
to the case of rules of duty clearly supported by 'common
consent.' Let us suppose then that after considering the
consequences of any such rule, a Utilitarian comes to the conclusion that a different rule would be more conducive to the
general happiness, if similarly established in a society remaining
in other respects the same as at present—or in one slightly
different (in so far as our forecast of social changes can be
made sufficiently clear to furnish any basis for practice). And
first we will suppose that this new rule differs from the old
one not only positively but negatively; that it does not merely
go beyond and include it, but actually conflicts with it. Before
he can decide that it is right for him (*i.e.* conducive to the
general happiness) to support the new rule against the old,
by example and precept, he ought to estimate the force of

---

[1] Cf. especially Book iii. chap. ii.

certain disadvantages necessarily attendant upon such innovations, which may conveniently be arranged under the following
heads.

In the first place, as his own happiness and that of others
connected with him form a part of the universal end at
which he aims, he must consider the importance to himself
and them of the penalties of social disapprobation which he
will incur : taking into account, besides the immediate pain of
this disapprobation, its indirect effect in diminishing his power
of serving society and promoting the general happiness in other
ways.   The prospect of such pain and loss is, of course, not
decisive against the innovation ; since it must to some extent
be regarded as the regular price that has to be paid for the
advantage of this kind of reform in current morality.   But
here, as in many Utilitarian calculations, everything depends
on the quantity of the effects produced ; which in the case supposed may vary very much, from slight distrust and disfavour
to severe condemnation and social exclusion.   It often seems
that by attempting change prematurely an innovator may incur
the severest form of the moral penalty, whereas if he had
waited a few years he would have been let off with the mildest.
For the hold which a moral rule has over the general mind
commonly begins to decay from the time that it is seen to be
opposed to the calculations of expediency : and it may be
better for the community as well as for the individual that it
should not be openly attacked, until this process of decay has
reached a certain point.

It is, however, of more importance to point out certain
general reasons for doubting whether an apparent improvement
will really have a beneficial effect on others.   It is possible that
the new rule, though it would be more felicific than the old one,
if it could get itself equally established, may be not so likely
to be adopted, or if adopted, not so likely to be obeyed, by the
mass of the community in which it is proposed to innovate.   It
may be too subtle and refined, or too complex and elaborate :
it may require a greater intellectual development, or a higher
degree of self-control, than is to be found in an average member
of the community, or an exceptional quality or balance of
feelings.   Nor can it be said in reply, that by the hypothesis
the innovator's example must be good to whatever extent it

operates, since *pro tanto* it tends to substitute a better rule for
a worse. For experience seems to show that an example of
this kind is more likely to be potent negatively than positively;
that here, as elsewhere in human affairs, it is easier to pull
down than to build up; easier to weaken or destroy the restraining force that a moral rule, habitually and generally.
obeyed, has over men's minds, than to substitute for it a new
restraining habit, not similarly sustained by tradition and
custom. Hence the effect of an example intrinsically good
may be on the whole bad, because its destructive operation
proves to be more vigorous than its constructive. And again,
such destructive effect must be considered not only in respect
of the particular rule violated, but of all other rules. For just
as the breaking of any positive law has an inevitable tendency
to encourage lawlessness generally, so the violation of any
generally recognised moral rule seems to give a certain aid
to the forces that are always tending towards moral anarchy
in any society.

Nor must we neglect the reaction which any breach with
customary morality will have on the agent's own mind. For
the regulative habits and sentiments which each man has received by inheritance or training constitute an important force
impelling his will, in the main, to conduct such as his reason
would dictate; a natural auxiliary, as it were, to Reason in its
conflict with seductive passions and appetites; and it may be
practically dangerous to impair the strength of these auxiliaries.
On the other hand, it would seem that the habit of acting rationally is the best of all habits, and that it ought to be the aim of
a reasonable being to bring all his impulses and sentiments
into more and more perfect harmony with Reason. And indeed
when a man has earnestly accepted any moral principle, those
of his pre-existing regulative habits and sentiments that are
not in harmony with this principle tend naturally to decay
and disappear; and it would perhaps be scarcely worth while
to take them into account, except for the support that they
derive from the sympathy of others.

But this last is a consideration of great importance. For
the moral impulses of each individual commonly draw a large
part of their effective force from the sympathy of other human
beings. I do not merely mean that the pleasures and pains

which each derives sympathetically from the moral likings and aversions of others are important as motives to felicific conduct no less than as elements of the individual's happiness : I mean further that the direct sympathetic echo in each man of the judgments and sentiments of others concerning conduct sustains his own similar judgments and sentiments.   Through this twofold operation of sympathy it becomes practically much easier for most men to conform to a moral rule established in the society to which they belong than to one made by themselves.   And any act by which a man weakens the effect on himself of this general moral sympathy tends *pro tanto* to make the performance of duty more difficult for him.   On the other hand, we have to take into account—besides the intrinsic gain of the particular change—the general advantage of offering to mankind a striking example of consistent Utilitarianism ; since, in this case as in others, a man gives a stronger proof of genuine conviction by conduct in opposition to public opinion than he can by conformity.   In order, however, that this effect may be produced, it is almost necessary that the non-conformity should not promote the innovator's personal convenience ; for in that case it will almost certainly be attributed to egoistic motives, however plausible the Utilitarian deduction of its rightness may seem.

The exact force of these various considerations will differ indefinitely in different cases ; and it does not seem profitable to attempt any general estimate of them : but on the whole, it would seem that the general arguments which we have noticed constitute an important rational check upon such Utilitarian innovations on Common-Sense morality as are of the negative or destructive kind.

If now we consider such innovations as are merely positive and supplementary, and consist in adding a new rule to those already established by Common Sense ; it will appear that there is really no collision of methods, so far as the Utilitarian's own observance of the new rule is concerned.   For, as every such rule is, *ex hypothesi*, believed by him to be conducive to the common good, he is merely giving a special and stricter interpretation to the general duty of Universal Benevolence, where Common Sense leaves it loose and indeterminate.   Hence the restraining considerations above enumerated do not apply to this case.   And whatever it is right for him to do himself, it is obviously right for him to approve and recommend to other persons in similar circumstances.   But it is a different question whether he ought to seek to impose his new rule on others, by express condemnation of all who are not prepared to adopt it; as this involves not only the immediate evil of the annoyance given to others, but also the further danger of weakening the general good effect of his moral example, through the reaction provoked by this aggressive attitude.   On this point his decision will largely depend on the prospect, as far as he can estimate it, that his innovation will meet with support and sympathy from others.

It should be observed, however, that a great part of the reform in popular morality, which a consistent Utilitarian will try to introduce, will probably lie not so much in establishing new rules (whether conflicting with the old or merely supplementary) as in enforcing old ones.   For there is always a considerable part of morality in the condition of receiving formal respect and acceptance, while yet it is not really sustained by any effective force of public opinion : and the difference between the moralities of any two societies is often more strikingly exhibited in the different emphasis attached to various portions of the moral code in each, than in disagreement as to the rules which the code should include.   In the case we are considering, it is chiefly conduct which shows a want of comprehensive sympathy or of public spirit, to which the Utilitarian will desire to attach a severer condemnation than is at present directed against it.   There is much conduct of this sort, of which the immediate effect is to give obvious pleasure to individuals, while the far greater amount of harm that it more remotely and indirectly causes is but dimly recognised by Common Sense.   Such conduct, therefore, even when it is allowed to be wrong, is very mildly treated by common opinion; especially when it is prompted by some impulse not self-regarding.   Still, in all such cases, we do not require the promulgation of any new moral doctrine, but merely a bracing and sharpening of the moral sentiments of society, to bring them into harmony with the greater comprehensiveness of view and the more impartial concern for human happiness which characterise the Utilitarian system.

§ 3. We have hitherto supposed that the innovator is endeavouring to introduce a new rule of conduct, not for himself only, but for others also, as more conducive to the general happiness than the rule recognised by Common Sense. It may perhaps be thought that this is not the issue most commonly raised between Utilitarianism and Common Sense: but rather whether exceptions should be allowed to rules which both sides accept as generally valid. For no one doubts that it is, *generally speaking*, conducive to the common happiness that men should be veracious, faithful to promises, obedient to law, disposed to satisfy the normal expectations of others, having their malevolent impulses and their sensual appetites under strict control: but it is thought that an exclusive regard to pleasurable and painful consequences would frequently admit exceptions to rules which Common Sense imposes as absolute. It should, however, be observed that the admission of an exception on general grounds is merely the establishment of a more complex and delicate rule, instead of one that is broader and simpler; for if it is conducive to the general good that such an exception be admitted in one case, it will be equally so in all similar cases. Suppose (*e.g.*) that a Utilitarian thinks it on general grounds right to answer falsely a question as to the manner in which he has voted at a political election where the voting is by secret ballot. His reasons will probably be that the Utilitarian prohibition of falsehood is based on (1) the harm done by misleading particular individuals, and (2) the tendency of false statements to diminish the mutual confidence that men ought to have in each other's assertions: and that in this exceptional case it is (1) expedient that the questioner should be misled; while (2), in so far as the falsehood tends to produce a general distrust of all assertions as to the manner in which a man has voted, it only furthers the end for which voting has been made secret. It is evident, that if these reasons are valid for any person, they are valid for all persons; in fact, that they establish the expediency of a new general rule in respect of truth and falsehood, more complicated than the old one; a rule which the Utilitarian, as such, should desire to be universally obeyed.

There are, of course, some kinds of moral innovation which, from the nature of the case, are not likely to occur frequently;

as where Utilitarian reasoning leads a man to take part in a political revolution, or to support a public measure in opposition to what Common Sense regards as Justice or Good Faith. Still, in such cases a rational Utilitarian will usually proceed on general principles, which he would desire all persons in similar circumstances to carry into effect.

We have, however, to consider another kind of exceptions, differing fundamentally from this, which Utilitarianism seems to admit; where the agent does not think it expedient that the rule on which he himself acts should be universally adopted, and yet maintains that his individual act is right, as producing a greater balance of pleasure over pain than any other conduct open to him would produce.

Now we cannot fairly argue that, because a large aggregate of acts would cause more harm than good, therefore any single act of the kind will produce this effect. It may even be a straining of language to say that it has a *tendency* to produce it: no one (*e.g.*) would say that because an army walking over a bridge would break it down, therefore the crossing of a single traveller has a tendency to destroy it. And just as a prudent physician in giving rules of diet recommends an occasional deviation from them, as more conducive to the health of the body than absolute regularity; so there may be rules of social behaviour of which the general observance is necessary to the well-being of the community, while yet a certain amount of non-observance is rather advantageous than otherwise.

Here, however, we seem brought into conflict with Kant's fundamental principle, that a right action must be one of which the agent could " will the maxim to be law universal." [1] But, as was before [2] noticed in the particular case of veracity, we must admit an application of this principle, which importantly modifies its practical force : we must admit the case where the belief that the action in question will not be widely imitated is an essential qualification of the maxim which the Kantian principle is applied to test. For this principle,—at least so far as I have accepted it as self-evident—means no more than that an act, if right for any individual, must be right on general grounds, and therefore for some *class* of persons ; it therefore

---

[1] Cf. Book iii. chap. i. and chap. xiii.
[2] Book iii. chap. vii. § 3.

cannot prevent us from defining this class by the above-mentioned characteristic of believing that the act will remain an exceptional one. Of course if this belief turns out to be erroneous, serious harm may possibly result; but this is no more than may be said of many other Utilitarian deductions. Nor is it difficult to find instances of conduct which Common Sense holds to be legitimate solely on the ground that we have no fear of its being too widely imitated. Take, for example, the case of Celibacy. A universal refusal to propagate the human species would be the greatest of conceivable crimes from a Utilitarian point of view;—that is, according to the commonly accepted belief in the superiority of human happiness to that of other animals;—and hence the principle in question, applied without the qualification above given, would make it a crime in any one to choose celibacy as the state most conducive to his own happiness. But Common Sense (in the present age at least) regards such preference as within the limits of right conduct; because there is no fear that population will not be sufficiently kept up, as in fact the tendency to propagate is thought to exist rather in excess than otherwise.

In this case it is a non-moral impulse on the average strength of which we think we may reckon : but there does not appear to be any formal or universal reason why the same procedure should not be applied by Utilitarians to an actually existing moral sentiment. The result would be a discrepancy of a peculiar kind between Utilitarianism and Common - Sense morality ; as the very firmness with which the latter is estab-lished would be the Utilitarian ground for relieving the individual of its obligations. We are supposed to see that general happiness will be enhanced (just as the excellence of a metrical composition is) by a slight admixture of irregularity along with a general observance of received rules ; and hence to justify the irregular conduct of a few individuals, on the ground that the supply of regular conduct from other members of the community may reasonably be expected to be adequate.

It does not seem to me that this reasoning can be shown to be necessarily unsound, as applied to human society as at present constituted : but the cases in which it could really be thought to be applicable, by any one sincerely desirous of pro-

moting the general happiness, must certainly be rare. For it
should be observed that it makes a fundamental difference
whether the sentiment in mankind generally, on which we rely
to sustain sufficiently a general rule while admitting exceptions
thereto, is moral or non-moral; because a moral sentiment is
inseparable from the conviction that the conduct to which it
prompts is objectively right—*i.e.* right whether or not it is
thought or felt to be so—for oneself and all similar persons in
similar circumstances; it cannot therefore coexist with approval
of the contrary conduct in any one case, unless this case is
distinguished by some material difference other than the mere
non-existence in the agent of the ordinary moral sentiment
against his conduct. Thus, assuming that general unveracity
and general celibacy would both be evils of the worst kind, we
may still all regard it as legitimate for men in general to remain
celibate if they like, on account of the strength of the natural
sentiments prompting to marriage, because the existence of
these sentiments in ordinary human beings is not affected by
the universal recognition of the legitimacy of celibacy: but
we cannot similarly all regard it as legitimate for men to tell
lies if they like, however strong the actually existing sentiment
against lying may be, because as soon as this legitimacy is
generally recognised the sentiment must be expected to decay
and vanish. If therefore we were all enlightened Utilitarians,
it would be impossible for any one to justify himself in making
false statements while admitting it to be inexpedient for
persons similarly conditioned to make them; as he would have
no ground for believing that persons similarly conditioned
would act differently from himself. The case, no doubt, is
different in society as actually constituted; it is conceivable
that the practically effective morality in such a society, resting
on a basis independent of utilitarian or any other reasonings,
may not be materially affected by the particular act or expressed opinion of a particular individual: but the circumstances are, I conceive, very rare, in which a really conscientious
person could feel so sure of this as to conclude that by
approving a particular violation of a rule, of which the *general*
(though not *universal*) observance is plainly expedient, he will
not probably do harm on the whole. Especially as all the
objections to innovation, noticed in the previous section, apply

with increased force if the innovator does not even claim to be introducing a new and better general rule.

It appears to me, therefore, that the cases in which practical doubts are likely to arise, as to whether exceptions should be permitted from ordinary rules on Utilitarian principles, will mostly be those which I discussed in the first paragraph of this section : where the exceptions are not claimed for a few individuals, on the mere ground of their probable fewness, but either for persons generally under exceptional circumstances, or for a class of persons defined by exceptional qualities of intellect, temperament, or character.   In such cases the Utilitarian may have no doubt that in a community consisting generally of enlightened Utilitarians, these grounds for exceptional ethical treatment would be regarded as valid ; still he may, as I have said, doubt whether the more refined and complicated rule which recognises such exceptions is adapted for the community in which he is actually living ; and whether the attempt to introduce it is not likely to do more harm by weakening current morality than good by improving its quality.   Supposing such a doubt to arise, either in a case of this kind, or in one of the rare cases discussed in the preceding paragraph, it becomes necessary that the Utilitarian should consider carefully the extent to which his advice or example are likely to influence persons to whom they would be dangerous : and it is evident that the result of this consideration may depend largely on the degree of publicity which he gives to either advice or example. Thus, on Utilitarian principles, it may be right to do and privately recommend, under certain circumstances, what it would not be right to advocate openly ; it may be right to teach openly to one set of persons what it would be wrong to teach to others ; it may be conceivably right to do, if it can be done with comparative secrecy, what it would be wrong to do in the face of the world ; and even, if perfect secrecy can be reasonably expected, what it would be wrong to recommend by private advice or example.   These conclusions are all of a paradoxical character :[1] there is no doubt that the moral conscious-

---

[1] In particular cases, however, they seem to be admitted by Common Sense to a certain extent. For example, it would be commonly thought wrong to express in public speeches disturbing religious or political opinions which may be legitimately published in books.

ness of a plain man broadly repudiates the general notion of an esoteric morality, differing from that popularly taught; and it would be commonly agreed that an action which would be bad if done openly is not rendered good by secrecy. We may observe, however, that there are strong utilitarian reasons for maintaining generally this latter common opinion; for it is obviously advantageous, generally speaking, that acts which it is expedient to repress by social disapprobation should become known, as otherwise the disapprobation cannot operate; so that it seems inexpedient to support by any moral encouragement the natural disposition of men in general to conceal their wrong doings; besides that the concealment would in most cases have importantly injurious effects on the agent's habits of veracity. Thus the Utilitarian conclusion, carefully stated, would seem to be this; that the opinion that secrecy may render an action right which would not otherwise be so should itself be kept comparatively secret; and similarly it seems expedient that the doctrine that esoteric morality is expedient should itself be kept esoteric. Or if this concealment be difficult to maintain, it may be desirable that Common Sense should repudiate the doctrines which it is expedient to confine to an enlightened few. And thus a Utilitarian may reasonably desire, on Utilitarian principles, that some of his conclusions should be rejected by mankind generally; or even that the vulgar should keep aloof from his system as a whole, in so far as the inevitable indefiniteness and complexity of its calculations render it likely to lead to bad results in their hands.

Of course, as I have said, in an ideal community of enlightened Utilitarians this swarm of perplexities and paradoxes would vanish; as in such a society no one can have any ground for believing that other persons will act on moral principles different from those which he adopts. And any enlightened Utilitarian must of course desire this consummation; as all conflict of moral opinion must *pro tanto* be regarded as an evil, as tending to impair the force of morality generally in its resistance to seductive impulses. Still such conflict may be a necessary evil in the actual condition of civilised communities, in which there are so many different degrees of intellectual and moral development.

We have thus been led to the discussion of the question

which we reserved in the last section; viz. how Utilitarianism should deal with the fact of divergent moral opinions held simultaneously by different members of the same society.   For it has become plain that though two different kinds of conduct cannot both be right under the same circumstances, two contradictory opinions as to the rightness of conduct may possibly both be expedient ; it may conduce most to the general happiness that A should do a certain act, and at the same time that B, C, D should blame it.   The Utilitarian of course cannot really join in the disapproval, but he may think it expedient to leave it unshaken ; and at the same time may think it right, if placed in the supposed circumstances, to do the act that is generally disapproved.   And so generally it may be best on the whole that there should be conflicting codes of morality in a given society at a certain stage of its development.   And, as I have already hinted, the same general reasoning, from the probable origin of the moral sense and its flexible adjustment to the varying conditions of human life, which furnished a presumption that Common-Sense morality is roughly coincident with the Utilitarian code proper for men as now constituted, may be applied in favour of these divergent codes also : it may be said that these, too, form part of the complex adjustment of man to his circumstances, and that they are needed to supplement and qualify the morality of Common Sense.

However paradoxical this doctrine may appear, we can find cases where it seems to be implicitly accepted by Common Sense ; or at least where it is required to make Common Sense consistent with itself.   Let us consider, for example, the common moral judgments concerning rebellions.   It is commonly thought, on the one hand, that these abrupt breaches of order are sometimes morally necessary ; and, on the other hand, that they ought always to be vigorously resisted, and in case of failure punished by extreme penalties inflicted at least on the ring-leaders ; for otherwise they would be attempted under circumstances where there was no sufficient justification for them : but it seems evident that, in the actual condition of men's moral sentiments, this vigorous repression requires the support of a strong body of opinion condemning the rebels as wrong, and not merely as mistaken in their calculations of the chances of success.   For similar reasons it may possibly be expedient on the whole that certain special relaxations of certain moral rules should continue to exist in certain professions and sections of society, while at the same time they continue to be disapproved by the rest of the society. The evils, however, which must spring from this permanent conflict of opinion are so grave, that an enlightened Utilitarian will probably in most cases attempt to remove it ; by either openly maintaining the need of a relaxation of the ordinary moral rule under the special circumstances in question ; or, on the other hand, endeavouring to get the ordinary rule recognised and enforced by all conscientious persons in that section of society where its breach has become habitual. And of these two courses it seems likely that he will in most cases adopt the latter ; since such rules are most commonly found on examination to have been relaxed rather for the convenience of individuals, than in the interest of the community at large.

§ 4. Finally, let us consider the general relation of Utilitarianism to that part of common morality which extends beyond the range of strict duty ; that is, to the Ideal of character and conduct which in any community at any given time is commonly admired and praised as the sum of Excellences or Perfections. To begin, it must be allowed that this distinction between Excellence and Strict Duty does not seem properly admissible in Utilitarianism—except so far as some excellences are only partially and indirectly within the control of the will, and we require to distinguish the realisation of these in conduct from the performance of Duty proper, which is always something that *can* be done at any moment. For a Utilitarian must hold that it is always wrong for a man knowingly to do anything other than what he believes to be most conducive to Universal Happiness. Still, it seems practically expedient,—and therefore indirectly reasonable on Utilitarian principles,—to retain, in judging even the strictly voluntary conduct of others, the distinction between a part that is praiseworthy and admirable and a part that is merely right : because it is natural to us to compare any individual's character or conduct, not with our highest ideal—Utilitarian or otherwise—but with a certain average standard and to admire what rises above the standard ; and it seems ultimately conducive to the general happiness that such natural sentiments of admiration should be encouraged and developed. For human nature seems to require the double stimulus of praise and blame from others, in order to the best performance of duty that it can at present attain : so that the 'social sanction' would be less effective if it became purely penal. Indeed, since the pains of remorse and disapprobation are in themselves to be avoided, it is plain that the Utilitarian construction of a Jural morality is essentially self-limiting; that is, it prescribes its own avoidance of any department of conduct in which the addition that can be made to happiness through the enforcement of rules sustained by social penalties appears doubtful or inconsiderable. In such departments, however, the æsthetic phase of morality may still reasonably find a place ; we may properly admire and praise where it would be inexpedient to judge and condemn. We may conclude, then, that it is reasonable for a Utilitarian to praise any conduct more felicific in its tendency than what an average man would do under the given circumstances :—being aware of course that the limit down to which praiseworthiness extends must be relative to the particular state of moral progress reached by mankind generally in his age and country ; and that it is desirable to make continual efforts to elevate this standard. Similarly, the Utilitarian will praise the Dispositions or permanent qualities of character of which felicific conduct is conceived to be the result, and the Motives that are conceived to prompt to it when it would be a clear gain to the general happiness that these should become more frequent : and, as we have seen,[1] he may without inconsistency admire the Disposition or Motive if it is of a kind which it is generally desirable to encourage, even while he disapproves of the conduct to which it has led in any particular case.

Passing now to compare the contents of the Utilitarian Ideal of character with the virtues and other excellences recognised by Common Sense, we may observe, first, that general coincidence between the two on which Hume and others have insisted. No quality has ever been praised as excellent by mankind generally which cannot be shown to have some marked felicific effect, and to be within proper limits obviously conducive to the general happiness. Still, it does not follow that such qualities are always fostered and encouraged by society in the proportion

[1] Cf. chap. iii. § 2 of this Book.

which a Utilitarian would desire : in fact, it is a common observation to make, in contemplating the morality of societies other than our own, that some useful qualities are unduly neglected, while others are over-prized and even admired when they exist in such excess as to become, on the whole, infelicific. The consistent Utilitarian may therefore find it necessary to rectify the prevalent moral ideal in important particulars. And here it scarcely seems that he will find any such Utilitarian restrictions on innovation, as appeared to exist in the case of commonly received rules of duty. For the Common-Sense notions of the different excellences of conduct (considered as extending beyond the range of strict duty) are generally so vague as to offer at least no definite resistance to a Utilitarian interpretation of their scope : by teaching and acting upon such an interpretation a man is in no danger of being brought into infelicific discord with Common Sense : especially since the ideal of moral excellence seems to vary within the limits of the same community to a much greater extent than the code of strict duty. For example, a man who in an age when excessive asceticism is praised, sets an example of enjoying harmless bodily pleasures, or who in circles where useless daring is admired, prefers to exhibit and commend caution and discretion, at the worst misses some praise that he might otherwise have earned, and is thought a little dull or unaspiring : he does not come into any patent conflict with common opinion. Perhaps we may say generally that an enlightened Utilitarian is likely to lay less stress on the cultivation of those negative virtues, tendencies to restrict and refrain, which are prominent in the Common-Sense ideal of character ; and to set more value in comparison on those qualities of mind which are the direct source of positive pleasure to the agent or to others—some of which Common Sense scarcely recognises as excellences : still, he will not carry this innovation to such a pitch as to incur general condemnation. For no enlightened Utilitarian can ignore the fundamental importance of the restrictive and repressive virtues, or think that they are sufficiently developed in ordinary men at the present time, so that they may properly be excluded from moral admiration ; though he may hold that they have been too prominent, to the neglect of other valuable qualities, in the common conception of moral Perfection. Nay, we may even venture to say that, under most circumstances, a man who earnestly and successfully endeavours to realise the Utilitarian Ideal, however he may deviate from the commonly-received type of a perfect character, is likely to win sufficient recognition and praise from Common Sense. For, whether it be true or not that the whole of morality has sprung from the root of sympathy, it is certain that self-love and sympathy combined are sufficiently strong in average men to dispose them to grateful admiration of any exceptional efforts to promote the common good, even though these efforts may take a somewhat novel form. To any exhibition of more extended sympathy or more fervent public spirit than is ordinarily shown, and any attempt to develop these qualities in others, Common Sense is rarely unresponsive ; provided, of course, that these impulses are accompanied with adequate knowledge of actual circumstances and insight into the relation of means to ends, and that they do not run counter to any recognised rules of duty.[1] And it seems to be principally in this direction that the recent spread of Utilitarianism has positively modified the ideal of our society, and is likely to modify it further in the future. Hence the stress which Utilitarians are apt to lay on social and political activity of all kinds, and the tendency which Utilitarian ethics have always shown to pass over into politics. For one who values conduct in proportion to its felicific consequences, will naturally set a higher estimate on effective beneficence in public affairs than on the purest manifestation of virtue in the details of private life : while on the other hand an Intuitionist (though no doubt vaguely recognising that a man ought to do all the good he can in public affairs) still commonly holds that virtue may be as fully and as admirably exhibited on a small as on a large scale. A sincere Utilitarian, therefore, is likely to be an eager politician : but on what principles his political action ought to be determined, it scarcely lies within the scope of this treatise to investigate.

[1] We have seen that a Utilitarian may sometimes have to override these rules ; but then the case falls under the head discussed in the previous section.

CONCLUDING CHAPTER

THE MUTUAL RELATIONS OF THE THREE METHODS

§ 1. In the greater part of the treatise of which the final chapter has now been reached, we have been employed in examining three methods of determining right conduct, which are for the most part found more or less vaguely combined in the practical reasonings of ordinary men, but which it has been my aim to develop as separately as possible. A complete synthesis of these different methods is not attempted in the present work: at the same time it would hardly be satisfactory to conclude the analysis of them without some discussion of their mutual relations. Indeed we have already found it expedient to do this to a considerable extent, in the course of our examination of the separate methods. Thus, in the present and preceding Books we have directly or indirectly gone through a pretty full examination of the mutual relations of the Intuitional and Utilitarian methods. We have found that the common antithesis between Intuitionists and Utilitarians must be entirely discarded: since such abstract moral principles as we can admit to be really self-evident are not only not incompatible with a Utilitarian system, but even seem required to furnish a rational basis for such a system. Thus we have seen that the essence of Justice or Equity (in so far as it is clear and certain), is that different individuals are not to be treated differently, except on grounds of universal application; and that such grounds, again, are supplied by the principle of Universal Benevolence, that sets before each man the happiness of all others as an object of pursuit no less worthy than his own; while other time-honoured virtues seem to be fitly explained as special manifestations of impartial benevolence under various circumstances of human life, or else as habits and dispositions indispensable to the maintenance of prudent or beneficent behaviour under the seductive force of various non-rational impulses. And although there are other rules which our common moral sense when first interrogated seems to enunciate as absolutely binding; it has appeared that careful and systematic reflection on this very Common Sense, as expressed in the habitual moral judgments of ordinary men, results in exhibiting the real subordination of these rules to the fundamental principles above given. Then, further, this method of systematising particular virtues and duties receives very strong support from a comparative study of the history of morality; as the variations in the moral codes of different societies at different stages correspond, in a great measure, to differences in the actual or believed tendencies of certain kinds of conduct to promote the general happiness of different portions of the human race: while, again, the most probable conjectures as to the pre-historic condition and original derivation of the moral faculty seem to be entirely in harmony with this view. No doubt, even if this synthesis of methods be completely accepted, there will remain some discrepancy in details between our particular moral sentiments and unreasoned judgments on the one hand, and the apparent results of special utilitarian calculations on the other; and we may often have some practical difficulty in balancing the latter against the more general utilitarian reasons for obeying the former: but there seems to be no longer any theoretical perplexity as to the principles for determining social duty.

It remains for us to consider the relation of the two species of Hedonism which we have distinguished as Universalistic and Egoistic. In chap. ii. of this Book we have discussed the rational process (called by a stretch of language 'proof') by which one who holds it reasonable to aim at his own greatest happiness may be determined to take Universal Happiness instead, as his ultimate standard of right conduct. We have seen, however, that the application of this process requires that the Egoist should affirm, implicitly or explicitly, that his own greatest happiness is not merely the rational ultimate end for himself, but a part of Universal Good: and he may avoid the proof of

Utilitarianism by declining to affirm this. It would be contrary to Common Sense to deny that the distinction between any one individual and any other is real and fundamental, and that consequently " I " am concerned with the quality of my existence as an individual in a sense, fundamentally important, in which I am not concerned with the quality of the existence of other individuals : and this being so, I do not see how it can be proved that this distinction is not to be taken as fundamental in determining the ultimate end of rational action for an individual. And it may be observed that most Utilitarians, however anxious they have been to convince men of the reasonableness of aiming at happiness generally, have not commonly sought to attain this result by any logical transition from the Egoistic to the Universalistic principle. They have relied almost entirely on the Sanctions of Utilitarian rules ; that is, on the pleasures gained or pains avoided by the individual conforming to them. Indeed, if an Egoist remains impervious to what we have called Proof, the only way of rationally inducing him to aim at the happiness of all, is to show him that his own greatest happiness can be best attained by so doing. And further, even if a man admits the self-evidence of the principle of Rational Benevolence, he may still hold that his own happiness is an end which it is irrational for him to sacrifice to any other ; and that therefore a harmony between the maxim of Prudence and the maxim of Rational Benevolence must be somehow demonstrated, if morality is to be made completely rational. This latter view, indeed (as I have before said), appears to me, on the whole, the view of Common Sense : and it is that which I myself hold. It thus becomes needful to examine how far and in what way the required demonstration can be effected.

§ 2. Now, in so far as Utilitarian morality coincides with that of Common Sense—as we have seen that it does in the main—this investigation has been partly performed in chap. v. of Book ii. It there appeared that while in any tolerable state of society the performance of duties towards others and the exercise of social virtues seem *generally* likely to coincide with the attainment of the greatest possible happiness in the long run for the virtuous agent, still the *universality* and *completeness* of this coincidence are at least incapable of empirical proof :

and that, indeed, the more carefully we analyse and estimate the different sanctions—Legal, Social, and Conscientious
—considered as operating under the actual conditions of
human life, the more difficult it seems to believe that they
can be always adequate to produce this coincidence. The
natural effect of this argument upon a convinced Utilitarian
is merely to make him anxious to alter the actual conditions
of human life: and it would certainly be a most valuable
contribution to the actual happiness of mankind, if we could so
improve the adjustment of the machine of Law in any society,
and so stimulate and direct the common awards of praise and
blame, and so develop and train the moral sense of the members
of the community, as to render it clearly prudent for every individual to promote as much as possible the general good. However, we are not now considering what a consistent Utilitarian
will try to effect for the future, but what a consistent Egoist is
to do in the present. And it must be admitted that, as things
are, whatever difference exists between Utilitarian morality
and that of Common Sense is of such a kind as to render the
coincidence with Egoism still more improbable in the case of
the former. For we have seen that Utilitarianism is more
rigid than Common Sense in exacting the sacrifice of the agent's
private interests where they are incompatible with the greatest
happiness of the greatest number: and of course in so far as
the Utilitarian's principles bring him into conflict with any of
the commonly accepted rules of morality, the whole force of the
Social Sanction operates to deter him from what he conceives
to be his duty.

§ 3. There are, however, writers of the Utilitarian school [1]

---

[1] See J. S. Mill's treatise on Utilitarianism (chap. iii. *passim*): where, however,
the argument is not easy to follow, from a confusion between three different
objects of inquiry : (1) the actual effect of sympathy in inducing conformity to
the rules of Utilitarian ethics, (2) the effect in this direction which it is likely to
have in the future, (3) the value of sympathetic pleasures and pains as estimated
by an enlightened Egoist. The first and third of these questions Mill did not
clearly separate, owing to his psychological doctrine that each one's own
pleasure is the sole object of his desires. But if my refutation of this doctrine
(Book i. chap. iv. § 3) is valid, we have to distinguish two ways in which
sympathy operates : it generates sympathetic pleasures and pains, which have to
be taken into account in the calculations of Egoistic Hedonism ; but it also may
cause impulses to altruistic action, of which the force is quite out of proportion
to the sympathetic pleasure (or relief from pain) which such action seems likely

who seem to maintain or imply, that by due contemplation
of the paramount importance of Sympathy as an element of
human happiness we shall be led to see the coincidence of
the good of each with the good of all.   In opposing this view,
I am as far as possible from any wish to depreciate the value of
sympathy as a source of happiness even to human beings as at
present constituted.   Indeed I am of opinion that its pleasures
and pains really constitute a great part of that internal reward
of social virtue, and punishment of social misconduct, which in
Book ii. chap. v. I roughly set down as due to the moral sentiments.
For, in fact, though I can to some extent distinguish sympathetic from strictly moral feelings in introspective analysis of
my own consciousness, I cannot say precisely in what proportion
these two elements are combined.   For instance: I seem able
to distinguish the " sense of the ignobility of Egoism " of which
I have before spoken—which, in my view, is the normal
emotional concomitant or expression of the moral intuition that
the Good of the whole is reasonably to be preferred to the Good
of a part—from the jar of sympathetic discomfort which attends
the conscious choice of my own pleasure at the expense of pain
or loss to others; but I find it impossible to determine what
force the former sentiment would have if actually separated
from the latter, and I am inclined to think that the two kinds
of feeling are very variously combined in different individuals.
Perhaps, indeed, we may trace a general law of variation in the
relative proportion of these two elements as exhibited in the
development of the moral consciousness both in the race and in
individuals; for it seems that at a certain stage of this development the mind is more susceptible to emotions connected with
abstract moral ideas and rules presented as absolute; while
after emerging from this stage and before entering it the feelings that belong to personal relations are stronger.[1]   Certainly
in a Utilitarian's mind sympathy tends to become a prominent
element of all instinctive moral feelings that refer to social

to secure to the agent. So that even if the average man ever should reach such
a pitch of sympathetic development, as never to feel prompted to sacrifice the
general good to his own, still this will not prove that it is egoistically reasonable
for him to behave in this way.

[1] I do not mean to imply that the process of change is merely circular.   In
the earlier period sympathy is narrower, simpler, and more presentative; in the
later it is more extensive, complex, and representative.

conduct; as in his view the rational basis of the moral impulse must ultimately lie in some pleasure won or pain saved for himself or for others; so that he never has to sacrifice himself to an Impersonal Law, but always for some being or beings with whom he has at least some degree of fellow-feeling.

But besides admitting the actual importance of sympathetic pleasures to the majority of mankind, I should go further and maintain that, on empirical grounds alone, enlightened self-interest would direct most men to foster and develop their sympathetic susceptibilities to a greater extent than is now commonly attained. The effectiveness of Butler's famous argument against the vulgar antithesis between Self-love and Benevolence is undeniable: and it seems scarcely extravagant to say that, amid all the profuse waste of the means of happiness which men commit, there is no imprudence more flagrant than that of Selfishness in the ordinary sense of the term,—that excessive concentration of attention on the individual's own happiness which renders it impossible for him to feel any strong interest in the pleasures and pains of others. The perpetual prominence of self that hence results tends to deprive all enjoyments of their keenness and zest, and produce rapid satiety and *ennui*: the selfish man misses the sense of elevation and enlargement given by wide interests; he misses the more secure and serene satisfaction that attends continually on activities directed towards ends more stable in prospect than an individual's happiness can be; he misses the peculiar rich sweetness, depending upon a sort of complex reverberation of sympathy, which is always found in services rendered to those whom we love and who are grateful. He is made to feel in a thousand various ways, according to the degree of refinement which his nature has attained, the discord between the rhythms of his own life and of that larger life of which his own is but an insignificant fraction.

But allowing [1] all this, it yet seems to me as certain as any conclusion arrived at by hedonistic comparison can be, that

---

[1] I do not, however, think that we are justified in stating as *universally* true what has been admitted in the preceding paragraph. Some few thoroughly selfish persons appear at least to be happier than most of the unselfish; and there are other exceptional natures whose chief happiness seems to be derived from activity, disinterested indeed, but directed towards other ends than human happiness.

the utmost development of sympathy, intensive and extensive, which is now possible to any but a very few exceptional persons, would not cause a perfect coincidence between Utilitarian duty and self-interest. Here it seems to me that what was said in Book ii. chap. v. § 4, to show the insufficiency of the Conscientious Sanction, applies equally, *mutatis mutandis*, to Sympathy. Suppose a man finds that a regard for the general good— Utilitarian Duty—demands from him a sacrifice, or extreme risk, of life. There are perhaps one or two human beings so dear to him that the remainder of a life saved by sacrificing their happiness to his own would be worthless to him from an egoistic point of view. But it is doubtful whether many men, "sitting down in a cool hour" to make the estimate, would affirm even this: and of course that particular portion of the general happiness, for which one is called upon to sacrifice one's own, may easily be the happiness of persons not especially dear to one. But again, from this normal limitation of our keenest and strongest sympathy to a very small circle of human beings, it results that the very development of sympathy may operate to increase the weight thrown into the scale against Utilitarian duty. There are very few persons, however strongly and widely sympathetic, who are so constituted as to feel for the pleasures and pains of mankind generally a degree of sympathy at all commensurate with their concern for wife or children, or lover, or intimate friend: and if any training of the affections is at present possible which would materially alter this proportion in the general distribution of our sympathy, it scarcely seems that such a training is to be recommended as on the whole felicific.[1] And thus when Utilitarian Duty calls on us to sacrifice not only our own pleasures but the happiness of those we love to the general good, the very sanction on which Utilitarianism most relies must act powerfully in opposition to its precepts.

But even apart from these exceptional cases—which are yet sufficient to decide the abstract question—it seems that the course of conduct by which a man would most fully reap the rewards of sympathy (so far as they are empirically ascertainable) will often be very different from that to which a sincere desire to promote the general happiness would direct

[1] See chap. iii. § 3 of this Book, pp. 432-33.

him. For the relief of distress and calamity is an important part of Utilitarian duty : but as the state of the person relieved is on the whole painful, it would appear that sympathy under these circumstances must be a source of pain rather than pleasure, in proportion to its intensity. It is probably true, as a general rule, that in the relief of distress other elements of the complex pleasure of benevolence decidedly outweigh this sympathetic pain :—for the effusion of pity is itself pleasurable, and we commonly feel more keenly that amelioration of the sufferer's state which is due to our exertions than we do his pain otherwise caused, and there is further the pleasure that we derive from his gratitude, and the pleasure that is the normal reflex of activity directed under a strong impulse towards a permanently valued end. Still, when the distress is bitter and continued, and such as we can only partially mitigate by all our efforts, the philanthropist's sympathetic discomfort must necessarily be considerable ; and the work of combating misery, though not devoid of elevated happiness, will be much less happy on the whole than many other forms of activity ; while yet it may be to just this work that Duty seems to summon us. Or again, a man may find that he can best promote the general happiness by working in comparative solitude for ends that he never hopes to see realised, or by working chiefly among and for persons for whom he cannot feel much affection, or by doing what must alienate or grieve those whom he loves best, or must make it necessary for him to dispense with the most intimate of human ties. In short, there seem to be numberless ways in which the dictates of that Rational Benevolence, which as a Utilitarian he is bound absolutely to obey, may conflict with that indulgence of kind affections which Shaftesbury and his followers so persuasively exhibit as its own reward.

§ 4. It seems, then, that we must conclude, from the arguments given in Book ii. chap. v., supplemented by the discussion in the preceding section, that the inseparable connexion between Utilitarian Duty and the greatest happiness of the individual who conforms to it cannot be satisfactorily demonstrated on empirical grounds. Hence another section of the Utilitarian school has preferred to throw the weight of Duty on the Religious Sanction : and this procedure has been partly adopted by some of those who have chiefly dwelt on sympathy as a motive. From this point of view the Utilitarian Code is conceived as the Law of God, who is to be regarded as having commanded men to promote the general happiness, and as having announced an intention of rewarding those who obey His commands and punishing the disobedient. It is clear that if we feel convinced that an Omnipotent Being has, in whatever way, signified such commands and announcements, a rational egoist can want no further inducement to frame his life on Utilitarian principles. It only remains to consider how this conviction is attained. This is commonly thought to be either by supernatural Revelation, or by the natural exercise of Reason, or in both ways. As regards the former it is to be observed that—with a few exceptions—the moralists who hold that God has disclosed His law either to special individuals in past ages who have left a written record of what was revealed to them, or to a permanent succession of persons appointed in a particular manner, or to religious persons generally in some supernatural way, do not consider that it is the Utilitarian Code that has thus been revealed, but rather the rules of Common-Sense morality with some special modifications and additions. Still, as Mill has urged, in so far as Utilitarianism is more rigorous than Common Sense in exacting the sacrifice of the individual's happiness to that of mankind generally, it is strictly in accordance with the most characteristic teaching of Christianity. It seems, however, unnecessary to discuss the precise relation of different Revelational Codes to Utilitarianism, as it would be going beyond our province to investigate the grounds on which a Divine origin has been attributed to them.

In so far, however, as a knowledge of God's law is believed to be attainable by the Reason, Ethics and Theology seem to be so closely connected that we cannot sharply separate their provinces. For, as we saw,[1] it has been widely maintained, that the relation of moral rules to a Divine Lawgiver is implicitly cognised in the act of thought by which we discern these rules to be binding. And no doubt the terms (such as ' moral obligation '), which we commonly use in speaking of these

---

[1] See Book iii. chap. i. § 2 : also Book iii. chap. ii. § 1.

rules, are naturally suggestive of Legal Sanctions and so of a Sovereign by whom these are announced and enforced. Indeed many thinkers since Locke have refused to admit any other meaning in the terms Right, Duty, etc., except that of a rule imposed by a lawgiver. This view, however, seems opposed to Common Sense; as may be, perhaps, most easily shown[1] by pointing out that the Divine Lawgiver is Himself conceived as a Moral Agent; *i.e.* as prescribing what is right, and designing what is good. It is clear that in this conception at least the notions 'right' and 'good' are used absolutely, without any reference to a superior lawgiver; and that they are here used in a sense not essentially different from that which they ordinarily bear seems to be affirmed by the *consensus* of religious persons. Still, though Common Sense does not regard moral rules as being *merely* the mandates of an Omnipotent Being who will reward and punish men according as they obey or violate them; it certainly holds that this is a true though partial view of them, and perhaps that it may be intuitively apprehended. If then reflection leads us to conclude that the particular moral principles of Common Sense are to be systematised as subordinate to that pre-eminently certain and irrefragable intuition which stands as the first principle of Utilitarianism; then, of course, it will be the Utilitarian Code to which we shall believe the Divine Sanctions to be attached.

Or, again, we may argue thus. If—as all theologians agree —we are to conceive God as acting for some end, we must conceive that end to be Universal Good, and, if Utilitarians are right, Universal Happiness: and we cannot suppose that in a world morally governed it can be prudent for any man to act in conscious opposition to what we believe to be the Divine Design. Hence if in any case after calculating the consequences of two alternatives of conduct we choose that which seems likely to be less conducive to Happiness generally, we shall be acting in a manner for which we cannot but expect to suffer.

To this it has been objected, that observation of the actual world shows us that the happiness of sentient beings is so imperfectly attained in it, and with so large an intermixture of pain and misery, that we cannot really conceive Universal

[1] Cf. Book i. chap. iii. § 2.

Happiness to be God's end, unless we admit that He is not Omnipotent. And no doubt the assertion that God is omnipotent will require to be understood with some limitation; but perhaps with no greater limitation than has always been implicitly admitted by thoughtful theologians. For these seem always to have allowed that some things are impossible to God: as, for example, to change the past. And perhaps if our knowledge of the Universe were complete, we might discern the *quantum* of happiness ultimately attained in it to be as great as could be attained without the accomplishment of what we should then see to be just as inconceivable and absurd as changing the past. This, however, is a view which it belongs rather to the theologian to develop. I should rather urge that there does not seem to be any other of the ordinary interpretations of Good according to which it would appear to be more completely realised in the actual universe. For the wonderful perfections of work that we admire in the physical world are yet everywhere mingled with imperfection, and subject to destruction and decay: and similarly in the world of human conduct Virtue is at least as much balanced by Vice as Happiness is by misery.[1] So that, if the ethical reasoning that led us to interpret Ultimate Good as Happiness is sound, there seems no argument from Natural Theology to set against it.

§ 5. If, then, we may assume the existence of such a Being, as God, by the *consensus* of theologians, is conceived to be, it seems that Utilitarians may legitimately infer the existence of Divine sanctions to the code of social duty as constructed on a Utilitarian basis; and such sanctions would, of course, suffice to make it always every one's interest to promote universal happiness to the best of his knowledge. It is, however, desirable, before we conclude, to examine carefully the validity of this assumption, in so far as it is supported on ethical grounds

---

[1] It may perhaps be said that this comparison has no force for Libertarians, who consider the essence of Virtue to lie in free choice. But to say that *any* free choice is virtuous would be a paradox from which most Libertarians—admitting that Evil may be freely chosen no less than Good—would recoil. It must therefore be Free choice of good that is conceived to realise the divine end: and if so, the arguments for the utilitarian interpretation of Good—thus freely chosen—would still be applicable *mutatis mutandis*: and if so, the arguments for regarding rules of utilitarian duty as divinely sanctioned would be similarly applicable.

alone.   For by the result of such an examination will be
determined, as we now see, the very important question whether
ethical science can be constructed on an independent basis; or
whether it is forced to borrow a fundamental and indispensable
premiss from Theology or some similar source.[1]   In order
fairly to perform this examination, let us reflect upon the
clearest and most certain of our moral intuitions.   I find that I
undoubtedly seem to perceive, as clearly and certainly as I see
any axiom in Arithmetic or Geometry, that it is 'right' and
'reasonable' for me to treat others as I should think that I
myself ought to be treated under similar conditions, and to do
what I believe to be ultimately conducive to universal Good or
Happiness.   But I cannot find inseparably connected with this
conviction, and similarly attainable by mere reflective intuition,
any cognition that there actually is a Supreme Being who will
adequately[2] reward me for obeying these rules of duty, or
punish me for violating them.[3]   Or,—omitting the strictly
theological element of the proposition,—I may say that I do
not find in my moral consciousness any intuition, claiming
to be clear and certain, that the performance of duty will be
adequately rewarded and its violation punished.   I feel indeed
a desire, apparently inseparable from the moral sentiments,
that this result may be realised not only in my own case but
universally; but the mere existence of the desire would not go
far to establish the probability of its fulfilment, considering the

[1] It is not necessary, if we are simply considering Ethics as a possible
independent science, to throw the fundamental premiss of which we are now
examining the validity into a Theistic form.   Nor does it seem always to have
taken that form in the support which Positive Religion has given to Morality.
In the Buddhist creed this notion of the rewards inseparably attaching to right
conduct seems to have been developed in a far more elaborate and systematic
manner than it has in any phase of Christianity.   But, as conceived by enlightened Buddhists, these rewards are not distributed by the volition of a
Supreme Person, but by the natural operation of an impersonal Law.

[2] It may be well to remind the reader that by 'adequate' is here meant
'sufficient to make it the agent's interest to promote universal good'; not necessarily 'proportional to Desert.'

[3] I cannot fall back on the resource of thinking myself under a moral necessity to regard all my duties *as if they were* commandments of God, although not
entitled to hold speculatively that any such Supreme Being really exists.   I am
so far from feeling bound to believe for purposes of practice what I see no
ground for holding as a speculative truth, that I cannot even conceive the state
of mind which these words seem to describe, except as a momentary half-wilful
irrationality, committed in a violent access of philosophic despair.

large proportion of human desires that experience shows to be
doomed to disappointment. I also judge that in a certain sense
this result *ought* to be realised: in this judgment, however,
'ought' is not used in a strictly ethical meaning; it only
expresses the vital need that our Practical Reason feels of
proving or postulating this connexion of Virtue and self-
interest, if it is to be made consistent with itself. For the
negation of the connexion must force us to admit an ultimate
and fundamental contradiction in our apparent intuitions of
what is Reasonable in conduct; and from this admission it
would seem to follow that the apparently intuitive operation
of the Practical Reason, manifested in these contradictory
judgments, is after all illusory.

I do not mean that if we gave up the hope of attaining a
practical solution of this fundamental contradiction, through
any legitimately obtained conclusion or postulate as to the
moral order of the world, it would become reasonable for us
to abandon morality altogether: but it would seem necessary
to abandon the idea of rationalising it completely. We should
doubtless still, not only from self-interest, but also through
sympathy and sentiments protective of social wellbeing, im-
parted by education and sustained by communication with
other men, feel a desire for the general observance of rules
conducive to general happiness; and practical reason would
still impel us decisively to the performance of duty in the more
ordinary cases in which what is recognised as duty is in harmony with self-interest properly understood. But in the rarer
cases of a recognised conflict between self-interest and duty,
practical reason, being divided against itself, would cease to be
a motive on either side; the conflict would have to be decided
by the comparative preponderance of one or other of two
groups of non-rational impulses.

If then the reconciliation of duty and self-interest is to be
regarded as a hypothesis logically necessary to avoid a fundamental contradiction in one chief department of our thought, it
remains to ask how far this necessity constitutes a sufficient
reason for accepting this hypothesis. This, however, is a profoundly difficult and controverted question, the discussion of
which belongs rather to a treatise on General Philosophy than
to a work on the Methods of Ethics: as it could not be

satisfactorily answered, without a general examination of the criteria of true and false beliefs. Those who hold that the edifice of physical science is really constructed of conclusions logically inferred from self-evident premises, may reasonably demand that any practical judgments claiming philosophic certainty should be based on an equally firm foundation. If on the other hand we find that in our supposed knowledge of the world of nature propositions are commonly taken to be universally true, which yet seem to rest on no other grounds than that we have a strong disposition to accept them, and that they are indispensable to the systematic coherence of our beliefs,—it will be more difficult to reject a similarly supported assumption in ethics, without opening the door to universal scepticism.

APPENDIX

THE KANTIAN CONCEPTION OF FREE WILL

[*Reprinted, with some omissions, from* MIND, *1888, Vol. XIII., No. 51.*]

MY aim is to show that, in different parts of Kant's exposition of his doctrine, two essentially different conceptions are expressed by the same word freedom; while yet Kant does not appear to be conscious of any variation in the meaning of the term.

[In the one sense, Freedom = Rationality, so that a man is free in proportion as he acts in accordance with Reason.] I do not in the least object to this use of the term Freedom, on account of its deviation from ordinary usage. On the contrary, I think it has much support in men's natural expression of ordinary moral experience in discourse. In the conflict that is continually going on in all of us, between non-rational impulses and what we recognise as dictates of practical reason, we are in the habit of identifying ourselves with the latter rather than with the former: as Whewell says, "we speak of Desire, Love, Anger, as mastering us, and of ourselves as controlling them"—we continually call men "slaves" of appetite or passion, whereas no one was ever called a slave of reason. If, therefore, the term Freedom had not already been appropriated by moralists to another meaning—if it were merely a question of taking it from ordinary discourse and stamping it with greater precision for purposes of ethical discussion—I should make no objection to the statement that "a man is a free agent in proportion as he acts rationally." But, what English defenders of man's free agency have generally been concerned to maintain, is that "man has a freedom of *choice* between good and evil," which is realised or manifested when he deliberately chooses evil just as much as when he deliberately chooses good; and it is clear that if we say that a man is a free agent in proportion as he acts rationally, we cannot also say, in the same sense of the term, that it is by his free choice that he acts irrationally when he does so act. The notions of Freedom must be admitted to be fundamentally different in the two statements: and though usage might fairly allow the word Freedom to represent either notion, if only one or other of the above-mentioned propositions were affirmed, to use it to represent both, in affirming both propositions, is obviously inconvenient; and it implies a confusion of thought so to use it, without pointing out the difference of meaning.

If this be admitted, the next thing is to show that Kant does use the term in this double way. In arguing this, it will be convenient to have names for what we admit to be two distinct ideas. Accordingly, the kind of freedom which I first mentioned—which a man is said to manifest more in proportion as he acts more under the guidance of reason—shall be referred to as 'Good' or 'Rational Freedom,' and the freedom that is manifested in choosing between good and evil shall be called 'Neutral' or 'Moral Freedom.' [1]

But before I proceed to the different passages of Kant's exposition in which 'Good Freedom' and 'Neutral Freedom' respectively occur, it seems desirable to distinguish this latter from a wider notion with which it may possibly be confounded, and which it would be clearly wrong to attribute to Kant. I mean the "power of acting without a motive," which Reid and other writers, on what used to be called the Libertarian side, have thought it necessary to claim. "If a man could not act without a motive," says Reid, "he could have no power"—that is, in Reid's meaning, no free agency—"at all." This conception of Freedom —which I may conveniently distinguish as 'Capricious Freedom'—is, as I said, certainly not Kantian : not only does he expressly repudiate it, but nowhere—so far as I know—does he unconsciously introduce it. Indeed it is incompatible with any and every part of his explanation of human volition : the originality and interest of his defence of Neutral Freedom—the power of choice between good and evil—lies in its complete avoidance of Capricious Freedom or the power of acting without a motive *in any particular volition.*

[This] distinction helps me to understand how [it is that] many intelligent readers have failed to see in Kant's exposition the two Freedoms—Good or Rational Freedom and Neutral or Moral Freedom—which I find in Kant. They have their view fixed on the difference between Rational or Moral Freedom, which Kant maintains, and the Freedom of Caprice, which he undoubtedly repudiates : and are thus led to overlook with him the distinction between the Freedom that we realise or manifest in proportion as we do right, and the Freedom that is realised or manifested equally in choosing either right or wrong. When we have once put completely out of view the Freedom of Caprice, the power of acting without a motive, or against the strongest motive when the competition is among merely natural or non-rational desires or aversions,—when we have agreed to exclude this, and to concentrate attention on the difference between Good Freedom and Neutral Freedom—I venture to think that no one can avoid seeing each member of this latter antithesis in Kant. It will be easily understood that, as he does not himself distinguish the two conceptions, it is naturally impossible for the most careful reader always to tell which is to be understood ; but there are many passages where his argument unmistakably requires the one, and many other

---

[1] The terms 'rational' and 'moral' seem to me most appropriate when I wish to suggest the affinity between the two notions : the terms 'good' and 'neutral' seem preferable when I wish to lay stress on the difference.

passages where it unmistakably requires the other. Speaking broadly, I may say that, wherever Kant has to connect the notion of Freedom with that of Moral Responsibility or moral imputation, he, like all other moralists who have maintained Free Will in this connexion, means (chiefly, but not solely) Neutral Freedom—Freedom exhibited in choosing wrong as much as in choosing right. Indeed, in such passages it is with the Freedom of the wrong-chooser that he is primarily concerned : since it is the wrong-chooser that he especially wishes to prevent from shifting his responsibility on to causes beyond his control. On the other hand, when what he has to prove is the possibility of disinterested obedience to Law as such, without the intervention of sensible impulses, when he seeks to exhibit the independence of Reason in influencing choice, then in many though not all his statements he explicitly identifies Freedom with this independence of Reason, and thus clearly implies the proposition that a man is free in proportion as he acts rationally.

As an example of the first kind, I will take the passage towards the close of chap. iii. of the "Analytic of Practical Reason,"[1] where he treats, in its bearing on Moral Responsibility, his peculiar metaphysical doctrine of a double kind of causation in human actions. According to Kant, every such action, regarded as a phenomenon determined in time, must be thought as a necessary result of determining causes in antecedent time—otherwise its existence would be inconceivable—but it may be also regarded in relation to the agent considered as a thing-in-himself, as the "noümenon" of which the action is a phenomenon : and the conception of Freedom may be applied to the agent so considered in relation to his phenomena. For since his existence as a noümenon is not subject to time-conditions, nothing in this noümenal existence comes under the principle of determination by antecedent causes : hence, as Kant says, "in this his existence nothing is antecedent to the determination of his will, but every action . . . even the whole series of his existence as a sensible being, is in the consciousness of his supersensible existence nothing but the result of his causality as a noümenon." This is the well-known metaphysical solution of the difficulty of reconciling Free Will with the Universality of physical causation : I am not now concerned to criticise it,—my point is that if we accept this view of Freedom at all, it must obviously be Neutral Freedom : it must express the relation of a noümenon that manifests itself as a scoundrel to a series of bad volitions, in which the moral law is violated, no less than the relation of a noümenon that manifests itself as a saint to good or rational volitions, in which the moral law or categorical imperative is obeyed. And, as I before said, Kant in this passage—being especially concerned to explain the possibility of moral imputation, and justify the judicial sentences of conscience—especially takes as his illustrations noümena that exhibit bad phenomena. The question he expressly raises is "How a man who commits a theft" can "be called quite free" at the moment of committing it ? and answers that it is in virtue of his "transcendental freedom" that "the rational being can justly say of *every unlawful action* that he performs that he could very well have left it undone," although as

[1] *Werke*, v. pp. 100-104 (Hartenstein).

phenomenon it is determined by antecedents, and so necessary; "for it, with all the past which determines it, belongs to the one single phenomenon of his character which he makes for himself, in consequence of which he imputes to himself" the bad actions that result necessarily from his bad character taken in conjunction with other causes. Hence, however he may account for his error from bad habits which he has allowed to grow on him, whatever art he may use to paint to himself an unlawful act he remembers as something in which he was carried away by the stream of physical necessity, this cannot protect him from self-reproach: —not even if he have shown depravity so early that he may reasonably be thought to have been born in a morally hopeless condition—he will still be rightly judged, and will judge himself "just as responsible as any other man": since in relation to his noümenal self his life as a whole, from first to last, is to be regarded as a single phenomenon resulting from an absolutely free choice.

I need not labour this point further; it is evident that the necessities of Kant's metaphysical explanation of moral responsibility make him express with peculiar emphasis and fulness the notion of what I have called Neutral Freedom, a kind of causality manifested in bad and irrational volitions no less than in the good and rational.

On the other hand, it is no less easy to find passages in which the term Freedom seems to me most distinctly to stand for Good or Rational Freedom. Indeed, such passages are, I think, more frequent than those in which the other meaning is plainly required. Thus he tells us that "a free will must find its principle of determination in the [moral] 'Law,'" [1] and that "freedom, whose causality can be determined only by the law, consists just in this, that it restricts all inclinations by the condition of obedience to pure law." [2] Whereas, in the argument previously examined, his whole effort was to prove that the noümenon or supersensible being, of which each volition is a phenomenon, exercises "free causality" in unlawful acts, he tells us elsewhere, in the same treatise, that the "supersensible nature" of rational beings, who have also a "sensible nature," is their "existence according to laws which are independent of every empirical condition, and therefore belong to the autonomy of pure [practical] reason." [3] Similarly, in an earlier work, he explains that "since the conception of causality involves that of laws . . . though freedom is not a property of the will depending on physical laws, yet it is not for that reason lawless; on the contrary, it must be a causality according to immutable laws, but of a peculiar kind; otherwise, a free will would be a chimæra (Unding)." [4] And this immutable law of the "free" or "autonomous" will is, as he goes on to say, the fundamental principle of morality, "so that a free will and a will subject to moral laws are one and the same."

I have quoted this last phrase, not because it clearly exhibits the notion of Rational Freedom,—on the contrary, it rather shows how easily this notion may be confounded with the other. A will subject to its own moral laws *may* mean a will that, so far as free, conforms to these laws; but it also *may* be conceived as capable of freely disobeying these

[1] *Werke*, **v.** p. 30.   [2] *Ibid.* p. 83.   [3] *Ibid.* p. 46.   [4] *Werke*, iv. p. 294.

laws—exercising Neutral Freedom. But when Freedom is said to be a "causality according to immutable laws" the ambiguity is dispelled; for this evidently cannot mean merely a faculty of laying down laws which may or may not be obeyed; it must mean that the will, *quâ* free, acts in accordance with these laws;—the human being, doubtless, often acts contrary to them; but then, according to this view, its choice in such actions is determined not "freely" but "mechanically," by "physical" and "empirical" springs of action.

If any further argument is necessary to show that Kantian "Freedom" must sometimes be understood as Rational or Good Freedom, I may quote one or two of the numerous passages in which Kant, either expressly or by implication, identifies Will and Reason; for this identification obviously excludes the possibility of Will's choosing between Reason and non-rational impulses. Thus in the *Grundlegung zur Metaphysik der Sitten*,[1] he tells us that "as Reason is required to deduce actions from laws, Will is nothing but pure practical reason"; and, similarly, in the *Kritik der praktischen Vernunft*, he speaks of the "objective reality of a pure Will or, *which is the same thing*, a pure practical reason."[2] Accordingly, whereas in some passages[3] the "autonomy" which he identifies with "Freedom" is spoken of as "autonomy of *will*," in others we are told that the "moral law expresses nothing else than autonomy of the pure practical *reason*: that is, Freedom."[4]

I think that I have now established the verbal ambiguity that I undertook to bring home to Kant's account of Free Will; I have shown that in his exposition this fundamental term oscillates between incompatible meanings. But it may, perhaps, be thought that the defect thus pointed out can be cured by a merely verbal correction: that the substance of Kant's ethical doctrine may still be maintained, and may still be connected with his metaphysical doctrine. It may still be held that Reason dictates that we should at all times act from a maxim that we can will to be a universal law, and that we should do this from pure regard for reason and reason's law, admitting that it is a law which we are free to disobey; and it may still be held that the reality of this moral freedom is to be reconciled with the universality of physical causation by conceiving it as a relation between the agent's noümenal self—independent of time-conditions—and his character as manifested in time; the only correction required being to avoid identifying Freedom and Goodness or Rationality as attributes of agents or actions.

I should quite admit that the most important parts both of Kant's doctrine of morality, and of his doctrine of Freedom may be saved:—or I should perhaps rather say that the latter may be left to conduct an unequal struggle with the modern notions of heredity and evolution: at any rate I admit that it is not fundamentally affected by my present

---

[1] *Werke*, iv. p. 260 (Hartenstein).

[2] *Werke*, v. p. 58. See an acute discussion of Kant's perplexing use of the term "Will" in Prof. Schurman's *Kantian Ethics*, which has anticipated me in the above quotations.

[3] *E.g. Werke*, iv. p. 296.

[4] *E.g. Werke*, v. p. 35.

argument. But I think that a good deal more will have to go from a corrected edition of Kantism than merely the " word " Freedom in certain passages, if the confusion introduced by the ambiguity of this word is to be eliminated in the manner that I have suggested. I think that the whole topic of the " heteronomy " of the will, when it yields to empirical or sensible impulses, will have to be abandoned or profoundly modified. And I am afraid that most readers of Kant will feel the loss to be serious ; since nothing in Kant's ethical writing is more fascinating than the idea— which he expresses repeatedly in various forms—that a man realises the aim of his true self when he obeys the moral law, whereas, when he wrongly allows his action to be determined by empirical or sensible stimuli, he becomes subject to physical causation, to laws of a brute outer world. But if we dismiss the identification of Freedom and Rationality, and accept definitely and singly Kant's other notion of Freedom as expressing the relation of the human thing-in-itself to its phenomenon, I am afraid that this spirit-stirring appeal to the sentiment of Liberty must be dismissed as idle rhetoric. For the life of the saint must be as much subject—in any particular portion of it—to the necessary laws of physical causation as the life of the scoundrel : and the scoundrel must exhibit and express his characteristic self-hood in his transcendental choice of a bad life, as much as the saint does in his transcendental choice of a good one. If, on the other hand, to avoid this result, we take the other horn of the dilemma, and identify inner freedom with rationality, than a more serious excision will be required. For, along with 'Neutral' or 'Moral' Freedom, the whole Kantian view of the relation of the noümenon to the empirical character will have to be dropped, and with it must go the whole Kantian method of maintaining moral responsibility and moral imputation : in fact, all that has made Kant's doctrine interesting and impressive to English advocates of Free Will (in the ordinary sense), even when they have not been convinced of its soundness.

INDEX

517

SOME DOVER SCIENCE BOOKS

SOME DOVER SCIENCE BOOKS

WHAT IS SCIENCE?,
Norman Campbell
This excellent introduction explains scientific method, role of mathematics, types of scientific laws. Contents: 2 aspects of science, science & nature, laws of science, discovery of laws, explanation of laws, measurement & numerical laws, applications of science. 192pp. 5⅜ x 8.   60043-2 Paperbound $1.25

FADS AND FALLACIES IN THE NAME OF SCIENCE,
Martin Gardner
Examines various cults, quack systems, frauds, delusions which at various times have masqueraded as science. Accounts of hollow-earth fanatics like Symmes; Velikovsky and. wandering planets; Hoerbiger; Bellamy and the theory of multiple moons; Charles Fort; dowsing, pseudoscientific methods for finding water, ores, oil. Sections on naturopathy, iridiagnosis, zone therapy, food fads, etc. Analytical accounts of Wilhelm Reich and orgone sex energy; L. Ron Hubbard and Dianetics; A. Korzybski and General Semantics; many others. Brought up to date to include Bridey Murphy, others. Not just a collection of anecdotes, but a fair, reasoned appraisal of eccentric theory. Formerly titled *In the Name of Science*. Preface. Index. x + 384pp. 5⅜ x 8.
20394-8 Paperbound $2.00

PHYSICS, THE PIONEER SCIENCE,
L. W. Taylor
First thorough text to place all important physical phenomena in cultural-historical framework; remains best work of its kind. Exposition of physical laws, theories developed chronologically, with great historical, illustrative experiments diagrammed, described, worked out mathematically. Excellent physics text for self-study as well as class work. Vol. 1: Heat, Sound: motion, acceleration, gravitation, conservation of energy, heat engines, rotation, heat, mechanical energy, etc. 211 illus. 407pp. 5⅜ x 8. Vol. 2: Light, Electricity: images, lenses, prisms, magnetism, Ohm's law, dynamos, telegraph, quantum theory, decline of mechanical view of nature, etc. Bibliography. 13 table appendix. Index. 551 illus. 2 color plates. 508pp. 5⅜ x 8.
60565-5, 60566-3 Two volume set, paperbound $5.50

THE EVOLUTION OF SCIENTIFIC THOUGHT FROM NEWTON TO EINSTEIN,
A. d'Abro
Einstein's special and general theories of relativity, with their historical implications, are analyzed in non-technical terms. Excellent accounts of the contributions of Newton, Riemann, Weyl, Planck, Eddington, Maxwell, Lorentz and others are treated in terms of space and time, equations of electromagnetics, finiteness of the universe, methodology of science. 21 diagrams. 482pp. 5⅜ x 8.
20002-7 Paperbound $2.50

CHANCE, LUCK AND STATISTICS: THE SCIENCE OF CHANCE,
Horace C. Levinson
Theory of probability and science of statistics in simple, non-technical language. Part I deals with theory of probability, covering odd superstitions in regard to "luck," the meaning of betting odds, the law of mathematical expectation, gambling, and applications in poker, roulette, lotteries, dice, bridge, and other games of chance. Part II discusses the misuse of statistics, the concept of statistical probabilities, normal and skew frequency distributions, and statistics applied to various fields—birth rates, stock speculation, insurance rates, advertising, etc. "Presented in an easy humorous style which I consider the best kind of expository writing," Prof. A. C. Cohen, Industry Quality Control. Enlarged revised edition. Formerly titled *The Science of Chance*. Preface and two new appendices by the author. xiv + 365pp. 5⅜ x 8. 21007-3 Paperbound $2.00

BASIC ELECTRONICS,
prepared by the U.S. Navy Training Publications Center
A thorough and comprehensive manual on the fundamentals of electronics. Written clearly, it is equally useful for self-study or course work for those with a knowledge of the principles of basic electricity. Partial contents: Operating Principles of the Electron Tube; Introduction to Transistors; Power Supplies for Electronic Equipment; Tuned Circuits; Electron-Tube Amplifiers; Audio Power Amplifiers; Oscillators; Transmitters; Transmission Lines; Antennas and Propagation; Introduction to Computers; and related topics. Appendix. Index. Hundreds of illustrations and diagrams. vi + 471pp. 6½ x 9¼.
61076-4 Paperbound $2.95

BASIC THEORY AND APPLICATION OF TRANSISTORS,
prepared by the U.S. Department of the Army
An introductory manual prepared for an army training program. One of the finest available surveys of theory and application of transistor design and operation. Minimal knowledge of physics and theory of electron tubes required. Suitable for textbook use, course supplement, or home study. Chapters: Introduction; fundamental theory of transistors; transistor amplifier fundamentals; parameters, equivalent circuits, and characteristic curves; bias stabilization; transistor analysis and comparison using characteristic curves and charts; audio amplifiers; tuned amplifiers; wide-band amplifiers; oscillators; pulse and switching circuits; modulation, mixing, and demodulation; and additional semiconductor devices. Unabridged, corrected edition. 240 schematic drawings, photographs, wiring diagrams, etc. 2 Appendices. Glossary. Index. 263pp. 6½ x 9¼. 60380-6 Paperbound $1.75

GUIDE TO THE LITERATURE OF MATHEMATICS AND PHYSICS,
N. G. Parke III
Over 5000 entries included under approximately 120 major subject headings of selected most important books, monographs, periodicals, articles in English, plus important works in German, French, Italian, Spanish, Russian (many recently available works). Covers every branch of physics, math, related engineering. Includes author, title, edition, publisher, place, date, number of volumes, number of pages. A 40-page introduction on the basic problems of research and study provides useful information on the organization and use of libraries, the psychology of learning, etc. This reference work will save you hours of time. 2nd revised edition. Indices of authors, subjects, 464pp. 5⅜ x 8.
60447-0 Paperbound $2.75

A SOURCE BOOK IN MATHEMATICS,
D. E. Smith
Great discoveries in math, from Renaissance to end of 19th century, in English translation. Read announcements by Dedekind, Gauss, Delamain, Pascal, Fermat, Newton, Abel, Lobachevsky, Bolyai, Riemann, De Moivre, Legendre, Laplace, others of discoveries about imaginary numbers, number congruence, slide rule, equations, symbolism, cubic algebraic equations, non-Euclidean forms of geometry, calculus, function theory, quaternions, etc. Succinct selections from 125 different treatises, articles, most unavailable elsewhere in English. Each article preceded by biographical introduction. Vol. I: Fields of Number, Algebra. Index. 32 illus. 338pp. 5⅜ x 8. Vol. II: Fields of Geometry, Probability, Calculus, Functions, Quaternions. 83 illus. 432pp. 5⅜ x 8.
60552-3, 60553-1 Two volume set, paperbound $5.00

FOUNDATIONS OF PHYSICS,
R. B. Lindsay & H. Margenau
Excellent bridge between semi-popular works & technical treatises. A discussion of methods of physical description, construction of theory; valuable for physicist with elementary calculus who is interested in ideas that give meaning to data, tools of modern physics. Contents include symbolism; mathematical equations; space & time foundations of mechanics; probability; physics & continua; electron theory; special & general relativity; quantum mechanics; causality. "Thorough and yet not overdetailed. Unreservedly recommended," *Nature* (London). Unabridged, corrected edition. List of recommended readings. 35 illustrations. xi + 537pp. 5⅜ x 8.
60377-6 Paperbound $3.50

FUNDAMENTAL FORMULAS OF PHYSICS,
ed. by D. H. Menzel
High useful, full, inexpensive reference and study text, ranging from simple to highly sophisticated operations. Mathematics integrated into text—each chapter stands as short textbook of field represented. Vol. 1: Statistics, Physical Constants, Special Theory of Relativity, Hydrodynamics, Aerodynamics, Boundary Value Problems in Math, Physics, Viscosity, Electromagnetic Theory, etc. Vol. 2: Sound, Acoustics, Geometrical Optics, Electron Optics, High-Energy Phenomena, Magnetism, Biophysics, much more. Index. Total of 800pp. 5⅜ x 8.
60595-7, 60596-5 Two volume set, paperbound $4.75

THEORETICAL PHYSICS,
A. S. Kompaneyets
One of the very few thorough studies of the subject in this price range. Provides advanced students with a comprehensive theoretical background. Especially strong on recent experimentation and developments in quantum theory. Contents: Mechanics (Generalized Coordinates, Lagrange's Equation, Collision of Particles, etc.), Electrodynamics (Vector Analysis, Maxwell's equations, Transmission of Signals, Theory of Relativity, etc.), Quantum Mechanics (the Inadequacy of Classical Mechanics, the Wave Equation, Motion in a Central Field, Quantum Theory of Radiation, Quantum Theories of Dispersion and Scattering, etc.), and Statistical Physics (Equilibrium Distribution of Molecules in an Ideal Gas, Boltzmann Statistics, Bose and Fermi Distribution. Thermodynamic Quantities, etc.). Revised to 1961. Translated by George Yankovsky, authorized by Kompaneyets. 137 exercises. 56 figures. 529pp. 5⅜ x 8½.
60972-3 Paperbound $3.50

COLLEGE ALGEBRA, *H. B. Fine*
Standard college text that gives a systematic and deductive structure to algebra; comprehensive, connected, with emphasis on theory. Discusses the commutative, associative, and distributive laws of number in unusual detail, and goes on with undetermined coefficients, quadratic equations, progressions, logarithms, permutations, probability, power series, and much more. Still most valuable elementary-intermediate text on the science and structure of algebra. Index. 1560 problems, all with answers. x + 631pp. 5⅜ x 8. 60211-7 Paperbound $2.75

HIGHER MATHEMATICS FOR STUDENTS OF CHEMISTRY AND PHYSICS, *J. W. Mellor*
Not abstract, but practical, building its problems out of familiar laboratory material, this covers differential calculus, coordinate, analytical geometry, functions, integral calculus, infinite series, numerical equations, differential equations, Fourier's theorem, probability, theory of errors, calculus of variations, determinants. "If the reader is not familiar with this book, it will repay him to examine it," *Chem. & Engineering News*. 800 problems. 189 figures. Bibliography. xxi + 641pp. 5⅜ x 8. 60193-5 Paperbound $3.50

TRIGONOMETRY REFRESHER FOR TECHNICAL MEN, *A. A. Klaf*
A modern question and answer text on plane and spherical trigonometry. Part I covers plane trigonometry: angles, quadrants, trigonometrical functions, graphical representation, interpolation, equations, logarithms, solution of triangles, slide rules, etc. Part II discusses applications to navigation, surveying, elasticity, architecture, and engineering. Small angles, periodic functions, vectors, polar coordinates, De Moivre's theorem, fully covered. Part III is devoted to spherical trigonometry and the solution of spherical triangles, with applications to terrestrial and astronomical problems. Special time-savers for numerical calculation. 913 questions answered for you! 1738 problems; answers to odd numbers. 494 figures. 14 pages of functions, formulae. Index. x + 629pp. 5⅜ x 8. 20371-9 Paperbound $3.00

CALCULUS REFRESHER FOR TECHNICAL MEN, *A. A. Klaf*
Not an ordinary textbook but a unique refresher for engineers, technicians, and students. An examination of the most important aspects of differential and integral calculus by means of 756 key questions. Part I covers simple differential calculus: constants, variables, functions, increments, derivatives, logarithms, curvature, etc. Part II treats fundamental concepts of integration: inspection, substitution, transformation, reduction, areas and volumes, mean value, successive and partial integration, double and triple integration. Stresses practical aspects! A 50 page section gives applications to civil and nautical engineering, electricity, stress and strain, elasticity, industrial engineering, and similar fields. 756 questions answered. 556 problems; solutions to odd numbers. 36 pages of constants, formulae. Index. v + 431pp. 5⅜ x 8. 20370-0 Paperbound $2.25

INTRODUCTION TO THE THEORY OF GROUPS OF FINITE ORDER, *R. Carmichael*
Examines fundamental theorems and their application. Beginning with sets, systems, permutations, etc., it progresses in easy stages through important types of groups: Abelian, prime power, permutation, etc. Except 1 chapter where matrices are desirable, no higher math needed. 783 exercises, problems. Index. xvi + 447pp. 5⅜ x 8. 60300-8 Paperbound $3.00

NUMERICAL SOLUTIONS OF DIFFERENTIAL EQUATIONS,
H. Levy & E. A. Baggott
Comprehensive collection of methods for solving ordinary differential equations of first and higher order. All must pass 2 requirements: easy to grasp and practical, more rapid than school methods. Partial contents: graphical integration of differential equations, graphical methods for detailed solution. Numerical solution. Simultaneous equations and equations of 2nd and higher orders. "Should be in the hands of all in research in applied mathematics, teaching," *Nature*. 21 figures. viii + 238pp. 5⅜ x 8.   60168-4 Paperbound $1.85

ELEMENTARY STATISTICS, WITH APPLICATIONS IN MEDICINE AND THE BIOLOGICAL SCIENCES, *F. E. Croxton*
A sound introduction to statistics for anyone in the physical sciences, assuming no prior acquaintance and requiring only a modest knowledge of math. All basic formulas carefully explained and illustrated; all necessary reference tables included. From basic terms and concepts, the study proceeds to frequency distribution, linear, non-linear, and multiple correlation, skewness, kurtosis, etc. A large section deals with reliability and significance of statistical methods. Containing concrete examples from medicine and biology, this book will prove unusually helpful to workers in those fields who increasingly must evaluate, check, and interpret statistics. Formerly titled "Elementary Statistics with Applications in Medicine." 101 charts. 57 tables. 14 appendices. Index. vi + 376pp. 5⅜ x 8.   60506-X Paperbound $2.25

INTRODUCTION TO SYMBOLIC LOGIC,
S. Langer
No special knowledge of math required — probably the clearest book ever written on symbolic logic, suitable for the layman, general scientist, and philosopher. You start with simple symbols and advance to a knowledge of the Boole-Schroeder and Russell-Whitehead systems. Forms, logical structure, classes, the calculus of propositions, logic of the syllogism, etc. are all covered. "One of the clearest and simplest introductions," *Mathematics Gazette*. Second enlarged, revised edition. 368pp. 5⅜ x 8.   60164-1 Paperbound $2.25

A SHORT ACCOUNT OF THE HISTORY OF MATHEMATICS,
W. W. R. Ball
Most readable non-technical history of mathematics treats lives, discoveries of every important figure from Egyptian, Phoenician, mathematicians to late 19th century. Discusses schools of Ionia, Pythagoras, Athens, Cyzicus, Alexandria, Byzantium, systems of numeration; primitive arithmetic; Middle Ages, Renaissance, including Arabs, Bacon, Regiomontanus, Tartaglia, Cardan, Stevinus, Galileo, Kepler; modern mathematics of Descartes, Pascal, Wallis, Huygens, Newton, Leibnitz, d'Alembert, Euler, Lambert, Laplace, Legendre, Gauss, Hermite, Weierstrass, scores more. Index. 25 figures. 546pp. 5⅜ x 8.
20630-0 Paperbound $2.75

INTRODUCTION TO NONLINEAR DIFFERENTIAL AND INTEGRAL EQUATIONS,
Harold T. Davis
Aspects of the problem of nonlinear equations, transformations that lead to equations solvable by classical means, results in special cases, and useful generalizations. Thorough, but easily followed by mathematically sophisticated reader who knows little about non-linear equations. 137 problems for student to solve. xv + 566pp. 5⅜ x 8½.   60971-5 Paperbound $2.75

FIVE VOLUME "THEORY OF FUNCTIONS" SET BY KONRAD KNOPP

This five-volume set, prepared by Konrad Knopp, provides a complete and readily followed account of theory of functions. Proofs are given concisely, yet without sacrifice of completeness or rigor. These volumes are used as texts by such universities as M.I.T., University of Chicago, N. Y. City College, and many others. "Excellent introduction . . . remarkably readable, concise, clear, rigorous," *Journal of the American Statistical Association*.

ELEMENTS OF THE THEORY OF FUNCTIONS,
Konrad Knopp
This book provides the student with background for further volumes in this set, or texts on a similar level. Partial contents: foundations, system of complex numbers and the Gaussian plane of numbers, Riemann sphere of numbers, mapping by linear functions, normal forms, the logarithm, the cyclometric functions and binomial series. "Not only for the young student, but also for the student who knows all about what is in it," *Mathematical Journal*. Bibliography. Index. 140pp. 5⅜ x 8. 60154-4 Paperbound $1.50

THEORY OF FUNCTIONS, PART I,
Konrad Knopp
With volume II, this book provides coverage of basic concepts and theorems. Partial contents: numbers and points, functions of a complex variable, integral of a continuous function, Cauchy's integral theorem, Cauchy's integral formulae, series with variable terms, expansion of analytic functions in power series, analytic continuation and complete definition of analytic functions, entire transcendental functions, Laurent expansion, types of singularities. Bibliography. Index. vii + 146pp. 5⅜ x 8. 60156-0 Paperbound $1.50

THEORY OF FUNCTIONS, PART II,
Konrad Knopp
Application and further development of general theory, special topics. Single valued functions. Entire, Weierstrass, Meromorphic functions. Riemann surfaces. Algebraic functions. Analytical configuration, Riemann surface. Bibliography. Index. x + 150pp. 5⅜ x 8. 60157-9 Paperbound $1.50

PROBLEM BOOK IN THE THEORY OF FUNCTIONS, VOLUME 1.
Konrad Knopp
Problems in elementary theory, for use with Knopp's *Theory of Functions*, or any other text, arranged according to increasing difficulty. Fundamental concepts, sequences of numbers and infinite series, complex variable, integral theorems, development in series, conformal mapping. 182 problems. Answers. viii + 126pp. 5⅜ x 8. 60158-7 Paperbound $1.50

PROBLEM BOOK IN THE THEORY OF FUNCTIONS, VOLUME 2,
Konrad Knopp
Advanced theory of functions, to be used either with Knopp's *Theory of Functions*, or any other comparable text. Singularities, entire & meromorphic functions, periodic, analytic, continuation, multiple-valued functions, Riemann surfaces, conformal mapping. Includes a section of additional elementary problems. "The difficult task of selecting from the immense material of the modern theory of functions the problems just within the reach of the beginner is here masterfully accomplished," *Am. Math. Soc.* Answers. 138pp. 5⅜ x 8. 60159-5 Paperbound $1.50

PRINCIPLES OF STRATIGRAPHY,
A. W. Grabau
Classic of 20th century geology, unmatched in scope and comprehensiveness. Nearly 600 pages cover the structure and origins of every kind of sedimentary, hydrogenic, oceanic, pyroclastic, atmoclastic, hydroclastic, marine hydroclastic, and bioclastic rock; metamorphism; erosion; etc. Includes also the constitution of the atmosphere; morphology of oceans, rivers, glaciers; volcanic activities; faults and earthquakes; and fundamental principles of paleontology (nearly 200 pages). New introduction by Prof. M. Kay, Columbia U. 1277 bibliographical entries. 264 diagrams. Tables, maps, etc. Two volume set. Total of xxxii + 1185pp. 5⅜ x 8.   60686-4, 60687-2 Two volume set, paperbound $6.25

SNOW CRYSTALS, *W. A. Bentley and W. J. Humphreys*
Over 200 pages of Bentley's famous microphotographs of snow flakes—the product of painstaking, methodical work at his Jericho, Vermont studio. The pictures, which also include plates of frost, glaze and dew on vegetation, spider webs, windowpanes; sleet; graupel or soft hail, were chosen both for their scientific interest and their aesthetic qualities. The wonder of nature's diversity is exhibited in the intricate, beautiful patterns of the snow flakes. Introductory text by W. J. Humphreys. Selected bibliography. 2,453 illustrations. 224pp. 8 x 10¼.   20287-9 Paperbound $3.25

THE BIRTH AND DEVELOPMENT OF THE GEOLOGICAL SCIENCES,
F. D. Adams
Most thorough history of the earth sciences ever written. Geological thought from earliest times to the end of the 19th century, covering over 300 early thinkers & systems: fossils & their explanation, vulcanists vs. neptunists, figured stones & paleontology, generation of stones, dozens of similar topics. 91 illustrations, including medieval, renaissance woodcuts, etc. Index. 632 footnotes, mostly bibliographical. 511pp. 5⅜ x 8.   20005-1 Paperbound $2.75

ORGANIC CHEMISTRY, *F. C. Whitmore*
The entire subject of organic chemistry for the practicing chemist and the advanced student. Storehouse of facts, theories, processes found elsewhere only in specialized journals. Covers aliphatic compounds (500 pages on the properties and synthetic preparation of hydrocarbons, halides, proteins, ketones, etc.), alicyclic compounds, aromatic compounds, heterocyclic compounds, organophosphorus and organometallic compounds. Methods of synthetic preparation analyzed critically throughout. Includes much of biochemical interest. "The scope of this volume is astonishing," *Industrial and Engineering Chemistry.* 12,000-reference index. 2387-item bibliography. Total of x + 1005pp. 5⅜ x 8.   60700-3, 60701-1 Two volume set, paperbound $4.50

THE PHASE RULE AND ITS APPLICATION,
Alexander Findlay
Covering chemical phenomena of 1, 2, 3, 4, and multiple component systems, this "standard work on the subject" (*Nature,* London), has been completely revised and brought up to date by A. N. Campbell and N. O. Smith. Brand new material has been added on such matters as binary, tertiary liquid equilibria, solid solutions in ternary systems, quinary systems of salts and water. Completely revised to triangular coordinates in ternary systems, clarified graphic representation, solid models, etc. 9th revised edition. Author, subject indexes. 236 figures. 505 footnotes, mostly bibliographic. xii + 494pp. 5⅜ x 8.   60091-2 Paperbound $2.75

APPLIED OPTICS AND OPTICAL DESIGN,
A. E. Conrady
With publication of vol. 2, standard work for designers in optics is now complete for first time. Only work of its kind in English; only detailed work for practical designer and self-taught. Requires, for bulk of work, no math above trig. Step-by-step exposition, from fundamental concepts of geometrical, physical optics, to systematic study, design, of almost all types of optical systems. Vol. 1: all ordinary ray-tracing methods; primary aberrations; necessary higher aberration for design of telescopes, low-power microscopes, photographic equipment. Vol. 2: (Completed from author's notes by R. Kingslake, Dir. Optical Design, Eastman Kodak.) Special attention to high-power microscope, anastigmatic photographic objectives. "An indispensable work," J., Optical Soc. of Amer. Index. Bibliography. 193 diagrams. 852pp. 6⅛ x 9¼.
60611-2, 60612-0 Two volume set, paperbound $8.00

MECHANICS OF THE GYROSCOPE, THE DYNAMICS OF ROTATION,
R. F. Deimel, Professor of Mechanical Engineering at Stevens Institute of Technology
Elementary general treatment of dynamics of rotation, with special application of gyroscopic phenomena. No knowledge of vectors needed. Velocity of a moving curve, acceleration to a point, general equations of motion, gyroscopic horizon, free gyro, motion of discs, the damped gyro, 103 similar topics. Exercises. 75 figures. 208pp. 5⅜ x 8.   60066-1 Paperbound $1.75

STRENGTH OF MATERIALS,
J. P. Den Hartog
Full, clear treatment of elementary material (tension, torsion, bending, compound stresses, deflection of beams, etc.), plus much advanced material on engineering methods of great practical value: full treatment of the Mohr circle, lucid elementary discussions of the theory of the center of shear and the "Myosotis" method of calculating beam deflections, reinforced concrete, plastic deformations, photoelasticity, etc. In all sections, both general principles and concrete applications are given. Index. 186 figures (160 others in problem section). 350 problems, all with answers. List of formulas. viii + 323pp. 5⅜ x 8.
60755-0 Paperbound $2.50

HYDRAULIC TRANSIENTS,
G. R. Rich
The best text in hydraulics ever printed in English . . . by former Chief Design Engineer for T.V.A. Provides a transition from the basic differential equations of hydraulic transient theory to the arithmetic integration computation required by practicing engineers. Sections cover Water Hammer, Turbine Speed Regulation, Stability of Governing, Water-Hammer Pressures in Pump Discharge Lines, The Differential and Restricted Orifice Surge Tanks, The Normalized Surge Tank Charts of Calame and Gaden, Navigation Locks, Surges in Power Canals—Tidal Harmonics, etc. Revised and enlarged. Author's prefaces. Index. xiv + 409pp. 5⅜ x 8½.   60116-1 Paperbound $2.50

Prices subject to change without notice.

Available at your book dealer or write for free catalogue to Dept. Adsci, Dover Publications, Inc., 180 Varick St., N.Y., N.Y. 10014. Dover publishes more than 150 books each year on science, elementary and advanced mathematics, biology, music, art, literary history, social sciences and other areas.